www.wadsworth.com

wadsworth.com is the World Wide Web site for Wadsworth Publishing Company and is your direct source to dozens of online resources.

At *wadsworth.com* you can find out about supplements, demonstration software, and student resources.
You can also send e-mail to many of our
authors and preview new publications and exciting
new technologies.

wadsworth.com
Changing the way the world learns®

World Religions

 Third Edition

Warren Matthews
Old Dominion University

WADSWORTH PUBLISHING COMPANY

I(T)P® An International Thomson Publishing Company

Belmont, CA • Albany, NY • Boston • Cincinnati • Johannesburg • London • Madrid
Melbourne • Mexico City • New York • Pacific Grove, CA • Scottsdale, AZ • Singapore
Tokyo • Toronto

Religion Editor: Peter Adams	Designer: Donna Davis Graphic Design
Assistant Editor: Kerri Abdinoor	Copy Editor: Linda Purrington
Editorial Assistant: Mindy Newfarmer	Illustrator: Carto–Graphics
Marketing Manager: Dave Garrison	Cover Design: Jeanne Calabreese
Print Buyer: Stacey Weinberger	Cover Image: Sand Dune, Gary Faye/Graphistock
Permissions Editor: Robert Kauser	Compositor: Parkwood Composition
Production Coordinator: The Book Company	Printer: Transcontinental Printing, Inc.

Printed in Canada
1 2 3 4 5 6 7 8 9 10

For more information, contact Wadsworth Publishing Company, 10 Davis Drive, Belmont, CA 94002, or electronically at http://www.wadsworth.com

International Thomson Publishing Europe
Berkshire House
168-173 High Holborn
London, WC1V 7AA, United Kingdom

International Thomson Editores
Seneca, 53
Colonia Polanco
11560 México D.F. México

Nelson ITP, Australia
102 Dodds Street
South Melbourne
Victoria 3205 Australia

International Thomson Publishing Asia
60 Albert Street
#15-01 Albert Complex
Singapore 189969

Nelson Canada
1120 Birchmount Road
Scarborough, Ontario
Canada M1K 5G4

International Thomson Publishing Japan
Hirakawa-cho Kyowa Building, 3F
2-2-1 Hirakawa-cho, Chiyoda-ku
Tokyo 102 Japan

International Thomson Publishing Southern Africa
Building 18, Constantia Square
138 Sixteenth Road, P.O. Box 2459
Halfway House, 1685 South Africa

Library of Congress Cataloging-in-Publication Data
Matthews, Alfred Warren.
        World Religions / Warren Matthews.—3rd ed.
             p. cm.
        Includes bibliographical references and index.
        ISBN 0-534-56691-X
        1. Religions. I. Title.
    BL80.2.M355 1999
    291—DC21   98–16562

 This book is printed on acid-free recycled paper.

For Julia, Charles, Betty, Lucille, Louise, Robert, Virginia, Julie, Nancy, Alyson, Christopher, and John.

Brief Contents

INTRODUCTION 2

PART ONE   *Religions of Tribes and City-States*   19
1 Religions of the Americas   20
2 Religions of Africa   53

PART TWO   *Religions Arising in India*   81
3 Hinduism   82
4 Buddhism   127
5 Jainism and Sikhism   178

PART THREE   *Religions of China and Japan*   207
6 China and Japan   208

PART FOUR   *Religions that Influenced East and West*   255
7 Ancient Religions of Iraq and Iran   257

PART FIVE   *Religions of the Family of Abraham*   279
8 Judaism   280
9 Christianity   329
10 Islam   385

Contents

Preface to the Third Edition   xxi

INTRODUCTION   2
The Sacred and the Profane   2
   Sacred Space   3
   Sacred Stories   3
   Sacred Writings   4
   Rituals   5
   Dance   6
   Religious Drama   6
Organization of Studies   7
   Historical Development   8
   Worldview   9
   Consider This   14
   Resources for Study   15
The Point of View of the Text   15
Consider This: Definitions of Religion   17
Vocabulary   17
Notes   17
Readings   17

PART ONE

RELIGIONS OF TRIBES AND CITY-STATES   19

CHAPTER 1

RELIGIONS OF THE AMERICAS   20
   Introduction   20
Religions of North America   21
   The Naskapi   21
   The Kwakiutl People   26
   The Powhatan Peoples   27
   The Cherokees   31
   The Pueblo Peoples   35
   Peoples of the Great Plains   36
Common Features of Religions in North America   36
   The Absolute   37
   The World   37
   Humans   37
   The Problem for Humans   37

The Solution for Humans   38
Community and Ethics   38
An Interpretation of History   39
Rituals and Symbols   39
Life After Death   40
Relationship with Other Religions   40
Objections to Older Scholarship   40
Religions of Mesoamerica and South America   41
The Aztecs   41
The Incas   44
Common Features of Religions in Mesoamerica and South America   49

Consider This: A Point of View   50

Vocabulary   50
Questions for Review   51
Questions for Discussion   51
Notes   51
Readings   52

CHAPTER 2

RELIGIONS OF AFRICA   53
Introduction   53
The Egyptian Religion   54
Historical Development   55
Worldview of the Ancient Egyptians   56
The Basongye of Congo   63
Historical Development   63
Worldview of the Basongye   64
The Zulu Peoples   67
Historical Development of South Africa   67
Worldview of the Zulu Peoples   67
The Yoruba   71
Historical Development of Nigeria   71
Worldview of the Yoruba Peoples   71
Common Features of Religions in Sub-Saharan Africa   73
Worldviews   74

Consider This: Official and Folk Religions   77

Vocabulary   77
Questions for Review   77
Questions for Discussion   78
Notes   78
Readings   78

PART TWO

RELIGIONS ARISING IN INDIA   81

CHAPTER 3

HINDUISM   82
  Introduction   82
Historical Development   83
  Historiography   83
  The Origins of Hinduism   83
  Shruti: Revelation and Scriptures   85
  Gods of the Rig-Veda   85
  Three Collections of the Vedas   88
  The Brahmanas and Aranyakas   89
  The Upanishads   89
  Karma and Samsara   93
  Alternatives to the Vedas and Upsanishads   94
  Four Goals for Hindus   97
  The Laws of Manu   98
  Four Ways of Salvation   99
  The Laws of Manu   102
  Orthodox Hindu Systems of Philosophy   103
  Islam in India   104
  Christianity in India   105
  Hindu Responses to Western Influence   105
  Independent India   109
Consider This: The Law of Karma   112

Worldview   112
  The Absolute   112
  The World   113
  Humans   115
  The Problem for Humans   115
  The Solution for Humans   115
  Community and Ethics   116
  An Interpretation of History   117
  Rituals and Symbols   117
  Life After Death   119
  Hinduism and Other Religions   119
Vocabulary   123
Questions for Review   123
Questions for Discussion   123
Notes   124
Readings   125

CHAPTER 4

BUDDHISM   127

Introduction   127
Historical Development   128
  Historiography   128
  The Life of the Buddha   130
  The Development of Buddhism After the Buddha   142
  Two Ways of Experiencing the Buddha   143
  Buddhist Missionary Activities in Asia   148
  Recent Buddhism   158
  Some Recent Buddhist Political Leaders   159
  Buddhism and the West   162
  Buddhist Women   164
  Buddhism Today   164

Consider This: The Selfless Mind   165

Worldview   165
  The Absolute   165
  The World   166
  Humans   167
  The Problem for Humans   167
  The Solution for Humans   168
  Community and Ethics   170
  An Interpretation of History   171
  Rituals and Symbols   171
  Life After Death   172
  Buddhism and Other Religions   173
Vocabulary   173
Questions for Review   174
Questions for Discussion   174
Notes   175
Readings   176

CHAPTER 5

JAINISM AND SIKHISM   178
JAINISM   178

Introduction   178
Historical Development   179
  Historiography   179
  The Life of Mahavira   179
  Jain Scriptures   182

Consider This: Respect for All Living Things   183

Worldview   183
  The Absolute   183
  The World   184

Humans   185
    The Problem for Humans   185
    The Solution for Humans   186
    Community and Ethics   187
    Rituals and Symbols   188
    Jainism and Other Religions   189
Summary of Jainism   189

SIKHISM   190
Introduction   190
Historical Development   190
    Historiography   190
    The Life of Guru Nanak   191
    The Teachings of Guru Nanak   195
    The Nine Gurus After Nanak   196

Consider This: The Appearance of Monotheism   199

Worldview   200
    The Absolute   200
    The World and Humans   200
    The Problem and the Solution for Humans   200
    Community and Ethics   201
    Rituals and Symbols   201
    Life After Death   202
    Sikhism and Other Religions   203
Vocabulary   204
Questions for Review   205
Questions for Discussion   205
Notes   205
Readings   206

PART THREE

RELIGIONS OF CHINA AND JAPAN   207

CHAPTER 6

CHINA AND JAPAN   208
    Introduction   208

CHINA   208
The Religions of China   208
Background of the Religions of China   209
    Heaven   209

Daoism   210

Historical Development   211

Historiography   211
Laozi (Lao Tzu)   211
Zhuangzi (Chuang Tzu)   214
Religious, Sectarian Daoism   215

Consider This: Harmony with Forces of Life   216

Worldview   216
The Absolute   216
The World   216
Humans   216
The Problem for Humans   217
The Solution for Humans   217
Community and Ethics   218
Rituals and Symbols   218

Confucianism   219

Historical Development   219
Historiography   219
The Life of Confucius   220
The Teachings of Confucius   220
Challenges to the Teachings of Confucius   223
Confucius and Other Thinkers   225
Confucianism After Confucius   225
Mengzi (Mencius)   226
Xunzi (Hsun Tsu)   226
Han Support for Confucianism   227
Neo-Confucianism   227
Confucianism and Daoism in Korea and Japan   228
The Height and Downfall of Confucianism   229
Confucianism Under Mao Zedong (Mao Tse-tung)   229
Chinese Folk Religion   230

Consider This: Harmony with Society   231

Worldview   231
The Absolute   231
The World   232
Humans   233
The Problem for Humans   233
The Solution for Humans   233
Community and Ethics   233
Rituals and Symbols   234
Life After Death   235

JAPAN   235
Introduction   235
Historical Development   235
Historiography   236
Prehistoric Japan   236
Visitors from Korea   236
Myths of Japan   236

Buddhist Influence on Shinto   238
The Bushido Code   239
Reactions to Foreign Influence   239
State Shinto   240
Recent Shinto   240
New Religions   243
Consider This: Harmony in Japan   244

Worldview   244
The Absolute   244
The World   244
Humans   245
The Problem for Humans   245
The Solution for Humans   245
Community and Ethics   245
Rituals and Symbols   245
Life After Death   248
Shintoism and Other Religions   248
Vocabulary   249
Questions for Review   249
Questions for Discussion   250
Notes   250
Readings   251

✍ PART FOUR

RELIGIONS THAT INFLUENCED EAST AND WEST   255

CHAPTER 7

ANCIENT RELIGIONS OF IRAQ AND IRAN   257
Introduction   257

Mesopotamian Religion   258

Historical Development   258
Historiography   258
Recovering the History of Mesopotamia   258
Worldview   259
The Absolute   259
Myths   260
Gilgamesh   262
Rituals and Symbols   263
Relationship to Other Religions   264
Consider This: Mesopotamia in the Bible   265

Iranian Religion   267

Historical Development   267
Historiography   267

The Life of Zarathustra   267
Teachings of Zarathustra   268
Zoroastrianism After Zarathustra   269
Consider This: Persians in the Bible   270

Worldview   270
The Absolute   270
The World   271
Humans   271
The Problem for Humans   272
The Solution for Humans   272
Symbols and Rituals   272
Life After Death   273
An Interpretation of History   274
Zoroastrianism and Other Religions   274
Vocabulary   276
Questions for Review   276
Questions for Discussion   276
Notes   276
Readings   277

PART FIVE

RELIGIONS OF THE FAMILY OF ABRAHAM   279

CHAPTER 8

JUDAISM   280
Introduction   280
The Jewish Bible   281
Interpreting the Bible   281
Historical Development   282
Historiography   282
Abraham   283
Life Under the Egyptians   284
Moses   285
Settlement in Canaan   287
The Hebrew Prophets   288
Destroyed Kingdoms, Exiled Leaders   290
Life of Babylonian Exiles   290
Editing the Scriptures   291
An Alternative to Temple Worship   292
Postexilic Judaism   292
The Greeks   293
Wisdom Literature   294
The Maccabean Revolt   294
The Romans   295
Rabbinic Judaism   296

Philo   299
Medieval Judaism   300
Jewish Philosophy   300
Judaism, Christianity, and Islam   304
Judaism in the Modern Age   305
Forms of Judaism   306
The Holocaust   310
Israel   311
The Roots of the Arab-Israeli Conflict   311

Consider This: Authentic Observance   312

Worldview   313
The Absolute   313
The World   317
Humans   318
The Problem and the Solution for Humans   319
Community and Ethics   319
Rituals and Symbols   323
Life After Death   324
Judaism and Other Religions   324
Vocabulary   325
Questions for Review   326
Questions for Discussion   326
Notes   326
Readings   327

CHAPTER 9

CHRISTIANITY   329
Introduction   329
Historical Development   330
Historiography   330
Jesus of Nazareth   330
The Teachings of Jesus   331
Jesus' Authority   334
The Teachings and Authority of Jesus in John, the Fourth Gospel   334
The Last Week of Jesus   335
Three Thousand People Join the Church   327
Some Jews Feel Threatened by the Church   340
Saul of Tarsus   340
Romans Persecute Christians   344
Forming the New Testament   346
Christian Worship   347
Christian Platonists of Alexandria   347
Ecumenical Councils   348
Grace of God for the Sin of Man   350
Monasticism   351
Governance in Roman Catholic and Greek Orthodox Traditions   352
Greek Orthodox and Roman Catholic Paths of Service   353

St. Thomas Aquinas   355
The Crusades   357
The Arts   357
Protestant and Reformed Churches   358
The Catholic Reformation   361
Missions in North America   363
Eastern Orthodox Christianity in the New World   364
Religious Diversity in the United States   364
The Age of Reason   365
Emerging Forms of Protestant Christianity   365
Cooperation Among Protestants   367
Newer Forms of Christianity   368
Major Roman Catholic Reforms   369
Christianity and Liberation   369
Worldview   372
The Absolute   372
The World   373
Humans   374
The Problem and the Solution for Humans   374
Community and Ethics   375
An Interpretation of History   378
Rituals and Symbols   378
Life After Death   380
Christianity and Other Religions   380

Consider This: What Separates Jews and Christians?   381

Vocabulary   381
Questions for Review   382
Questions for Discussion   382
Notes   382
Readings   383

CHAPTER 10

ISLAM   385

Introduction   385
Historical Development   386
Historiography   386
The Background of Islam   386
The Life of Muhammad   388
The Teachings of Muhammad   395
The Successors of the Prophet   398
Sunni and Shi'a   398
The Expansion of Islam   399
The Shari'a   401
Greek Influences on Islam   401
Muslim Spiritual Experiences   402
Sufis   402
Al-Ghazali   404

Philosophy After Al-Ghazali: Ibn Arabi   405
Islam's Relationship with Other Religions   405
Ibn Rushd   408
Islam in India   409
The Baha'i Religion   410
Modernism in Islam   410
Muslim Responses to Modernism   411
Islam in the Last Half of the Twentieth Century   413
Islam in the United States   415
Worldview   417
The Absolute   417
The World   418
Humans   419
The Problem for Humans   420
The Solution for Humans   421
Community and Ethics   421
Rituals and Symbols   422
Life After Death   423
Islam and Other Religions   424
Islam and the Future   425

Consider This: What Separates Jews, Christians, and Muslims?   427

Vocabulary   427
Questions for Review   428
Questions for Discussion   428
Notes   428
Readings   429

CONCLUSION   431

Diversity and Common Ground   431
Learning More About World Religions   432
The Campus   432
Dialogue   432
Travel   433
Discovery of Values   433
Vocabulary   434
Notes   434
Readings   434

APPENDIX: CHARTS   435

Membership of Religions   435
Membership of Churches in Canada   435
Membership of Churches in the United States   435
Membership of Major Religions   436
Basic Tenets of Religions   436
Religions of the Americas   436
Religions of Africa   437

Hinduism   437
Buddhism   438
Jainism and Sikhism   438
Religions of China and Japan   439
Ancient Religions of Iraq and Iran   439
Judaism   440
The Books of the Jewish Bible   440
Christianity   441
Islam   441
Some Common Symbols of Various Religions   442

GLOSSARY   443

INDEX   457

Preface

PURPOSE

Why would a teacher who enjoys lively conversations with students choose the rigors of producing a text on world religions? My purpose has been to make those conversations more informative and rewarding for students. With only one semester to communicate the wealth of spiritual insights of the world's greatest religious leaders to students from every discipline awarding a degree, I sought to gather into one source the best ideas that I had found in more than twenty years of teaching. From my good experiences with authors, texts, resources, seminars, courses, and workshops, I wanted to select the best, most impressive ideas and methods for our students. Beginning with the first edition in 1991, many colleagues, readers, teachers, and students have studied *World Religions* and offered their suggestions for improvement. Dynamic education is ever changing, so we have been invited to include new scholarship, fresh interpretations, and more effective ways of learning. The third edition of *World Religions* helps fulfill my purpose at the turn of this century.

The choice of religions presented in my text reflects the needs and interests of students from most geographical areas and major religions of the world. Our graduates will be active participants in the social, political, business, and religious endeavors of the world community. Because their interests have become somewhat standardized in world religions courses, *World Religions* can contribute to most instructors' course plans.

METHOD

Each religion is presented in two major approaches, the historical and the comprehensive. The first approach, in the Historical Development sections, presents to students the historical facts of how each religion began, the persons whose insights inspired it, the teachings of founders and followers, the major divisions and forms of institutions, and events that have shaped contemporary expressions of the religion. The second approach, the the Worldview sections, presents students a coherent, systematic understanding of the current beliefs of each religion. The topics addressed in the Worldview sections are essentially the same for every major religion, helping students analyze the worldview of any religion and compare it with any other religions. These balanced approaches help students appreciate religious traditions, current beliefs, and continuing developments of living faiths. Students who use *World Religions* are prepared to engage in dialogues and cultural appreciation with members of any major world religion. They can continue a lifetime of learning about world religions.

PEDAGOGICAL FEATURES

Pedagogical features in *World Religions* have been well tested in experience. The third edition has refined many of these features according to student preferences.

QUOTATIONS FROM SCRIPTURES AND RELIGIOUS TEACHERS

Examples of scriptures and teachings of religious teachers are presented for most religions. Students learn to appreciate expressions of a faith by those who practice it. Most selections are chosen to present a complete thought or argument. References point to more complete sources of quotations. For most students, the amount of quoted material is sufficient, however, with my students I have recently used Robert E. Van Voorst, *Anthology of World Scriptures,* Second Edition, by Wadsworth Publishing Company, Belmont, CA 1997.

MASTERY OF VOCABULARY

For beginning students in a subject, the number and complexity of new terms can be overwhelming. Students need new terms and meanings in order to understand religions, but they also need some guidance in learning which terms are important and how they function. Introduction of useful terms has been carefully considered.

Terms are introduced as part of the historical story and the worldview. Sidebars (in the margin) next to **boldface** terms in the text help students learn to recognize, pronounce, and define terms in the context which they are used. A simplified pronunciation guide using capital letters and lower-case letters (e.g., ES-eens) has been preferred by students. At the end of each chapter, a list of terms used in the text is presented for review. A third resource for learning terms is given in the Glossary, where terms in the margin sidebars are repeated alphabetically. A fourth resource is the detailed Index, which gives numbers of pages where each term appears. As instructors know, vocabulary terms are only part of the story of any religion; nevertheless, learning a few terms well helps students relate the story and discuss the beliefs. Instructors may select among the terms presented; their choices for students are abundant.

CRITICAL THINKING AND DISCUSSION

Narrative presentation of facts and beliefs is often supplemented with material that invites students to reflect on the claims made by the religion. Although these topics do not weaken the overall appreciation of each religion, they do make students aware that not all adherents of the religion agree on all beliefs and practices.

Historiography is considered in each Historical Development section for a religion. In every religion there are at least two ways of selecting, grouping, and interpreting "facts" and beliefs. Each religion presents unique choices, but students are invited to think critically about any particular claims in the "story" of a religion's special history. Students soon realize that in any major faith, not all adherents agree on a single sacred story.

SIGNIFICANT ISSUES

In the presentation of each religion, a Consider This boxed section highlights a significant topic for students to consider critically. They can use these topics to engage in discussions with other students and with their instructor. Students are invited to step back from story and faith and reflect about the significance of some insight, claim, or activity. Although each topic begins in a particular religion, most topics raise issues applicable to many religions. The purpose is not to decide which religion is best, worst, right, or wrong, but how people of a religion reasonably disagree about their beliefs and practices.

END-OF-CHAPTER QUESTIONS

The third edition presents new questions for review and for discussion. Some of the questions invite students to reflect on larger significance of religious claims. Some topics encourage classroom discussion with the instructor. Students are stimulated to think beyond vocabulary and facts to some of the implications of the religion's beliefs.

SUGGESTED READINGS

Because I require a book report from each student, I continue to add recent titles to the bibliography. In their reports, students inform me of the books that they have found most interesting and useful. Reviews and recent books by scholars have suggested new titles for the list.

CHANGES IN THE THIRD EDITION

In the third edition of *World Religions* we have made changes that will increase interest, promote critical thinking, and present more recent information. New introductions to each chapter emphasize the story of the religion in relationship to prior religions discussed. More attention has been given to personalities that helped form the religion. Historiography considerations have been discussed in each Historical Development section. Boxed material has been included in each religion to promote critical thinking about some aspect of the religion's beliefs and practices. For example, in Buddhism Peter Harvey's study of *The Selfless Mind* has been introduced.

Help for students and instructors include a new pronunciation guide and new study questions for each chapter. Students have chosen the combination of capital and lower-case letters (e.g., CAN-on) as their most helpful pronunciation guide. Instructors who have used prior editions will appreciate all new questions for review and discussion at the end of each chapter. The lists of Readings have been brought up to date. Maps, timelines, and pictures have been revised to reflect current events and interests.

ANCILLARY MATERIALS FOR THE THIRD EDITION

The Study Guide to Accompany World Religions has proven its effectiveness since 1991. David Prejsnar, who prepared the first two editions, has used his experience to produce an even more effective guide for the third edition. Students seeking help find the guide a thorough preparation for objective and essay examination questions.

The *Instructor's Manual to Accompany World Religions*, Third Edition, has nearly all new material. The chapter summaries have been rewritten to present more of the author's views in preparing the text. Instructors can more quickly assess the author's presentations. The Sample Test Questions are new and include multiple choice, true or false, matching, and essay questions. A Test Bank of the questions is available from Wadsworth Publishing Company on request. Instructors of large sections or multiple sections will find test materials adequate for their needs. The list of resources for teaching world religions has been expanded; only the list of possible goals in teaching world religions has been condensed. Wadsworth Publishing Company makes available, also, Internet access to its site for additional ancillary materials. The address is www.wadsworth.com

An author's intention to present a stimulating, informative text for students from many different disciplines can only be fulfilled with help of other scholars and publishing professionals. My colleagues Professor David Putney and Dr. Thomas Neill have made many suggestions to improve the text. Peter Adams, the new philosophy and religion editor at Wadsworth Publishing Company, has brought a fresh appraisal, improved presentations, and added new features for critical thinking. His selection of readers to offer advice has also contributed to the quality of this new edition. Thank you for production of the book to Kerri Abdinoor of Wadsworth Publishing; Dusty Friedman of The Book Company and Betsy Martin of Emspace Artwork.

Readers whose insights have improved the text include:

Professor Christine M. Bochen
Nazareth College of Rochester

Professor Nathan Katz
Florida International University

Dr. David Damrel
Arizona State University

Professor Ramdas Lamb
University of Hawaii at Manoa

Professor Cynthia Ann Humes
Claremont McKenna College

Professor Donald Nolen
Parkland College

Professor Denis Janz
Loyola University

Improvement of a text, however, is an ongoing process. Although many of the suggestions that I received have been incorporated into the third edition, I have had to reserve some helpful comments for a later edition.

I hope that other instructors will find *World Religions* as helpful in their teaching as I have in my own, and that their students will be as enthusiastic about the subject as mine have been.

Warren Matthews
Old Dominion University
February 9, 1998

World Religions

Third Edition

Introduction

Welcome to the study of world religions. Perhaps you have heard about some of the interesting personalities in these religions. Confucius, the Buddha, Moses, Jesus, and Muhammad are a few of the persons who have attracted millions of people to religious views of the world. As you know, for many centuries they have influenced their followers as they have shaped whole cultures. Now you can look at their lives to see what experiences formed their beliefs and helped them address the deepest human problems of their times. Each charismatic leader set in motion organizations that continued to grow beyond the life of the founder. In addition to the wonderful stories about the founders of religions, we have accounts of the individuals who followed them and expanded their thoughts and influences over future generations.

As you learn the stories of personalities and religious organizations, you will also find answers to your questions about unusual beliefs and practices of their followers. You will learn how peoples of various religions act and what beliefs lead them to practice particular rituals. Beyond the stories, then, you will learn about beliefs and acts that are essential ingredients in the perpetual dramas of religion.

In this introduction to world religions you will learn, also, some of the methods and skills that will enable you to explore other facets of religions on your own. You will learn some terms used in discussing religions and some of the scholarly literature that can help you begin a lifelong appreciation of religious faiths. Throughout this text you will learn a lot about other peoples of the world. At the same time, you may learn a lot about yourself. As you see how other peoples respond to life, you may reflect on your own beliefs and practices. You will not be told what to believe, but you will find that your choices of beliefs have multiplied. Studying world religions will offer you more freedom to form your own opinions about religions.

In the next few sections of this Introduction you will learn a little more about the ingredients of any religion. As you read subsequent chapters, you will begin to see how the ingredients interact in religions that have attracted deep loyalty from millions of people.

THE SACRED AND THE PROFANE

sacred [SAY-crid]
Set apart for worship of a deity or as worthy of worship.

profane [proh-FANE]
Nonreligious. Outside the sphere of religion. Contemptuous of religion.

secular [SEK-u-lur]
Worldly. Not spiritual or religious.

From your experience, you know that some objects and activities are set apart as special, holy, or **sacred.** They are treated differently from objects and activities that are ordinary, secular, or **profane.** Mircea Eliade, an expert on world religions, has elaborated the difference. A visitor to Bangkok, Thailand, for example, may have her interest aroused by three different types of architecture of temples, by spirit houses on lawns of private residences, and by prohibitions against taking out of the country any Buddha images. These arrangements alert us to the sacred. In the same city, motor scooter taxis, canal boats that transport tourists past vendors in small boats, and modern fast-food restaurants are **secular** (worldly) or profane. Most peoples have sacred buildings or activities. Governments that have espoused atheism, such as the one in Moscow or the one in Beijing, have their own places, people, and activities that are set apart from ordinary life.

Some of the earliest human activities of which we have evidence may have had sacred as well as secular significance. Paintings on the walls of caves in Lascaux, France, have puzzled scholars who think that they may have been attempts to influence future events as much as to record the past. A statue of a primitive mother may have been carved not only to depict motherhood but also to ensure the fertility of those who sought to become mothers. Much of the beautiful art from Tutankhamen's tomb in Egypt reflects belief in life after death.

Sacred Space

The sacred is set apart, also, through establishing a center in space. A sacred hill, a sacred tree, or a special building may represent the center of sacred space. The farther one goes from the center, the less holy the space. For example, in Muslim countries, the mosque is at the center of the city; other institutions and houses are built around and away from it. In larger modern cities, such as Tashkent and Uzbekistan, Russians, Uzbeks, and hundreds of other ethnic groups have constructed a modern city to replace the old city destroyed by an earthquake in this century. The new city focuses on a modern complex of municipal buildings. The old city, or what remains of it, retains the mosque as the center of the Muslim community. Sacred structures, natural spaces enhanced by human art or craft, and space consecrated by deliberate arrangement or features can represent sacred space. The lofty Gothic cathedrals of medieval Europe enclose sacred space.

Sacred Stories

Peoples also organize their lives according to stories. Although details of a people's beginnings may be unclear or confused, most of them can trace

Primitive Paintings in Caves of Lascaux, France. Scholars differ on whether the paintings were records of past events or attempts to influence future activities.

Statue of a Primitive Mother. Some scholars think that statues of this sort were supposed to promote fertility.

myth [MITH]
A story dealing with supernatural beings that represents the worldview of a people.

epic [EP-ic]
A narrative poem celebrating the acts of a traditional hero.

scriptures [SKRIP-churs]
Sacred writings. A sacred scroll or book.

their story back to their grandfathers. Beyond that time, some accounts are vague; the details of others are remarkably clear. Because some of the stories have been preserved in the oral traditions of people who did not produce written accounts of their past, these sacred stories are even more remarkable. For example, the Aztecs told stories of their arrival at Lake Texcoco, but details of their having lived in caves before their journey to Texcoco have been difficult to confirm.[1] In the West, we are familiar with stories of Abraham, Isaac, Jacob, Joseph, and Moses, the earlier characters in the sacred stories of Israel, later embraced also by Christians and Muslims.

Often sacred stories attempt to trace peoples, animals, planets, and stars to their beginnings. Our investment of millions of dollars in the Hubble telescope in space demonstrates that we, no less than ancient peoples, search for the beginning of everything. What the universe was like before there were humans is a great puzzle. Sacred stories that answer these questions usually claim to precede any human witness. Creation stories have been "given" or "revealed" to humans. They take place in sacred, or special, times and places. A god, goddess, demon, or other spiritual being may be credited with starting the world. The Hebrew story reports that in the beginning God created heaven and earth. One Hindu account in the Rig-Veda reports that the world's commencement preceded the gods. Some stories of Native Americans explain that the world began when a little creature (various sorts are suggested) descended in water to the muddy bottom and brought up some earth to the surface. The Babylonian sacred story recounts the beginning when earth and water, fresh waters and salt waters were divided. Because these sacred stories preceded what could be known by direct human witness, scholars of world religions refer to them as **myths.** They may be true stories, attested by visions or voices, or hallowed by long usage, but they differ from what we consider history. Perhaps you have seen films of Bill Moyers interviewing Joseph Campbell, an expert on myths and author of *The Masks of God.*[2]

Differing from myths and sacred stories of peoples, **epics** are long, narrative poems about feats of legendary or traditional heroes. These characters represent values held dear by creators of the stories. The protagonists battle numerous antagonists in episodes of a journey or ordeal. Epics were forerunners of the modern television serial. In epics we discover what a people value, pursue, fear, dread, or enjoy. They help us see how they understood many of the most significant issues of human life. In India, for example, epics about Prince Rama and his wife, Sita, are told in the Ramayana and about Lord Krishna in the battle with his warring cousins in the Bhagavad Gita. These are earthly people, but they are more than human rulers or teachers. Popular Hinduism honors Rama and Krishna as incarnations of supreme deity, who fight for goodness on behalf of humans caught in a morass of evil.

Sacred Writings

In our study of world religions we will encounter many sacred books. Each major world religion has a collection of writings that its adherents believe came directly from God or from divinely inspired writers. These **scriptures** are revered above all other writings, forming the foundations for ritual, ethics, and law. Older writings usually carry more authority than later ones. Adherents generally believe that their sacred writings are the only ones needed for faith and practice of their religion. Scriptures of other religions that conflict with their scriptures cannot be equally true.

Peoples often revere writing itself. The technology of writing and reading has been considered sacred. In her book *Out of Africa*, Isak Dinesen (Baroness Blixen) described her early-twentieth-century experience managing her plantation in Africa.[3] Her written record of a decision of a people's council in favor of a black worker on her farm inspired the worker's wonder, awe, and power. He kept it in a leather bag hung from a strap around his neck. When he had the baroness read and reread the document to him (for he could not read), the wonder of the written account was renewed. We can imagine the awe that early writing inspired when scribes laboriously served kings and priests in northern Africa by recording major events and proclaiming important laws. Early pharaohs recorded their achievements, and early priests wrote guides for those who died seeking immortality. King Hammurabi (1792–1750 B.C.E.) of Babylon directed that laws be carved on stones, representing his receiving them from the god Shamesh. By 1000 B.C.E. oral traditions were finding their way into writings that became scriptures of Jews or of Hindus. In China, ancient texts of the Zhou (Chou) dynasty, perhaps preceding 1000 B.C.E., were honored long before the births of Laozi (Lao Tzu) or Confucius. Writing preserved oral traditions, helping stabilize future generations of a culture. Passing time deepened reverence for the accounts. Stories of gods, kings, and priests (sacred) were easily distinguished from secular business accounts and military orders.

In India, however, we find some exceptions to written words being considered more sacred than spoken words. Hindus prefer hearing sacred sounds, which they believe are violated when reduced to writing. To a lesser extent, Buddhists and Jains prefer to hear the sacred sounds of revelation. Reading scriptures does not convey the full import of spoken words.

Rituals

Actions, too, may be sacred or secular. Although groups may participate annually in repetitive actions such as fishing, hunting, gathering, migrating, fighting, and dancing, they may consider these activities either sacred or secular. Sacred actions, to be beneficial, must be performed exactly according to a prescribed pattern.

Rituals are applicable to the most important events in life. Segregation of women who manifest signs of the reproductive process is practiced in many tribal and village societies. In some religions, signs are posted outside temple precincts giving notice that menstruating women are prohibited from entering. Some actions, such as sexual intercourse in a sacred place, are prohibited for religious reasons. Some groups have foods that must be avoided: Jews and Muslims avoid pork, and Hindus avoid beef. Some actions may also be prescribed for religious reasons. Obligatory practices associated with **rites of passage** are sacred. Birth, adolescence, marriage, and death all require rites of passage. Rites can be prescribed, also, for annual solar or lunar seasons at new year, spring, summer, fall, and winter. In Judaism, Christianity, and Islam, rites may be associated with weekly observances of the Sabbath, Sunday, or Friday.

Rituals are repetitive actions performed as a social obligation. Religious traditions assign the first use of a ritual to a sacred time, person, or event.

rituals [RICH-oo-als]
Prescribed religious ceremonies.

rites of passage [riits-ov-PAS-ij]
A prescribed ceremonial act or series of acts. The sign that a person is passing from one stage of life to another.

For example, in Judaism, Passover began when God instructed Moses to free Hebrew slaves from Egyptian rule. In Christianity, Holy Communion began with Jesus' words and deeds at his last supper with his disciples. In Islam, the pilgrimage to Mecca points to the time when Abraham and his son Ishmael built the sacred Ka'bah. Repeating each prescribed set of actions, participants identify with original personalities, with later leaders who repeated the actions, and with the group that has benefited from the ideals of the ritual. To outsiders, the most shocking rituals have been those that required human sacrifice. These extreme acts, however, seldom have been part of ordinary rituals in any large group over a long period of time.

Dance

Dance can be either sacred or secular. The Sun Dance of the Sioux Indians is a good example of a sacred dance. Taking place in summer, it draws participants from a wide area to dance together for days in order to purify themselves. Most groups use visual arts and performing arts as dancers clothe themselves in costumes representing animals, birds, fish, or gods. Dancers paint their faces and bodies, transforming themselves into other characters. Wearing masks, they can conceal their identity for a few hours, while they become a deity, a demon, or a creature of the natural world. Or they may consider masks as divine, animated for a few hours by the dancers who wear them. Dancers and those who observe them are transported out of ordinary existence into dimensions shared with their ancestors. Past and present are joined in renewing life for the future. Australian aboriginal peoples, New Zealand Maoris, and Hawaiian peoples have been enthusiastic dancers.

Religious Drama

Religious drama is the medium that combines sacred stories and actions. Lasting from an hour to months, dramas may incorporate serial episodes played in each season of the calendar. In the Northern Hemisphere, Chris-

Ceremonial Dance of Aborigine Men.
Near Pepperminate, Australia, men perform stories of bush animals and spirits.

INTRODUCTION

Christian Pilgrimage to Lourdes, France.
Pilgrims from Glasgow, Scotland pass by
the statue of Our Lady.

tians celebrate the birth of Jesus when hours of sunlight increase. They celebrate Easter when new life begins to appear amid dead vegetation. Pentecost is celebrated when full growth of vegetation is apparent. Thanksgiving festivals acknowledge the ingathering of summer crops that sustain life through the winter. In Hindu communities of Africa and Indonesia, as well as in India, devotees of Rama and Sita hold festivals of the dance and story of the Ramayana, to celebrate Lord Rama's dramatic rescue of his kidnaped wife, Sita. Masses of devotees in world religions are so caught up in dramas that one could almost describe large world religions as perpetual dramas.

The drama of each major religion frames its sacred stories, writings, and examples of fine and performing arts. These media carry messages of the history and worldview of each people. In each drama, a people's view of themselves and their world is presented in their actions. Your curiosity about these features of world religions will be addressed throughout this text.

ORGANIZATION OF STUDIES

Let me describe how I have planned to help you learn about major world religions in only one semester. Understanding the organization of this text will help you anticipate what to look for as you study.

Although your experiences with a religion can be helpful as you seek to understand other religions, I have found it useful for students to begin their studies with religions that may be quite different from their daily experiences. This approach helps cultivate an objectivity that is useful in understanding world religions. I will first discuss some of the earliest religions of the Americas and of Africa. Many of these peoples still practice ancient forms of their religions. Other peoples have combined their traditional forms with a major world religion, such as Christianity or Islam. The next chapters will focus on religions of Asia, dealing first with the family of religions in India. Hinduism, Buddhism, Jainism, and Sikhism share a fascination with souls. The family of Chinese and Japanese religions emphasizes relationships with community and ancestors. Then I will move from the East toward the West, using ancient religions of Iraq and Iran, Mesopotamian religions and Zoroastrianism, as an approach to Western religions. In the Middle East, Palestine, and Arabia, we will examine three major religions that belong to the family of Abraham. Judaism, Christianity, and Islam, though different, are siblings that look to one father of faith, Abraham.

Because you want to know not only what people believe but also why they believe it, most chapters will discuss both the worldview of a religion and the history of its development. Beliefs of Hindus and Buddhists are more interesting when we know why they share some beliefs but not others. The history of each religion helps us understand how a common background gave rise to such different beliefs and practices. History and worldview are so closely related that one can help you understand the other. Together, history and worldview help you deepen your appreciation of each religion.

Beginning with Chapter 3, I will open chapters with the story of how a religion developed and then describe its beliefs and practices today. In the first two chapters, I will describe the beliefs and practices of groups within the Americas and Africa and then summarize some beliefs common to the peoples of each continent.

Historical Development

Although this text is not exclusively a history of world religions, one section of each chapter does discuss the religion's historical development. Major world religions do not suddenly appear fully developed. They evolve over many decades or centuries. Information is given, without the inclusion of overwhelming facts and interpretations, that is essential in understanding how a religion reached its present form.

In this edition I have included in each discussion of historical development a brief consideration of historiography. Historians of religions have their particular points of view of what counts as history, evidence, and analysis. Some historians write from within a religion, defending one point of view against a competing view within the religion. Other historians understand the religion from the view of an outsider. Some writers think that myths and wonder stories are important in describing religious developments, other writers want to consider only evidence that can be substantiated by artifacts or contemporary written records. Without entering lengthy discussions of scholarship, I try to present the main choices to be made by people relating the historical development of a religion.

In the beginning of a religion, there is often a charismatic person whose life and teachings attract followers to a new order. Many religions have sacred writings that are based on the life and teachings of their founders. These religions began earlier than 1200 B.C.E. It is important to know what the founder taught—the unique contributions that he or she made in the development of a distinct religion. The immediate disciples of the founder who carried on the work after his or her departure are of particular interest.

Over the centuries many personalities and events have changed the original teachings of founders. Outstanding thinkers and conflicting ideals have influenced changes in beliefs, practices, and interpretations. What major changes occurred in each religion from its inception to its practices

Ancient Egyptian Fresco of Deities and Snake. These fresco paintings appear in a tomb of The Valley of the Kings, Luxor, Egypt.

today? How did the major divisions of a religion develop? Why are beliefs and practices of various groups in the religion so different from the teachings and practices of the founder and the early followers? To understand most world religions, it is necessary to know some major personalities, events, and developments of history.

A historical study shows how a religion interacted with societies, resulting in changes for both the societies and the religion. Major world religions have influenced the arts, sciences, literature, economics, government, and social structure of the adherents. In turn, the adherents' societies have brought changes in the beliefs and functions of religions. Many students find a historical approach to religion enjoyable and rewarding.

In discussing historical development, you will find many academic subjects useful. The popular movies and television programs about archaeologists, anthropologists, and sociologists give a sense of adventure in studying world religions past and present. Texts in **cuneiform,** from Mesopotamia, and **hieroglyphics,** from Egypt, fascinate visitors to tombs or museums. Engineers, artists, and craftspeople are rewarded with intriguing structures, art forms, and technologies. Economists learn how progress in agriculture, mining, and textiles changed with religions after those of hunters, gatherers, and nomads.

cuneiform [kyoo-NEE-a-form] Wedge-shaped writing found on clay tablets in ancient Mesopotamia.

hieroglyphics [HII-er-u-GLIF-iks] A system of writing used in ancient Egypt. Pictorial symbols represented sounds or sounds and meanings.

Worldview

I have developed an outline to help you understand some of the essential components of world religions. In the major religions, most of the topics are addressed in some detail. As you learn this outline of topics under the Worldview heading, you will learn about a particular religion's beliefs and practices. Soon you will able to use this Worldview outline to compare religions for their similarities and differences. When you reach the end of the text, you will find that this distinctive Worldview feature has prepared you to compare all the religions you have studied. As you encounter religions that are new to you, you will be able to analyze them quickly and see how they compare to the established world religions.

A Clay Tablet with Cuneiform Writing. Ancient Mesopotamian city-states recorded their history, beliefs, and laws in writing that later scholars learned to translate into modern languages.

In a Worldview section each religion is examined under several topics. The systematic analysis of a religion helps in understanding its beliefs and practices in their most developed forms. How do the teachings and practices of religion fit together to form a coherent system for its adherents? To an outsider, isolated beliefs and practices may seem puzzling or strange. Within the context of other beliefs and practices as they are understood by adherents, the puzzling aspects may seem completely reasonable. Students attempt to view persons in the universe and in society as the adherents of the religion understand them.

In the next paragraphs you will find many topics that help us understand most people's beliefs. In each religion I will address the most relevant topics; however, seldom will I discuss all topics equally. Taken out of context, beliefs and practices of any people can seem unreasonable; placed within the context of their total belief system, the ideas and actions can make sense.

THE ABSOLUTE

A child may wonder who is in charge of the playground. An adult may ask who is in charge of the world. A scientist may ask what principles govern the universe. Most religions assure us that something or someone *is* in charge.

Most religions have something to say about an Absolute. There is a highest reality that precedes all else, on which everything else is dependent. For many religions the Absolute is a personal God—as in Judaism or Christianity. Sometimes the Absolute is beyond all personality and existence, as Nirguna Brahman is in Hinduism. Sometimes the Absolute is an impersonal Way or Force, as is the Dao in Daoism, a religion of China and Japan. Some religions deny that gods have any role in the most important con-

Archaeologists in Israel. To understand beliefs and practices of earlier cultures, archaeologists painstakingly uncover, catalog, and interpret artifacts.

INTRODUCTION

cerns of humans, as does Jainism, a religion of India. The Buddha, founder of Buddhism, in India, thought he needed no gods in his answer to the problem of life. Confucius, in China, participated in rites for heaven, but he said little about gods. Although each religion has some reality that it considers ultimate, religions do not agree on the nature of the Absolute.

THE WORLD

Each religion's view of the universe is discussed in the section titled "The World." Does the religion look at the universe as friendly or unfriendly, a place that is pleasant for humans or a place of suffering? Should adherents affirm the goodness of life in the universe, or should they seek to escape from its miseries? Is the world created by a beneficent God for the enjoyment of humans, or is it a happenstance that has no design, order, or purpose?

HUMANS

How we think of humans influences our conduct with them. If we consider them only objects, we can exploit them as tools to accomplish our purposes. If we think of them as animals, we have a greater moral responsibility to all other living beings. We should not indiscriminately exploit animals in experiments, manipulate them genetically, enslave them for labor, or exterminate them when they are no longer economically profitable. If humans are different from and more valuable than other animals, more akin to deities, then their thoughts, decisions, desires, purposes, loves, and lives should be respected and conserved.

What, essentially, are human beings? Are they only psychological impressions? Does the human soul endure through eternity individually, or can it be dissolved into a great world soul, an Absolute? Are humans by nature good, bad, or capable of both good and bad? Most religions say that humans have freedom and responsibilities; however, some religions see the range of choices severely restricted either by past events (for example, the fall of Adam and Eve) or by the nature of the Absolute.

THE PROBLEM FOR HUMANS

Many of the largest nations have experienced an increase in violent acts among citizens. Although a few people deny that evil exists anywhere outside our thoughts, most people think that acts or conditions that cause unnecessary human suffering are evil. What is wrong with our world? How did it become this way?

Most religions envision a central problem encountered by all humans. How does the religion conceive of the problem for humans? Judaism and Christianity see the problem as sin. Sin is both individual and corporate and is ingrained in the human species. In Islam, the problem is that humans refuse to submit to God. Hinduism sees the problem as a recurring cycle of rebirths—a soul's continuous return into a series of bodies. All the sufferings of lives in bodies are repeated until the wheel of rebirth is overcome. Buddhism views the problem of life as suffering. Confucianism phrases ignorance of how to live harmoniously with other humans as the problem. The problem is the human failure to live in harmony with nature, according to Daoism. Religions define a central problem in human existence. Having defined the human problem, the religion then offers a way of solving it.

THE SOLUTION FOR HUMANS

Most humans dream of a better life. What would be the ideal life? How would you change the world? Our answers show our understanding of salvation. Can crime be eliminated by schools or prisons? Can it be eliminated only by divine intervention? How much human suffering can be eradicated? Can humans of good will and intelligence solve the problems?

In conjunction with the problem for humans is the solution for humans. In Judaism and in Christianity the solution, salvation, is defined in terms of eradicating sin. Islam defines the solution for humans as submitting to God. Confucianism teaches one to attain harmonious social relationships. Daoism suggests ways for individuals to live in harmony with nature. In the Four Noble Truths, Buddhism gives the solution for suffering. Hinduism describes paths that lead to release from a potentially endless cycle of rebirths.

COMMUNITY AND ETHICS

Advancing technologies have solved some ethical problems and created others. We can feed everybody in the world. Many dreaded diseases, such as smallpox, have been eliminated. Should we, however, use artificial means to limit conceptions or induce abortions? Is voluntary euthanasia ever permissible? Should health care be limited to one's ability to pay for it? Should people of greater ability receive more rewards, or should everyone share equally? Ethical questions are ever before us; religions supply answers.

Most religions advocate participation in a religious community and practice of a code of ethics. Buddhism and Christianity invite people who seek to overcome the central problem of life to join a congregation of believers. In a group, adherents find support for living by ethical principles established by the exemplary teacher of the religion. In Judaism and in Hinduism, religions that humans enter by birth, there are ceremonies marking affirmation of membership in the community. In each religion, adherents accept responsibility for living by moral standards. Without requiring membership in a special group within society, Confucianism teaches ethical principles. Daoism emphasizes individual conduct but avoids social responsibilities. Although Jains support each other in ethical living, adherents must work out their own release from rebirth.

AN INTERPRETATION OF HISTORY

Are we concerned only with our own futures or with those of all humankind? Is the only significant story that of an individual life that appears, grows, and disappears? Or is each life interwoven with others, making each responsible to the creator for its care of others? Do humans move toward a future that can be better or worse? Religions interpret history as they address or avoid these questions. Judaism, for example, describes history from the beginning of God's creation of the world. It foresees a time when all nations will live together in peace and order, conducting life according to humanitarian principles. Christianity envisions a new heaven and a new earth—a perfect community ruled by God. Hinduism describes numerous creations and destructions of the universe, a cycle that repeats as far as can be imagined.

In Christianity, the arrival of a new period of a thousand years increases anxieties and anticipations. If responses to the year 1000 and 1001 C.E. are guides to the future, as this century ends we can expect prophets predicting that the day of judgment is near. Other prophecies will predict either an age of greater suffering or the dawn of better living. Few people accept unexamined events in their lives; most of us want to organize our experiences into a meaningful pattern. Religions often provide such patterns.

RITUALS AND SYMBOLS

The psychiatrist Sigmund Freud and his successors reemphasized what world religions teach: Although humans are sometimes rational creatures, they are more deeply affected by feelings and habits. Holidays, weddings, or commencements stir us deeply. Our memories, fears, desires, and hopes are emotions that matter more than our reasons. We are creatures of rituals and symbols.

Most religions emphasize the importance of rituals and symbols. Adherents must repeat certain actions in order to restore their place in the universe. There are symbols that bring humans into a proper relationship with the Absolute, with themselves, and with the community. Each religion advocates a best way to worship or conduct rituals of life. Each religion has drawings, carvings, music, phrases, or natural objects that have been set apart as sacred. Through these symbols the individual and the community are drawn closer to the Absolute. Although adherents can give rational explanations for their rituals and symbols, those rituals and symbols have meaning that cannot be fully articulated.

LIFE AFTER DEATH

The ultimate question may be "When I die, will I live again?" Most religions answer yes to this question. They differ in what form they think life will take. Atoms continue to exist, but does the mind? Does the soul live on in a new body, outside any body, or in a renewed body? Most religions agree that life before death influences or decides life after death.

Religions offer their adherents explanations of what happens when a human dies. For most religions, the death of a human body is not the end of a person. In ancient Egypt, kings believed that they would live in another land, enjoying their earthly wealth and servants. Hindus hope that their devotion will be rewarded with release from the wheel of rebirth. Some Hindus think that their individual souls will become at one with the Soul of the universe. Many Muslims think of life after death as residing in a pleasant oasis. Confucians and Shintoists, of Japan, think that ancestors who live in heaven are aware of the activities of their descendants on earth.

RELATIONSHIP TO OTHER RELIGIONS

As people of diverse religions meet each other, they wonder how they will relate. People of some religions are accustomed to living in communities with diverse beliefs and practices. They can be open and inviting with peoples of other faiths. Through years of discussions, they understand beliefs and practices of other religions. In India, for example, Hindus, Jains, Sikhs, Muslims, and Christians have lived and worked together for more than a century. They understand each other's preferences and religious responsibilities.

Peoples of some religions share concepts with those of other religions. For example, most Jews and Christians in the United States are aware of their common traditions in the Bible. They are also aware that they differ on whether Jesus is the Christ, or Messiah. In comparison, only a few Jews,

Students at an Urban University. Many institutions attract students of all races from many nations. In these settings, comparing beliefs and practices of world religions can be an informal student activity.

Christians, and Muslims are aware that they share a religious tradition that derives from a common patriarch of faith, Abraham.

In a world where people of different faiths are constantly brought together in business, education, and government, it is helpful to know how peoples of those faiths regard each other. How does one become an adherent of a particular faith? Can peoples of that faith associate freely with peoples of another faith? What are the limitations on social cooperation?

Evidence suggests that many peoples of diverse religions can live and work together peacefully. To understand current events, however, we need to be aware that sometimes religious beliefs are offered as reasons for peoples to punish or exterminate each other. These religious differences can be exploited to keep animosities alive for decades. In the interest of peace and cooperation, it is helpful for us to know where there are grounds for agreement in religions and where, at best, peoples can only agree to disagree.

A POINT OF VIEW

CONSIDER THIS

For each major religion I have suggested a topic that is important in understanding the religion. You can think about these issues in light of your reading in the religion. Although you can form your opinions privately, you may find it helpful to discuss these issues with your classmates and your instructor. As you study the information in the chapter in light of your thoughts on issues in the "Consider This" sections, you will be more likely to make the information your own. The rewards of your course will last longer if you can transfer information from short-term recall to long-term retention.

INTRODUCTION

There are other resources in the text to make learning easier. In the text and the margins are definitions of important terms. A guide to pronunciation can help you use the terms in conversations. If you are studying this text with an instructor, listen to his or her pronunciation of each term. If your instructor is a specialist in a religion, pay particular attention to sounds. Realize that among adherents of any religion pronunciations of the same term may differ. Do try to pronounce words aloud, for speaking the terms will help you remember them.

Time lines, maps, and pictures supplement words of text. At the end of each chapter, there are terms for building vocabulary of world religions, questions for review, and questions for discussion. At the end of each chapter are notes and readings to assist students who want to read more deeply about subjects that have been introduced. The readings are divided into a short, annotated bibliography and a longer list of books and articles that can assist in research and reports. A glossary is provided for a quick reference to meanings of terms that have appeared in the text, in margins, and in the vocabulary lists. The index guides readers to pages where each subject is discussed. Readers who use these resources often should find it easier to understand and retain information in the text.

THE POINT OF VIEW OF THE TEXT

Beginning a study of world religions is easier if you can decide on a point of view. How will you approach each religion studied for the first time? How should you think about the more familiar religions?

Students can approach each religion as objectively as possible, examining the facts that adherents offer to explain their beliefs and practices. They can seek to understand the values that adherents place on facts. Although the attempt in this text has been to refrain from expressing judgments about a religion, on a particular concept or practice one religion is often compared with another. There are no conclusions regarding which religion is better or worse, worst or best. The reader may consider and then draw or avoid drawing any conclusions about the truths or values of a religion.

The objective approach, however, involves empathy. Without taking sides or being overcome with emotions, students can understand the emotions of adherents. Adherents present their feelings and interpretations of their religion. The meaning that they find in their faith can sometimes be expressed in scriptures, stories, commentaries, actions, and explanations. Many quotations express in adherents' own terms the meaning of their faith for them.

Readers who participate emotionally in what they read will find religions as fascinating as the world that contains them. World travelers discover, nevertheless, that no matter how wonderful the scenery is, they cannot comprehend everything at once. The world must be explored a day at a time, with rest and reflection between days. Seen in stages, the world keeps the traveler looking forward to each new day. Students, also, find that world religions are best studied a day at a time. Time is required to read carefully the new information that is provided. Almost as important, students need time to assimilate and reflect on what they have read.

I hope that the text will awaken in you an interest in world religions that will reward you throughout the course. More important, I hope that you will discover an exciting area of learning to explore for a lifetime.

At this point, you will find it helpful to consider some of the meanings of the term *religion*. The "Consider This" section will discuss some types of definition of religion.

Students Visit a Temple in Bangkok, Thailand. The Buddhist temples in Thailand are so beautiful and so numerous that a traveler would need many days to visit and appreciate all of them.

CONSIDER THIS: DEFINITIONS OF RELIGION

As you study world religions, you may think about finding a good definition of religion. You may be surprised that few scholars agree on any "essential" definition of religion. There are a few types of definition to examine before you decide which one seems to work best in your experience. Unlike *essential* definitions, *normative* definitions attempt to describe what a religion "ought" to be. *Functional* definitions describe how religions "work" in individuals and society. *Descriptive* definitions "describe" a particular religion or several religions.

Each kind of definition has been supported by good scholars. Although in Hinduism the Bhagavad Gita accepts various paths of salvation, the way of salvation through love of the Lord is offered as the highest form. For some people this love of the lord is a *normative* standard. Psychologist of religion Walter H. Clark attempted to describe what happens most of the time when a person is religious; he offered an *essential* definition. Sociologists of religion such as Thomas Luckmann, Peter Berger, Clifford Geertz, and Emile Durkheim have preferred *functional* definitions of how religion works in society. Paul Tillich, theologian; William James, psychologist, and Sigmund Freud, psychotherapist; defined religion as it is *experienced* in individuals.

As you develop your own understanding of the basic ingredients of religions, you will form opinions of how they affect individuals and societies. From time to time you can attempt to state a definition that expresses what you have learned. Exchange opinions with your fellow students and with your instructor. When you reach the end of this text, perhaps you will have developed a definition that not only satisfies you but is shared by other members of your class.

☞ VOCABULARY

cuneiform [kyoo-NEE-a-form]
epic [EP-ic]
hieroglyphics
   [HII-er-u-GLIF-iks]

myth [MITH]
profane [proh-FANE]
rites of passage [riits-ov-PAS-ij]
rituals [RICH-oo-als]

sacred [SAY-crid]
scriptures [SKRIP-churs]
secular [SEK-u-lur]

☞ NOTES

1. David Carrasco, "Aztec Religion," in *The Encyclopedia of Religion*, vol. 2, ed. Mircea Eliade (New York: Macmillan, 1987), pp. 23–29.

2. Robert A Segal, *Joseph Campbell: An Introduction* (New York: Garland, 1987), pp. 31–32.

3. Isak Dinesen, *Out of Africa* (New York: Random House, 1985), pp. 128–130.

☞ READINGS

Berger, Peter L., and Thomas Luckmann. *The Social Construction of Reality*. Garden City, NY: Doubleday, 1966.

Eliade, Mircea. *A History of Religious Ideas*. Chicago: University of Chicago Press, 1978.

————. *The Sacred and the Profane*, trans. Willard Trask. New York: Harcourt, Brace, and World, 1959.

Eliade, Mircea, and Joseph M. Kitagawa. *The History of Religions: Essays in Methodology*. Chicago: University of Chicago Press, 1959.

Geertz, Clifford. *The Religion of Java*. New York: Free Press, 1960.

Smith, Wilfred Cantwell. *Towards a World Theology*. Philadelphia: Westminster Press, 1981.

Tillich, Paul. *What Is Religion?* ed. James Luther Adams. New York: Harper & Row, 1969.

Tyler, Edward B. *Primitive Cultures*. New York: Gordon Press, 1974.

Wulff, David M. *Psychology of Religion*. New York: Wiley, 1991.

Yinger, J. Milton. *The Scientific Study of Religion*. New York: Macmillian, 1970.

Religions of Tribes and City-States

Chapter 1 RELIGIONS OF THE AMERICAS

Chapter 2 RELIGIONS OF AFRICA

In the first part of our study, we look at some interesting places of the Americas and Africa to encounter exciting peoples whose practices of religion may, at first, seem mysterious or frightening. From groups of two or three families living within the Arctic Circle, to the vast nations of the Plains Indians, to the cities of the Andes, to the highly civilized Egyptians in northern Africa to peoples of sub-Sahara Africa we encounter people whose handling of the hidden forces of universe seem far removed from the established rituals of world faiths today. Yet in the elaborate ceremonies of the Incas and in the divination of the Yoruba babalawo (see definition on page 20), we find essential elements that are present in the most sophisticated beliefs of our contemporary society. With a few exceptions, we look primarily at peoples whose names and practices have not been widely known in text or film.

Personalities of charismatic people draw us to their faiths and entice us to appreciate their ways of seeing and responding to the awesome forces of nature and secret ways of human minds and hearts. Tutankhamen of Egypt and Powhatan of Virginia are familiar names, but the Naskapi hunters, the kachina dancers, the Yoruba practitioner of Ifa divination may provide us deeper insight into why ordinary humans practice their religions.

Our story of world religions begins with peoples whose religions have been overshadowed by major world religions, it introduces us to some of the essential religious experiences that endured and entered more dominant religions. Although it would be desirable to have written accounts of practices of peoples prior to the arrival of Europeans, we are dependent on these early explorers and settlers whose views were biased by their own religions. Later methodologies in archaeology, sociology, and anthropology can inform us about earlier stages of religion and correct some misinformation of the earlier writers, but impressions of earliest visitors from the outside are still valuable. Using more recent methods of scholarship, later insiders and visitors alike have corrected earlier misunderstandings and supplied a background of wider meaning not available to outside observers or to devoted members of particular groups.

Religions of the Americas

Mexican Feast Costume. In Huachinago, Mexico, this man dressed as a bird celebrates a feast.

---

babalawo [bah-BAH-lah-wu]
The one who practices Yoruba, Ifa divination.

Introduction

More than most areas on earth, the Americas have been seed beds for wide varieties of religions. Their seminal forms have arrived on wind and tide from around the globe, germinated, put down roots, and flowered with variegated blossoms. Each has contributed to the beauty and fragrance of religions in the Americas. One shrub, or young tree, grew so quickly that is sometimes threatened the health of others. Christianity, in the Americas, has extended its roots and branches widely, tempting some observers to oversimplify, writing that the Americas are Christian. More careful observation reveals that even among the nominal Christians there are people who practice the rituals and share the concepts of the Native Americans. In this chapter we will look at some of these non-Christian beliefs and practices.

In exploring Native American beliefs, we enter a world far removed from the Internet, chips, screens, and binary languages that comprise the mysteries of the twenty-first century. From miniaturization we turn to the world of big sky, big seas, big ice, big mountains, and big threats to human life. In this different world, human intuition, seasoned by long traditions of each people, actively tests forces of nature, the spirits in animals of earth, sky, and sea; these forces measure resources within the human spirit to survive and endure.

In this world of encounter between big world and small people, we are rewarded with designs that flow from dreams, totems that represent peoples, wrapped dried bodies of human leaders, myths of creation of the world and humans, and masks of kachina dancers. No less than the early conquistadores we are terror-struck by Aztec rituals to replenish the life-giving sun and greed-struck by the hoards of gold reflecting the brilliance of the sun. Curiosity moves us to explore why prior Americans fashioned these particular forms of ordering their lives. We begin to discover not only answers about them but also about our own needs and how religions offer to satisfy them.

Although we will describe practices of Native Americans before they were significantly changed by their encounters with Europeans, we remember that many of these American groups are among us today. Since their encounters with invaders of their lands, they have continued to adjust and compromise with outside challenges. Some Native Americans live successfully in their own communities, still observing many of the traditions of their ancestors. Others are active leaders in Christianity. Many are very much part of the business, professional, and political life of their nation. Occasionally they may choose to preserve their traditions by gathering with their families and tribes to observe the old ways. Increasingly, many non-Native Americans are impressed with the older traditions that bring rewards of spiritual living.

RELIGIONS OF NORTH AMERICA

The Naskapi

The Naskapi home, the land between Hudson Bay and the Atlantic Ocean, was once known as the Labrador peninsula. In summer it is a picturesque composition of open sky, impressive forests, and beautiful lakes. In winter it is almost as forbidding as the Arctic itself. Except for a few weeks in summer, the subarctic climate challenges the survival of any humans who must live off the land. Although the eastern shore is in Newfoundland, most of the Naskapi territory lies in Canada's province of Quebec. The Montagnais-Naskapi have shared the area with the Eskimo.

The account of the religion of the Naskapi Indians is based on a study published by anthropologist Frank G. Speck in 1935. According to scholar J. E. Michael Kew, Speck's methods are up-to-date, and his information remains valuable.[1] Many changes since 1935 have modernized the area where the Naskapi live, so the study helps us understand the lifestyle of a nonliterate hunting people before their means of economic support was altered. The strength of Speck's study lies in his listening carefully and recording accurately the information offered by the Naskapi, who were his hosts.

As a hunting people seeking survival in a very cold environment, the Naskapi spent most of their time in isolated groups of two or three families. Only in summer when food was plentiful did families camp together in small communities. Their portable homes were wigwams, wooden poles covered by skins. They moved about their territory in pursuit of the wild game on which their survival depended. Of special importance to the Naskapi were the caribou, the bear, and the beaver. Of lesser importance were fish and birds.

Although Speck discovered that the Naskapi knew of Christianity to the extent that they could participate in Christian rituals with Christian missionaries, they had their own vital religion that was an essential part of

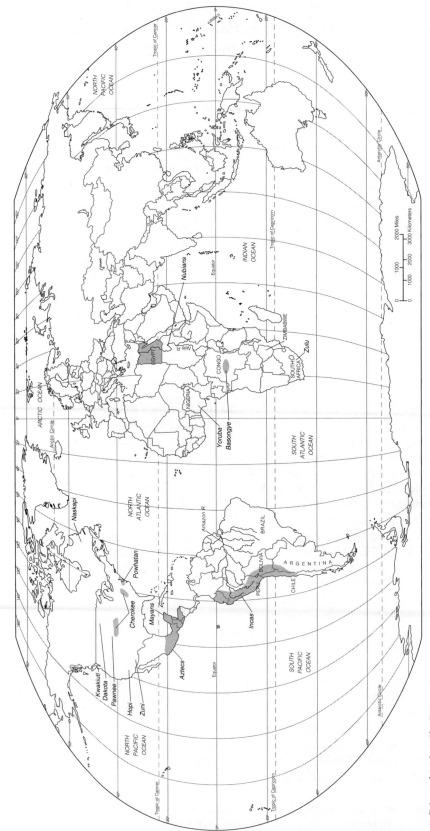

Religions of Ancient City-States.

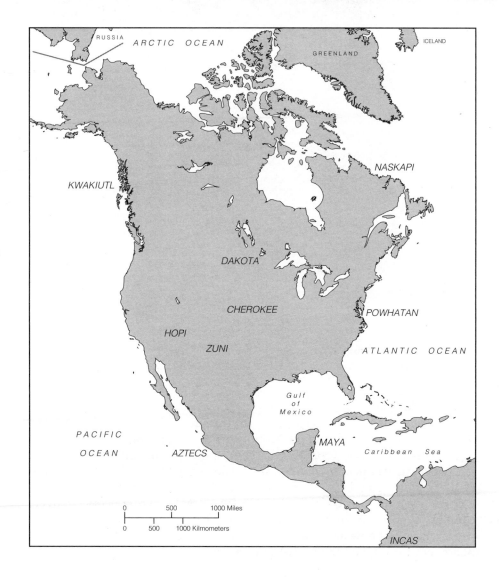

RUSSIA ARCTIC OCEAN   ICELAND
GREENLAND

NASKAPI

KWAKIUTL

DAKOTA

CHEROKEE   POWHATAN

HOPI

ZUNI   ATLANTIC OCEAN

Gulf
of
Mexico

PACIFIC

OCEAN   AZTECS   MAYA   Caribbean Sea

0   500   1000 Miles

0   500   1000 Kilmometers

INCAS

Selected Native Peoples of the Americas.

their hunting and fishing. In summer, when they gathered near larger communities, they participated for a few weeks in Christianity. Speck found they had little interest in the Christian deity or creeds; they were much more concerned with understanding souls—their own and those of the animals who kept them alive. The major problem of the Naskapi was to find enough food to stay alive; their ancient religion—not Christianity—helped them meet and overcome that problem.

THE SOUL

For the Naskapi, the whole world is filled with soul, **Mantu.** The physical world is real, but just as real are the souls that animate it. Stars, trees, wind, thunder, fish, birds, animals, and humans are all activated by souls. Knowing how to influence souls in their favor is essential to the survival of individuals and families. Individuals must be on friendly terms with all souls, their own and those of all other beings. Offended souls can withdraw their support, leaving hunters open to weakness, illness, and death. A **shaman,** a person who knows how to control souls, is as important to the Naskapi

Mantu [MAHN-too]
Among the Naskapi, the soul of nature, animals, and humans. The soul of a person is referred to as the "Great Man."

shaman [SHAH-man]
A Siberian term for people who have been initiated in rituals that enable them to control spirits. Shamanlike men were found among Indians of North America. In Asia, some shamans were women. Today, the term is applied to persons of many cultures.

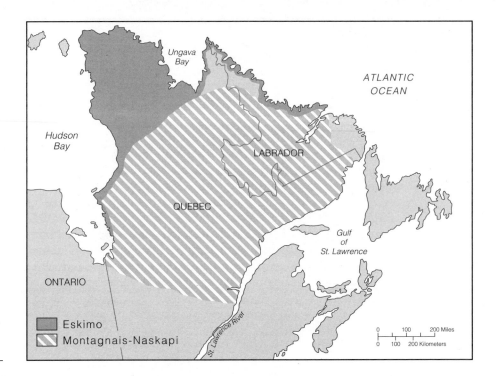

Area of Naskapi Inhabitation. The Naskapis' territory was so far north that for most of the year survival was their central problem.

Legend:
- Eskimo
- Montagnais-Naskapi

Map labels: Ungava Bay, ATLANTIC OCEAN, Hudson Bay, LABRADOR, QUEBEC, Gulf of St. Lawrence, ONTARIO, St. Lawrence River

Scale: 0 100 200 Miles / 0 100 200 Kilometers

Mista'peo [mis-TAH-pe-oh]
Among the Naskapi, the Great Man—an individual's soul that lives in the heart; it is a person's essential self. It reveals itself in dreams.

Tsaka'bec [tsah-KAH-bec]
Among the Naskapi, a hero figure. He was a trickster who altered the natural world. He exhibited a craftiness admired by the Naskapi.

trickster [TRIK-stur]
A male character found among stories of North American Indians. Although the trickster was not the creator, he audaciously performed deeds that altered creation. He represents the canniness admired by nonliterate peoples.

reincarnation
[REE-in-cahr-NAY-shun]
A belief, widely shared among world religions, that a soul that has departed a body can, after a period of respite, return in the body of a newborn child.

survival as a chemist or a physicist is for the survival of industrial peoples. All successful Naskapi hunters study ways of influencing souls.

The Naskapi primary contact with soul is through the soul of the individual person, **Mista'peo,** the Great Man.[2] The Great Man is the active, living soul of each person. Located in the heart, it is the essential person. Individuals can meet the Great Man in their dreams. Besides aiding people in overcoming the souls of hunted animals, the Great Man also assists them in becoming moral and helpful. At times, the Naskapi can smoke, drink, and dance, not to entertain themselves, but to reward the Great Man in them.

THE UNIVERSE

The Naskapi explain their views of the universe by reciting myths. In their myths, the earth is depicted as a hill floating above water. There is no story of its genesis. A central figure in the myths is **Tsaka'bec,** a human personage endowed with the cleverness and altruistic spiritual powers valued by the Naskapi.[3] He was able to snare the sun and the moon; he became the man in the moon after getting into it. This type of figure, a **trickster,** appears in stories of other nonliterate peoples. The souls of all persons, between the times when they reside in bodies, live among the stars. This concept of **reincarnation,** souls returning to life in another body, is found in religions of both nonliterate peoples and literate peoples, particularly in Hinduism. The four winds, rainbows, the aurora borealis, and the Milky Way are incorporated into the mythology of departed ancestors.

Recognizing that soul is the absolute of the Naskapi universe leads to an understanding of the essential nature of the universe and humans. Knowing how to live with souls is fundamental to survival, the essential problem for the inhabitants of subarctic regions. Accidents, exposure, illness, and

Naskapi Indians. These inhabitants of the Labrador peninsula lived in wigwams. They rewarded the Great Man in themselves with a pleasant smoke.

starvation are ever-present reminders that life can end at any moment. Only with help from the environment and its inhabitants can a person survive.

THE HUNT

Naskapi perceive a strong presence of grace in the universe. Animals give themselves to the hunters. In return, hunters must express gratitude to the animals by respecting their carcasses and using them in the most economical way. Hunters and fishers revere their environment, knowing that they will starve if they offend the souls that guard the animals and fish. The technical implements and skills of the hunters and fishers are only minor means of their success; the generous souls of the animals and fish are paramount.

As hunters sleep, the souls of animals appear in dreams to show where they can be found and how they can be taken. Through dreams, the Naskapi learn the proper designs to work into their art, the kind of drums to make, the required rhythms to use in beating them, and the right way to dance. The traditions of the people are passed along from fathers to sons and daughters, for women also hunt and fish. But the general wisdom of the group is supplemented by timely information given by souls of game to individuals who will seek and take them for food, clothing, and shelter.

The Naskapi distinguish between appropriate and inappropriate food. In so harsh an environment, the Naskapi think domestic animals and Virginia deer are inappropriate food. The woodland Naskapi avoid the fish and animals of the sea. Freshwater fish are their choice. The caribou is their most important animal, with bear and beaver coming second and third. In hunting, killing, dressing, and consuming these revered animals, rituals are obligatory.

Humans must respect animals, for humans and animals are closely related. The Naskapi believe that animals could once talk. Now animals can communicate with humans only through dreams and signs. The caribou are under the guardianship of Caribou Man, a former hunter devoted to seeing that only the caribou that are needed by hunters are taken from the vast herds that live in a reserve set apart from all humans. Carelessness in hunting, ignoring communications in dreams, or disregarding rituals of handling a caribou carcass will cause Caribou Man to withhold animals from the hunter. The moose fly oversees fishing, hovering over each catch to make sure that fishers do not violate the rituals appropriate for fish.

The ritual surrounding bears demonstrates the relationship of hunter and hunted. In winter, hunters, responding to information in dreams, locate a hibernating bear. Emphasizing their kinship of souls, they call him Grandfather, inviting him to come out for a smoke of tobacco. When the bear emerges, it is killed. But none of the bear bones are broken, and dogs are not allowed to eat them. The hunter carefully follows a ritual for preserving the bear skull. It is painted on the brow, a piece of tobacco is placed in its mouth, and its jaw is fastened shut. The skull is placed on a stick set in the ground, positioned so that the bear can view the scenery and watch its kind pass in their travels. This respectful, friendly treatment of the bear assures hunters that they will receive favors of other bears offering themselves.

By studying animal bones, skilled interpreters can divine the future. Speck carefully observed animal bone interpretations. Although many hunters were capable of reading signs, a shaman could give much more information about them.

OTHER BELIEFS AND RITUALS

Speck did not find among the Naskapi rites of passage, those ceremonies that mark the important stages of life. The few families hunting together were too preoccupied with their survival to engage in initiations of boys into adult hunters. The rituals of adolescence found among other tribes of Algonquian (Algonkian) Indians to the south were missing. Death, however, was treated with reverence. Weather permitting, burial was the preferred means of disposing of a body. An alternative was placing it on a platform. It was positioned a certain way, facing an appropriate scene. The Naskapi believed in reincarnation; good people lived among the stars until they entered a womb again to be reborn.

Although the Naskapi's relationship to other peoples and religions was one of tolerance, Speck found they sought glory in wars. The Naskapi were accepting, in a limited way, of the teachings of Christian missionaries. The Christian religion, however, was for dwellers in herding, agricultural, and manufacturing societies. The religion that was helpful in Naskapi economy—hunting and fishing—was that of their own traditions. Their religion offered survival; moreover, it inspired people to live moral, humane lives. The Naskapi had a reverence for life usually not associated with those who survive only by killing animals.

The Kwakiutl Peoples

The west coast of Canada was home for the often-studied Kwakiutl peoples, famous for their carved **totems,** ancestorlike figures of clans, and their gift-distributing gatherings—**potlatches.** Their land, adjacent to the sea, was forested. The climate, warmed by the sea, produced ample rain for growth of timber. Trees yielded permanent houses, dugout canoes, and totem poles. The sea and rivers produced fish for immediate consumption or preserving against winter hunger. Caribou and bear were plentiful, and diets could be supplemented with seeds, berries, and roots. Agriculture was not necessary.

totem [TOW-tem]
An animal, plant, or object serving as the symbol of a traditional people's clan or tribe.

potlatch [POT-lach]
A practice among Kwakiutl peoples of distributing gifts at ceremonial feasts according to social order.

The Kwakiutl shared with other peoples of the Americas the theme of a keeper of animals and a keeper of fish who must not be offended. Animals and fish allowed themselves to be caught. Because hunters and fishers depended on the generosity of animals and fish, they honored their prey. Offending the game could bring about human starvation.

The potlatch custom, where hosts gave away as much wealth as possible, has been subject to different interpretations among anthropologists. The self-sufficient Kwakiutl needed little trade with other peoples. They used their crafts to enrich their own lives. Giving away their possessions not only stimulated production of other goods but also demonstrated social position, wealth, and power. Recipients desired to reaffirm their own positions by redistributing their goods. Giving away goods to demonstrate superior status appeared also in Powhatan's generosity to his English guests in Virginia.

The Powhatan Peoples

In two sources, an earlier book by Ben C. McCrary and a more recent book by Helen C. Rountree, readers are informed about the Powhatan peoples of

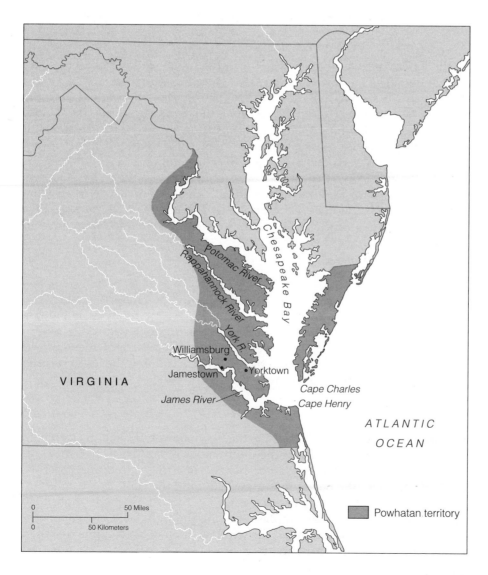

Seventeenth- and Eighteenth-Century Territory of the Powhatans. The settlers of the first permanent English colony intruded on the hunting and agricultural society of the Powhatans.

Virginia as the English settlers found them after 1607.[4] Eyewitness accounts by John Smith, William Strachey, Henry Spelman, and others are supplemented by that of Rev. Samuel Ames, who interviewed in England Uttamatomakkin, an Indian priest sent to represent Powhatan in 1616–1617. Although these accounts are limited in that none of the observers were anthropologists trained in writing objective reports, they do describe the American Indians before they were greatly influenced by Europeans.

The settlers at Jamestown met Algonquian-speaking Indians who were members of tribes dominated by a **mamanatowick,** a "great king" or paramount chief, called Powhatan. He ruled a vast territory of southeastern Virginia through a number of **weroances,** who were commanders, or petty chiefs. Rather than a confederacy, this group of tribes was an empire ruled by Powhatan. He claimed four of every five deer killed by his subjects. All the copper, iron, and useful metals belonged to him. He used this material and the agricultural products grown by forced laborers in his fields to reward his weroances, to buy services of warriors for battles, or to impress his English guests. Most descriptions of Powhatan indicate that although he was sometimes a generous host, he could be temperamental and vengeful.

HUNTING

The Powhatans hunted deer in at least three ways. The most difficult method, perhaps, was that used by the individual bowman stalking a small herd of deer. The bowman would carry a deerskin stuffed to look like a live deer. By skillfully manipulating the head and parts of the stuffed deer, the hunter could imitate a grazing deer. With this disguise, he could get close enough to a grazing herd to take a shot. Hitting a deer, he had to pursue it until it dropped—no matter where it went. An individual hunter might also use a special concoction of smells to attract animals to the range of his bow. In the fall, Powhatan parties surrounded areas four or five miles in circumference with fire, driving animals to a small area where all were killed. Animals were not spared because of their sex or age or saved for reproduction. As a result, many areas were severely depleted not only of deer but also of other animal life.

GATHERING

Gathering took place on land in fresh and salt waters. Berries, nuts, and roots were available for food and medicine. Fish were often taken in ingeniously crafted pens or traps. Shellfish, such as oysters, were gathered for food, ornaments, and cutting implements. These foods supplemented deer and turkey, which were preferred by the Powhatans, and the lesser desired animals that could be trapped by boys.

FARMING

Having entered the agricultural age, the Powhatans burned and cleared, in rough fashion, small fields. In the depressions of soft earth left after tree stumps were removed, they planted maize—or corn—and beans. After the cornstalk formed, the bean vines grew, climbing the stalk. Each stalk produced approximately two ears of corn. The Powhatans made more than one planting, keeping their supplies growing through the frost-free months of the year. Women who tended the gardens often cooked staple dishes of succotash, a mixture of corn and beans.

mamanatowick
[ma-ma-na-TOW-wick]
The supreme king or chief of the Algonquian-speaking peoples of eastern Virginia. Powhatan was the first mamanatowick that the English settlers dealt with at Jamestown.

weroances [WEH-row-ances]
The subchiefs, or commanders, of the Powhatan empire. Female commanders were known as **weroansquas**.

The Powhatans of Virginia (left). The English settlers recorded their impressions of the dress and activities of the Algonquian-speaking peoples of southeastern Virginia. **A Powhatan Village (right).** Corn is growing near the houses. A religious ritual is celebrated near the field.

RELIGION

In the Powhatan way of classifying activities, medicine and religion were grouped together. The same men often practiced in both areas.[5] **Wisakon** was the Powhatan word for medicine and bitter substances that tasted like medicine. As Native Americans found herbs that effected cures for them, they took them to their priests, who kept a supply in the temple. Thus the priests became keepers of the store of knowledge and medicines. Using their knowledge of cures and their rituals of divination, the priests retained a place of superiority in the tribal hierarchy. In addition to using drugs, the priests could perform minor surgery. They also supervised the "sweat house," a kind of sauna, that drove out illness. The user exited the sweat house to take a bath in a cold stream and then covered his or her body with an oil paint prepared for decoration, which also kept away insects and other pests.

Although the Powhatans and whites lived separately, there were some intimate contacts. White male guests of Native American chiefs were entertained

wisakon [WI-sa-kon]
The Powhatan term for medicine and substances tasting like medicine. The priests controlled all medicines of significance.

royally with food, gifts, and female Native Americans to share their beds, in separate quarters, for the night. White guests considered Native Americans promiscuous. Some Native Americans considered these acts ways of removing threats from foreigners and bringing them into the community. The stories of settlers and archaeological study of Native Americans skeletal remains reveal that syphilis was widespread among the Native Americans. As diseases of the whites afflicted the natives, they eagerly sought the sweat baths and medicines of the priests. Epidemics of smallpox more than decimated the Powhatans, for treatments by Powhatan priests were ineffective against diseases introduced by the English.

Each weroance had a loaf-shaped building, about twenty by a hundred feet, that served as a temple. Some temples had a pole carved with deities at each corner. On a platform at the western end of the interior, the Powhatans kept the bodies of their dead weroances. (There were sometimes women rulers; these were known as weroansquas.) Under the platform was a carved figure of the god **Okeus.** Although the Powhatans believed in a good god, **Ahone,** who brought forth the sun and fruits from the earth, they gave most of their attention to a malevolent deity, Okeus, seeking to turn away his wrath. The black figure, sometimes dressed in pearls, wore an angry expression. He was flanked by images of stuffed animals whose traits the Indians wanted to gain. One writer, Beverley, risked his life to study a temple without the Powhatans' knowledge. He reported that the image of Okeus could be manipulated in the dark by priests so that in the dim light ordinary Powhatans perceived the god as living.[6]

The Powhatan priests also practiced divination and magic. Soon after his arrival, the intrepid Capt. John Smith was taken prisoner by a Powhatan hunting party. Afraid that he would be tortured and killed—the way Powhatans disposed of their war prisoners—he was anxious for three days while numerous Native Americans made their magic about him. Their priests practiced divination in his presence to learn whether the English were friends of the Native Americans and what future they would bring.[7] Seven priests participated in the ritual that lasted more than three days. Cornmeal was spread in a circle around Smith. The chief priest counted out kernels of corn and led the other priests in songs and dances. The answer they received was that the English would not harm them. Smith was freed and lived to have many more experiences with the Powhatans.

Although the English were generally skeptical of Native American claims of magic, they occasionally witnessed results that made them believe that the Native Americans were in league with the devil. Native Americans, however, admitted that often their magic did not apply to the English as it did to their enemies among the Native Americans. In addition to all the problems of the Naskapi, the Powhatans had the added problem of surviving attacks from other Native American tribes and the encroachment of English settlers. Wherever they could, the Powhatans used magic to help improve the odds over their enemies.

The Powhatans believed in life after death. Although bodies of ordinary Powhatans were buried, bodies of their weroances were wrapped and dried. Their bones were preserved on platforms in their temples. According to Strachey's account, at death, souls of people of high status journeyed to the west to pleasant fields. Without work they could feast, dance, and live in peace. Eventually they would die there and then enter into a woman's womb on earth to be born again.[8]

The accounts of McCrary and Rountree may seem strange, for there is no evidence that the English Christians took seriously any sustained pro-

Okeus [OH-kee-us]
Among the Powhatans, a god, or group of gods, that caused suffering. His counterpart is the beneficent deity, Ahone.

Ahone [A-hone]
The beneficent deity of the Powhatans, whose powers were of less concern than those of the malevolent Okeus.

CHAPTER ONE

gram to convert the Native Americans. One famous convert, however, was Pocahontas, a daughter of Powhatan. At age twelve, this "playful one," according to John Smith, saved his life by placing her head over his on the killing block when Powhatan was about to bash his skull with a club of stone. During a war between whites and Indians, she was imprisoned on an English ship. While she was on the ship, she fell in love with John Rolfe, an English settler. Although she had married a Powhatan chief at fourteen, Pocahontas converted to Christianity, married Rolfe, and made a trip to England. They had a son, Thomas. Developing smallpox in England, she died before the return voyage.

The early English thought that the Native Americans were so different that they seldom considered them suitable for converting to Christianity. Native Americans seemed utterly cruel. For example, whites had heard stories that the Native Americans initiated their sons into manhood in a ceremony known as the **huskanaw**.[9] The boys were paraded before their families and mourned as if they were dead. Then they were led off into the deep woods. The English, who were not allowed to witness the entire procedure, thought that the boys were actually killed. Further study indicates that they were given drugs to expunge their minds of childhood memories. When, after several weeks, they were released, they returned to the tribe showing no recognition of their fathers and mothers. They were warriors accountable only to the weroance and to Powhatan. Not only did Native Americans deal harshly with their own sons; they tortured their war prisoners to death. From the point of view of the English, the stately ritual of the Church of England hardly seemed compatible with that of the howling, leaping savages.

For their part, the Powhatans did not see anything in the Christian message that replaced the need to appease Okeus. In creation stories there may be some parallels between the Christian God and Ahone, but the Native Americans life of hunting and fighting depended on divination and averting the ill will of Okeus. The whites seldom had enough game or other food; periodically they sought more from the Native Americans. What advantage was there to worshiping the God of the whites?

The Powhatans' animosity for the whites made it difficult for anyone to do missionary work among them. However, over a period of time, the Native Americans did learn many religious concepts from the whites. Rountree thinks that since no flood story was recorded among the Native Americans until the late seventeenth century, they borrowed the story from the whites.[10] Powhatan's death in 1618 did not help communication between whites and Native Americans, for he was succeeded by his vindictive brother Opechancanough. The new chief led a massacre of settlers in 1632 that took a reported 347 lives and brought constant warfare and bitterness on both sides.[11]

We turn now to another Native American people encountered by the colonists as they moved westward in Virginia and North Carolina. Today, Cherokees make their homes in North Carolina and Oklahoma.

The Cherokees

In the beautiful ridge of mountains rising from the Piedmont Plateau of the East Coast of the United States, Europeans found the home of the Cherokees. The Cherokees who lived in western Virginia and the mountains of North Carolina were part of the Iroquois peoples. Cherokees, however, were concentrated in the Appalachian Mountains in western North Carolina and Tennessee. Constant encroachment by new white settlers under-

huskanaw [HUS-ka-now]
The Powhatan rite of passage for adolescent boys. They left their families, "died," and returned as warriors who were under command of their weroances and Powhatan.

Commander in Chief of the Cherokee Nation. This engraving of 1762 is a portrait of Austenaco, a great warrior, in his native clothing.

mined any agreements Indians made with colonists; wars were frequent. No less than the Powhatan group, the Cherokees suffered from smallpox.

Animosity between the whites and the Cherokees expressed itself during the Revolutionary War. The Cherokees took their revenge by fighting on the side of the British against the colonists.

Relationships between whites and Native Americans improved for a short period after the war. Some Christian missionary groups attempted to work among the Cherokees. The United States Congress, in 1792, appropriated funds to teach Cherokee men agriculture and women domestic arts. The Cherokees, in return, formed in 1827 a "nation under God," with a constitution patterned after that of the United States. The friendship of the nations grew.

When gold was discovered on Cherokee lands, friendships were strained. Whites wanted the gold. In order to get it, they pressured the United States government to force the Indians to sell their lands and move. In 1838–1839, government troops organized military escorts and marched the Cherokees, on foot, to the Indian Territories, now Oklahoma. A few Cherokees managed to stay behind; they eventually negotiated a reservation, where many of them live today.[12]

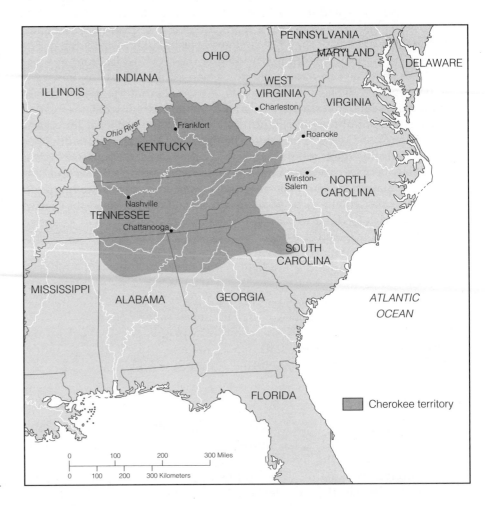

Area of Early Cherokee Habitation. The Cherokees attempted to adjust to white culture, but immigrants coveted the wealthy Cherokee lands.

The Cherokees present a different aspect of Native American life from the Powhatans. Some of their fascinating stories were recorded at the end of the nineteenth century by James Mooney in *Myths of the Cherokee*.[13] Stories of creation were not told by ordinary members of the tribe. Initiates could hear the stories only after participating in a proper ceremony. Keepers of the sacred stories and priests met at night in a low, log house to recite the stories around a fire. Hearers were admitted by appointment for initiation to the **myths.** At daybreak, the party went to a running stream where the hearers stripped themselves and had their skin scraped by a bone-tooth comb held by a priest. While the priest recited prayers, they dipped themselves seven times in the water. The creation stories were part of a ritual of remembrance and new beginnings.

In the story of the creation of the world, there was a great arch; the animals lived above it and below it was water. Because the animals were crowded, they wanted a place to live below the arch. They could find nothing but water. A water beetle darted over the water without finding a place to rest. It dived to the soft bottom of the water and brought up some mud. Now, at the bottom of the sky of stone vault, an island, the earth, floats on the water. It is held up at the cardinal points by cords attached to the sky vault. No one remembers who made or tied the cords. Over time the cords would wear and the island would sink, drowning the people on it.

The sun was placed on a track above the earth but below the sky. Through experimentation, the sun was adjusted for the right heat by running it seven handbreadths high, just under the sky vault. Each day it runs under the arch from east to west; at night it returns on the upper side of the arch to begin again the next day. There is also an underworld, similar to the world above ground, but with different seasons. It can be entered through openings in the earth where waters come out a different temperature from those above the land.

When the animals came to earth they were instructed to keep watch for seven nights. Most animals fell asleep too soon. Only the panther, the owl, and a few more were awake the full period; they can see to hunt at night. The cedar, pine, spruce, holly, and laurel trees stayed awake, so they retain their green and medicinal qualities all year. All other trees lose their "hair" each winter.

A brother and a sister were the first humans. He struck her with a fish; seven days later a child was born. A child was born every seven days until there was a danger of excessive population. Now a child is born only every year.

Fire came to earth when lightning struck a sycamore tree—the fire burned at the base of the hollow trunk. Animals were cold and wanted to reach the fire, but even though they could see its smoke, they could not reach it. The raven tried and failed when its feathers were scorched black. The screech owl tried and failed when its eyes were burned red. The hoot owl and horned owl failed when the smoke blackened rings around their eyes. The black racer snake failed when its body was burned black; its burns cause it to double back on its track. The black water spider with downy hair and red stripes on its body made a bowl of web and carried it on its back. It was able to obtain a small coal from the fire, which it gave to animals and humans. To this day, the water spider keeps its bowl on its back.

myth [MITH]
A story of gods acting in a different time. Creation myths are stories of how the gods acted before humans were created, how they created humans, and how they communicate with humans. The word *myth* in religious studies does not mean untrue.

Dolls. Examples of Native American craftsmanship.

Why do Cherokees have to hunt for game and work in agriculture? Cherokees blame two boys whose curiosity was too much for them. Near Pilot Knob lived a hunter, Kana'ti, and his corn wife, Selu. With their son's help, they captured a wild boy to live with them. But the Wild Boy led the son of Kana'ti to spy on his father. They found that when the father wanted meat, he opened a stone door and took from a cave whatever animal he wanted and then closed the opening. A few days later, the boys, having made arrows, opened the stone gate to try their hand at hunting. Failing to close the door again, they allowed all the game to escape and wander the earth. After that incident, hunting became a more uncertain venture.

The boys then spied on the mother, Selu, when she went to the store-house for corn and beans. She produced corn for the basket by rubbing her stomach and beans by rubbing her armpits. Convinced that Selu was a witch, the boys killed her. Before her death, she had instructed the boys to drag her body seven times in a circle over cleared ground in front of the house. The boys failed to clear all the land; they prepared only seven small spots. That is why corn grows in only a few places. They dragged her body only twice; that is why Native Americans plant only twice a year.

In the beginning of time, animals could talk and lived well. Humans crowded them and made their lives miserable by hunting them. The animals held council to determine measures to protect themselves. Only the ground squirrel spoke well of humans; the others were so angry that they tore the ground squirrel's back—the stripes are there to this day. The other animals devised deadly ailments for humans. The plants, friendly to humans, devised cures for each of the diseases. Weeds, as well as trees, shrubs, and herbs, agreed to help humans—they only have to learn how plants can help.

Cherokees prized the curative role of tobacco, for it was the one plant that served all human needs. The Dagulku geese stole it and carried it far away to the south. The various animals attempted to steal the plant and return it, but each was killed by the geese. At last the hummingbird succeeded; it was so small and fast that it obtained the top leaves and seeds before the Dagulku geese knew what had happened. An old woman who

Navajo Hogan. Navajo peoples of the Southwest sometimes occupy a distinctive house. Herding sheep is one vocation that can be done close to home.

CHAPTER ONE

was nearly dead from lack of tobacco was revived when the hummingbird blew smoke into her nostrils. The Cherokees, as well as the Aztecs and the Incas, who are discussed later in the chapter, had great respect for the amazing little bird.

To stories about the sun, moon, thunder, and stars, the Cherokees add one about the Milky Way. Indians in the South had a corn mill where they ground the corn to powder. Each night someone stole the meal. Keeping watch, the owners discovered a dog eating the meal. They fell upon the animal, whipping it as it ran away. As it ran, it left a trail of meal to the north. That is why the Cherokees call the Milky Way "Where the Dog Ran."

The Cherokees have many stories about how the animals came to be as they are. These stories have lost their sacred character, so they can be told by anyone in the tribe for entertainment. Scholars have discussed whether stories of Native Americans and African Americans developed separately or influenced each other. Cherokees also have some interesting historical accounts of the Native Americans' first encounter with white people, but James Mooney believes these stories have little religious significance.

The Pueblo Peoples

THE ZUNI

The Zuni peoples of the Southwest were studied for about eight years by a shipwrecked Spaniard, Cabeza de Vaca, until his compatriots found him in 1536. Interested primarily in gold, Spaniards such as Coronado launched expeditions to locate the fabled wealth of the Zuni. The Zuni valued not gold but the land to which they had been led. The land, its natural environment, and their cities were treasures to the Zuni. They had wandered far to locate just the right place to practice their rituals according to the summer and winter solstices. The appropriate place was blessed with abundant rains, enabling the Zuni to prosper through agriculture. Their sacred stories spoke of **Awanawilona,** the creator manifested in the sky stretching from horizon to horizon.[14] Because all life was a gift from the creator, the Zuni considered themselves rich.

Awanawilona
[u-WAH-nah-wi-LOW-nu]
The Zuni god of the wide sky.

THE HOPI

Another Pueblo people, the Hopi, lived in houses with many rooms. Underground chambers used for religious rituals, **kivas,** were places where **kachinas** danced. (These traditional figures still appear in ceremonies today.) Kachinas were costumed and masked figures that represented animals, ancestors, or spirits; there were more than five hundred types. Wearing sacred masks, dancers animated them. Uninitiated Hopi were not permitted to see the dancers out of costume; masks were hidden from view when they were not being worn. Until older children were initiated, between ages ten and twelve, everyone impressed on them that the kachinas were gods.

kivas [KEE-vas]
Underground chambers used by the Hopi for religious ceremonies.

kachinas [ka-CHI-nas]
Among the Hopi, masked, costumed dancers that represent gods, ancestors, or spirits.

Kachinas have played a major role in teaching children to obey their parents and to behave according to the preferences of the Pueblo. Wayward children have been disciplined not by their parents but by kachinas who visited their home. Parents have sided with their children to protect them from the kachinas. Together, parents and kachinas have impressed on children the importance of conforming to the rules of Pueblo society.

Two features of North America deeply impressed the first Europeans to see the Great Plains: thousands of acres of grass and millions of buffalo that grazed on them. Many Native American peoples combined farming with hunting buffalo. To them, the earth, the sky, and the animals were manifestations of great spirits. Acquiring Spanish horses, these peoples of the plains were able to travel farther and faster, increasing their take of meat from buffalo. Their spiritual orientation allowed them to take only the animals they needed for food, clothing, shelter, and trade. They were appalled with the Europeans' massive slaughter of these animals only for decorative hides.

The Dakota peoples had no one supreme god, but worshiped a hierarchy of spirits headed by the sun. Sharing equality were sky, earth, and rock. These were the **Wakan tanka,** the sacred ones. Buffalo, bear, the four winds, and the whirlwind were a lower level of spirits.[15]

Pawnee tribes revered the North Star as a good creator god; they feared a magical South Star, symbol of the underworld. The Morning Star led the sun into the sky, but the Evening Star drove the sun down to darkness. Out of their beliefs developed a myth with an impressive ritual.

In the myth the ritual of the Morning Star and the Evening Star Girl was observed every four years. Young warriors began the ritual by kidnaping a maiden from an enemy tribe. Returning with her to their camp, they treated her well for many days. At the appointed time, they brought her into the open, stripped her naked, and painted half her body black and half red, symbolizing the Morning Star and the Evening Star. They tied her high on a scaffold that they had built and then shot her body full of arrows. Her blood, they believed, would renew their past blessings and ensure their well-being in the future.

Our moral standards today urge us to inquire whether this was only a myth or whether the myth was acted out in ritual. Evidence for the practice is sketchy. Discussing human sacrifice among Indians of North America, Harold E. Driver, a scholar who assembled a comprehensive view of many peoples, summarized the subject this way:

> The Pawnee Indians of Nebraska were the only other people north of Mexico to practice human sacrifice. . . . They used to sacrifice a maiden of their own tribe by tying her to a rectangular frame and shooting her with arrows.[16]

If the human sacrifice took place, it was for religious reasons and not cruelty. The interval between sacrifices was four years, indicating that human life was of considerable value to the gods and to tribes.

COMMON FEATURES OF RELIGIONS IN NORTH AMERICA

Assessing and summarizing common features of religions of North America has become more controversial among scholars. In this section, I have listed some of the common features discussed by numerous scholars of Native American religions. More recently, more scholars have arisen to challenge not only earlier conclusions but also assumptions that there ever were common features. Scholars from within Native American traditions have disagreed with views presented by outsiders. After presenting the views of common features, I will conclude the section with some recent objections.

Wakan tanka [WAH-kan-TAHN-ka] Among the Dakota peoples, the collective name of "the sacred ones," a hierarchy of spirits.

CHAPTER ONE

The Absolute

Although many peoples had a chief god, few peoples agreed on the name of that deity. Rather than a god who ruled alone, however, as one finds in **monotheism,** the high god was first among many spirits, an arrangement known as **henotheism.** Cottie Burland's summary of North American Indian mythology provides charts of some of their gods and spirits. The variety of names, characters, and functions is impressive. Correlating names, spirits, functions, and rankings in hierarchy, however, would be a formidable task. Most animals, forces of nature, natural objects, and heavenly bodies can qualify as spirits; different tribes assign the same objects different ranks in their hierarchies. Some of the most impressive spirits combined features of animals and nature. The thunderbird of the Northwest Coast, though mythical, is awe inspiring. The flesh-eating antelope, Delgeth, appears among peoples of the Southwest.[17] Spirits could be good, like Ahone of the Powhatans, or evil, like his counterpart Okeus. A good creator was sometimes offset with an evil twin or brother who deliberately distorted a good creation. The fluid organization of spirits among most peoples reflected the somewhat open organizations of their own tribal hierarchies.

monotheism [MON-u-the-IS-um]
A belief that there is only one deity.

henotheism [HEN-o-thee-ISM]
A belief that one deity is supreme over other deities.

The World

The earth rises above the waters and separates them from the sky, as the Cherokee myth, which is typical, illustrates. The world is not so much a finished creation, fashioned once, long ago; it is a manifestation of active spirits ever involved in its changes. Winds, directions, clouds, seasons, and day and night are signs that spirits participate in changes of the earth.

The story of emergence of humans and animals from a region beneath the earth is a common feature of stories of North American peoples. The Zuni, for example, claim to have emerged from the womb of the earth.[18] Kinship of animals and humans is affirmed in the belief that animals could once talk and that they willingly give themselves to hunters and fishers who treat them well. Plants are cared for by spirits and, properly honored, can provide food and medicine for humans and animals.

Humans

Humans and animals are so closely related that kinships abound. Small groups of tribes have customarily chosen a bird or an animal as their symbol. A buffalo dance of Plains Indians depicts a time when buffalo hunted humans. This theme of role reversal is repeated in stories of various human activities. Although most tribes emphasized that physical strength and endurance are prized, strength of spirit, the highest part of a human, is essential.

The Problem for Humans

Most peoples of North America were well aware that the world could have been designed so that humans would suffer less. As illustrated by the story of the boys who carelessly released the animals from a cave so that they have to be hunted, some problems result from human ignorance or carelessness. The story of infertile soil resulting from boys carelessly dragging the mother on the earth illustrates the failure to follow directions. Other problems can be traced to the impulsive trickster, whose delinquent behavior amused humans but made their lives more difficult. The California peoples referred to the trickster as Coyote; as we have read, the Naskapi called him Tsaka'bec. Acting out rebellious impulses, though temporarily enjoyable, introduces the disorder of an imperfect world.

The Solution for Humans

From the viewpoint of our urban civilizations, lives of North American peoples may seem to have been remarkably free and enjoyable. Survival, however, was seldom easy. Societies were highly traditional, governing all lives with customs and regulations. Violators of prohibitions were severely punished, even to death. Most North American peoples, however, valued both group solidarity and individual insight that contributed to public welfare. The Naskapi hunter's dream was individual, but it contributed to survival of the group. The widespread value of the adolescent's vision quest encouraged individuals to exercise insight and resourcefulness for the good of the tribe. The isolation of the youth in lonely places, restriction of food and drink, and dedicated search for a vision all emphasized individual responsibility within the context of the tribe. Differing from dreams at night, visions revealed a spirit's unique relationship with an individual. Without his own vision, a young man was not ready to contribute to adult society.

Healing has been part of the religion of every people in North America. Physical illness manifested spiritual disorder. Healing required gaining assistance from benevolent spirits, or appeasing vengeful spirits. The old shaman figure of Asia, the person on speaking terms with spirits, occurred often among peoples in the Americas. Lower in the hierarchy, medicine men and women also depended on visions of spirits. Medicine bundles, wrapped objects that appeared ordinary but possessed great powers, were used in many societies. Healing plants were valued by peoples who trusted priests and medicine people to master their uses. Directions for using drugs and diets were given to practitioners through dreams and voices of spirits. In the Southwest, peoples used sand paintings on the earth that could create powerful healing forces in the person who sat in the middle of the painting. Healing and religion were closely related.

Community and Ethics

Individuals and communities had shared responsibilities. The tribe enforced its expectations on all members through custom and rigorous training. Children and youth learned from parents and elders conduct that was expected in the tribe.

Women, no less than men, were indoctrinated in proper conduct. At adolescence, young women learned conduct with men, distinguishing what was prohibited, permitted, or prescribed. Sex outside marriage was usually condemned; only with the husband's approval could a wife have sex with someone else. In the Southwest, women had sex, symbolically at least, with any animal (for food) or human (scalp of enemy) that entered the house. Sex symbolized removing animosity and receiving a foreign object into the family. Illegitimacy was subject to scorn. Abortion was widely practiced on fetuses conceived outside marriage, in time of severe hardship, and when mothers had too many children to raise. Infanticide was practiced for similar reasons; it was considered merciful when an infant was too deformed to participate in the harsh requirements for survival in the tribe.

Killing members of one's own tribe was not permitted, but men were expected to kill enemies of the tribe. Freely wandering tribes maintained their identities through strong traditions. Chiefs could sometimes hold absolute power; more often, they were influenced by the collective will of their peoples.

An Interpretation of History

Recurring times were a common theme among peoples of North America. Sunrise and sunset recurred daily; the four seasons recurred each year. In the western mountains, medicine wheels, large circles of stones on the ground, marked the changing seasons. The myth of the Morning Star–Evening Star ritual of the Pawnees was on a four-year cycle. Recurrence over a period of years was as possible as daily and annual cycles. People and animals recurred on even longer cycles. For North Americans, time was circular.

Rituals and Symbols

Feathers were symbols appearing among all peoples of the Americas. Spirits of birds and humans were similar; perhaps humans envied the ability of birds to soar above the earth. The flights of eagles deeply impressed them. The full headdresses of the Shoshone circled their heads and trailed down their backs. The symbolism was so impressive that many other peoples adopted it. One or two feathers worn in the hair was an almost obligatory symbol.

Among religions of the Americas, rites of passage were particularly important. Birth, puberty, marriage, and death required rituals to ensure good lives and tribal success.

Birth required particular actions both before and after the infant arrived. Pregnant women were segregated from men and sometimes the larger family. Sometimes their cravings for food, thought to be those of the fetus, were indulged; in other groups women ate and drank sparsely until delivery. At birth, special care was taken to keep placentas from animals, and the umbilical cord might be carefully preserved for several months, ensuring the health of the infant. For health, convenience, and safety, children were often wrapped in bundles, sometimes strapped to a board. The mother or a wet nurse was the source of food; in the absence of either, the child usually died.

Puberty was carefully regulated. Because women's blood was considered especially dangerous to men, young women beginning menses were segregated from men. Sometimes they were isolated in separate structures for weeks, fed only by older women. At the end of the initiation some tribes held a festival or dance to celebrate the new life of an adult woman.

Initiation into puberty for boys could be quite harsh. The vision quest could end in injury or death, although supervision usually prevented permanent damage. Among the Sanpoil of eastern Washington State, young men counted on finding spirit-helpers so that they could succeed in society.[19] The severe ordeal of Powhatan youths does not seem to have been typical among peoples of North America.

Marriage customs varied widely, but some stories testify to romantic love as well as marriages for wealth or power. Monogamy was usual. In difficult circumstances, one woman might serve as wife for more than one man, usually among brothers. Husbands and wives had essential, if differing, roles. Men ruled the hunts, but women dressed game, preserved and cooked meat, and made clothes. Men fought wars. Women raised children, kept gardens, and cooked. Among the Pueblos the wife ruled the rooms inside the dwelling; she could order her husband to get out.

Death rites varied by region. Funerals were normal, followed by a period of mourning for weeks or months. Bodies were honored a few days and then disposed of according to tribal custom. Cremation was practiced, but it was not widespread. Burial could be alone; or among tribes in middle America, it could be in large mounds containing dozens of bodies. A few tribes preserved bodies by drying them. Bones of chiefs and medicine men could be kept for inclusion in medicine bundles.

Life After Death

Belief in reincarnation was widespread; the soul of the departed would be reborn as a child within the tribe. Transmigration of the soul to inhabit the body of an animal was a less common belief. The cycles of souls were not immediate or automatic, for a soul could enjoy an indefinite stay in a pleasant hunting ground.

Although living and dead were deliberately separated, ancestors were remembered and honored. Often the home of the deceased was disassembled and a new residence was fashioned for the survivors. As far as scholars have been able to tell, the peoples of North America considered death a mystery; few of them attempted to work out in detail exactly what happened to the soul of the departed.

Relationship with Other Religions

Because Native American peoples had distinctive beliefs, they expected other peoples to differ from them. Peoples practiced their own religions; all shared a belief in spirits, souls, and the value of rituals. Although many peoples of North America have affiliated with Christian groups, many continue to preserve their own traditional worship. The Native American Church, which has been granted legal use of peyote in worship, is a notable example of preservation of traditional worship.

Both Catholic and Protestant groups have benefited from converts among the peoples of North America. Not only have men, women, and children participated enthusiastically in Christian congregations, but many have become leading priests and pastors.

Objections to Older Scholarship

Some of the conclusions of older scholarship have been considered distorted or in error. One objection is to the belief that the religions were henotheistic, that is, worshipers of a "high god." The terms *good* and *evil* have been considered to be derived from "Christian" points of interpretation. Women are said to have had a much larger role in government than hithertofore and were not regarded as sometimes evil. Women also participated in vision quests. Finally, these cultures were not totalitarian, enforcing group will against individual freedom.

With new generations of scholars, particularly among Native Americans, new ways of understanding early traditions are being presented. This excising progress in scholarship has many rewards for inquiring readers.

RELIGIONS OF MESOAMERICA AND SOUTH AMERICA

The Spanish explorers were impressed with the highly developed civilizations in Mesoamerica and South America. Instead of mobile tribes numbering a few hundred, they found that whole peoples numbering thousands lived in well-designed cities. Towering pyramids were notable landmarks in these cities. Chiefs and priests communicated with gods and ruled the peoples of the cities. The surrounding countryside was highly developed in agriculture, providing support for inhabitants of the city. The city-state civilization represented the successful organizations found earlier in Mesopotamia, Egypt, and Greece. Explorers have been so impressed with similarities that occasionally someone attempts to prove conclusively that peoples of the Mediterranean area sailed west and settled in the Americas.

The Aztecs

Like the Mesopotamians, the Aztecs were builders of stone-covered mounds. In the central plaza of their major city, **Tenochtitlán,** which was built on one island in a lake, were pyramid-shaped structures, topped by temples to Aztec gods. Their chief deity was **Huitzilopochtli,** god of the sun.

When Spanish explorers first encountered Aztecs, they were appalled at their rituals of human sacrifice. We should not assume, however, that the Aztecs of that particular period of history were typical of Mesoamerican peoples or even of Aztecs. Some scholars think that large-scale practice of human sacrifice occurred in a period of only a century and a half. For most of history, Aztecs were, like their neighbors the Mayans, dedicated farmers of maize (corn), beans, squash, and other vegetables. Animal sacrifices, where practiced, excluded human victims.

Tenochtitlán [TEN-ok-TIT-lan]
The Aztec island city on Lake Texcoco. Hernando Cortez called it the Venice of the New World. It was the site of the major temple to the Aztec god Huitzilopochtli.

Huitzilopochtli
[HWEET-zi-low-POK-tli]
The chief god of the Aztecs. He was god of the sun who led his people, the Aztecs, to their home in Tenochtitlán.

The Mesoamerican Home of Aztecs and Mayans. Devotion to the sun was practiced by pyramid builders in Mesoamerica.

Precursors of the Aztecs were the Chichimec, who migrated in the thirteenth century. The Aztecs had a story that they once lived in caves far from their city on the lake. They journeyed from the northwest to the site of Tenochtitlán. The Aztec ancestors endured a long ordeal of travel, rejection and oppression from more powerful tribes already settled, and a struggle to make their home in the swampy area of Lake Texcoco. There they built a number of cities, Tenochtitlán being the most famous. Scholars date the settlement of Tenochtitlán at 1325 C.E. Scholars believe that between 1300 C.E. and 1521, all main roads led to the center of the Aztec capital. Because it had numerous canals in addition to its roads, Cortez called it the Venice of the New World. Its defenses relied on water and causeways with drawbridges.

From the writings of the early Spanish explorers and the studies of modern scholars, we have developed an understanding of the Aztec religion.

THE ABSOLUTE

The chief of the several gods of the Aztecs was Huitzilopochtli. Represented as a sacred bundle of potent symbols, he had led the Mexica, a branch of the Chichimec group that became the Aztecs, from Aztlan, their homeland, to the place where they built his shrine at the center of Tenochtitlán. In Aztec accounts, Huitzilopochtli was born miraculously from his mother, Coatlicue, on Coatepec (serpent mountain), near Tula.[20] Four hundred siblings, enraged at Coatlicue's pregnancy and birthing, attacked her. Huitzilopochtli was born armed with a magic weapon, "a fire serpent," with which he killed the siblings. Some scholars think that the story describes the sun conquering the moon and the stars. Huitzilopochtli was the god of war and the sun. He was considered leader of the Aztecs, who viewed themselves as the "chosen people." His symbol was the eagle, king of the birds. The Spanish learned that the symbol of the god was a wooden figure of a man sitting on a blue bench, heaven. His crown was of hummingbird feathers, and he was clothed in garments of feathers.[21] He was the lord of fertility and the regeneration of agriculture. In his holy place, a curtain separated him from the people who came to worship. Adjacent to his court was a room for the god **Tlaloc,** who was the original source of waters and vegetation. The rooms of these idols were at the top of a pyramid, which was reached by a climb of 120 steps. The sacred temple was set apart by a stone wall resembling serpents. The temple platform was flanked by row upon row of human skulls held in place by a rod running through their temples.

Female fertility deities were the mother goddesses. They were sources of abundant powers of earth, women, and fertility. One goddess (Tlazolteotl) was in charge of sexual powers and transgressions. Another goddess (Xochiquetzal), the nubile maiden of love, was goddess of pleasure. A third goddess (Coatlicue), "serpent skirt," both conceived stellar beings and devoured all beings in her repulsive form. Her statue was studded with sacrificial body parts and snake heads.

RITUALS AND SYMBOLS

The function of the Aztec temple is demonstrated in an event of 1487, when Ahuitzotl celebrated a military victory and dedicated the Great Temple. National leaders were invited guests, and lesser leaders were required to bring sacrificial victims for the service. Captives numbering in the thousands (perhaps an exaggeration) were lined up along the roadways for sacrifice to the god. Rulers and priests participated in slashing open the

Tlaloc [TLAH-loc]
The Aztec god of earth and rain.

prisoners' chests and ripping out their beating hearts to throw against the god of the Great Temple.[22] The Aztecs believed that human sacrifices, which furnished ample human blood, were necessary to nourish the sun, which was personified in **Tonatiuh.**

During the Flowery Wars of 1450–1519, the Aztecs perpetrated many attacks on their neighbors. Their purpose was to keep their warriors in training and to provide enough human flesh and blood to keep strong the source of all life, the sun. Tenochtitlán had eighty ritual temples and skull racks. After their hearts—"precious eagle cactus fruits"—were offered to the deity, victims were prepared for cooking and eating. Facial skin, with beard intact, was often flayed off victims and preserved like glove leather.

In the Toxcotl festival, the most admired warrior captured from the enemy was set apart for a privileged existence in the capital. In the last twenty days of his life, he enjoyed four wives. At the end of that time, he voluntarily ascended the steps to be sacrificed to **Tezcatlipoca.**

This bloodthirsty period of Aztec history is well attested, but it is inaccurate to think that these extreme practices were typical of the traditions of Mexican peoples, even Aztecs. Their practice of city-state religion focused on the forces necessary for agriculture: sun, soil, rain, and seasonal growth. The concept of nourishing the sun with blood drawn from hearts of human victims was an extreme concern to obtain favor from the sun.

WORLDVIEW

The Stone of the Sun, a flat stone twelve feet in diameter and approaching twenty-six tons in weight, rested at the top of the temple of Huitzilopochtli.[23] Symbolizing the Aztec cosmos, it was dedicated to the sun god, Tonatiuh,

Tonatiuh [TOE-na-TI-uh]
An Aztec sun god.

Tezcatlipoca [tez-CAT-li-POH-ca]
The Aztec lord of the night sky.

Aztec Calendar Stone. The Aztecs related themselves to ages of the sun. Their sacrifices supported continuation of the life-giving sun.

Quetzalcoatl [KWEET-zal-coatl]
The Aztec god known as the Plumed Serpent. He was god of civilization, teacher of the arts and priestcraft.

whose face is in its center. On the side are claws clutching human hearts for the sun god. There are symbols for the twenty-day calendar, the four creations and destructions of the world, and the struggle between **Quetzalcoatl,** the Plumed Serpent, and Tezcatlipoca, the Lord of the Night Sky. The people from the four destructions were transformed into jaguars, monkeys, fish, and birds. The sun of the fifth world is the Aztec sun. The world is not a permanent creation; it must be kept alive through great effort. The gods could be persuaded to keep the fifth sun alive only as long as the Aztecs kept them sufficiently supplied with the blood they demanded. Aztec life, indeed, all human life, depended on their dutiful conquest and sacrifice of slaves.

The Aztecs were not the only ones practicing human sacrifice when the Spanish explorers arrived in Mexico. When the Christian missionaries encountered them, the Maya of the Yucatan peninsula in Mexico were sacrificing humans. Although their early centuries were spent worshiping rather peaceful deities, Mayans reported to the Spaniards that they began to practice sacrifice to idols on orders of a captain called Quetzalcoatl. S. G. Morely, a scholar of the Mayans, concludes,

> In view of such evidence, documentary as well as archeological, there is little doubt that the sanguinary character of Maya religion as found by the Spaniards in the early sixteenth century was due chiefly to Mexican influence and was introduced into Yucatan by the Mexican invaders of the tenth century.[24]

The Aztec religion, then, was not so different from other religions of Mesoamerica in its use of sacrifice, including human, to keep the sun shining and civilization blooming. What was different was the extent to which human sacrifice and cannibalism were practiced in preference to that of other animals. In Aztec myth, the gods had sacrificed themselves to restore a revolving sun to the world. Mass sacrifice energizes the sun. Humans could do no less than the gods.[25]

THE INFLUENCE OF AZTEC RELIGION

The fall of the Aztec kingdom was due in part to their religion. In 1519, Montezuma, the Aztec king, welcomed Hernando Cortez (1485–1547), thinking he was the Plumed Serpent from beyond the sea who had returned to his people. The Plumed Serpent, who represented civilization as teacher of the arts and priestly learning, was usually a beneficent deity. When Cortez made Montezuma his prisoner, the Aztecs knew that Cortez was not their benefactor.

Archaeologists have devoted careful study to Aztec and Mayan religions. For many civilized peoples, however, the Aztecs' human sacrifices cast a shadow over their achievements in cosmology and architecture.

The Incas

The Incas of Peru made a lasting impression on the Spanish explorers who reached them in 1532 C.E. The personal secretary of Francisco Pizarro (1475–1541), Pedro Sancho de la Hoz, compared Cuzco, the capital of the Inca empire, to a Spanish city.[26] Streets were laid out at right angles, and the stonework of buildings was so closely fitted without mortar that a knife blade would not fit between stones.

Francisco Pizarro invaded Cajamarca, killed the followers of Atahualpa, their emperor, and made him a prisoner. In ransom for Atahualpa, the

The Empire of the Incas. The impressive mountains of South America were significant in the religion of the earthly representatives of the sun, the Incas.

Incas filled a room in the palace to the height of a man with gold and silver. Pizarro took the precious metals, but he strangled Atahualpa.

Located in central Peru, the Inca empire stretched 2,500 miles north and south into Ecuador and Chile. Their heart of the empire was located in the Andes mountains, but it was connected with the extremities by a system of paved roads not only in the mountains but also along the coast. The highway system has been admired by all who have studied it. In 1548, a young soldier, Pedro Cieza de Leon, wrote glowingly of the stone-paved highway as the longest, grandest highway in the world.[27]

HISTORICAL DEVELOPMENT

The religion of the Incas inspired their building of Cuzco and their expansion of empire. They were their god's people, called to rule the world. Like the Egyptians, the Incas worshiped the sun; the chief Inca was his representative on earth. The stone structures of Cuzco built by each succeeding emperor were their homes in life, their homes and tombs in death, and the places where they would return to life. The Coricancha, the great Temple of the Sun at Cuzco, was guarded by two golden pumas, and the walls were covered with gold and silver plaques. Statues of cosmic beings and the mummies of earlier kings and queens were housed in its halls.

THE ABSOLUTE

The Inca empire reached its height only shortly before the Spanish arrived. The tribes that initiated it may have begun two thousand years earlier; they had stories of having begun in caves and wandered, with the guidance of their god, to the sacred place where they were directed to build Cuzco among sacred streams of the Andes. Their god at that time, about 1200 C.E., was **Inti,** symbolized by a fetish (perhaps a dried hummingbird) in a closely woven basket. He was carried by priests who interpreted his directions. By the time of Atahualpa's reign, Inti had been superseded by **Viracocha,** the creator and sustainer, a more appropriate symbol for the emperor and lords who ruled the peoples of a world empire. The emperor Huascar had a gold image fashioned and named it Viracocha-Inti.[28] In older times, Incas thought that each tribe had been created by its patron god. Viracocha, originally a tribal god, was elevated to a larger office. He was associated with the water and foam of Lake Titicaca. Huari Viracocha created all gods and cosmic functions.

Closer manifestations of the holy were the **huacas,** unusual appearances in stones, plants, animals, or people. They were holy in their ability to communicate as well as appearance, for they spoke to humans who could interpret them. Another example of *huaca* was a stone place of divine appearances and sacrifices. Stars and constellations of the night sky are other examples; the Southern Cross was a llama spirit, and Sirius was a jaguar. Cuzco, the city, was also *huaca,* making holy those selected to live there. Sorcerers practiced magic, and priests had minor roles. Incas thought that the only proper person to approach the gods was the emperor.

The Incas also worshiped the earth mother, who was, for them, the peaks of the Andes. In her place of worship, Machu Picchu, emperors built houses and, after they died, stayed on as mummies. Their attendants were celibate women who served food and drink to the mother and to the mummified emperors, who were treated as if they were alive.

Other deities represented earthly or heavenly forces. Without listing the names of the deities, they can be summarized as regional family groups. For example, there was a family of deities for the mountains and another for the lowlands and seashore. Heavenly bodies had family relationships, and natural occurrences of weather were respected as deities. The serpent, which appeared often as a symbol, could stand for a lightning bolt.

RITUALS AND SYMBOLS

The generally beneficent Inca deities, who cared for both the living and the dead, could be satisfied with the sacrifice of sacred llamas and food shared by humans. The chief Inca represented the sun. Sometimes human infants were sacrificed to him, but most of the time his needs were met by priests and "virgins of the sun," who made cloth and beer for the cult and served as the Inca's concubines. The god of the sun and the Inca emperor were much alike, for the first emperor of the Incas was believed to have been the

Inti [IN-ti]
An early god of the Incas, probably symbolized by a hummingbird. Inti was a creator god who was later combined with Viracocha.

Viracocha [VI-rah-COH-cha]
A creator god of the Incas. He symbolized the sun.

huacas [HUAH-cas]
In Inca religion, natural phenomena that provide unusual manifestations of the holy. Unusual rocks, for example, could symbolize the presence of the holy.

offspring of the sun.[29] The "virgins of the sun," with whom the emperor mated, produced "children of the sun" to serve him. Because there was no metal trade, gold, which like the sun did not tarnish, was used to adorn the gods and royal personages.

Some festivals were religious rituals. The feast of salvation, the Situa, involved heavens, gods, humans, and *huacas* in a great ritual of forgiveness and healing. The Festival of the Queen, the moon goddess, occurred after the planting of seed. The chosen people of the creator expunged any disease or evil from among themselves and participated in the renewing of heavens. Brundage describes the drama in three acts.[30] The emperor Huascar ordered Cuzco purged of all foreign influences, so that only pure Incas were in the city. Gods were brought to Coricancha: the golden image of Viracocha, the creator; an ugly stone of Huanacauri, the Inca's manhood; and Inti, the sun god. Mother Earth and Mother Moon were present, attended only by women. Eleven ancestors—mummies—attended. At the end of the council, messengers announced to soldiers of the guard the good news of a splendid ceremonial celebration.

The second act of the drama required Inca knights in battle dress to go through the city and bring offenders to the boards of judges, who passed out sentences. Then four bodies of soldiers in mock battle went through the city carrying torches, chasing evil. Inhabitants came out and joined in the drive to rid the city of any evil spirits. The soldiers proceeded outside the city until they had driven all evil from the precincts. Returning, they ceremonially washed their weapons under starlight—the city was safe from evil for another year.

The third act of the Situa took place the next morning, when inhabitants in their best costumes and cosmetics participated in eating and wearing *yahuar sanco*, a kind of dough made with maize and the blood of a hundred sacred white llamas. The gods received the food, which was spread across their mouths. The emperor and his head wife, servants and representatives of the creator, entered wearing feather crowns. The sun god was paraded, and the mummies of prior emperors attended. The emperor prayed to the creator god. The people danced the *huayaya*, using a woolen rope of many

Scenes of Inca Cities. The mountain cities of the Incas were homes of deities and their earthly representatives.

Religions of the Americas in History

◆ **60,000–30,000 BCE** Native American groups migrate from northeast Asia

◆ **12,000** Paintings made in caves of France

1200 CE Incas build Cuzco in the Andes Mountains ◆

1325 Aztecs settle at Tenochtitlán, Mexico ◆

1487 Ahuizotl dedicates the Great Temple ◆

1492 Columbus sails from Spain ◆

1519 Montezuma welcomes Hernando Cortez ◆

1521 Cortez conquers the Aztecs ◆

1532 Francisco Pizarro finds the Incas ◆

1541 Francisco Vasquez Coronado, Spanish explorer, meets Zuni Indians ◆

1598 Franciscan missionaries bring Christianity to Zuni Indians ◆

1607 English settlers in Virginia encounter Powhatan Indians ◆

17th-century English hunters and traders encounter Cherokee Indians in Appalachian Mountains ◆

1776–1781 Revolutionary War; Cherokees join British in fight against colonists ◆

1792 US Congress appropriates funds to teach Indians agriculture and domestic arts ◆

1827 Cherokees describe themselves as "one nation under God" ◆
and adopt a constitution based on that of the United States

1838–1839 "Trail of Tears": US government troops force Cherokees to march ◆
on foot to the Indian Territories, now Oklahoma

1861–1865 American Civil War ◆

1914–1918 World War I ◆

1919 Introduction of Peyote religion on Wind River Reservation ◆

1935 Frank G. Speck studies Naskapi Indians of the Labrador peninsula ◆

1939–1945 World War II ◆

| BCE | 2000 | 1500 | 1000 | 500 | 0 | 500 | 1000 | 1500 | 2000 | CE |

colors, decorated with gold, symbolizing a giant anaconda. The celebration and worship to prepare for a successful year occupied four days.

The stone roads, magnificent buildings, and artifacts of the Incas remain today.[31] In them we can see a pre-Columbian civilization whose city-state was as impressive as some of those in the Mediterranean area. With the coming of Christianity, however, most of the beliefs and rituals faded away. Only those that could be reconciled with the religion of the invaders were retained and incorporated into a new culture.

Corpus Christi, Peru. These descendants of the Incas participate in Christian festivals today.

COMMON FEATURES OF RELIGIONS IN MESOAMERICA AND SOUTH AMERICA

Although each culture exhibited distinctive features, the worldviews of the city-states shared common features. We can summarize some of these similar features.

The absolute, the world, and humans were active participants in a cosmic drama. The absolute comprised interactive forces that were described in terms of personlike gods and goddesses. Heavenly bodies, phenomena of weather and seasons, and earth and water were perceived as deities who were characters in a perpetual drama. They were characters who struggled, loved, fought, won, lost, and sometimes died. The earth that produced crops, herds, and marine life to support city-state civilization was dependent on heaven for its increase. In its own way, however, it contributed to the annual cycles of animal and vegetable life. Humans, who received the benefits and the hardships of heaven and earth, were active partners in maintaining a productive balance between heaven and earth. Absolutes, the world, and humans depended on each other in ensuring the prosperity of civilization.

The interdependent relationship between the absolute, the world, and humans was the ground for both the problem for humans and the solution for humans. The problem for humans was to meet all the responsibilities required for maintaining a balance of forces necessary to produce food, clothing, shelter, arts, crafts, government, and effective military strength. Failure to meet their obligations brought humans anarchy, famine, slavery, or death. The solution for humans was to keep all the moral and ritual laws of their society. By observing all laws and rituals or by making proper amends for shortcomings, inhabitants of city-states ensured positive dynamics in the universe. Through public rituals, inhabitants guaranteed the annual renewal of sources of life. Through private rituals, they sought assurance of life after death. As long as the absolute, the world, and humans met their obligations, nature, society, and individuals would prosper.

Symbols and rituals of city-states were both distinctive and shared. Each city had a patron deity, and symbols and rituals were attached to it. The city-state thought of its religion as separate and distinct from religions of all other peoples. Nevertheless, deities, rituals, and symbols were often borrowed from other city-states and integrated into established beliefs and practices. Thus, as new city-states rose to power and extended their influence, the religion of the civilization changed to accommodate preferences.

The religions of peoples of city-states did not obliterate the religions of other peoples. Deities of hunting and gathering peoples were often included among the gods worshiped by peoples of advanced agricultural societies. With the division of labor possible in large city-states and the development of kingdoms, the functions and organization of gods reflected earthly developments. There were parallels between the organization of families on earth and the organization of families of gods over earth. Among the religions studied in this chapter, none developed an enduring concept of only one god, a monotheism. There were, however, attempts to conceive of a unified cosmic system of forces that interact in dramatic ways. Religion in the city-states sought the advantage of humans and their societies by integrating them positively into the perpetual dramas of the cosmos.

✍ A POINT OF VIEW

CONSIDER THIS

Describing a religion forces us to choose a point of view. Understanding how a point of view influences description of a religion deserves special consideration. An outsider has an outsider's point of view of a religion, a view influenced by her own religious tradition (or lack of any), time in history, and methodologies of observing and recording. An insider in a religion is accustomed to communicating with others inside a faith. Although she may communicate effectively with insiders, she may fail to communicate accurately with outsiders who are less familiar with the total culture of the religion. Professional apologists, or explainers, of religious groups tend to put a pleasant face on their faith to make it more appealing to outsiders or to exaggerate the impossibility for outsiders to understand the faith. Whatever the point of view, students of religions need to reflect on who is reporting and what influences are inherent in that point of view.

Inside, outside, and objective points of view of a religion select and group data that help us reconcile new information with our larger bodies of knowledge. Outsiders seldom think that insiders can be objective; insiders usually think that outsiders cannot fully appreciate what insiders experience. Scholars of religions who are trained in special methodologies are influenced by schools of study advocated by competing educational systems. Any reader who wants to understand a religion well must actively evaluate the various points of view that can contribute to his or her conclusions.

The religions of tribes and city-states have many examples among religions of the Americas. We can find more examples among the religions of Africa, which are discussed in Chapter 2.

✍ VOCABULARY

ahone [A-hone]
Awanawilona [u-WAH-nah-wi-LOW-nu]
babalawo [bah-BAH-lah-wu]
henotheism [HEN-o-thee-ISM]
huacas [HUAH-cas]
Huitzilopochtli [HWEET-zi-low-POK-tli]
huskanaw [HUS-ka-now]
Inti [IN-ti]
kachinas [ka-CHI-nas]
kivas [KEE-vas]

mamanatowick [ma-ma-na-TOW-wick]
Mantu [MAHN-too]
Mista'peo [mis-TAH-pe-oh]
monotheism [MON-u-the-IS-um]
myth [MITH]
Okeus [OH-kee-us]
potlatch [POT-lach]
Quetzalcoatl [KWEET-zal-coatl]
reincarnation [REE-in-cahr-NAY-shun]
shaman [SHAH-man]

Tenochtitlán [TEN-ok-TIT-lan]
Tezcatlipoca [tez-CAT-li-POH-ca]
Tlaloc [TLAH-loc]
Tonatiuh [TOE-na-TI-uh]
totem [TOW-tem]
trickster [TRIK-stur]
Tsaka'bec [tsah-KAH-bec]
Viracocha [VI-rah-COH-cha]
Wakan tanka [WAH-kan-TAHN-ka]
weroances [WEH-row-ances]
wisakon [WI-sa-kon]

QUESTIONS FOR REVIEW

1. What is your understanding of the word *shaman*? How is it related to *soul*?

2. How are "dreams" related to "souls"?

3. Why would people organize priests to dispense medicines?

4. What is a myth? How does it function in religions?

5. Give examples of masked dancers in religions and explain their functions.

6. What kinds of evidence indicate that people believe in life after death?

7. What is the relationship of rites of passage to religion?

8. Describe some rites of cleansing in religions.

9. What are the most important human concerns addressed by religions?

10. What conditions affect the forms that religions take?

QUESTIONS FOR DISCUSSION

1. When we read accounts of religions of the Americas written by early explorers, what allowances should we make?

2. What are the problems and rewards of attempting to find common features in religions of the Americas?

3. Who understands a religion better, an insider or an outsider? Which is in a better position to compare the religion with others?

4. What lasting impressions do you have of religions of the Americas? What questions remain for your further study?

5. What are some of the most common misconceptions about religions of the Americas? How could these misconceptions be corrected?

NOTES

1. Frank G. Speck, *Naskapi* (Norman: University of Oklahoma Press, 1977).

2. Ibid., p. 33.

3. Ibid., pp. 47–48.

4. Ben C. McCrary, *Indians in Seventeenth Century Virginia* (Williamsburg, VA: Virginia 350th Anniversary Celebration Corporation, 1957). Helen C. Rountree, *The Powhatan Indians of Virginia* (Norman: University of Oklahoma Press, 1989).

5. Rountree, p. 126.

6. Ibid, pp. 134–135.

7. Ibid., p. 132.

8. Ibid., p. 139.

9. Ibid., pp. 80–82.

10. Ibid., p. 137.

11. McCrary, p. 79.

12. John Ehle, *Trail of Tears* (New York: Doubleday-Anchor, 1988).

13. James Mooney, *Myths of the Cherokee* (St. Clair Shores, MI: Scholarly Press, 1970), pp. 239–427.

14. Sam D. Gill, *Native American Religions* (Belmont, CA: Wadsworth, 1982), p. 16.

15. Clark Wissler, *North American Indians of the Plains* (New York: Burt Franklin Reprints, 1974), p. 110.

16. See Alice Marriott and Carol K. Rachlin, *Plains Indian Mythology* (New York: Crowell, 1975), p. 15.

17. Cottie Burland, *North American Indian Mythology* (New York: Peter Bedrick Books, 1985), pp. 97–98.

18. William E. Coffer, *Spirits of the Sacred Mountain* (New York: Van Nostrand Reinhold, 1978), p. 99.

19. Harold E. Driver, *Indians of North America* (Chicago: University of Chicago Press, 1961), p. 506.

20. H. B. Nicholson, "Mesoamerican Religion: Postclassic Cultures," in *The Encyclopedia of Religion*, vol. 9, ed. Mircea Eliade (New York: Macmillan, 1987), pp. 419–428.

21. Fray Diego Duran, *Book of the Gods and Rites and the Ancient Calendar*, trans. Fernando Horcasitas and Doris Heyden (Norman: University of Oklahoma Press, 1971), p. 73.

22. Nigel Davis, *The Aztecs* (New York: Putnam, 1973), p. 165.

23. Ibid., pp. 143–145.

24. Sylvanus Griswold Morley, *The Ancient Maya*, rev. George W. Brainerd (Stanford, CA: Stanford University Press, 1956), p. 186.

25. David Carrasco, "Aztec Religion," in *The Encyclopedia of Religion*, vol. 6, ed. Mircea Eliade (New York: Macmillan, 1987), pp. 518–523.

26. Burr Cartwright Brundage, Lords of Cuzco (Norman: University of Oklahoma Press, 1967), p. 8.

27. Victor W. von Hagen, Highway of the Sun (Boston: Little, Brown with Duell, Sloan & Pearce, 1955), p. 3.

28. Brundage, p. 143.

29. Jean Rhys Bram, "Sun," in The Encyclopedia of Religion, vol. 14, ed. Mircea Eliade (New York: Macmillan, 1987), pp. 132–142.

30. Brundage, p. 198.

31. Von Hagen.

✍ READINGS

NORTH AMERICA

Burland, Cottie. North American Indian Mythology. New York: Peter Bedrick Books, 1985.

Calloway, Colin G. New World for All: Indians, Europeans, and the Remaking of Early America. Baltimore: Johns Hopkins University Press, 1997.

Coffer, William E. Spirits of the Sacred Mountain. New York: Van Nostrand Reinhold, 1978.

Driver, Harold E. Indians of North America. Chicago: University of Chicago Press, 1961.

Gill, Sam D. Native American Religions. Belmont, CA: Wadsworth, 1982.

Guitiérrez, Ramón A. When Jesus Came, The Corn Mothers Went Away. Stanford, CA: Stanford University Press, 1991.

Hultkrantz, Ake. Native Religions of North America. Hagerstown, MD: Torch Publishing, 1988.

Marriott, Alice, and Carol K. Rachlin. Plains Indian Mythology. New York: Crowell, 1975.

Mooney, James. Myths of the Cherokee. St. Clair Shores, MI: Scholarly Press, 1970.

Rountree, Helen C. The Powhatan Indians of Virginia. Norman: University of Oklahoma Press, 1989.

Speck, Frank G. Naskapi. Norman: University of Oklahoma Press, 1977.

Wissler, Clark. North American Indians of the Plains. New York: Burt Franklin Reprints, 1974.

MESOAMERICA AND SOUTH AMERICA

Austin, Alfredo Lopez. Tamoanchan, Tlalocan: Places of Mist., trans. Bernard and Thelma Ortiz de Montellano. Niwot: University Press of Colorado, 1997.

Brundage, Burr Cartwright. Two Earths, Two Heavens. Albuquerque: University of New Mexico Press, 1975.

———. Lords of Cuzco. Norman: University of Oklahoma Press, 1967.

Currasco, David. "Aztec Religion," vol. 2, pp. 23–29. In The Encyclopedia of Religion, ed. Mircea Eliade. New York: Macmillan, 1987.

Davis, Nigel. The Aztecs. New York: Putnam, 1973.

Duran, Fray Diego. Book of the Gods and Rites and the Ancient Calendar, trans. Fernando Horcasitas and Doris Heyden. Norman: University of Oklahoma Press, 1971.

Duviols, Pierre. "Inca Religion." In The Encyclopedia of Religion, ed. Mircea Eliade. New York: Macmillan, 1987.

Marcus, Joyce. Mesoamerican Writing Systems. Princeton, NJ: Princeton University Press, 1992.

Mason, J. Alden. The Ancient Civilizations of Peru. Baltimore, MD: Penguin Books, 1969.

Monaghan, John. The Covenants with Earth and Rain: Exchange, Sacrifice, and Revelation in Mixtec Sociality. Norman: University of Oklahoma Press, 1995.

Morley, Sylvanus Griswold. The Ancient Maya, rev. George W. Brainerd. Stanford, CA: Stanford University Press, 1956.

Nicholson, H. B. "Mesoamerican Religions." In The Encyclopedia of Religion, ed. Mircea Eliade. New York: Macmillan, 1987.

Skar, Sarah Lund. Lives Together, Worlds Apart: Quechua Colonization in Jungle and City. Oslo, Norway: Scandinavian University Press, 1994.

Religions of Africa

Karnah, Egypt. The site of ancient Thebes is on the right bank of the Nile River. Its remains include the Great Temple of Amen as well as statues of pharaohs.

Introduction

The continent of Africa has always excited Western imaginations. From ancient times Mesopotamians, Persians, Greeks, and Romans were fascinated with the peoples, animals, and places of Africa. The pyramids of Egypt and the religion that gave rise to them captivated visitors. Ancient pharaohs represented not only monarchs to be obeyed but also deities to be worshiped.

As ancient Egyptian civilization declined, new groups arrived and spread over the continent. In early days of Christianity converts multiplied in Egypt and sent missionaries north of the Sahara Desert. In the seventh century, Muslims swept out of Arabia, crossed North Africa, and eventually reached Spain. In the colonial period, British, French, and German interests studied Islam but promoted Christianity.

As the colonial powers moved into sub-Saharan Africa, their religion began to make converts to Christianity. Muslims also began missionary efforts in the southern regions. Through missionary activities many peoples of Africa have become officially either Christian or Muslim. We will study these religions in Chapters 9 and 10. In this chapter we will study some of the distinctively African religions that are still practiced, sometimes by people who are nominally members of either Islam or Christianity.

We will meet powerful figures in African religion who arouse both awe and fear. Witches are believed to have influence over forces that can bring either good or evil. Chiefs are not only earthly rulers but also controllers of spiritual forces of life and death. Believers who seem to be enjoying simple freedoms may feel encompassed by hundreds of prescriptions to avoid powers of evil.

In this chapter we will examine ancient Egyptian religion and three sub-Saharan religions still practiced today. Many people still regard the civilization of the ancient Egyptians as the finest example of what Africa has produced. The sub-Saharan religions are examples of traditional beliefs that have been subordinated to major world religions that arose in the Middle East. In these religions we will meet dozens of interesting deities and the humans who are believed to have influence over their powers.

THE EGYPTIAN RELIGION

The pyramid of the Pharaoh Cheops, in Giza, not far from Cairo, was a wonder of the ancient world; it remains so today. Ravages of weather, pollution, and looters have not destroyed the construction marvel of 2600 B.C.E.[1] Over two million blocks weighing an average of 2.5 tons were assembled to a height of more than 450 feet along the Nile River to provide an inviolable tomb for the body of a pharaoh who believed that he would live again in another world. What a staggering amount of labor and material to commit to a public work in the belief that it would ensure a good future life for a human representative of the gods!

Modern Africa. The African continent is home to many different religious traditions.

Written records of Egypt began about 3100 B.C.E. with a king named Menes, who ruled Memphis.[2] Because most of the surrounding country was desert, cities were clustered near the Nile River, the source of most of the fresh water in the country. Some Egyptians were fisherfolk and others were farmers who planted in the rich, black soil deposited on the banks of the Nile by its annual floods. The Egyptians invented hieroglyphics, a system of writing that used symbols or pictures to represent words or sounds, and recorded their history long before many other civilizations. Although there are references to Egypt in records of other peoples, scholars can know from the Egyptians themselves what they did, thought, and believed. Egyptian written records have provided archaeologists with reliable information about their ancient religion.

From the information on kingdoms and dynasties of Egypt for more than 2500 years, we know the trend of religious development. More powerful rulers imposed the beliefs and rituals of their cities on the peoples of the cities that they conquered. In the process, deities of two or more cities were often combined; deities of the victorious city usually dominated the deities of the conquered cities. Over time, however, a more national view of Egyptians affected their religious worldview. Among royalty, at least, deities, rituals, and beliefs were shared over much of the country. In this long history, peoples from the south, such as the **Nubians,** participated often, contributing their cultures as they assumed roles of leadership, even that of Pharaoh.

Nubians [NOO-bay-ans]
People of the southern Nile valley; neighbors of the ancient Egyptians. Their leaders formed the twenty-fifth dynasty of Egyptian pharaohs.

The period of the pyramid builders, the Old Kingdom (2700–2200 B.C.E.), was succeeded by the First Intermediate Period (2200–2050 B.C.E.), a time of chaos. Nobles from Thebes reunited Egypt during the Middle Kingdom (2050–1800 B.C.E.). During the Second Intermediate Period (1800–1570

The Sphinx and the Pyramids of Giza. All over the world people have marveled at these symbols of ancient Egyptian religion.

B.C.E.), local rulers were replaced by warrior rulers from Asia, the Hyksos. In the Early New Kingdom, (1570–1300 B.C.E.), Egyptians mastered the Hyksos's weapons of war and threw off the yoke of their foreign rulers. Queen Hatshepsut ruled over a peaceful period of building beautiful temples and cities.

In 1370 B.C.E., the Amarna Revolution began with King Amenhotep IV, who worshiped only one god, the sun. He named this one god Aton; he called himself Akhenaton. Naming a new city after himself, he moved his court there to avoid the old worship of Amon. Under Tutankhamen, a son-in-law of Akhenaton, Egyptians returned to the old polytheism. Howard Carter and Lord Carnarvon discovered King Tutankhamen's tomb in 1922; clearly, the splendors of his kingdom were dazzling. In the Later New Kingdom (1300–1090 B.C.E.), the Egyptians fought the Hittites and Philistines, recovering much of the territory they had lost in earlier centuries.

With the beginning of the iron age, about 1100 B.C.E., the Egyptians, who had no iron, began to lose territory to invaders armed with iron weapons. During the Period of Invasions to the coming of the Romans in 30 B.C.E., the Egyptians were often ruled by non-Egyptians. Libyans, Sudanese, Assyrians, Persians, and Greeks ruled the land. The Ptolemies brought about the revival of intellectual, cultural, and commercial activity. The Egyptian city Alexandria became a beacon for learning, gaining respect from scholars of many nations. During the Roman period, Christianity gained a foothold in Egypt. Egypt eventually became part of the Byzantine empire and later fell to the Muslims in 639 C.E. From that year, Islam played an increasing role in Africa.

Worldview of the Ancient Egyptians

THE ABSOLUTE

By the time Cheops built his tomb, Egyptian religion was well developed. Egyptians considered sky, earth, river, and sun sources of life. They were symbolized as humans, animals, and combined human–animal forms. The symbols of the sun, the highest god, had different names for different times of the day. Isis and Osiris were a husband and wife deified as the self-renewing vitality in nature. **Horus,** the son of Isis and Osiris, was symbolized by a falcon. As the king of the gods, he stood for light and heaven. **Amon-Re,** or Ra, combined the god of Thebes with the god of the noon sun. He was symbolized by a human form wearing a headdress or by an obelisk (the sun's ray). **Aton,** championed by Pharaoh Akhenaton, was the sun, symbolized by a disk. Akhenaton proclaimed that the sun god, Aton, was the only god.

The gods and goddesses who were patrons of cities had various symbols, but they were often depicted as combined human and animal forms in one figure.[3] In addition to the sun, the creator of the earth, **Hathor,** played an important role. Her symbol is a woman's body with the head of a cow. Jackals and crocodiles were combined with human bodies to represent scavengers. A feather at the scene of the final judgment symbolized **Mayet** (Maat), goddess of order and truth.

Ordinary people honored cats, for they knew that the goddess Sakhmet, a form of Hathor, was symbolized by a woman's body with the head of a

Horus [HER-us]
In Egypt, the son of Isis and Osiris who opposed his uncle, Seth. Horus was also the sun, symbolized by a falcon.

Amon-Re [AH-mun-ray]
A sun god of Egypt. His symbol was the obelisk, a ray of the sun. Amon, originally the god of Thebes, became highest god in 2000 B.C.E., when Thebes dominated all Egypt.

Aton [AHT-un]
In Egypt, this god's symbol was a disk, representing the sun. After Akhenaton established his throne in Akhetaton, Aton was the only god worshiped.

Hathor [HAH-thor]
The Egyptian goddess who created the world. Her symbol was a woman's body with the head of a cow.

Mayet [MU-yut]
(Maat) The Egyptian goddess of order and truth, who prompted the deceased at the time of judgment.

Religions of Africa in History

◆ **2700–2200 BCE** Old Kingdom in Egypt

◆ **2700** Pyramid of Cheops built

　◆ **2500** Document giving Ptah-hetep's concept of God

　◆ **2200–2050** First Intermediate Period in Egypt

　　◆ **2050–1800** Middle Kingdom in Egypt

　　　◆ **1800–1570** Second Intermediate Period in Egypt

　　　　◆ **1570–1300** The Early New Kingdom in Egypt

　　　　　◆ **1370** Akhenaton worships Aton, the Amarna Revolution

　　　　　◆ **1300–1090** Later New Kingdom of Egypt

　　　　　　　◆ **330** Alexander the Great in Egypt

　　　　　　　◆ **200** Septuagint, Greek translation of Hebrew Bible made

　　　　　　　◆ **31** Octavian, the Roman, conquers Egypt

1st century CE Christianity enters Egypt ◆

7th century Islam enters Egypt ◆

12th century Advanced cultures appear in Yoruba area of Nigeria ◆

15th and 16th centuries Portuguese and British slavers appear in Nigeria ◆

17th century Dutch settle in Cape of Good Hope (South Africa) ◆

1806 British seize Cape of Good Hope ◆

1897 Cecil Rhodes and British South Africa Company control Zimbabwe ◆

1899–1902 Anglo-Boer War of South Africa ◆

1923 British take over Southern Rhodesia ◆

1960 Nigeria becomes independent ◆

1963 Nigeria becomes a Republic ◆

1969 The Congo becomes independent ◆

1971 Republic of Zaire is proclaimed ◆

1979–1980 Zimbabwe gains independence ◆

1990 Nelson Mandela freed from 27 years in prison, South Africa ◆

1991 President de Klerk announces plans to end apartheid laws in South Africa ◆

1994 South Africa holds first election where all people can vote; Nelson Mandela elected president ◆

1996 Post-apartheid constitution becomes law of South Africa ◆

1997 General Laurent Kabila changes name of "Zaire" to "Congo" ◆

| BCE | 2000 | 1500 | 1000 | 500 | 0 | 500 | 1000 | 1500 | 2000 | CE |

lion and that the goddess Bast, who represented joy and fertility from the sun, was symbolized by the head of a cat atop a woman's body. Architects built temples to honor cats, and sculptors used them as models for statues. Embalmers preserved feline bodies, storing them in gold coffins. Jewelers sometimes put cat figures atop the **ankh,** the circle-topped Egyptian cross that symbolized immortality.

The numerous Egyptian representations of the deities may prevent modern observers from realizing the sophistication of their concept of the absolute. Egyptians admired some traits of animals, holding them in awe. They found these animals suitable vehicles for deities. Other symbols of the deities are Egyptian attempts to express the qualities, functions, and powers that they encountered in the annual cycle of life. From written records, we know that Egyptians conceived of the universe as a unit. Sky, earth, sun, and river united to bring forth fruits from the earth. These forces cooperated to sustain rewarding lives for humans. Body and soul were unified not only in this life but also in the life to come. As justice requires that goodness be rewarded and evil punished in this life, so will righteousness be compensated and immorality penalized in the world of the dead.

The unity of the Egyptian worldview emphasized an observable phenomenon of Egypt—dependability. The sun rose, sailing as a double-ended boat across the day sky. After sailing under the earth all night, it would return with its light and heat the next day. The shallow Nile River mysteriously increased its flow each year, flooding the lands along its banks. Although at times terrifying, the river brought not only food but also rich soil in which industrious farmers could produce the grain that has been for centuries the envy of other nations of the world. During its lifetime, the human body increased for years and then decreased to death. With preservation, however, the body could be maintained and restored to life. In Egypt, life was dependable.

RITUALS AND SYMBOLS

The Egyptian temple represented the mansion of the god, his home on earth. The priests of each temple cared for the statue of the god as if it were a live person. As the divine and intermediary of the divine, the pharaohs represented god to the people and the people to god. High priests assisted in making offerings, pouring libations, and burning sweet-smelling incense to the gods. The priests' other duties were to serve as judges on a tribunal headed by the vizier and to supervise the vast temple lands dedicated to the god. So important was the office that sometimes, as at the temple of Ptah in Memphis, royal princes served as high priests.[4] Other persons familiar with the sacred writings, the prophets and the scribes, also had official offices. Nevertheless, faithful worshipers themselves often performed duties in the temple for a month at a time. Some gave a total of three months a year in temple service. Women served as priestesses to Hathor, and it is reported that Queen Nefertiti made offerings to Aton. From the pharaoh to the lowliest subject, Egyptian society was unified through the service to the patron deity of the city.

As important as the temples to the patron deity were in each city, one story of the gods eventually captured the hearts of many Egyptians. Its theme is the one most often associated with the Egyptian religion—death and life after death.

Akhenaton Makes an Offering to the Sun.
For a brief time, this Pharaoh established in
Egypt the worship of only one god, Aton.

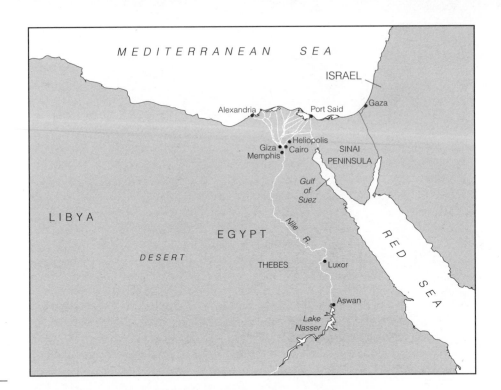

Nile Centers of Ancient Egyptian Civilization. The Nile River was a major symbol of fertility. Cities along the river developed religions that shared worldviews.

Osiris [oh-SI-ris]
In Egyptian myth, a king who became lord of the underworld. With his wife, Isis, he fathered Horus, the king of Egypt.

Isis [II-sis]
In Egypt, the wife of Osiris, god of the dead, and the mother of their son, Horus. She was the giver of life.

Seth [seth]
In Egyptian myths, the wicked brother of Osiris. He stole the third eye from Osiris. Horus, the son of Osiris, fought Seth and recovered the third eye, symbol of kingship in Egypt.

OSIRIS AND ISIS

The most memorable story for many visitors to Egypt was the account of a god who was killed and rose from the dead. The main characters were **Osiris**, reported to have been the king who brought a golden age to Egyptians, his devoted wife, **Isis,** and Osiris's evil brother, **Seth.** Seth tricked Osiris into lying down in a coffin, sealed it, and threw it into the Nile River. It floated down to the Mediterranean and landed in Byblos, off the coast of Lebanon.[5] Lodged in a tree, it became part of a pillar used in building a king's house. The grieving Isis searched for the body of Osiris. Locating it, she persuaded the king to give her the body. After taking Osiris's body to a secluded place and employing her magic powers, she embraced it. Osiris revived enough to impregnate her. In secrecy she bore Horus, protecting him from the threats of his uncle Seth. On reaching manhood, Horus organized supporters to avenge his father's murder. He fought and defeated Seth, recovering the third eye, a sign of kingship, which Seth had stolen from Osiris. The victorious Horus reigned sovereign over Egypt, and Osiris became lord of the underworld, the one who bestows immortality. Osiris symbolized the perfect king who gives life both on earth and after death, and Isis symbolized the queen who is a wise, devoted wife.

Although the Isis-Osiris myth circulated widely in Mediterranean cultures long enough to challenge Christianity, for the Egyptians it had meanings tied to the Nile and to birth, death, and life after death. From the beginning of recorded history, the annual rising and falling of the Nile River has provided the very staff of life for Egyptians. The agricultural cycle was associated with the events in the lives of Isis and Osiris. The myth was also associated with the birth and deaths of the pharaohs. The pharaoh was more than a representative of the divine; he was the divine.

Immortality, at first believed to be restricted to kings, was later extended to common people. The Egyptians considered the soul complex. There was a **ka,** a spiritual form that mirrored the body. It had physical needs that were met after death by food and drink left at the tomb. The **ba** was a spirit that flew as a bird to heaven. An **akh** or **ikhu** was a ghost of a person that went to the land of the blessed. When the ka departed, the body died. Through mummification and funeral rites, a person could be recreated. Mummification bound the ka and the body of the deceased to the world. Since living required eating, funerary meals had to be provided for the deceased. Then the Egyptians embalmed the body and made images of the deceased, servants, and loved ones. Sir Wallis Budge believed that the images of servants found in tombs represent servants who were actually buried, alive or dead, with their masters.[6] The servants were not embalmed or found with their masters, so it is difficult to confirm whether this actually occurred. Egyptians entombed possessions of the deceased, especially a boat, to help the person reach the land of paradise. The preserved body, images, possessions, and food served the needs of the soul immediately after death, in the tomb, and in the journey to the land of the blessed.

Egyptians did not consider immortality a guaranteed blessing. Each person had to appear for judgment before Mayet (truth) in the kingdom of Osiris. On entering the Hall of Mayet, the deceased greeted the goddess of truth and sought her clemency. He or she acknowledged the forty-two gods who kept watch over those who had done evil. The deceased then recited, even before his or her heart was weighed, a negative confession—the things he or she had not done:

1. I have not sinned against men.
2. I have not oppressed (or wronged) [my] kinsfolk.
3. I have not committed evil in the place of truth.
4. I have not known worthless men.
5. I have not committed acts of abomination.
6. I have not done daily works of supererogation (?).
7. I have not caused my name to appear for honours.
8. I have not domineered over slaves.
9. I have not thought scorn of the god (or God).
10. I have not defrauded the poor man of his goods.
11. I have not done things which the gods abominate.
12. I have not caused harm to be done to the slave by his master.
13. I have caused no man to suffer.
14. I have allowed no man to go hungry.
15. I have made no man weep.
16. I have slain no man.
17. I have not given the order for any man to be slain.
18. I have not caused pain to the multitude.
19. I have not filched the offerings in the temples.
20. I have not purloined the cakes of the gods.
21. I have not stolen the offerings of the spirits.

ka [KA]
In Egypt, divine breath that supported life. It is sometimes referred to as the soul.

ba [BAH]
In Egypt, a kind of human consciousness. It is sometimes described as the soul.

akh or **ikhu** [AHK]
A part of the soul of a person. It was the ghost that went to the land of the blessed.

Egyptian Final Judgment of the Dead. This court is based on Egyptian courts, but the characters in the drama are deities.

22. I have had no dealing with the paederast.

23. I have not defiled myself in the pure places of the god of my city.

24. I have not cheated in measuring of grain.

25. I have not filched land or added thereto.

26. I have not encroached upon fields of others.

27. I have not added to the weight of the balance.

28. I have not cheated with the pointer of the scales.

29. I have not taken away milk from the mouths of the babes.

30. I have not driven away the beasts from their pastures.

31. I have not netted the geese of the preserves of the gods.

32. I have not caught fish with bait of their bodies.

33. I have not obstructed water when it should run.

34. I have not cut a cutting in a canal of running water.

35. I have not extinguished a flame when it ought to burn.

36. I have not abrogated the days of offering the chosen offerings.

37. I have not turned off cattle from the property of the gods.

38. I have not repulsed the god in his manifestations. I am pure. I am pure. I am pure. I am pure.[7]

The judge ordered the heart of the deceased weighed in a balance; the lighter the heart, the better the life. A heart heavy with evil earned for the deceased the condemnation of being devoured by a composite monster that symbolized the most feared creatures in Egypt—the crocodile, the lion, and the hippopotamus. The light-hearted person was sent to a pleasant land that the Egyptians considered ideal. Speaking to the Four Apes sitting by the lake of fire near the throne of Osiris, the deceased said,

> Hail, ye Four Apes, who sit in the bows of the Boat of Ra, who convey truth to Neber-tcher, who sit in judgment on my weakness and my strength, who make offerings to the gods, and sepulchral meals to the Spirits, who feed upon truth, who are without deceit and fraud, to whom wickedness is an abomination, do away my evil deeds, put away my sin, which merited stripes upon earth, destroy

whatsoever evil is in me, and let there be nothing in me which shall separate me from you. Let me pass through the Ammehet, let me enter Re-stau, let me pass through the pylons of Amentet, give me of the bread, and beer, and dainty food which are given to the living Spirits, and let me enter in and come forth from Re-stau.

The Four Apes responded,

Advance, for we have done away thy wickedness, and we have put away thy sin, and thy sin committed upon earth, which merited stripes, and we have destroyed all the evil which appertained to thee upon earth. Enter, therefore, into Re-stau, and pass through the secret gates of Amentet, and bread, and beer, and dainty food shall be given unto thee, and thou shalt go in and come forth at thy desire, even as do the Spirits who are favoured of the god, and thou shalt be proclaimed each day in the horizon.[8]

Having satisfied the gods and goddesses of Egypt, the deceased was received into the kingdom of Osiris.

This organized religion developed along with diversified civilization. The lives of the ancient Egyptians are reflected in the words of the *Book of the Dead*. They found wealth in the Nile River and in the rich farmlands along its banks. The river irrigated their crops and provided fish and game. At the bottom of society, slaves provided a labor force that supported a class structure of poor and rich, dominated by royalty. Known as the land of two kingdoms, Upper and Lower Egypt, for many centuries Egypt held its own against neighboring countries.

RELATIONSHIP TO OTHER RELIGIONS

Although ancient Egyptian religion is no longer active, it lives on in the history of Western civilization. Greek philosophers marveled at Egyptian wisdom, and historians of Greece and Rome imported Egyptian stories, dramas, and beliefs. Roman soldiers, such as Mark Antony and Julius Caesar, were fascinated with Egypt and its goddess Isis. Egyptians made lasting impressions on Judaism and Christianity. Medieval visitors to Egypt were amazed at the temples and tombs of the pharaohs. Muslims and Jews, such as Maimonides, made their home near the Nile. The Sphinx, located near the pyramid of Cheops, symbolized the mysteries of ancient Egypt. Nineteenth- and twentieth-century archaeologists brought to light the beliefs and practices of a civilization that is as impressive to peoples of the world today as it was to ancient peoples. Throughout much of the world, ancient Egyptian religion continues to influence religious beliefs of new generations.

THE BASONGYE OF CONGO

Historical Development

The country of Democratic Republic of Congo, formerly called Zaire, has about forty million people. Almost half of them live in urban areas. The major ethnic group is Bantu, but about two hundred other tribes inhabit the country. Most people are Christians. About 10 percent are Muslims. When Portuguese explorers arriving in the fifteenth century found a kingdom of Bantus. From 1876, King Leopold of Belgium directed an international group in exploiting the resources of the Congo. In 1960, the country became independent, ruled by Patrice Lumumba. After a period of warfare, the country changed its name to Zaire in 1971. Shortly after that, people with Christian names were required to change them to African names.[9] In a revolution of 1997 the name Congo was revived.

In his *African Religions and Philosophy,* chapter 2, John S. Mbiti wrote that African peoples have both religion and magic. Although these two can be distinguished, they are closely related. Magic is part of the religious background. In our discussion of the Basongye of Congo (Zaire), after mentioning the beliefs about gods, I will emphasize magic, witchcraft, and divination. In discussions of the Zulu and Yoruba peoples, I will emphasize religions more than magic.

Alan P. Merriam, in a twentieth-century study of the Basongye of Congo (Zaire), shows that many of the perceptions of humans and the universe that antedated the coming of whites remain strong among peoples of isolated villages.[10] Part of the eastern Congo since the fifteenth century, the tribe was disrupted by Arabs and Europeans in the nineteenth century. Sweeping through the land, armed Arabs and Europeans took so many slaves that the survivors had difficulty maintaining community and agriculture. In the 1960s, Merriam and his family lived in Lupupa Ngye, a village of mud-and-thatched huts. The people were primarily engaged in agriculture, although they supplemented their produce with fishing and a little hunted game. The most interesting reports for our purposes are Merriam's accounts of metaphysical surroundings.

Worldview of the Basongye

Merriam describes the Lupupans' views of universe as static. They know a few constellations, the sun and the moon, and the earth. Everything is in the hands of their good deity, **Efile Mukulu.** The earth is a flat circle, resting on water below and covered by water in the sky. The Congo is in the center, and at the edges are the United States, Portugal, and Belgium. Efile Mukulu has assigned the masculine sun to dry things; that is good for

Efile Mukulu [E-fu-le mu-KOO-loo] Among the Basongye of Congo (Zaire), the chief god of good. His counterpart is the evil god, Kafilefile.

People of Congo (Zaire). An Efe man bottles honey to trade for food.

CHAPTER TWO

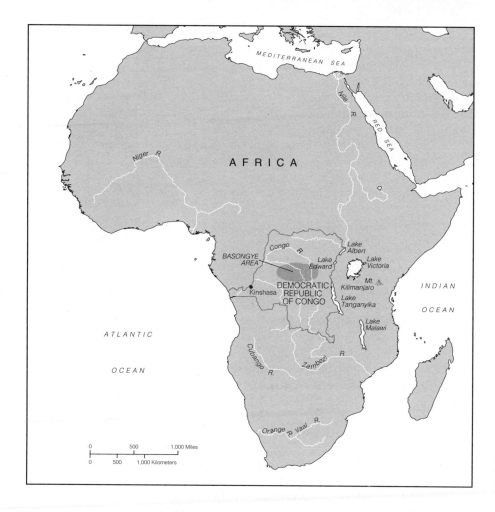

The Homeland of the Basongye Peoples.
Although Congo (Zaire) has many features of modern societies, some of its tribes preserve their traditional religions.

some purposes but perhaps bad for older people. The moon, usually feminine, has been assigned by Efile Mukulu to give light at night and be a mother of all. Mostly good, the moon symbolizes water, which, along with the sun, is needed for growing crops. On the first day of the new moon, the village protector and fertility figure is brought out and made the center of dances. It is the time to promote fertility in crops and women. Stars are friends and advisers of the moon. Shooting stars are symbols of babies to be born.

Inanimate objects and animals do not have spirits. A person can physically abuse animals, whether domestic dogs used in hunting or wild creatures, without fearing evil. Plates and spoons have essences that can accompany human spirits to Efile Mukulu. The villagers have a story, probably from the World War I era, that animals come from a hole in the ground that is near Lake Tanganyika.

BASONGYE RELIGION

Deities have spent little time on earth and, for the most part, have abandoned it. Opposite to the good god, Efile Mukulu, is the evil god, **Kafile-file.** He has departed, leaving his evil influence. Efile Mukulu rarely extends his beneficence, but in special circumstances he intervenes. Of much greater concern in daily living are four kinds of phenomena.[11]

Kafilefile [kah-FI-le-FI-le]
In Congo (Zaire), among the Basongye, the god of evil. His counterpart is the good god, Efile Mukulu.

Sorcerers are greatly feared and sometimes fought. They use enormous witless humanoids to carry out their evil purposes. Witches and *buchi* are persons of evil intent. Ancestral spirits are among the living; most are benevolent, but under some circumstances, a few do harm to humans.

A human comprises body, spirit, shadow, and perhaps a conscience. The essential part of a person is the spirit, which is incarnated up to three times as a human, perhaps a fourth time as a lion or leopard. Each incarnation is determined by Efile Mukulu. Happy ancestors can cause a human spirit to return to its family as a child. The human spirit, **kikudu,** can return as a child of either sex, carrying on family resemblances. The spirit informs the body through dreams and guides it in its responses to most circumstances—the body has no will of its own. Because the spirit knows Efile Mukulu, it always knows more than the body. The body knows only what is already known by the spirit. Consciousness, then, extends beyond the short span of a spirit in a body. A spirit can travel abroad from a sleeping body.

Because ancestors can help or hurt the living and receive or reject a spirit that has been separated from a body by natural death or by magic, they are remembered with gifts and sacrifices. The ancestors are part of Efile Mukulu, who is part of all things. Sacrifices of first fruits honor and please both Efile Mukulu and ancestors.

Basongye use small figures, **mankishi,** averaging about twelve inches tall, to bring about desired results. A couple desiring a child obtains a figure that is carved according to the sex they want. The figure is then named for the child. Obtaining children is the main use of the figures, but they can also bring success in hunting, fishing, personal magic, and guarding against witches and house fires. Although individuals can do much to influence their lives, in a last analysis it is fate that decides the outcome.

Humans, not gods, cause death. This concept is intertwined with a very active belief in witches, sorcerers, and their magic. To be distinguished from the small figures, mankishi, are human spirits bent on vengeance, **mikishi.** In contrast to good human spirits, these vengeful spirits cause a special illness that is different from illnesses caused by Efile Mukulu. To some extent, sorcerers control vengeful spirits; a person who wants protection from them can call on a sorcerer for help.

Magic influences every aspect of the Basongye's daily lives. It is so carefully studied and practiced that it could be classified by some observers as a kind of technology, a body of procedures that can be counted on to produce desired results. Merriam classifies four types of magic, each with subgroups and distinctive functions. One type of magic can be used in protecting crops, another type can be employed in producing rain, another can cause death by lightning, and another can destroy an enemy's crops. In addition to concocting recipes for all sorts of potions, members of Basongye cults wear sacred masks to obtain their desires.

Witches are creations of Efile Mukulu, but they do the work of Kafilefile. Being able to fly, they depart their houses at night, leaving their legs behind. Their intent is to cause mischief to humans. When people are visited by a witch who intends only harm, they see a special light—witch's fire—and are left paralyzed. A witch intent on killing a person can assume the form of an attacking wild animal. A chief is often assumed to be a witch. A deceased person is not free from witches, for at the cemetery a witch who has captured a person's last breath, the soul, can call the body out of the ground. The witch reduces its size, takes it home, and stores it in

kikudu [ki-KOO-doo]
The soul of a human being that may live after the death of the body.

mankishi [man-KI-shi]
Among the Basongye of Congo (Zaire), a small carved figure used to represent a child desired by a couple. The figure can also be used to effect good fishing and to protect homes and people from bad magic.

mikishi [mi-KI-shi]
Among the Basongye of Congo (Zaire), these are human spirits bent on doing harm. Sorcerers can control them.

a hanging calabash. The concept of witch changes among African traditional religions. The concept is different from historical usage in Christian cultures.

A person can become a sorcerer only by giving up a family member to be killed. Any kind of magic or power costs human lives. Sorcerers can see evil in others, foretell future events, prevent childhood illnesses in the village, and protect warriors against revenge from spirits of men they have killed in battle. Most important, they can locate and identify the source of a person's death. Because deaths are not natural but are caused by human designs, the sorcerer serves as the chief homicide investigator. In another role, sorcerers can provide magic to cause the death of an enemy.

Merriam's contemporary work, which uses approved methods of scientific cultural study, provides a judgmental view of magic. It should not be assumed that only African tribes believe in magic—it has been a part of every culture. When other religions have rituals and priests that replace sorcerers, it should not be concluded that all beliefs in witches, sorcerers, and magic have disappeared. A great deal of their lore has been subsumed in some religions, and unofficially belief in these powerful forces continues.

THE ZULU PEOPLES

Historical Development of South Africa

South Africa has approximately the same number of people as Congo, about forty million, most of whom live in cities. Christians are most numerous, followed by Hindus and Muslims. Bantus, including **Zulus,** had occupied much of the country before the seventeenth century, when Dutch settlers arrived. The British fought the Dutch and in 1910 formed the Union of South Africa. Apartheid, separation of races, which had been unofficial, was official from 1949 to 1991. In 1994 the first election open to all races was held. The first black president, Nelson Mandela, came to office on May 10, 1994.[12]

Zulu [ZOO-loo]
A member of the Bantu peoples of southeast Africa. Inhabitants of South Africa.

Worldview of the Zulu Peoples

Zulu religion and Zulu lives are one; for Zulu peoples all life has religious significance. A settled people, they live in kraals, circles of houses, and keep cattle. Their formal arrangement of simple houses is reflected in their ordering of personalities of religious significance.

The chief person of the kraal lives in the **umnumzane,** the chief house. He is both headman and priest. In his house is an **umsamo,** a place for communing with ancestors through objects of ritual significance. Other houses have similar sacred spaces.[13] The chief is responsible for communing with the important ancestors of the kraal, for ancestors know what is happening among their descendants and can help or hinder them.

umnumzane [oom-nam-ZAH-ni]
The head of the kraal in Zulu society.

umsamo [oom-SAH-mo]
In Zulu religion, the place where ancestors are communicated with.

Ancestors are helpful in healing patients. Below the chief, **diviners,** who are often women, are assisted by ancestors, who communicate with them by dream or vision. Diviners diagnose what spiritual powers are at work in patients so that healers can do their work. Herbalists (*izinyanga zemithi*) are often men who prescribe medicine for healing. As in other cultures, everyone has some general knowledge, or opinions, on diagnosing and

diviner [di-VII-nur]
A person, man or woman, who is spirit-possessed and knows how to discover people's destinies.

Zulu King Goodwill Zwelithini and Chief Mangosuthu Buthelezi.

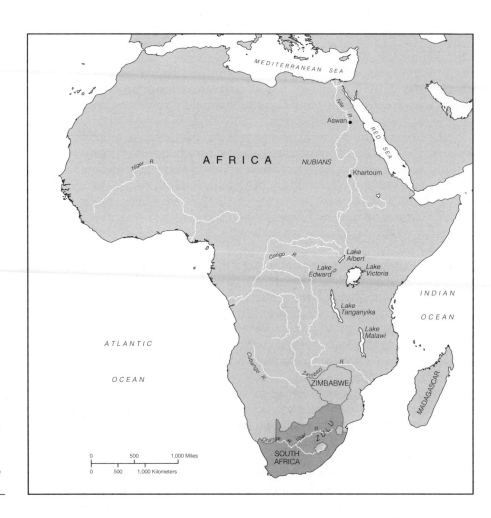

Area of Zulu Habitation. Today, Zulus are a vital part of South Africa.

Zulu Temple. An early 20th century temple in Maryloa, Zululand.

prescribing for patients. Medicine is any power that can change situations. Whether specific or abstract, it is respected.

Responsibilities for dealing with transcendent forces of the heavens are assigned to specialists known as **izinyanga zezulu,** herders of storms. As the Zulus herd cattle, so the sky specialists herd storms. They serve the God of the Sky. On uninhabited, sacred hills these specialists carry out their functions.

Some Zulu peoples, as do the Basongye, believe that the spiritual energies of the universe can be employed for purposes that are either beneficial or harmful. The dark side of the forces of healing employed by diviners and herbalists is cultivated by sorcerers. They use neutral forces for evil ends. An **abathakati** (translated "witch") also uses powers for evil purposes. They are believed to exist, but it is only conjecture as to who such persons are. Failure to honor ancestors may give an abathakati power to twist displeasure into forces of death. Witches are people who are "possessed," sometimes without their knowledge.

Ancestors, a source of power, are souls of people who sought to fulfill their moral obligations. Ancestors of the whole kraal are honored by the chief and all families. Ancestors of each family are honored by the head of the family, using rituals at the sacred place within the house.

izinyanga zezulu [iz-in-YAN**-ga ze-**ZOO**-loo]**
The deity in Zulu religion who herds weather or sky as boys herd cattle.

abathakati [u-bah-TAH**-kah-ti]**
In Zulu society, a person who uses spiritual forces for evil ends. A witch or wizard.

RITES OF PASSAGE

Although all life has religious significance, rites of passage call attention to moments of greatest religious importance in each person's life. The kraal, as well as the individual and the family, has an interest in keeping spiritual forces properly channeled. Many Zulus who have become Christians choose not to observe the traditional Zulu rites.

Birth of an infant requires its being bathed in the umsamo and treated with medicine. Because boys have responsibilities for cattle, a boy's first milk is from a cow. Only then is he fed his mother's milk. Mothers are required to observe many ritual precautions and to receive medicine.

Puberty is another time of rituals. Bathing, new clothes, and sacrifices of oxen mark this important event in the lives of young men. The days of open warfare between peoples that demanded fierce warriors with shields and spears have passed. The custom of young men being inducted into societies of warriors has less significance now, but the urge to be part of an exclusive group was traditionally met by these organizations.

Marriage is a special time not only for the bride and groom but also for their families. Powerful spiritual forces are at work, and they must be handled carefully, according to prescribed traditions. The prospective groom transfers cattle from his kraal to those of his prospective bride. After receiving permission from the prospective bride's family, the two kraals negotiate the terms of marriage. The bride then comes to the groom's kraal for the wedding events.

The father of the groom sacrifices an ox to the ancestors, and the families of the bride and the groom partake of the feast. The bride shares gifts with her new family, and symbolically leaves the kraal of her ancestors. The bride represents powers of different ancestors, so she must be especially careful and respectful of the ancestors of the new kraal. One requirement is that she cover her face when moving about the kraal. After a time, this requirement is eased.

ihlambo [ih-LAHM-boh]
The ceremony of washing spears after mourning the death of a Zulu chief.

ukubuyisa idlozi rite [oo-KOO-boo-YI-sa id-LOH-si]
The Zulu ritual of bringing home the ancestor after a period of mourning.

Death is also a threatening event for the kraal. Unless a person is old, there is always the question of what caused an untimely death. The death of a chief subjects the whole kraal to potential harm. The body of the chief is honored and buried within the kraal. People must take plentiful medicine to protect them from harmful forces. One medicine is made by sacrificing a goat. An **ihlambo** ceremony involves "washing the spears." Spears are "washed" by using them in a hunt, and women's hoes are "washed" by digging with them in earth. Ancestors are "brought home" with the **ukubuyisa idlozi rite,** which returns the ancestor's spirit to its rightful place in the kraal. With the killing and eating of an ox, the kraal closes the long period of mourning for a chief. During the mourning all rituals have to be carefully observed so that the ancestor or other forces do not turn against the people of the kraal.

DEITIES OF THE ZULU PEOPLES

u mueling angi [oo-MWE-ling-AHN-gi]
In the creation story of Zulus, the first "comer out," followed by humans, animals, and nature.

Inkosazana [in-KOH-sa-ZAH-na]
The Zulu princess of heaven who assists women and girls.

umnayama [oom-nay-YAH-ma]
Zulus use this term for a weakened state that makes a person vulnerable to environmental influences.

Inkosi Yezulu [in-KOH-si ye-ZOO-loo]
In Zulu religion, one name for the God of the Sky.

Having considered the lives of Zulu peoples, we can turn to a more detailed consideration of their traditional deities. The first being, according to them, was **u mueling angi,** who sent a chameleon to humans with a message that they would live forever.[14] He also sent a lizard with a message that all people would die. Because the lizard arrived first, humans die.

The creator god, who once was close to earth, is now so remote that he is not worshiped directly. The sky "above" is sharply delineated from the earth "below." Feminine forces of the universe are represented in the Princess of Heaven **(Inkosazana).** The sender of rains beneficial in growing crops, she protects women and girls who hoe the crops. Because they also grow children, Inkosazana protects them from the dangerous energies associated with human procreation. Contact with birth or death weakens a person with darkness or heaviness **(umnayama).** In this condition, women are particularly vulnerable to sorcery and malicious beings. The Lord of the Sky **(Inkosi Yezulu)** personifies heaven that sends thunder and lightning.

Deities and ancestors communicate with humans in various ways. Humans communicate their desires and respect with rituals. Deities, spirits, and ancestors communicate with humans through dreams and visions. Ancestors employ the medium of deep sleep (**ubuthongo**). A person can become spirit possessed, requiring the services of a diviner (**isangoma**) who can intercede with the spirit world.

The Zulu peoples have well-thought-out patterns of individual, family, and kraal life. They also have a reasoned system explaining how the powers of the universe impinge on their lives. There is a hierarchy of heaven as there is a hierarchy on earth. As there are rules for dealing with human powers, so there are rules for dealing with spiritual powers. Traditional rituals and customs maintain the vital balance among the living and their relationships with their ancestors and their deities.

ubuthongo [oo-boo-THON-go]
Zulu term for the deep sleep of persons in which ancestors can appear.

isangoma [I-san-GO-ma]
A Zulu woman who is a diviner.

THE YORUBA

Historical Development of Nigeria

Nigeria has about ninety million people, as many as Congo and South Africa combined. The Hausa, Yoruba, and Ibo groups form over half the population. Half the people are Muslims, followed closely by Christians. We know of cultures in the area from 700 B.C.E. In the fifteenth century C.E. Portuguese and British slave traders exploited the area. In 1861 a campaign against slavery began. In 1960, Nigeria gained independence, and in 1963 it formed a republic. Since then the population has been divided by civil war between competing governments.[15]

On the populous west coast of Africa, in Nigeria, the Yoruba peoples have developed an impressive civilization. Their central city, **Ife,** functioned as a city-state.[16] Although their farms provided much of their food, they entered into trade with other peoples. Their trade with the Europeans who came for slave trade and colonization did not exempt them from harsh treatment.

Ife [IF-fe]
The most sacred city of the Yoruba peoples of Nigeria.

Worldview of the Yoruba Peoples

The Yoruba of Ife considered their city particularly sacred, for there their god **Orisha-nla** began creation. On all important matters, a diviner (**aworo**) communicates with Orunmila, the deity of Ife. Like the Zulu, the Yoruba think that other deities, ancestors, and spirits play active roles in the universe and in human lives.

Orisha-nla [oh-REE-sha-nla]
A Yoruba creation god.

aworo [a-WOH-roh]
A priest of the Yoruba.

ORGANIZATION OF RELIGION

The basic unit of religion among the Yoruba is the household, dominated by the male head of family (olori ebi) who functions as a priest at the family shrine. The village, the town, and major cities are the next levels. The chief (**oba**) is responsible for sacred rites of the community.

The Yoruba peoples believe that the god **Olorun** gave them their fates at creation. Unfortunately, humans have forgotten their fates; through divination they can be learned again. An alter ego of Olorun, **Esu,** has functioned as both trickster and mediator for humans.

Ancestors are believed to be aware and active in Yoruba lives. Mediation enables living persons to receive powerful blessings from ancestors.

oba [OH-ba]
A chief or king of the Yoruba.

Olorun [OH-lu-roon]
Supreme deity of the sky in Yoruba religion.

Esu [E'S-zoo]
A Yoruba god who is amoral; he is a trickster deity and a messenger.

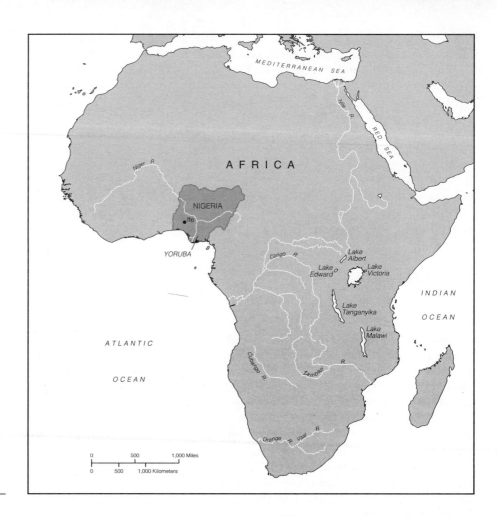

The Place of Yoruba Habitation. The Yoruba peoples today are prominent in southern Nigeria.

Prescribed rituals assist in the mediation. At the heart of ritual is a sacrifice, which may be only a prayer or a kola nut. A slaughtered animal is a more precious sacrifice, which can serve as food for the gods.[17]

COMMUNITY AND INDIVIDUAL RESPONSIBILITIES

Festivals involve the whole community in mediation with deities and ancestors. The Gelede festival celebrates the arrival of spring rains and cools the power of female witches. It honors the mothers **(awon iya wa),** a collective form of divine energy **(ase).** The deity **(orisha)** Agemo is represented by a chameleon in a festival of kings and priests. Sixteen chief-priests approach the city of Ijebu-Ode where they are invited by the *oba* Awajale. They mutually acknowledge the powers of kings and priests.

Individuals have particular duties toward various spirits *(orisha)* who have claim on them. In each person's head there is a personal orisha *(ori inun)* who represents an ancestral guardian of the soul. In heaven, one has an *ori* who serves as surity for one's destiny, its possibilities and limitations.

The hierarchy of deities of the Yoruba can be somewhat complicated. Olorun is the primary power of **Orun,** the sky. He is also known as **Olodumare.** His lofty status prevents direct approach, but he can be approached through the spirits, orisha. Ancestors, who occupy a somewhat lower level, are also subjects of veneration. According to Bolaji Idowu, each person has a double or guardian spirit.[18]

awon iya wa [u-WON-I-YAH-wa]
Yoruba term for "the mothers."

ase [AH-se]
Spiritual forces of the Yoruba; divine energy.

orisha [oh-REE-sha]
Various Yoruba spirits.

Orun [OH-roon]
In Yoruba religion, the supreme king; the sky. Also known as Olodumare.

Olodumare [oh-LOH-du-MA-ree]
In Yoruba religion, the sky.

Yoruba People.

The earth is *Aiye*, the home of humans, animals, and *omoraiye*, "the children of the world," who are responsible for sorcery and witchcraft. Communications between earth and heaven are facilitated by orisha, spirits, such as **Obatala.** He created earth and brought to it sixteen people already created by Olorun. Among the Yoruba, physically unfortunate people are considered sacred. At Ife, **Odudwa** is the deity credited with correcting Olorun's errors. Orisha-nla is head of the "white gods," named not for their skin color but for their white clothes. He prohibits drinking palm wine and associating with dogs.

The Yoruba peoples employ specialists for dealing with deities, orisha, and ancestors. A medium (*elegun*) is anyone possessed by divine powers. A specialist in medicine (*oloogun*) diagnoses and prescribes in curing illnesses. The masked dancers (*egungun*) represent ancestors for all festival and ritual occasions. Mediation between spirits and humans is a regular part of life among the Yoruba.

Although the Yoruba have a hierarchy of gods, spirits, and ancestors, theirs is a unified universe permeated by divine energy (*ase*). Religion is their way of channeling the energy for beneficial rather than dreadful results.

Obatala [OH-bah-TUH-lu]
Creator of earth, according to the Yoruba, who brought to it sixteen people created by Olorun.

Odudwa [oh-DOO-doo-wah]
A Yoruba creation god associated with the city of Ife.

COMMON FEATURES OF RELIGIONS IN SUB-SAHARAN AFRICA

The sub-Saharan peoples are too numerous and diverse to be described in detail. We have briefly examined only three examples of sub-Saharan

Ghanaian Drummers. Drumming can be used for communication, for recreation, or for religious rituals.

religion. The Basongye of Congo illustrated how a small group of people organized their lives around careful handling of energies of society and the universe. Powers had to be channeled into good or evil purposes. These energies were also recognized by Zulu and Yoruba peoples.[19] They were particularly concerned with powers of ancestors and with spirits above them in the hierarchy. All life was ritualized to maintain beneficial relationships between peoples "below" and the divine ones "above." Having looked at these three religions, let us consider more of their common features, remembering that in other peoples of sub-Saharan Africa there are exceptions to our conclusions.

Worldviews

THE ABSOLUTE

Sub-Saharan peoples of Africa are not mere animists, thinking that all things contain spirits, or polytheists, believing that many gods administer the world in a disorganized, unpredictable fashion. Some peoples, such as the Yoruba, Nuer, and Dinka, honor and fear one creator god; others honor one god who rules over a hierarchy of gods.

Although they respect a transcendent creator god, many peoples are more concerned with deities who are actively engaged in affecting their survival. We may think of Olorun (Olodumare), the high god of the Yoruba, or of Inkosi Yezulu, the Lord of the Sky of the Zulu. The female principle of the universe is worth noting in societies ordinarily giving dominance to men. Women play essential roles in powers of life in children and crops, as the Princess of Heaven (Inkosazana) of the Zulu illustrates.

These central deities, or chiefs of heaven, reign over spiritual beings of lesser sorts who have responsibilities for well-functioning heaven and societies. The 401 orisha living on the road to heaven, according to the Yoruba, come to mind. Ancestors, also, function as guards and guides of their descendants.

THE WORLD

Among sub-Saharan peoples, the world is filled with energies that can be used for beneficial or destructive purposes. The beginning of the world or

West Nigerian Village. Women pounding palm kernels.

CHAPTER TWO

of people is an important story in every African religion. In a story, one learns how to employ profitably the energies present "above" and "below." Life can be good or bad; resources can be bountiful or scarce. Although life is not so good that one would choose to live on earth forever, it is not so bad that people should shorten lives to become ancestors. Eventually, ancestors can be reincarnated.

HUMANS

For the sub-Saharan peoples, the soul or spirit is the essential part of a person, and the body is also good and useful. Sometimes a shadow of a person or a conscience is considered a separate entity. The physical body dies, is buried, and is protected. The person, however, disassociates from the body. Even in death, a soul can be captured by a sorcerer, according to the Basongye. People with atypical bodies can represent unusual powers that must be treated with extraordinary care. In Congo, twins and albinos are thought to possess the power to afflict disrespectful people; among the Yoruba, twins and albinos are considered sacred.[20]

Congo (Zaire). An Efe man announces a honey find by blowing a honey whistle.

THE PROBLEM FOR HUMANS

Among the Zulu and the Yoruba peoples, there is a belief that each human is assigned his or her own personal destiny. The gods know the destiny, but each human has forgotten it. Divination helps the person rediscover personal destiny. Priests and sorcerers can help influence powers that alter the destinies somewhat, ensuring more acceptable outcomes. The powers of ancestors can be problems for the living; neglected or offended ancestors can cause suffering or death. Generally, ancestors can be an important source of assistance.

THE SOLUTION FOR HUMANS

Communications between heaven and earth are essential to proper functioning of societies. Some, but not all, societies are organized with kings, priests, diviners, sorcerers, and rituals of mediation to ensure harmony between heaven and earth. Through divination, a person can recover memory of his or her destiny. Through sacrifice, he or she can alter some outcomes of destiny. In the absence of a dream or vision, an individual may consult a specialist in mediation. Victims of misdirected powers can employ a sorcerer for defense. Powers in the world must be harnessed for good purposes.

RITUALS AND SYMBOLS

The sub-Saharan peoples have abundant rituals and symbols. All their lives are lived aware that mediation with spiritual powers is essential. All activities of life are filled with prescribed steps to cultivate favor and avoid the wrath of spirits. As we noted among the Zulu wedding traditions, care must be taken by both kraals to keep ancestors favorable to the families. We noted that ending mourning for a chief is as prescribed as burial of his body. As Noel King has observed, among African peoples rites of passage are of major importance.[21]

Symbols fill all of life among these peoples. Each group has its own symbols; where symbols are the same, their interpretations sometimes differ.

Cameroon. Women's choir at a church service.

Chiefs, priests, diviners, sorcerers, prophets, and healers symbolize points of union between humans and spirits. Masks are symbols of deities, spirits, and ancestors. Except for creator gods, personalities of the upper world make themselves active on earth through masks and other dedicated symbols.

LIFE AFTER DEATH

Africans generally believe that the soul or spirit lives on after death. The Basongye fear their soul's being captured and badly used. If one is a particularly good person, one may become an honored ancestor or a minor deity.

RELATIONSHIP WITH OTHER RELIGIONS

Judaism, Christianity, and Islam have had many adherents in North Africa. Some Ethiopians had been Jews well before the birth of Jesus or Muhammad, and others were Christians from the sixth century C.E. In sub-Saharan Africa, Christianity arrived in force with missionaries of the colonial powers. Often African Christianity was European Christianity to which Africans were expected to conform. Islam became more popular on the west coast when Muslims stopped trading slaves. For more than five hundred years Islam has had indigenous leadership in most areas of Africa.

At the end of the twentieth century, conditions of these major world religions in Africa have changed. Leadership in Christian churches has become indigenous. Rites of Africans have influenced rites of Christianity and Islam. African peoples may work in cities with strong European influences; when they return to their home villages, they may participate in the traditional religions of their peoples. African traditional religions, however, have also absorbed some influences from Christianity and Islam.

In the Americas, many features of African traditional religion have accompanied those peoples forcibly taken from their homes. Whether in traditional form or mixed with Christianity or Islam, African beliefs and practices have entered the cultures of the Americas. Two practices of some African women, clitoridectomy and infibulation, have recently stirred controversies in the Americas. Although these customs are enforced by some women in Africa, they are not required of any major religion in the way that Judaism and Islam require circumcision of males. Female immigrants from Africa have sometimes resisted having their daughters receive these surgeries.

The diverse peoples of Africa celebrate different religions. Their richness and sophistication cannot be confined to the negative stereotypes spread by the old colonial powers. African peoples have experienced their universe as a meeting place of humans and spiritual powers. Most of them recognize that they live in a spiritual universe. At the close of the twentieth century, we are beginning to appreciate their religions' contributions to their achievements as African peoples. Alone or in cooperation with other religions, African traditional religions have made rich contributions to the perpetual dramas of world religions.

☞ A POINT OF VIEW

CONSIDER THIS: OFFICIAL AND FOLK RELIGIONS

Religions of Africa offer clear examples of differences between official religious beliefs and practices and the common, unofficial folk religions of ordinary peoples. Because written records and physical constructions make

CHAPTER TWO

official religions more visible, much of our understanding of religions is based on these public, ideal forms. In all religions, however, less well-known forms, perhaps even heretical practices, are nurtured by common folk. Deep-seated needs to overcome pain, suffering, evil, and death are sometimes deemed unmet by public, official religion. Which is the real religion of a people? Both public and private forms contribute to the whole picture of the religious life of a people. Because we generally know more about public, official forms of a religion, these forms are the ones that are discussed in most chapters of this text. Occasionally, however, we will indicate some of the heterodox expressions of a faith that are preferred in folk religion.

Having studied religions of the Americas and of Africa, we turn now to the subcontinent of India. In this area of South Asia, we will find religions that developed more than three thousand years ago. Most of them still influence the lives of millions of peoples in India and in other Asian countries. Our first consideration will be the family of religions that has given India a reputation as the mother of religions. The focus of the next chapter will be on one of those religions, Hinduism.

✐ VOCABULARY

abathakati [u-bah-TAH-kah-ti]
akh or ikhu [AHK]
Amon-Re [AH-mun-ray]
ankh [angk]
ase [AH-se]
Aton [AHT-un]
awon iya wa [a-WON-I-YAH-wa]
aworo [a-WOH-roh]
ba [BAH]
diviner [di-VII-nur]
Efile Mukulu
   [E-fu-le mu-KOO-loo]
Esu [E's-zoo]
Hathor [HAH-thor]
Horus [HER-us]
Ife [IF-fe]
ihlambo [ih-LAHM-boh]
Inkosazana [in-KOH-sa-ZAH-na]

Inkosi Yezulu
   [in-KOH-si ye-ZOO-loo]
isangoma [I-san-GO-ma]
Isis [II-sis]
izinyanga zezulu [iz-in-YAN-ga
   ze-ZOO-loo]
ka [KA]
Kafilefile [kah-FI-le-FI-le]
kikudu [ki-KOO-doo]
mankishi [man-KI-shi]
Mayet [MU-yut]
mikishi [mi-KI-shi]
Nubians [NOO-bay-ans]
oba [OH-ba]
Obatala [OH-bah-TUH-lu]
Odudwa [oh-DOO-doo-wah]
Olodumare
   [oh-LOH-du-MA-ree]

Olorun [OH-lu-roon]
orisha [oh-REE-sha]
Orisha-nla [oh-REE-sha-nla]
Orun [OH-roon]
Osiris [oh-SI-ris]
Seth [seth]
ubuthongo [oo-boo-THON-go]
ukubuyisa idlozi rite
   [oo-KOO-boo-YI-sa id-LOH-si]
u mueling angi [oo-MWE-ling-
   AHN-gi]
umnayama
   [oom-nay-YAH-ma]
umnumzane
   [oom-nam-ZAH-ni]
umsamo [oom-SAH-mo]
Zulu [ZOO-loo]

✐ QUESTIONS FOR REVIEW

1. In each of the four religions described, state the nature of the Absolute, using the most important names of deities.

2. In each of the four religions, describe the problem for humans and its solution.

3. In each of the four religions, describe some of the most important rituals and symbols.

4. In each religion, outline some of the moral obligations and prohibitions.

5. Choose one rite of passage from each religion to describe and explain.

6. Give examples of how each religion defines and deals with forces of evil.

7. Describe your impressions of how practices of sub-Saharan religions relate to practices of majority religions of their culture.

8. Can you generalize about the roles of women in religions of Africa? State reasons for your answer.

9. What attitudes do governments in African countries have toward minority religions of their countries?

10. Are sub-Saharan religions more oral or written? Does a written basis for a religion change its practices?

QUESTIONS FOR DISCUSSION

1. Is Egyptian religion an integral part of Africa, or does it seem to be closer to some other religions, such as those of the Americas? State reasons for your answer.

2. Comparing religions of North America with those of sub-Saharan Africa, what similarities and differences do you find?

3. How do religions of hunters and gatherers differ from religions of agricultural peoples?

4. How do rituals surrounding death reflect concepts of life after death?

5. Give examples of African religions that are practiced beyond the borders of the continent of Africa. Discuss some practices in these religions that supplement or conflict with the dominant religions of these areas.

NOTES

1. "Africa: History," in *Encyclopedia Britannica* (Chicago: Encyclopedia Britannica, 1986), pp. 74–85.

2. Ibid., p. 62.

3. H. Frankfort, *Ancient Egyptian Religion* (New York: Harper & Row, 1948), pp. 8–14.

4. Leonard Lesko, "Egyptian Religion: An Overview," in *The Encyclopedia of Religion*, vol. 5, ed. Mircea Eliade (New York: Macmillan, 1987), pp. 37–54.

5. David Kinsley, *The Goddesses' Mirror* (Albany: State University of New York Press, 1989), p. 166.

6. E. A. Wallis Budge, *Osiris*, vol. 1 (New Hyde Park, NY: University Books, 1961), p. 216.

7. Ibid., vol. 1., pp. 338–339. From chapter 126 of the *Book of the Dead*.

8. Ibid., vol. 1, pp. 346–347.

9. *The World Almanac and Book of Facts 1994*, ed. Robert Famighetti (Mahwah, NJ: Funk and Wagnalls, 1993), p. 827.

10. Alan P. Merriam, *An African World: The Basongye Village of Lupupa Ngye* (Bloomington: Indiana University Press, 1974).

11. Ibid., p. 111.

12. *The World Almanac*, p. 809.

13. E. Thomas Lawson, *Religions of Africa* (Hagerstown, MD: Torch Publishing, 1985), p. 19. For background information on ancestors, rites of passage, etc., see John S.

Mbiti, *African Religions and Philosophy*, 2nd ed. (Oxford, England: Heinemann International, 1990), chapters 9–14.

14. Eleanor Preston-Whyte, "Zulu Religions," in *The Encyclopedia of Religion*, vol. 15, ed. Mircea Eliade (New York: Macmillan, 1987), p. 591.

15. *The World Almanac*, pp. 795–796.

16. Lawson. For background on Nigerian religions, particularly that of the Yoruba, see also William Bascomb, *The Yoruba of Southwestern Nigeria* (New York: Holt, Rinehart and Winston, 1969), chapters 6, 7, and 8; R. E. Dennett, *Nigerian Studies* (London: Cass, 1968), chapter 3; J. S. Eades, *The Yoruba Today* (Cambridge: Cambridge University Press, 1980), chapter 6.

17. John Pemberton, "Yoruba Religion," in *The Encyclopedia of Religion*, vol. 15, ed. Mircea Eliade (New York: Macmillan, 1987), pp. 535–538.

18. E. Bolaji Idowu, *African Traditional Religion: A Definition* (London: S.C.M. Press, 1973), chapter 5.

19. Geoffrey Parrinder, *African Traditional Religion* (Westport, CT: Greenwood Press, 1970), pp. 20–28.

20. Wyatt MacGaffey, *Religion and Society in Central Africa: The Ba Konga of Lower Zaire* (Chicago: University of Chicago Press, 1986).

21. Noel Q. King, *Religions of Africa* (New York: Harper & Row, 1970), p. 62.

READINGS

Bascomb, William. *Ifa Divination: Communication Between Gods and Men in West Africa*. Bloomington: Indiana University Press, 1969.

———. *The Yoruba of Southwestern Nigeria*. New York: Holt, Rinehart and Winston, 1969.

Bronowski, Jacob. *The Ascent of Man*. Boston: Little, Brown, 1973.

Budge, E. A. Wallis. *Egyptian Religion*. New Hyde Park, NY: University Books, 1959.

Dennett, R. E. *Nigerian Studies*. London: Cass, 1968.

Eades, J. S. *The Yoruba Today*. Cambridge: Cambridge University Press, 1980.

Gleason, Judith. *Orisha: The Gods of Yorubaland*. New York: Atheneum, 1971.

Hammond-Tooke, W. D., ed. *The Bantu Speaking Peoples of South Africa.* London: Routledge & Kegan Paul, 1974.

Idowu, E. Bolaji. *African Traditional Religion: A Definition.* London: S.C.M. Press, 1973.

Josephy, Alvin M., Jr. *The Horizon History of Africa.* New York: American Heritage Publishing, 1971.

Kaplan, Irving, ed. *Zaire: A Country Study.* Washington, DC: American University Press, 1979.

King, Noel Q. *Religions of Africa.* New York: Harper & Row, 1970.

Lawson, E. Thomas. *Religions of Africa.* Hagerstown, MD: Torch Publishing, 1985.

MacGaffey, Wyatt. *Religion and Society in Central Africa: The Ba Kongo of Lower Zaire.* Chicago: University of Chicago Press, 1986.

Marwick, Maxwell Gay. "African Witchcraft." In *The Encyclopedia of Religion,* ed. Mircea Eliade. New York: Macmillan, 1987.

Mauss, Marcel. *A General Theory of Magic,* trans. Robert Brain. New York: Norton, 1975.

Mbiti, John S. *African Religions and Philosophy,* 2nd ed. Oxford England: Heinemann International, 1990.

Moore, Albert C. *Iconography of Religions: An Introduction.* London: S.C.M. Press, 1977.

Murphy, E. Jefferson. *The Bantu Civilization of Southern Africa.* New York: Crowell, 1974.

Parrinder, Geoffrey. *African Traditional Religion.* Westport, CT: Greenwood Press, 1970.

Ray, Benjamin C. *Myth, Ritual, and Kingship in Buganda.* New York: Oxford University Press, 1991.

Turner, Harold W. *Religious Innovation in Africa: Collected Essays on New Religious Movements.* Boston: Hall, 1979.

Whisson, Michael G., and Martin West, eds. *Religion and Social Change in Southern Africa.* Cape Town: David Philip, with Rex Collings, London, 1975.

Zahan, Dominique. *The Religion, Spirituality and Thought of Traditional Africa.* Chicago: University of Chicago Press, 1979.

Zuesse, Evan M. *Ritual Cosmos.* Athens: Ohio University Press, 1979.

PART TWO

Religions Arising in India

Chapter 3 HINDUISM

Chapter 4 BUDDHISM

Chapter 5 JAINISM AND SIKHISM

Except for Egyptian religion, most of our knowledge of the religions of Africa and the religions of the Americas comes from the Common Era (C.E.), the time since Jesus of Nazareth. The foundations of the religions of India, except for Sikhism, precede the birth of Christ. We have little knowledge of the third millennium B.C.E. of India, the period of the early pyramids of Egypt, we have some knowledge of the second millennium, the time of Abraham and Moses of the Jewish Bible, and a lot of information about the first millennium, the time since David, Solomon, and the great prophets of Judaism. Early in the first millennium B.C.E. in India, two powerful concepts took permanent root: karma and reincarnation. We have already encountered in religions of the Americas the concept of a permanent soul reborn in a new body after the death of the old body, so we know this concept was not confined to India. We may surmise that at some time reincarnation has been an accepted belief on most continents. In India, however, reincarnation has been a powerful belief of three religions and a stimulus for development of a fourth religion, Buddhism. Hinduism, Jainism, and Sikhism retain the belief in full form. Buddhism, however, retains the concept of karma that underlies the religions of Hinduism, Jainism, and Sikhism: All thoughts and deeds influence our future lives, bringing reward or punishment.

A third concept, caste, has also helped shape the religions of India. One is born according to one's karma in prior lives. Hindus and Jains regard caste as a fact of life. Buddhists and Sikhs ignored caste distinctions among their followers, but they did not seek to abolish the caste system of India. Now, in official India, distinctions of caste have been weakened to the point that even the lowest castes participate in government leadership.

In religions arising in India, these powerful concepts have guided some personalities who have inspired respect and awe. Peoples far beyond the borders of India still imitate and worship Siddhartha Gautama, the Buddha. Three million Jains of India regard Mahavira, as their role model for release from the Wheel of Rebirth. Sikhs praise Nanak for his faith that intended to transcend the separation of Hindus and Muslims. Although later literature supersedes the early personalities in Hinduism, millions of Hindus honor multiple gods of the Veda, such as Indra and Agni, and later gods of popular Hinduism, such as Shiva and Vishnu. In the twentieth century, personalities such as Mohandas K. Gandhi, Sri Aurobindo Ghose, Rabindranath Tagore, and Jawaharlal Nehru stimulated fresh expressions of Hinduism in independent India.

From India, some of the greatest religious insights of humans have arisen, and some of the richest traditions have endured. We turn now to the four great religions that have sprouted, taken root, and grown to maturity in the fertile soil of India.

Hinduism

Introduction

A Hindu Temple. The carvings represent divine characters in the Hindu religious dramas.

In the second millennium B.C.E., along the banks of the Indus River, Hinduism began with the dynamic encounter of two very different peoples. The darker-skinned inhabitants of well-developed cities of the Indus were overwhelmed by the lighter-skinned Aryans who were nomads from the area of Persia, and ultimately Greece. A priestly caste developed to tend the sacrificial fires that sent pleasant aromas to the heavens. Worshipers sang hymns, performed rituals, and established distinctions between sacred and profane. Over time, after the sacred sounds and actions had become engrained in society, inspired people gave them written form and permanent status as the Veda, the required guide of every Hindu.

Vital religion, however, ferments and expands, its popular elixir overflowing the boundaries of one caste or one set of rituals. Hinduism inspired gurus such as Yajnavalkya and Uddalaka Aruni, men who were revered by their wives, sons, and pupils as revealers of the Great Soul. The stories of the Mahabharata, including the beloved Bhagavad Gita, filled with stories of deities and their teachings, inspired ordinary men and women. Manu guided younger people into the more established rules for good Hindus. Meanwhile, great masses of people paid homage to hundreds of male and female deities whose images they could see, touch, bathe, and feed. Ascetics and pilgrims immersed themselves in the great rivers of India, such as the Ganges, and walked the river banks back to their sources in the lofty Himalayas. In the twentieth century, devotion to faith sometimes meant breaking the yoke of the British stronghold on India. It also included separating from the people along the Indus who had embraced a more recent faith from Arabia, Islam. Hindu leaders against the British government, such as Gandhi and Nehru, having served their time in British jails in India, in 1947 became leaders of a new India where Hinduism is still the dominant religion. The Sikhs have continued to press their case for a separate state, but Jains, Muslims, Christians, and Zoroastrians have been contented to remain as minorities among Hindus. Although Hinduism is no longer found in strength along the Indus River, now part of the Muslim state of Pakistan, it predominates in India and extends to those countries where its immigrants have established new homes.

HISTORICAL DEVELOPMENT

Hinduism has approximately 800 million adherents, so we can expect to find many different ways of understanding it. Over three thousand years, even scholars and teachers of the Hindu way of life have differed on what the most essential points of their faith are. Anyone who wants to understand Hinduism, then, has to evaluate whose views of Hinduism will receive priority. We begin with the priority of interpreting its historical development.

Historiography

Most Hindu teachers enthusiastically explain the history of Hindu beliefs and practices. Although scholars do not always agree on their interpretations of Hinduism, they do agree that foreigners cannot grasp the depths of their language and culture. Hindus may be comfortable pointing out similarities between their traditions and those of outsiders, but they are seldom comfortable with outsiders, even scholars, who find quick and easy comparisons with Western religions and philosophies. Hindus have particularly rejected accounts of "orientalists," scholars from the United Kingdom and Europe who studied languages of India and offered interpretations from a "scientific" point of view, placing little value on Hindu evaluations of their own faith and practice.

Both Hindu and non-Hindu writers can agree, however, that presenting the vast riches of Hindu tradition in the limited space of a world religions text is a formidable task. Even the best Hindu scholars would be challenged in deciding what to introduce here, and what to omit. The non-Hindu approaching from the view of comparative world religions may have a slight advantage. If we ask the questions that we ask of all religions and listen to Hindu answers, perhaps we can overcome some of the limitations of "orientalists" and reap some of the rewards that Hinduism offers. In recent years in colleges and universities of North America, a kind of agreement has emerged on how to present Hinduism. We will honor that informal agreement of pattern, trusting that in some way it will compensate for not offering the selectivity of individual Hindu teachers. Our goal, of course, is to introduce readers to Hinduism, hoping that they will continue to study, over their lifetimes, its richer varieties.

The Origins of Hinduism

Hinduism formed before anyone kept contemporary written records of its development. Oral traditions later preserved in the **Vedas** and remains studied by archaeologists provide sources for reconstructing the initial

Vedas [VAY-daz]
Knowledge or wisdom. Scriptures of the Hindus.

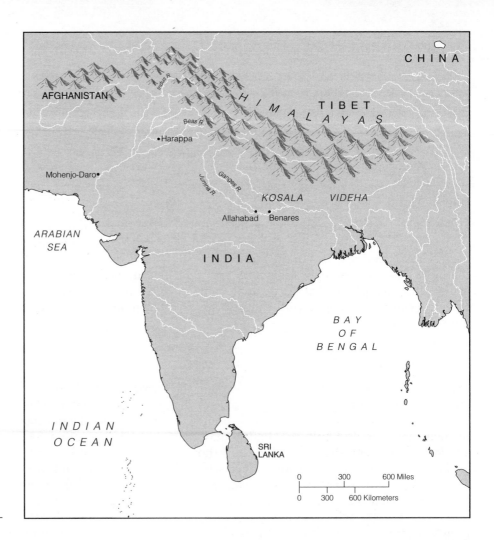

The Sacred Rivers of Early Hinduism. As sources of life, the rivers of India were considered sacred.

Dravidians [drah-VID-e-uns]
Dark-skinned inhabitants of India. They differed from the light-skinned Aryans who entered from the North-west.

Aryans [AHR-yuns]
Indo-Europeans who entered the Indus Valley prior to 1000 B.C.E. They expressed their evolving religion in the hymns of the Rig-Veda.

stages of the Hindu religion. Along the banks of the Indus River, in Pakistan, a **Dravidian** people lived in cities. Twentieth-century archaeological excavations in Mohenjo-Daro reveal a large city with houses, underground plumbing, and other refinements of a developed urban population. Some figurines indicate a concern with human fertility and other forces of nature. Also discovered was a tank, or large pool, similar to ones now used in Hindu temples. We do not know the full nature of their religion.

About 1000 B.C.E., **Aryans** migrated into Greece and India. Of Indo-European background, they traveled through what is now Iran, bringing with them the language and religious concepts of Persia and Greece. The Aryans (noble people) were herders, nomads who drove their animals ahead of them. Their deities were the natural powers of heaven and earth. The Aryans honored their gods by sacrificing animals and sharing the flesh with them in a meal. The god's portion was sent through smoke rising from the sacrificial fire; worshipers ate their portions during the service. The gods, or *devas*, were shining ones who represented things that are good for humans. *Asuras* were evil powers, representing things harmful to humans. Religion had an ethical concern to keep things on the right path, for good to be ascendant over evil.

As these Aryans mixed with the native peoples, they shared customs, traditions, rites, symbols, and myths. Each contributed and each received.

The earliest hymns of Hinduism reveal a worship that retained many Aryan practices. Later worship of Shiva reflects traditions of the Dravidians. Although scholars cannot say exactly when Hinduism began, they believe that it developed in an early period of interaction between Aryans and Dravidians.

During this period, groups and strata of Hindu society began to form. One theory is that the organization of Hindu society began as a result of **varna,** color. The invaded peoples were dark; the invading Aryans were light. Because the conquerors were lighter, light color was superior to dark. Some Hindus, however, see it differently. They think that stratification developed because of psychological preferences. The Aryans were militant, active, ruling types, and the invaded peoples were settled urbanites who preferred artisan and merchant activities. It is difficult for scholars to determine which is right, for in the early centuries stratification was neither rigid nor universally recognized. The firm **caste** system of India emerged later.

Shruti: Revelation and Scriptures

Because revelation is that which has been heard, **shruti,** and the scriptures are writings that record what has been heard, we may take a moment to describe how various forms of Hindu sacred writings are related.[1] The Vedas, the oldest part of shruti, have four collections of scriptures: the Rig-Veda, the Sama-Veda, the Yajur-Veda, and the Arthava-Veda. The second part of the shruti comprises the **Brahmanas,** or "explanations of sacrifices." The **Aranyakas,** or "forest treatises," are the later parts of the Brahmanas. The **Upanishads,** "sittings near teachers," are considered **Vedanta,** the end of the Vedas. Later Upanishads are considered **Agamas,** as ancient and as authoritative as the Vedas.

Shruti is distinguished from **smriti,** or that which has been remembered.[2] Among the smriti writings are **Manu** and the **Itihasa-Purana** comprising the epics of the **Mahabharata** and the **Ramayana.** We will look at these examples of Hindu literature a few pages later.

Gods of the Rig-Veda

AGNI

The Vedas offer varying explanations of beginnings of reality. Many of the passages speak of different gods active in the functioning of the universe. The *Purusha Sukta* describes **Purusha** as the All from which, through sacrifice, parts of the universe are formed. Gods, also, arise from Purusha. One of the gods arising from Purusha is **Agni,** the fire used in sacrifice.

I. 1.

1. Agni I call on, who is placed at the fore, the divine ministrant of the sacrifice, the invoker, who bestows the most gifts.
2. Agni is worthy of being called on by former seers and present: may he bring hither the gods!
3. Through Agni may he obtain wealth, prosperity, every day, splendid and abounding in heroic sons!
4. O Agni, the sacrifice and work of the sacrifice, which you encircle on every side—that alone goes unto the gods.

varna [VAR-na]
Color once associated with caste.

caste [CAST]
In Hinduism, the permanent social group into which a person is born. Social and religious obligations are determined for a lifetime by caste.

shruti [SHROO-ti]
Sacred writings, such as the Vedas, based on what Hindu writers "heard" in revelation. These writings are revealed knowledge.

Brahmanas [BRAH-muh-nus]
Commentaries and manuals prepared to instruct priests in the rites associated with the Vedas.

Aranyakas [ah-RAN-yu-kuz]
A philosophical section interpreting ritual of the Vedas for ascetics living in the forest.

Upanishads [oo-PA-ne-shads]
Sitting closely to a teacher; the last of the Vedas.

Vedanta [ve-DAHN-ta]
The end of the Vedas. A name for schools of philosophy founded on teachings of the Upanishads.

Agamas [AH-ga-mas]
Scripture from tradition. These writings divide according to the deity worshiped in each.

smriti [SMRI-ti]
Writings based on what their human authors "remembered" of revelations to Hindus. These works are less authoritative than revealed scriptures.

Manu [MAH-noo]
In Hinduism, the first man.

Itihasa-Purana [iti-HAHT-sah poo-RAH-na]
Ancient. Eighteen *puranas* honor Brahma, Shiva, and Vishnu.

Mahabharata [ma-HAH-BAH-ra-ta]
A long epic poem featuring activities of the god Krishna.

Ramayana [rah-MAH-ya-na]
An epic of the ideal man, Rama, and Sita, the ideal woman.

Purusha [PU-roo-sha]
Primal spirit, or soul of an individual.

Agni [AG-ni]
Fire. The Vedic god of fire.

5. May Agni, the invoker who has the powers of a sage, true and most brilliant in glory, come hither, as god with the gods!

6. Whatsoever favor you would bestow upon your worshipper, Agni, that favor of yours surely is unfailing, On Agniras.

7. You we approach every day, O Agni, you who gleam in the darkness, with devotion and bearing homage:

8. —you who are of the sacrifices, guardian of the Order, brightly shining, growing in your own abode.

9. Be accessible unto us, O Agni, as a father unto his son! Accompany us for our well-being.[3]

INDRA

Indra [IN-dra]
In Hinduism, a god of the Rig-Veda. The creator and ruler of the universe.

A quarter of the verses of the Rig-Veda are dedicated to the praise of **Indra,** and he is considered the most important deity of the hymns. He slays demons, such as Vritra, and hateful forces, but he preserves humans and gods. He is a warrior who fights for the Aryans against the aboriginal Dasas. He quenches his thirst with Soma, an invigorating drink.

I. 32

1. Now I shall proclaim the heroic feats of Indra, which the holder of the thunderbolt performed first: he slew the serpent, bored after the waters, split open the flanks of the mountains.

2. He slew the serpent reclining on the mountain. Tvaṣṭṛ fashioned for him the resounding thunderbolt. Running like lowing cows, the waters went quickly down to the sea.

3. Desiring manly strength, he chose the Soma: he drank of the extract in three brown vessels. Maghavan took his missile, the thunderbolt, slew him, the first-born of serpents.

4. When, Indra, you slew the first-born of serpents and then reduced to naught the wiles of the wily, causing to be born the sun, the heaven and the dawn, since then you have found no enemy at all.

5. With the thunderbolt, his great weapon, Indra slew Vṛtra, the arch-Vṛtra, the shoulderless: like a tree-trunk split asunder with an axe, the serpent lay flat on the ground.

6. For infatuated, like one who has not fought before, he challenged the great hero, distresser of the mighty, the onrusher. He did not survive the impact of his weapons: faceless from the clash, he whose enemy was Indra was completely crushed.

. . .

11. The waters whose master was a Dāsa, whose guardian was the serpent, had been penned up, as were the cows by Paṇi. Having slain Vṛtra, Indra opened up the orifice of the waters which had been closed.

12. You became a horse's hair, Indra, when he struck his fangs against you—you the one and only god! You won the cows, you won the Soma, O hero! You let go the seven streams to flow.

13. For him neither the lightning nor the thunder availed, nor the mist and the hail which he bestrewed. When both Indra and the serpent fought each other, Maghavan won out also for future days.

14. Whom did you see as the serpent's avenger, Indra, that fear entered your heart after you slew him and you crossed ninety-nine streams, as a frightened eagle the aerial spaces?

15. Indra is king of what moves and what has gone to rest, and of the tamed and the horned—he who has the thunderbolt in his arm. He indeed rules as king of the peoples: as a felly the spokes, he encompasses them.[4]

After Indra and Agni, **Soma,** the deified plant, is the most important god in the Rig-Veda. Its background can be found among the Haoma of the ancient Persians; perhaps its use came with European immigrants to India.

Soma [SOW-ma]
The Hindu deity of a plant that was intoxicating. In the Vedas, soma was used in worship.

VIII. 48

1. I, of good understanding, have partaken of the sweet potion, the well-minded, the best finder of bliss, which all the gods and mortals, calling it "honey," seek.

2. When you have proceeded within, you shall become Aditi, the appeaser of divine wrath. Enjoying the companionship of Indra, O Indu, as an obedient span of horses the wagon-pole, may you promote us to wealth hereafter.

3. We have drunk the Soma. We have become immortal. We have gone to the light. We have found the gods. What shall hostility do to us now? What, O immortal, shall the malice of mortal do?

4. Be comfort to our heart, when imbibed, O Indu, very kind, Soma, as a father to his son. Thoughtful as a friend to a friend, do you, of praise far and wide, extend our life, Soma, that we may live!

5. These splendid, freedom-giving drops, which I have drunk, have girt me together in the joints, as straps a chariot. May these drops protect me from the slippings of my foot and may they keep me from sickness!

6. Make me to flame like a kindled fire! Make us to see clearly, make us richer! For then, in my intoxication with you, O Soma, I'll think: 'As a rich man, move forward unto prosperity!'

7. With eager heart we would partake of your extract, as of one's father's wealth. O Soma, O king! prolong our lives, as does the sun the days of spring!

8. O Soma, O King! be gracious unto us for our well-being! We are devoted to you: of this be sure! Ill-will is arising and anger, O Indu: do not give us away to our foe, according to your pleasure!

9. For, as protector of our body, Soma, you have settled down in every limb as man's observer. When we infringe upon your ordinances, be gracious unto us as a good friend, O god, for our betterment![5]

VARUNA

Varuna, also, is among the more important deities of the Rig-Veda. The protector of Truth, the principal force of the universe, is **Rita,** which orders all things, preventing Chaos. The principle of order arose from chaos, the celestial waters, every drop of which contained Varuna.

Varuna [VA-roo-na]
In Hinduism, the Rig-Veda god of the high-arched sky.

Rita [RI-ta]
The Hindu god of order and principles.

VII. 87

1. Varuṇa traced the paths of the sun. Forth went the floods of the rivers to the sea, as does a charger unpenned to the mares. Conforming to the Ṛta, he has made the mighty courses for the days.

2. Your breath, the wind, roared and roared throughout the atmosphere, like a wild beast in search of fodder in the pasture. Within these two mighty, lofty worlds of your manifestations, Varuṇa, are dear.

3. Varuṇa's spies, simultaneously dispatched, look around both well-established worlds—sages, adhering to the Ṛta, versed in the sacrifice, mindful who shall send a prayer.

4. Varuṇa has said to me the understanding: "Thrice seven names the cow bears: let the one who had knowledge of the word tell them, like secrets—a sage helpful to the next generation!"

5. The three heavens are deposited within him, the three earths below, forming an arrangement of six. The wise king Varuṇa has made this golden swing in the sky for himself, in order to shine.

6. Like the day, Varuṇa has settled down to the sea—like the bright drop, a powerful beast. He, for whom there is profound praise, the traverser of the atmosphere, who has dominion over the sea—he is king of that which is.

7. May we be free of wrong toward Varuṇa, who will have mercy upon him who has done any wrong—we prospering in Aditi's ordinances! Protect us always with well-being![6]

MITRA

Mitra—closely allied with Varuṇa, Truth—personifies an agreement or contract. Individuals invoked his name as they entered binding agreements. Perhaps his name appeared later in Mithra worship, devotion to promise keeping.

III. 59

1. Mitra, being called, brings about agreements among people. Mitra sustains earth and heaven. Mitra watches with eye unwinking over the tillers. To Mitra pour an oblation rich in ghee!

2. May that mortal, Mitra, be ahead, endowed with food, who in accordance with his vow serves you, OĀditya! He is not smitten, he is not conquered, who is favored by you. Harm comes not to him from near, not from afar.

3. Free of illness, rejoicing in refreshment, firm-kneed on earth's expanse and abiding by the Āditya's vow, may we be in Mitra's good will!

4. This Mitra is worthy of homage, very dear. King of goodly rule, he has been born an upholder. May we be in the good will of him who is worthy of worship and in his auspicious good graces!

5. Mighty is the Āditya: to be approached with homage, who brings about agreements among people, to the singer very dear. For him the most praiseworthy, for Mitra, pour out this welcome oblation into the fire![7]

The gods of the Rig-Veda inspired worship through sacrifices. Devotees had priests, **Brahmins,** perform exactly rites that may have seemed simple when out-of-doors and attracting few people, but were profound in their influence. Three pits of fire, representing earth, air, and sky were dug; another pit was dug for utensils and offerings. Valuable items, such as vegetables, flesh, and clarified butter (ghee) were offered to deities on behalf of worshipers. Skilled priests influenced the universe to favor worshipers.

Three Collections of the Vedas

The Rig-Veda, although the best known of the Vedas, does not stand alone. With it, three other collections, *samhitas,* comprise the Vedas. The Yajur-Veda is a collection of litanies, prayers, and prose dedications used in devotions. The Sama-Veda repeats some of the hymns of the Rig-Veda in its collections of chants to be used by priests in the soma sacrifices. It helps purify the listeners and prepare them for receiving the spirit soma. The Artharva-Veda reflects the concerns of persons who have to wrestle day by day with the emotions of jealousy, lust, hatred, and fear. Charms and spells are written for ordinary people to use to improve their chances for decent life in a hostile environment.

By preserving the Vedas, the Hindus have retained something for everyone, a vital ingredient for literature that is to remain alive for each new generation. The Laws of Manu, 2.6, states that the root of religion is the entire Vedas.

The Brahmanas and Aranyakas

Those who want to understand the meaning of the Vedas for early Hindus without reading into them experiences of later centuries and cultures must turn to the Brahmanas for their interpretations. These commentaries, which began to appear about 800 B.C.E., to guide priests in their sacrifices, helped worshipers appreciate the deeper meanings and traditions of the rituals. Priests, however, began to encourage the belief that correct sacrifice, rather than the whim of deities, brought desired results. The Brahmanas not only provide access to the theology of the Vedic period but also understanding of how priests gained increased status in society.

Careful attention to details made the rituals of the priests effective. The Satapatha Brahmana instructs priests how to set up the Vedic sacrifices by building three fires, whose essence is Agni. Besides gathering combustibles, the priest also pours water on the lines of the fireplaces. The text teaches that water is the female element that joins with the male element, Agni, in procreation of food for the world.

The Aranyakas are the last part of the Brahmanas. These forest treatises sometimes teach practices that require special tutoring from a guru, for they are too esoteric for individual seekers. Some of the Aranyakas are referred to as Upanishads.

The Upanishads

Some Hindus branched out from the tradition of the Brahmins and the Vedas. They never denied these traditions, but they did go beyond them. They explored other paths of speculation about the universe, and they concentrated their investigations on the place of humans in it. Humanity is a gateway to the cosmos. As **Brahman** is behind the changes of the universe, so **Atman** is behind changes in the individual. Atman, which is essentially Brahman, can be found sustaining the core of the individual.

The experience of Atman and Brahman as different is based on **Maya,** illusion. The two may be differentiated in speaking, for that is their appearance. In reality, they are essentially one. The Vedas teach that sacrifices of meat and vegetables bring harmony between gods and humans; the Upanishads seek a sacrifice of many psychological aspects to unite the Atman in humans with Brahman, the absolute of the universe.

Many Hindus look on the Upanishads as natural developments of thoughts already suggested in the Vedas. According to their theory, no social upheavals were necessary to bring about an evolution of religious thought. Outsiders suggest that the Upanishads developed as a result of some castes rebelling against the rigid Brahmin control of all life. In the Upanishads, there is considerable speculation about the nature of the universe without agreement among various gurus. On the whole, the Upanishads have a

Brahman [bram-MUN]
In Hinduism, the name of the highest deity, the Absolute.

Atman [AHT-man]
The essence of Brahman that is present in individuals. The universal self.

Maya [MAH-ya]
Appearance or illusion; power of creation.

common spirit of inquiry. Their answers are not all the same, but they tend to be similar.

Another theory is that the Upanishads began in response to an increasing belief that humans die not only at the end of this life but also at the end of the next life. Wendy O'Flaherty states that "the theory of rebirth does not appear in the Vedas; but the theory of re-*death* appears at a very early stage indeed."[8] The pleasant prospects of living another life, an idea that brought comfort in the sadness of death, was balanced with the dismal thought of having to die another death. How many cycles of birth and death would an individual have to face? What caused the cycle of births and deaths? Was there a way to break free from these animal existences? As the strengths of these fears increased during the period of the Upanishads, so did the solutions offered by spiritual teachers.

The Upanishads began as oral tradition. In the period between 800 and 300 B.C.E., several Upanishads were saved in writing. As a body of literature, they offer ways that religion can supplement other practices of the Vedas.

THE GURUS

guru [GU-RU] or [GOO-ROO]
A Hindu teacher of religious duties. For a student, the guru represents the divine in human form.

The **gurus,** or teachers of the Upanishads, are more seers than prophets or priests. They are not fortune tellers nor do they warn of wrath from the gods that will certainly befall the unfaithful. Neither do they officiate at rituals, bringing together gods and humans. They are thinkers whose insights and reasoning lead others to believe that they have been illumined by the gods or God. The gurus present thinking that is neither cold logic nor warmed-over principles; their insights and explanations are warmed by a personality illumined by divine light. A guru's student finds the teacher more than human; the student, at least, sees in the teacher the very presence of the divine. The guru's words, then, are akin to the word of God—truth through personality. Their offering made to the gods or God is not external or material—it is the offering of the very soul and mind.

Some gurus of the Upanishads were married. Some of them were depicted as teaching their sons or wives. Many of them lived ascetic lives, having no more use of riches than did Socrates; indeed, they went beyond him in renouncing rich food and intoxicating drinks. Wealth for gurus is knowledge—the certainty of the soul's relationship with God.

One famous guru of the Upanishads is Yajnavalkya. In one scene, he discusses death with his wife, Maitreyi. As he prepares to go away and dwell in the forest, he proposes to leave her with property. But she does not want property; she wants knowledge of immortality. Yajnavalkya patiently lists many things that humans hold dear and then explains that each is dear only because it has the Self in it. The being behind all these changes is pure knowledge. Knowing oneself is to know this being. Wisdom is knowing that oneself and the Being of the universe are the same. A person cannot cease to be:

1. "Maitreyi," said Yajnavalkya, "verily, I am about to go forth from this state (of householder). Look, let me make a final settlement between you and that Katyayani."

2. Then said Maitreya: "If indeed, Venerable Sir, this whole earth filled with wealth were mine, would I be immortal through that?" "No," said Yaj-

navalkya: "Like the life of the rich even so would your life be. Of immortality, however, there is no hope through wealth."

3. Then Maitreyi said: "What should I do with that by which I do not become immortal? Tell me that, indeed, Venerable Sir, of what you know (of the way to immortality)."

4. Then Yajnavalkya said: "Ah, dear, you have been dear (even before), and you (now) speak dear words. Come, sit down, I will explain to you. Even as I am explaining reflect (on what I say)."

5. Then he said: "Verily, not for the sake of the husband is the husband dear but a husband is dear for the sake of the Self. Verily, not for the sake of the wife is the wife dear but a wife is dear for the sake of the Self. Verily, not for the sake of the sons are the sons dear but the sons are dear for the sake of the Self. Verily, not for the sake of wealth is wealth dear but wealth is dear for the sake of the Self. Verily, not for the sake of brahminhood is brahminhood dear but brahminhood is dear for the sake of the Self. Verily, not for the sake of ksatriyahood is ksatriyahood dear but ksatriyahood is dear for the sake of the Self. Verily, not for the sake of the worlds are the worlds dear but the worlds are dear for the sake of the Self. Verily, not for the sake of the gods are the gods dear but the gods are dear for the sake of the Self. Verily, not for the sake of the beings are the beings dear but the beings are dear for the sake of the Self. Verily, not for the sake of all is all dear but all is dear for the sake of the Self. Verily, O Maitreyi, it is the Self that should be seen, heard of, reflected on and meditated upon. Verily, by the seeing of, by the hearing of, by the thinking of, by the understanding of the Self, all this is known."[9]

In another scene, Yajnavalkya has a public discussion with Gargi Vacaknavi. Responding to her question about the foundation of existence, he answers that it is space. She then wants to know on what space depends. He responds that space depends on Brahman, which is not itself a being but is the imperishable in which everything is grounded. Personal existence is grounded in Brahman. The wisdom of Yajnavalkya's answers wins him a wealthy prize, which he gladly accepts.

Uddalaka is another guru of the Upanishads. His conversation with his son Svetaketu, who has completed his Vedic studies with a different teacher, reveals that Svetaketu has missed some important lessons. Uddalaka tells him that by a thorough study of the basic elements of the universe a person can understand the whole. All separate forms have their ground in the same Brahman. In the Chandogya Upanishad, Uddalaka instructs his son:

1. Then Uddalaka Aruni said to his son, Svetaketu, "Learn from me, my dear, the true nature of sleep. When a person here sleeps, as it is called, then, my dear, he has reached pure being. He has gone to his own. Therefore they say he sleeps for he has gone to his own.

2. Just as a bird tied by a string, after flying in various directions without finding a resting-place elsewhere settles down (at last) at the place where it is bound, so also the mind, my dear, after flying in various directions without finding a resting-place elsewhere settles down in breath, for the mind, my dear, is bound to breath.

3. Learn from me, my dear, what hunger and thirst are. When a person here is hungry, as it is called, water only is leading (carrying away) what has been eaten (by him). So as they speak of a leader of cows, a leader of horses, a leader of men, so they speak of water as the leader (or carrier of food). On this, my dear, understand that this (body) is an offshoot which has sprung up, for it could not be without food.

4. And what else could its root be than food? And in the same manner, my dear, with food as an offshoot, seek for water as the root; with water, my dear, as an offshoot, seek for heat as the root; with heat, my dear, as an offshoot, seek for Being as its root. All these creatures, my dear, have their root in Being. They have Being as their abode, Being as their support.

5. Now when a person here is thirsty, as it is called, heat only is leading (or carrying off) what has been drunk (by him). So as they speak of a leader of cows, a leader of horses, a leader of men so one speaks of heat as the leader of water. On this, my dear, understand that this (body) is an offshoot which has sprung up, for it could not be without a root.

6. And what else could its root be than water? With water, my dear, as an offshoot, seek for heat as the root; with heat, my dear, as an offshoot, seek for Being as the root. All these creatures, my dear, have their root in Being. They have Being as their abode, Being as their support. But how, verily, my dear, each of these three divinities, on reaching the human, becomes threefold has already been said. When my dear, a person departs from hence, his speech merges in his mind, his mind on his breath, his breath in *heat* and heat in the highest divinity.

7. That which is the subtle essence (the root of all) this whole world has for itself. That is the true. That is the self. That art thou, Svetaketu. "Please, Venerable Sir, instruct me still further." "So be it, my dear," said he.[10]

The phrase "That art thou" *(tat tvam asi)* emphasizes the divine nature of the human soul.

Monism or Dualism?

The move toward unity in the Upanishads does not reach an absolute monism—saying that there is only one fundamental reality—nor does it deny some dualism—that there are two irreducible realities. The Shvetasvatara Upanishad speaks of a dualism consisting of physical nature, **prakriti;** and soul or spirit, Atman. In contrast, the Chandogya Upanishad emphasizes the unity of human and divine. The most common name for ultimate reality used in the Upanishads is Brahman. Brahman is the ground of being behind all things. The individual soul of humans is Atman. Although distinctions can be made between Brahman and Atman, they are, if not the same in essence, very similar. The Atman of the self is essentially like the Atman of all living creatures. This is a foreshadowing of the doctrine of Maya, for what appears to humans as ultimately different is ultimately the same. In the Upanishads, such speculation is not idle curiosity but a dedicated search for ways to unite the Atman in individuals with Brahman. Klaus K. Klostermaier has written,

> A person must learn to distinguish the self from what is not the self, reality from appearance, and must be strong enough to reject all that is nonessential and nonreal. Through this, the students gain access to new depth and to new horizons that enable them to understand the true meaning of the words used to express the higher knowledge. Self-realization can be neither gained nor taught vicariously; everyone has to gain it personally. The guru points the way, supervises the training, clarifies doubts.[11]

How can the Atman become one with God? The Upanishads teach that insight into the nature of gods and humans is a first step toward overcoming the separation between Atman and Brahman. A person who recognizes that the nature of Atman in living things is very similar to Brahman, the ground of all existence, has an insight into his or her own identity. Humans

prakriti [pra-KRI-ti]
In Hinduism, it refers to matter, as opposed to *purusha*, spirit.

are not *prakriti*, essentially physical and radically different from the divine. Their true nature is not physical but spiritual. They are Atman rather than body. Their closest kin is not physical matter but the Atman of all living things. The Atman of living things is rooted and grounded in Brahman. Atman striving to be at one with God is not seeking an object strange and different; it is, rather, seeking to be one with itself. Atman returning to God is overcoming a separation, an alienation, that does not need to become permanent. The doctrine of Brahman–Atman recognizes that self and God are ultimately a unity. The release of Atman from the body so that it can join Brahman is **moksha.**

What is the experience of the Atman joining Brahman? Brahman can be considered personal, a God among gods. In this mode, Brahman is **saguna Brahman,** God with attributes. In the role of ultimate reality, Brahman is **nirguna Brahman,** Brahman impersonal, without attributes. The analogy sometimes employed to explain Atman joining Brahman is falling asleep. As there are levels of sleep, so there are levels of experience in joining Brahman. The purest form of the Atman joining Brahman is the obliteration of distinction between them—Atman and Brahman become one.

When can devotees experience this joining? They can approach it closely by living well in this life so as to attain release, *moksha.* Some Hindus believe that the universe comes into being, evolves for a period, and then dissolves, releasing all souls into suspended being. Then another **kalpa,** or age of creation, begins, bringing souls back among the living in the universe. In the Upanishads, there is no absolute end for either humankind or the universe. Their conceptions of the universe's age come close to those of geologists and astronomers today.

Prior to its final release to join Brahman, the Atman survives as an individual. The Upanishads mention the soul's **reincarnation** in different bodies until it is worthy to join Brahman. They also mention the **Law of Karma,** the law that every act, either in thought or deed, has a consequence for future reincarnations.

Instead of replacing the Vedas, the Upanishads offer an additional way for Hindus to reach God. Together with the Vedas and the Brahmanas, the Upanishads are shruti, revealed, rather than smriti, the product of human authors remembering revelation. For a thoughtful approach to religion, the Upanishads are one of the richest sources available. They have given rise to several different schools of philosophy in Hinduism, some emphasizing monism and others rejecting it for dualism.

Karma and Samsara

After the Upanishads were completed, the doctrines of karma and **samsara** played a more important role in Hindu thinking. The Vedas and the Upanishads project a positive view of the universe. The world can be a good place for those who seek to please the gods or God. But before the beginning of the Common Era, the Hindu doctrines of karma and samsara had combined with the doctrines of caste to form a view of the world that displeased many Hindus. The Law of Karma states the principle that people reap what they sow. This principle of justice requires that every thought or deed—good or bad—counts in determining how a person will be born in his or her next life on earth. A person with bad karma could be reborn many times into lower castes of humans, or even lower animals, and then not be released until he or she has been reborn in the Brahmin, or priestly,

moksha [MOWK-sha]
In Hinduism, the release of the soul from a cycle of rebirths. It is one of the four acceptable goals of life for Hindus.

saguna Brahman [SA-goo-na]
In Hinduism, Brahman as he is known with his attributes. This form of Brahman has personlike qualities.

nirguna Brahman [NIR-goo-na]
In Hinduism, Brahman as he is in himself, beyond attributes. Nirguna Brahman is impersonal.

kalpa [KAL-pa]
In Hinduism, a long period of the created world. One world ends and a new period begins with another creation.

reincarnation [REE-in-cahr-NAY-shun]
The soul leaves one body at death and is reborn in a new body. Although bodies are replaced, the soul remains essentially the same.

Law of Karma [KAHR-ma]
The inexorable principle in Hinduism that a person's thoughts and deeds are followed eventually by deserved pleasure or pain.

samsara [sam-SAH-ra]
The Hindu concept of the wheel of rebirth that turns forever. Souls are reborn until they reach perfection.

Shudra [SHOO-dra]
In Hinduism, the fourth caste, the caste of laborers. Shudras were not permitted even to hear the reading of the Vedas.

Vaishya [VAI-shya]
The third Hindu caste, that of merchants and artisans. Its members participate in the Vedic practices of religion.

Kshatriya [KSHA-tri-ya]
A Hindu caste of warriors and administrators. Originally, this caste was the highest, but it was later subordinated to the Brahmins.

caste. The doctrine of samsara is that the soul is reborn on earth many times, each time in a different body appropriate to a person's karma. The permanent soul changes bodies just as a person changes worn-out clothes.

The **Shudras,** the castes of laborers, were not permitted to practice the religion of the Vedas or even to hear the books being read. The **Vaishyas** and the **Kshatriyas,** the merchant and military castes, were able to listen to the Vedas and practice the Vedic religion, but they, too, lost enthusiasm for an endless wheel of rebirths. Some Hindu thinkers gave highest priority to discovering ways of gaining release from rebirth.

Alternatives to the Vedas and Upanishads

Two systems of thought and practice offered alternatives to the Brahmin view of the universe. Mahavira, a leader of the Jains who lived about 599 to 527 B.C.E., was regarded by his followers as the latest of many Tirthankaras (ford finders), whose example, if followed, could lead to release from the wheel of rebirth. Jainism practiced reverence for life, celibacy, and moral conduct. In turning from the animal drives of the body to the higher intellectual and spiritual potentialities of humans, it sought a path of release for the soul in one lifetime. The Jain religion will be described more fully in a later chapter.

The other system was Buddhism. Siddhartha Gautama (563–483 B.C.E.) sought a way of release that did not depend on the teachings of the Vedas and the rituals of the Brahmins. He first subscribed to Jain teachings, but he did not find release in them. In a sudden enlightenment, he saw a different view of the problem and different means for release. His teachings will be described in the next chapter. Buddha's answer of renouncing the world and practicing nonattachment to anything had an impact not only on his followers but also on Indians who remained loyal to the Vedas and the Brahmins.

THE BHAGAVAD GITA

The classic Bhagavad Gita, consisting of 700 verses (a variation gives 701), which is a part of the longer Mahabharata, presents a variety of options for those who would find release from rebirth. Although the Mahabharata is part of Itihasa-Purana, combining what is remembered and what is heard, this more popular literature is often attributed to the same source as the Vedas.[12] The "Song of the Blessed Lord" is regarded by Hindu philosophers and masses of other people as a book of profound spiritual insight that can revitalize spiritual life. In its earliest form, the Gita probably dates from the fourth century B.C.E. The setting for the dialogue is a field of battle in which Arjuna and his chariot driver (really the god **Krishna** in human disguise) are drawn up in formation against Arjuna's cousins. Arjuna protests to his driver that he would rather be killed or live as a beggar than be guilty of taking the lives of his kinsmen. Lord Krishna reminds Arjuna that as a member of the Kshatriya caste, it is his duty to fight in order to bring good out of a bad situation. Kshatriyas must protect the right by fighting if necessary. Arjuna would be rejecting the duty of his caste if he were to lay down his arms.

Krishna [KRISH-na]
An incarnation of Vishnu, who is also the chariot driver of the warrior Arjuna of the Bhagavad Gita.

WORK

yoga [YOH-ga]
In Hinduism, a path of discipline. Four disciplines lead to release from rebirth.

Krishna opens the way to other possibilities for deliverance. Humans can find release through doing their caste duties. Karma **yoga,** the yoke of

Krishna at Hour of Cowdust. Lord Krishna, with flute, is admired by women as he comes home with the cows at dusk.

work, is an acceptable way of approaching God. Useful knowledge is that which is inward and not merely academic. The motivation for work should be duty, and not an attachment to results, to maintain its saving effect. The measure of a person's deed is at the point of intention rather than in the results. According to the Bhagavad Gita, a person should renounce any attachment to the deed itself or to its results. An individual who can approach his or her caste duties in a spirit of detachment is closer to release than an ascetic who renounces all action:

> No one exists for even an instant without performing action; however unwilling, every being is forced to act by the qualities of nature. (5) When his senses are controlled but he keeps recalling sense objects with his mind, he is a self-deluded hypocrite. (6) When he controls his senses with his mind and engages in the discipline of action with his faculties of action, detachment sets him apart. (7) Perform necessary action; it is more powerful than inaction; without action you even

Vishnu at Rest on the Serpent of Eternity.
Vishnu is experienced through his avatars, such as Rama and Krishna.

fail to sustain your own body. (8) Action imprisons the world unless it is done as sacrifice; freed from attachment, Arjuna, perform action as sacrifice! (9)[13]

KNOWLEDGE

jnana yoga [JYNAH-na]
Jnana means knowledge or wisdom. The Hindu path of release based on intellectual knowledge. Jnana yoga appeals to people who emphasize rational understanding of religious beliefs.

Krishna declares that **jnana yoga** is also helpful for obtaining release. The yoga of knowledge does not demand original thought; a person has only to internalize the lessons taught by the ancient masters. Rediscovering the truths of earlier masters is enough to lead a person to salvation. There is no joy in doubt. A person who has knowledge finds pleasure in this world and even knows how to enjoy sense objects so as to make a pleasurable experience a sacrifice to God. The very essence of sacrifice is restraint, so restraint in enjoying the senses is considered a sacrifice. The avatar of Vishnu, Krishna, is perfection who has assumed imperfection in order to inaugurate a new world; he begins by imparting to Arjuna a knowledge that can save him:

> Though myself unborn, undying, the lord of creatures, I fashion nature, which is mine, and I come into being through my own magic. (6) Whenever sacred duty decays and chaos prevails, then, I create myself, Arjuna. (7) To protect men of virtue and destroy men who do evil, to set the standard of sacred duty, I appear in age after age. (8) He who really knows my divine birth and my action, escapes rebirth when he abandons the body—and he comes to me, Arjuna. (9)[14]

The most important thing to learn is renunciation that leads to release from the wheel of rebirth so that an individual can come to God. Renunciation need not mean leaving home or caste duties or turning from knowledge of the world. Whether a person chooses karma yoga or jnana yoga, the results can be the same if his or her attitude is one of renunciation.

> Learned men see with an equal eye a scholarly and dignified priest, a cow, an elephant, a dog, and even an outcaste scavenger. (18)[15]

YOGA

Raja yoga, the yoga of disciplining the body and the mind through correct postures and breathing, is also presented by Krishna as an acceptable way of release. It requires *brahmacharya*, which means celibacy.

LOVE

To the other three ways of release, Krishna adds **bhakti yoga,** devoted love for God. For individuals attaining union with the God whom he or she loves is the very highest goal of living.

> He who sees me everywhere and sees everything in me will not be lost to me, and I will not be lost to him. (30)[16]

Krishna reveals that God is not dependent on the universe, for he lives even when the universe ceases. The true self is not the doer; it is only the witness. It is a spectator rather than an actor. Nothing in the subject world is true reality. Suffering is the process through which humans fight for their true nature. The great Brahman is the father of all beings, giving rise to everything that exists. As is any other creature, man is dependent on God. Although any person has the freedom to refuse the grace of God, surrender to him is the easiest way of release. The Blessed Lord said,

> *Lord Krishna[:]* Eternal and supreme is the infinite spirit; its inner self is called inherent being; its creative force, known as action, is the source of creatures' existence. (3) Its inner being is perishable existence; its inner divinity is man's spirit; I am the inner sacrifice here in your body, O Best of Mortals. (4) A man who dies remembering me at the time of death enters my being when he is freed from his body; of this there is no doubt. (5) Whatever being he remembers when he abandons the body at death, he enters, Arjuna, always existing in that being. (6)[17]

Four Goals for Hindus

A Hindu is not required to seek the highest goals of release in this lifetime. In its breadth and tolerance, Hinduism permits four major goals in living:

bhakti yoga [BAHK-ti]
Personal devotion to deity. In Hinduism, a path that leads to salvation.

A Hindu Wedding. These Hindus of a high caste participate in traditional rites. Parents usually arrange marriages for their children.

kama, artha, dharma, and *moksha.* A person can choose a life in search of pleasures, kama. Those who seek the pleasure of the literary arts can turn to the Natyasastras for guidance. The more fleshly pleasure of making love can be guided by the Kamasutra. Pursuing politics or the materialism of commercial competition is the goal of artha. All Hindus are expected to choose the goal of dharma and live according to the duties of their caste. Moksha, release, is the goal of those who have grown tired of the other pursuits in previous lifetimes and who now seek release from the wheel of rebirth.

The Laws of Manu

Laws of Manu [MAH-noo]
A Hindu code of conduct compiled about 200 B.C.E. to 200 C.E.

The **Laws of Manu** is part of smriti tradition, perhaps the most accepted of all codes of conduct. As ancestor of the human race, Manu received the law and applied it to the different classes of society. The code allows readers to understand the duties and responsibilities of ancient Hindus as their leaders envisioned them. Scholars think that this code dates from about 200 B.C.E.

THE FOUR CASTES

Manu assumes that humans are divided between those who are twice-born and those who are not. Among the twice-born are the Brahmins (priests), Kshatriyas (kings), and Vaishyas (commoners). Those not twice-born are Shudras.

FOUR STAGES OF LIFE

Hinduism has different duties for a person according to his or her stage in life. The first stage is student. A young man between ages eight and twelve, but no later than age twenty-four, is introduced to study of the Vedas. A sacred cord is placed over his shoulder, signifying that as a member of one of the three highest castes, he has been reborn as a spiritual person. Studies with his guru may last through his twenty-fourth year.

When the former student marries and becomes a householder at age twenty-five, he lives as closely to the ideals of wisdom as he can. He tries to observe the rituals required of householders and, at the same time, tries to avoid unnecessary injury to living things. Above all, he tries to observe caste duties in marriage, in his occupation, and in raising children. He follows the model of a spiritual man who has the duties of earning a living, raising children, supporting parents, and maintaining a household. He is also expected to meet the obligations of entertaining guests and supporting holy men. Only when he has a son to whom he can turn over responsibilities can he cease being a householder and move to the next stage of life.

The Laws of Manu, which will be described later in this chapter, describes the next stage:

6.1–5

[1] After he has lived in the householder's stage of life in accordance with the rules in this way, a twice-born Vedic graduate should live in the forest, properly restrained and with his sensory powers conquered. [2] But when a householder sees that he is wrinkled and grey, and (when he sees) the children of his children, then he should take himself to the wilderness. [3] Renouncing all food cultivated in the village and all possessions, he should hand his wife over to his sons and go to the forest—or take her along. [4] Taking with him his sacrificial

fire and the fire-implements for the domestic (sacrifice), he should go out from the village to the wilderness and live (there) with his sensory powers restrained.

[5] He should offer the five great sacrifices with various sorts of the pure food of hermits, or with vegetables, roots, and fruit, ritually prepared.[18]

This period of life enables the aging householder to reflect on earlier studies and duties without having to engage in them. The essential orientation is away from home, family, human endeavors, and worldly concerns and toward Brahman, with whom he hopes to unite. Although the percentage of men who take this drastic step is small, many other men use this stage of life to retire from day-to-day responsibilities. They devote their time to the study of sacred writing and mediate on uniting their souls with God.

The goal of the optional fourth stage is **samadhi,** the release of the soul from the body so that it can unite with Brahman. Raja yoga, disciplines based on a special psychology developed by Hindus, trains the body to be subservient to the soul. In the later stages of life, this exercise can assist in meditation and liberation of the soul from the body. Ultimate success is uniting the Atman with Brahman.

samadhi [sa-MAH-di]
Concentration that unifies; absorption.

Women observe three stages of life. As a student, a woman is instructed in religious duties. As a householder, she has a separate set of duties that complement those of her husband. She may join him as a forest dweller in the third stage. In India, a woman is not expected to become a **sannyasin,** a wandering ascetic, though some indeed do.

sannyasin [san-NYAH-sin]
One in the last stage of renunciation or detachment.

Four Ways of Salvation

Hinduism has welcomed all the ways of salvation set forth in the Bhagavad Gita. The ways suggested by the Bhagavad Gita have developed into well-established paths that many Hindus walk today. The Puranas and Tantras add further information on deities and ways to serve them. Popular Hinduism's understanding of the four ways offers more varieties than those outlined in the Bhagavad Gita.

Karma Yoga

Karma yoga, the Way of Works, is valued, in part, because it is praised by Krishna in the Bhagavad Gita. Those who perform the proper rituals every day and at the turning points in their passage of life can fulfill all of their religious obligations. Although not the highest road to salvation, it nevertheless leads to the goal of release. The Vedas guide in the proper hymns and sacrifices to be used in greeting the rising sun or in marking birth, marriage, and death. The Vedic sacrifices are the heart of the path of works.

For men and women, there are distinctive duties. A man has special duties as priest in the home, remembering daily offerings of food to the gods. But his most essential duties come in the *shraddha* rites to ancestors. Besides keeping the rites of the funeral pyre, a male descendant is required to make additional offerings to nourish the souls of ancestors and keep them from the wheel of rebirth. Women cannot perform these rites, so the birth of a son is a particular blessing to Hindu families. Women, also, have their duties to perform. They prepare the food that is used in sacrifices or offerings to the gods in daily remembrance and on the special yearly religious festivals. Beyond that, the Laws of Manu prescribes many duties for women. In contemporary Hinduism, the laws that require a woman to be under the control of some man and to be almost worshipful toward her husband have been relaxed. Higher education for women and employment outside the home in business and government have made the old ways seem repressive.

Jnana Yoga

The Way of Knowledge, jnana yoga, is based on a method developed in the Upanishads and refined through the centuries. The Sankhya system of Hindu philosophy, in its dualism, emphasizes freeing Atman from *prakriti*. There is perhaps a stronger emphasis on the nondualism of Brahman–Atman. Although these two aspects of ultimate reality can be experienced separately, they are one. A human's alienation from God rests on ignorance—not knowing *(avidya)* or not seeing that the human soul (Atman) is ultimately of the same essence as Brahman.

The ignorant soul, not knowing its nature, thinks that the self is identified with the world rather than with the universal soul. The misconception involves the individual soul in a long series of rebirths, in which it experiences not only the sufferings of human existence but also estrangement from its true nature. In this state of ignorance, humans' identity can never be complete—they are always separated from themselves. The Way of Knowledge in the Upanishads indicates that knowledge can overcome ignorance. The truth that liberates is that Atman and Brahman are as similar as river and sea or as the ocean wave and the spray that the wind blows from it.

Salvation lies in a person's recognizing that his or her identity is grounded not in the world but in Brahman–Atman. In this realization lies homecoming for the soul, the release from rebirth. The home of the soul is an unchanging realm of being, Nirvana. Insight is of utmost importance, but training and guidance can help a person move more quickly toward release.

Bhakti Yoga

The Way of Devotion provides a third means for helping overcome the vicissitudes of human existence and gaining release from them. *Bhakti yoga*, the Way of Devotion, is strongly emphasized in the Bhagavad Gita. Those who serve God through *bhakti* passionately embrace him, in love. The grace of God is far more effective in salvation than is any law or ritual. A person need only trust and love God in order to be preserved in eternity. A person who trusts the ultimate deity cannot perish.

The roots of this path of loving God can be found in the hymns of the Rig-Veda. The later Upanishads offer treatises on bhakti, and the **Puranas** and the Ramayana are popular sources of its inspiration. Bhakti was widespread among the masses of Hindus during the reign of the Gupta emperors, 300–500 C.E. These eighteen treatises explain beliefs in *trimurti*, the triad of Gods: Brahma, Vishnu, and Shiva.

Those who want to follow the Way of Devotion can commit themselves to one of several Hindu gods. Brahman is regarded as the one God, who may appear in popular Hinduism as many gods. One of three gods is **Brahma,** the creator. His responsibilities are shared with **Vishnu,** the preserver, and **Shiva,** the destroyer. Vishnu is worshiped in his incarnation as Krishna as the personification of divine love. Although Shiva destroys life in order to make room for new creations, he can be generous to his devotees. In popular Hinduism, most people usually choose to serve either Shiva or Vishnu.

Puranas [pu-RAHN-as]
"Ancient Lore" treatises or the deities of popular Hinduism.

Brahma [bram-HAH]
Ultimate reality; the creator.

Vishnu [VISH-noo]
The Supreme Lord; the preserver.

Shiva [SHEE-va]
The Auspicious. Ultimate Lord; the destroyer.

Shiva with His Consort Parvati. Parvati is the symbol of young love.

Those who choose to serve Shiva in the Way of Devotion may also worship one of his consorts. Shiva, the one who brings death and destruction, is also powerful in creating new life. By joining with his consorts, he can generate life-giving forces. Parvati is his kind and gentle consort; Kali is a terrifying figure who can spread disease and death. Durga is pictured as requiring sacrifices—even human sacrifices. She is a warrior superior to male gods, for after they failed, she subdued the demon Mahisha. Nevertheless, these personalities of wrath have attracted their devotees. To a non-Hindu, Kali, who wields a sword and wears a necklace of skulls, while her mouth drips blood, may seem altogether frightening, but thousands of women look upon her as the deity who can be kind and helpful to them. In various contexts, Kali and Shiva are partners in dance. In Kapalakundala's hymn in Bhavabhuti's Malatimadhava, they "appear as mad partners in a cosmic dance that is destined to destroy the worlds."[19] Devoted men have called her the Divine Mother. Ganesh, the son of Shiva and Parvati, is the elephant-headed god who can work like an elephant to lift heavy burdens and clear the road of life. Nandi, the bull, guards Shiva's temples and protects four-footed beasts. A person may practice bhakti with Shiva or with one of his consorts. Only a minority of Shaivites have worshiped Shiva through **tantrism,** a religious practice that includes sexual intercourse as a ritual to generate the power of the spirit.

Vaishnavites choose to serve Vishnu or one of his avatars, or incarnations. As the preserver, Vishnu is kind and compassionate. Lakshmi, his beloved consort, exhibits loyalty and love for him. Vishnu is divine love that redeems the world from evil. In times of human troubles, he has assumed human forms in order to come to the aid of his people. Among his better-known incarnations is Lord Krishna, the one who reveals himself in the Bhagavad Gita. Krishna is the Divine Child, the embodiment of Beauty of Grace who plays his flute to attract women in divine love, particularly his beloved Radha.[20] Rama, the hero of the Ramayana, is also an incarnation of Vishnu, and Rama's wife, Sita, is an incarnation of Lakshmi. Rama is the perfect ruler and husband, and Sita is the perfect wife. Their love

tantras [TUN-trus]
Religious treatises for developing latent powers in persons. Dialogues between Shiva and Shakti.

Kali, a Consort of Shiva. Her fierce appearance indicates that she can destroy forces of evil that attack her devotees.

story, which ends tragically when, after renewing their love, Rama, due to public suspicion, sends Sita away, draws masses of Hindus in devotion to the divine pair. Judged before the gods, Sita is praised for her innocence in a miracle:

> From the earth rose a marvelous celestial throne supported on the heads of Nagas of immeasurable power, their bodies adorned with divine gems. The Goddess Dharani, bidding her welcome, took Maithili in her arms, causing her to be seated on that celestial seat and, while she occupied the throne, a shower of blossoms fell without ceasing from the sky. Then the Gods burst into loud acclamations, crying "Excellent! Excellent! O Sita, thy virtue is supreme!"[21]

When Buddhism developed in India, many Hindus incorporated Buddha's teachings into their own faith, looking on Siddhartha Gautama, the founder of Buddhism, as an incarnation of Vishnu. Some Hindus do not hesitate to regard both Muhammad and Jesus as incarnations of Vishnu. Hindus who find the qualities of their god Vishnu in these persons of other religions help devotees of other religions understand the qualities of love and compassion they find in Vishnu.

RAJA YOGA

The Way of Physical Discipline, *raja yoga,* is often identified with the Yoga Sutra, attributed to Patanjali about the second century C.E. The goal of raja yoga is training the physical body so that the soul can be free. Samadhi comes after restraint of all physical and mental activity. The system set forth by Patanjali is not one that can give desired results to those who approach it lightly while doing routine work in the world. As the Bhagavad Gita teaches, the first step is to embrace an ethic that emphasizes detachment from the world. A person who is serious about approaching God must concentrate on cleanliness and strong control over bodily desires. The third step concentrates on forming the body into the correct posture—learning to sit in the lotus position until the body is no longer of any concern. The fourth step teaches controlling breathing in order to attain serenity of mind. The fifth step is withdrawal from all stimulation of the senses. In the sixth step, a person concentrates on only one object until it fills his or her whole mind. The seventh step requires withdrawing the object that has filled the mind until the person is no longer conscious of it. The eighth step extinguishes all consciousness of the world.

The Laws of Manu

We have seen in the discussion of four ways of release and four castes that the Laws of Manu played an important role. Between 200 B.C.E. and 200 C.E. new literary forms appeared that developed full discussions around a thread of precepts, or sutra. The Brahmins designed moral codes that set the standards of conduct for every Hindu. Hindus had great freedom in what they believed; they had little freedom in what they could do. Attributed to Manu, the Laws of Manu describe an ideal code of behavior for Hindus. Here readers find described the Brahmin ideals for each caste and for each member of society. For example, before giving details on women in society, the Laws of Manu sketch a general attitude that men should take toward women:

[1] I will tell the eternal duties of a man and wife who stay on the path of duty both in union and in separation. [2] Men must make their women dependent day and night, and keep under their own control those who are attached to sensory objects. [3] Her father guards her in childhood, her husband guards her in youth, and her sons guard her in old age. A woman is not fit for independence. [4] A father who does not give her away at the proper time should be blamed, and a husband who does not have sex with her at the proper time should be blamed; and the son who does not guard his mother when her husband is dead should be blamed.[22]

These directions are balanced by another section (3.55–59):

[55] Fathers, brothers, husbands, and brothers-in-law who wish for great good fortune should revere these women and adorn them. [56] The deities delight in places where women are revered, but where women are not revered all rites are fruitless. [57] Where the women of the family are miserable, the family is soon destroyed, but it always thrives where the women are not miserable. [58] Homes that are cursed by women of the family who have not been treated with due reverence are completely destroyed, as if struck down by witchcraft. [59] Therefore men who wish to prosper should always revere these women with ornaments, clothes, and food at celebrations and festivals.[23]

Hindu conduct today is not determined by Manu, but the Laws still have some influence. For faithful Hindus, this code is still a standard to be considered.

Orthodox Hindu Systems of Philosophy

Indian philosophy is a way of perceiving the universe. The Hindu philosopher is one who intuits reality, who knows the basis of the universe and the purpose of human life. From intuitions, the philosopher reasons a systematic understanding of the universe and humanity. Philosophers are concerned with both metaphysics, the general understanding of reality, and ethics, the principles that direct human conduct.

THE SANKHYA

The Sankhya system of philosophy is attributed to Kapila, who lived at the beginning of the period of the Upanishads. However, the earliest written statement of the six systems that we have may come from the second or third century of the Common Era. The Sankhya system is dualistic and explains the universe without employing gods; it argues that there are two irreducible realities in the universe. Prakriti is matter; it is real and not an illusion. Purusha is the stuff of souls or spirits. Purusha is composed of individual souls rather than one undifferentiated soul. These souls attract prakriti to themselves. The souls are in a foreign environment, imprisoned by their attachment to matter. Only by enlightening souls so that prakriti dissolves can they be released. Living in ways that do not involve the soul with matter leads to release. The purpose of Sankhya philosophy is to free souls from bondage to matter.

OTHER PHILOSOPHICAL SYSTEMS

Advaita Vendanta, part of the Vendanta system, refers to itself not as a monism but as a nondualism, advaita. Set forth by Shankara (788–829 C.E.)

avidya [a-VID-ya]
In Hinduism, the term means
"ignorance," or not seeing things as
they are.

in a commentary on the Vendanta Sutra, the system rests on Brahman. The phenomenal world is not as we experience it. What we experience is Maya; things, though real, are not what they seem to be. Appearances are not ultimate reality. It is ignorance, **avidya** (not seeing), that keeps individuals from the reality of Brahman. Believing in the independent human soul is also avidya. Belief in the various gods of Hinduism demonstrates an ignorance of Brahman–Atman, the one reality. The world can be overcome through rituals and worship as well as ascetic living. The key to release is recognition that Atman and Brahman are not ultimately separate.

The other four systems of Hindu philosophy are also concerned with knowing how humans can best attain spiritual maturity. Yoga, which was discussed in this chapter as raja yoga, is dualistic. The classical explanation of this philosophy was given by Patanjali in the second century C.E. Yoga, often allied with the Sankhya system, is the choice of people who experiment in liberating the soul from the body. Nyaya focuses on intellectual analysis and logic in understanding obligations for humans. It is attributed to a person named Gautama, who emphasized that all knowledge must be empirically tested, for most suffering in life comes through false notions. Vaisheshika philosophy studies the external world and understands it in terms of atoms. Kanada, its founder, believed that atoms and soul are both eternal. The entire process of souls entering and leaving the world is governed by the power of Advishta, an unseen force or deity. Purva-Mimamsa emphasizes the literal truth of the Vedas, which sets forth the whole *dharma*, or duty, of humans. Founded by Jaimini, the system maintains that the Vedas are uncreated and eternal. It is the ground of Being itself. The Purva-Mimamsa system is closer to the priestly interests of the Brahmanas than to the speculations of philosophers.

These four systems, as well as Sankhya and Advaita Vedanta, focus on the ways humans can best realize their spiritual potentialities. All of the six orthodox systems of Hindu philosophy aim to release humans from the suffering involved at the animal level of life.

Islam in India

Muslim invaders arrived in Debul (Pakistan) in the early eighth century C.E., less than a century after the inception of Islam. Soon Muslims controlled much of the Indian subcontinent. Strict monotheists, believing that the only God is Allah, they opposed Hindu polytheism, though for the most part they took the practical course of toleration.

For nearly five hundred years, Muslims controlled much of India. Moguls, followers of Babur, who conquered India in 1526, established a Muslim empire that lasted until the mid-nineteenth century. The Mogul influence can still be seen in many architectural remains of India.

As different as Islam and Hinduism were, there were men of spiritual insight who thought a harmony could be achieved. Through the efforts of Kabir (1440–1518), a Muslim, Hindu and Muslim ideas were combined. He taught that complete love for God is sufficient to release anyone from the Law of Karma. Nanak (1469–1538), a Hindu, found ways for Hindus to participate in monotheism. This guru became the founder of a new religion, the Sikh, which sought to attract both Hindus and Muslims. It was rejected by both. Islam and Sikhism are still important religions in India. Both religions will be discussed in other chapters.

Christianity in India

Christians of the Thomas Church of India claim that their church began with a visit of Jesus' apostle Thomas. Although that claim has not been supported to the satisfaction of all historians, there is evidence of Christian congregations in India from the third century. Located in Kerala, Southwest India, the Thomas Church broke with Rome and affiliated with the Jacobite Christians.[24]

Christian influence arrived in another form with Europeans seeking trade. The Portuguese were followed by Dutch and French traders. But from 1757 to 1947, the British controlled India. Under their rule, Christian groups felt free to establish numerous missions. Through educational and other activities, Christians made some impact on Hinduism, if only to have Hindus search their tradition for responses to Christian teachings. Unitarianism, for example, also believed that many different paths lead to one God. Some Hindus deny that Christians were successful in making many converts in India, except among the lowest castes. Christianity will be discussed in a later chapter.

Hindu Responses to Western Influence

British rule in India separated educational, governmental, and humanitarian concerns from religion. Hindus were free to accept certain aspects of Western culture while at the same time rejecting Christianity. Although they might dislike Christian doctrine and missionaries, they evaluated other aspects of Western culture on their own merits. Hindu responses to the British lifestyle varied widely; some rejected it, whereas others embraced it. The more interesting responses were those that combined both Hindu and Western traditions in new approaches to a better world.

RAM MOHAN ROY

Although Ram Mohan Roy (1772–1833) lived during the early years of British rule in India, in many ways he was the forerunner of the Hindu reformers who created modern India. His work was limited among the Hindus because he moved too fast, gave up too much Hindu tradition, and was influenced too much by Unitarianism. The Unitarian denomination is a Protestant Christian group that broke with the Congregationalists by abandoning belief in the Trinity of Father, Son, and Holy Spirit; by viewing Jesus as only an exemplary social reformer; and by emphasizing the value of human reasoning.

The Brahmo Samaj founded by Ram Mohan Roy turned to the Dharma Shastras and the Upanishads for teachings that paralleled those of the Unitarians. He denounced polytheism, abandoned a belief in reincarnation, and emphasized the power of the human intellect to bring about better living conditions for all humans. He searched for a humanitarian ethics that would reform the practices of infanticide of females, burning live widows on the funeral pyres of their husbands, and child marriage. He found the model for a new India in Hindu sacred writings. But it was clear to his Hindu critics that the inspiration and standards for his ideas came from Unitarianism, which was essentially Western and nominally Christian. The Brahmos were influential through the nineteenth century, but they failed to become the nucleus of the new India. One leader of the Brahmo Samaj was Debendranath Tagore, who abandoned claims to orthodoxy and evaluated all scriptures asserting to the judgment of a light within the human heart.

DAYANANDA SARASVATI

Hindus eagerly received the Arya Samaj of Dayananda Sarasvati (1824–1883). He turned away not only from Western influences but also from post-Vedic developments of Hinduism. Raised a Shaivite, he defied his parents' plan for his marriage and became a *sannyasin*, or celibate wanderer, at the age of twenty-one. He mastered the life of the yogin, and then he studied Sanskrit grammar to the point that he was a sound scholar of the Vedas. He became a champion of the Vedas; the Vedas, he held, are the only true scripture. They are the only standard that Hindus should follow.

His views of the Vedas had some radical implications for both Hinduism and other religions. He said that since the Vedas do not mention the *jatis*, occupational castes that bound Hindus, they should have no application in modern Hinduism. Rama and Krishna are not gods. All knowledge is given in the Vedas; knowledge claimed by the Western cultures and religions was first presented in the Vedas. He carefully argued that the Vedas are superior to the false claims of Christian and Muslim scriptures. He asked Hindus to return to the pure, active, positive lives of the Aryans. His surprising combination of raja yoga and social activism set an example for later reformers.

RAMAKRISHNA

Ramakrishna (1836–1886) is the holy title for Gadadhar Chatterji, who lived most of his Brahmin life in a temple of Kali near Calcutta. Neither an organizer nor an ardent social reformer, he was, nevertheless, a model for a different approach to harmony among religions and cultures. His absolute devotion to Kali led him to repeated experiences of samadhi. In a direct vision of the goddess, he came to understand that all divinities experienced by humans are manifestations of the one God. Through experiments, he found God in the worship not only of Krishna, Sita, and Rama but also of Allah and Christ.

> Different creeds are but different paths to reach the Almighty. Various and different are the ways that lead to the temple of Mother Kali at Kalighat (Calcutta). Similarly, various are the ways that lead to the house of the Lord. Every religion is nothing but one of such paths that lead to God.[25]

Ramakrishna's views were spread in India by people who came to visit him and by disciples who gathered about him in his later years. Swami Vivekananda, a young law student, organized a Ramakrishna movement. Through his speech at the Parliament of Religions in Chicago in 1893, he was instrumental in forming societies in the United States and other countries. At Ramakrishna centers in India and abroad, he instilled in visitors the insights and conclusions of his teacher, the mystic Ramakrishna.

RABINDRANATH TAGORE

The son of Debendranath Tagore, who was a leader of the Brahmo Samaj, Rabindranath Tagore (1861–1941) departed from the Brahmos to emphasize mysticism in his experience with a personal God. His poems reflect his intuitive experiences with God. He presents a Hindu view of life that wins the appreciation of peoples from many countries. He received a Nobel Prize for his book of poems, *Gitanjali*.

In 1941, nearing death, Rabindranath Tagore wrote of the end of British rule in India:

> I live today in the hope that the Saviour is coming, that he will be born in our midst in this poverty-shamed hovel which is India. I shall wait to hear the message he brings with him, the supreme word of promise he speaks unto man from this eastern horizon to give faith and strength to all who hear.
>
> I look back on the stretch of past years and see the crumbling ruins of a proud civilization lying heaped as garbage out of history! And yet I shall not commit the grievous sin of losing faith in Man, accepting his present defeat as final. I shall look forward to a turning in history after the cataclysm is over that the sky is again unburdened and passionless.
>
> Perhaps the new dawn will come from this horizon, from the East where the sun rises; and then, unvanquished Man will retrace his path of conquest, despite all barriers, to win back his lost heritage.[26]

Rabindranath Tagore. His poems depart from the rationalism of the Brahmo Samaj and emphasize his mystical experiences with a personal God.

MOHANDAS K. GANDHI

In contrast to the earlier Hindu reformers, Mohandas K. Gandhi (1869–1948) studied in Britain and practiced law in South Africa. He was keenly aware of the social injustices imposed by the British; he became aware of the injustices imposed by Hindus, especially against **untouchables.** Untouchables were Hindus, often of the Shudra caste, who were considered by higher castes too defiling to contact physically. He referred to them as Harijans, "Children of God." In life he worked for their welfare, and in death he inspired continuing care for them.

Gandhi neither embraced Western culture nor rejected it. He sought to use its resources to help India. At the same time, he tried to kindle by example the light of truth available in the simple virtues of Hinduism.

The outside world saw a small, ascetic man who kept the British rulers in India in turmoil by organizing mass demonstrations against injustices. That his followers were nonviolent resisters was sometimes ignored in the British show of force and arrests of demonstrators. His fasting in prison until others did his bidding was a new weapon in the arsenal of social reform. The British lion was not amused at being bearded in public; the masses of Hindus loved Gandhi for it. What many observers overlooked was that he had a sound spiritual foundation for his program of reform.

Gandhi was influenced by the Isha Upanishad. Two doctrines shaped his personal commitments and public actions. *Satyagraha* can be translated "truth force." For Gandhi, God is truth. A person's whole life should be a commitment to seek and fulfill truth. The other doctrine is *ahimsa*, which is usually translated "noninjury" or "nonviolence," but it can also mean "love." To love God is also to love the beings in whom God dwells. From these doctrines it follows that there is no room for hatred and violence among any humans. Before anyone can correct the impurities and injustices of the world, they must first purify themselves. Gandhi is, perhaps, the best-known example in the twentieth century of using spiritual force to effect political change.

> He said that having rejected the sword, he had nothing to offer his opposition but love. He lived in expectation that in some future life he would be able to hug all humanity as friends.[27]

untouchable
In Hinduism, a person, often a Shudra, who is considered by upper castes to be too impure to allow physical contact. Untouchability has been abolished.

Mohandas K. Gandhi. He is the Hindu pacifist leader who demonstrated against British rule in India.

Gandhi's spiritual approach was influential in moving the British government to grant independence to India in 1947.

Aurobindo Ghose, now referred to as Sri Aurobindo (1872–1950), received his education in Cambridge, England. His studies of European languages did not sever his ties with Hindu friends. Once back in India, he soon joined Bal Gangadhar Tilak (1856–1920) in political action for nationalism. Between 1906 and 1950, he led a group that published the *Bande Mataram* (Hail to the Mother), espousing noncooperation, passive resistance, boycott, and national education. Although Sri Aurobindo did not participate in active guerrilla warfare, he endorsed and inspired it. Eventually, he was arrested by the British and served time in prison. While there, he had a mystical experience that changed his life. He abandoned his Western ways and spent the last years of his life in Pondicherry practicing yoga exercises and writing his philosophy in English. Not abandoning the struggle against imperialism, he intended to find the source of spiritual power that would defeat India's enemies.

Sri Aurobindo thought of the universe as essentially spiritual. There are gradations of spirituality from the insentient up the scale of conscious being until the highest levels *sat-chit-ananda*, or being-consciousness-bliss. Through yogin practices a person can become conscious of the universal spirit that resides within. Being conscious of God's dwelling within opens up possibilities for freedom and the full realization of bliss. Through spiritual discipline, a person comes to experience the life divine:

> The Divine that we adore is not only a remote extracosmic Reality, but a half-veiled Manifestation present and near to us here in the universe. Life is the field of a divine manifestation not yet complete: here, in life, on earth, in the body . . . we have to unveil the God-head.[28]

The spiritual world has a firm order, the Rita of the Vedas. As the soul comes to know itself, it becomes aware of universal principles that govern conduct leading to life divine. Thus, the moral law is not a foreign regimen to be suffered but a realization of principles deep within the self. By practicing spiritual discipline, a person discovers the freedom and bliss of life divine.

World reform comes through spiritual development of the self. Secular education that ignores the spirit can lead only so far; students always fall short of the level that they could reach if they were taught the spiritual concerns of humans. Through spiritual awakening of individuals, society is reformed. With a reformed society, the environment changes to help liberate souls for life divine. Sri Aurobindo teaches that those who would change the world must first change themselves. To make any significant changes in the physical world, a person must first realize its roots in the spirit:

> If there is, as there must be in the nature of things, an ascending series in the scale of substance from matter to spirit, it must be marked by a progressive diminution of those capacities most characteristic of physical principle and a progressive increase of the opposite characteristics which will lead us to the formula of pure spiritual self-extension. . . . Drawing away from durability of form, we draw towards eternity of essence; drawing away from our poise in the persistent separation and resistance of physical matter, we draw near to the highest divine poise in the infinity, unity and indivisibility of spirit.[29]

Sri Aurobindo has had a profound effect on many current Hindu philosophers and religious leaders. His influence continues through his voluminous writings and his ideal community at Pondicherry.

Sarvepalli Radhakrishnan (1888–1975) bridged the world between Britain and India. He wrote extensively of both Western and Hindu philosophy. He was at home lecturing anywhere in the world. His personal philosophy was a development of Vivekananda's Vedanta that sought a common spiritual ground for all peoples and religions. He had faith in human potential to make a better world, for humans are spiritual as well as physical. Their spiritual capacities make it possible for humans to cooperate in achieving a harmony in political, economic, and religious life.

> It is the aim of religion to lift us from our momentary meaningless provincialism to the significance and status of the eternal, to transform the chaos and confusion of life to that pure and immortal essence which is its ideal possibility. If the human mind so changes itself as to be perpetually in the glory of the divine light, if the human emotions transform themselves into the measure and movement of the divine bliss, if human action partakes of the creativity of the divine life, if the human life shares the purity of the divine essence, if only we can support this higher life, the long labour of the cosmic process will receive its crowning justification and the evolution of centuries unfold its profound significance. The divinising of the life of man in the individual and the race is the dream of the great religions.[30]

Independent India

In 1947, India gained independence from Britain. For the first time in a thousand years, its peoples were free to develop their own government, laws, economy, and educational systems. Independent India has guaranteed freedom of religion for all the faiths in its borders. Hindus and Muslims are large groups, and Jains and Sikhs are important native religions. Although they came from other countries, Parsis and Christians have been in India for many centuries. All these religions have a place of respect in India.

At the same time, the insights of the reformers have been retained in modern India. India's constitution guarantees freedom of religion, life, liberty, and due process of law. It makes illegal practices of untouchability, forced labor, and discrimination due to caste, race, sex, belief, and place of birth.[31] As in other countries, laws are not always observed. Humanitarian and educational concerns have changed practices from the old ideals of the Laws of Manu. As experience helps evaluate old answers, India changes, revises, and redesigns programs. Having rid the country of imperialism, Indians still have to wrestle with the new ideologies of communism, socialism, and capitalism.[32] A trend toward secularism throughout India undermines the spiritual worldviews of all its religions. Whatever the problems and accomplishments of India, they are India's; Indians want to do their own analyses and propose their own solutions. Outsiders are welcome to observe, to encourage, and, when invited, to participate in ways stipulated by the peoples of India.

Since the independence of India, traditional roles for Hindu women have been greatly expanded. The Constitution made women equal in

◆ **1500** Aryans move into India

◆ **1200** Vedas recorded

◆ **800** Upanishads begun; Kapila, Sankhya philosophy

◆ **599** Birth of Mahavira

◆ **563** Birth of Buddha/Bhagavad Gita written

◆ **326** Alexander the Great invades India

◆ **300** Upanishads completed

◆ **200** Laws of Manu begun

200 Laws of Manu completed ◆

711 Muslims reach Dabul (Pakistan) ◆

788 Birth of Shankara, Advaita Vedanta ◆

1440 Birth of Kabir ◆

1469 Birth of Nanak ◆

1526 Baber establishes Mogul Empire ◆

1757 British East India Company gains control of Bengal ◆

1772 Birth of Rob Mohan Roy, Brahmo Samaj ◆

1824 Birth of Dayananda Sarasvati, Arya Samaj ◆

1858 British control government of India ◆

1861 Birth of Rabindranath Tagore ◆

1863 Birth of Ramakrishna of Calcutta ◆

1872 Birth of Sri Aurobindo ◆

1885 Indian National Congress formed ◆

1888 Birth of Sarvepalli Radhakrishnan ◆

1890 Birth of Mohandas K. Gandhi ◆

1920 M.K. Gandhi leads Indian National Congress ◆

1940 Moslem League demands that a Muslim country, Pakistan, be carved out of India ◆

1947 India independent of Britain; Pakistan formed for Muslims ◆

1948 M.K. Gandhi assassinated ◆

1950 India becomes a republic ◆

1962 Chinese Communist forces invade India, then withdraw ◆

1966 Indira Gandhi, daughter of Nehru, becomes Prime Minister of India ◆

1984 Golden Temple of Sikhs invaded by Indian Army; Indira Gandhi assassinated by Sikhs ◆

1992 Hindus and Muslims clash over sacred site in Ayodhya ◆

1995 Shiv Sena leader Bal Thackera changes "Bombay" name to Mumbai; opposes secular constitution ◆

| BCE | 2000 | 1500 | 1000 | 500 | 0 | 500 | 1000 | 1500 | 2000 | CE |

Recent India and Its Neighboring States.
The partition of India in 1947 created a separate country for Muslims, Pakistan. Other neighboring states of India are largely Buddhist.

matters of social, political, and economic acts. Health and education became matters of state and central governments, which sought to improve the status of women. Marriage, divorce, and inheritance fell to the Hindu Code Bill.[33] Indira Gandhi's service as leader of India proved a role model for women. Many women, however, stay home, performing traditional roles of house-holders. Some women study the traditional subjects in universities. A few women are active in the sciences and professions. A few exceptional women have assumed roles as religious leaders, roles not generally open to women. One example of a present-day guru is Ma Jnanananda, of Madras, a mother of five who studied Advaita Vedanta. She taught that women who love God should find their roles in life no obstacle.[34]

The independence of India has permitted religious rivals to express themselves more freely. The first clashes were between Hindus and Muslims when Pakistan was set aside for a Muslim state. More recently, in 1980, Sikhs have demonstrated, sometimes violently, for a separate state in the Punjab. The Bharatiya Janata party in the 1990s has pushed hard for Hindu rights as representing the majority of the population. In Ayodhya, Hindus destroyed a Muslim mosque to erect a temple to Lord Rama, claiming that Muslims had earlier destroyed a Hindu temple on that spot. The incidents prolong a dispute over who shall have ascendancy in India.

HINDUISM

CONSIDER THIS: THE LAW OF KARMA

Does the Law of Karma promote resignation to one's present status in life or accepting responsibility for one's freedom? Sometimes students think of the Law of Karma as a sentence that cannot be commuted, punishment for deeds in past lives. Another interpretation may be more rewarding. Although a person's present condition is determined by past thoughts and deeds, the Law of Karma implies that by changing one's *present* thoughts and deeds one can change one's future. Rather than sentencing us to a future that we cannot change, the Law of Karma challenges us to exercise our very real freedom and responsibility. By making good choices now, we can assure ourselves a good future.

Because we can change our futures, the Law of Karma differs from either fate or predestination in other religions. Fate is an unalterable road to a determined end; predestination guarantees a foreordained finish. The Law of Karma, however, permits us, here and now, to choose our futures.[35] We can choose a goal, modify our thoughts and deeds, and through responsible actions arrive at a destination that we have chosen.[36] Instead of victims, we are victors.[37] We are free and responsible for our own destinies.[38]

WORLDVIEW

Since its earliest centuries, Hinduism has encouraged a variety of beliefs and practices. Hindus start with guidance from the Vedas; from that scriptural basis is freedom to develop manifold expressions of faith and action. As we have seen, describing what Hindus believe and practice is difficult, for there are many Hindus, many sources, and many types of belief and practice. Although there can be exceptions to almost any statement made about Hinduism, there is value in summarizing the understanding of many Hindus. The following generalizations are offered as introductions to Hindu beliefs. Those who read widely in Hindu literature will become aware of variations from these views.

The Absolute

Images of the Hindu gods are not intended to be understood literally. The well-known figure of Nataraja, or Shiva, as lord of the dance, serves as an example. Shiva has four arms and hands extending from his shoulders. The upper hands with drum and flame symbolize the forces of creation and destruction. The lower hands tell observers not to fear, for the Lord protects those who worship him. His right foot treads on the demon ignorance. The Lord's dance within a circle of fire represents the incessant dancing energy that supports the action of the universe. The universe exhibits rather than exhausts the Lord's power of creation and destruction. A. L. Basham writes of Indian dance,

> Indian dancing is not merely a thing of legs and arms alone, but of the whole body. Every movement of the little finger or the eyebrow is significant, and must be fully controlled. The poses and gestures are classified in detail, even as early as the *Bharata Natyasastra,* which mentions thirteen poses of the head, thirty-six of the eyes, nine of the neck, thirty-seven of the hand, and ten postures of the body. Later texts classify many more poses and gestures, every one of which depicts a specific emotion or object. With so many possible combinations the dancer can tell a whole story, easily comprehensible to the observer who knows the convention.[39]

When the hymns that became the written Vedas were being composed in oral form, the spiritual leaders of the Aryans had a problem describing the forces of the universe. They feared making the mistake of ascribing too many personalities to individual gods or, on the other hand, they could err in depicting an ineffable, unknowable ground of all existence. Hindu leaders, except for gurus of the Upanishads and saints of various groups, have thought it better to include many personalities. It is better to have people choose among images of many gods than to leave them unable to feel any devotion for an abstract principle. Hinduism, in contrast to Judaism and Islam, has not seen image worship as a threat. If a few people worship images as literal depictions of the gods, they are still better off than not worshiping at all. In time, if they have the capacity, they will come to know that the divine transcends the image. Able worshipers will realize that images are symbols of the various powers at work in the universe. Some sophisticated Hindus prefer one image or god to another—for example, either Shiva or Vishnu. Many more Hindus prefer one of the more personal deities, such as Kali or Krishna. Few images of Brahman are found. Intellectually, it can be understood that Brahman is the ground of all gods. How can Brahman be worshiped? Answering the question of how many gods there are, Yajnavalkya gave all sorts of figures, from 3 to 3,300. In the end, there is only one God; all the others are but manifestations of powers. Ramakrishna began by finding God through Kali; before he died, he could find God through either Hindu gods or the God of Christians or Muslims. He told a story of Shiva, who denounced one of his devotees because he refused to worship Vishnu. The devotee did not realize that all the gods are only powers of the one Brahman.

With studying Hinduism comes the realization that the traditional labels of polytheism, monotheism, or atheism are inappropriate. They are not helpful in understanding Hindu attitudes toward the divine. Perhaps the term **henotheism** is better, for it emphasizes one superior god in the presence of lesser gods. The traditional terms, however, are inadequate to Hindu attitudes toward the divine.

henotheism [HEN-o-the-ISM]
A belief that affirms one deity without denying the existence of others.

A distinctive attitude of Hinduism is that there is more to the universe than meets the eye. There is a reality that embraces all that we experience; to understand the universe and ourselves, its presence is necessary. Behind all the phenomena of life, there is a source of energy that makes it possible. This unit can be experienced, however, in a great variety of ways. No one way in itself is complete.

The World

The Hindu world, or the universe, is more complicated than in religions from the Middle East. The ancient Hindu writings speak of time and space in terms that stagger the imagination of all but modern astronomers and physicists. Other Hindu scriptures speak of cycles of expansion and collapse in the universe that are consistent with the big bang theory, except following the bang is another expansion phase followed by collapse and another bang. Hinduism has no problem with island universes or black holes. These theories support rather than threaten Hindu views of God and the universe.

Hinduism finds polarities of energy everywhere. Creation is balanced by destruction. Shiva is symbolized in both the phallus of creation and the trident of destruction. Kali wears a necklace of skulls, a symbol of death;

Shiva as Nataraja, Lord of the Dance. This figure is in bronze, from Tanjore, twelfth or thirteenth century.

she is also the divine mother who is gentle and kind to those who seek her help. The world is both good and bad. Life is followed by death, and out of decay comes life. Seasons repeat in cycles. Water from the sea goes to the sun and descends as rain that runs through the rivers of the sea—a process that never ends. In a balance of forces is peace; in the gods is a balance of forces. Although India has pollution problems, in Hindu ecosystems environmentalists could find much to cheer them. Recognizing both creation and destruction in nature, Hindus have been less enthusiastic than Westerners to conquer the natural world. Hindus believe that using and co-operating with nature is a wiser course of action.

Hindus are less prone than Westerners to judge the world in moral terms. It is hardly meaningful to speak of the world as good or bad. It is both and neither. Some things seem helpful to humans, and others seem destructive. These immediate human impressions and assessments made in the short term, however, may not be correct in the long term. In assessing processes over very long periods, it is difficult to judge whether a result is good or bad.

Hindus can speak of the universe as not being God. Most Hindus do not think that God is physical the way the universe is. Yet the physical universe exists because it is influenced by God. The universe may be atoms and space, but spirit is also a reality.

Humans

Hinduism teaches a lengthy existence for humans. The physical body is not the whole story of a human. The body that we see is only one chapter in a volume of a whole set of books on the life of a soul, or Atman. Our appearance now only hints of what we have been or will become. A human is a soul who wears, in succession, many different costumes. Each is appropriate to the human's current condition. When the soul reaches its destiny, it has no need of costumes. Should the released soul return sometime in the distant future to a cycle of births and deaths, it will not be exactly the same soul with the same self-consciousness.

The Law of Karma is the most important doctrine of Hinduism. More than any other religion, Hinduism emphasizes that people get exactly what they deserve. Humans cannot change the fact that they are exactly what they are supposed to be in life. In this life, however, people can change what they will become in future lives.

The Problem for Humans

The problem for humans, as Hindus understand it, is an immortal soul that continues to inhabit one body after another until it is freed from the wheel of rebirth. The soul is bound to the revolving wheel through karma, its own choices of thoughts and deeds. Karma does not end with a body's death, so its influence may extend through many incarnations of the soul, where other karma is generated. *Varna,* or caste, is the lifetime status in a body. Be it superior or inferior in the social order, one's caste is exactly the appropriate condition according to the karma that one has accumulated. A person is responsible for his or her own condition in this life, for though a person cannot change the effects of past decisions, he or she is free to change thoughts and actions now so as to alter lives in the future. Soul, karma, wheel of rebirth, and individual choice are the ingredients of the problem of humans; they are also the ingredients of its solution.

The Solution for Humans

For Hindus, the human solution is reconciliation with the Absolute; reconciliation is overcoming life's polar tensions. Purusha is liberated from prakriti; Atman is liberated from Maya. In raja yoga, the soul is liberated from the body; in jnana yoga, the mind is liberated from avidya, not seeing the truth of the universe. In bhakti yoga, the devotee is detached from the world and attached to God. Instead of being pulled apart by divided loyalties, reconciled people have a single base of identity. They come to themselves undivided, focused, and serene.

Paths of reconciliation are available for each type of personality. People differ, and their approaches to God differ. Some people need the emotional ties of personal relationships; bhakti yoga is their road. Some people are intellectuals, preferring mind over body and emotions; jnana yoga fulfills their desires. Some people need to be involved in activities with their family and community; karma yoga is the most rewarding path for them. In Hinduism, all these ways are of equal value.

Reconciliation is according to the Law of Karma. Bad actions produce alienation; good actions produce reconciliation. The four paths to reconciliation are four ways of good action that bring rewards according to the Law of Karma. There are no shortcuts, for only meritorious acts bring release and reconciliation. Meritorious acts are fueled by devotion to spiritual values.

For masses of Hindus, solution of their problem depends on assistance from a deity. For Shaivites, Shiva and his consorts are sources of help. For Vaishnavites, Vishnu and his avatars respond to human petitions. Of course, the great devas of the Vedas can still be approached through ancient sacrifices. The goal of the universe is the full realization of humans. Troy W. Organ writes,

> The greater the realization of the true nature of man, the less the separation of man and the world, and at the level of the Perfection of Man the essence of man and the essence of totality admit of no fundamental distinction—*Atman* is Brahman. The hominization of the universe is the goal of both man and the world.[40]

Community and Ethics

Hindus usually enter the religious community by birth. Males of the three higher castes participate in the *upanayana* rite, which invests them with the sacred thread that is a symbol of their being born a second time, of the spirit. Females have traditionally been dependent on males for their spiritual guidance, but they have their own responsibilities in worship, rites, fasts, and moral obligations. Hinduism allows great variety in paths of reconciliation. It has had strong control, however, over individual acts.

Hinduism has a rigid moral code, although it is not always the same as a Western moral code. In the Vedas, Rita is the principle of right order in the universe; all things conform to its control. For the individual, the principle of right action is dharma. Dharma is Rita incorporated into the life of individuals. Sri Aurobindo pointed out that correct moral action for individuals is not foreign to them—something imposed by society. Freedom comes through living according to the universal principle within humans. Being true to themselves, their own highest principles of the self, brings freedom to individuals.

In Hinduism, the family is sacred. Husbands and wives should be loyal to each other. They should be responsible in generating children, providing for their physical needs, and educating them in spiritual as well as secular disciplines. Younger people should care for older generations.

Hindus have obligations to the community. They are to do no harm to other people or their property. They are responsible to help holy people who have forsaken the world to seek God. Expressing compassion to all humans and animals, especially the cow, is of special merit. The cow, which gives milk and manure that serves as fuel, disinfectant, and building material, is a symbol of the value of all living things. Some Hindus act according to very strong humanitarian principles; the Brahmo Samaj taught that it was an obligation of their religion. For other Hindus, the humanitarian activities of the community are secular rather than religious obligations.

An Interpretation of History

History for Hindus differs from history in Western religions. Western religions think of a definite beginning of history, progress through centuries in which God intervenes in human lives, and a final judgment separating good from evil. Hindus honor the Vedas, ancient beliefs and practices, and acknowledge the appearance of deities in specific times and places. The big difference is that Hindu literature implies that the whole process can end and begin again for successive repetitions. What is true for the universe is also true for humans.

Rituals and Symbols

The most important rituals of Hindus are the **Samskaras,** the sacraments or rites by which a Hindu is fully integrated into the community.[41] The birth of a child and his or her name giving is assigned great importance.

The **upanayana** sacrament initiates a boy as a twice-born person, one who is responsible for his actions in religious regulations. It is the beginning of the student stage, or ashram. He is invested with a sacred thread, **janëu,** which he must wear at all times if he would remain in his caste. He must respect the janëu and his guru at all times.

Marriage, **vivaha,** symbolizes entry into the second stage, or ashram, that of householder. Monogamy is the most common form of marriage today. India now recognizes civil marriage and the right of divorce, which can be initiated by either man or woman. The marriage ceremony proper is usually culminated with a generous feast. The purpose of marriage, according to the Vedas, was to allow a man to produce a son who would continue the sacrifices. Today, various motives in marriage are acknowledged.

Funerals, **antyesti,** are the last rites observed by almost all Hindus. Although a few Hindus are buried, most are cremated in a **shraddha,** the last rites. The eldest son of the deceased is usually the one who performs the rites. The ideal wood used in the funeral pyre is sandalwood, which is

Samskaras [sam-SKAHR-as]
The sacraments or rites by which a Hindu is fully integrated into the community.

upanayana [oo-PA-na-YAH-na]
The initiation rite indicating that a boy is a twice-born person.

janëu [JAN-eu]
The sacred thread worn by the three upper castes.

vivaha [vi-VA-ha]
Marriage. The rite of entry into the second stage or ashram, that of householder.

antyesti [un-TYES-ti]
Funerals. Last rites.

shraddha [SHRAD-dha]
Last rites. The prescribed rituals for the deceased.

Lighting the Lamps for Divālī. This is the feast of lamps. Thousands of lamps are placed in homes, in temples, and along roads and rivers to illuminate the darkness.

pleasantly fragrant. These sacraments, at birth, second birth, marriage, and death, complete the obligations of a Hindu.

Between times of these major sacraments, Hindus practice many rituals and use many symbols.

Hindu worship in temples can be either individual or congregational. Worship may be assisted by a priest. Worshipers may recite Vedic hymns, light candles or other sacred flame, offer pure food to the gods, offer money to be used for religious purposes, and comment on a guru's insights regarding religious duties. The pool, or tank, found at some temples is used for ritual bathing. There may be only one god image or images of several different gods. Different acts of worship may be occurring at the same time in different parts of the temple.

Puja is a form of worship that an individual addresses to the image of a deity or a pair of deities. This devotion of a person to an image, then, becomes an important person in the residence, cared for with personal attention as one would care for a member of the family.

Other religious obligations may also be either individual or communal. It is quite common for different members of the same family to choose separate paths of duty for themselves. They may worship at different temples at different times, keep separate fast days, and meet different humanitarian obligations. There are festivals that bring local communities together, and there are observances that may bring together all the followers of a particular guru or saint. There are some national holy days.

Some of the nationwide festivals are described here as they appear in Dr. I. C. Sharma's *Ethical Philosophies of India*.[42] During Raksabandhana, Indians tie a thread around their wrists to symbolize the individual's obligation to sacrifice personal, family, and community interests to the welfare of the nation and all humanity. Everyone who has this concern for humanity is a Brahmin at heart. Vijayadasami celebrates the victory of Rama over

puja [POO-ja]
Worship. Worship of household deities. Hindu worship of deities. Brahmins often performed rituals desired by householders. The ritual worship of India.

Hindus Feed Sacred Cattle. In Sodupur Fairgrounds, near Calcutta, India, sacred cows for annual ceremonial worship receive food from worshipers.

Ravana. The celebrant rejoices in the victory of good over evil and assumes responsibility for being a keeper of righteousness. Deepavali is a festival of lights, awakening aesthetic appreciation. All castes recognize that the aesthetic gifts of the Vaisyas reside, in some measure, in them. During Holi, all castes become as Shudras. Through costume and actions, the roles of participants are temporarily reversed. Castes are a temporary condition; ultimately everyone has the same spiritual unity. Some Brahmins think that in mass celebrations the ideals of the festivals are often lost.

Life After Death

> He who thinks this self a killer and he who thinks it killed, both fail to understand; it does not kill, nor is it killed. (19) It is not born, it does not die; having been, it will never not be; unborn, enduring, constant, and primordial, it is not killed when the body is killed. (20) Arjuna, when a man knows the self to be indestructible, enduring, unborn, unchanging, how does he kill or cause anyone to kill? (21)[43]

In this passage of the Bhagavad Gita, the Lord Krishna assures the young warrior Arjuna that he can neither kill his family in warfare nor be killed by them. Each soul is indestructible. Inevitably it will endure the death of the present body and be reborn in another body. The soul changes bodies as a person changes worn-out clothes. Among the dozens of doctrines of Hinduism that have fascinated peoples all over the world, none is more interesting than the concept of reincarnation or, its Hindu term, *samsara*.

In Hinduism, reincarnation is expressed as samsara, a course or succession of states of existence. One author has translated samsara as "what turns round forever."[44] Hinduism has analyzed humans into many more parts than body and soul. Essentially, the Bhagavad Gita asserts that the self is unchanging, for it is of the essence of the Absolute. The embodied self, however, is subject to the changing conditions of life. Although the self is inviolable, the distinctive personality is involved in karma and the conditions of rebirth. Many Hindus found pleasures in life, but they realized that at some point they would desire release from the wheel of rebirth. As a person can tire of seeing a motion picture film too many times, so he or she can tire of birth, life, death, and rebirth. The Hindu sages differed in their opinions whether a person can find final liberation in an embodied state.

The last rites complete the sacraments required to prepare a Hindu for the next life. One who has followed the approved paths and completed the required sacraments can anticipate blessing one's family. The most holy can anticipate release from rebirth.

Hinduism and Other Religions

Hinduism's response to other religions has varied according to the religions and the circumstances of history. In general, Hinduism has gone its own way, independent of the religions of other peoples. Most often it has been tolerant of other religions in India. It has resisted religions that have tried to prove that Hinduism is wrong or insisted that Hindus should convert. Many Hindu religious leaders have pointed out the similarities between the teachings and practices of other religions and Hinduism. They are glad to have peoples of other religions gain insights from the sacred writings of the Hindus. Upper-caste Hindus, however, have been harsh to peers who abandon the faith of their birth. Hinduism has had centuries of experience in religious pluralism. More than any other religion, it has produced saints and teachers who have taught ways for peoples of many religions to find a common spiritual ground.

In practice, however, relationships between Hindus, Muslims, and Sikhs have erupted into violence. A decade after the partition of India and Pakistan, a young Akbar Adil said to Jan Myrdal, "Don't tell me about Hindus! They got hold of my aunt and hacked her to pieces. Before burying her we had to put the corpse together again from sixteen pieces. And still there were parts missing."[45] Myrdal shows that terrible murders were perpetuated by both Muslims and Hindus. The Sikhs, he reported, participated as well. More recently, some Sikhs revolted against President's Rule in the state of Punjab. On June 6, 1984, Indian Army troops invaded the Sikh

A Hindu Temple in Flushing, New York.
Hindus living in this metropolitan area express their faith in traditional Hindu yogas of release.

CHAPTER THREE

The Ganges at Benares. One of the seven most sacred centers of India is visited by Hindus, Buddhists, Jains, and other pilgrims.

Golden Temple at Amritsar in order to remove revolutionary followers of Sant Jarnail Singh Bhindranwale. On October 31, 1984, Sikh members of Mrs. Indira Gandhi's bodyguard assassinated her.[46] Many Hindus responded by murdering Sikhs. In Ayodhya, in 1990, Hindus clashed with Muslims over possession of the site of a sixteenth-century mosque. These reports were deeply shocking; they were even more shocking because Hinduism has a history of living peacefully alongside many different religious minorities. It is hoped that Radhakrishnan is current in his observation that although the history of religion is a record of conflicts of contradictory systems, there is a future of agreement. That truth is viewed in different ways by different groups does not deny that truth is ultimately one.[47]

Hinduism has inspired other religious expressions that incorporate its teachings and practices but whose devotees are not accepted by most

Brahmins as real Hindus. Two forms that appeared in the Western world, as well as in India, are of particular interest. They are Theosophy and the International Society for Krishna Consciousness (ISKCON) movements.

In Madras, India, residents are cognizant of the Theosophical Society, a group organized by Helena Petrovna Blavatsky (1831–1891) in the United States in 1875. Theosophy, which means "divine wisdom," played a role in promoting independent India by supporting Swami Dayananda Sarisvati in his Arya Samaj. Blavatsky's teachings appeared in *The Secret Doctrine* (1888) and *The Voice of Silence* (1889). The ancient masters of religion, she wrote, knew and taught a single, universal wisdom. In each person there is something eternal and divine that can be brought together with that wisdom, liberating the soul from endless deaths and births. Not limited to Hindu culture, Blavatsky claimed knowledge from Tibet and cooperated with Colonel Olcot in winning social reforms for Buddhists in Sri Lanka who felt discriminated against by their British rulers. After Bla-vatsky's death, the movement continued to grow and prosper, particularly in the United States and Great Britain.

The International Society for Krishna Consciousness began in the United States in 1966. Abhay Charyan De worked among the young men and women of the counterculture, involving them in the bhakti movement. He taught them kirtana, chanting the name of Lord Krishna. Dressed as Hindus, men and women lived separately until they married. Couples were taught to engage in sex only for procreation. Their activities are public chanting, offering food, distributing literature, collecting contributions, and talking with potential converts. Members of the society may practice puja and are sometimes seen in Hindu temples. Their most conspicuous temple is New Vrindavran in Wheeling, West Virginia.

HINDUISM IN THE UNITED STATES

Although literary Americans such as Ralph Waldo Emerson (1803–1882) and Henry David Thoreau (1817–1862) read Hindu scriptures, many Americans knew little about people from India. Through the World Congress on Religions in Chicago, in 1893, Swami Vivekananda disseminated the teachings of Ramakrishna. But prior to India's independence from Great Britain, people from India were not numerous in the United States. Indians who went abroad from India were more likely to go to England. After Indian independence, the United States changed its immigration laws to permit more people from India to enter the country. The immigration laws of 1968 gave preference to large groups of Indian professionals. The status of all Indians in the United States was improved by the independence of India.

Most of the major religions of India have adherents in the United States. Where there are large groups of adherents of a single religion, there is likely to be a cultural center that serves, also, as a place of worship. After a few more decades in the United States, the religions of India are likely to be more visible to the public. The distinctive architecture of Hindu temples attracts attention.

Having introduced Hinduism, the largest religion in India, we now turn to Buddhism, a distinctive faith that had its roots in Hinduism. Buddhism retained many Hindu concepts, but it added fresh insights and practices. In turn, Buddhism helped influence later Hinduism. Through efforts of missionaries, however, Buddhism spread its influence across Asia and now touches all parts of the world.

☙ VOCABULARY

Agamas [AH-ga-mas]
Agni [AG-ni]
antyesti [un-TYES-ti]
Aranyakas [ah-RAN-yu-kuz]
Aryans [AHR-yuns]
Atman [AHT-man]
avidya [a-VID-ya]
bhakti yoga [BAHK-ti]
Brahma [bram-HAH]
Brahman [bram-MUN]
Brahmanas [BRAH-muh-nus]
Brahmin [BRAH-men]
caste [CAST]
dharma [DAR-ma]
Dravidians [drah-VID-e-uns]
guru [GU-RU] or [GOO-ROO]
henotheism [HEN-o-the-ISM]
Indra [IN-dra]
Itihasa-Purana
   [iti-HAHT-sah poo-RAH-na]
janëu [JAN-eu]
jnana yoga [JYNAH-na]

kalpa [KAL-pa]
Krishna [KRISH-na]
Kshatriya [KSHA-tri-ya]
Law of Karma [KAHR-ma]
Laws of Manu [MAH-noo]
Mahabharata
   [ma-HAH-BAH-ra-ta]
Manu [MAH-noo]
Maya [MAH-ya]
Mitra [MI-tra]
moksha [MOWK-sha]
nirguna Brahman
   [NIR-goo-na]
prakriti [pra-KRI-ti]
puja [POO-ja]
Puranas [pu-RAHN-as]
Purusha [PU-roo-sha]
Ramayana [rah-MAH-ya-na]
reincarnation
   [REE-in-cahr-NAY-shun]
Rita [RI-ta]
saguna Brahman [SA-goo-na]

samadhi [sa-MAH-di]
samsara [sam-SAH-ra]
Samskaras [sam-SKAHR-as]
sannyasin [san-NYAH-sin]
Shiva [SHEE-va]
shraddha [SHRAD-dha]
shruti [SHROO-ti]
Shudra [SHOO-dra]
Soma [SOW-ma]
smriti [SMRI-ti]
tantras [TUN-trus]
untouchable
upanayana [oo-PA-na-YAH-na]
Upanishads [oo-PA-ne-shads]
Vaishya [VAI-shya]
varna [VAR-na]
Varuna [VA-roo-na]
Vedanta [ve-DAHN-ta]
Vedas [VAY-daz]
Vishnu [VISH-noo]
vivaha [vi-VA-ha]
yoga [YOH-ga]

☙ QUESTIONS FOR REVIEW

1. How did Hinduism begin? What were its characteristics in its formative stages?

2. How do gods of the Rig-Veda differ from gods of later, popular Hinduism?

3. What is the setting for the Bhagavad Gita? What are the most important truths that Krishna reveals to Arjuna?

4. What is a yoga? How are the four yogas distinguished? How is a yoga chosen?

5. Why are there four goals, four yogas, four stages of life, and four major castes? What terms do Hindus use in this important discussion?

6. In Hinduism, is reality reducible to one element, or are two required? What terms are used in this important discussion among Hindus?

7. What Indian leaders have helped define Hinduism's relationship to Western civilizations? What did each one contribute to the independent state of India?

8. How are Theosophy and the International Society of Krishna Consciousness related to Hinduism? What religions have conflicted with Hinduism in India?

9. Explain how the elements of caste, karma, and samsara are related in Hinduism.

10. Describe how roles of Hindu women have changed and how they have remained the same in recent centuries.

☙ QUESTIONS FOR DISCUSSION

1. Is a Hindu's life predetermined forever, or is there room for some freedom in the future? How much responsibility does a Hindu have for his or her place in society?

2. What evidence could you offer to support a belief in reincarnation? What evidence could you offer to weaken belief in reincarnation?

3. What doctrines and practices of Hindus do you think are most misunderstood by non-Hindus? How would you correct these misunderstandings?

4. What beliefs and practices in Hinduism are similar to some beliefs and practices of another religion known to you, perhaps your own? Which concepts of these two religions do you find most attractive? most unattractive?

5. In Hinduism, which predominate, the teachings affirming life in the world or the teachings denying life in the world? Is there a way of balancing the two emphases?

✒ NOTES

1. Klaus K. Klostermaier, *A Survey of Hinduism* (Albany: State University of New York Press, 1989), p. 63.

2. Ibid., p. 67.

3. Walter H. Maurer, *Pinnacles of India's Past: Selections from the Ṛgveda* (Philadelphia: John Benjamins, 1986), p. 12.

4. Ibid., pp. 42–43.

5. Ibid., pp. 76–77.

6. Ibid., p. 99.

7. Ibid., p. 108.

8. Wendy Doniger O'Flaherty, ed., *Karma and Rebirth in Classical Indian Traditions* (Berkeley, CA: University of California Press, 1980), p. 3.

9. S. Radhakrishnan, *The Principal Upanishads* (London: Allen & Unwin, 1968), Brhadaranyaka Upanishad, Fourth Brahmana, II. 4,3. Pp. 195–197. Copyright by Unwin Hyman, an Imprint of HarperCollins Publishers Limited. Reprinted by permission.

10. Ibid., Chandogya Upanishad, VI. 8, 1–7. Pp. 456–458.

11. Klostermaier, p. 193.

12. Ibid., pp. 68, 94.

13. *Bhagavad-Gita*, trans. Barbara Stoller Miller (New York: Columbia University Press, 1986), 6:5-9, pp. 41, 42. Copyright © 1986 by Columbia University Press. Reprinted with permission of the publisher.

14. Ibid., 4:6–9, p. 50.

15. Ibid., 5:18, p. 59.

16. Ibid., 6:30, p. 67.

17. Ibid., 8:3–6, pp. 77–78.

18. Wendy Doniger and Brian K. Smith, *The Laws of Manu* (London: Penguin Books, 1991), p. 117. Copyright © 1991 by Wendy Doniger and Brian K. Smith. Reproduced by permission of Penguin UK Ltd.

19. David R. Kinsley, *The Sword and the Flute* (Berkeley: University of California Press, 1975), pp. 104–105.

20. Ibid., pp. 41ff.

21. Hari Prasad Shastri, trans., *The Ramayana of Valmiki*, vol. 3 (London: Santi Sadan, 1959), p. 617.

22. Doniger and Smith, p. 197.

23. Ibid., pp. 48–49.

24. Stephen C. Neill, *The Encyclopedia of Religion*, vol. 3 (New York: Macmillan, 1987), p. 422.

25. Swami Abhedananda, ed., *The Sayings of Sri Rama-krishna* (New York: Vedanta Society, 1903).

26. Rabindranath Tagore, *Towards Universal Man* (Bombay: Asia Publishing House, 1961), p. 359.

27. Louis Fischer, ed., *The Essential Gandhi* (New York: Random House, 1962), p. 309.

28. June O'Connor, *The Quest for Political and Spiritual Liberation* (Rutherford, NJ: Fairleigh Dickinson University Press, 1977), p. 95.

29. Sri Aurobindo, *The Life Divine* (New York: Greystone Press, 1949), p. 233. Radhakrishnan and C. A. Moore, *A Source Book in Indian Philosophy* (Princeton, NJ: Princeton University Press, 1957), p. 599.

30. S. Radhakrishnan, *An Idealist View of Life* (London: Allen & Unwin, 1929), as quoted in S. Radhakrishnan and C. A. Moore, p. 635.

31. Richard F. Nyrop, *India: A Country Study* (Washington, DC: U.S. Government Printing Office as represented by the Secretary of the Army, 1985), p. 72.

32. Jan Myrdal, *India Waits*, trans. Alan Bernstein (Chicago: Lake View Press, 1986).

33. Katherine K. Young, "Hinduism," in *Women in World Religions*, ed. Arvind Sharma (Albany: State University of New York Press, 1987), p. 97.

34. Denise Lardner Carmody, *Women and World Religions* (Englewood Cliffs, NJ: Prentice-Hall, 1989), pp. 63–64.

35. Klostermaier, p. 203.

36. Wendy Doniger O'Flaherty, *The Rig Veda* (London: Penguin Books, 1981), p. 51.

37. Klostermaier, p. 205.

38. Bruce R. Reichenback, *The Law of Karma* (Honolulu: University of Hawaii Press, 1990), pp. 13ff.

39. A. L. Basham, *The Wonder That Was India* (New York: Grove Press, 1959), p. 385.

40. Troy Wilson Organ, *The Hindu Quest for the Perfection of Man* (Athens: Ohio University, 1970), p. 154.

41. Klostermaier, p. 175.

42. I. C. Sharma, *The Ethical Philosophies of India* (Lincoln, NB: Johnsen, 1965), pp. 83–85.

43. Barbara Stoller Miller, trans., *The Bhagavad-Gita*, 2:19-22, p. 32. Copyright © 1986 by Columbia University Press. Reprinted with permission of the publisher.

44. R. J. Zwi Werblowsky, "Transmigration," in *The Encyclopedia of Religion*, vol. 15, ed. Mircea Eliade (New York: Macmillan, 1987), pp. 21–26.

45. Myrdal, p. 25.

46. Nyrop, p. 377.

47. J. G. Arapura, "India's Philosophical Response," in *Modern Indian Responses to Religious Pluralism*, ed. Harold G. Coward (Albany: State University of New York Press, 1987), pp. 171–194, 181.

READINGS

Doniger, Wendy, and Brian K. Smith. *The Laws of Manu.* London: Penguin Books, 1991. A recent introduction and translation of a classical Hindu guide to life.

Fischer, Louis, ed. *The Essential Gandhi.* New York: Random House, 1962. An older work that is still an enjoyable account of the life of Mohandas Gandhi.

Isherwood, Christopher. *Ramakrishna and His Disciples.* New York: Simon & Schuster, 1965. A study of the fascinating devotee of Mother Kali, Ramakrishna.

Kinsley, David. *Hinduism: A Cultural Perspective.* Englewood Cliffs, NJ: Prentice Hall, 1982. A good, recent introduction to Hinduism in a cultural context.

Klostermaier, Klaus K. *A Survey of Hinduism.* Albany: State University of New York Press, 1989. A scholarly overview of Hinduism.

Koller, John M. *The Indian Way.* New York: Macmillan, 1982. A recent study of the religious philosophies of India.

Maurer, Walter H. *Pinnacles of India's Past: Selections from the Rgveda.* Philadelphia: John Benjamins, 1986. A scholarly presentation by a professor of Sanskrit.

O'Flaherty, Wendy Doniger. *The Rig Veda.* London: Penguin Books, 1981.

Radhakrishnan, S. *The Hindu View of Life.* London: Allen & Unwin, 1964. An older work by a respected Hindu scholar and political leader.

————., ed. and trans. *The Bhagavadgita.* New York: Harper Colophon Books, 1973. This devotional classic is translated and explained by a noted Hindu scholar.

Sharma, I. C. *Ethical Philosophies of India.* Lincoln, NB: Johnsen, 1965. The ethical ideals that govern Hindu lives are discussed by a Hindu scholar and religious leader who has taught often in the United States.

READINGS FOR RESEARCH AND REPORTS

Aurobindo, Sri. *Bande Mataram.* 29 vols. Pondicherry: Sri Aurobindo Ashram, 1972.

Basham, A. L. *The Wonder That Was India.* New York: Grove Press, 1959.

Bondurant, Joan Valerie. *Conquest of Violence; The Gandhian Philosophy of Conflict.* Berkeley: University of California Press, 1965.

Borman, William. *Gandhi and Non-violence.* Albany: State University of New York Press, 1986.

Buhler, Georg, trans. *The Laws of Manu.* New York: Dover, 1969.

Christie-Murray, David. *Reincarnation.* London: David and Charles, 1981.

Coward, Harold G., ed. *Modern Indian Responses to Religious Pluralism.* Albany: State University of New York Press, 1987.

Gandhi, Mohandas. *All Men Are Brothers*, ed. Krishna Kripalini. New York: Columbia University Press, 1958.

Griffith, Ralph T. H., trans., J. L. Shastri, ed. *The Hymns of the Rgveda.* Delhi: Motilal Banarsidass, 1973.

Grimes, John. *A Concise Dictionary of Indian Philosophy.* Albany: State University of New York Press, 1989.

Keys, Charles F., and E. Valentine Daniel, eds. *Karma.* Berkeley: University of California Press, 1983.

Kinsley, David R. *The Sword and the Flute.* Berkeley: University of California Press, 1975.

Koller, John M. *The Indian Way.* New York: Macmillan, 1982.

Long, J. Bruce. "Reincarnation." In *The Encyclopedia of Religion*, vol. 12, ed. Mircea Eliade. New York: Macmillan, 1987. Pp. 265–269.

Mahoney, William K. "Karman: Hindu and Jain Concepts." In *The Encyclopedia of Religion*, vol. 8, ed. Mircea Eliade. New York: Macmillan, 1987. Pp. 261–266.

McDermott, Robert A. *Six Pillars: Introduction to the Major Works of Sri Aurobindo.* Chambersburg, PA: Conococheaque Associates, Wilson Books, 1974.

Moreland, W. H., and Atul C. Chatterjee. *A Short History of India.* New York: David McKay, 1957.

Myrdal, Jan. *India Waits*, trans. Alan Bernstein. Chicago: Lake View Press, 1986.

Narayan, Shriman. *The Selected Works of Mahatma Gandhi.* Ahmedabad, India: Navjivan, 1968.

Nyrop, Richard F. *India: A Country Study.* Washington, DC: U.S. Government Printing Office, represented by the Secretary of the Army, 1985.

O'Connor, June. *The Quest for Political and Spiritual Liberation.* Rutherford, NJ: Fairleigh Dickinson University Press, 1977.

O'Flaherty, Wendy Doniger, ed. *Karma and Rebirth in Classical Indian Traditions.* Berkeley: University of California Press, 1980.

Organ, Troy Wilson. *The Hindu Quest for the Perfection of Man.* Athens: Ohio University Press, 1970.

Panikkar, K. M. *Hindu Society at Cross Roads.* Bombay: Asia Publishing House, 1961.

Radhakrishnan, S. *The Principal Upanishads.* London: Allen & Unwin, 1968.

————. *Indian Philosophy,* 2nd ed., 2 vols. London: Allen & Unwin, 1962.

Raju, P. T. *The Philosophical Traditions of India.* London: Allen & Unwin, 1971.

The Ramayana of Valmiki, trans. Hari Prasad Shastri. London: Shanti Sadan, 1959.

Reichenback, Bruce R. *The Law of Karma.* Honolulu: University of Hawaii Press, 1990.

Sharma, Arvind. *Women in World Religions.* Albany: State University of New York Press, 1987.

Stevenson, Ian. *Children Who Remember Previous Lives.* Charlottesville: University Press of Virginia, 1987.

————. *Twenty Cases Suggestive of Reincarnation.* New York: American Society for Psychical Research, 1966.

Tagore, Rabindranath. *Towards Universal Man.* Bombay: Asia Publishing House, 1961.

Upadhyaya, K. N. *Early Buddhism and the Bhagavadgita.* Delhi: Motilal Banarsidass, 1983.

Werblowsky, R. J. Zwi. "Transmigration." In *The Encyclopedia of Religion,* vol. 15, ed. Mircea Eliade. New York: Macmillan, 1987.

Buddhism

Buddhist Monks. Father and son monks keep a Buddhist temple in South Korea. The temple, from 982 C.E., is maintained by revenue from its own lands and from contributions of parish families.

Introduction

About the time that some of the Upanishads were being written, a handsome young prince appeared among the Shakyas of northern India. His proud parents, King Suddhodanna and Queen Maya, named him Siddhartha Gautama. Hidden and protected from the harshness of the world, he grew up surrounded by luxury and sensual pleasures. Later, when he did make his brief excursions outside his palace, into the environment of common people, he became so disturbed by their suffering that he wanted to devote his life to relieving them of their pain. Beginning his search in his late twenties, he found his answers in his mid-thirties. Having discovered how to accomplish release of humans from suffering, he became known as the Buddha, the enlightened one. During the remainder of his eighty years he was revered as Shakyamuni, the sage of the Shakyas, and as the compassionate Buddha.

In India, about two centuries later, the Four Noble Truths of the Buddha's message reached the remorseful heart of the powerful monarch Ashoka Maurya. As penance for his wanton destruction of the kingdom of Kalinga some years earlier, he reformed his own court, making it more compassionate for living creatures, and taught his people the Buddha's message that emphasized family and community values. He was so devoted a follower that he enlisted his family in carrying the Buddha's teachings to the neighboring island of Ceylon (Sri Lanka).

The monks and nuns who had left their homes to follow the Buddha took his teachings also to the isolated heights of Tibet. In that mountainous region they initiated a form of Buddhism that eventually produced a twentieth-century celebrity, the Dalai Lama. When monks took their message to China, Chinese peoples learned that sons who became monks could help both ancestors and living relatives. Buddhism joined Confucianism and Daoism as vital religions in China. From China, missionaries influenced the Koreans, who, in turn, introduced the Buddha's <u>dharma</u> in Japan. From China and Japan immigrants brought their Buddhism to Canada and the United States, where it continues to grow from its Asian roots.

Buddhism has rewarded both its ordinary and its exceptional followers. On the surface, there are no religious teachings easier to appreciate than the Four Noble Truths of the Buddha. In depth, there are no religious teachings more profound. For gifted followers who have patience and persistence, Buddhism has offered some of the most challenging doctrines found in religions. What could be more challenging than to understand the meaning of a "selfless mind"? From its simplest rites to its greatest philosophies, Buddhism has offered a faith to motivate millions of followers around the world.

HISTORICAL DEVELOPMENT

Buddhism introduces a feature not present in the nascent forms of Hinduism. The Vedas, forming the foundation of orthodox Hinduism, rise from the dim mists of prehistoric times as full-blown traditions of a culture. If there were major authors, most were either anonymous or long forgotten. Buddhism, however, began in history with a founder. Indeed, along with Buddha are the first reliable dates of history in India.[1] The personality of Buddha in history is absolutely essential to understanding the character of Buddhism.

The appearance of a central person with whom believers can identify introduces fresh possibilities for varieties of interpretation. The task is complicated because believers themselves are divided about interpretation.[2]

Historiography

Within Buddhism, believers in two major points of view contend to tell the "correct" story of the Buddha. The more conservative view, the Theravadin, which will be described later, emphasizes the down-to-earth, practical example of an exceptional man, Siddhartha Gautama, the Buddha. The more creative view, the Mahayana, also to be described later, emphasizes the divine character of the Buddha who revealed to his precocious followers profound insights of human minds, heavens, and hells. Both these views are represented in the dynamic tradition of a powerful, living faith. From widely differing points of view, devoted Buddhists interpret the same facts in the history of the Buddha.

Writers comparing world religions, however, have a task beyond satisfying Theravadin and Mahayanist views of history. Shall we relate the story of a religion's founder from a natural, humanistic perspective, or shall we include sacred stories of angels, demons, signs, wonders, and miracles as part of historical development? Either choice requires some reasonable compromise.

At stake is our point of view of all world religions. If we accept all religious stories of faithful followers at their face value, we can become lost in vast seas of wonder stories, legends, and beliefs that are rejected even by some followers of the religion involved. If we insist on our objectivity and

Bodhgaya. The temple commemorates the central religious experience of the Buddha, Siddhartha Gautama.

reject all stories that cannot be easily explained in natural and humanist terms, we discard much that believers in a particular religion find essential to its understanding. Although we want to listen to followers as they tell stories that motivate their faith, we want, also, to retain enough objectivity not to become lost in one religion at expense of the others.

In attempting to give a balanced view of the history of each religion, including Buddhism, I will try to present the accounts of faithful followers with understanding and respect. At the same time, I will try to present fairly both the humanistic and sacred histories of each religion, as well as with the conflicting claims of many religions.

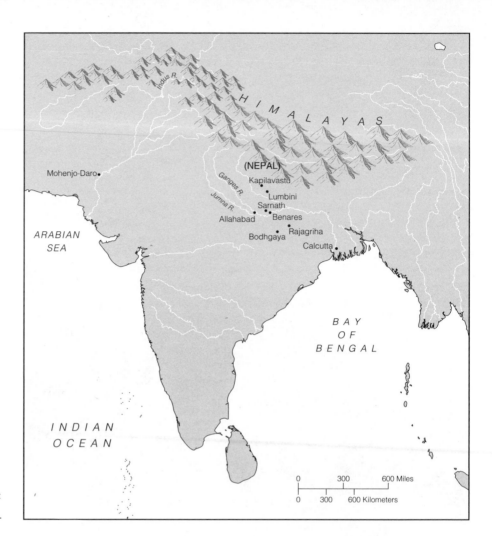

Centers of Early Buddhism. Buddhism began in northeast India. The Buddha's first sermon was in Sarnath.

The Life of the Buddha

Some facts about the adored Buddha are generally accepted. He began life on earth as Siddhartha Gautama about 563 B.C.E (some scholars say 560) in northern India at Lumbini Grove, about a hundred miles from Banares. As pictured in Buddhist art, his mother, Queen **Maya,** stood holding with her right hand the branch of an ashoka tree as she gave birth to the future Buddha.[3] Being from the Shakya clan, he was later known, particularly to the Chinese, as **Shakyamuni** (sage of the Shakyas). His father, **Suddhodana,** was a powerful lord, a Kshatriya, in the feudal system.

THE BIRTH OF THE BUDDHA

Beyond these facts, there are many different interpretations. To many faithful Buddhists, Siddhartha's birth was brought about by a sacred elephant who entered the side of Queen Maya and inserted the one who was to be the Buddha.[4]

Queen Maya dreamed, the night before conceiving the Buddha, that she lay on a heavenly couch in a golden mansion in the Himalayas. The Buddha became a beautiful white elephant, bearing in his trunk a white lotus flower. He seemed to touch her right side and enter her womb. From this

Maya (queen) [MAH-ya]
The mother of Siddhartha Gautama, the Buddha.

Shakyamuni [SHAH-kya-MOO-nee]
The sage of the Shakya clan, Siddhartha Gautama, the Buddha. The term is widely used in China and Japan.

Suddhodana [SUD-DHOH-da-na]
The king who was father of Siddhartha Gautama. He is said to have kept Siddhartha ignorant of human suffering.

dream, Buddhists believe that is how the Buddha was incarnate into Queen Maya. At the time of her deliverance, she was traveling from Kapilavastu to Devadaha. In a Sal grove along the way she stood as she delivered the child. Angels received the new baby in a golden net. The child stood, walked, and cried, "I am supreme in the world. This is my last birth: henceforth there shall be no more birth for me!"[5]

There are also accounts of consternation among forces of evil who attempted to destroy such a power for good in the world. In order to provide a contrast to Buddha's later monastic life, his family's riches are described in detail. Another story tells about Suddhodana's being informed that if Siddhartha could be prevented from becoming a monk, he would become a powerful king.

PRINCE SIDDHARTHA

Siddhartha moved through the Brahmanical (Hindu) steps as a student and then as a householder, marrying a neighboring princess, **Yashodhara,** when he was nineteen. From that union was born a son, Rahula. Siddhartha had done his duty according to Brahmanic custom. He had all the riches of a prince and everything he needed to fulfill the expectations of an orthodox member of the Kshatriya caste. Restless, he wanted to see the world beyond his palace.

Yashodhara [ya-SHOW-dha-ra] The wife of Siddhartha Gautama and mother of Rahula. She is said to have been a neighboring princess chosen for Prince Siddhartha.

THE FOUR PASSING SIGHTS

Siddhartha's father, thinking of his son's potential as a ruler, tried to prevent him from seeing any painful human experiences; instead, he surrounded him with every kind of pleasure. His plan was thwarted when Siddhartha went out into the community and, on separate occasions, saw four sights that deeply disturbed him. He saw an old man and learned from his chariot driver that all human beings must grow old. He saw a sick person and learned that sickness and suffering are part of human existence. Siddhartha saw a corpse and learned that death is an experience that befalls every human. His deep concern and anguish caused by the first three sights was relieved only when he saw a wandering ascetic; to his mind this figure offered the only way to deal with the sufferings of humanity. The seed of his future identity was planted.

THE GREAT RENUNCIATION

Having learned of the suffering that is entailed in birth, Siddhartha could not find comfort in the palace. His father did everything he could to distract him from his preoccupation with human suffering—to no avail. Within the confines of his princely life, Siddhartha could not find a way out of human suffering. After looking for a last time upon his beloved Yashodhara and Rahula, who were sleeping, he departed at night. Having gone some distance, he sent home his horse, Kanthaka, and his servant, Channa. He was twenty-nine when he began his search for release from the wheel of rebirth. His arduous quest was to last six years.

Shaving his head, Siddhartha put on the clothes of a wandering ascetic. Eventually he reached Rajagaha, a royal city, and went in succession to the caves of two Brahmin yogins, whom he chose in turn as gurus. Alara Kalama and Uddaka Ramaputta attempted to teach him through intellectual order and discussions the way to the realms of nothingness.

Siddhartha gave each of them an opportunity to help him, but he did not think that he was making progress. Perhaps a more rigorous form of asceticism, the type being practiced in India by the Jains, could bring him to his goal.

Artists and writers devoted to the Buddha have depicted him in the grove of Uruvela as emaciated from six years of fasting. As long as a person is enjoying the pleasures of the flesh, Siddhartha reasoned, he or she cannot find the light of truth or release from rebirth. The anecdotes of his devotion are truly impressive. He held his breath until his head roared, ate little food—and what he did eat was sickening—endured painful body positions for lengthy periods, became encrusted with filth, and lost weight until his bones protruded and he could feel his spine by pressing on his abdomen. The five ascetics who were his friends during this ordeal thought that he would die from his privations.

He did lose consciousness. One tradition claims that his life was saved by a village maid, Sujata, who gave him a little food. As he gained the strength necessary to return to life, he concluded that he had followed the extreme path of asceticism as far as he could go, and it had brought no release for him.

THE ENLIGHTENMENT

Bodhgaya [bowd-GAH-ya]
A temple that commemorates the grove where the Buddha found enlightenment.

He moved on to a grove (now **Bodhgaya**; see photo on page 111), where he found a pipal tree under which he could sit in isolation. The paths suggested by others had not worked for him. Abandoning the path of rigid asceticism, he practiced a form of meditation that did not cause such bodily pain. It was in that state of meditation that he became enlightened, the Buddha. For under the Bo tree, the tree of enlightenment, he saw why he had not attained release.

In one account of his meditation, Buddhist tradition describes the steps of his awakening.[6] His mind cleansed and concentrated, Siddhartha remembered his former existences—his names, roles in life, and sufferings. Early in the night he found knowledge dispelling ignorance. Concentrating his powerful vision on the order of beings coming into existence and passing away, he interpreted the process in terms of their karma. In a third exploration, during the third watch, he concentrated on destruction of binding influences of desire that caused suffering. He realized that destroying desire would eliminate suffering, leaving him free, awake, and enlightened.

Mara [MAH-rah]
The evil one who tempted the Buddha at Bodhgaya.

According to Buddhist tradition, the incident is full of godly and demonic characters who enter Buddha's struggle to aid or mislead him from his goal. **Mara** tempted him to return to the Kshatriya duties of the Shakyas. When he had withstood the temptations, the Buddha experienced the blessings of the gods. Tradition says that he stayed under the tree for seven weeks.

The enlightened one knew that he had overcome the ignorance that leads to suffering with the knowledge that brings release. He could now experience a glimpse of what it would be like to escape rebirth. He was ecstatic, enlightened, and released. Filled with joy and compassion, the Buddha wanted to share his good news with the five ascetics who had endured the ordeal that had ended in fortune for him. Tradition says that he waited seven weeks before he began to teach.

THE FIRST SERMON AT BANARES

Siddhartha's enlightened state changed his outward appearance to the extent that the five reluctant ascetics accepted him again, curious to learn what had happened to him. In the Deer Park of Sarnath, outside Banares, the Buddha, the enlightened one, delivered his first sermon. Essentially he presented the Middle Path between the two extremes of self-indulgence and self-mortification. He went on to list the four truths of his enlightenment.

Monks, these two extremes should not be followed by one who has gone forth as a wanderer. What two?

Devotion to pleasures of sense, a low practice of villagers, a practice unworthy, unprofitable, the way of the world (on the one hand); and (on the other) devotion to self-mortification, which is painful, unworthy and unprofitable.

By avoiding these two extremes the Tathāgata has gained knowledge of that middle path which giveth vision, which giveth knowledge, which causeth calm, special knowledge, enlightenment, Nibbāna.

And what monks, is that middle path which giveth vision . . . Nibbāna?

Verily it is this Ariyan eightfold way, to wit: Right view, right aim, right speech, right action, right living, right effort, right mindfulness, right concentration. This, monks, is that middle path which giveth vision, which giveth knowledge, which causeth calm, special knowledge, enlightenment, Nibbāna.

Now this monks, is the Ariyan truth about Ill:

Birth is Ill, decay is Ill, sickness is Ill, death is Ill: likewise sorrow and grief, woe, lamentation and despair. To be conjoined with things which we dislike: to be separated from things which we like,—that also is Ill. Not to get what one wants,—that also is Ill. In a word, this body, this fivefold mass which is based on grasping,—that is Ill.

Now this monks, is the Ariyan truth about the arising of Ill: In a word, this body, this fivefold mass which is based on grasping, that is Ill.

Now this monks, is the Ariyan truth about the arising of Ill:

It is the craving that leads back to birth, along with the lure and the lust that lingers longingly now here, now there: namely, the craving for sensual pleasure, the craving to be born again, the craving for existence to end. Such, monks, is the Ariyan truth about the arising of Ill.

And this monks, is the Ariyan truth about the ceasing of Ill:

Verily it is the utter passionless cessation of, the giving up, the forsaking, the release from, the absence of longing for this craving.[7]

Convinced of his doctrine, the five ascetics became his disciples. Their identification with Gautama's experience was the beginning of Buddhist religion. The **Sangha,** the Buddhist religious order that included ascetics and, eventually, laypeople, was the first organization.

After the five ascetics joined the Buddha, fifty-five men of good families joined the order. All became **arhats,** ones instructed in the dharma, teachings, and attained enlightenment. They would not be reborn. These men became the vanguard of monks wandering the countryside, villages, and towns, teaching the dharma. Brahmins, also, such as Sariputra, a chief disciple, joined the order. Caste was not abolished, but in the sangha it was accepted without distinction.

At a grove in Uruvela, the Buddha met three Brahmin monks who worshiped the sacred flame. He received them and their disciples into his order. The most important of the three was Uruvela Kashyapa. To these fire worshipers the Buddha delivered his famous sermon on fire. Everything is on fire, or burning, he said. Everything burns with desire and suffering. The true monk despises sensations, desires, and suffering. He is freed from sensations, desires, and suffering. Kashyapa (Mahakashyapa) understood and became one of the Buddha's leading disciples. He appeared at the great turning points of Buddhism, when his leadership was most needed.

Sangha [SANG-ha]
The Buddhist monastic order. Buddhism accepted both monks and nuns. The term can also include laity.

arhat [UR-hut]
An enlightened, holy person.

The Buddha Addressing Monks at Sarnath.
The newly enlightened Siddhartha
Gautama delivers his sermon to ascetics.

On his early missions, the Buddha traveled through the powerful kingdoms of Koshala and Magadha, along the river Ganges. Recognizing Siddhartha Gautama as a prince, the lords generously welcomed him and
provided for his needs. His charisma attracted men and women of all
castes. When he returned to his father's home in Kapilavastu, he was honored in his own country.

Members of the Buddha's family, who had missed his presence, now
responded warmly to his spiritual leadership. Suddhodana, his father,
embraced his teachings. Rahula, his son, entered monastic life. His cousin
Ananda joined the order and became his faithful companion. Although his

cousin Devadatta, brother of Yashodhara, joined, he was often portrayed as acting from resentment toward his brother-in-law. Perhaps the most influential person on the future of Buddhism, however, was Mahajapati, a wife of Suddhodana and sister of Queen Maya, who had died shortly after the birth of the Buddha.

Seeing that most of her family had entered the order, Mahajapati earnestly requested that she be allowed to join. The Buddha denied her request. Again and again she implored him to admit her to an order for women. A story relates that rather than accept as final his decision, she organized a group of women who dressed as ascetics and traveled a far distance in bare feet to entreat the Buddha. When he saw their suffering, he was impressed with their earnestness and relented. Buddhism accepted into the monastic order men, and separately, women. The Buddha was reluctant to upset family life; he was already criticized for it.

The Buddha attracted social classes as different as that of a barber and a wealthy courtesan. The great success of the order, however, flowed from devotion of householders who wanted to support the monks, nuns, and the Buddha. Householders could observe the first five of the Ten Precepts, and in lieu of observing the second five, could support the monks who observed all ten.

1. not taking life
2. not stealing
3. being chaste
4. not lying
5. not drinking intoxicants
6. eating moderately and not after noon
7. avoiding spectacles such as singing or dramas
8. not using flowers, perfumes, or jewelry
9. using simple beds
10. accepting no gold or silver

Monks in the Sangha practiced the lives of wandering ascetics or of Hindu forest dwellers. Although a distinction arose between monks who lived near villages and those who avoided villages, they all observed the Ten Precepts. All of them received their daily food from nature or from offerings of laypeople. In return, monks taught the dharma, offered chants, and practiced simple forms of medicine. Each day a monk spent time in meditation. The plain, yellow robes of the monks, also, were donated by the laity.

Buddha was an example for his monks; he lived as simply as they did. For forty-five years the winsome person comforted and taught wayfarers he met, entered conversations, and offered lectures to people of high or low social standing. He never lost sight of his mission: to overcome suffering and to help all who would receive the Noble Truths, find Nirvana. Annually he renewed the serious commitment of monks in the Sangha.

In the rainy season, the Buddha and the monks gathered to renew the Sangha. New monks were presented and initiated. Rules of the order were recited. Dialogues on the dharma and its implications were held frequently. Daily meditation was practiced, keeping the holy ones free from undesirable traits. Monks gained further insights into the Three Jewels of Buddhism, reciting, "I take refuge in the Buddha, I take refuge in the Dharma, and I take refuge in the Sangha."

The foundations of the Buddha's teaching are found in the Four Noble Truths. First, all of life is suffering, **dukkha.** Second, the cause of suffering is craving, **tanha.** Third, the end of suffering is getting rid of craving and grasping. Fourth, the method to use in overcoming suffering is the **Eightfold Path:**

1. *Right view.* The disciple gains proper knowledge about illness—how he or she becomes ill, endures illness, and is released from illness.

2. *Right aim.* The disciple must be prepared to renounce attachment to the world and give benevolence and kindness.

3. *Right speech.* The disciple must not lie, slander, or use abusive or idle talk.

4. *Right action.* The disciple must abstain from taking life, from taking what is not given, and from carnal indulgence.

5. *Right living.* The disciple must put away wrong livelihood, acts that are condemned in the fourth step, and seek to support him- or herself by right livelihood.

6. *Right effort.* The disciple applies the force of his or her mind to preventing potential evil from arising in him- or herself, to getting rid of evil that has arisen in him- or herself, and to awakening and sustaining good potentials within him- or herself.

7. *Right mindfulness.* The disciple looks on the body so as to remain ardent, self-possessed, and mindful. The disciple has overcome the craving and dejection common in the world. The disciple also looks on each idea, avoiding craving and dejection common in the world.

8. *Right concentration.* Aloof from sensuous appetites and evil desires, the disciple enters the first **jhana** (meditative state), where there is cognition and deliberation born of solitude, joy, and ease. The disciple moves a step toward the fourth jhana—purity of mind and equanimity where neither ease nor ill is felt.

The Buddha developed his basic teachings similarly to the way a physician diagnoses an illness. What are the symptoms? What causes the suffering? Can anything be done about the patient's distress? What is the treatment that can bring relief or a cure? Buddha was more a physician than a priest, prophet, or metaphysician.

The dharma, which is used in Buddhism as religious teaching of the Buddha, focuses on two terms and a path. Because suffering is the problem, understanding what suffering is requires much attention.

DUKKHA

By suffering *(dukkha),* Buddha meant more than having pain in body or mind. Dukkha pervades all human existence.[8] It is having to endure physical and mental phenomena that are unpleasant, that humans want to avoid, and it is losing those things that humans want to keep, such as parents, loved ones, and possessions. These sufferings are balanced by pleasures that are found in other people and possessions. But the one who enjoys people and possessions is just as impermanent as they are. There is no permanence either in the world that is experienced or in the one who experiences it. The search for permanence in any experience leads to dukkha.

---

dukkha [DUK-kah]
The Buddhist term for the suffering of humans and other sentient beings.

tanha [TAN-ha]
In Buddhism, the thirst or craving that leads to suffering. In the second Noble Truth, it is identified as the cause of suffering.

Eightfold Path
The fourth Noble Truth, the path of deliverance in Buddhism.

jhana [JHAH-na]
Buddhist meditation, or the states reached in Buddhist meditation.

CHAPTER FOUR

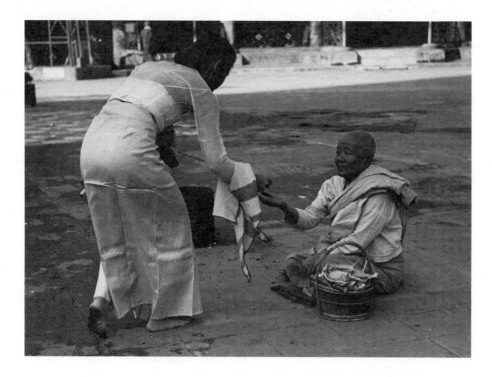

Burmese Nun Receives Gift of Food. Since Buddhist nuns have no money, they depend on local women for gifts of food for their once-a-day meal.

There is no permanent self to experience anything. Instead, the appearance of a self is generated by five basic groups, or *skandhas*, of experience. There are activities in humans' physical bodies and sense organs. There is the process of feeling. The mind that receives the sensations is part of the perceiving activity. There are responses to sensations in the form of impulses toward action. Accompanying these sensations and responses is consciousness. None of the skandhas, including consciousness, exists alone.

The Buddha differed sharply with Hindu belief in an eternal self that continues on through a series of bodies. Consciousness is not identical with self. A person is an aggregation of psychological activities, all temporary. In death, the aggregation comes apart. These five skandhas make up what we refer to as a person. Those who seek permanence of the self suffer, for no self exists.

In Buddhism, no self exists over and beyond the five skandhas, nor can a self be identified in any skandha or group of skandhas. Even consciousness cannot be identified with the self, for consciousness arises out of groups of factors. Without matter, sensations, perceptions, and mental activities, consciousness cannot arise.

TANHA

"Grasping," "craving," and "coveting" are better translations of *tanha* than is "desire." Simple desires of the body are not, in themselves, causes of suffering. A deep craving or grasping to make permanent what is impermanent is the cause of suffering. Assuming a permanent ego when there are only psychological processes produces suffering. Trying to keep objects, persons, and processes, which are impermanent, produces suffering. A craving to make a permanent ego that can grasp and hold all things produces suffering, for there is no ego to grasp the impermanent psychological processes.

Our thinking that over and above processes of body and mind we are permanent selves increases our suffering. For thinking that we are permanent selves, we seek to attach the world of experience to ourselves. What we cannot befriend, we fear. We are caught between grasping and aversion. Changes fuel our attempts to rearrange and enlarge what we grasp or avoid. The more we seek permanence, the more we suffer.

The whole existence of humans is becoming. Birth depends on death. All the psychological processes that make a person depend on birth. Cravings, grasping, and the desires to continue existence depend on psychological processes. Old age leads to death, which leads to rebirth, which initiates a repetition of the process. Early in his ministry, Buddha carried on a careful analysis of dependent origination, **pratitya-samutpada,** with his disciple Ananda:

> Ananda, if it be asked, "Do old age and death depend on anything?" the reply should be, "Old age and death depend on birth."
>
> Ananda, if it be asked, "Does birth depend on anything?" the reply should be, "Birth depends on existence."
>
> Ananda, if it be asked, "Does existence depend on anything?" the reply should be, "Existence depends on attachment."
>
> Ananda, if it be asked, "Does attachment depend on anything?" the reply should be, "Attachment depends on desire."
>
> Ananda, if it be asked, "Does desire depend on anything?" the reply should be, "Desire depends on sensation."
>
> Ananda, if it be asked, "Does sensation depend on anything?" the reply should be, "Sensation depends on contact."
>
> Ananda, if it be asked, "Does contact depend on anything?" the reply should be, "Contact depends on the mental and physical phenomena."
>
> Ananda, if it be asked, "Do the mental and physical phenomena depend on anything?" the reply should be, "The mental and physical phenomena depend on consciousness."
>
> Ananda, if it be asked, "Does consciousness depend on anything?" the reply should be, "Consciousness depends on the mental and physical phenomena."
>
> Thus, Ananda, on the mental and physical phenomena depends consciousness;
> On consciousness depends the mental and physical phenomena;
> On mental and physical phenomena depends contact;
> On contact depends sensation;
> On sensation depends desire;
> On desire depends attachment;
> On attachment depends existence;
> On existence depends birth;
> On birth depend old age and death, sorrow, lamentation, misery, grief, and despair. Thus does this entire aggregation of misery arise.[9]

This wheel of becoming fuels our suffering as long as we ignorantly assume that we are selves independent of the processes. Our clinging to the processes, either to grasp or to avoid them, extends our suffering.

THE END OF SUFFERING

Knowledge or enlightenment puts an end to suffering. Seeing clearly the nature of a person—that there is no permanent self—helps bring an end to craving. Realizing that everything is only part of impermanent psychological processes makes grasping foolish. There is nothing to have and nothing to be had. Individuals can simply let go. Destiny is each person's decision. Letting go is the end of suffering.

pratitya-samutpada [pra-TEET-ya sam-ut-PAH-da]
The Buddhist doctrine of dependent origination. It explains the experienced universe without resorting either to lawlessness or a first cause.

Letting go, however, does not mean obliteration of our lives. The purpose of overcoming suffering is liberation for living, not eradication of the processes of living. The processes of living do not cause suffering; the cause of suffering is unwarranted attachment to the processes. Through recognition that there is no permanent self, one can eventually overcome unreasonable attachment, craving, and desire. We can replace attachment with detachment.

THE MIDDLE PATH

The Middle Path of the Buddha was the path that he discovered between two extremes. The Brahmins who practiced Vedic rituals in temples and homes appeared too much identified with worldly endeavors. The wandering ascetics with whom he had lived were too dedicated to denying their bodies. The path that leads to Nirvana, the cessation of suffering, avoids these two extremes. It allows a person to experience life free from the suffering that ensues from attachment to extreme practices.

The Middle Path, the Eightfold Path, is marked by observing all the precepts at the same time. As psychological creatures, humans require more than insight to free themselves from dukkha. The first two requirements are right understanding and intention, a kind of wisdom. Unless humans understand the nature of suffering and release and that they can do something about it, they will not make an effort. Understanding does not require being an expert in metaphysics; humans need concentrate only on the goal of ending suffering. Unless humans intend to put an end to grasping, there can be no end to suffering. Intention must include proper conduct. Those who seek an end to suffering are careful in speaking and avoid lying, slander, abusive language, and gossip. Injury to any living being must be avoided. Dishonesty, stealing, drinking intoxicating beverages, and illicit sex lead to suffering. Earning a living in any way that injures or exploits other people is prohibited. Prostitution, trading weapons or intoxicants, or killing animals cannot be engaged in by anyone who is dedicated to ending suffering. Correct meditation or contemplation comprises effort, mindfulness, and concentration. The mind is the center of suffering and release; those who would escape suffering must learn to control all thoughts. When humans are fully aware of all psychological processes and bodily functions, they can be released to a sense of joy and contentment. The goal of contemplation is direct insight, an equanimity above all suffering.

SAMSARA AND KARMA

The Buddha agreed with the Hindu idea of samsara, in that he believed that birth follows death. Like the Hindus, he saw the cycle of rebirths as a prison to be escaped. He differed with them in that he believed a righteous person, regardless of caste, could escape in his or her present lifetime from suffering rebirth. Moreover, it was not necessary to follow the Vedas, the Brahmin priests, or the rigors of Jain asceticism. By concentrating on the Four Noble Truths, a man or a woman could attain release from suffering in this life.

Karma, in Buddha's understanding, is psychological instead of physical. Grasping, desires, and intentions bind the psychological processes. Humans become what they intend. In grasping for the impermanent

karma [KAHR-ma]
The law that a person's thoughts and deeds are followed eventually by deserved pleasure or pain. In Hinduism, it is an explanation for caste. In Buddhism, karma is primarily psychological; in Jainism, it is understood in primarily physical terms.

world, the psychological processes become attached. At death, something carries over to influence another psychological aggregation. The psychological processes that are detached from this world and its persons have nothing to carry over to another aggregation. The lighted candle is extinguished. Where does it go? Nothing passes over to another candle and nothing remains. When grasping ceases, humans pass beyond suffering to the state of **Nirvana.**

Nirvana [ner-VAH-na]
In Buddhism, the state of being free of egocentrism and the suffering that it causes. Positively, it is joy and peace.

The Theravadin Buddhist tradition preserves a dialogue between Nagasena, a Buddhist saint, and King Menander (Milinda):

> "Reverend Nagasena," said the king, "does the Buddha still exist?"
> "Yes, your Majesty, he does."
> "Then is it possible to point out the Buddha as being here or there?"
> "The Lord has passed completely away in Nirvana, so that nothing is left which could lead to the formation of another being. And so he cannot be pointed out as being here or there."
> "Give me an illustration."
> "What would your Majesty say—if a great fire were blazing, would it be possible to point to a flame which had gone out and say that was here or there?"
> "No, your Reverence, the flame is extinguished, it can't be detected."
> "In just the same way, your Majesty, the Lord has passed away in Nirvana . . . he can only be pointed out in the body of his doctrine, for it was he who taught it."
> "Very good, Reverend Nagasena!"[10]

THE BUDDHA AND METAPHYSICS

The Buddha's teachings concentrated on the pragmatic means of relieving human suffering. Metaphysical questions that intrigued the Hindu gurus, such as whether the world is infinite and eternal and whether a person continues to exist after death, did not seem to hold any speculative attraction for the Buddha. Human psychology that leads to pain and suffering, on the other hand, attracted his careful analysis and exposition. He did not need to quote gurus, saints, or scriptures; he had been there, and he spoke from the authority of firsthand experience. He did not find the traditional religious devotion of prayer and ritual sacrifices worth practicing or advocating.

He explained these points to a monk, Malunkyaputta, who had tried to engage him in a discussion of metaphysics. The Buddha compared metaphysical queries to someone who, wounded by an arrow, wanted to know all the details of being wounded. The physician focused only on removing the arrow and healing the suffering person. The Buddha declared that he concentrated on suffering, its nature, cause, and cure. He concluded,

> Accordingly, Malunkyaputta, bear always in mind what it is that I have not elucidated, and what it is that I have elucidated. And what, Malunkyaputta, have I not elucidated? I have not elucidated that the world is not eternal; I have not elucidated that the world is finite; I have not elucidated that the world is infinite; I have not elucidated that the soul is one thing and the body another; I have not elucidated that the saint exists after death; I have not elucidated that the saint does not exist after death; I have not elucidated that the saint both exists and does not exist after death; I have not elucidated that the saint neither exists nor does not exist after death. And why, Malunkyaputta, have I not elucidated this? Because, Malunkyaputta, this profits not, nor has to do with the fundamentals of religion, nor tends to aversion, absence of passion, cessation, quiescence, the supernatural faculties, supreme wisdom, and Nirvana; therefore have I not elucidated it.

And what, Malunkyaputta, have I elucidated? Misery, Malunkyaputta, have I elucidated; the origin of misery have I elucidated; the cessation of misery have I elucidated; and the path leading to the cessation of misery have I elucidated. And why, Malunkyaputta, have I elucidated this? Because Malunkyaputta, this does profit, has to do with the fundamentals of religion, and tends to aversion, absence of passion, cessation, quiescence, knowledge, supreme wisdom, and Nirvana; therefore have I elucidated it. Accordingly Malunkyaputta, bear always in mind what it is that I have not elucidated, and what it is that I have elucidated.[11]

Buddhists tell the story of Kisagotami, a woman who carried her dead baby to the Buddha that he might heal it. The Buddha told her that he could heal the infant if she could find some mustard seed that came from a home where there had never been a death. Householders gladly offered the young mother mustard seed, but every family had experienced death. Kisagotami learned what the Buddha was trying to teach—death comes to everyone. She placed her dead baby in a forest and returned to learn more from the Buddha.

The Buddha's Ministry

For forty-five years, the Buddha moved from kingdom to kingdom, leader to leader, and people to people in northern India. He appointed monks to care for territories. The scriptures present his dialogues with kings, princes, military leaders, ordinary people, and monks. Firm in discipline, the Buddha set high standards for conduct. Compassionate, he understood human suffering and the difficulty encountered in converting to his teachings. He was a winsome person, eagerly sought and eagerly followed.

From his early ministry, the Buddha's loyal companion had been his cousin Ananda. But his most renowned disciple was Mahakashyapa. The teacher's doctrines remained with his pupils; they had learned their lessons well. In the classification of Buddha's principal disciples, there are lists of disciples who became Bhikkus (monks), women who became mendicant sisters, laymen, and laywomen.[12] The Buddha continued to travel and teach until his eightieth year. Some food, perhaps spoiled, brought on a short illness and his death in 483 B.C.E. (or 480). Among his last words to Ananda were

2.25. But, Ānanda, what does the order of monks expect of me? I have taught the Dhamma, Ānanda, making no "inner" and "outer": the **Tathāgata** has no "teacher's fist" in respect of doctrines. If there is any one who thinks: "I shall take charge of the order," or "The order should refer to me," let him make some statement about the order, but the Tathāgata does not think in such terms. So why should the Tathāgata make a statement about the order?

Ānanda, I am now old, worn out, venerable, one who has traversed life's path, I have reached the term of life, which is eighty. Just as an old cart is made to go by being held together with straps, so the Tathāgata's body is kept going by being strapped up. It is only when the Tathāgata withdraws his attention from outward signs, and by the cessation of certain feelings, enters into the signless concentration of mind, that his body knows comfort.

2.26. Therefore, Ānanda you should live as islands unto yourselves, being your own refuge, with no one else as your refuge, with the Dhamma as an island, with the Dhamma as your refuge, with no other refuge. And how does a monk live as an island unto himself, . . . with no other refuge? Here, Ānanda, a monk abides contemplating the body as body, earnestly, clearly aware, mindful and having put away all hankering and fretting for the world, and likewise with regard to feelings, mind and mind-objects. That, Ānanda, is how a monk lives as

Tathāgata [ta-TAH-ga-ta]
A title of the Buddha, meaning one who has thus gone.

an island unto himself, . . . with no other refuge. And those who now in my time or afterwards live thus, they will become the highest, if they are desirous of learning.[13]

Their serenity overcome with grief, the Buddha's disciples openly wept at his death. For six days they kept his body in the grove where he died. The monks honored it with music, hymns, dance, and flowers. On the seventh day, they carried the body out the eastern gate of the city to the shrine of the aristocratic Mallas, where it was cremated.

Buddhists relate that the fire did not catch until Mahakashyapa arrived with five hundred monks to salute the Buddha. When flesh and fluids of the body were consumed, rain extinguished the flames. Bones of the Buddha's body were honored in the council hall of the Mallas for another seven days. Then the remains were divided into eight parts and distributed to representatives from different territories. They took the remains away and built monuments to enshrine them. A great mound was erected over the ashes of the funeral pyre. Eight monuments, stupas, in different places witnessed to the life of the Buddha.

Through all the story of the Buddha radiates the light of a gifted, winsome leader. Rich and powerful people wanted to be near him; they offered him gifts that would support his ministry of compassion. Ordinary people, too, found their fulfillment in his service. A son of a humble family could honor his parents in following the Buddha. The courtesan Ambipali and the simple mother Kisagotami are exalted in stories not by their status in society but through their devotion to the ideals of the compassionate Buddha.

Artists and raconteurs sought to convey the importance of the one who offered release from the wheel of suffering. While he lived, no statues of his youth, ascetic struggle, or contented old age were required. Early symbols were footprints of the Buddha. Whether in the path he walked and taught or the paths he traveled for forty-five years through kingdoms of India, the Buddha's footsteps were revered. Stories of his birth include an account that a holy man, with keen spiritual insight, recognized on the soles of infant Siddhartha's feet the thousand-spoked wheel, the sign of a great man.

The Development of Buddhism After the Buddha

THE BUDDHIST SCRIPTURES

Like Hinduism, Buddhism has a manifold collection of sacred writings. Unlike Hindus, Buddhists are not bound to the Vedas, or to the entire collection of Buddhist writings. Tables listing Buddhist scriptures help us understand the impossibility of large numbers of people mastering all the scriptures. In the Pali collection, of the language the Buddha preferred, there are three groups, totaling fifteen collections. The Chinese collection has sixty-one volumes. The Tibetan collection comprises a hundred or more volumes in the *Kanjur* and two hundred and twenty-five in the *Tanjur*. Buddhists have been extraordinarily diligent and creative in collecting, preserving, and interpreting everything about the Buddha, the dharma, and the Sangha. In practice, Buddhist groups focus their attention on a few volumes, sometimes basing their central doctrines on one *sutra (sutta)*.

The first stories of the life of the Buddha and his teachings were preserved in the memory of his early disciples. In time, these oral accounts were compiled into written treatises that could be used to guide the faithful.

The **Tripitaka** (threefold basket), the collected Buddhist scriptures, was named in the early days when sayings were written in the Pali language on palm leaves and gathered into separate baskets *(pitakas)*. The first basket contains "Discipline Basket" ("Vinaya Pitaka"), the obligatory 227 rules for monks. Explanations are given in extensive detail so that laity and monks would have little doubt about how to conduct themselves. The teachings of the Buddha on various subjects are set forth in discourses and dialogues preserved in the "Discourse Basket" ("Sutta Pitaka"). One of the five sections contains stories of the Buddha's previous lives and devotees' poetry and songs to the Buddha. The third basket, "Further Teaching" ("Abhidhamma Pitaka") is an expansion and elaboration of the basic teachings in other places. In it are the fine points of advanced, nondiscursive analysis of the Buddha's teachings and an indication of differences of interpretation between Pali and Sanskrit scriptures.

Tripitaka [TREE-PI-ta-ka]
The "three baskets" collection of Buddhist scriptures. It is comprised of the "Vinaya Pitaka" (monastic rules), the "Sutta Pitaka" (discourses), and the "Abhidhamma Pitaka" (supplement to the doctrines).

THE FIRST BUDDHIST COUNCILS

Historians of religion do not usually accept as accurate the tradition reported in the "Vinaya" that soon after the Buddha's death, five hundred monks gathered at Rajagaha to recite the Tripitaka as it was remembered by Ananda and Upali. They think that the Buddhist scriptures continued to develop over several centuries. Although scholars using sources external to the "Vinaya" question the traditional account of the first council, they do generally agree on some of its results. Three results were the affirmation of the authority of the religious community; the purity of the monks; and the establishment of essential, official scriptures.[14]

A second council met a hundred years later at Vaisali to settle disagreements over the strictness of the Buddhist discipline. The council addressed the tensions between essentially conservative, rigorous views and traditions and progressive, relaxed views and practices. Whether emphasis should be placed on monasticism or the life of the laity was debated. The monks also considered the sacred community as opposed to the secular community. A breach between two opposing tendencies was, for a time, healed.

Other councils followed, many of them held in India. Under King Mahapadma, less than fifty years after the second council, a third, noncanonical, council was held at Pataliputra to debate orthodoxy. The larger party, the Mahasamghikas, withdrew. The minor party, the Sthaviras, or Elders, went its own way. Each party began to develop its own collection of scriptures and its own community. The third canonical council was held at Pataliputra in 247 B.C.E. under the reign of King Ashoka. The king chose a respected Buddhist monk to help restore orthodoxy by condemning those viewpoints that had introduced heretical views into the Buddhist doctrine. Influenced by the example of King Ashoka, King Kanishka (ca. 100 C.E.) sponsored a council that compiled a new "Vinaya" and a commentary, the *Mahavibhasa*.

Over the centuries, Buddhism continued its dynamic generation of alternative views and practices. Councils were held in various countries to reach agreement in faith and practice. A sixth Theravadin council was held in Rangoon, Burma, in 1954.

Two Ways of Experiencing the Buddha

The councils had confronted the deep feelings of monks and laity as they applied their creative questions and imaginations to living by the dharma

Theravadins [ter-a-VAH-dins]
The elders, monks who imitated the
Buddhas ascetic life to attain enlight-
enment.

Mahayanists [ma-HAH-YAH-nists]
Those of the great vehicle, who
emphasized universal Buddhist
enlightenment.

in their particular circumstances. The oldest continuous group was that of the elders, Sthaviras, who followed the path of the monks. They were the **Theravadins.** This group elevated the monk who, following the example of the Buddha, lived a strictly monastic life directed intently toward the experience of Nirvana, release from craving. Other people who revered the Three Jewels envisioned a larger order that included monks and laypeople. They became known as the **Mahayanists.** Which was more like the Buddha, the person who sought only his own release or the person whose compassion led him into the world to help release other beings from suffering? The Theravadins and the Mahayanists divided on the answer.

THERAVADIN BUDDHISM

The two major divisions of Buddhist religion, the Theravadin (Sthaviravadins) and the Mahayana (Mahasanghikas), differ according to where emphasis is placed in the life of the Buddha. Buddhism, as do most other religions, has a conservative branch (Theravadin) and a liberal branch (Mahayana). Theravadin devotees focus on the life of the monk Buddha. Thus they favor imitating the Buddha in monasticism or asceticism. They follow the one who worked out his own salvation through right aspiration and meditation. A monk who attains supreme enlightenment is an *arhat*. In the societies of southern Asia, this form of Buddhism glorifies the example of the monk, with many laypeople spending at least some period of life in monastic discipline. Monks can count on receiving gifts of food for their one meal a day from faithful Buddhist believers who admire their lifestyle, even though they cannot always practice it themselves.

Theravadins were always conservative, but through the centuries, they did change. They emphasized that the Buddha was a man and remembered him with symbols of a footprint, an empty throne, or a stupa for relics.[15] Eventually they accepted images of the Buddha and allowed placing flowers or fruit before them. They permitted temples to house the images. They included **Jatakas,** stories of the Buddha's previous lives. They spoke of Maitreya, the Buddha who awaits in Tusita heaven to descend to the earth in the future. But always they have emphasized that the monk's lifestyle is the ideal to follow, for the monk imitates the way of the Buddha. Salvation is through dedicated self-effort rather than through intervention of heavenly beings.

Jatakas [JAH-ta-kas]
Stories of the previous lives of the
Buddha, which were collected and
used in the teachings of Theravadin
monks.

MAHAYANA BUDDHISM

Mahayana, the large vehicle, offers a variety of ways to release from suffering; it appeals to laypeople and monks of widely differing personalities and cultural orientations.

It applies the derogatory term *hinayana*, lowly vehicle, to the Theravadin Buddhists. The Mahayanists find the Theravadins too fundamentally tied to the simple, basic acts of this world, a group of literalists compulsively bound to imitating one aspect of the Buddha's life. The Mahayana Buddhists think of themselves as having risen above such pedestrian concepts to the finer and higher teaching revealed or alluded to by the Buddha. They claim that Siddhartha Gautama pointed them toward far more beautiful truths than he ever discussed in detail for his first disciples. Mahayanists identify with the advanced insights of the Buddha, which he communicated to those disciples who were capable of receiving this higher knowledge.[16] Typically, Mahayana groups believe in heavenly beings who

Merit Through Gold. In a pagoda in Mandalay, Myanmar (formerly Burma), monks paste gold leaf to the image of the Buddha. The "coat" of gold is more than eight inches thick.

can assist human beings in escape from suffering here to beautiful lives beyond the grave. **Bodhisattvas** are beings who, although qualified for Nirvana, remain outside in order to assist humans in need. Although the Buddha may not have been interested in speculation about the universe and its spiritual inhabitants, these subjects became attractive to many of his followers in India. The development grew as Buddhism moved later into China, Korea, and Japan. Writings were introduced showing that the Buddha had taught a higher philosophy for those who were ready to move beyond the elementary experiences of the world of senses.

bodhisattvas [bow-dhee-SAT-tvas] In Buddhism, people who have qualified to enter Nirvana, but who, out of compassion for others, remain available to help others.

Guanyin (Kwan Yin), Goddess of Mercy. A very nontraditional presentation in Hong Kong of the goddess who extends help to those who call on her.

Soon after the death of Siddhartha Gautama, the Buddha grew in the eyes of many of his followers to be more than a human monk. The Mahayanists came to believe that there were many other Buddhas. They held that salvation is not simply a matter of escape through working off karma at the end of this life. Individuals are not dependent solely on their own resources or those of the Sangha; on the contrary, the heavens are populated with all sorts of enlightened beings, or Buddhas, who can help each generation as Gautama helped his. One example is a bodhisattva of mercy, a male, Avalokiteshvara (the Lord Who Looks Down), in India; and a female, Guanyin (Kwan Yin) in China. Moreover, everyone is a potential Buddha.

A COMPARISON OF THERAVADIN AND MAHAYANA BUDDHISM

Although Theravadin and Mahayana Buddhism developed a multitude of doctrines and practices over the centuries, from the early years people viewed differently how individuals related to the Sangha. We have emphasized their early differences over whether laypeople should be valued in the Sangha. Mahayanists favored wide participation; Theravadins preferred only those who observed the monastic ideal. Theravadin monks believed that in imitating the practices of the Buddha, they alone, as individuals, could work out their own experiences of enlightenment, Nirvana. If they followed his path in every respect, they, also, would experience release from suffering. Early Mahayanists, whose householder obligations altered the ways that they could participate in the Buddha's teachings, found merit in deeds that householders could offer the Buddha. Acts of giving food, clothing, shelter, and medicines were surely of merit that would bring reward. Their obligations to families concentrated their sense of being individual selves. Detachment from obligations could not be so extreme as to allow their very selves to disperse. The Buddha's body had been burned and his bones distributed for memorials. Even the elders thought that the relics retained Buddha power. Mahayanists thought the Buddha continued beyond death; surely the compassionate one would respond to their suffering. Help, thought the Mahayanists, is available from the Buddha who knows and cares about each suffering creature.

The Mahayanists' value of the Buddha's compassion extended to other people who demonstrated compassion. Mahayanists did not value the wise monk seeking to become an arhat as highly as a compassionate person who qualified for Nirvana, but who remained available to hear the prayers of suffering humans. As offering of food, clothing, and shelter had aided the Buddha on earth, so ritual offerings and supplications could reach him and his compassionate associates in heaven. The Mahayanists sought explanations of how earth and heaven could communicate and cooperate. The Theravadins who looked within themselves in meditation could renounce metaphysics; the Mahayanists who looked heavenward needed metaphysical teachings. Let the Theravadin slavishly imitate the earthly Buddha; the Mahayanists preferred to communicate with the Buddha who is now liberated from the confines of a body. Mahayanists were sure that the Buddha had taught many more exciting doctrines to those who were open to spiritual insights.

Inspired by the Buddha, Theravadins and Mahayanists were all Buddhists. They sought to board rafts of the dharma that would take them to the farther shore. They differed on the size and accommodations of the preferable raft. As Buddhists reached out in compassion to share their good news with other peoples of India and other countries, passengers chose one of the two rafts. We could simplify the picture, for clarity of concept, by saying that the Theravadin raft sailed south and east in India, Sri Lanka, Burma, Thailand, and Indonesia. The Mahayana raft sailed first north, then east and west. It gathered passengers in the central Asian regions such as Uzbekistan; it loaded millions of Buddhists in China, Korea, and Japan. In Tibet, it attracted a distinctive group of passengers. That is how the two different visions of Buddhism were enacted in history.

In the development of these two ways of following the Buddha, two schools of Mahayanist philosophy contributed their insights. Before turning to Buddhist missionary outreach, we should consider how the insight of philosophers contributed to Mahayanist interpretations of dharma.

THE MADHYAMIKA SCHOOL

Nagarjuna, of the second century C.E., is associated with the **Madhyamika** school of philosophy. The Buddha had taught that there is no ego, no soul; there is only a temporary gathering of skandhas. Nagarjuna's ideas were based on the Middle Way, a path between asceticism and hedonism and between teachings of absolute reality and nonreality. To teach the impermanence and interrelatedness of all existing things, he eliminated ties to ideas, even those of revered Buddhist doctrine.[17] He asserted that all existing things are empty of absolute reality. Nagarjuna is most remembered for his teaching on emptiness, which he identified with interdependent origination, *pratitya-samutpada.*

To understand the theory behind Buddhist practices of meditation, pratitya-samutpada, the doctrine of dependent origination, must be understood. *Samutpada* means "co-arising" or "arising in combination." *Pratitya* means "moving toward." The combined term means "dependence" or "dependent arising."[18] The Buddha's understanding of human existence avoided many traditional metaphysical questions, but his theory explained human experiences without relying on an ultimate, first cause. His accounting for the continuity of human experience on the one hand allows nothing to be permanent, but on the other hand, there is not complete discontinuity. The doctrine is so important that some Buddhists consider understanding it tantamount to enlightenment. "In it an entire complex of notions about moral responsibility, human freedom, the process of rebirth, and the path to liberation coalesce."[19]

The discussion of dependence addresses both the process of human bondage and freedom. As devotees understand dependent origination they pacify their dispositional tendencies and understand their own personality and the experienced world. The impermanence of the experienced world, when seen for what it is, makes foolish any craving for an attachment to it. As devotees abandon craving and attachment, suffering diminishes and they are freed to lead a happy life. Through meditation, devotees replace avidya with jnana, or compassion, and freedom.

THE YOGACARA SCHOOL

Asanga, of the fourth century C.E., is associated with the **Yogacara** school, which goes farther than the Madhyamika position. Even the individual mind and mental constructs of the phenomenal world are not real. There is

Nagarjuna [NAH-GAHR-ju-NAH]
The Buddhist philosopher of the second century C.E. who established the Madhyamika school of philosophy.

Madhyamika [ma-DYAM-ee-ka]
The Buddhist philosophy that the phenomenal objects that one experiences are not ultimately real. Nagarjuna was the founder of the Madhyamika school.

Asanga [a-SANG-a]
Made famous in the fourth century C.E., the Yogacara school of Buddhist philosophy that was founded by Maitreyanatha.

Yogacara [YOH-ga-CHAH-ra]
The Buddhist school of philosophy that teaches that neither the phenomenal world nor the mind is real. Founded by Maitreyanatha in the third century C.E., it was made famous in the fourth by Asanga.

a great single consciousness that holds all experiences and ideas. These ideas rise to the surface of consciousness and give the impressions that humans have of the phenomenal world. However, even this consciousness is not ultimate reality. Ultimate reality is a void that cannot be comprehended by the human mind. Those who would identify with ultimate reality must abandon phenomena and ideas and become released into the Void. Differing with many scholars, David Kalupahana, an authority on Buddhism, does not find these ideas in the works of Vasubandhu.

In later development, those who were adept at practicing yoga conjured up visions that had the same appearance as subjective experiences of the world. They realized that when they imagined themselves a mighty god leading lesser gods against Mara, the Evil One, god of desire and death, their visions were just as real as their perceptions of the external world. Both exist only in consciousness, which is also only apparent in what is really a void.

From a consideration of the various early Buddhist schools, we turn now to an exploration of the development of Buddhism in other countries. We first discuss the missionary activities in Asia. Then Buddhism's development in China, Korea, Japan, Tibet, and later India will be traced through recent times.

Buddhist Missionary Activities in Asia

Buddhist monks had begun their missionary activities under supervision of the Buddha. After his death, monks wandered ever farther from the Ganges Valley, carrying the dharma to larger India. As the Theravadins and the Mahayanists diligently pursued implications of their views of the dharma, new groups formed to emphasize their particular interpretations. Buddhist enthusiasm steadily increased. The young faith attracted thousands of believers and stimulated reexamination of Hinduism and Jainism, India's other ancient religion.

An emperor, however, enjoyed the highest visibility in promoting Buddhist missions. **Ashoka** Maurya came to the throne in Magadha in 273 B.C.E. and was formally crowned four years later. As grandson of Chandragupta, who defeated the garrisons left in India by Alexander the Great, Ashoka had strength to expand his empire through conquest. His violent attack on the kingdom of Kalinga brought him that prize of the east coast. Ashoka controlled most of India except the extreme south. His military success, however, left him discontented. With passing time, his remorse over the suffering his conquest caused soldiers and captives deepened. To remove his guilt, he initiated a program of contrition. First, he publicly proclaimed, by carving in stones erected in highly visible places, his guilt for causing suffering in so many peoples. He would henceforth pursue a course of peace. Second, he severely limited, and then altogether eliminated, killing animals for sport or for food on his own table. He instituted a program that would preserve the lives of many species of creatures. Third, Ashoka had stones carved so that rules to direct his people's values and morality would be easily observed. He emphasized ideals of family, school, and community; respect and gentleness should be extended to persons and animals. These rules did not quote Buddhist dharma and mentioned other religions too, so one could argue that they were not particularly Buddhist. Their ideal, however, was the spirit of Buddhist life. Fourth, Ashoka required civil servants to teach laypeople the dharma and

Ashoka [a-SHOW-ka]
This king, who reigned in India 273–232 B.C.E., sponsored Buddhist missionary activities.

supervise their conduct. Fifth, he promoted Buddhism as an international religion, sending representatives as far west as Egypt and members of his own family to the island of Sri Lanka (Ceylon).

The *Chronicles of Ceylon* support tradition that Ashoka's family brought Buddhism to the island. The mixture of legend and history has not been definitely determined, but the story reflects the high esteem that Buddhists had for Ashoka. He sent his son Mahendra to teach Buddhism in Ceylon. The king of Ceylon and thousands of his subjects embraced Buddhism. At the request of the Ceylonese leader, Ashoka sent his daughter Sanghamitta bearing a slip of the sacred Bodhi tree to be planted in Ceylon. Sanghamitta ordained princess Anula, who became an arhat. These persons formed the nucleus of a cell that grew into a major branch of Theravadin Buddhism; it overshadowed all religions on the island except that of the Tamils, who established a kingdom in the northern part around the tenth century C.E.[20]

Theravadin Buddhism won the allegiance of peoples in southeast India, Sri Lanka, Burma, Thailand, and Indonesia, but its venture into China was less successful. In northern and eastern Asia, the Mahayanists enrolled the converts to Buddhism.

BUDDHISM IN CHINA

Buddhism in China did not have a promising beginning, for Chinese peoples of the first century found Theravadin Buddhism unattractive. In the year 65 C.E., the emperor Ming Ti (58–75) permitted a statue of the Buddha to be erected. The Theravadin emphasis on the monk was not accepted by the Chinese people, who wanted their sons to marry and raise families. Ancestor worship in China made essential the continuation of male heirs. When invaders from Mongolia introduced a Mahayanist form of Buddhism, the Chinese people responded favorably. The Mahayanists described many heavenly beings and features that supplemented ancestor worship. Sons who became Buddhists could help their ancestors.

Soon Mahayana Buddhism flourished in China. Pagodas dotted the landscape; images of Gautama and other Buddhas were housed in numerous temples; and monasteries became part of country, village, and city life. Many new schools of thought were formed to teach particular approaches to salvation.

In spite of the Chinese people's rejection of Theravadin Buddhism, the Mahayana forms continued to grow in China. Under the Southern Dynasties (420–589 C.E.), there were dialogues between representatives of Chinese thought and representatives of the Buddhist doctrine. *The Disputation of Error* (Li-huo lun) provides an example of these debates. In them, Mou Tzu responds to questions such as why Buddhism is not mentioned in the Chinese classics, why Buddhist monks injure their bodies (by shaving their heads), and why monks do not marry.[21]

Buddhism in China reflected some philosophies and schools found elsewhere, but it developed into a number of schools of thought that excited for centuries and were later transported to Japan. Among the most important schools are the Lotus, the Flower Garland, Pure Land, and Meditation.

Tian Tai (Tyian-Tai)

Tian Tai (Tyian-Tai) is based on the Lotus Sutra as interpreted by the Chinese monk **Zhiyi** (538–597), who taught on the Tian Tai (Heavenly Terrace) Mountain in Chekiang province. As Zhiyi (Chi Kai) interpreted the Lotus,

Tian Tai [TYIAN-TAI]
The Mahayana Buddhist sect of China (and Japan) that is based on the Lotus Sutra. All beings can actualize their Buddha nature and become Buddhas.

Zhiyi (Chi-kai or Chi-i) [ZHIR-YEE]
The monk who founded the Tian Tai sect of Buddhism in China.

it was a guide to salvation. He combined a philosophical content with meditative practice. Wm. Theodore de Bary summarizes the teaching on the Lotus:

> In short, this is a philosophy of One-in-All and All-in-One, which is crystallized in the celebrated saying that "Every color or fragrance is none other than the Middle Path." Every dharma is thus an embodiment of the real essence of the Ultimate emptiness, or True Suchness. It follows that all beings have the Buddha-nature in them and can be saved. This is the great message of the Lotus.[22]

Hua-Yen

The scriptural basis was the Avatamsaka Sutra, which means "wreath" or "garland." The Tian Tai (Tyian-Tai) had identified absolute Buddha nature with each phenomenon. The **Hua-Yen** emphasized that all phenomena interpenetrate each other. Fa Zang (Fa Tsang), a teacher who used mundane examples to explain the most difficult doctrines, delighted the Empress Wu with a Buddha image and eight mirrors. In an octagonal pattern around the image he placed the mirrors so that the Buddha image appeared in each mirror and each mirror reflected the other seven. Ultimate reality and particular phenomena are interrelated at every moment! Through meditation one realizes the great truth.

Jingtu (Ching-T´u)

The complex philosophical schools attracted some students, but the masses of people needed more easily understood, attractive interpretations of Buddhism. A heaven ruled by a loving god who welcomed all who called his name attracted millions of suffering people.

Pure Land Buddhism, or **Jingtu** (Ching-t´u), in India known as Sukhavati, is based on a belief that in the present age there is a sphere, Sukhavati, ruled over by Buddha **Amitabha.** After each Buddha is incarnated and has attained Nirvana, his dharma gradually declines until the hope of salvation lies only in faith. Based on the Sukhavativyuha Sutra, the teaching is that a person can be saved by faith in Amitabha.

The Pure Land believers find little merit in a life devoted to deeds of holiness. They emphasize that one is saved by faith rather than works. A person can be saved by calling on Amitabha Buddha, A-mi-t´o-fo. This is the easy path to the Pure Land, ruled by Amitabha, who sits on a lotus throne accompanied by **Guanyin** (Kwan-yin), the bodhisattva of Mercy.[23]

Chan (Ch´an)

One of Buddha's sermons consisted only of his holding a flower.[24] Because Kashyapa smiled, indicating that he understood, he was given the True Law. It was brought to China in 520 C.E. by **Bodhidharma.** Although his teachings were based on the Lankavatara Sutra, he emphasized that meditation is more important than expounding scriptures. The **Chan** (Ch´an) school emphasized that through meditation alone can a person come to Truth. By discovering his or her own nature, a person becomes a Buddha. Although all Buddhist groups value meditation, its practice in Chan is unique. In Japan, as we shall see, the school became known as **Zen** Buddhism.

Buddhism grew and diminished over the centuries as other philosophies gained ascendancy in China. The neo-Confucians attacked it for its

---

Hua-Yen [HWAH-YEN]
The Chinese Buddhist sect whose primary Buddha is Vairocana. The school had a holistic view of Buddha nature and the universe.

Jingtu (ching-t'u) [JING-too]
Pure Land, or Western Paradise, Buddhism. It believes in Sukhavati, which is ruled by Amitabha Buddha. [In Japan the sect is Jodo.]

Amitabha (Amida) [a-mee-TAH-ba]
The Buddha who presides over Western Paradise. Hozo Bosatsu is the Japanese name for a legendary monk who long ago took a vow to become a Buddha if his merits could be used to help others. After fulfilling 48 vows, he became Amitabha.

Guan Yin (Kwan-yin) [GUAHN-YIN]
Guanyin, bodhisattva of mercy, is also known as Avalokiteshvara. In Pure Land Buddhism, he is placed beside Amitabha as his attendant.

Bodhidharma [BOW-dee-DAHR-ma]
The monk who brought meditative Buddhism to China. His example inspired Chan (Zen) Buddhism.

Chan (Ch'an) [CHAHN]
The Chinese Buddhist school of meditation founded by Bodhidharma.

Zen [ZEN]
The Japanese Buddhist meditation sect (in China, Chan) that was based on the practices of the Indian Buddhist, Bodhidharma.

---

world-denying pessimism. The Maoists of the twentieth century attacked it for its lack of practical application in reforming society. In the early twentieth century, Buddhism was active in a great network of monasteries that supervised farming, education, and morality of the laity. It provided charitable services and often furnished homes for orphans. Holmes Welch's two-volume study reports many interviews with monks who experienced monastic life in the first half of the twentieth century in China.[25] Found there is an institutional life that, although often corrupted by human weaknesses, nevertheless provided a general softening of the miseries of life for the common Chinese people. A third volume, based on interviews with monks who endured the policies of Mao Tse-tung, reveals a period that ranged from neglect to outright persecution of monks and destruction of monasteries.[26] Under the successors of Mao, Buddhism has enjoyed some revival. The position of the Chinese government, however, is to espouse atheism. Buddhism does not enjoy the government support that often helped it in the past.

BUDDHISM IN KOREA

The earliest religion of Korea, as reflected in histories written much later in the twelfth and thirteenth centuries C.E., was called *mu*. The earliest spiritual leaders, often women, were known as *mudang*, religious specialists. Among the early gods were the mountain god, earth god, dragon-king god, smallpox god, seven-star god, god of luck, god of house site, kitchen god, and house god.[27] These deities were neither good nor bad; they could be influenced according to circumstances. The *mudang* helped people worship the gods through offerings of food. Evidence supports belief in life after death and the rites of ancestor worship.

Buddhism arrived in Korea in stages, beginning with the work of individual monks. Sundo brought Buddhist images from an earlier Chin state in northeast China in the year 372 C.E. His place of mission in Korea was Koguryo. Twelve years later, the monk Malananda brought Buddhism to Paekche from the Yangtze valley of the eastern Chin state. The monk Ado brought Buddhism to Silla. Thus, in the Three Kingdoms period (fourth through seventh centuries C.E.), Buddhism was received peacefully by the royal houses of Korea. Official recognition of Buddhism came in the year 535 C.E.[28]

To the important function of ministering to the needs of individuals, Buddhism added the ministry of protecting the state. Royal houses relied on Buddhism to preserve their rulerships. The Buddhist school known as Vinaya, which emphasized the rules of Buddhist monastic life, was especially supported by the monk Kyomik of Paekche and the monk Chajang of Silla. Chajang became chief abbot of state, ruling all Buddhist establishments in the district. Tantric Buddhism, however, offering miraculous cures, existed alongside the official version. The Mahayana doctrine, that there is Buddha nature in all creatures, was promoted by the monk Podok of Koguryo to answer the Taoist appeal to immortality. Buddhists had a long history of leadership in Korea, but in 1406, the emperor T´aejong severely persecuted Buddhism, dealing it a blow that brought its decline while Confucianism ascended as the state religion.

BUDDHISM IN JAPAN

The date usually given for Buddhism's entering Japan is 552 C.E., during the reign of the Emperor Kimmei. Popular stories focus on the Soga clan, of which the prime minister was a member, who were entrusted with caring for the image of the Buddha. Although powerful clans had opposed Buddhism, the Soga clan prospered to the extent that other Japanese accepted Buddhism.

After a civil war, the Soga clan seized the emperor's throne in 592 C.E. The Empress Suiko, placed on the throne by the Sogas, was a devout Buddhist. Her regent was Prince Shotoku, under whose brilliant rule Japanese culture matured, the state consolidated, and Buddhism was made the national religion.[29] He founded the first major national Buddhist temple, Horuji Temple, outside Nara, in 607.

Several of the Mahayana sects of China found their ways into Korea and then into Japan by the seventh century C.E. There they established a place among the practices of Shinto, the native Japanese religion of patriotic belief structure. Along with Buddhism came other aspects of Chinese culture such as writing, literature, and art. Buddhism brought substantial advancement to the whole Japanese civilization. In turn, Japan provided an environment for some of the most creative ideas in the ongoing drama of Buddhism. There Chinese sects took hold and were transformed. In Japan, new groups formed around charismatic personalities who gave Buddhism the rich varieties of expression so visible in the twentieth century. Some of these schools will be briefly described to show the many implications of the Buddha's teachings for some of his followers.

Tendai

In Japan, the Tendai school of Buddhism expanded from Indian Buddhism into a Buddhist drama for all people who would participate in it. A. K. Reischauer dates Tendai from the ninth century C.E., when it was introduced by **Saicho. (Dengyo Daishi** was his posthumous name.)[30] In China, the sect was known as Tian Tai (Tyian Tai). Its founder in China, Zhiyi, regarded all teachings, whether of Theravadin or Mahayana, as coming directly or indirectly from the thoughts of the Buddha. In his mind, the various sects simply developed different aspects of the Buddha's thoughts. He made provisions for salvation through philosophic wisdom or through faith in Amitabha Buddha, a salvation coming through faith rather than knowledge. A third means is the way of meditation alone or contemplation. Tendai was almost all things for all people, but it did emphasize the value of the Saddharma-Pundarika-Sutra (the Lotus), which presents Gautama as a manifestation of the eternal Buddha.

Saicho brought from China what he considered the very best elements of all the Buddhist schools. The Tendai sect still claims to harmonize the truths from all of the Buddhist sects; yet even in Tendai temples there are variations, and certain Buddhas are singled out for honor. Amida (the Japanese form of Amitabha Buddha) is a common figure of honor in all temples of Tendai. Japanese people could choose to identify according to their personality types, and they could still hold to Shinto, the native, patriotic religion of Japan, while being Buddhists.

Shingon

Also entering Japan in the ninth century C.E. was the Shingon sect, established by **Kukai (Kobo Daishi),** a contemporary of Saicho. These two men shared insights in the beginning of their careers but later parted on bitter

Saicho (Dengyo Daishi) [SAI-CHOH] The monk who introduced Tendai (T'ien-T'ai) Buddhism in Japan. He helped the emperor Kwammu establish a new capital at Kyoto, diminishing the power of Buddhists at Nara.

Kukai (Kobo Daishi) [KOO-KAI] The ninth-century C.E. founder of the Japanese Buddhist Shingon sect. All Buddhas are emanations of the great sun, Vairocana or, in Japan, Dainichi.

terms. Kukai brought the insights of the Chinese Chen Yen School, which became in Japanese the **Shingon,** or True Word, sect. Besides meditating on pure intellectual concepts, Kukai is sometimes credited with establishing schools for public education and the industry of silk worm cultivation. In Buddhist doctrine, the sect emphasizes mystery and magic, the Secret Teachings, which are in essence the truth that a person can attain Buddhahood in this life because he or she and the eternal Buddha are essentially one. Whereas Saicho had five steps to salvation, Kukai had ten steps on an intellectual ladder or ten steps on a moral ladder. At the pinnacle joining the real world of ideas and its phenomenal counterpart is the All, Buddha **Vairocana,** also known as Dainichi or Great Sun. Matter and other Buddhas emanate from Vairocana.

Kukai made another move that helped Shingon gain a wide acceptance quickly in Japan. He identified Vairocana with the Japanese Shinto goddess of the Sun, Amaterasu. In Ryobo Shinto (double aspect), Buddhism and Shinto are only two different sides of the same reality. Human beings and gods and goddesses are all only aspects of one central reality, Vairocana. Amitabha was also admitted along with other figures and symbolized by the sun.

The most important mystery of Shingon, the True Word, is transmitted by speech, a word or phrase, which, in religious terms is called a **mantra.** Body positions, **mudras,** are a second way to truth, and a third way is meditation upon a sacred picture, a **mandala.** Fire and water ceremonies are also used to help devotees reach Buddhahood.

In addition to educational and industrial contributions, Shingon imported cultural improvements from China such as words, symbols, and signs. Fine arts in painting and sculpture arrived during the period when the sect was in Nara and Kyoto. Music and literature also helped amplify the teachings of Shingon and enrich the whole court culture of Japan. Beauty enhanced the mysterious intellectual doctrines of the True Word and attracted former Shinto followers who could worship Amaterasu and Vairocana and also become wonderful Buddhas in this lifetime.

Jodo

Amida worship in Japan seems to have been inspired by **Ryonin** (1072–1132). Although he studied Tendai and Shingon, he began to seek his own path by reading and reciting the phrase of adoration of Amida Butsu, the Buddha of eternal light. He eventually had a vision of Amida, who asked him to teach others to say the "Namu Amida Butsu" and thus enter paradise. Through the power of another person, individuals can enter paradise.

The **Jodo** sect began with **Genku (Honen Shonin).** He was first a student of the Tendai sect. He discovered that salvation depends not on a person's own efforts but on the grace of Amida. The way of working out salvation through virtue and wisdom was replaced with the way of faith in Amida.[31] Jodo is also known as the Pure Land or Paradise sect. Another interesting feature of this sect is the belief that salvation comes through the vicarious suffering of **Hozo Bosatsu,** a supremely good man, who became Amida Buddha.

Shinran

Whereas Jodo was revolutionary in concentrating on salvation by grace through faith rather than through works of individual wisdom or virtue, **Shinran,** a disciple of Genku, introduced even more radical practices

Shingon [SHIN-GOHN]
Japanese for the Chinese Chen Yen school of Buddhism. It taught that matter and other Buddhas emanate from Vairocana.

Vairocana [vai-ROH-cha-na]
In Japanese Buddhism, the Sun, who is also the Buddha. It is also Dainichi and Amaterasu.

mantra [MAN-tra]
A special formula of words recited in worship.

mudras [MUD-ras]
Special positions of hands used in worship.

mandala [MAN-da-la]
A geometric pattern used in worship.

Ryonin [RYO-neen]
In the early twelfth century C.E., founder of Amida worship in Japan.

Jodo [JO-DO]
The Japanese sect of the Pure Land. It was founded in the twelfth century C.E. by the monk Genku. Salvation comes by grace, through faith.

Genku (Honen Shonin) [GEN-koo]
Twelfth-century C.E. founder of the Jodo Buddhist sect in Japan. He was the monk Genku, who had been trained at Tendai monasteries on Mt. Hiei.

Hozo Bosatsu [ho-zo-bo-SAHT-soo]
In Shinran Buddhism, a meritorious person who became Amida Buddha.

Shinran [SHIN-RAN]
Genku's disciple, who established the Jodo-Shin sect of Buddhism in Japan.

Buddhist Priestess at Prayer. In the ancient monastery of Jakko-In overlooking Kyoto, Japan, the senior priestess reads prayers that are more than a thousand years old.

Dhyana [DYAH-na]
In Buddhism, mental concentration. It is the term for Buddhist meditation.

through the Shinran sect. His vision at about age thirty was of Kwannon, the bodhisattva of mercy. Through the influence of his vision, he took the drastic step of marrying a princess. He also broke Buddhist tradition by eating meat. Through him, Buddhism established a separate branch of tradition, with temple priests serving as heads of families, living much closer to the practices of laypeople. For his troubles, he was exiled to Hitachi. Twenty-eight years later, he returned to Kyoto, having made many converts and established many temples after his six-year ban was lifted. Shinran did not offer alternative methods of salvation; he said that in recent times, the golden age being over, human beings could no longer save themselves. Only by faith in Amida could a person be saved. Through Hozo Bosatsu, people could receive the merit needed for their own salvation. Differing from the Theravadin view that one can work out one's own salvation, Shinran looked on human beings as depraved, dependent on grace from someone other than themselves.

Zen

The sect that has most captured the attention of Westerners is Zen. It has its roots in the meditative practices of India, where this particular form of Buddhism was called the **Dhyana.** The personality often connected with its spread abroad is Bodhidharma (probably from the fifth century), who shocked the Chinese emperor Wu Ti by claiming that studying sacred Buddhist scriptures and building monasteries are worthless acts and good works performed for fellow humans do not provide merit for salvation. Only comprehending our real nature is of value. The way of salvation for Bodhidharma was demonstrated when he retired to Shao Lin Monastery and sat in meditation facing a wall for nine years. The whole purpose of meditation is self-knowledge and an inward vision.

In China, the meditative sects went by the name of Ch´an. Its teachings are based on the Heart Sutra, which is presented here as the Shingyo (Prajnaparamitahridaya).

> Homage to the Perfection of Wisdom, the lovely, the holy! Avalokita, the holy Lord and Bodhisattva, was moving in the deep course of the wisdom which has gone beyond. He looked down from on high; he beheld but five heaps; and he saw that in their own being they were empty. Here, O Sariputra, form is emptiness and the very emptiness is form; emptiness does not differ from form, nor does form differ from emptiness; whatever is form, that is emptiness, whatever is emptiness, that is form. The same is true of feelings, perceptions, impulses and consciousness. Here O Sariputra, all dharmas are marked with emptiness, they are neither produced nor stopped, neither defiled nor immaculate, neither deficient nor complete. Therefore, O Sariputra, where there is emptiness there is neither form, nor feeling, nor perception, nor impulse, nor consciousness; no eye, or ear, or nose, or tongue, or body, or mind; no form, nor sound nor smell, nor taste, nor touchable, nor object of mind; no sight-organ element, and so forth, until we come to: no mind-consciousness element; there is no ignorance, nor extinction of ignorance, and so forth, until we come to, there is no decay and death, no extinction of decay and death; there is no suffering, nor origination, nor stopping, nor path; there is no cognition, no attainment and no non-attainment.
>
> Therefore, O Sariputra, owing to a Bodhisattva's indifference to any kind of personal attainment, and through his having relied on the perfection of wisdom, he dwells without thought-coverings. In the absence of thought-coverings he has not been made to tremble, he has overcome what can upset, in the end sustained by Nirvana. All those who appear as Buddhas in the three periods of time—fully

Tentokuin Garden in Koyasin, Japan. In this temple garden, patterns have been raked into the sand surrounding the rocks.

awake to the utmost, right and perfect enlightenment because they have relied on the perfection of wisdom. Therefore one should know the Prajnaparamita as the great spell, the spell of great knowledge, the utmost spell, the unequaled spell, allayer of all suffering, in truth,—for what could go wrong? By the Prajnaparamita has this spell been delivered. It runs like this: Gone, gone, gone beyond, gone altogether beyond, O what an awakening, all hail![32]

The seven initial Ch´an sects eventually focused on two basic approaches. The Lin Chi used rigorous methods and abrupt tactics to produce enlightenment, whereas the Ts´ao-tung took a longer, more gradual path through instruction and practices of meditation to reach enlightenment.

Zen entered Japan when the Buddhist monk Dosho (628–670) brought it from China. He had studied in China in 653, learning Yogacara philosophy from his Chinese teacher, Hsuan-tsang.[33]

The Japanese pronounced *Ch´an* as *Zen.* Lin Chi became Renzai and Ts´ao-tung became Soto. The enlightenment experience in Japan is called **satori.** Problems used in meditation, designed to destroy ordinary logical ways of thinking, are known in Japan as **koans.** The word *kung-an* in Chinese referred to a public law case, so it is likely that the problems were first argued in public.[34] A few examples of koans illustrate that focusing the mind on a problem can destroy usual forms of logic and, perhaps, bring a flash of insight into the nature of self and world. Consider these cited by Christmas Humphries: "If all things are reducible to the One, to what is the One reduced?" "A man hangs over a precipice by his teeth, which are clenched in the branch of a tree. His hands are full and his feet cannot reach the face of the precipice. A friend leans over and asks him, 'What is Zen?' What answer would you make?"[35] By destroying paths of customary logic, Zen seeks to proceed beyond them.

The rigorous Zen form of Buddhism is practiced by only a dedicated minority of Buddhists. However, its principles of rigid control of body and strength of mind have appealed to Japanese athletes and warriors. There is Zen influence in the beautiful art forms of *hai-ku,* the seventeen-syllable Japanese poem, and in flower arranging. The Japanese tea ceremony is also expressive of the controlled spirit of Zen.

satori [SAH-TOH-ree]
The Japanese term for the Zen Buddhist experience of enlightenment.

koan [KO-an]
A problem used by Zen Buddhists to reduce dependence on ordinary ways of thinking about self and the universe.

Nichiren

Nichiren [NEE-chee-REN]
A monk in Japan who established a school based on the Lotus Sutra.

Nichiren Buddhism began as a vigorous reform movement. **Nichiren** was a prophet of the thirteenth century in Japan who attempted to restore the pure Buddhism taught by Dengyo. He thought this could be done by reciting the sacred title of the scripture, the Lotus. He announced the formula on the morning he launched his reform movement, using the sun as his witness—"Namu Myoho-renge-kyo," adoration be to the scripture of the Lotus of the perfect truth.[36] As he explained later in the day to protesting monks at his monastery on Kyozumi, those who recite this scripture are in possession of the Buddha's golden body. The divine beings in the scriptures are more than helpers to believers; they provide examples of behavior believers are to practice in their own lives.

Nichiren's old comrades rejected his ideas. The local lord sought to take his life for such radical doctrines. At Kamakura, then the seat of the government, Nichiren demanded that all other forms of Buddhism be stamped out as heretical. This position earned him the enmity of all other Buddhist organizations. It is easy to understand why he was, both in his lifetime and afterward, a very controversial figure among Japanese Buddhist schools.

In Japan, Buddhism flowered into a religion that appealed to every personality type. To the Theravadin appeal, which had attracted Southeast Asians, the Chinese and Japanese added the myriad opportunities of Mahayana. Monasticism was available for those who sought it in several sects, but Shinran opened the door for family life. Several sects attracted

Japanese Flower Arrangement. Ikebana gracefully combines themes of heaven, earth, and humans in one flowing harmony.

mystics, and Zen appealed to those who were rigorous about meditation. The moralist, the ritualist, and the world reformer all had models in the various Japanese schools. Each group had its intellectuals who developed theory and explanations. There were no exclusions based on sex, class, nationality, or even membership in other religions. Buddhism was available for all who found it helpful.

BUDDHISM IN TIBET

Srong Tsan Gampo, a ruler of Lhasa who had two Buddhist wives, sent an invitation to Buddhists in India in 630 C.E. to introduce Buddhism into his realm. The Tibetans, however, found the new religion difficult to understand and remained with their native religion, **Bon** (pronounced *pain*). The word *Bon* meant "murmuring spells."[37] Bon was a kind of animism, a worship of spirits in nature. It took another century before exciting teachers from Bengal arrived with a brand of Buddhism that captured the attention of the Tibetans. In the eighth century, Shantarakshita, a wandering yogin, taught Tantric Buddhism. Tantrism invites human males and females to experience, through disciplined sexual energy, cosmic forces present in the individual. About the same time, Padma-Sambhava urged the Tibetans to build monasteries.

In the works of Stephan Beyer is a myth about the origins of the Tibetan peoples that may show their preparation for receiving Indian tantrism.[38] According to the *Red Annals* of the fourteenth century C.E., Tibetans descended from the monkey bodhisattva, Avalokiteshvara incarnated, and the rock ogress, an incarnation of **Tara.** Her Tibetan adherents call Tara "mother." Her worship spread along with Buddhist law; she became a folk figure worshiped beyond any particular Buddhist sect. The two wives of King Srong Tsan Gampo were canonized as incarnations of Tara, the savioress, or goddess of mercy.[39]

The drama of Tibetan Buddhism combined features of Hinduism in Hatha Yoga and tantrism with Buddhist deities of Mahayana. Tantric books emphasize the masculine and feminine aspects of gods, goddesses, and the universe. Creation is through pairs of deities, male and female, who generate the whole process of the universe through their sexual intercourse. Human beings also reflect the universe and can participate in its forces. The **Kalachakra** (time and space) doctrine is that the whole universe moves in a cycle and that there is "a correspondence between the flow of the vital currents in the body and the flow of time in the universe."[40] It postulated that the experience of time is only the functioning of the vital currents.

Humans have a pure consciousness or transcendent self in a reservoir at the base of the spine, and through special postures, they can pass beyond the limits of the physical body to experience the pure consciousness. Exercises of controlled sexual energy are believed to purify the nervous system so that humans can experience pure consciousness. Monks required nuns or consorts to aid them in this form of worship. Special words are spoken in formulas, or mantras; and dramas of the gods take place in abstract geometric constructions, or mandalas; in special positions formed by the hands, or mudras; and in the act of worship, **puja.** But the culmination of the lengthy worship in tantrism, which some books regard as primarily figurative rather than literal, is the copulation of a man and a woman as an act of worship, to generate power and perhaps a spiritual enlightenment.[41] The heightening of all energies is the goal rather than relaxation or

Bon [PAIN]
The ancient animistic religion of Tibet.

Tara [TAH-rah]
The popular mother goddess of Tibet, associated with Avalokiteshvara, the Lord Who Looks Down.

Kalachakra [kah-lah-CHAK-ra]
The space–time doctrine in Tibet. The whole universe is related in its flow to the vital currents of the human body.

puja [POO-ja]
Hindu worship of deities. The ritual of worship in India.

Nyingmapa [ning-MAH-pa]
The Red Hat Buddhists of Tibet.
Their Buddhism retained an element
of pre-Buddhist beliefs and practices.

Gelugpa [ge-LUG-pa]
The Buddhists of Tibet known as
Yellow Hats. They reformed the
practices of the Nyingmapa, or Red
Hat Buddhists.

lama [LAH-mah]
The term means "supreme being,"
comparable to the term *guru* in
Indian Buddhism. A priest in
Tibetan Buddhism.

expending energies. Indeed, some Indian tantrists believe that yogins can recover any energy lost during tantric exercises. The older tantric form of Tibetan Buddhism, the **Nyingmapa,** was known as the Red Buddhism because the monks wore red garments instead of the usual yellow. A later reform movement opposed some of the practices of Red Buddhism. The **Gelugpa** monks wore yellow hats and belts to signify their differences from the monks of the old order and practices, who continued to wear red.

Both the Gelugpa and the Nyingmapa form of Buddhism contain some tantric elements. However, the Gelugpa form was initiated as a protest against the sexual abuses and lax practices of the Nyingmapa, who ate meat and consumed much alcohol. The Gelugpa advocated celibacy, vegetarianism, and restricted use of alcohol. It is at this point that a second striking feature in the Tibetan drama of Buddhism occurs.

How could the Gelugpa find replacements for their order if they did not have sons to take their places? The answer went beyond mere recruitment to promotion from within their ranks. They held that the head **lama** would be reborn shortly after death. Thus they conducted an elaborate drama to search out a newborn male child who would bear on his body markings of the deceased lama and also show familiarity with a few of his personal belongings. The child, when found, would become the next lama, a living Buddha.

BUDDHISM IN LATER INDIA

Buddhism in India, to which we now return, seldom had royal support as enthusiastic as that of Ashoka's. Occasionally rulers opposed the Buddhists, who did not subscribe to the Vedas and the Brahmin order of worship, in favor of orthodox Hindu practices. Other considerations, such as the isolation of Buddhist monasteries from support of the Hindu population and the invasion of foreign religions, were not as important as the vitality of Hinduism. The insights of Buddhism, although introduced in vital new forms, were not foreign to the Hindu traditions. It was easy for Hindu leaders to incorporate the insights of the Buddha into the orthodox Hindu teachings and practices. If the peoples of India could find everything the Buddhists had to offer within Hinduism, what need did they have for a separate, nonorthodox religion? Buddhism faded in northern India by the thirteenth century and in southern India by the fifteenth century. There are small sects in India still practicing their own forms of Buddhism, which are sometimes associated with Hindu shakti cults.[42]

Recent Buddhism

Buddhism was challenged in most Asian countries by the colonial powers of Europe. Western industries, the technologies associated with them, and scientific education challenged traditional Buddhist ways of looking at the universe, humans, and society. Japanese imperialism had some impact, but because the Japanese were accustomed to Buddhism, they did not set out to destroy the religion. The most devastating threat to Buddhism came from Marxism.

Communist movements inspired by the philosophy of Karl Marx (1818–1883 C.E.) believe that all religion keeps humans from seeing the world as it is and from working to introduce a more humane social order. The most threatening form of Marxism for Buddhism was that introduced by Mao Zedong (Tse-tung) of China. Maoism attacked all religions and advocated atheism, a doctrine that claims there is no God. Wherever Maoism influenced Asian leaders, Buddhists had problems. In China, monasteries were closed and monks were sent to the work force, many on collective farms. In Tibet, severe restrictions were placed on the practice of Buddhism, and after a rebellion of the Gelugpa, led by the Dalai Lama, reprisals were enforced. The Dalai Lama and his associates fled to India and have continued to live in exile since 1960. The Nyingmapa adjusted, with difficulties, to their conquerors and managed a restricted practice of Buddhism.

After the death of Mao Zedong, the government of the People's Republic of China relaxed some of its restrictions on Buddhism. A few of the more important temples were opened for worship and visits by Chinese peoples and their guests. The state continues to advocate atheism.

Although Burma and Sri Lanka have maintained their Buddhism in all aspects of life, in other countries Marxist governments have placed severe strains on official institutions. Buddhists in Vietnam and Cambodia have suffered great hardships for maintaining the full practice of their faith.

Elsewhere, Buddhism has fared better. Taiwan and Japan have continued a vigorous practice of Mahayana Buddhism. Thailand and Sri Lanka have exhibited impressive examples of Theravadin Buddhism. Other countries of Southeast Asia have had political upheavals, but most have managed to practice their traditional Theravadin Buddhism.

The Present Dalai Lama. The leader of millions of Tibetan Buddhists participated in an interfaith service for world peace at the Cathedral Church of St. John the Divine in New York City.

Some Recent Buddhist Political Leaders

For much of its history, Buddhist leaders were monks who were dependent on the whims of political leaders for their survival and welfare. In the twentieth century, there have been some notable exceptions; the world has seen the rise of political leaders who are dedicated Buddhists. They have used their Buddhism in association with political power to influence the directions of their governments.

U NU OF BURMA

In 1948, Burma became independent. Just prior to that event, Aung San was assassinated and **U Nu** was invited to form a new government. He made Buddhism an essential ingredient of his political program. In his answers to the problems of Burma, he joined socialism and Buddhism. He combined a Buddhist desire for a perfect society under a Buddhist ruler with socialism's classless society.[43]

His personal life was that of an exemplary Buddhist layman. From 1948 to his death he practiced sexual abstinence. He often entered a Buddhist monastery for a period of meditation. Each morning he arose before dawn to spend two hours in meditation.

U Nu [U NOO]
A twentieth-century Buddhist leader of Burma, who was active in the United Nations.

BUDDHISTS OF VIETNAM

The Buddhists of Vietnam helped topple the regime of Diem in 1963. In 1964, the United Buddhist Association established two leaders of their affairs. They appointed Thich Tri Quang as leader of religious affairs and Thich Tam Chau as leader of secular affairs. The organization was able to make social improvements for the masses. In 1966, Thich Tri Quang and Thich Thien Minh led demonstrations against the government. To date, Vietnam is the most vivid example of Buddhist monks taking an active role in political leadership. Few people who were alive in the era of the

◆ **563** Siddhartha Gautama born

◆ **483** The Buddha dies

◆ **327–25** Alexander the Great in northwest India

◆ **273** Ashoka begins reign

◆ **247** Third Buddhist Council at Paliputra

◆ **200** Mahayana Buddhism begins rise

◆ **140–115** King Milinda (Menander), a Greek, reigns

65 Ming Ti of China permits Buddha statue to be erected ◆

2nd Century Nagarjuna begins Madhyamika philosophy ◆

399 Buddhism introduced to Korea ◆

5th Century Buddhaghosa ◆

520 Bodhidharma brings Chan (Zen) meditation to China ◆

538 Zhiyi, founder of Tian Tai (T'ien-T'ai) Buddhism in China ◆
Buddhism introduced to Japan by Korea

552 Buddhism enters Japan under reign of Emperor Kimmei ◆

630 Srong Tsan Gam Po invites Buddhist missionaries to Tibet ◆

740 King Khri-strong establishes Mahayana Buddhism in Tibet ◆

845 Wu Tsang of China persecutes Buddhists ◆

9th Century Dengyo Daishi (Saicho) introduces Tendai in Japan ◆
Kobo Daishi (Kukai) establishes Shingon in Japan

1200 Muslims destroy Buddhist centers in north India ◆

1212 Honen, founder of Jodo in Japan, dies ◆

1262 Shinran, founder of Jodo Shin in Japan, dies ◆

1282 Nichiren, founder of Nichiren Sect in Japan, dies ◆

1898 Jodo Shinshu sect comes to America with Japanese immigrants ◆

1931 Zen Buddhist society formed in New York ◆

1937 Makiguchi Tsunesaburo founds Soka Gakkai in Japan ◆

1945 Hiroshima, Japan, destroyed by atomic bomb ◆

1948 U Nu leads Burma ◆

1949 Mao Tse-tung controls People's Republic of China ◆

1950 North Korea invades South Korea ◆

1960 Nichiren Shoshu Chapter founded in California ◆

1964 Tich Tri Quang leads United Buddhist Association in Viet Nam ◆

1995 Dalai Lama recognizes 6 year old boy as reincarnated Panchan Lama; ◆
People's Republic of China disagrees, names own choice

| BCE | 2000 | 1500 | 1000 | 500 | 0 | 500 | 1000 | 1500 | 2000 | CE |

Vietnam War can erase the memory of individual Buddhist monks sitting in a street, dousing themselves with gasoline, and burning themselves alive—protests against the evils of their government.

The communist government overcame the resistance of south Vietnam and imposed the usual restrictions on the practice of religion. Passing years have brought a relaxation in the suppression of religions. Now a viable practice of Buddhism is permitted, and as Vietnam courts better relationships with other countries, increasing tolerance of religion seems likely.

SOKA GAKKAI

In Japan, a laypeople's association of Nichiren Sho Shu called **Soka Gakkai** was started in 1937 by **Makiguchi** Tsunesaburo. Other leaders, Josei Toda and Daisaku Ikeda, made it a powerful religious-political movement in modern Japan. The Komeito, or Clean Government, party advocated a middle path between capitalism and communism. It was a kind of Buddhist socialism. The party had notable political success in winning seats in

Soka Gakkai [SOH-ka GAHK-kai]
In Japan, a group of Buddhist laypeople known as the Value Creation Society.

Makiguchi (Tsunesaburo) [MAH-ke-GOO-chee]
Founder of Soka Gakkai (Value Creation Society) of Japan in 1937.

U Nu. The Prime Minister of Burma visits United Nations headquarters in New York in 1955. In 1989 Burma was renamed "Myanmar."

the Japanese Diet.[44] Its trend of increasing power, however, changed in the
1970s, and by the 1980s, many people in Japan thought their influence in
government ended.

Buddhism and the West

In its early encounters with Buddhism, the West emphasized the religion's
strangeness. Christians viewed Buddhists as pagans ripe for conversion. Buddhists, responding to the challenge, revived the missionary emphases of their
religion. They sent their monks to Europe, South America, and North America. There they supported the practice of Buddhism among the immigrants
from Asia. They did more. They reached out to non-Asians to inform them of
the teachings of Buddhism. D. T. Suzuki was particularly successful in foster-

ing an appreciation for Zen Buddhism among peoples of the West. Buddhism is a minority religion in most Western countries, but a respected one.

In the global community, Buddhism has followed Asians to Europe and North and South America. It has continued to minister to Buddhists living in predominantly Christian countries. It has also reached out to Christian societies to explain its position. Many Christians have responded favorably to the profound insights of the Buddha on the nature of suffering and release.

Buddhism entered Hawaii in 1889 with a Jodo Shinshu priest, Soryu Kaghi. Hawaii was, at that time, neither an American possession nor one of the states. In the mid-nineteenth century, Buddhism reached the West Coast of the mainland United States with the Chinese who settled in San Francisco. The first temples provided Buddhist worship, but their Buddhism was not a pure, exclusive form. The World Parliament of Religions in Chicago, 1893, focused attention on world religions. Renzai Zen Buddhism was promoted in America by Soyen Shaku. Arriving in San Francisco in 1898, two priests brought Pure Land Buddhism from Kyoto. Its first movement was the Buddhist Mission of North America; in 1942, it became known as the Buddhist Churches of America. The Jodo Shinshu Group is the largest Buddhist group in America. Aside from this group, the history of Buddhism in America is largely the story of Zen Buddhism.

After 1960, conditions were favorable for the establishment of other Buddhist groups in the United States. The war with Japan having ended fifteen years earlier, Japanese peoples were more appreciated. More Americans had traveled abroad; they were curious about Buddhism. With America's involvement in the Vietnam War, even more citizens became curious about the teachings of the various Buddhist schools. Other schools of Buddhism appeared.

Among these newly arrived forms of Buddhism were schools from Japan. They were joined by groups from Tibet and China. Nichiren Shoshu Sokagakkai came to South America and California through the efforts of Daisaku Ikeda. Its program was similar to that in Japan; it promised better living for its adherents, who had only to chant "Namu Myoho Renge Kyo" ("Hail to the holy law of the Lotus Sutra"). In Washington, D.C., serving the international community, Theravadin Buddhism was represented from 1966 through the efforts of the Buddhist Virha Society. A few other small Theravadin groups, some of them Thai, have prospered in Massachusetts, California, and Chicago. Two Tibetan centers have expanded rapidly since their beginnings about 1970. The Tibetan Nyingma Meditation Center in California and Karme-Choling of Barnet, Vermont, have attracted many followers. Chinese Buddhism has been especially active in making American monks and nuns; the Sino-American Buddhist Association of San Francisco has been quite successful.

Charles Prebesh, a historian of Buddhism in America, has found Buddhist groups combining traditional elements of Asian culture with new movements in the United States. Buddhist groups tend to be separated from mainstream society; many of their teachings and practices are hidden from the larger community. Some of the people who participate in the groups have little knowledge of the larger teachings of the Asian schools. But each group emphasizes the importance of individuals participating in the group; group solidarity is promoted. Chanting in traditional Asian ways provides non-Asians with opportunities for participating in the mysteries of the faith. Individuals are rewarded with a sense of belonging, of being helped by higher powers, and of personal growth through principles in harmony with modern psychology and sociology. Prebish thinks that the groups will have to make their witness more public before Americans in general will think of Buddhism as a religion that is also American.

Buddhist Women

Buddhism, no less than other religions, is challenged by women in the industrial and business work force. In industrial countries such as Japan, women are gaining employment outside the home. Their progress in the management hierarchies of corporations has been slow, but their educational preparation has qualified them for greater roles in the future. Diana Y. Paul's study of women in Mahayana Buddhism shows that although Buddhism allowed women to participate as nuns and laypeople, it regarded them as second in order to the elite males, the monks.[45] Indeed, one exercise recommended to help monks escape temptation in the presence of a woman was to imagine her as a rotting corpse in a cemetery. Laymen were comfortable with nuns or childless widows but fearful of the generative forces of mothers. Paul concludes that a religion with these traditions needs to make some changes to maintain its relevance for women in the contemporary world.

A woman with an unusual experience in Buddhism is Tsultrim Allione. Born in New England as Joan Ewing, she indulged her curiosity about Buddhism by going to Nepal in 1967 to study. Eventually she was ordained as a Buddhist nun in Bodhgaya. After spending more than three years in monastic life, she returned to the Western world, married, and had four children. While living in the world as a married mother, she continued practicing her Buddhist life of meditation.[46]

An English woman, Jiyu Kennett Roshi, was born of Buddhist parents. She experienced Theravadin Buddhism and then studied with teachers in the Zen tradition. In 1962 she was ordained a priest of the Renzai tradition in Malaysia and then became a disciple of the chief abbot in a Soto Zen monastery in Yokohama, Japan. Licensed as a teacher of Zen, she founded Shasta Monastery in California.[47]

Although the West may be more open to leadership from Buddhist women, Asian women are becoming more active and visible as teachers and examples. Asian women in the past have been accepted as Buddhist leaders; as Asian women participate more widely in their cultures, more of them are likely to influence the practices of Buddhism.

Buddhism Today

What conclusion about Buddhism as a religion in the modern world can be drawn? The variety of subplots and dramas within Buddhism help mark it as a major world religion, one that is fulfilling for all types of people. The colorful temples and statues; the picturesque monks and monasteries; the prayer wheels of Tibet and prayer rocks of Japan; the serene contemplation of the Zen master; the scholarship of the students of the *Tripitaka;* laypeople visiting monasteries to hear lectures, to participate in prayers, or to spend a few weeks or months in monastic discipline; and a family's quiet moments before the Butsu-dan in their home are all facets of a tradition of rich religious experiences.

In some of its manifestations, Buddhism may seem to an outsider to have strayed far from the deep, quiet, regulated monasticism of the Gautama Buddha. There is, however, a theme running through Buddhism that is present in all of its forms. The drama is driven by individual human beings who seek a way out of the sufferings that are part of every human experience. The Buddha left a powerful stamp of practicality on all his followers: escape from human suffering is more important than any other pursuit in life or death.

CONSIDER THIS: THE SELFLESS MIND

Peter Harvey, in *The Selfless Mind* (Richmond, Surrey, England: Curzon Press, 1995, p. 251), concludes that the Buddha's Middle Way regarding the "self" falls between eternal existence and annihilation. He writes,

> In this work I have tried to show that the "early suttas" through both hints and explicit passages, see *nibanna,* in life or beyond death, as unsupported, objectless discernment, thus avoiding these partial extremes. . . . [O]ne should not cling to any view, however "purified" or "cleansed" it is; how much more so to one that may fall short in these regards! All views are not-Self.

In terms of *skandhas, anatta,* and *anicca,* people can refer to the five skandhas, the empirical signs of a person, as a self, but the configuration of skandhas is impermanent. The impact of skandhas in one life may carry over to skandhas in another life, but the skandhas are impermanent. The referent for self, then, is impermanent. In Pritya-samutpada, consciousness is the apex of all arisings; consciousness is not restricted or confined by any permanent self. To escape all dukkha and experience Nirvana, the "self" of mind, or consciousness, must be recognized as also impermanent.

Does the concept of no permanent self make Buddhism seem more attractive or less attractive to sufferers? Does retaining the concept of a self's mind make escape from dukkha impossible? What does "mind" mean apart from "self"?

WORLDVIEW

The Absolute

In learning that Buddha did not worship a god, many people have concluded that he was an atheist. His doctrine that there are no permanent entities in the universe (**anicca**) removed any ground for traditional beliefs in gods. A more careful reading of his conversations with his monks indicates that he had not had an experience with any god that he found worth describing. He also asked whether the Brahmins who taught so much about gods and sacrifices knew from experience what they were teaching or were only repeating hearsay and tradition. He did not denounce belief in gods; he taught that belief in gods was not essential to his mission of finding release from suffering.

> 10. "Concerning the true path and the false, Gautama. Various Brahmans, Gautama, teach various paths. . . . Are all those saving paths? Are they all paths which will lead him, who acts according to them, into a state of union with Brahma? . . ."
> 12. "But then, Vasettha, is there a single one of the Brahmanas versed in the Three Vedas who has ever seen Brahma face to face?"
> "No, indeed, Gautama! . . ."
> 13. "Well, then Vasettha, those ancient rishis of the Brahmans versed in the Three Vedas, the authors of the verses, the utterers of the verses, whose ancient

🖎 A POINT OF VIEW

anicca [a-NICH-cha]
Impermanence. The Buddhist doctrine that there are no permanent entities. All phenomena continuously change.

form of words so chanted, uttered, or composed, the Brahmanas of to-day chant over again or repeat; intoning or reciting exactly as has been intoned or recited . . . did even they speak thus, saying: We know it, we have seen it, where Brahma is, whence Brahma is, whither Brahma is?"

"Not so, Gautama!"

14. "Then you say, Vasettha, that none of the Brahmanas, or their teachers, or of their pupils, even up to the seventh generation, has ever seen Brahma face to face. . . . So that the Brahman versed in the three Vedas have forsooth said thus: What we know not, what we have not seen, to a state of union with that we can show the way, and can say: 'This is the straight path, this is the direct way which makes for salvation, and leads him, who acts according to it, into a state of union with Brahma!' "

"Now what think you, Vasettha? Does it not follow, this being so, that the talk of the Brahmans, versed though they be in the Three Vedas, is foolish talk?"[48]

Buddha's followers, however, were less careful to avoid discussing deities. Theravadins still deny that the Buddha is a god—he is a man, but such a man! Westerners visiting a Theravadin temple, if uninstructed, would conclude that the devotees are worshiping the Buddha. Theravadins' beliefs include spiritual beings who can influence human lives and be influenced by humans. Mahayanists speak of three bodies of Buddha **(Trikaya).** One is the body of Siddhartha Gautama, which is the Transformation Body (Nirmanakaya). Another is the spiritual reality in all things. It is the Body of Essence (Dharmakaya). Some philosophical schools identified it with Nirvana, or the World Soul—Brahman of the Upanishads. The third is the combined body of Siddhartha and spiritual reality; he is the incarnation of spiritual reality. It is the body of Bliss (Sambhogakaya).[49]

Mahayanists opened the door for all sorts of spiritual beings. Bodhisattvas are saints qualified for Nirvana who remain in contact with the world in order to help those who are suffering. Devotees can pray to them and offer adoration. There are figures such as Avalokiteshvara and Guanyin (Kwan Yin), Vairocana, and Amitabha. There are countless Buddhas and Buddha fields. There is a "Suchness" in which all Buddhas participate. All humans who now live can become Buddhas. Although Buddhism did not emphasize salvation through gods of the Vedas, its spirit deified persons and ideals. Mahayana Buddhism appeals to masses who prefer to personify aspects of the Absolute.

The World

Buddhists shared with Hindus many aspects of interpreting the world. The Brahmin emphasis on sacrifices according to the Vedas seemed to the Buddha too worldly; the sannyasin emphasis on denying the world, and especially the human body, seemed too harsh. The Middle Path led him to accommodation with the world, its creatures, and its householders. The world can be accepted, appreciated, and valued. The cause of suffering is not the world but individuals' attachment to it.

Theravadins and Mahayanists differed in their interpretation of detachment from the world. Theravadins emphasized the ideal of the arhat who turned away from the householders' involvement in creative processes of life. Mahayanists emphasized that the world of experience is only appearances. The real world is one revealed in the enlightenment experience. According to Zen Buddhism, one can experience this insight into the nature of reality in this lifetime; for other Mahayana groups, the insight comes after death.

Trikaya [tre-KAH-ya]
According to Buddhist doctrine, the three bodies of Buddha. The first body was indescribable, the second body is the almost divine body in which the Buddha appeared to the Mahayana faithful, and the third body was his appearance as a human being.

How, then, do Buddhists relate to modern scientific studies of the world? T'ai Hsu, in his lectures on Buddhism given in Paris in 1928, said,

> Buddhism . . . holds that science does not go far enough into the mysteries of nature and that, if it were to go further, the correctness of the Buddhist doctrine would be even more evident. The truths contained in the Buddhist doctrine concerning the real nature of the universe could make a real contribution to science and tend to bring about a union between it and Buddhism.[50]

Considering the view of the world held by most university graduates since the advent of modern atomic physics, the quotation seems to be particularly relevant. There is an impermanence in the physical world that is denied by our subjective formation of permanence in the universe.

Humans

The Hindu division of a human into body and soul, a view shared by many world religions, was too simplistic for the Buddha. These two entities suggested more permanence to humans than he could find in his enlightenment experience. He agreed with Hindus that the human body is not permanent. He differed with them by denying that there is any permanent soul, or purusha. His doctrine is labeled **anatta,** no soul. The soul and the body of the Hindus could best be analyzed as psychological experiences. The skandhas of psychological activities arise and fall without any permanence. Even mind or consciousness is dependent rather than absolute.

anatta [a-NAT-ta]
The Pali word for no soul or Sanskrit no Atman.

The Buddha acknowledged that karma influences each life; one must live with results of cravings of the past. Choice, however, can change the future. One can choose how to see oneself and the world and how to interpret experiences. The *Anguttara-nikāya* V, 147 says,

> By getting rid of three mental states: passion, aversion and confusion, one is able to get rid of birth, ageing and dying. By getting rid of three mental states: false view as to "own body," doubt and dependence on rite and custom, one is able to get rid of passion, aversion and confusion. By getting rid of three mental states: unwise reflection, treading the wrong way and mental laziness, one is able to get rid of false view as to "own body," doubt and dependence on rite and custom.[51]

The Problem for Humans

The problem for humans is suffering. Suffering is primarily humans' ignorance of the impermanence of the world, people, and even their own psychological processes. Assuming that the world and its contents are permanent, humans crave and grasp in order to possess and control. Because psychological experiences and things experienced are impermanent, efforts to make permanent and to control are futile. Suffering is the symptom of alienation due to ignorance.

The problem is also ignorance that something can be done about suffering. A common response of suffering persons is to assume that they can overcome suffering by increasing their possessions or by introducing permanence into their living conditions. Proceeding along these lines leads humans to greater suffering and intensifies the vicious circle. Humans may conclude, wrongly, that there is no way out of suffering and become resigned to it. The *Samyutta-nikāya* II, 19–21 says,

"Is suffering wrought by oneself, good Gotama?"

"No, Kassapa."

"Then by another?"

"No."

"Then by both oneself and another?"

"No, Kassapa."

"Well then, has the suffering that has been wrought neither by myself nor by another come to me by chance?"

"No, Kassapa."

"Then, is there not suffering?"

"No, Kassapa, it is not that there is not suffering. For there *is* suffering."

"Well then, the good Gotama neither knows nor sees suffering."

"It is not that I do not know suffering, do not see it. I know it, I see it."

"To all my questions, good Gotama, you have answered 'No', and you have said that you know suffering and see it. Lord, let the Lord explain suffering to me, let him teach me suffering."

"Whoso says, 'He who does (a deed) is he who experiences (its result)', is thereby saying that from the being's beginning suffering was wrought by (the being) himself—this amounts to the Eternity-view. Whoso says, 'One does (a deed), another experiences (the result)', is thereby saying that when a being is smitten by feeling the suffering was wrought by another—this amounts to the Annihilation-view.

"Avoiding both these dead-ends, Kassapa, the Tathagata teaches Dhamma by the mean: conditioned by ignorance are the karma-formations . . . *and so on.* This is the origin of this whole mass of suffering. By the utter stopping of that very ignorance is the stopping of the karma-formations . . . *and so on.* Thus is the stopping of this whole mass of suffering."[52]

The Solution for Humans

The solution for humans is found in knowledge. They learn the cause of suffering and know that something can be done about it. The Buddha taught the Middle Path that leads to release from suffering. Theravadins emphasize that humans must work out their own salvation. The Buddha is a model to follow, but his Eightfold Path requires a disciplined life.

Buddhists believe that meditation is the primary solution to the problem for humans. Mahayanists regard the Theravadin form of meditation as elementary instruction for unimaginative followers. The Buddha taught many lessons over a forty-five-year period. To those capable of receiving a higher knowledge, he revealed better ways of release. The essence of the higher knowledge is that there are savior beings who will help those who call on them. These wonderful beings have looked over the wall of the garden of Nirvana, and, although they had every right to enter, turned back to help others find the way. Humans in distress can call on one of these bodhisattvas to come to their assistance. Release comes not so much from ceasing to be as from ceasing to grasp. Freed from attachment that produces suffering, humans can experience joys of life, joys figuratively described in terms of physical heavens. The *Pañcaviṃśatisāhasrikā*, 40–51 says,

> *The Lord:* What do you think, Sariputra, does it occur to any of the Disciples and Pratyekabuddhas to think that "after we have known full enlightenment, we should lead all beings to Nirvana, into the realm of Nirvana which leaves nothing behind"? [Note: This is also translated as "Nirvana without any residue."]
>
> *Sariputra:* No indeed, O Lord.
>
> *The Lord:* One should therefore know that this wisdom of the Disciples and Pratyekabuddhas bears no comparison with the wisdom of a Bodhisattva. What

do you think, Sariputra, does it occur to any of the Disciples and Pratyekabuddhas that "after I have practised the six perfections, have brought beings to maturity, have purified the Buddha-field, have fully gained the ten powers of a Tathagata, his four grounds of self-confidence, the four analytical knowledges and the eighteen special dharmas of a Buddha, after I have known full enlightenment, I shall lead countless beings to Nirvana"?

Sariputra: No, O Lord.

The Lord: But such are the intentions of a Boddhisattva. A glowworm, or some other luminous animal, does not think that its light could illuminate the Continent of Jambudvipa, or radiate over it. Just so the Disciples and Pratyekabuddhas do not think that they should, after winning full enlightenment, lead all beings to Nirvana. But the sun, when it has risen, radiates its light over the whole of Jambudvipa. Just so a Bodhisattva, after he has accomplished the practices which lead to the full enlightenment of Buddhhahood, leads countless beings to Nirvana.[53]

Although Nirvana is spoken of in religions of India, Buddhism's use of the term has acquired specific usage. In general, Nirvana is the state that the Buddha achieved, the end of the spiritual path that all Buddhists seek. In various times, places, and groups, Nirvana acquired distinctive features. Perhaps in the beginning it meant enlightenment, the bodhi experience, an awakening beyond the powers of speech to describe.[54]

In Theravadin Buddhism, the connotations of Nirvana were both negative and positive. Negatively, Nirvana meant the extinction of samsara, what can be reborn. Positively, it meant direct insight into truth, bypassing language distinctions between Nirvana and samsara. The arhat, who has achieved Nirvana, can experience it but not express it in language. Nirvana is the dying out of the three fires: Greed, Anger, and Illusion. It is best described as not this or not that.[55]

Mahayana schools and philosophies sought a common ground for samsara and Nirvana. Yogacara Buddhism thought that the mind was the common ground, a core of Buddhahood in each person. Chinese Mahayanist schools of Tian Tai (T'ien T'ai) and Hua-Yen made the difference apparent. Tian Tai sought immersion into the pure mind; Hua-Yen taught that there is no underlying mind. Fa Zang (Fa-tsang) argued that all phenomena reflect all other phenomena (as his demonstration of the Buddha image and the eight mirrors illustrated).

Mahayanists emphasized an ideal that combined enlightenment and compassion, a life exemplified by a bodhisattva. Enlightenment is open to everyone in this lifetime. Its experience is lived out in one's harmony with the universe.

Other Buddhist schools emphasized slightly different dimensions of Nirvana. Chan, or Zen, sought to pass the Buddha's enlightenment experience from master to disciple in an unbroken chain. The newest experience of enlightenment, then, was the end of a series of experiences that began with the Buddha. Pure Land Buddhism thought that humans were incapable of achieving Nirvana by their own power; relying on Amida's compassion enabled them to experience it.

In Tantric Buddhism, the enlightenment, Nirvana, experience is participation in the Buddha's reality. Shingon Buddhism emphasized experiencing the Buddha's enlightened activity through his body. Participating in the world, one exemplifies the Buddha's enlightened action.

Nirvana's two aspects run through the course of Buddhist history. Negatively, Nirvana is the burning out of the craving that brings suffering from lifetime to lifetime.[56] Positively, Nirvana is the enlightenment that inspires compassion for all living beings and a sense of harmony with the universe.

A Japanese Tea Ceremony. In Mobara Agricultural High School, Japan, students learn proper etiquette of this ancient practice.

Some philosophers conceive Nirvana to be . . . a state where there is no recollection of the past or present, just as when a lamp is extinguished, or when a seed is burnt, or when a fire goes out. . . . But this is not Nirvana, because Nirvana does not consist in simple annihilation and vacuity. . . .

Nirvana is where the manifestation of Noble Wisdom expresses itself in Perfect Love for all; it is where the manifestation of Perfect Love that is Tathagata-hood expresses itself in Noble Wisdom for the enlightenment of all;—there, indeed, is Nirvana![57]

Community and Ethics

Buddhism maintains an interesting balance between adherent and society. The Sangha was a close organization of monks, but it involved laypeople in monastery activities. Where Buddhism flourished over the centuries, it developed a strong social organization built on cooperation between laity and monks. At the same time, Buddhism has emphasized individual responsibility in community living.

The Law of Karma is recognized by Buddhists; there is a consequence for every thought or deed. All thoughts and deeds make impacts on the universe.[58] Impacts of deeds carry over from one lifetime to another. There is no self to be reborn, but impulses from an individual's life carry over into another life. Individuals have a responsibility to the future to live an exemplary life now. In the Buddhist teaching of *karuna*, or compassion, there is a strong social concern. Buddhism has taught compassion for all living creatures, animal life as well as human. Those who have compassion are not attached or moved toward a given creature. They have an impersonal good will toward all living beings. Expressed in terms of counseling, Buddhist compassion is more empathy than sympathy. Out of respect for living things, most Buddhist monks avoid eating meat or fish—they are vegetarians. Many Buddhist laypeople follow their examples.

Buddhist morality avoids theft, drunkenness, careless speech, and injury to others. With the exception of tantric rituals, Buddhists require celibacy for monks and nuns and loyalty in marriage for laypeople. Fornication and adultery are usually condemned.

Buddhist morality is deserving of rich praise; it is a greater resource than has often been acknowledged. Traditionally, Buddhism has been more concerned to avoid inflicting suffering than it has been to changing society's environments and institutions to improve living conditions. Compassion could be interpreted in a larger context and be extended to social reform; indeed, there are examples of Buddhist governments taking this approach. The Buddha did not fight to eliminate the caste system or the inferior status given to women. He did set an example in his own order for all the world to see; he made no caste distinctions, and he recognized that women can be as holy as men.

An Interpretation of History

In Buddhism there is no overpowering vision of the end of history, so an interpretation of history as one finds it in Western religions is a false category. As in Hinduism, one finds in Buddhism emphasis on progress of a person toward release rather than fulfillment of some purpose in history. In popular Buddhist thought, however, there is anticipation of future developments.

Marjorie Topley describes the beliefs in Buddhist folk religion among the Kueiken (Return to the Root) sect of twentieth-century Singapore:

> The third major cycle, that of **Maitreya,** has already begun and [its] own present patriarch is Maitreya incarnate . . . [To avoid the end of the world in a great catastrophe] the patriarch must be given the opportunity for reaching the masses to teach them the Truth. This can be achieved only if there is a return to the dynastic system and the patriarch sits on the Dragon Throne as emperor. . . .
>
> Truth cannot reach the people, moreover, if the head of the state does not hold Heaven's Mandate to rule. Ideally, Maitreya himself should head the earthly state as the Buddhas did in Tibet. Then he could easily reach all the people.[59]

In spite of its universal missionary outreach, Buddhism has been more concerned with the progress of the individual toward release than it has with the progress of society or the world toward some final judgment or disposition. In theory, as the individual overcomes attachment to becoming, so the universe can overcome the generation of opposites. In either case, there is peace and stability, the end of becoming.

Rituals and Symbols

Buddhism's extension into many nations and cultures makes it difficult to describe its rituals. Almost everywhere, the central figure of devotion is an image of Buddha. Placed in open air, housed in a great temple hall, or seated in a small temple room, the figure of the meditating Buddha is approached by devotees who bring candles, fruit, flowers, or even a gold leaf. At times, large congregations kneel before an image; most times individuals or families approach for a few moments of bowing or kneeling. At times, a monk assists in worship; at other times, no assistance is given to the devotee. Although the figure is usually inspired by Siddhartha Gautama, it may be one of the other Buddhas or bodhisattvas.

Another symbol is the wheel of the law, or the dharma. It is not so much an object of worship as a reminder of the perfect way of release offered by the Buddha. Although the term *dharma* has both general and technical meanings in Buddhism, the wheel stands for the Buddha's teaching. It

Buddhist Dharma Wheel. A metal emblem near Baudhanath Stupa in Kathmandu, Nepal.

Maitreya [mi-TRAY-ya]
In the tradition of East Asia, the next Buddha to appear on earth.

includes his exposition of the general order of nature and his proclamation of the path toward deliverance. The shortest dharma was the Buddha's first sermon, in which he set in motion the wheel, or lore, of dharma.

Devotees enter the Buddhist faith by repeating the three refuges. They take refuge in the Buddha, in the Dharma, and in the Sangha. In the Theravadin countries of Southeast Asia, small boys may go through the ritual of becoming a monk—their heads are shaved and they put on the saffron-colored robes of monks. Older males may spend several weeks as monks who listen to the law and go out with bowls to receive their food from laypeople. Initiation into the monastic life of most Buddhist orders is very rigorous and extensive. In China and Japan, short-term stays and temporary status as a monk are discouraged. Monastic life has several rituals associated with the laws of entrance and conduct. The "Vinaya" governs the monastic practice of dharma.

In Mahayana countries, there are other interesting observances in life and death. In life, Buddhist monks offer the faithful several ways of discovering the wish of the Buddha for their lives at the moment. To an unsympathetic outsider, the process may appear to be commercial fortune telling offered in a temple. To the devout, the systems offer very practical ways of learning what the Buddha would have individuals do about personal problems or opportunities. In death, families are assured that the deceased has experienced a satisfactory process to a good resting place in heaven and to a comfortable life once he or she has arrived. Buddhism teaches that karma can be removed by a religious professional chanting verses for the deceased.

Life After Death

In theory, there is nothing to carry over from one life to another. Yet the Buddha believed in samsara. Unless humans cease all grasping in this life, something carries over. A consciousness of former existence or a personal identity is not what carries over; what carries over is an individual's moral impact in personal and social life.

Mahayana Buddhism had great success in China, Korea, and Japan because it was concerned with the life of the person after death. The body might be buried or cremated, but the person may retain identity as an ancestor in a spiritual realm. Many Buddhists would explain that the symbols of heavens and beautiful lands of paradise are not to be taken literally. They stand for the ancestor's psychological and spiritual states. It seems that for the typical adherent of Mahayana Buddhism, however, joys after death are found in heavens similar to ideal physical places on earth.

A short quotation from the *Sukhāvativyūha*, 21–27 gives a view of Pure Land Buddhists:

> 21. . . . And the beings who are touched by the winds, which are pervaded with various perfumes, are filled with a happiness as great as that of a monk who has achieved the cessation of suffering.
>
> 22. And in this Buddha-field one has no conception at all of fire, sun, moon, planets, constellations, stars or blinding darkness, and no conception even of day and night, except (where they are mentioned) in the sayings of the Tathagata. There is nowhere a notion of monks possessing private parks for retreats.
>
> 24. And all the beings who have been born, who are born, who will be born in this Buddha-field, they all are fixed on the right method of salvation, until they have won Nirvana. And why? Because there is here no place for and no

conception of the two other groups, i.e., of those who are not fixed at all, and those who are fixed on wrong ways. For this reason also that world-system is called the 'Happy Land.' . . .

26. And further again, Ananda, in the ten directions, in each single direction, in Buddha-fields countless like the sands of the river Ganges, Buddhas and Lords countless like the sands of the river Ganges, glorify the name of the Lord Amitabha, the Tathagata, praise him, proclaim his fame, extol his virtue. And why? Because all beings are irreversible from the supreme enlightenment if they hear the name of the Lord Amitabha, and on hearing it, with one single thought only raise their hearts to him with a resolve connected with serene faith.

27. And if any beings, Ananda, again and again reverently attend to this Tathagata, if they will plant a large and immeasurable root of good, having raised their hearts to enlightenment, and if they vow to be reborn in that world system, then, when the hour of their death approaches, that Tathagata Amitabha, the Arhat, the fully Enlightened One, will stand before them, surrounded by hosts of monks. Then, having seen that Lord, and having died with hearts serene, they will be reborn in just that world-system Sukhavati. And if there are sons or daughters of good family, who may desire to see that Tathagata Amitabha in this very life, they should raise their hearts to the supreme enlightenment, they should direct their thought with extreme resoluteness and perseverance unto this Buddha-field and they should dedicate their store of merit to being reborn therein.[60]

Buddhism and Other Religions

From its inception, Buddhism has had to live among other religions. As a missionary religion, it has reached out peacefully to win converts through meeting their needs and desires rather than through force. It has been more ready to cooperate than to condemn. When it has not agreed with another position, it has quietly gone its own way. Hinduism absorbed or emphasized many of its ideals. Chinese ancestor worship found it supportive. For a time, Taoists and Buddhists cooperated. For most of Buddhism's history in Japan, Shinto and Buddhism have lived together peacefully, even sharing the same temple compound. Christians have been instrumental in helping translate Buddhist scriptures for other cultures and in promoting dialogues between Buddhists and Christians. One person involved in this dialogue is Father Thomas Merton, who was interested in Buddhism—especially Zen. From time to time and place to place there have been militant Buddhists who opposed all doctrines and practices except their own. The general spirit of Buddhism, however, has been peaceful and cooperative with other religions.

Having considered Buddhism, the great religion that arose in response to Hinduism, we turn now to two other religions of India. The older, Jainism, claims that its beginnings can be traced to the Vedic period. The younger, Sikhism, arose centuries later, after Islam and Hinduism had shared allegiance of India's peoples for a number of centuries. Through encounters with explorers, traders, and emigrants, these vital religions have made an impact on Western civilization.

✍ VOCABULARY

Amitabha [a-mee-TAH-ba]
anatta [a-NAT-ta]
anicca [a-NICH-cha]
arhat [UR-hut]
Asanga [a-SANG-a]

Ashoka [a-SHOW-ka]
Bodhgaya [bowd-GAH-ya]
Bodhidharma
   [BOW-dee-DAHR-ma]

bodhisattvas
   [bow-dhee-SAT-tvas]
Bon [PAIN]
Chan [CHAHN]
dharma [DAR-ma]

Dhyana [DYAH-na]
dukkha [DUK-kah]
Eightfold Path
Gelugpa [ge-LUG-pa]
Genku [GEN-koo]
Guan Yin [GUAHN-YIN]
Hozo Bosatsu
    [ho-zo-bo-SAHT-soo]
Hua-Yen [HWAH-YEN]
Jatakas [JAH-ta-kas]
jhana [JHAH-na]
Jingtu [JING-too]
Jodo [JO-DO]
Kalachakra [kah-lah-CHAK-ra]
karma [KAHR-ma]
koan [KO-an]
Kukai [KOO-KAI]
lama [LAH-mah]
Madhyamika
    [ma-DYAM-ee-ka]

Mahayanists
    [ma-HAH-YAH-nists]
Maitreya [mi-TRAY-ya]
Makiguchi [MAH-ke-GOO-chee]
mandala [MAN-da-la]
mantra [MAN-tra]
Mara [MAH-rah]
Maya [MAH-ya]
mudras [MUD-ras]
Nagarjuna [NA-GAHR-ju-NA]
Nichiren [NEE-chee-REN]
Nirvana [ner-VAH-na]
Nyingmapa [ning-MAH-pa]
pratitya-samutpada
    [pra-TEET-ya sam-ut-PAH-da]
puja [POO-ja]
Ryonin [RYO-neen]
Saicho [SAI-CHOH]
Sangha [SANG-ha]
satori [SAH-TOW-ree]

Shakyamuni [SHAH-kya-MOO-nee]
Shingon [SHIN-GOHN]
Shinran [SHIN-RAN]
Soka Gakkai [SOH-ka GAHK-kai]
Suddhodana [SUD-DHOH-da-na]
tanha [TAN-ha]
Tara [TAH-rah]
Tathagata [ta-TAH-ga-ta]
Theravadins [ter-a-VAH-din]
Tian Tai [TYIAN-TAI]
Trikaya [tre-KAH-ya]
Tripitaka [TREE-PI-ta-ka]
U Nu [U-NOO]
Vairocana [vai-ROH-cha-na]
Yashodhara [ya-SHOW-dha-ra]
Yogacara [YOH-ga-CHAH-ra]
Zen [ZEN]
Zhiyi [ZHIR-YEE]

✒ QUESTIONS FOR REVIEW

1. How did Hinduism help form the early life of Siddhartha Gautama?

2. What beliefs and practices of Hinduism did the Buddha reject?

3. What were the central teachings of the Buddha? What religious questions were of little interest to him?

4. Who were some of the people who helped the Buddha establish a new religious order? What were their individual contributions?

5. Buddhism is a missionary religion; describe some of its early missionary ventures. What leaders helped expand the influence of Buddhism?

6. What are the similarities and differences among Mahayana, Theravadin, and Tibetan Buddhism? What points can be used for making comparisons?

7. How did the Buddha's views on what a human being is differ from views of Hindus? In teachings of the Buddha, do Mahayanists and Theravadins differ in their views of humans?

8. Describe various Buddhist beliefs about what happens at death.

9. Compare the Buddhist worldview with the Hindu worldview.

10. Has Buddhist influence remained in India, or is it to be found only in other countries?

✒ QUESTIONS FOR DISCUSSION

1. How does the Buddha's method of overcoming suffering compare with the "step" programs that are employed today?

2. Why do some pictures and statues of the Buddha show him fat and others show him skinny? Do the Theravadins, Mahayanists, and Tibetans have different ideals in symbols, or can the differences be explained purely by age of the subject?

3. How do the Four Noble Truths differ from the practices of Raja yoga? What role did tantrism play in Hinduism and in Buddhism?

4. Today, could Buddhism assist modern medical and mental health practices, or have the teachings of the Buddha been left behind with other primitive treatments of human health?

5. Are meditation and contemplation compatible with empirical and rational approaches to knowledge? Explain your answer.

6. Can you think of ways that Buddhism and other religions can cooperate to relieve human suffering?

◌ NOTES

1. W. H. Moreland and A. C. Chatterjee, *A Short History of India* (New York: David McKay, 1957), p. 40.

2. Richard F. Nyrop, *India: A Country Study* (Washington, DC: U.S. Government Printing Office as represented by the Secretary of the Army, 1985), p. 156.

3. René Grousset, *In the Footsteps of the Buddha,* trans. J. A. Underwood (New York: Grossman, 1971), p. 140.

4. Robert O. Ballou, *The Portable World Bible* (New York: Penguin Books, 1967), p. 90.

5. Ananda Coomaraswamy, *Buddha and the Gospel of Buddhism* (New Hyde Park, NY: University Books, 1969), p. 14.

6. Robert C. Lester, *Buddhism* (San Francisco: Harper & Row, 1987), p. 23. Majjhima Nikaya, 1. 247–249.

7. F. L. Woodward, trans. *The Book of the Kindred Sayings* (*Sanyutta-Nikaya.* Part V: Maha-Vagga) (London: Pali Text Society; distributed by Routledge & Kegan Paul Ltd. London, Henley and Boston, 1979), pp. 356–357. Copyright © 1979 by The Pali Text Society. Reprinted with permission.

8. John M. Koller, *The Indian Way* (New York: Macmillan, 1982), pp. 148–161.

9. "Maha-Nidana-Sutta," Digha-Nikaya, *Buddhism in Translations,* ed. Henry Clarke Warren (Cambridge, MA: Harvard University Press, 1915).

10. Milindapanha, in Wm. Theodore de Bary, ed., *Sources of Indian Tradition* (New York: Columbia University Press, 1958), p. 114.

11. Majjhima Nikaya, *Buddhism in Translations,* ed. Henry Clarke Warren (Cambridge, MA: Harvard University Press, 1915), Sutta 63.

12. J. G. Jennings, *The Vedantic Buddhism of the Buddha* (London: Oxford University Press, 1948), pp. 158–164.

13. Maurice Walshe, trans., *Thus Have I Heard: The Long Discourses of the Buddha, Digha Nikāya* (London: Wisdom Publications, 1987), p. 245.

14. Charles S. Prebesh, "Buddhist Councils," in *The Encyclopedia of Religion,* vol. 4, ed. Mircea Eliade (New York: Macmillan, 1987), pp. 119–124.

15.. Grousset.

16. John Blofeld, *The Jewel in the Lotus* (Westport, CT: Hyperion Press, 1948), chapter 3.

17. Frederick J. Streng, "Nagarjuna," in *The Encyclopedia of Religion,* vol. 10, ed. Mircea Eliade (New York: Macmillan, 1987), pp. 290–293.

18. David J. Kalupahana, "Prattiya-Samutpada," in *The Encyclopedia of Religion,* vol. 11, ed. Mircea Eliade (New York: Macmillan, 1987), pp. 484–488, 485.

19. Ibid.

20. Coomaraswamy, pp. 180–186.

21. Wm. Theodore de Bary, ed. *The Buddhist Tradition in India, China, and Japan* (New York: The Modern Library, 1969), pp. 131–138.

22. Ibid., p. 157.

23. Ibid., pp. 198–199. See also Hajime Nakamura, *Indian Buddhism* (Delhi: Motilal Banarsidass, 1987), p. 180.

24. A. V. Grimstone, ed., *Two Zen Classics,* trans. Katsuki Sekida (New York: John Weatherhill, 1977).

25. Holmes Welch, *The Practice of Chinese Buddhism 1900–1950,* 2 vols. (Cambridge, MA: Harvard University Press, 1967).

26. Holmes Welch, *Buddhism Under Mao* (Cambridge, MA: Harvard University Press, 1972).

27. Yim Suk-Jay, Roger L. Janelli, and Dawnhee Yim Janelli, "Korean Religion," in *The Encyclopedia of Religion,* vol. 8, ed. Mircea Eliade (New York: Macmillan, 1987), pp. 367–376.

28. Ki-baik Lee, *A New History of Korea* (Cambridge, MA: Harvard University Press, 1984), pp. 59–61.

29. Robert Ellwood and Richard Pilgrim, *Japanese Religion: A Cultural Perspective* (Englewood Cliffs, NJ: Prentice Hall, 1985), pp. 23–24.

30. A. K. Reischauer, *Studies in Japanese Buddhism* (New York: AMS Press, 1970), p. 91.

31. Ibid., pp. 106–107.

32. Edward Conze, ed., *Buddhist Texts Through the Ages* (New York: Philosophical Library, 1954), pp. 152–153. Copyright © 1954 by Mushiram Manoharial Publishers Pvt. Ltd. Reprinted by permission.

33. Heinrich Dumoulin, *Zen Buddhism: A History,* vol. 2, trans. James W. Heisig and Paul Knitter (New York: Macmillan, 1988), p. 5.

34. de Bary, pp. 208–209.

35. Christmas Humphries, *Buddhism* (Baltimore: Penguin Books, 1951), p. 184. Copyright © 1951 by Christmas Humphries. Reproduced by permission of Penguin UK Ltd.

36. Masaharu Anesake, *Nichiren, The Buddhist Prophet* (Gloucester, MA: Peter Smith, 1966), p. 16.

37. S. K. Ramachandra Rao, *Tibetan Tantrik Tradition* (Atlantic Highlands, NJ: Humanities Press, 1978), p. 1.

38. Stephan Beyer, *The Cult of Tara* (Berkeley, CA: University of California Press, 1973), pp. 4–5.

39. L. Austine Waddell, *Tibetan Buddhism* (New York: Dover Publications, 1972), p. 22.

40. Rao, p. 57.

41. Ibid., p. 100.

42. Nyrop, p. 157.

43. Donald K. Swearer, *Buddhism in Transition* (Philadelphia: Westminster Press, 1970), pp. 40, 41.

44. Ibid., pp. 58, 59.

45. Diana Y. Paul, *Women in Buddhism* (Berkeley, CA: Asian Humanities Press, 1979).

46. Tsultrim Allione, *Women of Wisdom* (Boston: Routledge & Kegan Paul, 1984).

47. Denise Lardner Carmody, *Women and World Religions* (Englewood Cliffs, NJ: Prentice Hall, 1989), pp. 88–89.

48. *Buddhist Suttas,* trans. T. W. Rhys Davids (New York: Dover Publications, 1969), pp. 171–173. Republication of *The Sacred Books of the East,* vol. 11 (Oxford, England: Clarendon Press, 1881).

49. de Bary, p. 76.

50. T'ai Hsu, *Lectures in Buddhism,* Paris, 1928, in Blofeld, p. 177.

51. Conze, p. 81.

52. Conze, pp. 68–69.

53. Conze, p. 119.

54. Thomas P. Kasulis, "Nirvana," in *The Encyclopedia of Religion,* vol. 10, ed. Mircea Eliade (New York: Macmillan, 1987), pp. 448–456.

55. Humphries, p. 156.

56. Coomaraswamy, p. 117.

57. Lewis Browne, *The World's Great Scriptures* (New York: Macmillan, 1961), pp. 198, 200. The Lankavatara Sutra [Mahayana text] reprinted from a translation by Suzuki and Dwight Goddard in *A Buddhist Bible,* ed. Dwight Goddard (Thetford, VT: 1938), pp. 352, 356).

58. Mizuno Kogen, "Karman: Buddhist Concepts," in *The Encyclopedia of Religion,* vol. 8, ed. Mircea Eliade (New York: Macmillan, 1987), pp. 266–268.

59. Marjorie Topley, "Great Way," in *Folk Buddhist Religion,* by Daniel L. Overmyer (Cambridge, MA: Harvard University Press, 1976), p. 159.

60. Conze, pp. 205–206.

⚭ READINGS

Burtt, E. A., ed. *The Teachings of the Compassionate Buddha.* New York: New American Library, 1955. A concise, readable introduction to the teachings of the Buddha.

Conze, Edward. *Buddhist Meditation.* New York: Allen & Unwin, 1956. An important consideration of meditation in Buddhism.

Coomaraswamy, Ananda. *Buddha and the Gospel of Buddhism.* New Hyde Park, NY: University Books, 1969. An older work that interprets experiences of the author, who was born in Ceylon and educated in Britain.

de Bary, Wm. Theodore, ed. *The Buddhist Tradition in China, India, and Japan.* New York: The Modern Library, 1969. A sound presentation by a noted scholar of sacred writings of Asia.

Ellwood, Robert S., Jr., and Richard Pilgrim. *Japanese Religion: A Cultural Perspective.* Englewood Cliffs, NJ: Prentice Hall, 1985. Buddhism is included in this analysis of religion in Japanese culture.

Gyatso, Tenzin (fourteenth Dalai Lama). *The Buddhism of Tibet and the Key to the Middle Way,* trans. Jeffrey Hopkins and Lati Rimpoche. New York: Harper & Row, 1975. A view of Tibetan Buddhism from the Dalai Lama.

Jayatillike, K. N. *The Message of the Buddha,* ed. Ninian Smart. New York: The Free Press, 1975. The views of a major scholar have been prepared for Western readers by an editor who is an authority on world religions.

Lester, Robert C. *Buddhism.* Hagerstown, MD: Torch Publishing Group, 1987. A concise, readable introduction to Buddhism.

Robinson, Richard H., and Willard L. Johnson. *The Buddhist Religion.* Belmont, CA: Wadsworth, 1982. A concise study of the historical development of Buddhism.

Suzuki, D. T. *Manual of Zen Buddhism.* New York: Grove Press, 1960. Students have found most of D. T. Suzuki's books fascinating reading.

Welch, Holmes. *The Practice of Chinese Buddhism 1900–1950.* Cambridge, MA: Harvard University Press, 1967. This study, based on interviews with monks, gives a wonderful picture of Buddhist monastic life in China to the mid-twentieth century.

READINGS FOR RESEARCH AND REPORTS

Allione, Tsultrim. *Women of Wisdom.* Boston: Routledge & Kegan Paul, 1984.

Anesake, Masaharu. *Nichiren, The Buddhist Prophet.* Gloucester, MA: Peter Smith, 1966.

Bapat, P. V. *2500 Years of Buddhism.* New Delhi: Government of India, 1956.

Beyer, Stephan. *The Cult of Tara.* Berkeley: University of California Press, 1973.

Blofeld, John. *The Jewel in the Lotus.* Westport, CT: Hyperion Press, 1975.

Carmody, Denise Lardner. *Women and World Religions.* Englewood Cliffs, NJ: Prentice Hall, 1989.

Chan, Wing-Tsit. *A Source Book in Chinese Philosophy.* Princeton, NJ: Princeton University Press, 1963.

Cobb, John B. "The Meaning of Pluralism for Christian Self Understanding." In *Religious Pluralism,* ed. Leroy S. Rouner. Notre Dame, IN: University of Notre Dame Press, 1984.

Collins, Steven. *Selfless Persona: Imagery and Thought in Theravada Buddhism.* Cambridge, England: Cambridge University Press, 1982.

Conze, Edward, ed. *Buddhist Texts Through the Ages.* New York: Philosophical Library, 1954.

de Bary, Wm. Theodore. *East Asian Civilizations: A Dialogue in Five Stages.* Cambridge, MA: Harvard University Press, 1988.

———, ed. *Sources of Chinese Tradition.* New York: Columbia University Press, 1960.

———, ed. *Sources of Indian Tradition.* New York: Columbia University Press, 1958.

Dharma Publishing Staff. *Dhammapada.* Berkeley, CA: Dharma Publishing, 1985.

Dumoulin, Heinrich. *Zen Buddhism: A History.* Vol. 2: *Japan,* trans. James W. Heisig and Paul Knitter. New York: Macmillan, 1988.

Goodman, Steven D., and Ronald M. Davidson, eds. *Tibetan Buddhism: Reason and Revelation.* Albany: State University of New York, 1992.

Grimstone, A. V., ed. *Two Zen Classics: Mumonkan and Hekiganroku,* trans. Katsuki Sekida. New York: John Weatherhill, 1977.

Grousset, René. *In the Footsteps of the Buddha,* trans. J. A. Underwood. New York: Grossman, 1971.

Harvey, Peter. *The Selfless Mind.* Richmond, Surrey, England: Curzon Press, 1995.

———. *An Introduction to Buddhism.* Cambridge, England: Cambridge University Press, 1990.

Humphries, Christmas. *Buddhism.* Baltimore: Penguin Books, 1951.

Jennings, J. G. *The Vedantic Buddhism of the Buddha.* London: Oxford University Press, 1948.

Johnson, Sandy. *The Book of Tibetan Buddhism.* San Francisco: Harper & Row, 1995.

Kalupahana, David J. *A History of Buddhist Philosophy.* Honolulu: University of Hawaii Press, 1992.

———. "Pratitya-Samutpada." In *The Encyclopedia of Religion,* vol. 11, ed. Mircea Eliade. New York: Macmillan, 1987, pp. 484–488.

———. *The Principles of Buddhist Psychology.* Albany: State University of New York Press, 1987.

———. *Nagarjuna, the Philosophy of the Middle Way.* Albany: State University of New York Press, 1986.

———. *Causality: The Central Philosophy of Buddhism.* Honolulu: University Press of Hawaii, 1975.

King, Winston L. *Theravada Meditation: The Buddhist Transformation of Yoga.* University Park: The Pennsylvania State University Press, 1980.

Kogen, Mizuno. "Karman: Buddhist Concepts." In *The Encyclopedia of Religion,* vol. 8, ed. Mircea Eliade. New York: Macmillan, 1987. pp. 266–268.

Lee, Ki-baik. *A New History of Korea,* trans. Edward W. Wagner with Edward J. Schiltz. Cambridge, MA: Harvard University Press, 1984.

Levinson, Claude B. *The Dalai Lama, A Biography,* trans. Stephen Cox. London: Unwin, Hyman, 1988.

Moreland, W. H., and A. C. Chatterjee. *A Short History of India.* New York: David McKay, 1957.

Myōdō, Satomi. *Journey in Search of the Way,* trans. Sallie B. King. Albany: State University of New York Press, 1993.

Nakamura, Kyoko Motonochi, trans. *Miraculous Stories from the Japanese Buddhist Tradition: The Nihon Ryoiki of the Monk Kyokai.* Richmond, Surrey, England: Curzon Press, 1997.

Nyrop, Richard F. *India: A Country Study.* Washington, DC: U.S. Government Printing Office, Secretary of the Army, 1985.

Oldenberg, Dr. Hermann. *Buddha: His Life, His Doctrine, His Order,* trans. William Hoey. Veranasi: Indological Book House, 1971.

Overmyer, Daniel L. *Folk Buddhist Religion.* Cambridge, MA: Harvard University Press, 1976.

Paul, Diana Y. *Women in Buddhism.* Berkeley, CA: Asian Humanities Press, 1979.

Payutto, Phra Prayudh. *Buddhadhamma: Natural Laws and Values for Life,* trans. Grant A. Olson. Albany: State University of New York Press, 1995.

Rao, S. K. Ramachandra. *Tibetan Tantrik Tradition.* Atlantic Highlands, NJ: Humanities Press, 1978.

Ray, Reginald. *Buddhist Saints in India: A Study of Buddhist Values and Orientations.* New York: Oxford University Press, 1994.

Reischauer, August Karl. *Studies in Japanese Buddhism.* New York: AMS Press, 1970.

Rhys Davids, T. W., trans. *Buddhist Suttas.* New York: Dover Publications, 1969. Republication of *Sacred Books of the East,* vol. 11. Oxford, England: Clarendon Press, 1911.

Saha, Dr. Kshanika. *Buddhism and Buddhist Literature in Central Asia.* Calcutta: Firma K. L. Mukhopadhyay, 1970.

Skoroupsi, Tadeusz. "Buddhist Dharma and Dharmas." In *The Encyclopedia of Religion,* vol. 4, ed. Mircea Eliade. New York: Macmillan, 1987, pp. 332–338.

Smart, Ninian. "Buddhism, Christianity, and Critique of Ideology." In *Religious Pluralism,* ed. Leroy S. Rouner. Notre Dame, IN: University of Notre Dame Press, 1984, pp. 145–157.

Suzuki, Daisetz Teitaro. *Essays in Zen Buddhism.* New York: Grove Press, 1961.

Swearer, Donald K. *Buddhism in Transition.* Philadelphia: Westminster Press, 1970.

Tanabe, George J., and Willa Jane Tanabe. *The Lotus Sutra in Japanese Culture.* Honolulu: University of Hawaii Press, 1989.

Thurman, Robert A. F. *Essential Tibetan Buddhism.* San Francisco: Harper & Row, 1995.

Tuck, Donald R. *Buddhist Churches of America.* Lewiston, NY: Edwin Mellen Press, 1987.

Waddell, L. Austine. *Tibetan Buddhism.* New York: Dover, 1972.

Walshe, Maurice, trans. *Thus Have I Heard: The Long Discourses of the Buddha (Digha Nikaya).* London: Wisdom Publications, 1987.

Welch, Holmes. *Buddhism Under Mao.* Cambridge, MA: Harvard University Press, 1972.

Woodward, F. L., trans. *The Book of the Kindred Sayings (Sanyutta-Nikāya).* London: Pali Text Society, 1979.

CHAPTER FIVE

Jainism and Sikhism

After the Rig-Veda was committed to writing and gurus were teaching the union of Brahman–Atman, a Jain spiritual leader appeared who offered his followers a way to "cross the stream." Parshva, who is less well known than the Buddha he preceded in India, receives honor from Jains as their first Tirthankara, or "ford finder." Although deities had little role in salvation of Jains, karma and reincarnation were important concepts. The best way to avoid bad karma and increase good karma was to revere all soul present in living things, human or not. Despite its lack of deities, Jainism influenced Hinduism through its high priority of reverence for all life.

About the time that Christopher Columbus sought to add Asia to the possessions of Queen Isabella and King Ferdinand of Spain, Nanak, a young Hindu of the Punjab, saw God. He astonished his friends, when he rejoined them after his walk in a forest, by announcing that there is no Hindu and no Muslim. Instead of salvation without gods or with many gods, he taught salvation through only one God. As did Hindus, he believed in reincarnation; unlike Jains, his followers employed swords in preserving their faith. As he traveled with his friend Mardana, a professional singer, he helped stir the hearts of converts with songs of love for God. In the twenty-first century, Sikhism is a vital religion of India.

The Golden Temple of Amritsar. A Sikh in the Holy Lake at the Golden Temple in Amritsar.

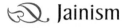 Jainism

Introduction

Jainism, although a minority religion of India, is considered so much a part of the religious scene that some people regard it as a subcaste of Hinduism. Since its views on the Vedas and deities differ from those of Hindus, it must be considered a separate religion. Its views on karma and samsara, however, are evidence of its origins in the fertile climate of India's religions.

HISTORICAL DEVELOPMENT

In Jain temples, twenty-four role models, Tirthankaras, are often represented by statues. The first, Parshva, is believed to have lived from the early days of the written Vedas; the last, Mahavira, was born about 599 B.C.E. The focal point of Jain beliefs and practices today is Mahavira.

Historiography

In writing the history of Jainism, beginning with Mahavira, one is confronted with two conflicting views of essential facts. Two groups of Jain monks disagree sharply about the life of their Tirthankara. Their points of view reflect their own choices of how to practice their faith. The more numerous, liberal monks and nuns, **Shvetambaras,** are clothed in white garments. The more conservative monks, the **Digambaras,** are "sky clad," which means "without clothing." Each group is sure that Mahavira set the example for their particular practices. As I tell the story of Mahavira, I will give both interpretations, so that at the end of the account readers will have a more complete view.

Shvetambaras [SHVAY-TAHM-ba-ras] The Jains who follow the tradition that allows monks to wear clothes. Shvetambaras believe that women can obtain release from life without being reborn as a man.

Digambaras [di-GAHM-ba-ras] The Jains who believe that a true monk is "sky clad." These monks think that women cannot become liberated until they are reborn as men.

The Life of Mahavira

Clothing is a symbol that expresses the different beliefs of the Digambaras and the Shvetambaras. Digambaras believe that wearing clothes demonstrates a person's attachment to the physical world. Because sal-

A Jain Temple in Calcutta, India. Worship of temple images of the Jinas is an important part of Jain devotion.

vation is achieved through renouncing the physical world and karma, which has physical attributes, Digambaras symbolize their renunciation by being only "sky clad." India accepts the nudity of its holy men, but holy women are not permitted nudity. The Digambara practice prevents women from becoming nuns in their order. Digambaras deny that women can, from this lifetime, become **Tirthankaras.** Only by being reborn as a man can a woman become a Tirthankara. The Shvetambaras disagree, believing that wearing clothes is irrelevant to a person's commitment to freeing the soul from the body. Accepting nuns in their practices, Shvetambaras believe that women can, in this lifetime, become liberated. These attitudes are manifested in the traditions and stories of each group.

The difference between Digambaras and Shvetambaras extends into their beliefs about their twenty-fourth Tirthankara. Both claim, of course, that there were twenty-three Tirthankaras prior to the twenty-fourth, Mahavira. They agree that he was born as Jnatrputra Vardhamana about 599 B.C.E. However, they are divided over his life in the womb of his mother, Trishala, and over the role of his father, Siddhartha, a Kshatriya chieftain of the Jnatr clan, in his birth. For the Shvetambaras, everything was as it appeared on the surface except that Trishala had fourteen dreams

Tirthankara [ter-TAN-ka-ra]
In Jainism, a spiritual leader who has found the crossing to the farther shore.

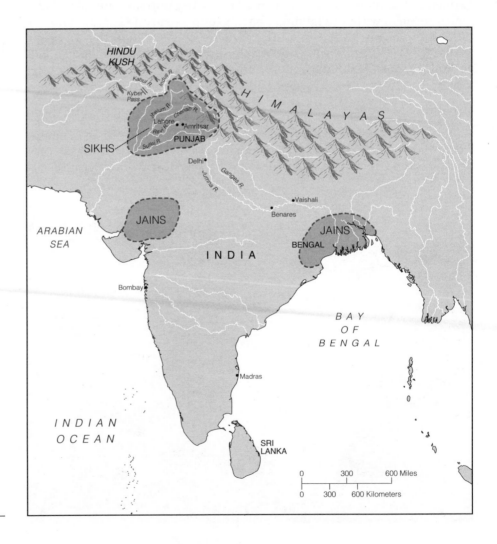

The Homes of Jains and Sikhs in India.
Although these faiths may be found in various places in India, the map indicates areas of concentrations.

that predicted the greatness of her son even before his birth. The dreams illustrate the attention to detail that devotees lavished on their sacred hero. The subjects of her dreams were

- a white elephant
- a white bull
- a lion
- Sri, the goddess of beauty
- garlands of Mandara flowers
- the full moon
- the rising sun
- a beautiful flag
- a vase of precious metal
- a lake of lotuses
- an ocean of milk
- a beautiful house in the heavens
- a pile of jewels
- a fire

To these dreams the Digambaras add

- a throne
- two fish in a lake[1]

All of these dreams indicate to the faithful that Mahavira was destined to be either a monarch or a saint. This account demonstrates the importance of dreams in prophecy, Jain symbols of a Tirthankara, and the elevation of Jnatrputra Vardhamana to that rank. It is interesting to compare this account with the stories surrounding the birth of the Buddha or the Christ.

The Shvetambaras tell an astonishing story of an embryo transfer. Mahavira was conceived through the union of a Brahman couple, Rshabhadatta and Devananda. Shakra, king of the gods, intervened and exchanged the embryo with that in the Kshatriya woman Trishala. The Jains thus rejected Brahmins in favor of Kshatriyas, who could become either spiritual or temporal monarchs. Shvetambaras believe that the embryo transplant was an auspicious moment in the life of Mahavira. The value that Jains place on ahimsa, or nonviolence toward living things, is seen in a story that the baby in the womb did not kick his mother but only stirred gently so that she would not worry. He was born in the Bihar region, near Vaishali.[2]

The two Jain groups are divided over whether Mahavira ever became a householder—the Digambaras deny it and the Shvetambaras profess it. According to Shvetambaras, Mahavira married Princess Yashodhara and fathered a daughter, Priyadarshana. The Digambaras insist that Mahavira never married.

Both groups agree that Mahavira renounced the world at age thirty. He tore out his hair in five handsful. The Digambaras claim that the gods came and removed his clothes and made him a naked wanderer. The Shvetambaras think that when his tattered garment was torn away by a thorn bush thirteen months after his wanderings began, Mahavira became "sky clad."

What is there in the philosophy of Jains that makes the issue of clothing so important? The Digambaras, disagreeing with the Shvetambaras, argue that although the absence of clothing does not necessarily signify a true monk, the presence of clothing on a monk indicates residual shame, a character flaw that is not found in a true monk. All the previous Tirthankaras, and not only Rshabha, the first one, were nude, say the Digambaras. They believe that only Digambaras can attain *moksha*, release from bondage to the world.

Mahavira's search for enlightenment lasted twelve years. Without clothes or home, he wandered, detached from the world. He did not answer questions put to him by villagers; they responded by siccing their dogs on him. He was attacked by animals and by humans who drove nails into his body to test the depths of his meditation. Eventually he experienced Nirvana. He was then known as a **Jina,** or conquerer. The word *Jain* means a follower of a **Jina.**

Jina [JI-na]
In Jainism, a person who has conquered rebirth. Mahavira was a Jina.

Once Mahavira attained enlightenment, he escaped from the cycles of human biological and psychological needs and weaknesses, say the Digambaras. Sitting in a lotus posture, he maintained an omniscient trance, sending forth only a divine sound. Above his head was a white umbrella, a symbol that nothing can be higher or holier than he. The Jain community around him, attracted by his Tirthankara nature, consisted of monks, nuns, laymen, and laywomen and was formed by efforts of his closest disciples. A Brahmin, Indrabhuti Gautama, came to him seeking an interpretation of a revelation of Jain teachings sent by the king of gods, Indra. In the presence of Mahavira, all of the teachings became clear.

The Shvetambara account is somewhat different, although in it, also, Mahavira astonished Brahmins with his holiness. Eleven of them were converted to be his followers. However, according to the views of this sect, Mahavira continued to eat sparingly of human food and to preach sermons on not harming life. He continued his teaching for thirty years. His omniscient cognition was not disturbed in this activity.

Both groups recognize that after his renunciation of the world, Mahavira attracted a very large congregation of devotees. According to the Shvetambaras, there were some 14,000 monks; 36,000 nuns; 159,000 laymen; and 318,000 laywomen.[3] His ranks of followers were deeply impressed with his holiness. At his death in 527 B.C.E. (other authorities date his life from 540 to 468 B.C.E.), a number of kings decided to celebrate a festival of lights to mark the passing of his internal light, which had gone to Nirvana.[4] They also celebrated the enlightenment of Indrabhuti Gautama to supreme knowledge. Jains believe that Mahavira is now in the blissful state of **ishatpragbhara,** beyond life and death.

ishatpragbhara
[ee-shut-PRAHG-bu-ru]
The Jain state beyond life and death.

Jain Scriptures

When Mahavira entered Nirvana, forever free from embodiment, his earthly impact was left in the care of his inner circle of eleven disciples, who were all Brahmins. In some way the "heavenly sounds" of Mahavira are translated by them into holy scriptures to enlighten followers in future generations. Collectively, the canon is known as the **Agamas,** written in Ardhamagadhi, an ancient Magadhan language. It is subdivided into three categories: *Purva, Anga,* and *Angabahya.* Jains claim to have been in existence before their twenty-fourth Tirthankara, Mahavira, and they logically carry their scriptures back to the time of Parshva, an earlier Tirthankara.

Agamas [AH-ga-mas]
The collection of Jain scriptures. It is subdivided into three categories: *Purva, Anga,* and *Angabahya.*

Nevertheless, these *Purvas,* or ancient texts, no longer exist, and the contents of the fourteen books are known only by references in later writings, such as the *Angas,* which originated with Mahavira.

The *Angas,* or limbs, consisted of twelve books, eleven of which are still in existence. Their composition, under critical analysis, seems to cover a long era and to contain material from different authors. Among this material are some of the basic teachings of Mahavira. The *Acaranga* contains the life of Mahavira and rules of conduct for monks and nuns. Other *Angas* give warnings against heretical doctrines, questions on systematic philosophy, tales of edification for laypeople, and as much as possible, an explanation of the rigorous Law of Karma.

The *Acaranga* states that anyone who does not refrain from injuring animals and who does not teach others not to harm animals continues to sin. A sage is one who knows that injuring animals is a sin.[5]

CONSIDER THIS: RESPECT FOR ALL LIVING THINGS

In Jainism, *Jiva,* living, is superior to everything *ajiva,* not living. Other religions place a high value on humans and many animals; Jains revere life in any form. The extent of Jain consistency troubles outsiders who first encounter Jains' care for living things. Having difficulty believing what they have seen, outsiders ask how Jains can value life in rats, grasshoppers, vegetables, and weeds to the same extent as they do life in humans and higher animals. They are particularly disturbed by practices in popular Jainism of caring for vermin and avoiding killing plants for food. Would consistency demand that Jains preserve the lives of all living organisms, such as bacteria, that threaten human life?

Deciding which forms of life are of no value and can be destroyed may be no less of a problem for non-Jains. Where should reverence for life begin and end? Is viability of a fetus outside a womb the test of life, or a fertilized egg, or a nonfertilized egg the dividing point between life to be revered and life to be discarded? Can we confidently distinguish between which life form is to be preserved and which is not? If we are going to value the lives of porpoises and whales, can we disregard lives of plankton, krill, and seaweeds? If we value lives of birds, can we destroy the insects and plants on which they depend? Although in practice we make distinctions, we can appreciate that Jain monks and nuns choose to include all living things among their higher values. Are we absolutely sure that we know enough to decide which forms of life should be preserved and which should be destroyed? Do we agree with those assessments of past generations within our own cultures? Will generations coming after us agree with where we drew the dividing line? Perhaps a Jain approach to life is not so ridiculous as some outsiders think.

WORLDVIEW

The Absolute

The Jains think that the universe is without beginning, so they do not believe in a creator god. They do believe that their doctrines originate from an omniscient and omnipotent being. Referring to their Jinas collectively as "the Jina," they mean God. Thus they do not require or seek any verification of doctrines

A POINT
OF VIEW

from any other source. Consider the selection from the *Great Legend* (Maha-purana) of the Digambara teacher Jinasena of the ninth century C.E.:

> Some foolish men declare that Creator made the world
> The doctrine that the world was created is ill-advised, and should be rejected.
>
> If God created the world, where was he before creation?
> If you say he was transcendent then, and needed no support, where is he now?
>
> No single being had the skill to make this world—
> For how can an immaterial god create that which is material?
>
> How could God have made the world without any raw material?
> If you say he made this first, and then the world, you are faced with an endless regression.
>
> If you declare that this raw material arose naturally you fall into another fallacy,
> For the whole universe might thus have been its own creator, and have arisen equally naturally.
>
> If God created the world by an act of his own will, without any raw material,
> Then it is just his will and nothing else—and who will believe—this silly stuff?
> If he is ever perfect and complete, how could the will to create have arisen in him?
>
> If, on the other hand, he is not perfect, he could no more create the universe than a potter could.
>
> If he is formless, actionless, and all-embracing, how could he have created the world?
> Such a soul, devoid of all modality, would have no desire to create anything.[6]

Jains do not deny that there is some truth in the doctrines of other philosophies; however, other philosophers who claim any sort of absolute truth are going to extremes. To Jains, statements depend on time, place, and circumstances for the truth they contain. And for each statement of fact, there can be an almost opposite statement that can also be true. After all, times change, and places and circumstances change so that more than one statement of fact becomes possible. Several authors claim the story of the blind men and the elephant is a Jain story told to illustrate exactly this point.

A king had five blind men examine an elephant and tell him what they had encountered. One, feeling the trunk, identified it as a huge snake. The second, feeling the tail, thought it was a rope. The third, feeling a leg, called it a tree trunk. The fourth, examining an ear, called it a winnowing fan. The fifth, feeling the side, called it a wall.[7] The point of the story is that human knowledge, limited and relative, is likely to be misleading.

loka [LOW-ka]
The universe where categories of sentient beings are reborn.

triloka [tri-LOW-ka]
The areas of the universe considered together: upper, middle, and lower.

jiva [JEE-va]
In Jainism, the soul. The term is opposite of ajiva, body. A monad is a single unit of basic substance.

The World

The **loka** is the emptiness of the vast but finite universe in which entities interact. The **triloka** is the triple world, seen by the omniscient ones. In the Middle World one finds the habitation of humans. Below it are hells; above it is Ishatpragbhara, where liberated souls live.

Five fundamental entities permeate the loka, providing the essentials of life. The most important is the **jiva,** which can be translated soul, or perhaps, "life monad."[8] Non-soul is divided into four entities: motion, rest, atoms, and space. Jiva acts through the mechanism of the four entities.

Jiva is characterized as eternal, consciousness, and will, in purity without form. Because Jiva is identical with knowledge, it can be immediately known.

In a world of experience, jiva is enmeshed with **ajiva,** or nonjiva. Karma, a sticky substance, binds jiva to nonjiva. The goal of jiva is to act so as to wear away nonsoul, including karma.

The world comprises individual souls. Some souls inflict suffering on other souls. There are many individual souls, not one undivided soul.[9]

ajiva or non-jiva [AH-JEE-va]
Category of existence that is insentient; lacking soul.

Humans

An example of how miserable and fruitless human life in the world can be is given in *The Story of Samaraditya,* by Haribhadra, of the seventh century C.E. A man left home to seek another country. Becoming lost, he was hungry and thirsty. A mad elephant charged at him. A demoness with a sharp sword appeared before him. He sought to reach refuge in a distant banyan tree. Unable to climb the tree, he dove into a well:

A clump of reeds grew from its deep wall, and to this he clung,
While below him he saw terrible snakes, enraged at the sound of his falling;
And at the very bottom, known from the hiss of its breath, was a black and
    mighty python
With mouth agape, its body thick as the trunk of a heavenly elephant, with terrible red eyes.
He thought, "My life will only last as long as these reeds hold fast,
And he raised his head; and there, on the clump of reeds, he saw two large mice,
One white, one black, their sharp teeth ever gnawing at the roots of the reed-
    clump.
Then up came the wild elephant, and enraged the more at not catching him,
Charged time and again at the trunk of the banyan tree.
At the shock of his charge a honeycomb on a large branch
Which hung over the old well, shook loose and fell.
The man's whole body was stung by a swarm of angry bees,
But just by chance, a drop of honey fell on his head,
Rolled down his brow, and somehow reached his lips,
And gave him a moment's sweetness. He longed for other drops,
And he thought nothing of the python, the snakes, the elephant, the mice, the
    well, or the bees,
In his excited craving for yet more drops of honey.[10]

After Haribhadra translates for a prince the story of the evils of the world, he concludes by saying that the drops of honey are the trivial pleasures for which humans cling to life in spite of its hardships.

The Problem for Humans

Jains share with Hindus and Buddhists the doctrine of an absolute law of karma. The other side of the doctrine for Jains is the absolute nature of soul (jiva), for even in the very lowest form of life, the soul is present, no matter how oppressed with the weight of karma. Moreover, as the soul can fall through accumulation of karma, so it can rise by release from karma. The soul accumulates karma through a creature's selfish desires; it loses karma by unselfish desires. Karma is the glue that binds humans to the cycle of rebirth—it is the operative element in samsara, the recurring rebirth of the soul. Of Hinduism, Buddhism, and Jainism, the Jains have the most physical analogies to the nature of karma.

Although Jains think that souls journey through infinite reincarnations in lower forms as well as human, they think that the human incarnation is the most important. Only from human form can a person obtain release, and only from human form can a person choose and carry out those thoughts and actions that can bring escape from eons of drudgery. Indeed, a person must know thoroughly the nature of karma in order to deal with it effectively. Jains have arrived at eight major types of karma, each with defined subsets. The four destructive karmas are (1) *mohaniya*—insight and conduct deluding; (2) *jnanavaraniya*—knowledge obscuring; (3) *darshanavaraniya*—perception obscuring; and (4) *antaraya*—restricting of energy. The four nondestructive karmas are (1) *vedaniya*—feeling producing; (2) *nama*—identifying the individual creature; (3) *ayu*—the longevity of a birth; and (4) *gotra*—the family environment. The final karmas can be destroyed only on the fourteenth *gunasthana,* or step on the ladder of deliverance.[11] This analysis of types of karma is evidence of the careful attention that Jain holy men have given to what they consider the central problem for human existence.

A person who seeks glory and honor is kept from happiness and wisdom. A person who causes pain on earth or who permits others to harm earth is deprived of happiness and wisdom.[12]

The Solution for Humans

Salvation comes through the soul's active desire and labor for its own release. From the depths of delusion, the soul begins a climb up fourteen steps of a ladder until at the top it achieves knowledge and freedom. Salvation is through a person's own effort; the only reward promised in worship is focusing the mind on release. A priest is not required; humans can worship alone or with other laypersons. Some exception is found in the form of Digambaras in the south of India who have Jaina-Brahmins residing at temples to take care of rituals. Even here they are not comparable to the role of Brahmins among the Hindus, and they do not replace the freedom of laymen to worship.

One who follows Mahavira in good works without deceit will eventually attain final liberation. Dedication and hard work in following the right path will bring reward.[13]

All the wise men have taught an unchanging law, teaches The Book of Good Conduct. No living things should be injured or slain.[14]

ahimsa [u-HIM-su]
The Sanskrit word that is translated "nonviolence." In Jainism, it is a reverence for all living things.

Ahimsa, the doctrine of nonviolence, is often associated with Mohandas K. Gandhi, who attributed his practice to Jain influence. The Jains practiced it centuries before Gandhi appeared in history to exemplify it for the rest of the world. *Ahimsa* is a Sanskrit word that is appropriately translated "nonviolence."[15] The doctrine appeared in the Upanishads; about 500 B.C.E. in India many people among the Brahmins, the Buddhists, and the Jains emphasized reverence for all life instead of the sacrifices of animals. Contemplative values superseded ritual values. Ahimsa, also, became ritualistic. It included self-control that arose from self-purification.

Jains practiced chastity, renunciation of possessions, and identification with all living beings.

Some scholars point to a Vedic belief in an "inverted" order in the "world to come," a situation in which a person would have to endure any pain that he or she had inflicted on other beings. It seemed to many holy men that in the light of such belief, a person should abstain as far as possible from injuring other beings. The doctrine of Brahman–Atman illustrated a fellow-feeling with all living creatures. The Law of Karma taught that a person could not escape the consequences of any act. Compassion became a virtue of those who sought liberation from rebirth. Ascetics of the three major religions of India agreed that "life should not be destroyed, whether in mind, in words, or in deeds."[16]

The Jains, including laypeople as well as ascetics, hold that all forms of violence, including passions, keep the soul from attaining perfection. Violence turns against those who do not refrain from it. The extreme examples in Jainism are holy men who believe that care should be exercised to avoid taking life from any living thing. Water is strained to removed any creatures in it. Masks are worn to prevent breathing in insects. Paths are swept before taking a step, to avoid killing an insect.[17] The only acceptable food is that which does not cost a life. To avoid eating all living creatures and cutting any vegetable, the most holy men survive only on fruits that have fallen naturally from trees.

Although the pain and suffering of earth bodies is not seen, it is real. A sage avoids sinning against earth.[18]

Respect for all living beings distinguishes Jain emphasis on the importance of soul. The Buddha had escaped the problem of redeath by declaring that there is no permanent soul. Hindus focused on the redeath of souls of humans. Jains emphasized respect for life itself in all living things. Sikhs emphasize the soul's relationship to God.

Community and Ethics

Jain ethics begin with principles of reverence for soul and detachment from physical things. Every Jain is expected to revere life, for beneath the karma that distinguishes individual creatures, all life, human or animal, is the same. Proper speech is a second requirement. Truthfulness (*satya*) is required, lest one injure another person and the community. Complete honesty in all relationships is so ingrained in the Jain community that its business and professional leaders are highly regarded by all people of India. The requirement not to steal (*asteya*) includes not taking anything that belongs to another. Sexual purity (*brahmacarya*) is a requirement for monks and laity. For monks and nuns, it means no sex at all; for laity it means no sex except in marriage. The requirement of nonattachment (aparigraph) is to avoid actions that lead to attachments to the physical world. The extreme form of nonattachment is a holy death **(sallekhana),** which is death by fasting. These requirements are accepted by people who take vows in becoming Jains. The vows help Jains make progress toward release from karma; they help the Indian community respect the moral principles of the Jain faith.

sallekhana [sal-lek-HAN-na]
In Jainism, a holy death achieved by fasting.

A wise person concentrates on liberation from rebirth. Avoiding attachment, a sage subdues the body, using only plainest food. This person will be liberated from rebirth.[19]

Rituals and Symbols

On a green plain northwest of Delhi, a temple of white stone reflects the rays of the dazzling sun. The dome impresses on visitors the sacredness of the building. Monks greet visitors and receive their offerings. Outside the walls, visitors remove their shoes and wash their hands and feet in water flowing from taps. The shadowy interior is cool, and the terrazzo floor comforts bare feet. Between the walls and the roof there is an open space that admits light and fresh air; birds fly in and out, celebrating with song. Under the dome is a life-size statue of a nude man. Jains and their guests walk slowly around the statue a number of times. A solitary devotee stands in one place at the pedestal of the statue, reading from a book and looking up to the dome. Although Jainism has no creator god, it does have temples for worshipers and meditating on the lives of its Tirthankaras (pathfinders or ford builders) to release their followers from the pain of rebirth.

What, then, is the point of worship if humans do not pray to a god for help and the twenty-four Tirthankaras are beyond reach? The images in the temple, sometimes twenty-four or only one, remind humans to approach as if in the presence of a living Jina, who is omniscient and sends forth a heavenly sound of inspiration and guidance to those who seek their own moksha. The images focus the human's physical eyes so that the mind can visualize the image of the kind of being he or she seeks to become. In the seventeenth century C.E., a third group of Jains, the **Sthanakvasis,** broke from the Shvetambaras, protesting against idolatry and temple worship.

Sthanakvasis [STAHN-AK-va-sees] A group of Jains that separated from the Shvetambaras over use of idols in worship.

What other actions can Jains take to illustrate their devotion to the example of Mahavira? Erecting a Jina image and caring for it by bathing it is one acceptable demonstration. Walking around an image of a Tirthankara in a Jain temple, bathing it, or waving a lighted lamp before it are also rituals of devotion. Celebrating the birthday of Mahavira in the spring and his liberation in the fall are customary. Or a Jain may recall in late spring Prince Shreyamsa's giving food to the mendicant Rshabha, establishing a model for laypeople to give food to wandering monks.

Sthanakvasi Jain Nuns. They cover their mouths to avoid taking lives of small creatures through breathing.

Devotees may go on pilgrimages to sacred places and worship there, participating in an annual rite of confession, fasting, and giving alms.

Jainism and Other Religions

Jainism and Buddhism appeared side by side with Hinduism and have often been confused with each other. Jains, however, claim that Mahavira and Buddha may have lived in the same century but that many Tirthankaras preceded Mahavira. Jainism is a much older religion, according to Jain claims, than Buddhism. Texts show, they argue, a separate Jain religion at the time Buddhism began. Buddhism and Jainism are two additional religions besides Hinduism with distinctive ways of dealing with karma and release. Although some Jains have claimed to be part of Hinduism, most scholars place them outside orthodox Hinduism. Jains do not, they argue, have Vedas for their scriptures.

Although Jains have coexisted in peace with Hindus and Buddhists for most of their history, one seventh-century C.E. king who was a Jain convert to Shiva worship, attempted to convert Jains in southern India to the worship of Shiva. When they refused, he impaled thousands of martyrs.[20]

SUMMARY OF JAINISM

There is a gentleness in the Jain view of life that commands respect. In a violent world, people who practice ahimsa seem as welcome as an oasis in a desert. There is a similarity with Theravadin Buddhism, for the meditating monk is an example of the devotion of life that even laypeople hope to encourage and, perhaps, one day achieve. A religion that inspires a person to work out his or her own salvation by imitating a model requires great fortitude. It is a cool life indeed where humans are not warmed by the glow of divine grace. But Jains know where responsibility lies and need not waste efforts on rituals and myths that may not yield results. Release comes to those who earn it.

In spite of the absence of a creator deity in Jainism, it shares some beliefs with Hinduism. The Law of Karma; the existence of the soul, which is reincarnated; and the cycle of rebirths until moksha is earned are similar to Hinduism. The extremes of depriving the body of clothing and food are closer to Hinduism than to the Middle Path chosen by Buddha. Like Buddha, however, the Jains can obtain release without deities. The focus is on humans and human models for them to follow. Jainism, too, has a logic that takes into account the relative truths and knowledge of humans. What we experience and reason as humans is more relative than absolute. Jainism requires of humans a commitment in faith long before they can know whether they will obtain release.

Jains are widely respected in India, sometimes regarded as a sect of Hindus. Very much a part of the modern world, Jains took advantage early of Western education. In general, they are prosperous urban dwellers. In a twentieth-century revival, Jains have adapted their older beliefs to current events. Through education of their priests, restoration of their numerous temples, and publication of periodicals, they have widely disseminated their renewed views of the world.[21]

⟨Ɋ Sikhism

Introduction

Approximately two thousand years after Jainism was firmly established in India, Nanak appeared as the first guru of the Sikhs. After receiving a revelation from God, he challenged the numerous gods and castes of Hinduism, the reverence for life in Jainism, and denial of the world in Buddhism. He denied also the revelation of Allah to Muhammad, the Quran. The initial response to Nanak's audacity was confusion and puzzlement. His success in establishing a rival faith, however, brought animosity from most other faiths, particularly the Mogul (Muslim) leaders. Some of them attacked particular successors of Guru Nanak.

Although Nanak's vision once seemed to offer a meeting ground for polytheistic Hindus and monotheistic Muslims, it eventually brought rejection from both. Only single-minded devotion to the Sikh faith preserved later gurus. Their determination to bear arms to preserve their religion was successful in their times, and inspires many of their followers today.

HISTORICAL DEVELOPMENT

The birth of Nanak, the first guru, in the fifteenth century, is for Sikhs the proper beginning of Sikhism. To understand the reception that he received, however, it is helpful for us to refer to the life of the Prophet Muhammad in Arabia, his recitations of Allah's revelation in the Quran, and Muslims who at various times and places introduced their faith to India. In particular, the presence of Muslim mystics, the Sufis, in the Punjab region helps us understand the climate in which Nanak's revelations were received. How to balance his unique contribution with general cultural influences is the subject of historiography in Sikhism.

Historiography

Two views of the historical development of Sikhism circulate today. Older scholarship describes Sikhism as Nanak's attempt to develop a religion that would incorporate the best spiritual insights of both Hinduism and Islam. More recent scholarship represents Sikh views of their own history; it emphasizes that Sikh religion is not a syncretism of two prior religions but a response to a new revelation to Nanak. Sikhism begins, according to more recent scholarship, with God's revelation to Guru Nanak. Although preference will be given to Sikhs' understanding of themselves, both views will be presented so that readers may know the difference.

Sikhism appeared in the sixteenth century C.E. as Moguls came with Babur in 1526. Muslims made their way to India shortly after the death of their prophet, Muhammad. From time to time, Muslim rulers tried to force monotheism on the polytheistic Hindus, with tragic results for Hindus and bitter disappointments for Muslims. Although an occasional ruler of the Muslim faith, such as Akbar (1542–1605), respected Hindu beliefs and practices, Hindus were not swift to reciprocate with foreigners. The two faiths were separate, and separate they have remained.

The Punjab, the region of northwest India bounding the five or six rivers that flow together to form the Indus River, was always subject to invasions of peoples from the West. Crossing the Hindu Kush mountains of the Sulaiman range at passes such as the Khyber, foreigners poured into the rich lands among the rivers. The Aryans had entered the Dravidian culture that way. Hinduism declined as Brahmins set about preserving caste and rituals. The Hindu kings showed little inclination to unite and defeat forces coming through the western countries of Afghanistan or Baluchistan. In the Punjab, the coexistence of cities such as Lahore and Multan and vast jungles filled with a variety of game animals allowed a mixture of cultures to develop side by side.[22] From the Vedic period, Hinduism allowed for many different approaches to deity. As Pratima Bowes wrote,

> The Hindus did think of religious reality in a variety of modes and it seems that they were willing to try any concept or approach to see if it was going to get them any closer to the mystery which fascinated them. The Hindu attitude seems to be that the more the ways in which we, with our inevitable limitations, try to fathom that which is all and beyond, the better is our chance to catch a glimpse of it in its inexhaustibility.[23]

Muslim invasions began with the Gaznavis in the 980s. They came in waves of warriors who settled and married local women. By the fifteenth century, these foreigners had identified with a region that they considered home, the Sindh, presently southwest of Pakistan.[24]

Older scholarship has identified prior religious movements that may have contributed to Sikhism. Sikhs, however, reject any notion that their religion formed as an attempt to syncretize other religious traditions, such as Hindu and Muslim. For example, the story of **Kabir** (1440–1518), the Muslim who could worship with Hindus, is rejected on grounds that no evidence supports a meeting of Guru Nanak and Kabir. It is not part of the history of Sikhism any more than the **Sant** tradition of northern India that worshiped a formless God. It does seem likely that Guru Nanak came from a Hindu family devoted to the worship of the god Vishnu.

Kabir [ku-BEER]
A Muslim who believed that God can save anyone of any caste from the Law of Karma.

Sant [sant]
A Punjabi tradition based on Bhakti worship of Vishnu.

The Life of Guru Nanak

Nanak (1469–1539 C.E.) was born a Hindu in the town of Talwandi in the Lahore district of the Punjab. His father, Kalu, was an accountant, and his mother, Tripta, was a very religious woman.

As other religions, Sikhism has a pious biographical tradition of its founder. In the *Janamsakhi* is a reconstruction that scholars do not classify as reliable history. Stories, however, help us understand the spirit of many people who have embraced the faith.

Sikh tradition reports that the astrologer who visited the infant soon after birth worshiped him, saying that he would grow up to sit under the umbrella, the symbol of prophetic dignity.[25] The astrologer also regretted that he would not live to see the great accomplishment that would be brought about by Nanak—the common worship of both Hindus and Muslims.

The next incident of some importance occurred when Nanak's father invited Hardial, the family priest and a Brahmin, to initiate the boy into Hinduism. This ceremony was attempted when Nanak was nine years old and consisted of having him invested with the sacrificial thread placed on his neck. Nanak rejected the thread, or janeu, even though the priest explained that it was a part of Vedic ritual required of all Hindus. Nanak was more

Sikh Homage to Guru Nanak. In Lahore, Pakistan, these Sikhs pay homage to the founder of Sikhism.

Japji [JAP-ji]
A Sikh hymn recited in devotions every morning. A guide for Sikh conduct.

interested in pure conduct than in traditional symbols made of materials that decayed and never did anything to keep a person morally upright.

Nanak's parents arranged a marriage for him when he was twelve. Sulakhani was the bride selected from Batala, a distant town. She came to live with him when he was nineteen. Nanak's duties then were those of a herdsman. He was not involved in great responsibility looking after buffaloes, but even in that occupation he is said to have shown miraculous powers. On one occasion, the shadow in which he was sleeping during the day did not move with the passing of time, and on another occasion a large cobra protected him by shading him with its hood. Two sons were born to this marriage.

Invited by his married sister, Nanak left his home and journeyed to Sultanpur, where he entered the service of the governor, Daulat Khan. He carried out the duties appropriate to his profession, which was an accountant.[26] The governor not only praised his work but also hired friends of Nanak who came to live and worship with him. When Nanak was thirty years old, he reached his spiritual crisis. Even his pious life was too closely identified with the business of the world.

One morning, after his ritual bathing in a river, he disappeared in a forest and there had a direct vision of God. Receiving a cup of nectar, he was given a promise of God's blessing for those who took his name and remained uncontaminated by the world. Nanak responded with these words of the **Japji,** the meditation:

Proem

There is one God,
Eternal Truth is His Name;
Maker of all things,
Fearing nothing and at enmity with nothing,
Timeless is His Image;
Not begotten, being of His own Being:
By the grace of the Guru, known to men.

Jainism and Sikhism in History

◆ **799–700 (8th Century)** Parshva

◆ **599–527** Mahavira (Shvetambara dates)

◆ **563–483** The Buddha

◆ **510** Mahavira (Digambara date)

1221 Mongols invade Iran ◆

[**1440–1518 Kabir of Northwest India**] (not Sikh tradition) ◆

1469–1539 Nanak, first Sikh Guru ◆

1504–1552 Angad, second Sikh Guru ◆

1479–1574 Amar Das, third Sikh Guru ◆

1534–1581 Ram Das, fourth Sikh Guru ◆

1563–1606 Arjan, fifth Sikh Guru ◆

1595–1644 Har Gobind, sixth Sikh Guru ◆

1605–1627 Emperor Jahanger persecutes Sikhs ◆

1630–1661 Har Rai, seventh Sikh Guru ◆

1656–1664 Harkishan, eighth Sikh Guru ◆

1621–1675 Tegh Bahadur, ninth Sikh Guru ◆

1666–1708 Gobind Rai, tenth Sikh Guru ◆

1687 Bombay becomes seat of English rule in India ◆

1757–1769 Ahmad Shad Abdsali of Afghanistan repeatedly ◆
invades the Punjab in a "holy war" against Sikhs

1858 British take over government of India ◆

1920 Mohandas K. Gandhi leads Indian National Congress ◆

1939–1945 World War II ◆

1947 Partition of Pakistan and India ◆

1984 Indian Army invades Golden Temple in Amritsar ◆
Mrs. Indira Gandhi assassinated; police accuse two of her Sikh bodyguards
In India, many Hindus riot against Sikhs

BCE 2000	1500	1000	500	0	500	1000	1500	2000 CE

AS HE WAS IN THE BEGINNING: THE TRUTH,
SO THROUGHOUT THE AGES,
HE EVER HAS BEEN: THE TRUTH,
SO EVEN NOW HE IS TRUTH IMMANENT,
SO FOR EVER AND EVER HE SHALL BE TRUTH ETERNAL.[27]

Guru [GU-ru] or [GOO-ROO]
In Sikhism, one of ten early spiritual leaders or, after their times, the Adi Granth. God is the one, true Guru.

In response, God appointed Nanak his Supreme **Guru.**

Nanak withdrew from his duties and wandered in the forest. His acquaintances called a Muslim *mulla* in hopes of exorcising the demon that they believed to be in Nanak. After a time, many concluded that Nanak was insane. He rejected any claims of the Khan. Moreover, he uttered the shocking and puzzling statement, "There is no Hindu and no Musalman [Muslim]." He cut all geographical ties and became a wanderer.

After his renunciation of the world, Nanak entered the most productive phase of his life. Sikh scholars believe that he had, during his three days in the forest, a genuine encounter with God and was called to evangelize India in the one True Name. He began to do this, accompanied by his constant companion, Mardana, a member of the Dums, or hereditary minstrels. The northern part of India was gradually covered as he went from town to town singing and reciting in marketplaces, street intersections, and places of Hindu or Muslim pilgrimage. Usually he made a few disciples, or Sikhs, before he had to move on, due either to hostility from local religious leaders or to his mission to reach many places. According to the *Janamsakhi,* his clothing was distinctive: he wore the lower garments of a Hindu and painted a saffron Hindu mark on his forehead, but on his torso and on his head he wore Muslim garments. He was a walking symbol of a religion that could receive both Hindus and Muslims. However, it was a symbol that could confuse and anger as well as impress and attract. He seems to have accepted caste as a civil custom and made no religious effort to combat it. His methods did, nevertheless, inevitably offend the Brahmins when he did not keep their priesthood or ceremonies or base his teachings and actions on the Vedas.[28]

In one intriguing account, Nanak and Mardana made a journey to Arabia and actually went to Mecca. According to the story, he ran afoul of Muslim customs and went to sleep with his feet directed at the sacred Ka'bah. Muslims awakened him and said that he should not point his feet toward God. He told them to try to point his feet where God is not, because God is everywhere.

Pious Sikhs tell many stories to illustrate either Nanak's clever insights or his miraculous powers. Seeing pilgrims bathing in the Ganges and throwing water into the air to bathe their ancestors thousands of miles away, Nanak threw water into the air to water his garden miles away. When the Hindus said that he was crazy, he asked how their practice was any more effective than his. When he came on a group of elephant keepers mourning the death of the emperor's elephant, which had provided them employment, the guru raised it to life. The emperor came and wanted Nanak to do the trick again for him. The elephant died, but Nanak did not revive it; he pointed out that God is the only one who gives life and death.

Nanak did believe in the Hindu ideas of karma and samsara. In a Sikh story of two shopkeepers, one chose to visit his guru and the other to visit his own mistress; the evildoer finds gold and the good man injures his foot.

Nanak explained that in a previous life the adulterer had done good deeds by giving alms to a holy man and the guru-visitor had sinned and deserved to be impaled. Karma from previous lives are worked out in the present life, and present deeds can modify the rewards and penalties for former lives. In these respects Nanak agreed with Hindus, although he did not regard the Vedas as binding on his beliefs and practices. He found the Vedas and the Quran both false. Nanak emphasized liberation through divine grace.

Old age, illness, and death caught up with the wanderers, and they settled in Kartarpur. Mardana died first, seated by a river. Nanak took the responsibility for appointing his own successor so that there should be no dissension after his death. His choice was Angad, chosen above Nanak's sons, whom he considered to be unworthy.[29] When Nanak died at the age of 70 in 1539, there was a question of what to do with the body. The story told for Kabir was repeated for Nanak—the body disappeared and flowers from Muslims and Hindus that surrounded it remained fresh. The Sikhs erected a shrine to him and the Muslims made a tomb; both memorials have been destroyed by the river.

The Teachings of Guru Nanak

The most important teaching of Nanak was on the nature of God. God is one (Ek Oankar), preceding all divisions. God is known directly by experience through encounter within the believer. God has the character of Nirguna Brahman, except that he wills to be Saguna Brahman, making himself known to individuals in a relationship of love. His unity includes the world, which manifests his glory. God is too great to be identical with the world; the world is in him, but he exceeds its greatness. God is one reality. Apart from him there is no happiness or immortality.

> He cannot be installed like an idol,
> Nor can man shape His likeness.
> He made Himself and maintains Himself
> On His heights unstained for ever;
> Honored are they in His shrine
> Who meditate upon Him.
>
> Sing though, O Nanak, the psalms
> Of God as the treasury
> Of sublime virtues.
> If a man sings of God and hears of Him,
> And lets love of God sprout within him,
> All sorrow shall depart;
> In the soul, God will create abiding peace.
>
> The Word of the Guru is the inner Music;
> The Word of the Guru is the highest Scripture;
> The Word of the Guru is all pervading.
> The Guru is Siva, the Guru is Vishnu and Brahma,
> The Guru is the Mother Goddess.
>
> If I knew Him as He truly is
> What words could utter my knowledge?
> Enlightened by God, the Guru has unravelled one mystery
> "There is but one Truth, one Bestower of life;
> May I never forget Him."[30]

Humans are essentially souls in bodies. The soul has functions of Atman, mind, and emotions. The soul is made for communion with God; when it is separated from God it suffers. For a soul that loves God, being in the body does not cause suffering. However, for a soul that is self-centered, loving only the self, the body and the world can intensify suffering. The world can be a place of beauty for the soul who loves God properly; it is a place of suffering for a soul that loves self more than God. Through their love, humans are either drawn to God or separated from him. By their wills, humans control their lives.

How do humans know God? The Word of God is his sound vibrating in creation. The Word is both the means of knowing God and a path leading to him. Focusing on the Word, which is present in everything, leads to personal experience of God. God's name is his personal being and the means by which he is known. God is the essential Guru, the one who brings truth that leads to salvation. The earthly guru, Nanak, imparts what he has experienced directly from the original Guru. God also expresses his truth through the divine law, Hakum. It regulates all order of the universe, and those who learn it are led to God. God seeks to make himself known by all these ways, so humans learn of him. He does not abandon humans to their own efforts; God's grace comes to assist them on their path.

The focus of Sikhism is God, who exists in the human heart. Humans turn inward to their own heart to find God. By meditating on God's name and listening to the original Guru, humans begin to know God and love him. The grace of God then helps humans love God more and the world less. Sin is weakened and goodness is strengthened. Sikhism is so internal that Nanak cared little for the external ceremonies of the Hindus or Muslims. He replaced their rituals with hymns—singing praises to God.

Guru Nanak thought that there are five stages in a person's progress toward union with God. The first stage is a piety that honors God and his law and seeks to help others. The second stage increases knowledge. Sikhs learn that the world is beyond comprehension and that other people have experienced God in their hearts. This knowledge leads Sikhs beyond self-centeredness to a greater love of God. The third stage is effort or humility, which focuses on knowing God within the heart. Sikhs listen to God's Word in creation. The fourth stage is being filled with the power of the spirit. Sikhs realize God in their heart, experience peace and fulfillment, and know that beyond death they can join God. The fifth stage is an experience of Truth. Sikhs enter into union with God.

> It is not through thought that He is to be comprehended
> Though we strive to grasp Him a hundred thousand times;
> Nor by outer silence and long deep meditation
> Can the inner silence be reached;
> Nor is man's hunger for God appeasable
> By piling up world-loads of wealth.
> All the innumerable devices of worldly wisdom
> Leave a man disappointed; not one avails.
>
> How then shall we know the Truth?
> How shall we rend the vails of untruth away?
> Abide thou by His Will, and make thine own,
> His will, O Nanak, that is written in thy heart.[31]

The Nine Gurus After Nanak

Angad (1504–1552 C.E.), the second guru, had many of the spiritual qualities of devotion found in Nanak. Formerly a devout Hindu, on hearing

Sikh Woman Meditating. Near Espanola, New Mexico, U.S.A. a Sikh woman meditates in privacy.

CHAPTER FIVE

Guru Nanak he abandoned his idols and his business to devote his life to the Sikh community. He composed hymns and served as a teacher and an example to the faithful. Guru Nanak had seen in him the highest virtue required of a leader of the order, namely, self-sacrifice on behalf of the faithful. Rejecting his sons as successors, he appointed Angad.

Amar Das (1479–1574), the third guru, departed only slightly in spiritual devotion by introducing the practice of making pilgrimages to the sacred well at Goindwal on the Beas River. He was so famous as a teacher that the emperor Akbar visited him and assigned income from some villages to his daughter, Bibi Bhani. Amar Das's choice for successor was his son-in-law, Ram Das, the husband of Bibi Bhani.

Ram Das (1534–1581), the fourth guru, although dedicated to spiritual life, found that wealth came under his control. Some of the material worth was through Akbar's gifts; other income came from Ram Das's inviting tradesmen to set up business in the center where he built a tank of water in a place of worship. Enjoying the favor of Emperor Akbar, Ram Das had a sacred pool and village developed at Amritsar. The villages that Ram Das's wife had received from the emperor she deeded to him. Using his wealth for the Sikh order, Ram Das sent missionaries to other parts of India, and the distinguished Bhai Gurdas went to Agra. In all, it was a rather happy, progressive time for the guru, his family, and the Sikh order.

Arjan (1563–1606), the fifth guru, was the youngest son of Ram Das. After becoming leader in 1581, he developed the large tank, or pool, at Amritsar and began construction of the Golden Temple in that area. Unlike Hindu temples, which opened only on one side toward the rising sun, it had openings on all sides, in part to indicate that Sikhism was open to all castes of Hindus. He also gathered the hymns of the first four gurus and compiled them into the Adi Granth to be enshrined in the Golden Temple. He was firm in his devotion to one God and refused to adopt either Hindu or Muslim religious practices. A new ruler, Jahangir (1605–1627), found him objectionable. He was progressively tortured with various methods of burning his skin and muscles. However, when he was so covered with broken blisters and deeply burned areas that he could scarcely walk, he was allowed to go bathe in the nearby Ravi River, where he died.

The lesson was remembered by his son, Har Gobind (1595–1644), who armed himself with two swords, one representing spiritual power and the other temporal.[32] He held court seated on a throne. Sikhism would from his time on take a military stance to defend itself against the armed forces of either Muslims or Hindus. He gave up the customary necklace of the Sikh gurus as too pacifistic and adopted instead a sword belt. In his turban he wore a royal aigrette. Moreover, he formed a Sikh bodyguard for himself, built a stronghold, and recruited an army of able soldiers, which he clothed, fed, and armed, using proceeds from the temple.

The first battles between the Sikhs and the Moguls under Jahangir were not very successful. The Moguls recognized the threat of the Sikhs to the balance of power in northwest India, especially when they were consolidated and armed as almost a separate nation. So Jahangir captured and imprisoned Har Gobind, but he lived to fight other battles. He seemed to live a charmed life, for even in infancy he had escaped an attempt by Prithia, who aspired to be guru, to have his nurse poison him during breastfeeding.

The next two gurus of the Sikhs, Har Rai (1630–1661) and Harkishan (1656–1664), were rather successful in avoiding abuse from the Moguls while they built an armed community; the ninth guru, however, Tegh Bahadur (1621–1675), was imprisoned by Emperor Aurangzeb. The emperor gave orders that Tegh Bahadur was to be tortured until he accepted Islam. Refusing to give up Sikhism, Tegh Bahadur was beheaded by a sword.

The fate of his predecessor had profound impact on the tenth and last guru, Gobind Rai (1666–1708), better known by the name he acquired in office, Gobind Singh (Lion). He startled the pacifists with this hymn: "Hail, hail to the Creator of the world, the Savior of creation, my Cherisher, hail to Thee, O Sword!"[33] He did seem to deify steel swords and to assert his own divinely inspired authority. The ensuing ritual he innovated was baptism with the sword, an initiation into the Khalsa.

In 1699, Guru Gobind emphasized the fierce struggle Sikhs had to face with the world and the need for sacrifice. He invited anyone willing to sacrifice his life to the sword to come to his tent. After the first man entered the tent, Gobind emerged with a bloody sword. Another man entered and again Gobind came out with a bloody sword. Five men entered the tent, all expecting death. Then Guru Gobind brought them out alive, for the blood of an animal had been on his sword.

Five men were baptized first as **Singhs.** Gobind Singh baptized the five men ready to die for their faith in water mixed with spices in an iron pot and stirred by a double-edge sword. The water was sprinkled five times into their eyes and on their hair. The five men in turn baptized Gobind. They repeated the war cry of the Sikhs, "The Khalsa are of God, and the victory is to God." They were members of the Khalsa, Singhs, or Lions. They wore the five *K*s, which are

1. Kesh—long, uncut hair on head and chin
2. Kangha—comb
3. Kach—short drawers
4. Kara—steel bracelet
5. Kirpan—sword

Further disciplines of the Singhs included a requirement to worship only the one God, to revere the Granth, to bathe in cold water at dawn and pray, and to renounce alcohol and tobacco. In turn, they were allowed to eat the meat of animals slain by a single stroke of the sword. They were not to molest any Muslim women. It was a rigorous order of fighting men, but it welcomed all castes who could accept the discipline.

Gobind Singh declared himself the last of the Sikh gurus—after his death Sikhs were to honor only the Adi Granth as their guru. He also abolished any caste distinctions among Sikhs and directed them to avoid other Hindu practices of worship. A Muslim assassin stabbed him, and in spite of efforts by the emperor's surgeons to save him, he died several days later. Since the death of the tenth guru, Sikh worship has centered around the **Adi Granth,** the perpetual guru. It is ritually honored and read on a daily schedule.

Under the British, the Sikhs attained international fame as warriors and policemen. However, they have not fared particularly well since colonial rule ended. In the partition of Pakistan and India, they lost to Pakistan several holy places, the most important being the birthplace of Nanak. Sikhs are now primarily in India. They regard themselves as so different from Hindus and Muslims that many of them still press for a separate Sikh state.[34] The issue has not been completely resolved to their satisfaction at

Singh [sing]
A "lion" of the Sikhs. The term was initiated by Guru Gobind, the tenth guru, in 1699 C.E.

Adi Granth [AH-di-grunth]
The scriptures and perpetual guru of the Sikhs. Hymns by the Sikh gurus are recorded in the Adi Granth.

CHAPTER FIVE

Recitation of the Guru Granth Sahib. The text is ritually honored and read on a daily schedule.

this time, although the Indian government has made some concessions that tend to recognize the import of Sikh claims.

Sikh customs today are largely community reinforced in Punjab, but there are many Sikhs residing in other countries. Anyone can become a Sikh by believing in one God, the teachings of the ten Gurus, and the Adi Granth. Beyond that, Sikhs are to live a life of prayer and meditation, recite or read hymns each day, and generally support the community of the faithful. Their guide to this life is the *Rahat Maryada,* the Sikh Way of Life, approved by Sikh authorities in Amritsar in 1931.

CONSIDER THIS: THE APPEARANCE OF MONOTHEISM

The appearance of monotheism among polytheists was not without precedent. It is remarkable, however, that despite persecution, Nanak's successors preserved monotheism's purity and intensity in their own hymns, teachings, and lives. Perhaps the presence of small numbers of Jews, Christians, and Zoroastrians helped create a climate of support for monotheism. Islam, with greater numbers of followers, is a more conspicuous contributer to monotheism in India. The Sikh gurus, however, rejected the Quran as they rejected the Vedas.

Although Buddhists had not observed caste distinctions in India, Sikhs, who came many centuries after the caste system was so well established, had to be courageous to ignore it. Their eating together without observing caste distinctions must have been as offensive as eating meat in the

☞ A POINT OF VIEW

presence of religions that practiced vegetarianism. Was the way prepared by Muslims of India?

Among the ingrained practices of religions of India we have remaining those based on karma and reincarnation. These vital concepts were emphasized in Sikhism. The newest religion had some continuity with its predecessors. Can some of the success of Sikhism in India be attributed to preparations of Hindus, Buddhists, Jains, and Muslims? Or is Sikhism best explained by the power of God's revelation to Sikh gurus? Among Sikh scholars today, one answer is preferable.

WORLDVIEW

The Absolute

The Sikh understanding of God is based on direct experience of a personal God in the human heart. God is as close to a person as his or her heart, but God is a unity unlimited in time and space. The Hindu deities and the Muslim deity are human experiences of God, but they are more limited than God himself. God cares for humans and approaches them through his Word. Through his Word he is known, and the way to him is made clear.

God is both Impersonal (Nirguna) and Personal (Saguna). Impersonal and formless, God is beyond reach. Relating to his creation, he is personal. Although no finite form, even the guru, can be worshiped as God, all forms come from the formless source. Formless, God became NAM, the divine name, and created nature.

The World and Humans

The world and humans are not essentially opposed to God. God is immanent in the world, but he also transcends it. God is available in the human heart, but he is also beyond complete human comprehension. According to the indication of a person's soul, the world can be experienced as good or evil. A person who is making progress toward unity with God finds the world a beautiful place that witnesses to God's glory. A person who is absorbed in self-love finds the world an enemy. The human soul has potential to live in peace and harmony with God; unfortunately, most humans are more in love with physical possessions than God.

The Problem and the Solution for Humans

Karma affects the lives of all people, but God can forgive the worst of sinners. One who turns toward God can be forgiven. The unaided individual cannot succeed. Seeing or hearing the guru is insufficient. One must become committed to God in one's heart. Salvation is available only through baptism.

The human soul can choose to love itself rather than God. Absorbed in self-centeredness, the soul is alienated from God. This alienation is exhibited in sin, immorality, and refusal to help others. By seeking to turn outward to God and to others, the soul overcomes the self-centeredness that alienates it from God. In turning to God and seeking to experience him in the heart, humans find that God graciously makes himself known as guru. He sheds an illumination that leads humans, in stages, along a path of salvation. The ultimate goal for a Sikh is to experience union with Truth, or

God. Peace, joy, and unity endure for eternity for humans who have found union with God.

Among the hymns of Guru Gobind Singh is this exhortation:

> O man, practise asceticism after the following manner:
> Think no more of thy house in the city
> Than as if it were a forest abode;
> And remain always a hermit in thine heart!
> Instead of matted hair, cultivate continence;
> Wash thyself daily in unity of will with God;
> Let thy daily religious duties be thy long growing nails!
> Let divine wisdom be thy Guru and enlighten your soul
> As with ashes, smear thy body with the love of God!
> Eat little, sleep little; be compassionate and forgiving;
> Be calm and contented;
> Then will you pass beyond the Three States.
> Hold not close in your heart
> Lust, anger, greed, obstinate selfhood or love of worldly things.
> Then shalt thou behold that which is real
> And attain to the One Lord.[35]

Community and Ethics

Sikhs have an affirmative attitude toward creation. The world is good and to be enjoyed. Although they can eat meat as well as vegetables, they do not use tobacco, a substance that many other peoples also regard as harmful to the body. The human body is good and to be strengthened. Aggressive behavior is not prohibited by any doctrine of ahimsa—force can be used where needed in warfare and in civil life. Besides guarding the *gurdwaras*, the *nihangs* attend fairs and stage mock battles, skills of horsemanship, and other martial arts. Belief in God and in the teachings of the gurus and the Adi Granth can give strength for victory over enemies. Sikh attitudes toward the world are more likely to conquer it than to befriend it.

Sikhs admit people of various castes and economic circumstances, for these distinctions are made by humans, not God. The first Sikhs baptized into the Khalsa represented different castes. In the Khalsa, members acknowledge ethical and religious duties for all humans.

Women in the Sikh religion have experienced both high and low status, depending on customs in India. Because women are not considered unclean or impediments to salvation, association with them or marriage to them does not make a man lower or higher. The householder is superior to the ascetic. Women, who give birth to men, including kings, cannot be considered obstructions to salvation. Early Sikhs avoided older Hindu practices of committing infanticide, burning widows on their husband's funeral pyre, and making women wear veils. Widows were allowed to remarry. Women's relationship to sons and husbands influences their status in the community.

Rituals and Symbols

The Golden Temple at Amritsar houses the object of veneration of all Sikhs, the Adi Granth, the scriptures. Worshipers approach the golden-domed building by crossing a bridge over a pool (tank) of water. The building, open on all sides, welcomes all people. Before entering the shrine, worshipers are expected to remove their shoes, wash their feet, and cover their heads. Inside, people assemble to listen to the reading of scriptures, the combined insights of the ten gurus, beginning with Nanak.

Sikhs learned from Guru Nanak that salvation, overcoming separation from God, is achieved through meditation, charity, and hard work. A spiritual union takes place; it is not dependent on external rituals. Nanak rejected both Islam and Hinduism for emphasis on rituals. The Sikhs who attend their places of worship and listen to the Adi Granth, however, have established patterns of correct behavior.

Worship at the **gurdwaras,** symbolical home of the guru, the Adi Granth, is recommended often. These centers of worship are marked by the yellow flag of Sikhism regardless of the style of architecture. The center of worship inside the building is the Adi Granth, placed on a dais in the center of a room on cushions and usually under a canopy. The faithful remove their shoes on entering the building, as is the custom in the East. Out of respect, men and women cover their heads in the presence of the Adi Granth and do not turn their backs on it. Worship in a congregation can be at any time, and the hymns of the gurus are important in worship. As from their earliest days, Sikhs enjoy singing with accompaniment by musical instruments.

Eating is a symbolic act emphasized in the activities in the gurdwara. Sikhs can bring sweets into the regular service and give them to one of the **bhais,** or brothers, who places them in the common collection. The worshiper is then given other sweets from the collection. Eating together from a common source removes any caste distinctions among worshipers. At the end of the service, sweets made from wheat flour, ghee, water, and brown sugar that were cooked beforehand are distributed. The mixture is kept near the Adi Granth during the service. At the conclusion of the service, it is stirred with a *kirpan* (sword) and served to worshipers, symbolizing the sustenance drawn from the guru.[36] A free kitchen prepares and serves meals outside the area of the Adi Granth to all who come. Bhais, wearing white, attend the temple. As the bhais represent the spiritual side of Sikhism, the **nihangs** represent the military side. Murray J. Leaf writes,

> As one important practical application of religious ideas, the relation of *nihang* to *bhai* and of the weapons to the book in the gurdwara has a symbolic parallel in the current practice of seeing the Sikh community as a single, "national," political entity.[37]

In addition to routine worship, there are special occasions when religion is an essential part of the drama of life. Rites of passage include the celebration of births as joyous occasions. Funerals, held the day after death, end usually in cremation of the body. The birthdays of Guru Nanak and Guru Gobind are days of rejoicing, and a memorial day is set aside to mark the martyrdom of Guru Arjan. On the days of remembering the gurus, the Adi Granth may be read through in its entirety.

Life After Death

Although Nanak believed in reincarnation, he also believed that a person can, in this lifetime, find a way of release. The body is not needed for personal identity after death; cremation in the Hindu fashion is commonly practiced. Sikhism seeks a mystical union of the soul with God; that is the only reward worth seeking. Being separated from God is as severe a punishment as can be endured.

---

gurdwara [GUR-dwah-ra]
A place of Sikh worship, fellowship, and hospitality. It is a temple, the dwelling of the guru.

bhais [BA-iz]
The brothers of a Sikh gurdwara who assist in worship. It is also the title used for a Sikh priest.

nihangs [NI-hangs]
The Sikhs with military skills who are always ready to fight for the community.

There can be no peace for man
So long as he thinketh that of himself he can do anything;
He shall wander from womb to womb in the cycle of births;
So long as he deemeth one man a friend and another an enemy,
So long shall he have no rest for his mind;
So long as man is in love with the illusory goods of the world
So long shall Dharmraj, the Justiciar King, continue to punish him.
It is by God's Grace that many can be freed from bondage;
And by the Guru's grace, saith Nanak, pride and self-will are removed![38]

Sikhism and Other Religions

Sikh temples are open to all who observe respect for the holy place and the Adi Granth. The gurdwaras in rural areas provide food and lodging for travelers. Sikhism welcomes men and women from any economic or social class—caste does not matter. Gurus shared beliefs of Hinduism and Islam. But Nanak's position that both the Vedas and the Quran are wrong angered Hindus and Muslims. That fact makes it difficult to maintain that he sought a harmony of Hinduism and Islam. His mysticism shares experiences of Muslim sufis and Hindu yogins, but the hymns of the Adi Granth reveal that the experiences of God reported by the Sikh guru were original.

Sikhs have had their bloody conflicts with both Hindus and Muslims. Their military stature developed as a defense for survival rather than a desire to overcome other religions. There is nothing in Sikhism that makes it use force to convert peoples of other religions. Sikh religion makes it possible for people of different religions to worship the same God. Although it has elements from both Islam and Hinduism, Sikhism should be considered a separate religion. R. W. Neufeldt has emphasized that Sikh exclusiveness does not denigrate other traditions:

> Sikh exclusiveness is related specifically to the question of deliverance or liberation. With respect to this question, a true Sikh is asked to say no to other scriptures, practices, and beliefs, and is to seek deliverance through belief in the *Adi Granth*, the teachings of the Gurus and the cultivation of meditation on the words of the *Adi Granth* and the Gurus.[39]

The most recent issue for Sikhism has been a fight by some of its members for an independent Sikh state in the Punjab. Sikh rebels seized the Golden Temple in Amritsar; Indira Gandhi, the prime minister of India, ordered troops to remove them from the temple. Several hundred Sikhs were killed, including Sant Jarnail Singh Bhindranwale, a leader of the rebels.[40] Sikhs protested her violation of their sacred temple. Sikhs in Gandhi's bodyguard later turned their weapons on her in a successful assassination. In revenge, Hindus went on a rampage, murdering Sikhs. Sikh rebels again seized the Golden Temple. Again Indian troops removed them. Many Sikhs demand that the government grant them a separate state. The Indian government has refused, although it has made some concessions of independence. Tensions between Hindus and Sikhs have remained high. Commenting on the changing role of the Sikh shrines, Richard G. Fox wrote in a postscript to his preface:

> One has to note how much Sikh shrines have changed in character over the last half-century. Until late in the Raj, they were staunchly loyalist institutions, but at present some of them have become centers of dissent from government.[41]

Aside from the political struggle, Sikhism has been threatened by secularism. Many of its adherents are not committed to practicing the daily prayers that distinguish the religion. As Sikhs emigrate from India to other countries where they are more a minority than in India, they feel pressure to give up their distinctive customs and dress. On the other hand, those who remain faithful and energetic in practice and witness may attract converts in new places. Sikhism may have a new growth in many countries outside India.

Considering Jainism and Sikhism along with Hinduism and Buddhism helps us realize what a fertile country India has been for religious life. A rich ground of religions germinates a wide variety of beliefs and practices. There are crude practices that may appear ridiculous; but there are also beliefs that are among the most sublime in the world. India has made provisions for the most worldly people, but in its religious life it has outlined systems that can absorb the most dedicated intellectuals.

Jainism offers several beliefs that impress peoples from other religions. The most important idea is the sacredness of life, whether or not it is human. Causing pain or death snares humans in a net of suffering. Another idea is that the physical world is always subordinate to the soul and should not be embraced. A third idea is that humans can have only relative knowledge—there is no absolute proof that God exists. Humans best find release for the soul in following the example of a person who has already demonstrated the way. Those who are wise accept full responsibility for their actions and destiny.

Sikhism contributes to discussions of religion the idea that there is only one ultimate deity, which is worshiped by different names. Sikhism demonstrates that ideas from different faiths can be borrowed and combined to yield a rewarding faith. It also demonstrates that bridging a gap between major religions, even those within the same country, is not easily accomplished. A religious syncretism can result in an additional faith that divides human loyalties.

We have concluded our discussion of religions that began in India. Hinduism, Buddhism, Jainism, and Sikhism are pearls on a single strand; they are concerned with the soul, karma, redeath, and rebirth. Of the four, only Buddhism has denied a permanent soul. It has retained the idea of karma and influence of each life on subsequent lives. All believe that suffering in the world can be overcome by renouncing attachment to changing phenomena that have the maya of permanence.

The next family of religions, the Chinese and Japanese, have seen the human problem in different terms. Their goal is not escape but harmony.

✐ VOCABULARY

Adi Granth [AH-di-grunth]
Agamas [AH-ga-mas]
ahimsa [u-HIM-su]
ajiva [AH-JEE-va]
bhais [BA-iz]
Digambaras [di-GAHM-ba-ras]
gurdwara [GUR-dwah-ra]
Guru [GU-ru] or [GOO-ROO]

ishatpragbhara
   [ee-shut-PRAHG-bu-ru]
Japji [JAP-ji]
Jina [JI-na]
jiva [JEE-va]
Kabir [ku-BEER]
loka [LOW-ka]
nihangs [NI-hangs]

sallekhana [sal-lek-HAN-na]
Sant [sant]
Shvetambaras [SHVAY-TAHM-ba-ras]
Singh [sing]
Sthanakvasis
   [STAHN-AK-va-sees]
Tirthankara [ter-TAN-ka-ra]
triloka [tri-LOW-ka]

QUESTIONS FOR REVIEW

1. Why have some religious writers thought that Mahavira and the Buddha were about the same in their religions? What responses would Jains make to establish that Jainism is a much older religion than Buddhism?

2. Why would Hindus disagree with the statement that Jains are only a subcaste of Hindus?

3. Why is ahimsa so important for Jains? Can Hindus or Sikhs support Jain views on ahimsa? Can ahimsa be a practical guide in our time?

4. What apparent contradictions do people find in the Jain understanding of the Absolute? How are these apparent contradictions related to conceptions of the world and the universe?

5. Explain how traditional views of Sikhism's development differ from contemporary Sikh views of their history.

6. List some of the turning points in Sikhism's development of a militant stance in India.

7. On what points do Sikhs and Hindus agree? Where do they differ?

8. Explain the similarities and differences between the concepts of Tirthankara and Guru.

9. How do Jains and Sikhs differ on their views of the Absolute?

10. Given that both Jains and Sikhs believe in reincarnation, how do they regard caste?

QUESTIONS FOR DISCUSSION

1. What Jain doctrines are most attractive to outsiders? Which of their teachings are most difficult to accept?

2. What Sikh doctrines are most attractive to outsiders? Which of their teachings are most difficult to accept?

3. What problems seem most common for peoples of minority religions in India? How do members of minority religions deal with these difficulties?

4. What have been the advantages and disadvantages of religious tolerance among peoples of India?

5. What are the advantages and disadvantages of forming separate states for peoples of different religions?

NOTES

1. Padmanabh S. Jaini, *The Jaina Path of Purification* (Berkeley: University of California Press, 1979), pp. 6, 7.

2. Wm. Theodore de Bary, ed., *Sources of Indian Tradition* (New York: Columbia University Press, 1958), pp. 45–46. Copyright © Columbia University Press, New York. Reprinted with permission of the publisher.

3. Jaini, p. 37. For further comparisons of the groups, see S. Gopalan, *Outlines of Jainism* (New York: Halsted Press, 1973).

4. W. H. Moreland and A. C. Chatterjee, *A Short History of India* (New York: David McKay, 1957), p. 40.

5. Hermann Jacobi, trans., "Jaina Sutras," in *Sacred Books of the East*, vol. 22, ed. Max Muller (Delhi: Motilal Banarsidass, 1968), pp. 12–13.

6. Quoted in de Bary, pp. 79–80.

7. John M. Koller, *The Indian Way* (New York: Macmillan, 1982), p. 123.

8. Paul Dundas, *The Jains* (London: Routledge, 1992), pp. 77–83.

9. Hermann Jacobi, trans., *Jaina Sutrās*, Part I (Delhi: Motilal Banarsidass, 1964), *Âkârâṅga Sûtra*, Bk. 1, lect. 1, lesson: verse 2:3. (First published Oxford University Press, 1884.)

10. Quoted in de Bary, pp. 56–58.

11. Jaini, p. 133.

12. Jacobi, p. 4.

13. Ibid., p. 5.

14. Quoted in de Bary, pp. 61–62.

15. Colette Caillat, "Ahimsa," in *The Encyclopedia of Religion*, vol. 1, ed. Mircea Eliade (New York: Macmillan, 1987), pp. 152–153.

16. Ibid., p. 153.

17. Mark Juergensmeyer, "Nonviolence," in *The Encyclopedia of Religion*, vol. 10, ed. Mircea Eliade (New York: Macmillan, 1987), pp. 463–468.

18. Jacobi, pp. 4–5.

19. Ibid., Bk. 1, lect. 5, lesson: verse 4:46–47.

20. Moreland and Chatterjee, p. 109.

21. Richard F. Nyrop, *India: A Country Study* (Washington, DC: U.S. Government Printing Office, Secretary of the Army, 1985), pp. 159–160.

22. Kushwant Singh, *A History of the Sikhs*, vol. 1 (Princeton, NJ: Princeton University Press, 1963), chapter 1.

23. Pratima Bowes, *The Hindu Religious Tradition: A Philosophical Approach* (London: Routledge & Kegan Paul, 1977), pp. 35–36.

24. Singh, vol. 1, pp. 13, 14.

25. Max Arthur Macauliffe, *The Sikh Religion* (London: Oxford University Press, 1909), vol. 1, p. 1.

26. A. Barth, *The Religions of India*, trans. J. Wood (Delhi: S. Chand, 1969), p. 243.

27. *Selections from the Sacred Writings of the Sikhs*, trans. Dr. Trilochan Singh et al. (London: Allen & Unwin, 1973), p. 28.

28. Singh, vol. 1, p. 43.

29. Macauliffe, vol. 2, p. 11, reports an interesting anecdote on this subject.

30. *Selections from the Sacred Writings of the Sikhs*, pp. 31–32.

31. Ibid., p. 29.

32. Singh, vol. 1, p. 63.

33. Macauliffe, vol. 5, p. 286.

34. Singh, vol. 2, chapter 18.

35. *Selections from the Sacred Writings of the Sikhs*, vol. 271, number. 9.

36. Murray J. Leaf, *Information and Behavior in a Sikh Village* (Berkeley: University of California Press, 1972), p. 157.

37. Ibid., p. 160.

38. *Selections from the Sacred Writings of the Sikhs*, vol. 168, number 36.

39. R. W. Neufeldt, "The Sikh Response," in *Modern Indian Responses to Religious Pluralism*, ed. Harold G. Coward (Albany: State University of New York Press, 1987), pp. 269–285.

40. Nyrop, p. 170.

41. Richard G. Fox, *Lions of the Punjab: Culture in the Making* (Berkeley: University of California Press, 1985), p. xiv.

✍ READINGS

Cole, W. Owen, and Piara Singh Sambhi. *The Sikhs: Their Religious Beliefs and Practices*. London: Routledge & Kegan Paul, 1978. A discussion of Sikh beliefs by a Sikh author.

Dundas, Paul. *The Jains*. London: Routledge, 1992. A recent, up-to-date presentation of Jain views on their beliefs and practices.

Folkert, Kendall W. *Scripture and Community: Collected Essays on the Jains*, ed. John E. Cort. Atlanta, GA: Scholar's Press, 1993. Presents some of the most recent scholarship on the Jains.

Fox, Richard G. *Lions of the Punjab*. Berkeley: University of California Press, 1985. A more recent account of Sikh struggle for a distinct faith.

Jaini, Jagmanderal. *Outlines of Jainism*. Cambridge, England: Cambridge University Press, 1916. An older, but still valuable, interpretation of Jainism.

Jaini, Padmanabh S. *The Jaina Path of Purification*. Berkeley: University of California Press, 1979. A more recent account of Jainism.

Singh, Khushwant. *A History of the Sikhs*. 2 vols. Princeton, NJ: Princeton University Press, 1966. A more complete account of Sikh history and doctrine.

READINGS FOR RESEARCH AND REPORTS

Archer, John Clark. *The Sikhs*. Princeton, NJ: Princeton University Press, 1946.

Bowes, Pratima. *The Hindu Religious Tradition: A Philosophical Approach*. London: Routledge & Kegan Paul, 1977.

Caillat, Colette. "Ahimsa." In *The Encyclopedia of Religion*, vol. 1, ed. Mircea Eliade. New York: Macmillan, 1987 pp. 152–153.

Coward, Harold G., ed. *Modern Indian Responses to Religious Pluralism*. Albany: State University of New York Press, 1987.

de Bary, Wm. Theodore, ed. *Sources of Indian Tradition*. New York: Columbia University Press, 1958.

Ferguson, John. *War and Peace in the World's Religions*. London: Sheldon Press, 1977.

Frost, S. E., ed. *The Sacred Writings of the World's Great Religions*. New York: McGraw-Hill, 1972.

Hawley, John Stratton, and Gurinder Singh Mann, eds. *Studying the Sikhs: Issues for North America*. Albany: State University of New York Press, 1993.

Jaina Sutras, trans. Hermann Jacobi. Part 1, vol. 22. Part 2, vol. 45. In *Sacred Books of the East*, ed. Max Muller. Delhi: Motilal Banarsidass, 1968.

Jaini, Padmanabh S. *Gender and Salvation*. Berkeley: University of California Press, 1991.

Juergensmeyer, Mark. "Nonviolence." In *The Encyclopedia of Religion*, vol. 10, ed. Mircea Eliade. New York: Macmillan, 1987, pp. 463–468.

Koller, John M. *The Indian Way*. New York: Macmillan, 1982.

Leaf, Murray J. *Information and Behavior in a Sikh Village*. Berkeley: University of California Press, 1972.

Macauliffe, M. A. *The Sikh Religion: Its Gurus, Sacred Writings and Anthems*. London: Oxford University Press, 1909.

Madan, T. N. *Religion in India*. Delhi: Oxford University Press, 1991.

McLeod, W. H. *Guru Nanak and the Sikh Religion*. Oxford: Clarendon Press, 1968.

Moreland, W. H., and A. C. Chatterjee. *A Short History of India*. New York: David McKay, 1957.

Nyrop, Richard F. *India: A Country Study*. Washington, DC: U.S. Government Printing Office, Secretary of the Army, 1985.

Pal, P. *The Peaceful Conquerors: Jain Art from India*. Los Angeles: Los Angeles County Museum of Art, 1994.

Radhakrishnan, Sarvepalli, and Charles A. Moore. *A Sourcebook in Indian Philosophy*. Princeton, NJ: Princeton University Press, 1957.

Schomer, Karine, and W. H. McLeod. *The Sants*. Berkeley: Religious Studies Series and Motilal Banarsidass, 1987.

Selections from the Sacred Writings of the Sikhs, trans. Trilochan Singh et al; rev. G. S. Fraser. London: Allen & Unwin, 1960.

Singh, Harbans. *The Heritage of the Sikhs*. New York: Asia Publishing House, 1964.

Singh, Harjinder. *Authority and Influence in Two Sikh Villages*. New Delhi: Sterling Publishers, 1976.

———. *The Life of Guru Nanak Dev*. Lahore, 1958.

PART THREE

Religions of China and Japan

Chapter 6   CHINA AND JAPAN

In the religions of China and Japan, we meet two Chinese teachers whose own distinctive views have been added to the insights of the Buddha, who lived almost at the same time. Laozi is as remote and mysterious as some of his followers who preferred solitude in the mountains over social relations in villages or cities. Confucius, ever seeking the centers of political power, impresses us as a wise man of the world. Laozi preferred nature, and Confucius preferred society. Both renewed ancient traditions of China, which, as we will see, had a different spirit from those in India.

As religions of India emphasize karma and reincarnation, so religions of China emphasize reverence for lands and ancestors. Instead of numerous deities, as Hindus honor, Chinese and Japanese religions honor millions of ancestors with vital relationships to their descendants on earth.

Peoples of India tended to find life in the world primarily suffering; peoples in China and Japan found it primarily good. As well as being a home for good spirits, nature itself is good. Rewards of living can be enjoyed here and now.

Among religions of India, harmony is to be found beyond this life, after one escapes from samsara. In religions of China and Japan, harmony with nature, families, neighbors, and ancestors can be realized in this life, on earth. India supported a relaxed, long-term view of finding oneself; China and Japan support an urgency brought on by termination of opportunities at one's death. One has only this lifetime in which to find the way, to follow it, and to take one's place in the larger scheme of things.

In India, salvation is primarily for the individual, for karma is in the sheath of the soul or in the skandhas that affect future lives. In China and Japan, salvation of persons involves families, communities, and a state or nation. The concept of an isolated, individual person is more common in the West than in China and Japan.

You may find some exceptions to these generalizations about religions in China and Japan, but you are more likely to find examples that support them. You can find similarities between religions of India and religions of China and Japan; however, if you are like most people, you will sense a shift of interpretation of human life in the world.

CHAPTER SIX

China and Japan

Torii of Shinto Shrine. This torii of
Nagasaki survived the atomic blast of 1945.

Introduction

When Buddhist missionaries from India arrived in China and Japan, people there were of course already practicing their own traditional religions. In China, concepts of heaven, ancestors, and forces of nature long preceded the individual religions of Daoism and Confucianism. In Japan, villagers already worshiped kamis and paid homage to the goddess of the sun. When Buddhism joined these nature religions, each tradition affected the others. Because accommodation was mutually beneficial, China retained three Asian religions, and Japan four, having added Daoism and Confucianism to Buddhism and Shinto. We have already discussed Buddhism in China and Japan; in this chapter, we focus on religions that began in those countries.

 China

THE RELIGIONS OF CHINA

China honors two "sages," or very wise ancestors, as founders of its religions. The more mysterious sage, Laozi, is reflected in the lines of the cryptic classic the *Dao De Jing (Tao Te Ching)*. He is believed to have written about the time of the Gurus of the Upanishads, perhaps preceding the enlightenment of Siddhartha Gautama. Although it is unlikely that they met each other, Confucius, the more widely known sage, is thought to have been a contemporary of the Buddha. Confucius's emphasis on good education for government eventually placed his teachings at the core of education and government in China. His successful disciples assured him a prominent role in the life of China until the beginning of the twentieth century.

Toward the end of that century, Chinese peoples again embraced many of his values. In this chapter we discuss the background of Chinese traditions that influenced both sages and their particular interpretations that established separate traditions for their students.

BACKGROUND OF THE RELIGIONS OF CHINA

The Chinese had developed religious beliefs, rites, and literature long before the births of the founders of Daoism and Confucianism. Chinese peoples believe that three dynasties preceded the birth of Confucius. The legendary Xia (Hsia) kingdom is considered to date from about 2000 B.C.E. The emperor Yu claimed to be the sky god, and his successors considered themselves "sons of heaven."[1] The Shang dynasty, 1500 to 1027 B.C.E., was located in the valley of the Yellow River. Ancestor worship was clearly important to that historical family. The famous Zhou (Chou [in the Pinyin system of romanization, spelled *Zhou*]) dynasty ruled from 1027 to 256 B.C.E. The founders of the Zhou family exerted such strong leadership that Confucius looked back to it as an example of how society should be governed. What beliefs did the Chinese peoples hold prior to the birth of Confucius?

Heaven

In Chinese thought, heaven is not radically separated from earth. Heaven is **Yang** and earth is **Yin**—both exist in balance, seeking harmony. Humans may be male, predominantly Yang, or female, predominantly Yin, but as philosopher-psychologist C. G. Jung noted, there are always some feminine characteristics in males and some masculine characteristics in females. In Chinese thought, there must be harmony in Yang and Yin, male and female, if there is to be peace in the family. Heaven, which is Yang, contains living ancestors who are both Yang and Yin. Earth, Yin, is inhabited by males (Yang) and females (Yin) who will one day become ancestors in heaven, Yang. All of these dynamic manifestations in balance, harmony, and peace flow in **Dao (Tao),** the way of the universe. Is this concept philosophy or religion? It is both. It is the canopy on which, to borrow an image from sociologist Peter Berger, the religions and philosophies of China project their interpretations of individuals and social groups.

The **Yijing (I Ching)** is so much a part of Chinese culture that in its earliest forms it predates even the earliest sages who are assigned names. Its present form may date from the third century B.C.E. It attempts to relate the day-by-day life of the individual to the ways of the universe. How does the Yijing function? Around the symbol of Yin-Yang are sixty-four (2^6) hexagrams. Each hexagram comprises six lines. The patterns include all possible mixtures of long lines and divided lines. For example, at one extreme is a hexagram of six long lines; at the other is a hexagram of six divided lines. Using either a coin or yarrow stalks, an interpreter is guided to the appropriate figure of lines. In the hands of a skillful interpreter, the Yijing can offer guidance in the choices available to an individual so that he or she can obtain the support of heaven and nature, or at least avoid offending them. Chung-ying Cheng maintains that both Daoism and Confucianism could assume in their formative stages that the Yijing was an established guide for Chinese life.

Yang [YAHNG]
In China, the male side of the Dao. It is exemplified in bright, warm, and dry conditions. Its opposite is Yin, the female side of the Dao.

Yin [YIN]
In China, the female side of the Dao. It is exemplified in dark, cool, and moist conditions. Its opposite is Yang, the male side of the Dao.

Dao (Tao) [DOW]
In China or in Daoism (Taoism), the path, course, or way of the universe. Although its influence is in nature, the eternal Dao is believed to be hidden from empirical experience.

Yijing (I Ching) [YEE-jing]
An ancient book of China that assists people in deciding how to plan their lives in accord with the forces of the universe. The *Yijing* influenced both Daoism and Confucianism.

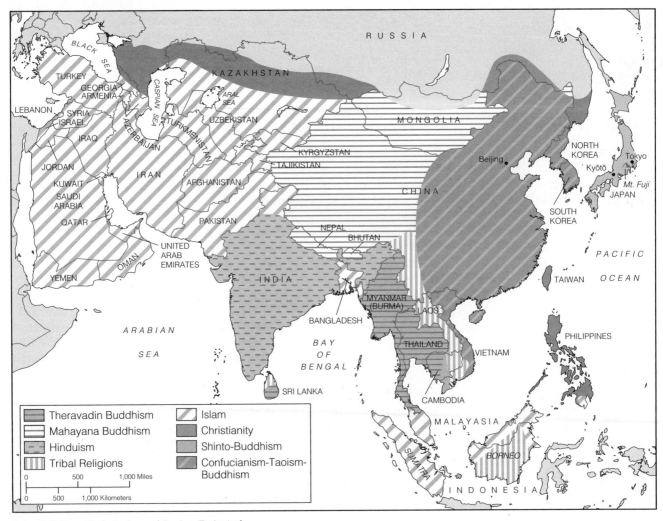

Asian Religions. Confucianism and Daoism (Taoism) of
China and Korea influenced Shinto of Japan. Buddhism
affected all these religions. Islam of Arabia touched the lives
of Jains, Zoroastrians, Sikhs, and Hindus.

Daoism

Daoism's *Dao De Jing* has stimulated a variety of responses in its readers.
Philosophers of China have emphasized its teachings about going with the
flow of nature rather than resisting it in artificial structures of culture.
Priests, responding to challenges from Buddhism, built temples for a religion based on Daoist ideals. Dietitians and pharmacists engaged in experiments of folk remedies that gave Daoism a reputation for magic. Before
the advent of mid-twentieth-century medicine, who could afford to ignore
remedies that might affect health, healing, and long life, perhaps even
immortality?

Daoism's teachers expounded their own doctrines as they criticized the
principles of Confucius and his disciples. Along with Mohists and Fajias,
Daoists became rivals to the way of the Confucians.

A viewer knows that a Daoist painting is definitely from China. In the barest number of brush strokes the viewer sees an expanse of space with trees, waterfall, and rising mist. After studying the painting for several seconds, the viewer discovers a human figure sitting on the ground, contemplating the scene. This painting depicts the Daoist philosophy in one of its most symbolic forms with its emphasis on nature and its minimization of the human's place in it.

Wang Wei, a Tang dynasty poet, wrote of painting,

> Gazing upon the clouds of autumn, my spirit takes wings and soars. Facing the breeze of spring, my thoughts flow like great, powerful currents. Even the music of metal and stone instruments and the treasure of priceless jades cannot match [the pleasure of] this. I unroll pictures and examine documents, I compare and distinguish the mountains and seas. The wind rises from the green forest, and foaming water rushes in the stream. Alas! Such paintings cannot be achieved by the physical movements of the fingers and the hand, but only by the spirit entering into them. This is the nature of painting.[2]

HISTORICAL DEVELOPMENT

The beginnings of Daoism are more obscure than its later achievements. The date of publication of the **Dao De Jing** is disputed. Legends attribute it to a wise old man who, as he left China, deposited it with a gatekeeper. Another interpretation reports that Laozi was a wise man who left the manuscript behind at his death. The accounts of earliest Daoism, then, present a puzzle.

Dao De Jing (Tao Te Ching)
[dow-du-JING]
The Way and Its Power. A book attributed to Laozi, founder of Daoism.

Historiography

From early writings of some Daoists we have accounts of an elderly sage, Laozi, being visited by an awestruck neophyte, Confucius. Their accounts of the conversations flatter Laozi's Daoist traditions at the expense of Confucius's teachings and practices. Scholars dispute the reliability of these accounts on facts of history. If they are reliable, then Laozi's life and teachings were firmly established before Confucius began his campaign for good government. Confucius, then, would be the impetuous innovator. If the Daoist accounts are not reliable, perhaps they represent only attempts of Daoists to hold their own against Confucian disciples. Without attempting a final judgment, we will present something of a consensus of scholars, acknowledging that the earliest days of Daoism are open to conjecture.

Laozi (Lao Tzu)

Its beginning as a philosophy in the sixth century B.C.E. has been attributed to the old sage **Laozi (Lao Tzu),** or Lao Tan. Speculations about his life have inspired many legends. Was he an elderly sage who left a deep impression on the young Confucius?[3] Did the two masters ever meet, or are their dialogues the dreams of devoted disciples imagining what their teachers might have said? Scholars do not agree on an answer. Some scholars retain the sixth-century B.C.E. date, and others prefer a later date, in the fourth, third, or later centuries B.C.E. Another possibility is that the *Dao De Jing (Tao Te Ching)* contains the teachings of Laozi but was compiled later by more than one person.[4] However, tradition does attribute to Laozi authorship of the classic *Dao De Jing (The Way and Its Power)*. The

Laozi (Lao Tzu) [LAHOW-dzi]
The sage of China once believed to have been the author of the *Dao De Jing (Tao Te Ching)*. He is regarded as the founder of Daoism.

Landscape with Waterfall and Two Figures. This hanging scroll in ink on paper by Zhao Jin (Chou Chin) of the Ming dynasty illustrates a common theme in Daoist art.

circumstances of the writing were that Laozi, tired of living in society, journeyed to the West on a water buffalo. Before Laozi's departure, the gatekeeper persuaded him to write down and leave behind his most important ideas. The book has been passed down for centuries in Chinese civilization, and its author, believed to have been Laozi, has been deeply revered.

The *Dao De Jing* focuses on the harmony of opposites within the peaceful flow of the Dao. Beneath phenomenal changes of the natural order, there is a relentless flow, or way, which is neither entirely visible nor open to full knowledge. Nevertheless, it influences the process of the changes that can be observed. The way of the Dao includes a peaceful harmony of opposites.

To these ideas, which were a part of Chinese beliefs before Laozi lived, the *Dao De Jing* adds the concept of the individual's relationship to society and nature. Although it may be too extreme to label Daoists anarchists, they do emphasize values of the solitary individual rather than organized society.[5] Daoist philosophy renounces many of society's expectations. In summary, the *Dao De Jing* argues that the natural course of things is the best; left undisturbed, the natural course leads to harmony and perfection. Artificial structures among persons or in societies eventually bring discord.

What can be said about the Dao? Although no one can define exactly the full dimension of the way of the universe, the Dao is the mysterious cosmic power present in all human experiences. The Dao is not only the actuality of experiences but also the potential activity of the universe unfolding itself; it is the nonbeing that gives rise to phenomenal reality. Hidden, the Dao nevertheless manifests itself to those who patiently observe and reflect. Enough can be known of the Dao that a person can choose to live in harmony with it.

> The Tao (Way) that can be told is not the unchanging Tao;
> The name that can be named is not the unchanging name.
> The Nameless is the origin of Heaven and Earth;
> The Named is the mother of all things.
> Therefore let there always be non-being so we may see their subtlety,
> and let there always be being so we may see their outcome.
> The two are the same.
> But after they are produced, they have different names.
> They both may be called deep and profound (*hsuan*).
> Deeper and more profound,
> The door of all subtleties![6]

Societies suffer when they disregard the Dao. History shows that societies often base standards on principles at odds with the Dao. Eventually, human efforts are destroyed and human purposes are thwarted, bringing misery on entire societies. Humans can gradually intuit the Dao's strength and undeterred direction. If they develop wisdom in the face of the Dao's inevitability, they learn to abandon their petty desires and designs and resign themselves to the flow of the Dao. Those who insist on their own way or who force society into their own plan may seem to succeed for a while, but inevitably the pendulum will swing the other way.

The sage, or the wise person, comes to realize that in the long run, humans cannot conquer nature. They can do much better by planning their lives so as to use the natural cosmic force and direction. The individual who harmonizes his or her purposes with the way of the Dao can reach the highest possible achievement. There is a learning process for humans that involves their realizing that life cannot always be as they would have it. For the sage, there is a certain amount of learning to accept frustrated desires and purposes, of bending to the inevitable course of events. Although Daoism is more than a philosophy, an intellectual exercise, it lacks some of the features often associated with a religion. No formal worship or prayer is necessary, for communication is limited between a human and an impersonal force (or perhaps a force that far transcends the limits of persons). Laozi sometimes refers to the Dao as the "Mother" of all living things. Daoism requires the response of a whole person. Contemplation and meditation in a quiet way of life are most helpful in intuiting the way of the Dao.

A central concept of Daoism is **wuwei.** Humans can learn to practice wuwei, a lifestyle that emphasizes quietism and avoids aggression. Sages act without acting, accomplishing without motion, influencing without seeming to exert themselves. Humans need not run about the world to know the way of the Dao. Sages do not seek to polish their personality for society in order to gain status, but seek to discover the natural, undistorted self. In all things, the sage seeks to be good, even returning good for evil. Many people in society may consider sages fools, but sages know that although water may seem the most pliable or unresisting element of the world, over time it can wear down even mountains of the most solid rock. The *Dao De Jing* explains,

> The softest things in the world overcome the hardest things in the world.
> Non-being penetrates that in which there is no space.
> Through this I know the advantage of taking no action.
> Few in the world can understand teaching without words
>   and the advantage of taking no action.[7]

A further explanation reads:

> There is nothing softer and weaker than water,
> And yet there is nothing better for attacking hard and strong things.
> For this reason there is no substitute for it.
> All the world knows that the weak overcomes the strong and the soft
>   overcomes the hard.
> But none can practice it.
> Therefore the sage says:
>   He who suffers disgrace for his country
>   Is called lord of the land.
>   He who takes upon himself the country's misfortunes
>   Becomes the king of the empire.
> Straight words seem to be their opposite.[8]

Disciples of Daoist sages argue that humans can develop mysterious powers to the extent that wild animals will not attack. On the other hand, these sages would never engage in offensive warfare; they know the wisdom of pacifism.

Daoism scorned social institutions. Education corrupts the natural goodness of humans.

> Abandon sageliness and discard wisdom;
> Then the people will benefit a hundredfold.
> Abandon humanity and discard righteousness;

wuwei (wu wei) [WOO-WAY] The Daoist principle of accomplishing tasks without assertion. Individuals in harmony with the flow of the Dao can accomplish more than individuals who assert themselves.

Zhuangzi (Chuang Tzu). This later disciple of Laozi avoided political appointments.

Then the people will return to filial piety and deep love.
Abandon skill and discard profit;
Then there will be no thieves or robbers.
However, these three things are ornament *(wen)* and not adequate.
Therefore let people hold on to these:
  Manifest plainness,
  Embrace simplicity,
  Reduce selfishness,
  Have few desires.[9]

Social conventions and governments are artificial, at odds with the natural flow of people in the universe. The ideal society is a small village where each family tends to its own affairs. People in the village know that other villages exist, for they hear roosters crowing and dogs barking there. They do not exchange visits. That government is best that governs least, so the best situation is not to have any government. If there must be government, rulers should remember that "ruling a big country is like cooking a small fish."[10] They should be careful not to overdo it.

Zhuangzi (Chuang Tzu)

Zhuangzi (Chuang Tzu, c. 369–286 B.C.E.), a champion of the **Daoists,** expanded on the teachings of the *Dao De Jing*. He, too, exalted nature above culture, the individual above society, and freedom to flow above rigid social forms. He accepted changes brought by the Dao; indeed, he may be said to have enjoyed them, seeking to ride the crests of the waves of change. Even the simple task of making a rack to hold a suspended bell can involve Daoism. By concentrating on their own nature—the nature of self—on the nature of a tree, and on the nature of heaven that brings them together in harmony, humans turn a practical task into a Daoist experience. The government can be handled in a similar way. Zhuangzi is reported to have turned down a civil service post in order to remain free from the constraints of society, even those that carried veneration.

> Once Chuang Tzu was fishing the P'u River when the King of Ch'u sent two of his ministers to announce that he wished to entrust to Chuang Tzu the care of his entire domain.
>
> Chuang Tzu held his fishing pole and, without turning his head, said: "I have heard that Ch'u possesses a sacred tortoise which has been dead for three thousand years and which the king keeps wrapped up in a box and stored in his ancestral temple. Is this tortoise better off dead and with its bones venerated, or would it be better off alive with its tail dragging in the mud?"
>
> "It would be better off alive and dragging its tail in the mud," the two ministers replied.
>
> "Then go away!" said Chuang Tzu, "and I will drag my tail in the mud!"[11]

Zhuangzi is also known for the philosophical questions he raises regarding the experience of dreaming. Beneath the apparently simple questions lie some profound questions about what is real and how to know what is real.

> Once upon a time, Chuang Chou [Chuang Tzu] dreamed that he was a butterfly, a butterfly fluttering about, enjoying itself. It did not know that it was Chuang Chou. Suddenly he awoke with a start and he was Chuang Chou again. But he did not know whether he was Chuang Chou who had dreamed that he was a butterfly, or whether he was a butterfly dreaming that he was Chuang Chou. Between

Zhuangzi (Chuang Tzu)
[JYAHNG-dzi]
A later Daoist. Zhuangzi wrote, in part, to distinguish Daoism from Confucianism.

Daoists (Taoists) [DOW-ists]
Followers of a philosophy or religion expressed in the *Dao De Jing*, attributed to Laozi, a sage of ancient China.

Chuang Chou and the butterfly there must be some distinction. This is what is called the transformation of things.[12]

Zhuangzi applied the experience of dreaming to all human experiences in living. Perhaps life is a delusion.

Those who dream of the banquet may weep the next morning, and those who dream of weeping may go out to hunt after dawn. When we dream we do not know that we are dreaming. In our dreams we may even interpret our dreams. Only after we are awake do we know we have dreamed. Finally there comes a great awakening, and then we know life is a great dream. But the stupid think they are awake all the time, and believe they know it distinctly. Are we (honorable) rulers? Are we (humble) shepherds? How vulgar! Both Confucius and you were dreaming. When I say you were dreaming, I am also dreaming. This way of talking may be called perfectly strange. If after ten thousand generations we could meet one great sage who can explain this, it would be like meeting him in as short a time as in a single morning or evening.[13]

Religious, Sectarian Daoism

Historically, Daoism developed forms that included common people as well as intellectuals. Some Daoists sought special ways to healing and health, some sought magical and political power, and others sought immortality through alchemy.

Zhang Daoling, of about the first century C.E., founded a secret society that promoted faith healing, health, and long lives. His male descendants organized many groups that exorcised illnesses. They used confession of sins to remove the cause of illnesses. Then they gave believers consecrated water and ashes of burned writings to drink. So numerous were their followers that they developed significant political power. Zhang Daoling was deified as "Celestial Master" and praised for having found the secret formula for immortality.

One promoter of magical Daoism is Ge Hong (Ko Hung), of the fourth century C.E., who spent many years as a soldier and civilian gathering diets and formulas that could either help humans fly to heaven as a genie or attain immortality. His *Baopuzi (Pao P'u-tzu)* is an example of the folk beliefs that led to experiments with drugs obtained from mountains, such as Dragon Tiger or Lofu Mountain. In developing pills of immortality, the alchemists preferred using gold. The theory was that because gold does not tarnish or decay, ingesting it can lead to immortality. Often unable to obtain gold, the alchemists used mercury to turn base metals into gold. Ingesting mercury, however, led to the deaths of many researchers. On the other hand, those who know the Dao can change the bodies of animals, ride on a phoenix or a crane, and caress crocodiles and whales.[14] Charms can prevent all sorts of evils, such as weapons and wild animals.[15] This form of Daoism still survives in Chinese cultures but is rejected by many Chinese intellectuals.

Daoism had a sect that emphasized worship in its own temples. During the Han dynasties (206 B.C.E to 220 C.E.) Laozi was elevated to the status of a god, Taishang Laojun, "Lord Lao on High." During the Song dynasty, shortly after 1000 C.E., Daoists, claiming to have received a recent revelation, identified the **Shang Di,** ruler of heaven, with Huang Di, the **Jade Emperor.** The popular revival of Daoism was also enhanced with the addition of teachings of heaven and hell. Ling Bao, leader of supernatural beings, was

Shang Di [shang-DI]
In China, the lord of heaven. Ancestors are believed to be obedient to Shang Di as living persons are to the emperor.

Jade Emperor
A mythical emperor of ancient China. In 1012 C.E., the emperor (Chen Tsung) claimed to have received revelation from Huang Di (Yu Huang), the Jade Emperor.

added to Laozi and the Jade Emperor to form the Three Purities of Daoism. Daoist priests led worship of the Eight Immortals. Folk religion elevated the god of the stove, **Zaoshen (Tsao Shen),** to a level that he received recognition of the emperor. Nevertheless, Buddhism eventually eclipsed Daoism.

A POINT OF VIEW

CONSIDER THIS: HARMONY WITH FORCES OF LIFE

In religions of China and Japan, peace and harmony are rewards for having practiced traditional faith. Daoism's tradition has emphasized harmony of organs within a person's body and harmony with forces of nature. Although Daoists have minimized structures of society and government, they have emphasized harmony with forces of life. Harmony in eating, drinking, and exercising enlists nature's support for a longer, healthier life. Old age is preferred to beauty, for those who have lived long know more about living well.

WORLDVIEW

The Absolute

The Dao is impersonal, an invisible way that the universe follows, a harmony of tensions between opposites. This powerful force is indifferent to human desires and artificial structures. It is not influenced by prayer, hymns, or rituals. Humans can only seek to discern it, for it does not reveal itself.

The **Three Purities** of sectarian Daoism, although incongruous with the *Dao De Jing,* were not foreign to Chinese tradition. Humans who died became ancestors who were worshiped as gods. If families worshiped departed grandfathers, why should the country not worship illustrious emperors and rulers of spirits? These personal deities satisfied the masses and fulfilled their need for folk heroes. The development was not too different from what happened in Mahayana Buddhism as it departed from the way of the elders.

Three Purities
In China, three deities of Daoism: Ling Bao, the Jade Emperor, and Laozi.

The World

The Daoists were enthusiastic about the universe. It is hardly proper to think of it as either good or evil. It is beyond good and evil—it just is. It provides all that humans and animals need. By living close to nature and studying its ways, humans can learn to remain healthy and wise. Trying to conquer nature or to improve on it is futile.

Humans

The best human is the natural human. Humans are essentially good and can enjoy a good life in the world. They should seek to live as long as possible, for old age is a sign of wisdom in fulfilling the proper human role. People should not be forced into education, rituals, social organizations, and etiquette. Humans are best when they remain as they were born—weak and simple.

The Problem for Humans

The problem for humans is their disharmony with the universe. The more humans depart from the simple, natural way of the universe, the more they are alienated from the Dao and from each other. Suffering comes from trying to conquer nature, altering the way of the universe, and establishing artificial human organizations. Artificial needs develop, and values foreign to natural order entice humans away from the source of their peace and harmony. Civilization is an enemy of the contented human.

The Solution for Humans

Humans solve their problem by returning to a simple life. Living in harmony with nature, either in a forest or in a small village, is the best way for a person to resolve tensions and experience peace of body and soul. A good, long life is the reward of those who learn to go with the flow of the Dao. Apart from the philosophies of Laozi and Zhuangzi, Daoist religion developed techniques of meditation.

> The breathing of the Sage, we read in many passages, must be like that of an infant. Later Taoist writers go a step further, saying that it must be like that of a child in the womb.[16]

> Embryonic respiration and *nei tan* are essentially mental operations, since it is thought processes that make the breath circulate through the body and that manipulate the internal alchemical symbols. One particular technique of concentration makes it possible to "gaze inward." While the breath circulates through the body, the eyes fix on it and follow its movement. Since the pupils of the eyes—small concretions of pure Yang—have illuminating power, they put darkness to flight and cause the triumph of the Yang, the principle of light and life.[17]

Daoists use techniques in contemplation that are similar to some of those used by Hindus. The most interesting, perhaps, is described as embryonic breathing, **taixi (t'ai-hsi),** that is, becoming like an infant who breathes through the umbilical cord in its mother's womb. Essentially, it is a technique that Daoists use to hold their breath for extended periods. Accompanying breathing is inward vision, which enables Daoists to experience light and the divinities of the human organs. Other techniques include engaging in sex without ejaculation and practicing alchemy, the marriage of elements of the universe.

taixi (T'ai-hsi) [tai-SHEE]
In Daoism, the art of embryonic breathing, a method of holding one's breath in contemplation.

In Daoist religion, contemplation of nature is a technically developed art. Daoists do more than simply sit at some vantage point and gaze at the landscape. Daoists guide the practice of **shouyi (shou-i),** which means "to preserve meditating on the One."[18] Preserving the One means to return to the origin, to unite with the Dao. Having arisen from the Dao, the One is both emptiness and nonbeing. The One is also the cosmos, mother, matrix, primordial breath, and origin of all things. The One divided into the Three, and the Three divided into the Ten Thousand Things. Thus, multiplicity is accounted for as well as the unity of all things.

shouyi (shou-i) [shoo-yi]
In Daoism, to preserve the One or to meditate on the One. It includes methods of meditation on the One.

Contemplation recognizes the relationship of the human to the cosmos. In contemplation, the One is thought of in human terms. The person who contemplates visualizes the light of the One and concentrates on the three primordial breaths, the Sanyi (San I), three ones. Although the three primordial breaths exist apart from humans, the breaths can also dwell in

Shrine for worship of ancestors, in pre-revolutionary China.

them in the Three Cinnabar Fields. Visualizing them during contemplation causes them to descend into the body of the meditator. According to the Mao Shan sect, if a person does not practice contemplation, the divinities that inhabit the bodies of individuals return to heaven. Their departure brings about illness or death. Daoists may also contemplate the Nine Palaces or the Nine Divinities from the Nine Heavens, which represent the One in totality.

The Daoist theory of contemplation of nature asserts that each organ of the human body is energized by a divinity. Those who recite sacred texts can stimulate this hierarchy of divinities. Another beneficial visualization is contemplation of heavenly bodies and planets. As meditators visualize the light of heavenly bodies, their own body increases in luminescence, becoming like the heavenly bodies.

The goal of Daoist meditation is the harmony of the human, the divine, and the cosmos. In contemplating nature, the Daoist seeks to internalize the energies of the universe to promote health and a long, rewarding life.

Community and Ethics

Nothing is so bad that action will not make it worse. Inaction is the secret of good life, not only for the Daoist but also for any neighbors. Trying to do good leads only to trouble. Live and let live is the best guide to conduct. By doing nothing, humans have a positive influence on society, according to the *Dao De Jing*.

> Here are my three treasures. Keep them and cherish them. The first is mercy, the second is frugality; the third is never to take the lead over the whole world. Being merciful, one has courage; being frugal, one has abundance; refusing to take the lead, one becomes the chief of all vessels. If one abandons mercy in favor of courage, frugality in favor of abundance, and humility in favor of prominence, he will perish.
>
> Mercy will be victorious in attack and invulnerable in defense. Heaven will come to the rescue of the merciful one and with mercy will protect him.[19]

Rituals and Symbols

Rituals are not needed, except in magical and sectarian Daoism. The alchemist's stove was once a symbol of Daoism. Charms, formulas, and drugs continue to be a part of folk Daoism. But philosophical Daoism had no rituals, for they were useless. The symbol of the Dao, the Yin and Yang in harmony, was sufficient for many Daoists. Artists' paintings of humans absorbed in nature were acceptable.

Daoist priests in Taiwan learn esoteric rituals that are carefully hidden from all except initiates. Studying with a master, disciples learn singing, dancing, ceremonial texts, and other matters of standard ritual. Students excel in priesthood when they learn cures for illness, exorcism of evil spirits, and magic. The most powerful priests learn to contact at least one of the other ancient spirits listed as deities; the more spirits contacted, the higher the rank of the priest.[20]

Confucians disagreed with some of the claims of philosophical Daoism. Granted, some individuals find the social world overpowering. Is government necessarily bad? Are social organizations disruptive of harmony in the universe? Is it necessary to abandon conventional social rituals in order to find peace? Are social contracts self-defeating? Although there are many examples that support what the Daoists say, can there also be some exceptions to their principles?

Although Daoism has been a part of the philosophies of China and, later, Japan, for many centuries, the most influential philosophy of China has been Confucianism. Wherever Chinese peoples have lived, they have been influenced by their greatest teacher, **Confucius** (**Kongfuzi**, 551–479 B.C.E.). [This text will use conventional references to Confucius and Confucianism.]

CONFUCIANISM

Despite numerous attacks over their long history, Confucian ideals have withstood the tests of time. Chinese peoples, in both the People's Republic of China and beyond the mainland, have maintained their respect for the basic values taught by Confucius. Like Daoism, Confucianism has been seen sometimes as more a philosophy than a religion. Other readers have thought it a political science or a system of education. It has been all these things and more, for the Confucian classics present a leader who was larger than life. Confucius's brilliance still inspires awe and reverence. In the minds of Chinese peoples, Confucius is at least as great as Muhammad, Jesus, Moses, and Siddhartha Gautama, some of the most influential leaders in history.

HISTORICAL DEVELOPMENT

In the long history of China, Confucianism has interacted with many different philosophies, religions, and political systems. From the days of Confucius we can look backward to the Zhou dynasty, his choice for the golden age that degenerated into his time of warring states. From him, also, we can look forward to a time of good government, the product of an educated and dedicated civil service. Princes did appear who were obedient to Heaven and worthy of imitation by their subjects. Children did grow up in homes with honor for father and mother. If on the day of his death Confucius had doubts about his success, today he could count himself as one of the most successful teachers of all time.

Historiography

Although we seem to know so much more about Confucius than Laozi, some scholars of Confucius, such as D. C. Lau, challenge our assumptions. They would classify much of our information about the biography of Confucius as legend or tradition rather than fact. The supposed conversations of Laozi and Confucius are only minor problems compared with some of the stories of Confucius's success in his various appointed positions. Did crime really disappear when he was "chief of police"? Is it only conjecture that he would have had two wives to demonstrate his skill at maintaining harmony in his own home? These stories and others like them support the status of a great man of history, but what is the strength of the evidence for them? Historians today are not so tolerant of tales and legends. If we follow our pattern of describing the lives of other religious leaders, however, we can see Confucius through the eyes of his devoted followers. To be

Confucius [kun-FYOO-shus] Kongfuzi, the Chinese founder of Confucianism. Primarily a teacher, he sought to develop good government through a responsible ruler and ethical people.

Confucius. For centuries this teacher was the moral ancestor for many Chinese peoples.

consistent, we should include some of the stories recounted by Confucians. From time to time, however, we will present the opposing views of his critics. In activities of rival philosophies, we find evidence of Confucius's effectiveness.

The Life of Confucius

Master Kong, Kongfuzi, or Confucius is definitely a historical figure, but the process of time has won him a place among legendary heroes. Dates given for his birth vary somewhat, but 551 B.C.E. seems likely to many scholars. The "official biography" set forth in the Historical Records (Shiji) by Sima Quin, about 100 C.E., supplies information on the family of Confucius. Today, critical historians doubt the reliability of the records.

The son of a tall, old soldier, Confucius was born to a young woman in the state of Lu, or Shantung province. He was only a child when his father died, leaving the young widow of a genteel but poor family to raise her son in the tradition of gentlemen. Confucius became a lover of literature, art, music, archery, traditional ceremonies, and life at the courts of nobles. Carl Crow wrote, "At the age of seventeen he secured his first employment, the task of keeping the granary accounts of the Chi family, one of the three great baronial houses in the ducal state of Lu."[21] Although the job was of limited status, the experience it provided was sufficient to open his eyes wide to the injustices of systems that burdened peasants with heavy taxes in order to support leisure and luxury for the extremely small ruling class.

Confucius married and had a son to carry on the family name. He also had a daughter. After mourning the death of his mother for twenty-seven months, counted as three years in China, Confucius spent his days as a teacher for young men from some of the finest families in Lu. Teaching was always his best-received activity; nevertheless, he believed that his greatest impact on social change could be made in government posts. From age fifty to fifty-five, he served under the Duke of Lu in several posts. Tradition says that he was disappointed with the Duke's neglect of government in favor of pleasant living with women. Leaving office in Lu, Confucius traveled to various districts in search of other positions. At times he was rejected. Once he was chased, and once he was imprisoned. The powerful official Huan Tui attempted to have him assassinated. But usually the traveling scholar, who brought his students with him, was received with courtesy and even honor. Nevertheless, through pride or fear on the part of their civil servants, nobles in other provinces did not give him a position. In 484 B.C.E., Duke Ai of Lu invited him to come home and act as his advisor. He returned home, but he spent his closing years as a scholar editing the classics. In 479 B.C.E he died.

The Teachings of Confucius

Confucians think that Confucius had a fundamental belief—humans are by nature good. Observing the province known to him, he had to have a strong faith in humans to make such an assumption. He was surrounded all his life by cruel wars; unjust societies; numerous forms of humans' inhumanity to each other; discord in families; and neglect of scholarship, writing, and the fine and performing arts. What had gone wrong?

Beginning with his foundational principle of human goodness, Confucius added a second principle. Humans, who are naturally good, learn best through example. The great need in every society is a model human being—a person who will set an example for others to follow. Confucius called his model person a **junzi (chun-tzu).** Translators use words such as *gentleman* or *superior man* to convey the idea. These words may be poor choices now, for they also carry other meanings. The junzi is opposite to the narrow-minded person, the selfish, petty, or aggressive person. The two are contrasted in the following passages from the *Analects* (Lun Yu).

> The Master said, "The gentleman understands what is moral. The small man understands what is profitable."[22]
>
> 23. The Master said, "The gentleman agrees with others without being an echo. The small man echoes without being in agreement." . . .
>
> 25. The Master said, "The gentleman is easy to serve but difficult to please. He will not be pleased unless you try to please him by following the Way, but when it comes to employing the services of others, he does so within the limits of their capacity. The small man is difficult to serve but easy to please. He will be pleased even though you try to please him by not following the Way, but when it comes to employing the services of others, he demands all-round perfection."
>
> 26. The Master said, "The gentleman is at ease without being arrogant; the small man is arrogant without being at ease."[23]

Confucius tried to be the kind of model he wanted his students to become.

> The Master said, "At fifteen I set my heart on learning; at forty I came to be free from doubts; at fifty I understood the Decree of Heaven; at sixty my ear was attuned; at seventy I followed my heart's desire without overstepping the line."[24]

When Confucius became a role model as well as a reciter of wisdom, he exhibited some characteristics of a reformer inspired with a religious zeal. Confucius's goal was not only to inform but also to form and reform. He taught principles of conduct that could be measured in human social interaction. His goal was to reform corrupt societies through princes, nobles, and civil servants who based their lives on the example of the junzi.

In *Li Ji (Li Chi),* Confucians present **li** as the principle of harmony that should rule the home, the society, and the empire. Li has to do with ritual, the correct formal way to behave in religious rites or in court ceremonies. Words associated with it are *propriety*, *appropriateness*, and *conformity* (to prevailing customs). It is the opposite of confusion. Confucius recommended li for every area of life—as in the five relationships between superior and inferior persons. They are ruler–subject, husband–wife, elder brother–younger brother, elder friend–junior friend, and father–son. Although the persons are unequal, each has a formal responsibility to carry out toward the other. The husband has responsibility for li toward his wife as she has an obligation for li toward him. The family is formally structured among males. Friendships outside the family are ritually governed. Relationships between ruler and subject entail obligations on each side. The junzi always acts from the internalized principle of li and is never at a loss on how to behave in any situation. Younger people learn from their elders, and the elders learn from observing the junzi. Li applied to the naturally good human being yields **yi,** which is the personalization of li.

Yi is internalized li. When humans internalize the rites, selfishness is overcome and benevolence takes its place. The personal self becomes orderly, and humans regulate themselves appropriately in society. They act on what is appropriate to themselves and to their position in society. They attain the mean that gives harmony.

junzi (chun-tzu) [JUN-dzi]
In Confucianism, the gentleman or superior man. He was a role model for the conduct of the Chinese people.

Li Ji (Li Chi) [LEE-jee]
The Chinese classic on rites supposedly edited by Confucius. Although it is one of five Confucian classics, it is now regarded as coming from a period later than Confucius.

li [LEE]
The Confucian principle of righteousness or propriety. Li can refer to ritual and correct conduct in society.

yi [YEE]
In Confucianism, internalized li, or righteousness; li as it has become a part of an individual's conduct.

Confucius taught that li is learned in studying rites and music, which included poetry. "Music was a required study, as its performance accompanied all ceremonies, whether religious sacrifice, court assembly, or family entertainment."[25] Harmony in music reflected harmony in society and the universe.

The junzi also exhibits **ren (jen).** Essentially, ren is humaneness, the quality of being a genuine human being to other human beings. This quality of human kindness is in balance with li and yi to keep formalism from destroying the highest and best possibilities of human personalities. Ren seeks the good of others as well as the self. Compassion for others is the mark of a good person.

> Fan Ch'ih asked about benevolence. The Master said, "Love your fellow men."
>
> The Master said, "One who is not benevolent cannot remain long in straitened circumstances, nor can he remain long in easy circumstances.
>
> "The benevolent man is attracted to benevolence because he feels at home in it. The wise man is attracted to benevolence because he finds it to his advantage."[26]

Confucius is known for his emphasis on reciprocity.

> Tsu-kung asked, "Is there a single word which can be a guide to conduct throughout one's life?" The Master said, "It is perhaps the word **shu.** Do not impose on others what you yourself do not desire."[27]

In summary, there are five distinctive qualities or virtues in the junzi. First, humans exert their own uprightness regardless of outward circumstances. Second, humans are magnanimous, expressing forgiveness toward others. Humans are not to be ruled by laws but follow an internal principle. Third, humans are sincere in speech and action and are not a mouthpiece for hire; their word is their bond. Fourth, humans are earnest. They want to be rather than seem to be. Genuine good work replaces the mere appearance of it. Fifth, humans are benevolent, always generous in their relationships with people.

Confucius was clearly a teacher of political philosophy and ethics. Is it appropriate for us to think of his work as religion as well as philosophy? In his teachings, Confucius did not speculate much about heaven. In the *Analects,* Confucius says, "When you have offended against Heaven, there is nowhere you can turn to in your prayers."[28] That statement shows reverence for heaven. His actions, his love for the Chinese classics, and his participation in traditional rituals indicate a reverence for worship. Ancestor worship was a duty of every person in China—whether peasant or prince. As Confucius mourned at the grave of his mother for three years, his disciples, when he was gone, spent many months at his grave honoring him. Confucius enjoyed participating in religious ceremonies—for him they were an essential part of life, the basis for an orderly society. He insisted that they be performed correctly and in the old traditions. Confucius could assume religion in his life; to teach its importance he needed only to participate in it. His ethics were for humans engaged in practical life; his ethical principles, however, were derived from a tradition that transcended present time and the confines of earth. In his own life he knew, at age fifty, the mandate *(ming)* of heaven.[29] As a man who felt a sense of mission, Confucius thought that the mandate of heaven was especially important. He sensed that heaven had given him the mission to restore morality to China, to help everyone achieve the virtues of ren and li.

ren (jen) [RUN]
In Confucianism, the humane principle, based on fellow-feeling. It is having deep empathy or compassion for other humans.

shu [SHOO]
In Confucianism, reciprocity; individuals treating others as they would like to be treated. They do not do to others what they would not want done to themselves.

Challenges to the Teachings of Confucius

THE MOHISTS

Some philosophies challenged Confucius's point of view. The **Mohists,** followers of **Mozi (Mo Tzu),** who lived sometime between 479 and 381 B.C.E., taught that if everyone would love each other, society would be transformed.[30]

Little is known about Mozi aside from his writings. Fung Yu-Lan believes that he was born before Confucius died and that he died before Mencius was born. He was a native of either Song or Lu and was once the chief officer of Song. Perhaps he was at one time a follower of Confucianism. He had about three hundred disciples. Yi-Pao Mei summarizes his attempts to serve as an adviser to princes in this way:

> But for all his efforts he succeeded in holding a state office only once. That was in Sung and apparently for a short time; it was put to an end when the Lord listened to Tse Han and imprisoned Motse.[31]

Mozi's teachings are centered on the requirement for humans to love one another. Through love, the evils of the world could be abolished. Of universal love (*jainai*) Mozi said,

> It is the business of the benevolent man to try to promote what is beneficial to the world and to eliminate what is harmful. Now at the present time, what brings the greatest harm to the world? Great states attacking small ones, great families overthrowing small ones, the strong oppressing the weak, the many harrying the few, the cunning deceiving the stupid, the eminent lording it over the humble—these are harmful to the world. So too are rulers who are not generous, ministers who are not loyal, fathers who are without kindness, and sons who are unfilial, as well as those mean men who, with weapons, knives, poison, fire, and water, seek to injure and undo each other.
>
> When we inquire into the cause of the various harms, what do we find has produced them? Do they come about from loving others and trying to benefit them? Surely not! They come rather from hating others and trying to injure them. And when we set out to classify and describe those men who hate and injure others, shall we say that their actions are motivated by universality or partiality? Surely we must answer by partiality, and it is this partiality in their dealings with one another that gives rise to all the great harms in the world. Therefore we know that partiality is wrong.
>
> Mo-tzu said: Whoever criticizes others must have some alternative to offer them. To criticize and yet offer no alternative is like trying to stop flood with flood or put out fire with fire. It will surely have no effect. Therefore Mo-tzu said: Partiality should be replaced with universality.
>
> But how can partiality be replaced with universality? If men were to regard the states of others as they regard their own, then who would raise up his state to attack the state of another? It would be like attacking his own. If men were to regard the cities of others as they regard their own, then who would raise up his city to attack the city of another? It would be like attacking his own. If men were to regard the families of others as they regard their own, then who would raise up his family to overthrow that of another? It would be like overthrowing his own. Now when states and cities do not attack and make war on each other and families and individuals do not overthrow or injure one another, is this a harm or a benefit to the world? Surely it is a benefit.[32]

As did Confucius, Mozi looked to an ancient society for an example, but he preferred the Hsia to the Zhou dynasty. Life should be lived on a basic

Mohists [MOW-hists]
Followers of Mozi (Mo Tzu). They advocated curing the ills of society by practicing mutual love among people. Confucians objected to Mohist universal love because it did not allow for special feelings for kin.

Mozi (Mo Tzu) [MOW-dzi]
Founder of the Mohist philosophy, which advocated brotherly love. Brotherhood meant sharing equally the essentials of food, clothing, and shelter.

level of share and share alike. Mozi believed in the firm discipline of society to achieve this sharing of life's goods. Although he permitted defensive wars, he condemned warfare as state policy. He was thoroughly utilitarian; the good must be practical. What is good brings pleasure to society and what is evil brings pain.

How can people learn to love each other? Confucius did not believe people should do good to their enemies, for what would they then be able to do for their friends? Do not do unto others what you would not have done to you was principle enough in those situations. Parallels to Confucius's position on the Golden Rule can be found in the Bible. Confucius believed that in relationships relatives are superior to others and that they deserve more than others. Love did not necessarily mean share and share alike, thought Confucius.

THE FAJIA (LEGALISTS)

The **Fajia** (**Legalists** or perhaps Realists) school of philosophy argued that human nature respects only strong laws and rigorous enforcement. Formal statement of this position dates from the third century B.C.E., but some scholars think that the philosophy predated Confucius. Burton Watson thinks that the Legalist philosophy dated from the statesman Guan Zhong (Kuan Chung) (d. 645 B.C.E.).[33] A prince should rule by causing fear in his subjects. He must control laws, methods, and all powers of state. The individual exists for the state, not the state for the individual. Confucians did not agree with the Legalists' assessment of human nature. Nevertheless, prior to the Han dynasty (206 B.C.E. to 220 C.E.), princes preferred caution and usually agreed with Legalist philosophy rather than with the faith of Confucius.

Because he stuttered, **Han Feizi (Han Fe Tzu)** (d. 233 B.C.E.) preferred to write. Being from a noble family of the state of Han, he was jailed by the king of Qin. The king admired Han Feizi's work but had him imprisoned as a threat: the Qin had designs on Han territory. Unable to appeal his innocence to the Qin ruler, Han Feizi drank poison provided for him by the man who had led the Qin ruler to have him imprisoned.[34] The writings he left show how his philosophy competed with that of Confucius as he sought a position of leadership with a prince.

Han Feizi believed that humans were not to be trusted. The king had to rule by a firm system of rewards and punishment. As did the Italian political theorist Niccolo Machiavelli (1469–1527 C.E.) in *The Prince*, Han Feizi urged rulers to support fully law and order.

> The enlightened ruler in bestowing rewards is as benign as the seasonable rain; the dew of his bounty profits all men. But in doling out punishment he is as terrible as the thunder; even the holy sages cannot assuage him. The enlightened ruler is never overliberal in his rewards, never overlenient in his punishments. If his rewards are too liberal, then ministers who have won merit in the past will grow lax in their duties; and if his punishments are too lenient, then evil ministers will find it easy to do wrong. Thus if a man has truly won merit, no matter how humble and far removed he may be, he must be rewarded; and if he has truly committed error, no matter how close and dear to the ruler he may be, he must be punished. If those who are humble and far removed can be sure of reward, and those close and dear to the ruler can be sure of punishment, then the former will not stint in their efforts and the latter will not grow proud.[35]

Confucians could not agree with the Fajia understanding of humans. The difference in their advice grew out of their different estimates of human

Fajia (Fa-Chia or Legalists)
[fah-JEE-a]
In China, the Legalist school of philosophy that taught governance by reward and punishment. An example of a Fajia philosopher is Han Feizi.

Han Feizi (Han Fei Tzu)
[hahn-FAY-dzi]
A representative of the Fajia, or Legalist, school of philosophy in China. He taught that people were governed best by a ruler who harshly enforced rigid laws.

nature. The Fajia thought that by nature all men are evil; Confucians thought that by nature all men are good.

THE DAOISTS (TAOISTS)

The Daoists and Confucius disagreed about the desirability of government and social conventions. Literature describes visits between Laozi and Confucius. In their conversations, Laozi is very critical of the social conventions advocated by Confucius, and Confucius makes some rather confused responses. Many scholars think the conversations never occurred but that they do reflect the differences between the Daoists and the Confucians. The writings of Zhuangzi, also, report conversations in which Confucius is portrayed as embracing a position, such as being rid of body and mind, that is quite different from the thrust of his teachings.

Confucius and Other Thinkers

Confucius can be contrasted with Daoists, Legalists, and Mohists in his concept of the good ruler. Confucius envisioned a reciprocal, though unequal, relationship between ruler and people. The ruler, a polestar around which others circulate, must, in his moral behavior, set an example of the superior person. In all things he abides by propriety and ritual. His conduct is so correct that all people, from ministers to peasants, must follow him. He does not permit the anarchy of Daoism or the harsh law-and-order government of the Legalists. He rectifies names, keeping the position and function of persons clear; he does not follow the Mohist principle of equality. He is economical in his expenditures, and he employs people in proper tasks according to the seasons. Above all, he loves his people, for the people's confidence in the ruler is more important to the success of the state than either food or military equipment. The evidence of a happy state, which begins in a good ruler–subject relationship, is that people within the state are happy, and those outside are eager to enter it.[36]

When Confucius speaks of the mean, **zhongyong (chung yung)**, attained by the junzi, does he intend the same thing that Aristotle (384–322 B.C.E.) referred to as the mean? There are some similarities. Both Confucius and the Daoists assumed the reality of the Dao. They differed only on how best to relate to it. For Confucius it is found in self and society; for Daoists it is found in self and nature. It is possible that the mean referred to by Confucius is the standard of the Dao. Aristotle thought that the mean is a choice lying between two extremes, which are vices. The prudent man, through reason, chooses a middle course, a mean, between extremes of too much and too little.

During his lifetime, it was difficult for Confucius to keep his faith in his life and teaching—he had not been appointed to many of the administrative positions that he sought. Would history judge him to have been a complete failure?

Confucianism After Confucius

It is beyond question that the academic work of Confucius was useful. He was a one-man faculty. He collected and revised Chinese classics, composed and performed music, and competed in archery tournaments. In his leisure he liked to hunt or fish with a pole and line. His rewards in life were

zhongyong (chung yung)
[JONG-YONG]
In Confucianism, the doctrine of the constant mean, the path between extremes of conduct. Confucius taught that a superior man avoids excesses in his conduct.

good friends and good conversations. The long list of accomplishments of generations of students demonstrates that his faith in them was justified. Generations later, **Mengzi (Mencius,** about 371–289 B.C.E.) added his own examples based on the teachings of Confucius and gave yet another source for seeing wisdom unfold from Master Kong. Tradition has attributed to Confucius the revision of five Chinese classics: the *Shujing*, or *Book of History*; the *Shijing*, or *Book of Poetry*; the *Liji*, or *Book of Rites*; the *Yijing*, or *Book of Changes*; and the *Ch'un Ch'iu*, or *Annals of Spring and Autumn*. The details of Confucius's teaching as they are remembered by his disciples are presented in the Confucian "Four Books." The *Analects (Lun Yu)*; the *Great Learning, Daxue (Ta Hsueh)*; the *Doctrine of the Mean, Zhongyong (Chung Yung)*; and the *Book of Mencius, Mengzi (Meng-tze)*.

Mengzi (Mencius)

Mengzi surpassed Confucius in emphasizing the internal goodness of the individual. A pupil of Confucius's grandson, according to the legend, Mengzi was more concerned for the individual than for the state. Humans must have security of employment in order to live a moral, productive life and make a contribution to society. They must first be a member of a family, for the family rests on the individual and the state and the empire rests on families. Government has a duty to treat its subjects well; if not, heaven gives a mandate for subjects to remove and replace the ruler. The ruler who abides by the will of heaven governs by virtue.

> Mencius said, "When the Way prevails in the Empire men of small virtue serve men of great virtue, men of small ability serve men of great ability. But when the Way is in disuse, the small serve the big, the weak serve the strong. Both are due to Heaven. Those who are obedient to Heaven are preserved; those who go against Heaven are annihilated."[37]

As A. C. Graham has put it, for Mengzi moral inclinations belong to nature in the same way as the physical growth of the body. They germinate spontaneously and can be fed or starved; they cannot be forced.[38]

Mengzi stated it this way:

> As far as what is genuinely in him is concerned, a man is capable of becoming good. . . . That is what I mean by good. As for his becoming bad, that is not the fault of his native endowment. The heart of compassion is possessed by all men alike; likewise the heart of shame, the heart of respect, and the heart of right and wrong. The heart of compassion pertains to benevolence, the heart of shame to dutifulness, the heart of respect to the observance of the rites, and the heart of right and wrong to wisdom. Benevolence, dutifulness, observance of the rites, and wisdom are not welded on to me from outside; they are in me originally. Only this has never dawned on me. That is why it is said, 'Seek and you will find it; let go and you will lose it.' There are cases where one man is twice, five times or countless times better than another man, but this is only because there are people who fail to make the best of their native endowment.[39]

Xunzi (Hsun Tsu)

Xunzi (Hsun Tsu, 298–230 B.C.E.) differed with Mengzi on the nature of human beings. Xunzi could not agree that all men are by nature good. Burton Watson writes,

> As a philosophical system, Hsun Tzu's thought rests upon the harsh initial thesis that man's nature is basically evil . . . it flatly contradicts the view of Mencius, who

---

Mengzi (Mencius) [MENG-dzi]
A later disciple of Confucius who emphasized an inborn goodness of humans. He differed from Xunzi (Hsun Tzu), who argued that men are born evil.

Xunzi (Hsun Tsu) [SHUN-dzi]
A Confucian who argued that humans are evil by nature and must be taught good rather than evil. He differed from Mengzi (Mencius), who believed that humans are born good.

CHAPTER SIX

taught that man is naturally inclined to goodness, and in later centuries, when Mencius' view came to be regarded as the orthodox one, it led to an unhappy clouding of Hsun Tzu's entire system of thought.[40]

This conclusion is supported by the words of Xunzi:

> Man's nature is evil; goodness is the result of conscious activity. The nature of man is such that he is born with a fondness for profit. If he indulges his fondness, it will lead him into wrangling and strife, and all sense of courtesy and humility will disappear. He is born with flings of envy and hate, and if he indulges these, they will lead him into violence and crime, and all sense of loyalty and good faith will disappear. Man is born with the desires of the eyes and ears, with a fondness for beautiful sights and sounds. If he indulges these, they will lead him into license and wantonness, and all ritual principles and correct forms will be lost. Hence, any man who follows his nature and indulges his emotions will inevitably become involved in wrangling and strife, will violate the forms and rules of society, and will end as a criminal. Therefore, man must first be transformed by the instructions of a teacher and guided by ritual principles, and only then will be able to observe the dictates of courtesy and humility, obey the forms and rules of society, and achieve order. It is obvious from this, then, that man's nature is evil, and that his goodness is the result of conscious activity.[41]

Xunzi taught that all humans are born equal in every respect. Only through training can a person become good. Society has a responsibility for education so that everyone will be trained in desirable morality. A person must be taught to cultivate the proper conduct and aspire to be wise. He did not believe in gods or spirits; heaven is indifferent to the needs of humans. He was, perhaps, too much of a naturalistic philosopher to win the love and devotion of the masses—his work is not considered one of the Confucian classics.

Han Support for Confucianism

The reverence that Confucius's students expressed for him both in his life and in his death continued to increase in succeeding generations. Early in the Han dynasty (206 B.C.E. to 220 C.E.), an emperor offered animal sacrifices at the grave of Confucius. Images, and more often, memorial tablets were placed in his honor. Through the centuries, schoolchildren recited his teachings. Until the twentieth century, civil servants in China had to pass a test on his teachings. The revered teacher in heaven became a revered ancestor, and temples were built so that everyone in China could worship him. The teacher who had once seemed such a failure in influencing the politics of a single province later influenced whole dynasties of emperors of China.

Neo-Confucianism

Neo-Confucianism was a revival of declining Confucianism, which began with Han Yu (768–824 C.E.). He opposed the Buddhist influence on a Tang emperor. Mahayana Buddhism and Daoism had so embraced folk religion that Confucians had only weak public support. Only when the Sung (Song) dynasty was evidently impotent in military resistance did Confucians begin to recover. In reaction to the Yuan (Mongols) and other foreigners, the Chinese peoples returned to their cultural roots.

An outstanding leader of the revival was **Zhuxi (Chu Hsi**, 1130–1200 C.E.). He was a scholar whose personal life epitomized the ideal of

Zhuxi (Chu Hsi) [JYOO-SHEE] The leader of the Neo-Confucian revival in the twelfth century.

Confucius. He examined the writings of Xunzi and concluded that they did not belong among the orthodox Confucian classics. More important, he concluded from the classics that the ancients advocated an objective study of nature and the universe. Everything comes into being by natural force, Qi, and natural order, li. Li in cosmic proportions can be called the great ultimate, **Taiji (Tai Chi).** This force stimulates natural matter to exercise the opposites of Yang and Yin and produce the elements of earth, fire, water, wood, and metal. There is only one Great Ultimate, which is also reason, but in all things the One is present. The same principle works in man, making him good.

In the Great Ultimate, Zhuxi found an impersonal absolute of the universe. It was more knowable than the hidden Dao of the Daoists. It was more positive than the Void of the Buddhists. Li can be seen at work in all things, and the Great Ultimate never ceases to stimulate matter to create.

> 115. *Question:* The Great Ultimate is not a thing existing in a chaotic state before the formation of heaven and earth, but a general name for the principles of heaven and earth and the myriad things. Is that correct?
>
> *Answer:* The Great Ultimate is merely the principle of heaven and earth and the myriad things. With respect to heaven and earth, there is the Great Ultimate in them. With respect to the myriad things, there is the Great Ultimate in each and every one of them. Before heaven and earth existed, there was assuredly this principle. It is the principle that "through movement generates the yang." It is also this principle that "through tranquility generates the yin."[42]

Zhuxi performed the function for Confucianism that Thomas Aquinas (1225–1274 C.E.) performed for Christianity. He interpreted prior centuries of doctrine for all succeeding generations.

Traditional Confucianism had emphasized individual virtue and opposed rule by laws. Zongzi (Huang Tsung-hsi, 1610–1695) argued that people's welfare could be guaranteed only by legitimate laws and institutions.[43] When good laws and institutions prevail, individual efforts and personal examples can be effective. However, the individual is of inherent worth and not to be subordinated to the state. Because his ideas could not be implemented under the Ming dynasty, they lay dormant until the nineteenth century. Neo-Confucianism was capable of conceiving a society in which rights of men would be protected by laws.

Confucianism and Daoism in Korea and Japan

Although Korean relationships with China in the Three Kingdoms period (220–265 C.E.) were predominantly conflicts, there were diplomatic and trade exchanges. During the Tang period of China (618–907 C.E.), there was extensive cultural interchange with the Koreans going to China to study Buddhism or Confucianism.[44] The Korean scholars brought home a knowledge of those two religions as they were taught and practiced under the Tang.

In the thirteenth century, during the Yuan dynasty, Mongol rulers subdued Korea. During the military rule, a new bureaucratic class appeared. The *sadaebu* were educated, learned men who were both literati and administrators of the state. They were advocates of Neo-Confucianism. Under the reign of King Ch'ungnyol, in the late thirteenth century, Confucian studies were supported to help rebuild the National Academy and the National Shrine of Confucius. Through their ties with the Yuan of China, the Korean Neo-Confucians strengthened their hold on Korea. Eventually they

Taiji (Tai Chi) [tai-shee]
The Great Ultimate in Zhuxi's (Chu Hsi's) Neo-Confucian philosophy. It is the rational law, or li, that works within everything.

attacked any corrupt practices of Buddhist monks and monasteries. Buddhism was denounced as harmful to the state, and Buddhist funeral and memorial rites were discontinued. Neo-Confucianism became the religion of the educated elite who administered the governments of Korea. Because the Neo-Confucians helped write the earliest histories of Korea, they gave their own interpretations to the earliest practices of Korean religion, some quite critical.

Daoism arrived in Korea through the informal exchanges of ideas. Its contemplation of nature attracted some Korean adherents. However, Daoism did not become the philosophy or religion of the established governments. It was overshadowed first by Buddhism and then by Confucianism. Nevertheless, Daoist ideas were absorbed by religious subgroups and artists, poets, and mystics.[45]

As Chinese ideas moved through Korea to establish Buddhism in Japan, they similarly moved to establish Confucianism and Daoism. Although the institutions of Confucianism and Daoism did not become as strong as those of Buddhism, Confucian and Daoist values mingled with those of Buddhism and Shinto.

The Height and Downfall of Confucianism

The traditional institution of Confucianism reached its height in 1906 when the Manchu rulers issued an edict to place sacrifices to Confucius on a level equal to those of heaven.[46] The edict was both an attempt to extend the highest honor to Confucius and to deify him. The Manchus fell and so did Confucianism as an institution. A republic was declared under **Sun Yat-sen** (1866–1925), and attempts to have Confucianism recognized as a state religion failed, due, in part, to objections from Confucians. Under **Chiang K'ai Shek,** leader of the Nationalist party Quomindang (Kuomin-tang), a New Life movement was launched in 1935 that emphasized Confucian virtues. When the Nationalists left the mainland of China for Taiwan (Formosa) in 1949, the government of **Mao Zedong (Mao Tse-tung,** 1893–1976) further weakened Confucian practices.

Confucianism Under Mao Zedong (Mao Tse-tung)

The most severe criticism of Confucianism has come in the twentieth century from the Chinese leaders of the People's Republic of China. Under Chairman Mao Zedong (Mao Tse-tung), Confucian ways were denounced as reactionary. Maoists thought Confucius looked backward to decaying feudalism instead of forward to a democracy or a republic. Among the criticisms found in the Maoist writers are that Confucius did not teach the masses of people; his education was theoretical rather than practical; he used education for political struggle; he educated only the talented; and he made students show respect for their teachers.[47] For a period of time, Red Guards, who publicly humiliated and condemned teachers, smashed many forms of surviving Confucianism and ridiculed Confucius's teachings and those of his followers. Given enough time, such persistent attacks could have eliminated most Confucian practices.

Confucius's influence, which had existed for centuries, was not to disappear so easily or quickly. It soon became evident to China's new leaders that families are basic units of Chinese society and that they are stronger when Confucian virtues are practiced. Mao Zedong died, and his wife was

Sun Yat-sen
The first leader of the republic in China after the fall of the Manchus. He reasserted Confucian virtues.

Chiang K'ai Shek [CHUNG-kai-SHEK]
The leader of Nationalist China who established a government in Taiwan. He was driven from mainland China by Mao Zedong.

Mao Zedong (Mao Tse-tung)
[MAOW-tse-DONG]
The Marxist leader of China who overthrew the Nationalist government of Chiang K'ai Shek in 1949. He established the People's Republic of China.

soon rejected. A new regime, although not abandoning its aim toward the future industrialization of China, restored Confucius to a place of honor. The power of the Confucians has been broken, but the strength of Confucius's virtues has been recognized.

How much Confucian influence remains among the Chinese people? In the mid-twentieth century, Wing-Tsit Chan found that although official, institutional Confucianism had collapsed, its fundamental doctrines endured in families.[48] In the light of Chinese family values and morals as they are practiced, it could be argued that Confucianism is still influential, even in the People's Republic of China. It is stronger in Taiwan and in Korea. Chinese people in Hong Kong are torn between secularism, Buddhism, and old family values that are essentially Confucian. Chinese scholars disagree whether Confucianism is still a moral force or only a memory incorporated in the culture of Chinese families.

At this time it seems unlikely that any government will reinstate Confucianism as a state religion or have its teachers train and examine civil servants. The values of Confucianism are still recognized by many Chinese peoples. If they decide to make an effort to give these values a greater place in the formal education of new generations, it would not be a complete surprise to those who recall the revival under Neo-Confucianism.

Chinese Folk Religion

Alongside the religion taught by scholars, priests, and official institutions of religion there exists in most cultures a religion understood and practiced by the general population. For ordinary people, the distinction between folk religion and the "official" versions of religions is often difficult to detect.

The Chinese peoples have a long tradition of appreciating myths and folktales. Creation and founding myths have been circulated along with stories about saviors, destroyers, goddesses, immortality, and the Yellow Emperor. Annie Birrell's collection of these myths in *Chinese Mythology* helps us understand much of the spirit of life in traditional Chinese communities.

Folk religion includes many practices beyond storytelling. Two examples selected from the many offered by David K. Jordan in *Gods, Ghosts, and Ancestors* show practices found not only in Taiwanese villages but also in large metropolitan areas of Chinese peoples. Methods of communication between ancestors, deities, and ordinary people are fascinating.

Satisfying the needs of departed humans is a constant concern in Chinese folk religion. Ancestors deserve attention and care, but "hungry ghosts," uncared for humans, can be a persistent problem if their needs are unmet. Chinese peoples can simply burn money as a way of sending it to the departed who need it, or they may send clothes and other material things in "care packages" assigned to the flames. Often, in conjunction with other celebrations, tables of food are prepared for hungry ghosts so that they will not consume the food prepared for ancestors or gods.

Deities can communicate with humans in various ways, one being the statistical devices known as *poe*. Crescent–moon–shaped blocks cut lengthwise, one side of each rounded and one side of each flat, form a device that a person can hold, drop, and interpret. One block landing rounded side up and one block landing rounded side down indicates a yes response to a question being decided by the *poe*. Three positive throws in a row indicate an affirmative answer. Other combinations indicate a no response or indefinite results. The seeker can keep trying until positive results are attained or quit the exercise.

In many large cities, such as Singapore or Hong Kong, Chinese individuals and families participate as enthusiastically in these folk practices as do peoples in small villages. Although these and other folk practices may not ascend to the highest levels of philosophy in the writings of the greatest Chinese sages, they do represent enduring cultural preferences among Chinese communities.

CONSIDER THIS: HARMONY WITH SOCIETY

Confucians differed with Daoists by emphasizing harmony within society. Without denigrating harmony with nature or Heaven, Confucius emphasized harmony within family and state. Confucian harmony was based on the assumption that humans are essentially good. It was structured with virtues of filial piety, humane considerations, reciprocity, and propriety. Role models honored for following established traditions could educate generations of Chinese peoples to live virtuous lives. Education in Confucian virtues instilled tradition that produced an enduring tradition of harmony. To this day, many Chinese peoples still seek it.

WORLDVIEW

The Absolute

Confucius participated in sacrifices to heaven, the home of ancestors who functioned as divine beings. That was the tradition in China that Confucius supported. Some scholars think that Confucius, following the Zhou beliefs of about 1000 B.C.E., conceived of heaven as a singular, personal deity; other scholars disagree. The sacrifices offered at the grave of Confucius during the Han dynasty could be construed as treating Confucius as a god. Perhaps it is more accurate, however, to say that he was honored as everybody's moral ancestor. He was revered as an educator.

Confucius said of heaven,

> The Master said, "There is no one who understands me." Tzu-king said, "How is it that there is no one who understands you?" The Master said, "I do not complain against Heaven, nor do I blame Man. In my studies, I start from below and get through to what is up above. If I am understood at all, it is, perhaps, by Heaven." (14/25)[49]

Neo-Confucianists were more likely to think of the Great Ultimate as impersonal, the source of li in nature and humans. Reverence for Confucius was expressed in imitating his example and honoring his teachings by practicing them in society.

Tian (T'ien), or heaven, often functioned as a moral absolute. Kings who prospered considered that they ruled by the mandate of heaven, **tianming (t'ien-ming).**[50] Humans believed that when they followed the mandate of heaven they prospered; when they disobeyed they suffered. Confucianism supported the concept that was among the beliefs of the Zhou dynasty and continued under the Han dynasty. From the early days after Confucius, there was disagreement among his followers whether heaven was

tianming (t'ien-ming) [TYIAN-MING] In Confucianism, the mandate of heaven. Zhou and Han emperors claimed to rule successfully because they followed the mandate of heaven.

impersonal—following its own course regardless of human desires—or of the nature of persons—able to respond to prayers and supplications.

The World

Confucians think that the natural world is a good place. When humans work with nature in accordance with the principles of heaven, the earth brings forth most things humans need. Humans need only to know and do the will of heaven. The Neo-Confucians were concerned with studying the natural world to find li in it. The search for order in nature was not properly science, but it was a concept that could be used when the scientific revolution extended to China.

Confucians supported developing technologies to make human life productive and enjoyable. Although their first concerns were ethical, Confucians encouraged the state to support good agriculture, transportation for commerce, and studies of the stars and planets. They favored using the earth for the benefit of humans.

Temple of Heaven, Beijing. As late as the Ming period, thirteenth century, the emperor was thought to stand between heaven and earth.

Humans

The controversy between Mengzi and Xunzi over the nature of humans was important, if sometimes exaggerated. Perhaps Xunzi did not think of humans as being born evil so much as he thought that they were born neutral, capable of becoming good or bad. But he agreed with Confucius and Mengzi that humans required education. More than his successors, Confucius thought that humans must have role models. They seek role models without being told. Confucius used that search to help humans develop their greatest moral potentials.

> The Master said, "I have no hopes of meeting a sage. I would be content if I met someone who is a gentleman."
>
> The Master said, "I have no hopes of meeting a good man. I would be content if I met someone who has constancy. It is hard for a man to have constancy who claims to have when he is wanting, to be full when he is empty and to be comfortable when he is in straitened circumstances.[51]

The Problem for Humans

The problem for humans is disharmony. Disharmony in Confucianism arises when humans think of their own advantage at the expense of others. Those who are small, mean, and petty think only of themselves. They forget their responsibilities to members of their family, their friends, and their ruler. They forget that they are both student and teacher of morals. To live without consideration of others is not only bad for the individual; it is also harmful to society—it sets a bad example.

The Solution for Humans

The solution for humans is harmony. They begin by not doing to others what they do not want done to themselves. Stated positively, reciprocity means taking your own feelings as a guide in how to treat others. Learning the lessons of propriety and setting good examples take most of a lifetime. Learning to fulfill obligations to parents, siblings, friends, and ruler requires constant vigilance. Little is said about the grace of heaven, although common belief holds that ancestors can help the living. Society supports humans in their quest for harmony, but they have to do most of the work themselves.

The individual subject should obey the good ruler. A good ruler embodies the Confucian virtues and loves his people. Because he has the mandate of heaven, the good ruler brings a good life to his subjects.

Confucius thought that harmony requires good government. A. C. Graham states, "An extremely remarkable feature of Confucius' thought is his conviction that all government can be reduced to ceremony."

> If you guide them by government, hold them even by punishment, the people will elude you and have no shame. If you guide them by Potency, hold them even by ceremony, the people will both have shame and draw near you. (2/3)[52]

Community and Ethics

Reciprocity is a good word for Confucian ethics. People should avoid doing to others what they would not want done to them. They should do those things that they would like done to themselves. People live their lives fulfilling their duty to superiors. Confucianism assumes an authoritarian father and an authoritarian ruler. It also assumes the authority of older persons. However, age does not free people from all responsibilities; they have to be kind to those who show deference, and they are always to be aware that they teach by their conduct. The emperor himself is not free from responsibility to heaven and his people.

> The Master said, "The rule of virtue can be compared to the Pole Star which commands the homage of the multitude of stars without leaving its place." (2/1)

> Someone said to Confucius, "Why do you not take part in government?"
> The Master said, "*The Book of History* says, 'Oh! Simply by being a good son and friendly to his brothers a man can exert an influence upon government.' In so doing a man is, in fact, taking part in government. How can there be any question of his having actively to 'take part in government'?" (2/21)[53]

Theresa Kelleher describes reciprocity in relationships of cosmic order and society. The harmonious interaction of the life-giving cosmos should influence society.[54] Humans have received life from their parents, who received it from the cosmos. Children owe their parents marriage and children. Marriage and childbirth are rituals of reverence and gratitude, part of ancestor worship. The monastic ideals of Theravadin Buddhism could not easily adapt to the Confucian society.

Men were seen in the context of family and state; women belonged in the context of family. As in Hinduism, a woman was always subject to a male: her father, her husband, or her son. A wife could not divorce her husband; if he died, she could not remarry, for she had ancestral obligations to the family into which she had married.

Rituals and Symbols

The Chinese calendar was full of festivals, both summer and winter. Season changes were marked in state ceremonies and in homes. There were activities associated with farming that had to be coordinated with the changes in the world. Some celebrations were religious; others were primarily social. The New Year celebrations, which lasted for many days, were very popular with ordinary people. Derk Bodde has written of the Chinese love of New Year festivals:

> The Han Chinese had no fewer than four major days of annual recurrence, plus a fifth of lesser importance, each of which in its own way could be regarded as inaugurating a new yearly cycle and therefore as constituting a New Year's Day. These beginnings, like their counterparts in other civilizations, expressed in varying degrees certain basic human concerns. They were times of religious activity—manifested by the Han Chinese primarily through sacrifices to the ancestors and the immediate household gods. They were also times of feasting, merriment, and relaxation, marking a break in the usual round of toil. And finally, they were times of *renewal*, when the old and bad was cast off and replaced by the new and good, and when omens were carefully studied to determine the good or bad fortune of the coming year. This last factor means that to some extent, at least, they were times of uncertainty and anxiety as well as of enjoyment.[55]

Confucius liked rituals and symbols; he supported those already observed in his society. He was the first full-time teacher in China for students who were not aristocrats, so it is not surprising that he became a symbol of the ideal Chinese gentleman, the junzi. He was also looked on as the ideal ancestor, a moral father of his country. It seems only a natural development that the rituals that were applied to other ancestors should be applied to him. He was a sage, a symbol of one who is more than human, a rare person who stands head and shoulders above centuries of people in his country. The first Han emperor honored Confucius at his grave; other emperors and governments gave him distinctive titles and ceremonies of recognition. Reflecting the Confucian doctrine of universal harmony, rites to honor Confucius include hymns of praise consisting of eight lines of four words each and orchestras of eight kinds of instruments.[56] For more than two thousand years, Confucius was a symbol that molded Chinese culture.

Life After Death

Confucius participated in rituals that honored ancestors, particularly parents. He observed mourning for his mother the prescribed time and lamented not having been old enough to mourn properly for his father. His emphasis was on duties of the living rather than speculation about the life of the dead.

> Chi-lu asked how the spirits of the dead and the gods should be served. The Master said, "You are not able even to serve man. How can you serve the spirits?"
> "May I ask about death?"
> "You do not understand even life. How can you understand death?" (11/12)[57]

Having discussed the religions of China, we will turn to Japan to see how Shinto developed as the distinctive religion of the Japanese people.

JAPAN

INTRODUCTION

We have no exact measurement of how long inhabitants of the islands of Japan worshiped *kami no michi,* the way of the gods. In the sixth century C.E., when Buddhism came from Korea to Japan, farmers and fishers already had a religion that honored spirits of sacred persons, places, or heaven and earth. Places were marked as sacred by a rope, a gateway (**torii**), or a small structure. To the **kami** of these places, people brought gifts of fruit, vegetables, or wine. Peoples of an area honored both a place and their ancestors who had inhabited it. Stories of local kami and cosmic kami mingled; the Japanese royal family traced their descent from a kami. The islands of the Japanese peoples were a special creation of kami. These vital traditions survived in oral forms until, inspired by Buddhist writings from Korea, leaders in Japan had their beliefs and practices described in writing. **Shinto** took its place among the world's religions that are based on written records.

torii [TOH-RE-EE]
In Shinto, a formal gate to a shrine. It marks the entrance to sacred space.

kami [KAH-mee]
Natural and supernatural persons and powers worshiped in Shinto. Kami are present everywhere, in nature and in people.

Shinto [SHIN-TOOH]
The Japanese religion of kami no michi, the way of the gods. Japanese people participate in Shinto, a combination of religion and patriotism.

HISTORICAL DEVELOPMENT

As with many other religions, Shinto's history stretches from prehistory until the twenty-first century. During that long period there have been many different ways of selecting and grouping aspects of Shinto's beliefs and practices. The upheavals of the nineteenth and twentieth centuries were as great as any that preceded them.

Historiography

Three periods of time brought changes in perspectives on the history of Shinto. The first change occurred when Shinto and Buddhism encountered and adjusted to each other. Buddhists found advantage in interpreting Shinto as supplementary to Buddhist doctrines of China and Korea. The second change came in the nineteenth century when, in response to Western challenges, the Meiji reinterpreted Shinto, purifying it of many Buddhist influences. The third major change occurred in the mid-twentieth century, after Emperor Hirohito denied his divinity. Historians within Shinto revised their views to reflect both ancient traditions and present political reality. Their changes have preserved the traditions of Shinto and ensured its vital role in contemporary culture of Japan.

Prehistoric Japan

From prehistoric times, Japanese peoples worshiped kami, powers in natural phenomena. Plants and stars, rain and wind, stream and sea, animals and mountains, forests and crops were all manifestations of powers that exceeded those of humans. Dead leaders who dominated and defended villages and districts also manifested these powers. The kami were manifestations of absolute power in the phenomenal world. Kami could become humans; humans could become kami. Worship was a formal communication between these distinct but interacting realms. Shamanism played an important role in these early communities, often with a woman serving as a shaman (in Japanese, a *miko*). A shaman is a person with priestly and healing powers. A book by Carmen Blacker, *The Catalpa Bow*, describes the practices that have lingered into recent times.[58]

Izanagi Creating the Japanese Islands.
The Japanese artist Kobayashi Eitaku (nineteenth century) painted a hanging silk scroll of Izanagi and Izanami.

Visitors from Korea

At the beginning of the Common Era, Japan was sparsely settled in numerous villages. There were regional rulers, but no one controlled the largest island. Although there was no national identity, the peoples were somewhat isolated from China and Korea. Later in the Common Era, however, visitors from Korea called on local rulers. Some of their receptions were friendly, and through them Buddhism came to Japan. Koreans also brought writing, books, paintings, and other art forms. Many Japanese leaders and their powerful allies were favorably impressed. The new, foreign culture that influenced Japanese in high places challenged the traditions of the native farmers and villagers. Adherents of the way of the gods, the kami no michi, responded by gathering the stories of Shinto.

Myths of Japan

Competition from Chinese writings in the eighth century C.E. stimulated the Japanese to record their own religious dramas. The islands of Japan have a special place in the written works of the *Kojiki* (712) and the *Nihongi* (720). The islands were generated from interaction of the male principle, **Izanagi** (He Who Invites), and the female principle, **Izanami** (She Who Invites), who descended from heaven on a bridge shaped like a rainbow.

> So the two Deities, standing upon the Floating Bridge of Heaven, pushed down the jewelled spear and stirred with it, whereupon, they had stirred the brine till it

Izanagi [ee-zah-NAH-gee]
In Shinto, the male-who-invites. Cocreator, with Izanami, of Japan.

Izanami [ee-zah-NAH-mee]
In Shinto, the female-who-invites. Cocreator, with Izanagi, of Japan.

went curdlecurdle, and drew [the spear] up, the brine that dripped down from the end of the spear was piled up and became an island.[59]

The couple, innocent as children, explored the differences in their bodies. Desiring offspring, they decided to attempt cohabitation. Unfortunately the woman spoke first, and their two offspring displeased them. Something was wrong! They had to ascend to the Sky-Kami for counseling.

> Then the Heavenly Gods divined this by the greater divination. Upon which they instructed them, saying:—"It was by reason of the woman's having spoken first; ye had best return thither again." Thereupon having divined a time, they went down. The two Deities accordingly went again round the pillar, the male Deity from the left, and the female Deity from the right. When they met, the male Deity spoke first and said, "How pretty! a lovely maiden!" The female Deity next answered and said:—"How pretty! a lovely youth!" Thereafter they dwelt together in the same palace and had children.[60]

After producing the islands, the couple produced many kami. The birth of the fire god killed Izanami, and she went to the land of the dead, Yomi. Seeking her in the corrupt land of the dead, Izanagi polluted himself. Ceremonial cleansing was required for him, and out of his act of cleansing, other deities were created who came to have a superior place of importance in Shinto. They were **Amaterasu,** the sun goddess, who was the highest; **Susanoo,** god of storms; and **Tsukiyomi,** the moon god.

Purification rites have played an important part in Shinto, and they are traced not only to Izanagi but also to the rites of Susanoo, who was, in the eyes of his sister Amaterasu, something of a delinquent. One story tells of her hiding in a cave, withholding her light from the world because she was unhappy with her brother's mischief. Several symbols of Shinto are attached to Susanoo's efforts to lure his sister from the cave. With the invention of music, he aroused her curiosity, and with the brilliance of jewels and a mirror, which became other sacred objects in Shinto, he persuaded her to come out of the cave and shed her light over the world again.

> Hereupon the Heaven-Shining-Great-August-Deity was amazed, and, slightly opening the door of the Heavenly Rock-Dwelling, spoke thus from the inside: "Methought that owing to my retirement the Plain of Heaven would be dark, and likewise the Central Land of Reed-Plains would all be dark: how then is it that the Heavenly-Alarming-Female makes merry, and that likewise the eight hundred myriad Deities all laugh?" Then the Heavenly-Alarming-Female spoke saying: "We rejoice and are glad because there is a Deity more illustrious than Thine Augustness." While she was thus speaking, His Augustness Heavenly-Beckoning-Ancestor-Lord and His Augustness Grand-Jewel pushed forward the mirror and respectfully showed it to the Heaven-Shining-Great-August-Deity, whereupon the Heaven-Shining-Great-August-Deity, more and more astonished, gradually came forth from the door and gazed upon it, whereupon the Heavenly-Hand-Strength-Male-Deity, who was standing hidden, took her august hand and drew her out, and then His Augustness Grand-Jewel drew the bottom-tied rope along at her august back, and spoke, saying: "Thou Heaven-Shining-Great-August-Deity had come forth, both the Plain of High Heaven and the Central-Land-of-Reed-Plains of course again became light."[61]

The struggle between Susanoo and Amaterasu continued with their descendants. Okunushi, of Susanoo, and Ninigi, grandson of Amaterasu, had a struggle for power, but Ninigi won, and through his great-grandson, **Jimmu,** began to dominate human affairs in Japan. The first human emperor, Jimmu, began his rule in 660 B.C.E. With the establishment of the Japanese state, the Japanese royal family, believed to be related to Jimmu,

Amaterasu [AH-MAH-te-RAH-su]
In Shinto, the goddess of the sun, created by purification of Izanagi. She is sister to Susanoo, the god of storms.

Susanoo [su-SAH-NOOH]
In Shinto, the storm god, who was brother of Amaterasu, the sun goddess.

Tsukiyomi [tsoo-ki-yoh-mi]
In Shinto, the moon god. He is related to Amaterasu and Susanoo.

Jimmu [jee-moo]
In Shinto, the first human emperor, a descendant of the gods. As part of the Shinto religion, the emperor of Japan has been revered.

took a divine aura. The shrine sacred to Amaterasu at Ise displays a mirror, beads, and a sword that belonged to Jimmu. Because he was a human with kami nature, he was able to communicate with the sun goddess. Humans and kami are involved together in the ebb and flow of natural phenomena and human dramas of life. "In the Shinto myth, all the stress is on immanence and the continuity between procreators and procreated. Everything is divine, *kami*-like. All things proceed from heavenly divine spirit."[62] Worship is not so much a human attempt to obtain a special gift or blessing as it is to share, through ritual, fellowship of life with the kami.

During the Nara (710–784 C.E.) and Heian, Kyoto, periods of the emperors' courts, Chinese influence was quite strong in literature, art, and architecture. Shinto, however, was kept as part of the ceremonies of the court, whereas Buddhism had to settle for other places of worship. Shinto was cared for by a department of government with a rank equal to all others.

Buddhist Influence on Shinto

Under Prince **Shotoku** (574–622 C.E.), cooperation between Shinto, Buddhism, and Confucianism was encouraged. He reasoned that Shinto helped Japanese peoples relate to their natural environment and Confucianism helped build solid families. Buddhism guided preparation for life after death. Although there was a brief attempt to restrict Buddhism to aristocrats, keeping it from peasants, all of the religions, including Daoism, became a part of folk practices. Japanese peoples responded well to the Chinese systems of holidays that the Daoists modified for them.

In the eighth century, the Emperor Shomu greatly expanded Buddhism by establishing kokubunji, official Buddhist temples, in every province. These temples were for monks and were used to support the government—they were not for missionary activities among common people. Shinto was still the native religion for the common people. As may be

Shotoku (Shotuku Taishi)
[SHOOH-TOH-ku]
The Japanese prince who supported the establishment of Buddhism in his country.

Amaterasu, the Sun Goddess. The goddess of light is shown in an encounter with other kami.

expected, Buddhism continued to strengthen its influence beyond the aristocracy. Common people combined kami and the spiritual beings of Mahayana Buddhism; in an emerging folk religion, Japanese peoples called on both kami and Buddhist deities.

We have discussed the Buddhist groups in Japan that developed third doctrines outside Kyoto on Mt. Hiei. In that remote area, they were beyond strict control of the court of the city. Japanese common people, who already associated kami and mountains in Shinto, could easily associate the Buddhas with the spirits of their native religion.

The Bushido Code

One development in Japan involving several religions working together in a way fascinating to Japanese and foreigners alike was the code of the feudal warrior or knight, **bushido.** This code, which emphasized absolute loyalty of the warrior to his lord, also included gratitude, courage, and justice. So fierce and devoted was the knight, that should he fail in his mission, the code required that he commit **hara-kiri,** ritual suicide. This unique code had its roots deep in Shinto, with extreme patriotism for emperor and country, but scholars find in it strong influences from Confucianism with emphasis on the ethics of the junzi. Individual self-discipline and harmony of self and duty bear the strong stamp of Zen Buddhism. Thus these religions influenced bushido, the warrior code; those who lived by it had a religious respect for it. Yamaga-Soko, given credit for establishing bushido, said: "The first and surest means to enter into communion with the Divine is by sincerity. If you pray to a deity with sincerity, you will surely feel the divine presence."[63]

bushido [bu-shi-DOOH]
A code of honor for Japanese warriors. It incorporated both Daoist and Zen Buddhist concepts and governed the samurai, the feudal military class.

hara-kiri (seppuku) [HAH-RAH-kee-ree]
In Japan, a ritual suicide to preserve or to restore a person's honor. It is considered an act of bravery rather than cowardice.

Reactions to Foreign Influence

Military leaders sought to reduce the influence of foreign religions and to restore native customs, including the emperor as a symbol of Japanese unity. Lord Nobunaga burned Buddhist buildings on Mt. Hiei and a fortress belonging to a Pure Land sect. Hideyoshi grew tired of Christian infighting. Jesuit missionaries had come in 1549 to help carry on trade with the West. But other Catholic and Protestant missionaries promoted competitive doctrines that divided Japanese loyalties. In 1587, Toyotomi Hideyoshi prohibited Christians from interfering with Shinto and Buddhists and from proclaiming their own doctrines. A crucifixion of Franciscan missionaries in Nagasaki in 1597 was followed in 1614 by a Tokugawa ban on the practice of Christianity.

But the Tokugawa regime, along with its strict policy of keeping foreigners out of Japan, established Neo-Confucianism and Buddhism as pillars to support the state. Neo-Confucianism was the philosophy of the civil service that required absolute loyalty to family and obedience to the ruler. Three principles governed the ideal sovereign. He should lead his people in conduct according to virtue conferred on them by heaven.[64] He should help them preserve pure heart and mind. He should preserve the ideal society that results from these principles. Buddhism, already established in every province, became a means of keeping contact with each family; each was required to belong to a Buddhist temple. Although Shinto priests had to become Buddhists, in the long run the move helped them. Through its ties with the state Buddhism became perfunctory, but Shinto priests strengthened their ties with folk religion and syncretized popular Buddhist ideas with vital Shinto practices.

State Shinto

One of the most significant changes in the status of Shinto is usually tied to a nonreligious event, the visit of Commodore Matthew C. Perry, who insisted in 1853 that Japan open its ports to the United States. Many scholars interpret this visit as the occasion when Japanese leaders decided to pursue Western technology in order to compete among nations of the West. The **shogun,** or military ruler, resigned in 1867, and the Emperor Meiji became the ruler of Japan in 1868. Immediately he imposed a sharper division between the Shinto and Buddhist priesthoods. From 1872, Buddhist priests could not teach that kami were really Buddhas. State Shinto was identified with the emperor, the government, and patriotism; citizens were required as a matter of national loyalty to participate. They could also participate in either Buddhism or sectarian Shinto, which did not receive state support. The Imperial Constitution of the Great Empire of Japan of 1889, the Meiji constitution, stated that within certain bounds of order and loyalty as subjects, Japanese peoples were to enjoy freedom of religion.[65] In the early twentieth century, the Japanese government maintained that state Shinto was not a religion.[66]

The popular form of state Shinto affirmed the connection of the nation with ancestors, the will of the emperor, and the goddess. The individual was not a free being or even primarily a unit of a family or class; the individual belonged to the state. In a half century, this powerful concept of roots and identity combined with a conscious plan to imitate the Western industrial and military powers to the point where the Japanese could compete successfully with them resulted in an astounding change in Japan. Shrines at Ise, in the Imperial Palace, and in various parts of the nation numbering a hundred thousand kept state Shinto before the people, promoting reverence for ancestors, patriots, and, above all, the emperor.

State Shinto went through a period of sharp decline, if not collapse, when the Japanese surrendered to the Allies in 1945. The emperor was no longer considered divine, at least officially. Although the Allies insisted on a separation of Shinto and state, the Association of Shinto Shrines has been instrumental in bringing Shinto ceremonies into the construction of government buildings and in obtaining government support for the periodic rebuilding of the shrine at Ise, as tradition requires. Of course, Shinto can still be found in Japanese homes in the **kami-dana,** or spirit shelf. The **butsudan,** a center for observing reverence for ancestors and departed members of the family, is not as prominent as it once was.

Recent Shinto

Traditional Buddhism and sectarian Shinto thrive in Japan. Buddhist temples of all sects are everywhere, and it is not unusual to find Shinto shrines even on the premises of some of Japan's most technologically advanced centers of communication. These religions still inspire the people of Japan.

SECTARIAN SHINTO

A publication of the Agency for Cultural Affairs classifies sectarian Shinto into three groups, giving their history and distinctive practices.[67] The three

---

shogun [SHOW-GUN]
In Japan, a military ruler serving, ostensibly, under the emperor.

kami-dana [KAH-mee-DAH-NAH]
In Japanese homes, a center of symbols honoring the kami. Sometimes the center is a shelf.

butsudan [Bu-tsu-DAH-NAH]
A Buddhist altar. Tablets commemorating ancestors are kept on it.

CHAPTER SIX

classifications are traditional sects, mountain worship sects, and sects based on revelation.

The traditional sects include six major organizations recognized by the government of Japan. Since 1886, *Shinto Taikyo* has worshiped the first three deities of the *kojiki* cosmogony, including Izanagi, Izanami, Amaterasu, and other kami. Its other principles of purification and services for the dead distinguish it little from shrine Shinto. Since 1883, there has been a sect, *Izumo Oyashirokyo*, dedicated to the worship of Okuninushi no Kami, the ruler of the nether world. The three major deities are subordinate to him. Okuninushi no Kami is the guarantor of happiness and the good life. *Shinto Shuseiha* worships the three deities and emphasizes living in accord with the Five Relations of Confucianism. *Shinto Taiseikyo*, established in 1882, emphasizes purification rituals, sitting quietly, and

A Kami-dana. Although small shelves are found often inside Japanese homes, this larger one is located in a garden.

Pilgrims Climbing Mt. Fuji. Several religious groups in Japan express their devotion by climbing the sacred mountain.

controlled breathing. Inspired by a mystical experience in the mountains, Yoshimura Masamochi, from a samurai family, founded *Shinshukyo* in 1880. Worshiping Honchi Taishin, a composite of the three deities, members of the sect practice purification rituals and physical exercises to attain spiritual discipline. *Shinrikyo* emphasizes worship of Amaterasu, obligations to the emperor, rituals, sacred music, flower arrangement, and the tea ceremony.

There are three mountain worship sects. *Ontakekyo* began with people who climbed Mt. Ontakekyo as a religious discipline. The sect seeks purity, divine virtues, and spiritual stability of the nation. The *Fusokyo* sect worships Sengen Daishin, the deity of Mt. Fuji. Its main activity is climbing Mt. Fuji as a ritual to benefit the individual and the nation. The *Jikkokyo* sect worships heaven, ancestral spirits, and earthly kami abiding on Mt. Fuji. In addition to the other Shinto goals, it seeks mystic unity with divine nature.

There are five sects based on revelation experiences. *Kurozumikyo* was founded when Kurozumi Munetada (1780–1850) experienced a revelation of Amaterasu and realized there is no distinction between divine and human other than eternal life. Honoring the founder, adherents seek to make his experience their own. Kawate Bunjiro (1814–1883), during an illness, experienced the dreadful golden kami, Konjin. In 1859, Kawate Bunjiro proclaimed himself Konko Daijin, a mediator between humans and the kami. Although there is a separate administrative head chosen from adherents of *Konkokyo*, the spiritual head of the sect is based on descent from the founder. *Misogikyo* was founded after Inoue Masakane (1790–1849) had a mystical experience. He discovered that the ritual of *misogi harai*, in which a Shinto priest waves a wand hung with strips of sacred paper over worshipers, delivers adherents from evil and impurities. Later adherents added controlled breathing to their rituals. *Omoto* was founded by a woman, Deguchi Nao (1836–1918). A product of grinding poverty, she had a revelation that inspired her to seek an ideal society. With her daughter Sumi and a master of shamanistic practices, Onisaburo (1871–1948), she created a religious sect. Adherents venerate the founder and Onisaburo.

An offshoot of the other religions, **Tenrikyo,** also honors **Miki Nakayama** (1798–1887), its foundress. The split of the Tenrikyo group came when Onishi, in 1913, announced that he was a mediator of a second dispensation of divine grace. Expelled from Tenrikyo, his adherents formed Honmichi.

Tenrikyo, a spiritual healing group, formed in the nineteenth century around a peasant woman (1798–1887), whose given name was Miki and whose married name was Nakayama. Experiencing the presence of the kami of Divine Reason when she reached middle age, she believed that she had been the medium of healing for her son in 1838. Her eldest son, Shuji, suffered a pain in his leg to the extent that he was unable to work. A yamabashi healer came to lead séances that helped Shuji. During one session, Miki took the place of the female assistant to the healer. In her trance, which lasted three days, she was the medium of a voice that claimed to be the true God who came down from heaven to save the world.[68] Of course she shared the secrets of her healing with her neighbors, and the Teaching of the Heavenly Reason was soon established. A person who lives reasonably, that is, in line with the Heavenly Reason, will have a prosperous and healthy life in the present world. For a period of time, she was opposed by her husband and her neighbors, who found her desire to give away her property evidence of her being possessed. She persisted, however, in her witness that illness could be overcome through a healthy belief. Her successes in healing mounted over the years, and her examples of virtue won her respect and adherents. She lived until January 26, 1887. Her teachings are passed down in four texts that her adherents consider scripture. Tenrikyo continues to thrive today in faith healings and voluntary work for public charity.

New Religions

Three new religions of Japan are developments based on the teachings of Omoto. P. L. (Perfect Liberty) Kyodan began in 1946. Miki Tokuchika emphasized aesthetic experiences and rites for healing. Seicho-no-Ie (House of Growth) emphasizes American positive thinking. Its founder was Taniguchi Masaharu. Suffering is not real; it is the result of bad attitudes. All beings are perfect children of God. These religions help complement the new religions of Japan based on Nichiren Buddhism: Soka Gakkai, Rissho Koseikai, and Reiyukai.[69]

Summarizing his views on the new religions of Japan, H. Paul Varley wrote,

> Despite the diversity of the new religions, they share certain general characteristics. For example, they have tended to spring up during times of intense crisis or social unrest, such as the early Meiji and post–World War II periods; their founders have typically been charismatic figures who have served as vehicles for the revelation of religious truth; they are highly syncretic, often partaking freely of Shinto and Buddhism, as well as Christianity; and they are millenarian in that they characteristically promise the advent of a paradise on earth. Also, the new religions have always appealed chiefly to people lower on the social and economic scales: to those who have in some sense been left behind in the march for modern progress.
>
> What makes the new religions most fascinating within the larger context of Japanese cultural history is the degree to which they reflect fundamental religious values and attitudes that have been held since ancient times. This can be seen perhaps most tellingly in the kinds of the charismatic figures who have found new religions, the most interesting of which are the female shamanistic types.[70]

Tenrikyo [TEN-ree-KYOOH]
A new religion of Japan based on the teachings of Miki Nakayama. It reveres the kami of Divine Reason.

Miki Nakayama [MI-ki NAH-KAH-YAH-MAH]
In Japan, founder of the new religion, Tenrikyo. She experienced divine healing through the kami of Divine Reason.

CONSIDER THIS: HARMONY IN JAPAN

In Shinto, a person seeks harmony with both nature and society. Harmony with nature is, in particular, harmony with the islands of Japan, which have a special place in stories of the kami who created a habitat for the Japanese people. Harmony with society includes relationships with family, community, and nation, but it also embraces members of those groups who now live beyond death as ancestors. "Extended family" includes relatives who are ancestors as well as those living on earth. Although the emperor of Japan no longer claims divinity, he is the symbolic apex uniting all the peoples of the islands. As H. Byron Earhart has written, "Japanese people" means a group of people united by common practices of religion, a religion that includes worship of kami and loyalty to the emperor.

WORLDVIEW

During its long history, Shinto has meant so many things to different people that it is difficult to describe its worldview. The worldview outline used to explain beliefs of other religions does not apply in every instance to Shinto.

The Absolute

Traditionally, Shinto has focused its worship on the goddess of the sun, Amaterasu-Omikami. The sun has been an object of veneration in many religions, for example, the Egyptian. But the Japanese have looked on Amaterasu-Omikami not so much as a universal deity but as a deity partial to the peoples of Japan. Nature kami are revered without any disrespect for Amaterasu. Emperors can be revered or worshiped at shrines because they have historically carried the title of descendants of the goddess of the sun. Emperor Hirohito, since 1945, denied descent from Amaterasu. In sectarian Shinto, such as Tenrikyo, other kamis or principles such as Divine Reason can be approached in reverence. Along with these powers an adherent can, without necessarily being disloyal, worship Confucius, the Dao, various Buddhas and Bodhisattvas, and his or her own ancestors.

Japanese people have a reverence for the extraordinary power and order immanent in nature and animals, including humans. Power and order are revered where they impinge on human experience. Although Shinto can be classified as polytheism, it is, perhaps, more accurately described today as a reverence for manifestations of power that have had special value for the Japanese people.

The World

Shinto reveres many natural phenomena. The Japanese islands as a group are regarded as sacred. The Japanese feel that their country is a special creation and gift of Amaterasu. Mt. Fuji, other mountains, streams, rivers, and the sea are all blessings bestowed on the Japanese people. The land belongs to the Japanese; it was made for them. There is still a feeling among some Koreans and other peoples who have lived in Japan for several generations that Japanese people will never accept them as Japanese and grant them a share in the country.

Humans

Shinto is concerned with Japanese peoples rather than with humanity. Humans are potentially kami. They came from acts of kami, and by acting heroically, they can become kami. As do Confucians, Japanese look on humans as servants of family, state, and ancestors. An individual is never isolated; he or she is always part of an extended family and a national people. People are expected to do their best for all these groups. To fail to do their best is disgraceful. There is freedom enough for individuals to have responsibility for their conduct, but they are never free to act with disregard for the welfare of all the constituent groups.

Denise Lardner Carmody has described the role of Japanese women in terms similar to those of Confucian family culture, as bushido woman, as shaman, or as court lady.[71] As a Japanese woman, she was subservient to father, husband, and son. As warrior, she was expected to die to protect her honor. As court lady, she cared for the aesthetic traditions of art, literature, and music. As shaman, she possessed status over men as well as women. Leaders in new religions, such as Tenrikyo, were honored as mediums of kami, elevating their status beyond that of ordinary humans. Although most Japanese women have attained more freedoms as they have participated in general education and employment, they still have lower status than men in their homes and workplaces.

The Problem for Humans

The problem for humans is alienation. Alienation can take several forms. Humans can be ritually unclean, in need of purification. They can be estranged from the kami, in need of communication. They can be alienated from family, ancestors, community, or emperor through loss of face—failure to do what has been expected.

The Solution for Humans

The solution for humans is reconciliation. Purification at a shrine can remove ritual pollution and permit humans to approach the kami. They can be reconciled by offerings and prayers. Reverence for ancestors and prayers to them can remove minor estrangements. Heroic deeds for the state can atone for some alienation from the nation. When all else fails, ritual suicide is considered an honorable way to atone for guilt.

Community and Ethics

Devotion to family and country governs all conduct. A person is part of a family, a school, a business organization, and a nation. Sacrificing impulses to selfishness for the good of these larger groups is a duty. Maintaining the honor of these groups guides conduct. If the existence of these groups does not influence a person's actions, he or she also has to consider that ancestors and kami are observing. For those who act unethically, or illegally, law enforcement officials may be the least of their worries.

Rituals and Symbols

Robert Ellwood and Richard Pilgrim have emphasized the importance of pilgrimages in Japanese religion, the need to move from one place to

◆ **1500–1027** Shang dynasty of China

◆ **1027–256** Zhou dynasty of China

◆ **660** Jimmu, the first human emperor of Japan

◆ **600–300** Laozi lived sometime during this period

◆ **551–479** Confucius

◆ **479–381** Mozi lived sometime during this period

◆ **369–286** Zhuangzi

◆ **371–289** Mengzi

◆ **298–230** Xunzi

◆ **215** Great Wall of China built

◆ **206** Han Dynasty begins

206–220 Han dynasty of China ◆

300s Ge Hong, the Taoist ◆

574–622 Prince Shotoku of Japan ◆

589–618 Sui dynasty of China ◆

618–907 Tang dynasty of China ◆

710 Nara period of Japan ◆

712 *The Kojiki* ◆

720 *The Nihongi* ◆

794 Heian period of Japan ◆

960–1279 Song dynasty of China ◆

1130–1200 Zhuxi, Neo-Confucian ◆

1186 Kamakura period of Japan ◆

1275–1292 Marco Polo visits China ◆

1279–1369 Kublai Khan, Yuan dynasty of China ◆

1336 Muromachi period of Japan ◆

| BCE | 2000 | 1500 | 1000 | 500 | 0 | 500 | 1000 | 1500 | 2000 | CE |

Religions of China and Japan in History

1368–1644 Ming dynasty of China ◆

1549 Jesuits enter Japan ◆

1600 Tokugawa period of Japan ◆

1610–1695 Huang Zongzi, Neo-Confucian ◆

1622–1685 Yamaga-Soko; Bushido ◆

1644–1912 Manchus rule China ◆

1798–1887 Miki Nakayama: Tenri-Kyo ◆

1842 Hong Kong transferred to British ◆

1853 Admiral Perry in Japan ◆

1868 Meiji period of Japan ◆

1900 Boxer Rebellion in China ◆

1912 Republic of China established ◆

1931 Japan invades China's northern provinces ◆

1941 Japanese bomb Pearl Harbor ◆

1945 United States drops atomic bombs on Japan; Emperor of Japan no longer divine ◆

1946 Civil war in China; Communists against Nationalists ◆

1947 Japan puts into effect democratic constitution ◆

1950 Chinese troops assist North Korea in fighting UN forces in South Korea ◆

1962 Chinese troops invade India, pull back ◆

1972 President Richard M. Nixon visits China, new relations established ◆

1976 Mao Zedong, People's Republic of China dies ◆

1989 Emperor Hirohito of Japan dies ◆

1993 Jiang Zemin president of People's Republic of China ◆

February, 1997 Deng Xiaoping dies ◆

July 1, 1997 Hong Kong returns to People's Republic of China ◆

BCE	2000	1500	1000	500	0	500	1000	1500	2000	CE

another.[72] One pilgrimage destination was the Grand Shrine of Ise. In the Heian era, only members of the imperial house and officials could worship there. A princess was chosen to be the priestess-shamaness to help lead the services to Amaterasu. In later periods, beginning with the Tokugawa, when common people could worship at Ise, it was important for people to go at least once during their lifetime. Those persons who could not go might help send a delegate to worship and bring back tokens.

Two forms of pilgrimage developed. One was an official pilgrimage undertaken by those with gifts and money. For these pilgrims there was a festival atmosphere in the inns, shops, and houses along the highway they traveled. Later, spontaneous pilgrimages occurred among thousands of poor people. Without permission or provisions, men, women, and children set out for the shrine, depending on the grace of the divine to provide for their safe arrival. Each day they traveled, holding aloft banners and dancing their way to Ise. When the Tokugawa era gave way to imperial rule, these pilgrimages to Ise ended. Today many worshipers observe traditions at Ise; other worshipers prefer to climb sacred mountains.

Shinto believes in the power of spoken words in prayer. The *Norito*, Shinto prayers, consist of words that praise the kami and list the offerings presented, persons reciting the prayer and those to be remembered, and any petitions. There are formal prayers for harvest and for the various shrines.[73]

Many of the other symbols of this religion have already been mentioned: the rising sun, a mirror, beads, a sword, the torii, a rope, and last, but by no means least, the emperor of Japan. All these symbols remind the Japanese of their community ties in their homes, villages, and nation.

Life After Death

The traditional Japanese view is that upon death, the body should be cremated. The departed joins his or her ancestors. Ancestors know what the members of their family are doing and can assist them when necessary. They can also receive honors and gifts from devoted members of the family.

Many Japanese families use Buddhist concepts, priests, and rituals to help them in times of bereavement. A popular way to express this eclecticism, which is more inaccurate than accurate, is that Japanese are Shintoists at the birth of a child or at the opening of a business, Christian for a wedding ceremony, and Buddhist at the death of a loved one.

A common belief, according to Robert J. Smith in *Ancestor Worship in Contemporary Japan*, is that at death each person becomes a "buddha." Some years pass before one is regarded as an ancestor. When no one in the family is alive who can remember the ancestor, that person is regarded as a kami of the community. The change of status proceeds with passing time.

Shintoism and Other Religions

Shinto has received rich blessings throughout its history from association with other religions. Traditionally it has cooperated, except for very brief periods, with Buddhism. Most Japanese can participate in Shinto and Buddhism without feelings of conflict. But Shinto is for Japanese people. It seeks no converts, but it is, today, generally tolerant of other religions. Christianity in Japan has only about 1 percent of the population. World religions, other than the early Chinese, have not made widespread converts.

With Shinto, we close our discussion of the religions of eastern Asia. We have studied only the best-known religions in that part of the world. Every country in Asia has its own history of religion that includes not only the major world religions but also lesser-known religions that preceded them. As you go beyond an introductory study of world religions, you may find it rewarding to explore religious developments in each country of eastern Asia.

We turn next to the religions of Mesopotamia, Babylonian religion, and Zoroastrianism. Many scholars of world religion have found in them a convenient bridge to study world religions that began in Central and West Asia (as some Asians call it), or, as it is known in the West, the Middle East. Although Mesopotamian religions help prepare us for study of Judaism, Christianity, and Islam, Zoroastrianism is also a living world religion, worthy of study for its influence in the modern world.

VOCABULARY

Amaterasu
  [AH-MAH-te-RAH-su]
bushido [bu-SHI-DOOH]
butsudan [bu-tsu-DAH-NAH]
Chiang K'ai-shek
  [CHUNG-kai-SHEK]
Confucius [kun-FYOO-shus]
Dao [DOW]
Dao De Jing [dow-du-JING]
Daoists [DOW-ists]
Fajia [fah-JEE-a]
Han Feizi [hahn-FAY-dzi]
hara-kiri (seppuku)
  [HAH-RAH-kee-ree]
Izanagi [ee-zah-NAH-gee]
Izanami [ee-zah-NAH-mee]
Jade Emperor
Jimmu [jee-moo]
junzi [JUN-dzi]

kami [KAH-mee]
kami-dana [KAH-mee-DAH-NAH]
Laozi [LAHOW-dzi]
li [LEE]
Li Ji [LEE-jee]
Mao Zedong
  [MAOW-tse-DONG]
Mengzi [MENG-dzi]
Miki Nakayama
  [mi-ki NAH-KAH-YAH-MAH]
Mohists [MOW-hists]
Mozi [MOW-dzi]
ren [RUN]
Shang Di [shang-DI]
Shinto [SHIN-TOOH]
shogun [SHOW-GUN]
Shotoku [SHOOH-TOH-ku]
shouyi [shoo-yi]
shu [SHOO]

Sun Yat-sen
Susanoo [su-SAH-NOOH]
Taiji [tie-JEE]
taixi [tai-SHEE]
Tenrikyo [TEN-ree-kyo]
Three Purities
tianming [TYIAN-MING]
torii [TOH-RE-EE]
Tsukiyomi [tsoo-ki-yoh-mi]
wuwei [WOO-WAY]
Xunzi [SHUN-dzi]
Yang [YAHNG]
yi [YEE]
Yijing [YEE-jing]
Yin [YIN]
Zaoshen [ZOW-SHEN]
zhongyong [JONG-YONG]
Zhuangzi [JYAHNG-dzi]
Zhuxi [JYOO-SHEE]

QUESTIONS FOR REVIEW

1. Describe the *Yi Jing* and its influences on China.

2. What are the differences among philosophical, religious, and magical forms of Daoism?

3. How did Daoists, Confucians, Mohists, and Fajia differ on the form of the ideal society?

4. How did Confucians design and implement their system of education?

5. How did Confucian ideals conflict with Buddhist ideals?

6. How did Shinto retain its ideals amid Daoism, Confucianism, Buddhism, and Christianity?

7. Name some groups in sectarian Shinto. What are some of the "new religions" of Japan? What explains the rise of so many different religious groups in one country?

8. Describe the differences between Mengzi and Xunzi. Whose views were closer to those of Confucius?

9. What virtues are displayed by the junzi?

10. Can you describe the "five relationships" in Confucianism?

QUESTIONS FOR DISCUSSION

1. Can society be changed for the better by educating role models? What are some of the possible consequences of a Confucian education?

2. What role could Daoism have in our world? Can it be a force for constructive changes? Give some examples to support your answer.

3. In your opinion, who was right about the nature of people, Mengzi or Xunzi? What examples would support your answer?

4. Can Japanese people really practice more than one religion? Explain your answer.

5. How do Chinese, Japanese, and Indian religions differ on the best way for people to live? Give examples from each culture to support your answer.

NOTES

1. James K. Feibleman, *Understanding Oriental Philosophy* (New York: New American Library, 1976), p. 79.

2. From Li-tai ming-hua chi, 6:5b–6b, in *Sources of Chinese Tradition*, ed. Wm. Theodore de Bary (New York: Columbia University Press, 1960), p. 295.

3. Farzeen Baldrian, "Taoism, An Overview," in *The Encyclopedia of Religion*, vol. 14, ed. Mircea Eliade (New York: Macmillan, 1987), pp. 288–306.

4. Wing-Tsit Chan, trans., *A Source Book in Chinese Philosophy* (Princeton, NJ: Princeton University Press, 1963), pp. 137–138.

5. Roger Ames, *The Art of Rulership* (Honolulu: University of Hawaii Press, 1983), p. 7.

6. Chan, p. 139.

7. *Tao Te Ching*, 43, as quoted in Chan, p. 161.

8. Ibid., 78; pp. 174–175.

9. Ibid., 19; p. 149.

10. Ibid., 60, l. 1; p. 168.

11. *Chuang Tzu*, chapter 17, as quoted in de Bary, p. 79.

12. Ibid., chapter 2, p. 75.

13. *Chuang Tzu*, chapter 2, in Chan, p. 189.

14. N. J. Girardot, *Myth and Meaning in Early Taoism* (Berkeley: University of California Press, 1983), p. 291.

15. James R. Ware, *Alchemy, Medicine and Religion in the China of A.D. 320* (Cambridge, MA: M.I.T. Press, 1966).

16. Arthur Waley, *The Way and Its Power* (London: Allen & Unwin, 1968).

17. Max Kaltenmark, *Lao Tzu and Taoism* (Stanford, CA: Stanford University Press, 1969), p. 136.

18. Baldrian, 14: pp. 288–306; 300.

19. Ed. de Bary, pp. 62–63.

20. Michael Saso, "Orthodoxy and Heterodoxy in Taoist Ritual," in *Religion and Ritual in Chinese Society*, ed. Arthur P. Wolf (Stanford, CA: Stanford University Press, 1974), pp. 325–336.

21. Carl Crow, *Master Kung* (New York: Harper, 1938), p. 62.

22. Confucius, *The Analects*, trans. D. C. Lau (New York: Penguin Books, 1979), p. 74. Copyright © 1979 by D. C. Lau. Reproduced by permission of Penquin UK Ltd.

23. Ibid., pp. 122–123.

24. Ibid., p. 63.

25. *The Sacred Books of Confucius and Other Confucian Classics*, trans. and ed. Ch'u Chai and Winberg Chai (New Hyde Park, NY: University Books, 1965). There is more information on music in the "Yoki" section of the *Li Chi*.

26. Confucius, p. 72.

27. Ibid., p. 135.

28. Ibid., p. 69.

29. Benjamin I. Schwartz, *The World of Thought in Ancient China* (Cambridge, MA: Belknap Press of Harvard University, 1985), pp. 117–126.

30. Fung Yu-Lan, *A History of Chinese Philosophy*, vol. 1, trans. Derk Bodde (Princeton, NJ: Princeton University Press, 1952), pp. 76–77.

31. Yi-Pao Mei, *Motse: The Neglected Rival of Confucius* (Westport, CT: Hyperion Press, 1973), p. 45.

32. *Basic Writings of Mo Tzu, Hsun Tzu, and Han Fei Tzu*, trans. Burton Watson, 1967. Copyright © Columbia University Press, New York. Reprinted with the permission of the publisher.

33. Ibid., p. 4.

34. Ibid., p. 3.

35. Ibid., p. 20.

36. Wing-Tsit Chan, "Confucian Thought: Foundations of Tradition," in *The Encyclopedia of Religion*, vol. 4, ed. Mircea Eliade (New York: Macmillan, 1987), pp. 15–24.

37. *Mencius*, trans. D. C. Lau (Baltimore: Penguin Books, 1979), p. 120. Copyright © 1979 by D. C. Lau. Reproduced by permission of Penguin UK Ltd.

38. A. C. Graham, *Disputers of the TAO* (La Salle, IL: Open Court, 1989), pp. 125–126.

39. *Mencius*, Book IV, Part A, 163.

40. *Basic Writings of Mo Tzu, Hsun Tzu, and Han Fei Tzu*, pp. 4–5.

41. Ibid., p. 157.

42. Chan, *A Source Book in Chinese Philosophy*, p. 638.

43. Wm. Theodore de Bary, "Human Rites: An Essay on Confucianism and Human Rights," in *Confucianism: The Dynamics of Tradition*, ed. Irene Eber (New York: Macmillan, 1986), pp. 109–132.

44. Ki-baik Lee, *A New History of Korea*, trans. Edward W. Wagner with Edward J. Schultz (Cambridge, MA: Harvard University Press, 1984), p. 73.

45. Wanne J. Joe, *Traditional Korea, A Cultural History* (Seoul: Chung'ang University Press, 1972), p. 102.

46. Wing-Tsit Chan, *Religious Trends in Modern China* (New York: Octagon Books, 1969), pp. 4–20.

47. Kam Louie, *Critiques of Confucius in Contemporary China* (New York: St. Martin's Press, 1980), chapter 5.

48. Chan, *Religious Trends in Modern China*, p. 20.

49. Confucius, p. 129.

50. *Sources of Chinese Tradition*, ed., Wm. Theodore de Bary, 1960, Copyright © Columbia University Press, New York. Reprinted with permission of the publisher.

51. Confucius, p. 89.

52. Graham, pp. 13, 14. Trans. A. C. Graham.

53. Confucius, pp. 63, 66.

54. Theresa Kelleher, "Confucianism," in *Women in World Religions*, ed. Arvind Sharma (Albany: State University of New York, 1987), pp. 137–143.

55. Derk Bodde, *Festivals in Classical China* (Princeton, NJ: Princeton University Press, 1975), p. 45.

56. Isabel Wong, "Music and Religion in China, Korea, and Tibet," in *The Encyclopedia of Religion*, vol. 10, ed. Mircea Eliade (New York: Macmillan, 1987), pp. 195–202.

57. Confucius, p. 107.

58. Carmen Blacker, *The Catalpa Bow* (London: Allen & Unwin, 1975).

59. *The Kojiki*, trans. Basil Hall Chamberlain (Rutland, VT: Tuttle, 1981), p. 19.

60. *Nihongi*, trans. W. G. Aston (Rutland, VT: Tuttle, 1972), pp. 15–16.

61. *The Kojiki*, p. 65.

62. Floyd Hiatt Ross, *Shinto: The Way of Japan* (Boston: Beacon Press, 1965), p. 19.

63. Ibid., p. 122.

64. *Japanese Religion, A Survey by the Agency for Cultural Affairs* (Tokyo and Palo Alto: Kodansha, 1972), p. 108.

65. Ibid., p. 26.

66. D. C. Holthom, *The National Faith of Japan* (New York: Paragon, 1965), chapter 19.

67. *Japanese Religion*, pp. 174–190.

68. Robert Ellwood and Richard Pilgrim, *Japanese Religion in a Cultural Perspective* (Englewood Cliffs, NJ: Prentice Hall, 1985), p. 81.

69. Ibid., pp. 150–151.

70. H. Paul Varley, *Japanese Culture* (Honolulu: University of Hawaii Press, 1984), p. 297.

71. Denise Lardner Carmody, *Women and World Religion* (Englewood Cliffs, NJ: Prentice Hall, 1989), pp. 115–120.

72. Ellwood and Pilgrim, pp. 56–60.

73. Joseph M. Kitagawa, *On Understanding Japanese Religion* (Princeton, NJ: Princeton University Press, 1987), p. 154.

✍ READINGS

CHINA

Confucius. *The Analects*, trans. D. C. Lau. New York: Penguin Books, 1979. A brief, scholarly introduction to the life of Confucius.

Graham, A. C. *Disputers of the TAO*. La Salle, IL: Open Court, 1989.

Koller, John M. *Oriental Philosophies*. New York: Scribner's, 1985. Compares philosophies of Hindus, Buddhists, and China.

Mencius, trans. D. C. Lau. Baltimore: Penguin Books, 1970. A brief, scholarly introduction to a Confucian thinker.

Overmyer, Daniel L. *Religions of China*. San Francisco: Harper & Row, 1986. An examination of Chinese religions in a cultural setting.

Schwartz, Benjamin I. *The World of Thought in Ancient China*. Cambridge, MA: Belknap Press of Harvard University Press, 1985. A thorough discussion of philosophy and religion in ancient China.

Thompson, Laurence G. *Chinese Religion*. Belmont, CA: Wadsworth, 1989. A short, readable introduction to Chinese religion.

JAPAN

Anesake, Masaharu. *History of Japanese Religion*. Rutland, VT: Tuttle, 1963. A helpful book by an outstanding scholar on Japanese religions.

Earhart, H. Byron. *Religions of Japan*. Hagerstown, MD: Torch Publishing Group, 1984. A brief introduction in a social context.

————. *Japanese Religion in the Modern Century*. Tokyo: University of Tokyo, 1980. A readable account by a scholar of modern Japan.

Ellwood, Robert, and Richard Pilgrim. *Japanese Religion: A Cultural Perspective*. Englewood Cliffs, NJ: Prentice Hall, 1985. The cultural side of Japan is explored as well as the religious.

Kitagawa, Joseph M. *On Understanding Japanese Religions.* Princeton, NJ: Princeton University Press, 1987. A master scholar of world religions writes on Japan.

Murakami, Shigeyoshi. *Japanese Religion in the Modern Century,* trans. H. Byron Earhart. Tokyo: University of Tokyo Press, 1980. A focus on recent religious developments in Japan.

Varley, H. Paul. *Japanese Culture.* Honolulu: University of Hawaii Press, 1984. A study of the cultural background of Japanese people.

READINGS FOR RESEARCH AND REPORTS—CHINA

Ames, Roger. *The Art of Rulership.* Honolulu: University of Hawaii Press, 1983.

Baldrian, Farzeen. "Taoism, An Overview," trans. Charles Le Blanc. In *The Encyclopedia of Religion,* vol. 14, ed. Mircea Eliade. New York: Macmillan, 1987. Pp. 288–306.

Basic Writings of Mo Tzu, Hsun Tzu, and Han Fei Tzu, trans. Burton Watson. New York: Columbia University Press, 1967.

Birrell, Anne. *Chinese Mythology: An Introduction.* Baltimore: Johns Hopkins University Press, 1993.

Bodde, Derk. *Festivals in Classical China.* Princeton, NJ: Princeton University Press, 1975.

Bush, Richard C., Jr. *Religion in Communist China.* New York: Abingdon Press, 1970.

Chai, Ch'u, and Winberg Chai, eds. *The Sacred Books of Confucius and Other Confucian Classics.* New Hyde Park, NY: University Books, 1965.

Chan, Wing-Tsit. *Chu Hsi Life and Thought.* New York: St. Martin's Press, 1987.

———. *Religious Trends in Modern China.* New York: Octagon Books, 1969.

Cheng, Chung-ying. *Tai Chen's Inquiry into Goodness.* Honolulu: East–West Center Press, 1971.

Ching, Julia. "Confucius." In *The Encyclopedia of Religion,* vol. 4, ed. Mircea Eliade. New York: Macmillan, 1987. Pp. 38–42.

Chiu, Milton M. *The Tao of Chinese Religion.* New York: University Press of America, 1984.

Creel, H. G. *Confucius: The Man and the Myth.* New York: John Day, 1949.

Crow, Carl. *Master Kung.* New York: Harper, 1938.

de Bary, Wm. Theodore. *East Asian Civilizations.* Cambridge, MA: Harvard University Press, 1988.

———. *The Liberal Tradition in China.* New York: Columbia University Press, 1983.

———, ed. *Sources of Chinese Tradition.* New York: Columbia University Press, 1960.

Eber, Irene, ed. *Confucianism: The Dynamics of Tradition.* New York: Macmillan, 1986.

Ebrey, Patricia Buckley. *The Cambridge Illustrated History of China.* Cambridge, England: Press Syndicate of the University of Cambridge, 1996.

Fung Yu-Lan. *A History of Chinese Philosophy,* trans. Derk Bodde. Princeton, NJ: Princeton University Press, 1952.

Gernet, Jacques. *A History of Chinese Civilization,* trans. J. R. Foster and Charles Hartmen. Cambridge, England: Press Syndicate for the University of Cambridge, 1996.

Giles, Herbert A. *Chuang Tzu.* Shanghai: Kelly & Walsh, 1926.

Girardot, N. J. *Myth and Meaning in Early Taoism.* Berkeley: University of California Press, 1983.

Joe, Wanne J. *Traditional Korea, A Cultural History.* Seoul: Chung'ang University Press, 1972.

Jordan, David K. *Gods, Ghosts, and Ancestors: The Folk Religion of a Taiwanese Village.* Berkeley: University of California Press, 1972.

Lee, Ki-baik. *A New History of Korea,* trans. Edward W. Wagner with Edward J. Shultz. Cambridge, MA: Harvard University Press, 1984.

Louie, Kam. *Critiques of Confucius in Contemporary China.* New York: St. Martin's Press, 1980.

MacInnis, Donald E. *Religious Policy and Practice in Communist China.* London: Macmillan, 1972.

Mei, Yi-Pao. *The Ethical Works and Political Works of Motse.* Westport, CT: Hyperion Press, 1973.

———. *Motse: The Neglected Rival of Confucius.* Westport, CT: Hyperion Press, 1973.

Moore, Charles A., ed. *The Chinese Mind.* Honolulu: East–West Center Press, 1967.

Needham, Joseph. *Science and Civilization in China.* Cambridge, England: Cambridge University Press, 1954.

Orr, Robert G. *Religion in China.* New York: Friendship Press, 1980.

Smith, D. Howard. *Confucius.* New York: Scribner's, 1973.

Thompson, Lawrence G. "Confucian Thought: The State Cult." In *The Encyclopedia of Religion,* vol. 4, ed. Mircea Eliade. New York: Macmillan, 1987. Pp. 36–38.

Waley, Arthur. *Three Ways of Thought in Ancient China.* New York: Barnes & Noble, 1953.

Weber, Max. *The Religion of China,* trans. Hans H. Gerth. New York: Free Press, 1951.

Weller, Robert P. *Unities and Diversities in Chinese Religion.* Seattle: University of Washington Press, 1987.

Wolf, Arthur P. *Religion and Ritual in Chinese Society.* Stanford, CA: Stanford University Press, 1974.

Wong, Isabel. "Music and Religion in China, Korea, and Tibet." In *The Encyclopedia of Religion,* vol. 10, ed. Mircea Eliade. New York: Macmillan, 1987. Pp. 195–202.

Yi-min, Henry Wei, and Suzanne Coutanceau. *Wine for the Gods.* Taipei, Taiwan: Ch'eng Wen Publishing, 1976.

Yutáng, Lin. *The Wisdom of Laotse.* New York: Modern Library, 1948.

READINGS FOR RESEARCH AND REPORTS—JAPAN

Aston, W. G. *Shinto.* New York: Longmans, Green, 1905.

Bach, Marchus. *The Power of Perfect Liberty.* Englewood Cliffs, NJ: Prentice Hall, 1971.

Blacker, Carmen. *The Catalpa Bow.* London: Allen & Unwin, 1975.

Genchi, Kato. *A Study of Shinto, The Religion of the Japanese Nation* Tokyo: Meiji Japan Society, 1926.

Griffiths, William Elliot. *The Religion of Japan.* Freeport, NY: Books for Libraries Press, 1972.

Holtom, D. C. *The National Faith of Japan.* New York: Paragon, 1965.

_____. *Modern Japan and Shinto Nationalism.* New York: Paragon, 1963.

Ichiro, Hori, ed. *Japanese Religion.* Tokyo: Kodansha, 1972.

Japanese Religion: A Survey by the Agency for Cultural Affairs. Tokyo and Palo Alto: Kodansha, 1972.

The Kojiki. *Records of Ancient Matters,* trans. Basil Hall Chamberlain. Rutland, VT: Tuttle, 1981.

Lu, David J. *Japan: A Documentary History.* Armonk, New York: Sharpe, 1997.

Mason, J. W. T. *The Meaning of Shinto.* New York: Dutton, 1935.

Moore, Charles A., ed. *The Japanese Mind.* Honolulu: East–West Center Press, 1967.

Naofusa, Hirai. "Shinto," trans. Helen Hardacre. In *The Encyclopedia of Religion,* vol. 13, ed. Mircea Eliade. New York: Macmillan, 1987. Pp. 280–294.

Nihongi. *Chronicles of Japan from the Earliest Times to A.D. 697,* trans. W. G. Aston. Rutland, VT: Tuttle, 1972.

Ono, Sokyo. *Shinto, The Kami Way.* Rutland, VT: Tuttle, 1963.

Ross, Floyd Hiatt. *Shinto: The Way of Japan.* Boston: Beacon Press, 1965.

Smith, Robert J. *Ancestor Worship in Contemporary Japan.* Stanford, CA: Stanford University Press, 1974.

Thomasen, Harry. *The New Religions of Japan.* Rutland, VT: Tuttle, 1963.

PART FOUR

Religions That Influenced East and West

For peoples in other lands, ancient Iraq and Iran were symbols of advanced civilizations. Their cities, agricultural systems, religions, and laws fascinated all who visited them. To such a rich area, immigrants brought their own ideals and values, and from it traders and adventurers carried away a wealth of ideas and produce.

The heart of Iraq is the land between the Tigris and the Euphrates rivers. These rivers brought the water and the silt that made possible abundant agriculture. Through use of irrigation, the land could support large populations concentrated in city-states. Scarcity of wood was overcome through use of abundant clay, which distinguished the architecture of the country.

Through the centuries, Mesopotamia has been home for many different peoples. Because it lacked sharply defined borders, migrating peoples could arrive from all directions. Arabia and Egypt were sources of many immigrants. As city-states formed in Mesopotamia, rulers of city-states organized hierarchies of deities that indigenous and immigrant peoples worshiped. These religions reflected the organization of city-states and inspired collections of literature, laws, and sciences. The Babylonians were famous for mathematics and astronomy.

Until recently, peoples of the West often referred to peoples of Iran as Persians. The land to the east of Iraq was distinguished by regions of mountains and plateaus. Its climate ranged from extreme heat, on the Persian Gulf, to extreme cold, near Azerbaijan. People who settled in different regions have emphasized their distinctive backgrounds and cultures. Today, about half the people speak Farsi. About a fourth of the people speak forms of Indo-European language, a gift from the Aryans who came and went in the second millennium B.C.E.

In the first millennium B.C.E., the Assyrians expanded their empire to encroach on peoples of Iran. The Medes and the Persians of Iran asserted their influence toward Mesopotamia. Cyrus the Great, the Persian king, defeated the Medes in 550 and overthrew the Mesopotamian city-state of Babylon in 538. His influence on Judaism is recorded in the Bible. The successors of Cyrus the Great developed Zoroastrianism, a distinctive religion of the Persians. Had the Greeks not defeated the Persians in battles such as Marathon and Salamis, Zoroastrianism may have had greater influence in the West.

In the first millennium C.E., important religious changes influenced peoples of Iraq and Iran. Jews of Babylon developed the Babylonian Talmud, the guidebook of rabbinic Judaism. Christians, especially the Nestorians, organized churches as they made converts ever farther east. In the seventh century, Islam expanded from Arabia, converting peoples of the Middle East and Central Asia. Seeking a more hospitable environment for their faith, many Zoroastrians moved into what is now Pakistan. Eventually, Zoroastrians formed large communities in India, where they are known as Parsees.

Although their religions could have exerted greater influences on the West and on the East, Iraq and Iran have helped shape beliefs of peoples in both areas. In Zoroastrianism, Iran has contributed an ancient religion that continues to serve thousands of believers.

Ancient Religions of Iraq and Iran

The Sacred Flame. This sacred fire in Zoroastrianism is the symbol of Ahura Mazda.

Introduction

As we move westward from southern and eastern Asia, we encounter the fascinating personalities of south-central Asia. Today we refer to these lands as Iraq and Iran. In Mesopotamia, the land between the Tigris and Euphrates rivers, we learn of deities such as Damuzi, Inanna, and Ishtar, the mother goddess of Babylonia. We meet Gilgamesh, the wandering king of Uruk, who met with Utnapishtim, the immortal who had made an ark to preserve pairs of all animals from a great flood. In Iraq, we learn of Zarathustra, the Persian who was released from prison to lead a new religion after he healed a favorite horse of Vishtaspa, his king.

On the Mesopotamian plain and the Persian plateau, we discover persons and religious beliefs that Jewish exiles of the sixth century B.C.E. may have encountered. In Babylon, Jews probably learned about the law code of Hammurabi. They probably saw sacred hills made by humans, ziggurats, that were crowned by temples to Babylonian gods. As Persians defeated Babylonians and freed exiled peoples, Jews may have learned of the sacred flame of the Zoroastrians, probably honored by Cyrus, the monarch honored in the Bible.

Our journey through south-central Asia helps us make the transition from religions of India, China, and Japan to religions of the Middle East, Judaism, Christianity, and Islam. From your studies of religions in earlier chapters, some of the religious concepts and parctices of ancient Iraq and Iran will be familiar. Other concepts will be new, or perhaps different; some of them will appear again in religions of Palestine and Arabia.

257

HISTORICAL DEVELOPMENT

Mesopotamia, the area along the banks of the Tigris and the Euphrates rivers in Iraq, was once the site of pyramidlike structures called **ziggurats.** The earth mounds, covered outside with baked bricks or with stones, were symbols of primal mountains; small temples crowned their summits. The impressive brickwork of Babylon can be seen in museums of Great Britain and Germany. In Iraq are ruins of city-states. The Mesopotamians developed sophisticated underground irrigation systems and designed cities that could accommodate thousands of people within fortress walls. With their advanced political structures, Mesopotamians developed integrated orders of gods and goddesses.

Historiography

Aside from the literature and carvings that have survived from ancient Mesopotamia, we receive most of its history through interpretations of outsiders. For example, the Hebrew Bible presents some history of Mesopotamia in the accounts of patriarchs in Genesis, in accounts of Babylon's overthrow of Egyptian rule in Palestine, and in accounts of the destruction of the Temple in Jerusalem. In the Hebrew prophets we have a view of Babylon through the eyes of Jews who were exiled there. The Persian defeat of Babylon is reflected in later books of the Bible. The Jewish scriptures stimulated interests of nineteenth- and twentieth-century orientalists, particularly British scholars. In the last half of the twentieth century, history by outsiders has been balanced by views of scholars living within Iraq. In recent years, Muslim interests have overshadowed appreciation of earlier religions of the area.

Recovering the History of Mesopotamia

Until the mid-nineteenth century, the glory of the ancient Mesopotamians was lost. Then archaeological works by Sir Austin Henry Layard and Sir Max (Edgar Lucian) Mallowan at Nineveh brought to light the thoughts of these ancient peoples. The discovery of the library of Ashurbanipal yielded thousands of cuneiform tablets for study. Cuneiform writing was done with a wedge-shaped stylus on clay tablets. On one set of tablets, George Smith of the British Museum recognized the Babylonian story of the flood, which included the story of Gilgamesh.[1]

In contrast to the predictable, recurring events of Egypt, events in Mesopotamia, a more accessible area, were unpredictable and often tragic. Floods could not be forecast as well as in Egypt. Borders were not clearly defined or easily defended. The climate sped deterioration of buildings and decay of bodies. Mesopotamians sought a good life on earth, for there was little in their experience that led them to expect a permanent existence after death.

A long succession of different peoples fiercely contested rights to control the water, land, and cities of Mesopotamia. There is scant information on the inhabitants before 4000 B.C.E., but after that time the Sumerians moved north and west from Arabia. Although the northern region, along the fertile

ziggurats [ZIG-gu-rats]
In Mesopotamia, pyramidlike structures used in worship. The brick- or stone-covered mounds were topped by a house that represented the court of the deity.

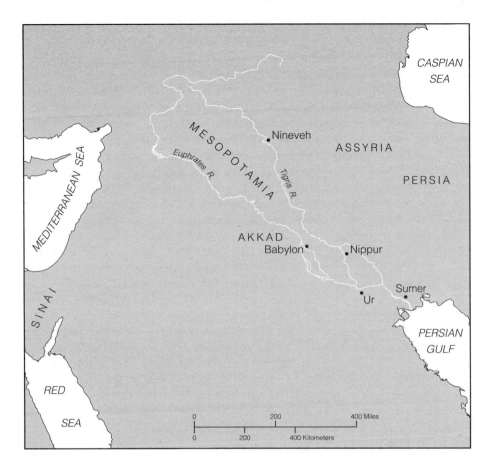

Ancient City-States of Mesopotamia. The land between the rivers was an ancient cradle of civilization.

plateau, receives some rain, the southern region could support agriculture only when the Sumerians built irrigation systems. From cuneiform records, historians can reconstruct a picture of their culture. An Akkadian-speaking group of Semites gained control by 2300 B.C.E, built cities, and consolidated, in order, the Akkadian, the Assyrian, the Babylonian, and the Chaldean empires. The Semitic domination ended in 538 B.C.E when Cyrus, a Persian, seized power. The next-to-last ruler of ancient times was Alexander the Great, who defeated the Persians in 331 B.C.E. When the Romans defeated the Greeks, the new rulers controlled the territory well into the Common Era.

WORLDVIEW

The Absolute

The earliest Mesopotamians symbolized the diversity of their universe in naming not one god, but many gods. Over thousands of years in Mesopotamia, the concepts of gods changed along with the fortunes of the peoples who worshiped them. One of the most systematic accounts of these changes is provided in the work of Thorkild Jacobsen.[2]

According to Jacobsen, the earliest gods of the agricultural peoples, in the fourth millennium, were names of forces of nature. The interaction of these forces was related in stories of courtship and marriage. One collection of stories described the courtship of **Damuzi,** a shepherd and god of grain, and **Inanna,** goddess of the storehouse. In the third millennium, as

Damuzi [du-MU-zi]
(Tammuz) The Mesopotamian god of fertility, who gave life to vegetation and children to women.

Inanna [in-AHN-nu]
In Mesopotamia, the goddess who was wife of Damuzi (Tammuz). She descended into the underworld to seek her husband's release.

Mesopotamian government changed, the gods were perceived as rulers, extending power not only over large city-states but also over the cosmos. In that period, the Mesopotamians developed concepts of individual divine figures. For example, An, god of the sky, was the force of authority and the power that gave being to all nature and gods. Enlil, an energy force of crop-growing weather, was god of the moist winds of springtime. Ninhursaga was the female deity manifest in the stony ground at the eastern and western boundaries of Mesopotamia. As giver of births, Ninhursaga governed wildlife and gave birth to kings. The cunning Enki, a rival of Ninhursaga, was the divine power of the sweet waters of rain, rivers, and marshes. There were other deities in the third millennium, but the triad of An, Enlil, and Ninhursaga, plus Enki, were the most important.

Gods of autonomous cities preceded those of the larger states. When the large city-states formed, these deities were sometimes combined into families. A political union of the city-states Sumer and Akkad brought about a unity of their gods. A triad of heavenly bodies appeared as Sin, the moon god; Shamash, the sun god; and **Ishtar,** the morning (and evening) star, Venus. The best-known and -loved deity was Ishtar, the goddess of fertility, whose popularity won her worship under other names in other cultures.

Jacobsen describes the second millennium as a time when the gods were given roles as parents. It was a time when personal gods served as objects of devotion in the religion of individuals. This was the period of the Enuma Elish myth of creation, which will be described in the next section. The **Gilgamesh** epic, which will also be described, was developed during this period as well. With the rise of Babylon, the deities of the earlier cities, such as Ur and Akkad, were combined in new stories that emphasized the superiority of Babylon.

Babylon had many claims to greatness. Hammurabi (eighteenth century B.C.E), its early builder, issued a famous code of laws, which were supposed to have come from the sun god, Shamash.[3] In his code, Hammurabi invited oppressed people to come before him to receive justice according to the inscribed law. Centuries later, Nebuchadnezzar rebuilt the city and made it a home for, among others, exiles from Jerusalem. Many Jews considered it a good place, for they maintained a creative community there well into the fifth century of the Common Era. The famous Babylonian Talmud, the book that governed Jewish life in medieval times, was produced by Jewish scholars in Babylon.

Myths

According to Babylonian myths, **Tiamat,** salt water, married Apsu, fresh water, and produced many divine descendants. Apsu, angry with their noisy play, tried to kill them. He was killed by Enki. The hero of the Enuma Elish myth of Babylon is **Marduk,** to whom all the gods delegated their authority. Tiamat went on a rampage of revenge until Marduk, the only god strong enough, subdued her. He split Tiamat in half, as if he were opening an oyster shell, the top forming heaven and the bottom earth. **Ea** helped him create humans from the blood of Kingsu, a husband of Tiamat. Marduk continued cosmic creation until he had completed the city of Babylon. The Enuma Elish creation myth was recited in the festival of the New Year as the king, priests, and people participated in the re-creation of the world.

An old story of the fertility god, Damuzi, and Inanna, the queen of heaven, became in later Babylonian accounts the story of **Tammuz** and

Ishtar [ISH-tar]
In Babylonia, a mother goddess who descended into the underworld. She was also known as Inanna.

Gilgamesh [GIL-gu-mesh]
A Mesopotamian king of Uruk about 2600 B.C.E. He searched for immortality, found the plant that was its source, and lost it to a serpent.

Tiamat [TYU-mut]
The Babylonian goddess of chaos. She was defeated by the god Marduk, who created the world.

Marduk [MAHR-dook]
The Babylonian god of creation. To create the world, he defeated the goddess of chaos, Tiamat.

Ea [eah]
A water god. He was sometimes known as Enlil.

Tammuz [TAM-muz]
The Babylonian version of Damuzi, the Mesopotamian god of springtime. He was a god of fertility.

Ishtar. The various versions of the story agree that Damuzi and Inanna, after a passionate courtship, consummated marriage. Through their marriage the vital forces of nature increased. Inanna, desiring to visit her sister, Ereshkigal, the ruler of the underworld, descended into the underworld of Hades. In her descent, she had to pass through seven guarded gates. At each gate she had to remove a piece of clothing. She arrived completely naked before the royal powers, bowing to submit to their judgment. Held hostage and subjected to indignities, Inanna was not released and resurrected until her father, Enki, sent gifts. During her absence underground, all vegetation on earth died. Inanna was permitted to return to earth for a few months each year, provided she could find another hostage to take her place during her absence. Angry that Damuzi had not rescued her, she had him sent underground as her replacement. Moved by the weeping of Damuzi's mother and sister, Inanna took pity on him:

> Inanna and Geshtinanna went to the edges of the steppe.
> They found Dumuzi weeping.
> Inanna took Dumuzi by the hand and said:
>> "You will go to the underworld
>> Half the year.
>> Your sister, since she has asked,
>> Will go the other half.
>> On the day you are called,

Ishtar Gate, Babylon. This gate and the Hanging Towers in the capital of Mesopotamia were famous in the ancient world.

That day you will be taken.
On that day Geshtinanna is called,
That day you will be set free."
Inanna placed Dumuzi in the hands of the eternal.[4]

Annually, during the New Year festival, Babylonians recounted this explanation of the changing seasons.[5]

The story of Inanna, however, affected the beliefs of Babylonians and Akkadians about the nature of the underworld. The land of Kigal, the subterranean realm, was entered where the sun sets. It could also be entered from the grave, for all graves led underground. The dead were ferried to the Great City of Ereshkigal. Her attendants included a plague god and seven judges called the Anunnaki. Demons spread pestilence and suffering among humanity, ensuring that there would always be new subjects for Ereshkigal.

Gilgamesh

Another story, the Epic of Gilgamesh, reveals a Mesopotamian concept of human destiny. Gilgamesh, king of Uruk, was opposed by a wild man of the wilderness, **Enkidu.**[6] Enkidu, a wild, hairy, naked creature from the wilderness, challenged Gilgamesh, who dwelled in urban luxury. Gilgamesh was an urban leader whose warrior skills had deteriorated somewhat in city life. Gilgamesh and Enkidu fought as enemies until they began to respect each other's strengths. They became good friends. Gilgamesh, realizing that he needed a physical challenge, invited Enkidu to join him in an expedition to slay the monster Huwawa in his cedar forest to the west. Death separated the friends soon after Enkidu killed Huwawa, who was part of the security force of Enlil. Enlil killed Enkidu. Gilgamesh mourned his friend and, grieving over his loss, began a journey to find immortality.

An interlude in the story of the journey recounts the tale of **Utnapishtim.** Because he was a just man, the gods warned him that Enlil was about to destroy the earth and its creatures in a great flood. Utnapishtim made an ark for his wife and a pair of all animals. They survived the flood, which wiped out all other living things. To make amends, Enlil conferred upon Utnapishtim and his wife the gift of immortality.[7]

Utnapishtim, being unselfish, told Gilgamesh how to find the plant of immortality, which grew at the bottom of the sea. Gilgamesh reached the place and recovered the precious plant. While he was resting from his exertions, a serpent ate the plant. Thus, the serpent, shedding his old skin, became immortal, and Gilgamesh returned to Uruk without a means of restoring his dead friend. The advice that Ishtar gave to Gilgamesh had merit:

O Gilgamesh, whither wilt thou go?
The life thou seekest thou shalt not find.
When the gods created mankind,
Death they prepared for man,
But life they retained in their hands.
Fill thou, O Gilgamesh, thy belly.
Be merry day and night.
Everyday prepare joyfulness.
Day and night dance and make music.
Let thy garments be made clean.
Let thy head be washed, and be thou bathed in water.
Give heed to the little one that takes hold of thy hand.

Enkidu [IN-ki-du]
In Mesopotamian tradition, a wild man befriended by Gilgamesh. He was killed by Enlil for slaying the monster Huwawa.

Utnapishtim [OOT-nu-PISH-tim]
In Mesopotamia, a just man whom the gods saved from the world flood and to whom they gave immortality. He informed Gilgamesh where he could find the plant of immortality.

Let a wife rejoice in thy bosom.
For this is the mission of man.[8]

The Mesopotamian stories that have been recovered emphasize human joys of this life rather than existence after death.

By 2400 B.C.E., Gilgamesh was named among the gods.[9] The stories made him king of the underworld, identifying him with Damuzi (Tammuz) or Nirgal. His statue was present at burial rites, in which his blessing was invoked. The point of the didactic Gilgamesh epic is that even the strongest humans are limited in what they can accomplish. Extending the good life of the earth after death is beyond the capabilities of kings.

Rituals and Symbols

Although the Mesopotamian religion did not satisfy the deep human longing for immortality, it did offer benefits in this life. The hierarchy of priests in state temples controlled large areas of land. Within the temple compounds, buildings and a ziggurat symbolized a meeting place for gods and humans. The room at the top of the ziggurat was the god's court. A wall with a door separated the courtroom from the god's private abode. Wood carvings in human form represented the gods. Priests provided food for the gods, who opened their eyes and mouths and took the nourishment offered to them. The priests taught that the deities were alive, so they were cared for as if they were living people. Worshipers praised and petitioned the gods, offering them libations and sacrificial animals in many temples.

Public festivals, involving the whole community, centered around dramas. In the drama of the sacred marriage, the ruler of Uruk became the god of the date palm, Amaushumgalana, and his wife became Inanna, goddess of the storehouse. Their marriage guaranteed powers that produced and

The King of Ur Offers Sacrifice. In this sculpture, Ur-Nammu, king of Ur, worships Sin, chief god of Ur, ca. 2300 B.C.E.

stored dates. The battle drama was the account of Marduk versus Tiamat, and the journey drama told the story of Emerkur, the founder of Uruk, who journeyed to Eridu to reconfirm his office as lord and provider.

The god ruled the community from his palace atop the ziggurat. The deities communicated through signs in stars, dreams, or signs on the entrails of animals offered in sacrifice. Humans communicated with gods through gifts, greetings, libations, and formal prayers, to which could be added private petitions. In the family home, parents could become habitations of the gods.[10]

The king represented the god, but the king was also subservient to the god. In one ritual that took place during the Babylonian New Year festival, the king took off his crown, scepter, ring, and ceremonial weapon so that they could be placed before Bel-Marduk. The priest struck the king's cheek and pulled his ears. Stripped of power, the king knelt before the god; there he recited,

> I have not sinned, lord of countries; I have not despised thy divinity;
> I have not destroyed Babel; I have not caused it to be scattered;
> I have not shaken Esagila; I have not forgotten its rituals;
> I have not smitten suppliants on the cheek;
> I have not humiliated them;
> I care for Babel: I have not broken down its walls.[11]

The priest then pronounced assurance of the god's blessing upon the king. People were under the law of the king, and the king was under the law of the god. The king was responsible to the god for conduct in his kingdom.

Relationship to Other Religions

The Mesopotamian concepts of deities changed over many centuries. Eventually Mesopotamians came to believe that life on the land was made possible when salt waters were divided from fresh waters. The sun of heaven and warm, moist breezes activated the forces of fertility in animals, plants, and humans. The process of growth was followed inexorably by death and the decay of all things on earth. The forces of life disappeared as if swallowed up by the earth. In nature, life would return annually; in humans, the periods of renewal, after a span of years, would end. Behind the myths of the gods were profound concepts of the universe. One of the most enduring contributions of the Mesopotamians was the concept that human life must be lived justly under the laws of the gods. The Mesopotamians believed, as did the later Hebrews, that all humans, including the king, must answer for their conduct toward fellow humans.

The Mesopotamians produced not only outstanding city-states but also powerful, unified kingdoms. Abraham, the ancestor of Judaism, Christianity, and Islam, came from Ur. In the thousand years before the Common Era, about the time of Abraham, Mesopotamian powers controlled the Fertile Crescent, the area that was also the homeland of the Hebrews. Mesopotamians were known for their laws, cities, irrigation, and geometry. Jews were divided, some preferring Egypt and some preferring Mesopotamia. Both countries developed significant populations of Jews and, through them, contributed to Western civilization.

The Mesopotamian religion, unlike the Egyptian religion, did not retain its hold on human imagination. It lacked the promise of immortality offered in Egyptian religion. But in the ancient world it carried considerable influ-

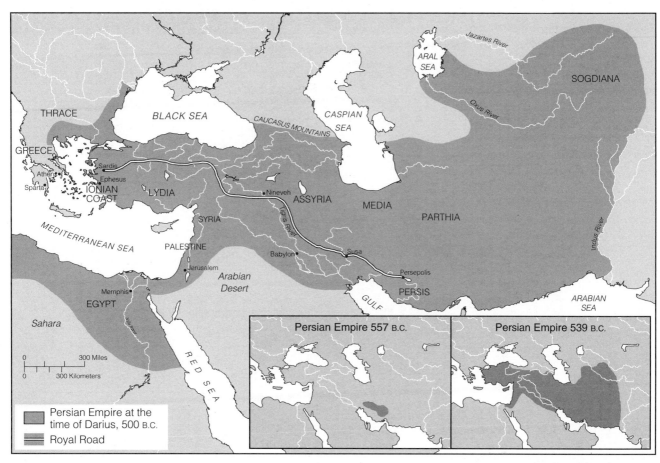

The map contains the following labels:

THRACE · GREECE · Athens · Sparta · IONIAN COAST · Sardis · Ephesus · LYDIA · SYRIA · PALESTINE · Jerusalem · Memphis · EGYPT · Sahara · BLACK SEA · CAUCASUS MOUNTAINS · CASPIAN SEA · ARAL SEA · Jazartes River · SOGDIANA · Oxus River · Nineveh · ASSYRIA · MEDIA · PARTHIA · Indus River · Tigris River · Babylon · Susa · Persepolis · PERSIS · GULF · MEDITERRANEAN SEA · Arabian Desert · RED SEA · ARABIAN SEA · Nile River

Persian Empire 557 B.C.

Persian Empire 539 B.C.

0   300 Miles
0   300 Kilometers

Persian Empire at the time of Darius, 500 B.C.
Royal Road

The Assyrian and Persian Empires.

ence with the Mesopotamians, with the peoples they conquered, and with the peoples who later conquered them: the Persians and the Greeks. Philosophers in other countries viewed Babylon as a center of learning and wisdom. Persians and Greeks were particularly attracted to Mesopotamian astronomy and astrology. The ancient Babylonian religion has passed away, but the civilization that it shaped has influenced modern times.

CONSIDER THIS: MESOPOTAMIA IN THE BIBLE

In the Jewish Bible, the prophet Ezekiel, a priest of Jerusalem who had been exiled in Babylon, had a vision in which he saw the influence of Babylonian religion in the occupied Temple of Jerusalem. Ezekiel's vision of 592 B.C.E. revealed women at the entrance of the north gate of the temple, weeping for Tammuz (Ezekiel 8:14). This syncretism of Babylonian worship in the temple of God was, for Ezekiel, an abomination, a sign of corrupt people of Judah.

The first exiles in Babylon saw Mesopotamian religion all about them, but they resisted it by reaffirming their own faith. The book of Daniel presents the story of heroes who miraculously overcame all attempts of Nebuchadnezzar to force Jews to abandon Judaism and worship deities of Babylon.

Although the religions of Mesopotamia are important for their own beliefs and practices, it is largely through the Hebrew Bible that they have become widely known in the West. As we read from that source, we become aware that its view of Babylonian religion is more negative than neutral or sympathetic.

⊘ A POINT OF VIEW

Ancient Religions of Iraq and Iran in History

◆ **c. 1700** Hammurabi establishes a law code for Babylon

◆ **c. 628–551** Zarathustra lived in Iran

◆ **586** Jews exiled from Jerusalem to Babylon

◆ **550** Cyrus the Great defeats the Medes

◆ **538** Cyrus the Great defeats the Babylonians

◆ **529–522** Reign of Cambyses II of Persia

◆ **522–486** Reign of Darius I of Persia

◆ **331** Parthians rule Persia

◆ **200s** Magi assert influence on Zoroastrianism in Persia

200s Manes, a Persian, teaches Manichean faith ◆

200s Priest Kartir establishes Zoroastrianism as Persian religion ◆

224–651 Sasanians rule Persia ◆

300s Christianity gains strength in areas of Persia ◆

431 Nestorian Christians flee to Mesopotamia-Persia ◆

480 Jewish scholars complete Babylonian Talmud ◆

632 Muhammad dies, successors launch expansion of Islam ◆

| BCE | 2000 | 1500 | 1000 | 500 | 0 | 500 | 1000 | 1500 | 2000 | CE |

HISTORICAL DEVELOPMENT

The religions of the peoples of Iran, or Persia, are probably reflected to an extent in the religions of India. The Aryans who arrived in India had lived for a time in the region of Iran. Aryan deities in the Vedas may recall some of the beliefs and practices of Iran, where common people worshiped *Ahuras*, or lords, and *Devas*, shining ones of the heavens.

Historiography

Zoroastrians, who preferred their own vision of the Absolute, had little favorable to report about the beliefs of people who had opposed them. Within Zoroastrianism, various groups sought to empower their versions of the true religion. They, also, had little good to say about their opponents. Christians and Muslims, in turn, had their particular criticisms of Zoroastrianism and pre-Zoroastrian religions. The best accounts of the history of Zoroastrian religion have emerged from Zoroastrians or from recent scholars sympathetic to that often-persecuted faith. Most Iranian views today favor Shi'ite Islam over other religions. Within Iran, at this time there is little incentive to pursue studies of pre-Islamic beliefs and practices.

The Life of Zarathustra

According to older scholarship, Zarathustra, known in the West by his Latin name, Zoroaster, was born in the seventh century B.C.E, as early as 660 or as late as 628—scholars disagree. R. C. Zaehner dates the life of the prophet from 628 to 551 B.C.E. More recent scholarship dates him from the end of the second millennium B.C.E.[12] According to Sir Rustom Masani, whose opinions are generally respected by Zoroastrians, his home was ancient Iran.[13] Of the warrior clan Spitama, his father was Pourushaspa and his mother was Dughdhova, of a noble family. Zarathustra grew up in the religion that shared some deities and concepts with the Aryans, who produced the hymns of the Rig-Veda. At fifteen, he received the sacred thread of initiation and lived an exemplary life, except that at age twenty he left his parents and the wife they had chosen for him. His religious upheaval began at age thirty.

Our legendary information on Zarathustra comes not from his hymns, the *Gathas*, preserved in the liturgy of the *Yasnas*, but from later sources. He had a vision, or revelation, of Good Thought, **Vohu Manah,** who appeared to him as a figure nine times human size. Leaving his body, Zarathustra responded to a command to come to the court of heaven. **Ahura Mazda,** Wise Lord, revealed the fact that immortality would be given to the followers of Zarathustra. Worshiped by the cattle owners and farm peoples, Ahura Mazda was opposed by **Angra Mainyu,** the spirit of evil, worshiped by rustlers. Zarathustra's vision was followed by six others containing angels, messengers of Ahura Mazda. The struggle between Ahura Mazda and Angra Mainyu could be aided by humans deciding to live moral lives. At the end of time, each would be judged according to his or her deeds and

Vohu Manah [VOH-hoo-MAH-nu]
In Zoroastrianism, Good Thought, one of the Amesha Spentas.

Ahura Mazda [u-HOOR-u MAZ-du]
The Zoroastrian god of light; the Wise Lord who is the highest deity.

Angra Mainyu [ANG-gra MIIN-yu]
In Zoroastrianism, the evil spirit who opposes Ahura Mazda.

rewarded in the pleasant courts of Ahura Mazda or the pits of Angra Mainyu.

The visions continued over a period of ten years, during which Zarathustra began to preach the message of the angels. Until he was about forty, he had only limited success with converts to his new message. His great success came two years later when he converted King Vishtaspa. Although scholars think that the king was a historical figure, they differ on whether he was the father of Cyrus the Great, ca. 585–529 B.C.E. Converting King Vishtaspa was not easy, for the monarch was surrounded by wicked ministers who had Zarathustra thrown into prison. When he was able to heal the favorite horse of King Vishtaspa, he was released. Zarathustra won his convert. The king brought his household into the new religion, and his subjects soon embraced it.

Zarathustra continued to teach and serve at the altar of the fire temple until he was seventy-seven. The kingdom was at war twice with Turanians; Zarathustra died in the second war, either serving at the altar or defending it from its enemies.

Teachings of Zarathustra

SCRIPTURES

The scriptures of Zoroastrianism were written over a period of several centuries. The Avesta, or book of the law, has the Gathas, or hymns, of Zarathustra in its oldest part, the Yasna. In addition are the Visperad, used to honor the ahuras, or lords; the Yashts, or hymns of praise; and the Vindevdat, or rituals against demons. The Avesta available to scholars is only the Videvdat, the one surviving book of 21.

PRINCIPLES OF ZARATHUSTRA

In the Gathas of the Avesta, Zarathustra declares that he has been dedicated to a divine mission of reform. He says in Yasna 43:7–8:

> (7) As the holy one I recognized thee, O Wise Lord,
> When he came to me as Good Mind and asked me:
> "Who art thou, whose art thou? Shall I appoint by a sign
> The days when inquiry shall be made about thy living possessions and
> thyself?"
> (8) I made answer to him: "I am Zarathustra, first,
> A true enemy to the wicked with all my might,
> But a powerful support for the righteous,
> So that I may attain the future blessings of the absolute Dominion
> By praising and singing thee, O Wise One!"[14]

A firm monotheist (one who worships only one god), Zarathustra taught his converts to worship only Ahura Mazda. He is served by six **Amesha Spentas,** who are Vohu Manah, Asha Vahista, Khshatra Vairya, Spenta Armaiti, Hourvatat, and Ameretat. These messengers bridge the gap between the holiness of God and human beings. Amesha Spentas are moral beings who set examples for human morality. They fight against Angra Mainyu and his daevas, or evil forces. R. C. Zaehner refers to them as "aspects of god, but aspects in which man too can share."[15]

These doctrines are essentially those outlined by Sir Rustom Masani, who represents a position acceptable to most Zoroastrians. Many scholars

Amesha Spentas

[u-MEE-shu SPIN-tas]
In Zoroastrianism, the higher spirits directly under Ahura Mazda. They are modes of divine being that bear names of ethical virtues, such as "Good Thought."

agree with Masani's interpretation, though others interpret the claim for Zarathustra's monotheism differently. For example, Jacques Duchesne-Guillemin finds the doctrine of Zarathustra to be that of a theologian. Disagreeing with the theories of J. Darmesteter and H. S. Nyberg, he thinks that Zarathustra's system of ordering the divine is sound philosophy. Zarathustra elevated the Wise Lord and made him the father of other members of a hierarchy. He is Father of Right, the Father of Good Mind. He is also Father of the Holy Spirit, also the Wise Lord—a kind of precursor of the Christian Trinity.[16] He finds this Trinity in the first stanza of Yasna 50:

> What help shall my soul expect from anyone,
> In whom am I to put my trust as a prosecutor for my cattle, in whom for
>   myself, in the invocation,
> But in the Right, in thee, Wise Lord, and the Best Mind?[17]

Humans have a choice between the way of the lie associated with Angra Mainyu and the way of good activity exemplified by the Amesha Spentas. What was the source of Angra Mainyu? For Masani, the evil one was not created by Ahura Mazda nor did he fall from grace. He was present from the beginning. This explanation does not satisfy Cyrus Pangborn that Zarathustra believed in monotheism rather than a dualism.[18] He thinks that Zoroastrian priests and scholars are not interested in settling a very real dispute for objective students of Zoroastrianism.[19]

At death, every person will be judged according to his or her morality and commitment and will be assigned either to Angra Mainyu or to Ahura Mazda. The soul of the person has to cross the **Chinvat Bridge,** which is an instrument of judgment. The followers of good will be rewarded with a life in paradise, and the followers of evil will be rewarded with a life of punishment.

Zoroastrianism After Zarathustra

Later Persian monarchs who embraced Zoroastrianism assisted its international influence.[20] Cyrus, who ruled from 558 to 530 B.C.E and was hailed by the Jewish prophet Isaiah as the Lord's anointed one, may have been a Zoroastrian. Darius, who claimed to be king by will of Ahura Mazda, and Xerxes were strong supporters of the kind of justice advocated by Zoroastrianism.[21] Some Biblical scholars think that belief in angels, heaven and hell, and the resurrection of the dead came to Judaism from Persian influence. A particular priestly group, the **Magi,** came to identify themselves with Zoroastrianism. They are known through their role in the Gospel of Matthew at the birth of the Christ.

The Magi made a very important contribution to the historical development of Zoroastrianism. Through their efforts, the faith was extended throughout the world that was under the influence of Iranian thought. They permitted older Zoroastrianism to be mixed with both Iranian and foreign religious concepts and practices. They emphasized dualism both in cosmic principles and in the conflicts of each human life. The Sassanians, who ruled Persia from the third to the seventh century C.E., were Zoroastrians who changed the faith to incorporate more of the elements rejected by Zarathustra and the Persian kings of the Achaemenid dynasty that began with Cyrus. Their essential refoundation of Zoroastrianism consisted of a revival of the concept of royalty that well served the monarch, the warrior aristocracy, and the priesthood. An Iranian nationalism was supported in a reorganization and canonization of tradition.[22]

Ahura Mazda. This relief sculpture stands on the Apadana at the ruins of Persepolis, residence of Persian kings beginning with Darius.

Chinvat Bridge [CHIN-vaht]
In Zoroastrianism, the bridge of judgment that a soul must walk over after death.

Magi [MAY-jii]
Among the ancient Persians, priests. Their doctrine reduced Ahura Mazda from a transcendent principle to a good spirit, opposed by an evil spirit.

Mani [MAH-nee]
A Persian teacher of religious dualism; he considered himself the Holy Spirit.

Zurvan [ZUR-van]
Among a minority of Zoroastrians, boundless time. It embraces both Ahura Mazda and Angra Mainyu.

Anahita [anna-HEE-tu]
In later Zoroastrianism, a mother goddess who was worshiped with fertility rites.

Haoma [HOE-mu]
In late Zoroastrianism, the divinity of the sacred elixir prepared during Zoroastrian ritual.

Mithra [MITH-ra]
The god of light in Zoroastrianism.

Zarathustra's monotheism was replaced with dualism, a fight between two equally powerful forces. Manichaeism developed from the teachings of **Mani** in the third century C.E. Mani's dualism was between flesh, which was evil, and spirit, which was good. He advocated denying flesh in order to free the spirits imprisoned in it. Manichaean dualism left a deep mark on the Roman Catholic saint Aurelius Augustine, who became bishop of Hippo at the end of the fourth century. Zurvanism attempted to overcome the dualism in Zoroastrianism. The theory was that **Zurvan** was boundless time or space transcending both Ahura Mazda and Angra Mainyu.[23] Zurvanism was rejected later by orthodox Zoroastrians.

Later Zoroastrianism added more deities. Zoroastrians regarded Zarathustra as a god who became a man. Evil forces struggled with the good forces to control the infant Zarathustra. The heavens and hells were filled with good and evil beings struggling over his supernatural deeds. A mother deity, **Anahita,** was added to receive fertility rites. **Haoma,** the recipient of animal sacrifices, and **Mithra,** the god of light, became part of ongoing Zoroastrianism. The final judgment was described in great detail and a kind of universal salvation replaced the sharp eternal division of good and evil.

At first, Muslims did not grant Zoroastrians the status reserved for Jews and Christians—people of the Book. Shortly after the death of Muhammad, Zoroastrians were extended protected status and allowed free practice of their religion. Either for trade or for religious freedom, Zoroastrians migrated to Gujarat in India. Most are now concentrated in Bombay, where they are a small minority among other religions of India.

✍ A POINT OF VIEW

CONSIDER THIS: PERSIANS IN THE BIBLE

In contrast with the Babylonians, Jewish biblical literature praised the Persians and Medes as instruments of God's goodness. They were responsible for humiliating the Babylonians who had burned the Jerusalem temple in 587 B.C.E. and held Judah's leaders in exile. Persian rulers are described in the biblical book of Nehemiah offering state support for rebuilding the walls of Jerusalem and preserving Judaism from encroachment of its enemies. That favorable view extended into the gospel of Matthew in the New Testament. Christians generally believe that the wise men from the East were from Persia.

Study of the religions of Persia are worthwhile apart from their relationships with Jews and Christians. Zoroastrianism in India, Pakistan, and the United States is a tradition from Persia. Much of it deserves praise in itself, apart from the favorable press given it by Jews and Christians. In the future, perhaps Zoroastrianism will be more appreciated within Iran.

WORLDVIEW

The Absolute

The deity worshiped by Zoroastrians is Ahura Mazda. The evil force that opposes God is Angra Mainyu. Whether these two forces are of equal strength is a question that has provided considerable variation in the concept of God throughout the history of Zoroastrianism. If God is ultimately the most powerful, then Angra Mainyu is not an equal force. However, if Angra Mainyu is of equal strength and the struggle is undetermined, then it seems that Zoroastrianism has two gods. This is a problem for any religion that claims both a single, all-powerful God and an opposing personality representing evil. Christianity and Islam have made the devil an opponent to God and subordinate to him. Although the devil may cause great mischief for a time, there is no doubt that in the end God will overcome him. The question remains, then, for non-Zoroastrians, why God ever allowed such a being to endure effectively for a period.

The World

Yasna 44 includes Zarathustra's question-assertions about the creation of the universe:

> 3. This I ask thee, O Lord, answer me truly:
> Who was the first father of Righteousness at the birth?
> Who appointed their path to sun and stars?
> Who but thou is it through whom the moon waxes and wanes?
> This I would know, O Wise One, and other things too!
>
> 4. This I ask thee, O Lord, answer me truly:
> Who set the Earth in its place below, and the sky of the clouds, that it shall
>   not fall?
> Who the waters and the plants?
> Who yoked the two steeds to wind and clouds?
> Who, O Wise One, is the creator of the Good Mind?
>
> 5. This I ask thee, O Lord, answer me truly:
> What artificer made light and darkness?
> What artificer sleep and waking?
> Who made morning, noon, and night,
> To remind the wise man of his task?
>
> 6. This I ask thee, O Lord, answer me truly:
> Whether things are such as I would make them known?
> Shall Devotion by her deeds support the Right?
> Is it as Good Mind that thou hast founded thy Dominion?
> For what men has thou fashioned the mother-cow, the source of good fortune?
>
> 7. This I ask thee, O Lord, answer me truly:
> Who created Devotion, sacred with the Dominion?
> Who made the son reverential in his soul towards his father:
> Thus I strive to recognize in thee, O Wise One,
> As Holy Spirit, the creator of all things.[24]

The world is clean and good. Zoroastrians will not permit a human corpse to contaminate earth, air, fire, or water. Ahura Mazda creates all things for the pleasure of humans. Unlike Mani, Zarathustra did not despise the body or its functions. He advocated responsible use of the world and its creatures, particularly cattle.

Humans

Humans are both soul and body. Personality involves the body as well as the mind. The body should remain under the control of the mind, which makes moral choices. Humans have choices in their actions; they are responsible to God for making moral decisions. Their choices can affect the outcome of the struggle between good and evil. The doctrine of the resurrection of the body emphasizes the importance of the body in personal identity. A living body can be clean and good; when governed by temperance, it is a means for doing good deeds, which are more pleasing to God than sacrifice.

The Problem for Humans

Humans are alienated from God when they choose to violate his law and follow the behavior of Angra Mainyu. There is no karma to build up and hold a soul to a body. Creation of the world and the fall of human beings are not identical. Humans are created by Ahura Mazda to abide by his laws. They can rebel against those laws and serve Angra Mainyu. In this life and in the world to come, there are penalties for those who persist in rebellion against Ahura Mazda.

The Solution for Humans

Reconciliation is effected through the worship of Ahura Mazda and keeping his commandments. Humans choose constantly between the way of good and the way of evil. Choosing good actions brings reconciliation with Ahura Mazda. Throughout life a person must continue to struggle, for final reconciliation is achieved only after a judgment that the individual is worthy of a place in paradise. According to Masani, the Zoroastrian code of ethics requires that humans cultivate civic virtues, **asha,** or spiritual truth, justice, chastity, self-help, planting corn, caring for cattle, compassion for the weak, charity for the poor, promotion of education, and good deeds.

> "Be Like God!" These are the three words in which the entire philosophy of life may be summed up. Likeness to God is the only way of communion with the Heavenly Father. There is no other path of Heaven.[25]

Symbols and Rituals

Hereditary priests are responsible for tending the holy fire in the temple and preparing the haoma every day. Today, Zoroastrians offer daily sacrifices of bread, milk, and sandalwood. New Year's day is a particularly important day for sacrifices. Dressed in their finest clothes, Zoroastrians bring to the fire temple their offerings for the fire, which is not an object of worship but the symbol of Ahura Mazda. During the sacrifice, the priest reads or recites from the Avesta. The priest, his face covered with a mask like a surgeon's, receives the offerings and places them on the fire. Small spoons of ashes are gathered and offered to the worshipers to rub on their foreheads. The priest offers a benediction, and the worshiper is free to depart.

Zoroastrians have a system of rituals for adherents at important points of passage. Adherents enter the religion by birth. Because Zoroastrians emphasize a strong family, they welcome children. After delivering a child, the mother must refrain from touching fire or water and from contacting the materials used in worship. In the seventh year, children participate in **Naozot,** in which they are vested with a sacred shirt called a **sudreh,** and a

asha [ASH-u]
In Zoroastrianism, spiritual truth. Some scholars equate Asha with the Hindu Rita.

Naozot [NAY-ow-zot]
Zoroastrian vesting of a child with a sacred shirt.

sudreh [SHOOD-reh]
The sacred shirt used in vesting a Zoroastrian child.

Parsi Haoma Ritual, India. Only the highest priests can perform this sacramental ritual with the sacred elixir.

sacred thread, or **kusti.** From that time on, the child is expected to offer prayers and fulfill other obligations of the religion. Asceticism is not advocated by Zoroastrians; the normal lifestyle for adults is marriage and family. Faithfulness in marriage is expected by both men and women.

To outsiders first encountering the study of Zoroastrianism, customs surrounding earth compel intense interest. Upon a person's death, the body is washed and placed on hard material, such as stone. The area is marked by a circle drawn with an iron bar or nail, segregating the corpse from the living. A dog with a black spot above each eye is brought to examine whether life in the body is extinct. A vase of fire burns fragrant wood as sacred texts of the Avesta are recited. During daylight hours, two or four corpse-bearers take the iron bier bearing the body to the Tower of Silence **(dakhma).** To avoid contaminating the soil, fire, or water with a corpse, Zoroastrians construct permanent circular towers about twenty feet high. Entering a door with the corpse, the bearers place it on one of three levels, according to whether it is a man, woman, or child. The bearers open the clothes of the corpse and leave. Within a few hours, vultures descend and strip the bones clean. When the bones are clean and dry, they are placed in a central pit of the tower where they crumble into harmless residue. Back at the home, priests pray to Sraosha, the guardian of souls after death. On the third afternoon, there is an Uthamna ceremony in which charity contributions are announced in memory of the deceased. On the dawn after the third night, the soul is prepared to cross the Chinvat Bridge.[26]

Life After Death

Zoroastrians believe that humans are born and die only one time. There is no concept of reincarnation. On the fourth day after death, humans must cross the Chinvat Bridge, the bridge of judgment. For the souls of good thought, the bridge is an easy path to heaven. To souls of evil thought, it is as narrow as the edge of a knife, causing them to fall to perdition. Souls can

kusti [KOOS-ti]
A sacred thread worn to indicate initiation into a religion. Hindus and Zoroastrians use the symbol.

dakhma [DAHK-ma]
A Zoroastrian Tower of Silence used for disposal of corpses of the faithful. It is believed to be necessary because a corpse cannot be allowed to contaminate either soil or fire.

The Navjote Ceremony. The number of holy participants emphasizes the importance of this Zoroastrian initiation.

continue to make progress after death; those who make enough progress will participate in life on a renewed earth. At the last judgment all forces of evil will be defeated, and souls cleansed by punishment will dwell together in a transformed world.

An Interpretation of History

The present struggle is a hard one, with each man's wise choice and actions being needed to sway it; but the issue to Zoroaster's mind was plainly not in doubt. Angra Mainyu and his legions are formidable and inflict harm generally, for even the man who is good by choice cannot escape cruelty and suffering at the hands of others, or afflictions such as famine, disease, bereavement and death. Yet in the end, the prophet was convinced, this dreadful power would be broken, defeated by the unity and positive force of the world of good. Zoroaster's radical dualism, of two separate principles from the beginning, thus ends with the destruction of the evil one, so that Ahura Mazda will finally reign supreme, his sway at last undisputed.[27]

Zoroastrianism emphasizes individual choice for salvation and adds the dimension of eschatology, the doctrine of last things, for all humans, spirits, and deities. In this aspect, Zoroastrianism is similar to the Abraham family of religions. As important as individual salvation is, there is overarching assurance that all history is moving toward a final decision between good and evil. The struggle is long and hard, but believers have no doubt that good will triumph over evil and that Ahura Mazda, the symbol of good, will reign supreme. The earth will be renewed, and all will dwell in a paradise on earth.

Zoroastrianism and Other Religions

J. Hinnells has described the persecution that Zoroastrians have experienced in their long history. They eagerly embraced English education in India and welcomed Christians who studied their religion and culture. In some cases, their tolerance for others has been limited. In particular, they

A Zoroastrian Dakhma. This Tower of Silence is atop a hill in Yard, Iran. According to Zoroastrians, this method of disposal of bodies preserves purity of fire and soil.

have been severe with heretics and have opposed any conversions to their religion. In March 1983, an American, Joseph Peterson, was initiated at the Zoroastrian center in New York. The action was widely opposed in Zoroastrian circles, particularly in Bombay. It must be said that general Zoroastrian sentiment is against any conversion of others to their religion. Hinnells wrote,

> But, if there is one common theme in Zoroastrian attitudes to religious pluralism, it is perhaps a general tolerance to outsiders (though not to others within the walls considered heretics). Throughout recorded history Zoroastrians have balanced a pride in their own religion with an acceptance of religious differences between races.[28]

In modern times, Zoroastrians from both India and Iran have had meetings in Tehran and Bombay. The interest in each other has provided some support and stimulation of faith. However, because Parsees participate in a hereditary tradition and seek no converts, political and sociological adversities have led to dwindling numbers of adherents. The faith that once was so vigorous at the eastern end of the Mediterranean Sea has made its contribution to the Western religions of Judaism, Christianity, and Islam. The emphasis on only one God, high moral laws, choice between good and evil, and rewards for good and punishment for evil influenced those three great religions. Through Persian influence on Judaism and through more direct influence, Zoroastrian thought entered religions of the West. In India, Hindus and Muslims have respected Parsees for their religious and moral integrity.

Our discussion of the ancient religions of Iraq and Iran has brought us to a discussion of Western religions, those from the Middle East. Although they are distinctive, the ancient religions of Iraq and Iran share some beliefs with religions of India and of the Middle East. Having studied the various religions of India and of China and Japan, we turn to three great religions of the West: Judaism, Christianity, and Islam. These three religions belong to one family, whose father, Abraham, descended from an inhabitant of Ur, in Mesopotamia.

VOCABULARY

Ahura Mazda
  [u-HOOR-u MAZ-du]
Amesha Spentas
  [u-MEE-shu SPIN-tas]
Anahita [anna-HEE-tu]
Angra Mainyu
  [ANG-gra MIIN-yu]
asha [ASH-u]
Chinvat Bridge [CHIN-vaht]
dakhma [DAHK-ma]
Damuzi [du-MU-zi]

Ea [eah]
Enkidu [IN-ki-du]
Gilgamesh [GIL-gu-mesh]
Haoma [HOE-mu]
Inanna [in-AHN-nu]
Ishtar [ISH-tar]
kusti [KOOS-ti]
Magi [MAY-jii]
Mani [MAH-nee]
Marduk [MAHR-dook]
Mithra [MITH-ra]

Naozot [NAY-ow-zot]
sudreh [SHOOD-reh]
Tammuz [TAM-muz]
Tiamat [TYU-mut]
Utnapishtim
  [OOT-nu-PISH-tim]
Vohu Manah
  [VOH-hoo-MAH-nu]
Zurvan [ZUR-van]
ziggurats [ZIG-gu-rats]

QUESTIONS FOR REVIEW

1. How did the land between the Tigris and Euphrates rivers affect the religions of city-states of the region?

2. How are Damuzi and Inanna related to Marduk and Tiamat?

3. What is the significance of Utnapishtim in the Epic of Gilgamesh?

4. How does the code of Hammurabi relate to other peoples of the Middle East?

5. Describe Zarathustra's encounter with the Absolute.

6. How did royal sponsorship assist in the development of Zoroastrianism?

7. How did Zoroastrianism relate to royal and popular interests in the Absolute?

8. Describe the importance of good thoughts and deeds in a person's life and death as a Zoroastrian.

9. How do Zoroastrians worship?

10. Describe rites of passage for Zoroastrians.

QUESTIONS FOR DISCUSSION

1. What similarities do you find between Asian religions and religions of ancient Iraq and Iran?

2. What are the major differences that you find between Asian religions and the religions of ancient Iraq and Iran?

3. What are the problems of maintaining monotheism in Zoroastrianism?

4. What is the Zoroastrian definition of the problem of evil, and what is the Zoroastrian solution for the problem?

5. Do you think it is an exaggeration to conclude that Zoroastrianism had considerable influence on religions such as Judaism, Christianity, Islam, and Hinduism? Give some reasons for your answer.

NOTES

1. S. H. Hooke, *Babylonian and Assyrian Religion* (Norman: University of Oklahoma Press, 1963), p. xi.

2. Thorkild Jacobsen, *The Treasures of Darkness* (New Haven, CT: Yale University Press, 1976).

3. James B. Pritchard, *Archaeology and the Old Testament* (Princeton, NJ: Princeton University Press, 1958), chapter 6.

4. Diane Wolkstein and Samuel Noah Kramer, *Inanna* (New York: Harper & Row, 1983), p. 89.

5. Tikva Frymer-Kenski, "Enuma Elish," in *The Encyclopedia of Religion*, vol. 5, ed. Mircea Eliade (New York: Macmillan, 1987), pp. 124–126.

6. William L. Moran, "Gilgamesh," in *The Encyclopedia of Religion*, vol. 5, ed. Mircea Eliade (New York: Macmillan, 1987), pp. 557–560.

7. Alexander Heidel, *The Gilgamesh Epic and Old Testament Parallels* (Chicago: University of Chicago Press, 1949), chapter 4.

8. Jack Finegan, *Light from the Ancient Past* (Princeton, NJ: Princeton University Press, 1946), p. 28.

9. Moran.

10. Thorkild Jacobsen, "Mesopotamian Religions: An Overview," in *The Encyclopedia of Religion*, vol. 9, ed. Mircea Eliade (New York: Macmillan, 1987), pp. 390–446.

11. Hooke, p. 110.

12. R. C. Zaehner, *The Dawn and Twilight of Zoroastrianism* (New York: Putnam's, 1961), p. 33.

13. Sir Rustom Masani, *The Religion of the Good Life* (London: Allen & Unwin, 1954), p. 25; Cyrus R. Pangborn, *Zoroastrianism: A Beleaguered Faith* (Delhi: Vikas, 1982).

14. Jacques Duchesne-Guillemin, ed., *The Hymns of Zarathustra*, trans. M. Henning (London: Murray, 1952), p. 135.

15. Zaehner, p. 46.

16. Duchesne-Guillemin, p. 16.

17. Ibid., p. 29.

18. Pangborn, p. 38.

19. Ibid., p. 48.

20. Jacques Duchesne-Guillemin, Introduction, in *Symbols and Values in Zoroastrianism* (New York: Harper & Row, 1970).

21. Zaehner, p. 155.

22. Gherardo Gnoli, "Zoroastrianism," in *Religions of Antiquity*, ed. Robert M. Seltzer, trans. U. F. Lubin (New York: Macmillan, 1989), p. 143.

23. R. C. Zaehner, *Zurvan* (New York: Biblo and Tannen, 1972), chapter 3.

24. Jacque Duchesne–Guillemin, *The Hymns of Zarathustra*, pp. 65–66.

25. Masani, p. 89, chapter 13.

26. Ibid., pp. 99–105.

27. Mary Boyce, *A History of Zoroastrianism*, vol. 1 (Leiden and New York: Brill, 1989), p. 233.

28. J. Hinnells, "Parsi Attitudes to Religious Pluralism," in *Modern Indian Responses to Religious Pluralism*, ed. Harold G. Coward (Albany: State University of New York Press, 1987), pp. 195–233, 224–225.

✒ READINGS

MESOPOTAMIAN RELIGION, READINGS FOR
RESEARCH AND REPORTS

Cumont, Franz. *The Mysteries of Mithra*. New York: Dover, 1956.

Frymer-Kenski, Tikva. "Enuma Elish." In *The Encyclopedia of Religion*, ed. Mircea Eliade. New York: Macmillan, 1987.

Gardner, John, and John Maier. *Gilgamesh: Translated from the Sin-leqi-unninni Version*. New York: Knopf, 1984.

Heidel, Alexander. *The Gilgamesh Epic and Old Testament Parallels*. Chicago: University of Chicago Press, 1963.

Hooke, S. H. *Babylonian and Asyrian Religion*. Norman: University of Oklahoma Press, 1963.

Jacobsen, Thorkild. *The Treasures of Darkness*. New Haven, CT: Yale University Press, 1976.

Long, J. Bruce. "Underworld." In *The Encyclopedia of Religion*, ed. Mircea Eliade. New York: Macmillan, 1987.

Moran, William L. "Gilgamesh." In *The Encyclopedia of Religion*, ed. Mircea Eliade. New York: Macmillan, 1987.

Ries, Julien. "Immortality." In *The Encyclopedia of Religion*, ed. Mircea Eliade. New York: Macmillan, 1987.

Thomas, Louis-Vincent. "Funeral Rites." In *The Encyclopedia of Religion*, ed. Mircea Eliade. New York: Macmillan, 1987.

ZOROASTRIANISM

Boyce, Mary. *A History of Zoroastrianism*. 2 vols. New York: Brill, 1989. A thorough, recent account of the history of Zoroastrianism.

Duchesne-Guillemin, Jacques. *Zoroastrianism*. New York: Harper & Row, 1970. A concise introduction to Zoroastrianism.

Masani, Rustom. *The Religion of the Good Life*. London: Allen & Unwin, 1954. This older account of Zoroastrianism is helpful, although it lacks the insights of the most recent scholarship.

Zaehner, R. C. *The Dawn and Twilight of Zoroastrianism*. New York: Putnam's, 1961. Zaehner has a clearly written account of the history of Zoroastrianism.

READINGS FOR RESEARCH AND REPORTS

Boyce, Mary, ed. *Textual Sources for the Study of Zoroastrianism*. Totowa, NJ: Barnes & Noble, 1984.

Duchesne-Guillemin, Jacques, ed. *The Western Response to Zoroaster*. Westport, CT: Greenwood Press, 1958.

————. *The Hymns of Zarathustra*, trans. M. Henning. London: Murray, 1952.

Gnoli, Gherardo. "Zoroastrianism." In *Religions of Antiquity*, ed. Robert M. Seltzer, trans. U. F. Lubin. New York: Macmillan, 1989.

Moulton, James Hope. *The Treasure of the Magi*. London: Oxford University Press, 1917.

Pangborn, Cyrus R. *Zoroastrianism, A Beleaguered Faith*. New Delhi: Vikas, 1982.

Zaehner, R. C. *Zurvan*. New York: Biblo and Tannen, 1972.

The Zend-Avesta, trans. James Darmesteter et al. In *Sacred Books of the East*, ed. Max Muller. Delhi: Motilal Banarsidass, 1969.

PART FIVE

Religions of the Family of Abraham

Chapter 8 JUDAISM

Chapter 9 CHRISTIANITY

Chapter 10 ISLAM

About the beginning of the second millennium B.C.E., in ancient Mesopotamia, land of the Tigris and Euphrates rivers, Terah, father of Abraham, set out for Haran, a city on the way to Canaan. At the age of seventy-five, Abraham responded to God's revelation that he should journey to Canaan and there become a great nation, a blessing to all peoples of the earth.

Abraham's two sons, Isaac through Sarah, and Ishmael through her servant Hagar, became patriarchs of nations. God blessed Ishmael as ancestor of the peoples of Arabia; God blessed Isaac as ancestor of the people of Israel. Through centuries of inspired leaders, the ancient faith of Israel developed into Judaism, and after the appearance of the Prophet Muhammad in Mecca in the sixth century C.E., Islam developed in Arabia. Beginning with a descendant of Israel, Jesus, and evolving through the efforts of Paul, Christianity emphasized that the faith of Abraham was a model for Christians to follow.

Only the temporary monotheism of Akhenaton of Egypt seems to have preceded the enduring faith in one God exemplified by Abraham and his descendants. That singleness of faith among descendants of Ishmael and Isaac emerged only after centuries of struggle with polytheism. Contrasted with other families of faith in this text, the family of Abraham was the earliest to emphasize that there is only one God who has no equals, partners, or rivals.

Missionary outreach was present in the faith of Abraham from its earliest days. Members of this family of faith believed that God wanted them to bring other peoples to worship him and follow his teachings. To this day Christianity and Islam fervently seek converts; Judaism, chastened by Christian and Muslim governments, is more subdued in its invitations but equally genuine in its welcomes. All three religions openly advocate, however, that all humans should live by the teachings of God, which are intended for all peoples of the world.

Judaism

Introduction

Before the Rig-Veda was written, the Buddha received enlightenment, Mahavira taught <u>ahimsa</u>, or Confucius revised and added the Chinese classics, Judaism experienced its inception when God appeared to its ancestors, challenging them to follow his commands. Although the written story of Judaism as we know it appeared some centuries later, the first ancestors received God's revelations in Mesopotamia about 1800 B.C.E.

Judaism sparkles with stellar personalities who have dazzled generations of peoples in Europe and the Americas. Abraham, the father of faith, raised sons Isaac, who became the father of Israel, and Ishmael, who became father of the Arab peoples. Joseph, son of Israel, sold as a slave, became second only to the pharaoh of Egypt, saving a whole region from starvation through his shrewd agricultural policies. After a period of decline and suffering of Hebrews in Egypt, Moses, under God, led his people from slavery to the threshold of abundant life in God's promised land to Israel, later known as Palestine. Joshua used strategy, tactics, and God's power to defeat many walled cities of the Canaanites, such as Jericho. David, the king, established Jerusalem as his center and incorporated the mighty Philistines into a peaceful coalition. His son, Solomon, negotiated with foreign leaders who brought religious, economic, and diplomatic forces to an apex unequaled before or since in Judaism. Great prophets such as Isaiah, Jeremiah, and Ezekiel inspired not only return to God's covenant in Torah, but also fresh visions of individual freedoms and responsibilities for the future. Psalms and songs from David and Solomon inspired poets, musicians, and religious leaders. All these men were supported, and sometimes led, by remarkable women such as Sarah, Rebekah, Deborah, Bathsheba, and Esther.

A Scribe Copies a Torah Scroll. Hebrew characters are read from right to left.

Because Judaism did not end with the closure of the text of the Bible, about 200 C.E., there are dozens of other outstanding personalities who have molded its faith and influenced larger civilizations. Yohannan ben Zakkai escaped Roman destruction of Jerusalem to organize rabbis in compelling discussions of Torah that culminated in the remarkable Babylonian Talmud. Maimonides wrote in both Hebrew and Arabic as he explained Judaism for medieval scholars, all the while supporting himself as the trusted physician to the Muslim emperor Saladin. Golda Meir was an influential prime minister of the young state of Israel. These names are only a sampling of the widely acclaimed persons who have influenced Judaism in its ancient and modern forms.

Fewer than twenty million Jews inhabit the earth. Their influence, and that of their ancestors, however, has been so immense, that Judaism is traditionally counted as one of the major world religions. Important in its own right, the study of Judaism is also needed to explain the development of both Christianity and Islam, which also worship the God of Abraham.

The Jewish Bible

The Jewish Bible **(Tanakh)** is the sacred book that interprets history as Jews have experienced it. Although it is proper to think of the Bible as a single book of scriptures, it is more accurate to describe it as a library of books assembled under three major headings. Most important is the **Torah,** which means divine instruction and guidance. Its books are Genesis, Exodus, Leviticus, Numbers, and Deuteronomy. The Prophets (Nevi'im) are divided into the former prophets: Joshua, Judges, First and Second Samuel, and First and Second Kings; and the latter prophets: Isaiah, Jeremiah, Ezekiel, and the twelve, who are Hosea, Joel, Amos, Obadiah, Jonah, Micah, Nahum, Habakkuk, Zephaniah, Haggai, Zechariah, and Malachi. The Writings (Kethuvim) are Psalms, Proverbs, Job, and the Festal Scrolls: Song of Songs, Ruth, Lamentations, Ecclesiastes, and Esther. Daniel, Ezra, Nehemiah, and First and Second Chronicles complete the list.[1] This is the canon (official collection) prepared by the rabbis in Yavneh about 90 C.E.

The Bible is the foundation on which a Jewish life is built. It traces God's activities in beginning the world, in calling a family from Mesopotamia who would respond to the progressive revelation of his will, and in establishing a nation of Jewish families responsible above all other peoples to demonstrate God's requirements and blessings for all peoples of the earth. It is the story of the education of a people who have a special mission to be

> A covenant people, a light of nations—
> Rescuing prisoners from confinement,
> From the dungeon those who sit in darkness. (Isaiah 42:6, 7)

In the Bible, maturity emerges through suffering, and leadership in faith is earned in schools of rigorous experience. In the rapidly vanishing moments of human lives, eternal truths are revealed.

Interpreting the Bible

The Bible has been understood in two very different ways. For most of history, and by most people today, it has been regarded as a document from

Tanakh [ta-NAK]
The complete Jewish Bible, comprising three parts: Torah, the five books of Moses; Nevi'im, the prophets; and Kethuvim, the writings. The first letters of the three terms yield Tanakh.

Torah [TOR-ah]
Teachings that comprise the first five books of the Bible: Genesis, Exodus, Leviticus, Numbers, and Deuteronomy.

God that is without error. Because it is not the product of humans, it is a reliable guide of God's requirements and promises. It is a factual account of history. This understanding of the Bible may be labeled "conservative" or "traditional."

The second way of understanding the Bible assigns a greater human role in its origin. The Bible, in this interpretation, is a record of human encounters with God. Their revelatory experiences and their responses to them form the traditions of the Bible. Although in this tradition the words of the Bible are not literal words of God, they are words expressing human understanding of God's revelation. Because it assigns to humans a more prominent role in producing the Bible, this approach has sometimes been labeled "liberal" or "critical." Many books, of which R. E. Friedman's *Who Wrote the Bible?* (1987) is only one example, have been produced over the last century and a half to explain this different interpretation. This interpretation will be described in more detail later.

Although people may differ on interpretation of the Bible, they begin with its accounts of events. Only when we know the accounts can we begin to interpret. In all the religions of the Near East, I will emphasize the account in the scriptures. All readers can recall that there are both conservative and liberal interpretations for every account. In Judaism, too, I will report the scriptural accounts at face value, allowing readers to decide how to interpret them.

The Bible orders accounts according to historical development. The worldview of Judaism grows out of the historical development. The worldview of Abraham was not the full-blown worldview of modern Judaism. The worldview of Judaism that began in the Bible has continued to develop for another two thousand years. To understand the worldview of Judaism, we study its historical development. In the Bible, however, we do not have history as historians today write it. German scholars had a word for biblical accounts—*heilsgeschichte*, salvation history. The Bible, they thought, is an interpretation of the events of history in light of their religious significance for Jews.

HISTORICAL DEVELOPMENT

Although Judaism's history is celebrated by both Jews and Christians, its interpretation has been divisive and controversial. One question is, When did Judaism begin? With creation of the world more than five thousand years ago, or with the exodus from Egypt? Did Judaism proper begin in Jerusalem after leaders returned from exile in Babylon, or only after the destruction of the Temple in 70 C.E.? All Jews agree that present-day Judaism is not confined to beliefs and practices that Christians read in their "Old Testament." Whether Orthodox in Israel or Reform in the United States, Judaism today is different from much of the religion that is reported in the Bible. Our challenge is to examine not only the biblical accounts but also the historical developments since the Bible was closed to new books.

Historiography

Two approaches dominate the historical studies of Judaism. One approach, which is more widely known and practiced, is traditional salvation history. God does all good things, and after the earliest days of creation, acts with and through individual humans to accomplish his purposes. Thus all events of history are influenced by God and cannot be understood apart from his will. In this view, the Bible itself, particularly Torah, is the word of God. Records of all events, including the creation of heaven and earth, are reliably provided by God. The other approach considers Judaism's development from the point of view of humanistic studies that include other peoples of the Middle East, Europe, and the Americas.

The more humanistic accounts of Jewish history emphasize a variety of oral traditions, periodic collecting, editing, and selecting for preservation. The achievements, failures, and sufferings of Jews are analyzed as humanists explain events in other cultures and histories. Although the humanist approach recognizes Judaism as a remarkable and impressive religion, it is hardly without parallels in development. These two different approaches to the history of Judaism also influence interpretation of its most important source, the Bible.

Abraham

The dramatic history of Judaism, which gives it a unique identity, focuses on encounter, a searching God confronting human beings in the progressing stream of time. In the third millennium B.C.E., God appeared in Haran and encountered Abraham, the son of Terah, a man who came there from Ur of the Chaldeans. God challenged Abraham to emigrate to the land surrounding the Sea of Galilee and the Dead Sea.

1. The Lord said to Abram, "Go forth from your native land and from your father's house to a land that I will show you.

2. I will make of you a great nation,
   And I will bless you;
   I will make your name great,
   And you shall be a blessing.

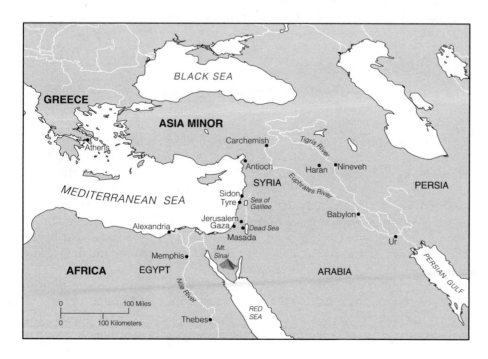

Locations of Biblical and First-Century C.E. Judaism. Although Jews settled primarily in the land around the Sea of Galilee, the Dead Sea, and the Jordan River, they also settled for periods of time in Egypt and in Mesopotamia.

3. I will bless those who bless you
And curse him that curses you;
And all the families of the earth
Shall bless themselves by you." (Genesis 12:1–3)

Having faith in God, Abraham, his wife Sarah, and Haran's son Lot began a migration to the land of promise located at the lower eastern end of the Mediterranean Sea. There he settled into a nomadic life among the local inhabitants, differing from them not only in his heritage but also in his covenant relationship with his God. If he would be faithful to his God, God promised that his descendants would inherit the land in which he was grazing his flocks. The covenant, a contract without a date of expiration, was sealed by the slaying of valuable animals, drawing their blood, and exposing their flesh to flames.

Sacrifice was the act of worship used by Abraham and his descendants. Something of value—sheep, goats, or cattle—the very means of survival for nomads, was killed, and its blood (life) was poured out to demonstrate the worshiper's bond to God, who gives life. The animal flesh was then placed on hot coals, so that its flames and smoke (essence) rose toward the sky. Sacrifice removed doubt, impediments, and any alienation between worshipers and God. It sealed a **covenant** in which each participant had duties to perform and rewards to receive. Only after the destruction of the Jerusalem temple by Romans in 70 C.E. did Judaism omit animal sacrifice as a central act of worship.

Abraham's covenant with God was continued through his son with Sarah, Isaac. God enabled Sarah, who had been barren, to bear Isaac.

The son of Hagar and Abraham, Ishmael, departed to another land, where he would become a respected leader of the Arabs. Isaac's son Jacob had twelve sons, and eventually he was also known as Israel. The covenant was preserved through the twelve sons of Israel, each of whom became head of a tribe of the children of Israel. Joseph, a favorite son of Israel, became viceroy of Egypt. During a time of famine, Pharaoh invited Joseph's father, his brothers, and their families to settle in Egypt. Due to a change of Pharaohs after the death of Joseph, the Egyptians enslaved the Israelites.

Life Under the Egyptians

The children of Abraham and of Israel lived often among the Egyptians. During the lifetime of Joseph they were honored residents who followed their own culture and religion. The Hebrews knew, from the days of Abraham, that Egyptians worshiped gods and goddesses that represented sun, earth, water, and changing seasons, the forces essential in agriculture. City-states along the Nile depended on the seasonal overflow of the river and the sun to sustain the lives of humans and domestic animals. Joseph, who married an Egyptian, may have used these Egyptian beliefs to build reserves of grain against years of drought, but there is no evidence that he abandoned his own God in favor of Egyptian deities. Hebrews explained the workings of the world in terms of the God of Abraham, Isaac, and Jacob; they did not require Egyptian explanations.

The center of attention of Egyptian religion presented in the Bible is Pharaoh. Egyptians considered any pharaoh both a god and a representative of the gods. The image of Pharaoh in the Bible is negative. The dynasty that elevated Joseph was overthrown; a new dynasty instituted a policy of

covenant [CUV-u-nunt] The binding agreement between God and his chosen people. The covenant was repeatedly renewed. Unlike a contract, the covenant had no date of expiration.

CHAPTER EIGHT

repressing Hebrews. Although the Bible describes Hebrew suffering in some detail, it fails to give enough evidence for modern scholars to identify with certainty the name and dynasty of the pharaoh who first turned against the Hebrews. Through the pathos of the biblical account it is clear that Pharaoh was so powerful that only God could prevail against him. The pharaoh of the exodus has been identified by many scholars as Ramses II, of the Nineteenth Dynasty, who lived about 1290–1224 B.C.E.

Moses

The laws that are part of the Torah were brought to the Hebrews by God's chosen leader, Moses. Moses was an exemplary man of God. As leader of the Hebrews, he not only received the Torah but also established a system to institute it among God's people. Born to Hebrew slaves and hidden in the bulrushes by his mother to escape annihilation, just as the Egyptian goddess Isis hid her child, Horus, from his hateful uncle, Moses grew up in Pharaoh's court, supervised by Pharaoh's daughter. Made an outlaw by Pharaoh for killing an Egyptian who harassed a Hebrew, Moses escaped to Midian, where he lived with a priest and his daughters. God came to Moses as he kept the flocks of Reuel, his father-in-law.

> 3:2. An angel of the Lord appeared to him in a blazing fire out of a bush. He gazed, and there was a bush all aflame, yet the bush was not consumed.
> 3. Moses said, "I must turn aside to look at this marvelous sight; why doesn't the bush burn up?" 4. When the Lord saw that he had turned aside to look, God called to him out of the bush: "Moses! Moses!" He answered, "Here I am."
> 5. And He said, "Do not come closer. Remove the sandals from your feet, for the place on which you stand is holy ground. 6. I am," He said, "the God of your father, the God of Abraham, the God of Isaac, and the God of Jacob." And Moses hid his face, for he was afraid to look at God.
> 7. And the Lord continued, "I have marked well the plight of My people in Egypt and have heeded their outcry because of their taskmasters; yes, I am mindful of their sufferings. 8. I have come down to rescue them from the Egyptians and to bring them out of that land to a good and spacious land, a land flowing with milk and honey, the region of the Canaanites, the Hittites, the Amorites, the Perizzites, the Hivites, and the Jebusites. 9. Now the cry of the Israelites has reached Me; moreover, I have seen how the Egyptians oppress them. 10. Come, therefore, I will send you to Pharaoh, and you shall free My people, the Israelites, from Egypt." (Exodus 3:2–10)

God revealed himself to Moses as Ehyeh-Asher-Ehyeh (Exodus 3:14). The Hebrew meaning is uncertain; it is variously translated "I Am That I Am"; "I Am Who I Am"; "I Will Be What I Will Be."[2] He called Moses to become leader of God's chosen people, to deliver them from Pharaoh. Moses became a successful instrument of theocracy, God's rule of a people through a human leader. Moses knew God as few men have known him, and God used him as few men have been used (Deuteronomy 34:10).

Moses was chosen by God to deliver the Hebrews from slavery in Egypt and was given divine assistance at crucial points. A series of ten plagues convinced Pharaoh that he should let the Hebrews go. The last plague, in which the angel of death killed all Egyptian firstborn sons but passed over the homes of Hebrews without harming them, is still recalled in their holiday **Passover.** By a mighty act of God, the Hebrews crossed the Red Sea on dry ground, but the waters returned in time to drown Pharaoh's army. The Hebrews were guided by a pillar of cloud by day and a pillar of fire by

Passover [PASS-o-ver]
A Jewish holiday in the spring. It celebrates God's deliverance of the Hebrews from slavery in Egypt during the time of Moses.

night as they crossed the Sinai Peninsula. They were fed by manna and quail on an almost daily schedule, and water was also provided miraculously. The Hebrews were not only chosen by God, according to Jewish sacred history, but also miraculously supported by him against enemies, both human and natural.

The events of the first Passover occurred in Egypt about 1300–1200 B.C.E. The Passover meal, based on the one in Exodus 12, is celebrated in the spring. Unleavened bread, called **matzah,** is baked to symbolize the bread prepared and eaten in haste before the Hebrew slaves escaped from Pharaoh. Other dishes of food in the meal symbolize the slaves' work with bricks and their tears shed because of the harsh treatment they received from slave masters. During each meal, the story of Hebrew deliverance from Egypt is recited and explained so that each new generation is incorporated into the covenant people whom God delivered through a power far superior to that of Egypt's Pharaoh or nature.

The summit of experience for the Hebrews under Moses was the receiving of the commandments of God, given by God to Moses on the top of Mt. Sinai. Essentially, the covenant between God and his people was renewed. If the Hebrews would serve God exclusively, he would give them a promised land and make them a great nation. If they accepted the promise, they had obligations to fulfill that were moral, ceremonial, and cultural. All life was to be lived under the command of God, a theocracy. God appointed human leaders through whom he was represented to the people. His mighty acts in history, however, are apparent to all humans. The symbol of his presence was the **Ark of the Covenant,** a wooden chest containing the stones bearing the Ten Commandments; in processions, the Ark was carried by priests. These commandments in Exodus were distinctive in the government of the Hebrews.

1. God spoke all these words, saying:

2. I the Lord am your God, who brought you out of the land of Egypt, the house of bondage:

3. You shall have no other gods besides Me.

4. You shall not make for yourself a sculptured image, or any likeness of what is in the heavens above, or on the earth below, or in the waters under the earth.

5. You shall not bow down to them or serve them. For I the Lord your God am an impassioned God, visiting the guilt of the parents upon the children, upon the third and upon the fourth generations of those who reject Me,

6. But showing kindness to the thousandth generation of those who love Me and keep My commandments.

7. You shall not swear falsely by the name of the Lord your God; for the Lord will not clear one who swears falsely by His name.

8. Remember the sabbath day and keep it holy.

9. Six days you shall labor and do all your work,

10. But the seventh day is a sabbath to the Lord your God: you shall not do any work—you, your son, or daughter, your male or female slave, or your cattle, or the stranger who is within your settlements.

11. For in six days the Lord made heaven and earth and sea, and all that is in them, and He rested on the seventh day; therefore the Lord blessed the sabbath day and hallowed it.

12. Honor your father and your mother, that you may long endure on the land that the Lord your God is assigning to you.

matzah [MUT-za]
(pl. *matzot*) Unleavened bread eaten by Jews during the Passover. During Passover, no leaven should be present in a Jewish home.

Ark of the Covenant
A box containing the Ten Commandments. Priests carried it in processions and then housed it in the tabernacle.

13. You shall not murder.
   You shall not commit adultery.
   You shall not steal.
   You shall not bear false witness against your neighbor.

14. You shall not covet your neighbor's house; you shall not covet your neighbor's wife, or his male or female slave, or his ox or his ass, or anything that is your neighbor's. (Exodus 20:1–14)

There were penalties for failing to keep the law that extended to several generations, just as there were rewards for keeping the law that extended to future generations.

The Ten Commandments and their interpretations are part of a larger discussion of moral, ceremonial, and cultural laws contained in four books of the Torah: Exodus, Leviticus, Numbers, and Deuteronomy. These books, together with Genesis, the book that describes the beginning of creation, humans, and the ancestors of the Jewish people, constitute the sacred books that Jews still read in their services of worship and study in their homes and schools.

A passage in the Torah known as the **Shema,** the commandment in Deuteronomy 6:4–9 that begins "Hear," directs adherents of Judaism:

> **Shema** [SHEE-ma]
> Hear. The beginning word of Deuteronomy 6:4, "Hear, O Israel!" A declaration of God's unity, it is recited twice daily.

4. Hear O Israel! The Lord is our God, the Lord alone.
5. You shall love the Lord your God with all your heart and with all your soul and with all your might.
6. Take to heart these instructions with which I charge you this day.
7. Impress them upon your children. Recite them when you stay at home and when you are away, when you lie down and when you get up.
8. Bind them as a sign upon your hand and let them serve as a symbol on your forehead;
9. Inscribe them on the doorposts of your house and on your gates.

Settlement in Canaan

The religion that developed in the Sinai Peninsula was an ideal form that was severely tested under practical conditions in Canaan. For the descendants of the former slaves in Egypt, their entry was a return of the children of Israel to join their people who remained in Canaan. The initial entry of the Hebrews into Canaan was announced by a series of battles against the Canaanites.

Under Joshua's leadership, the battles were won with assistance from God. However, few fortified cities were conquered immediately, and the nomadic Hebrews settled in open country, competing with the agricultural developments of the natives. Hebrew life was organized around twelve tribal leaders, descendants of the children of Israel.

> **Canaanites** [kay-nu-NIGHTS]
> The people among whom the Israelites settled on their return from slavery in Egypt. Canaan comprised the area bordered by the Sea of Galilee, the Jordan River, and the Dead Sea.

This loose federation was occasionally strengthened by the timely appearances of folk heroes, the judges, who championed the Hebrew cause against local oppressors. The real threat to Hebrew survival, which was centered in the worship of their God, came through the fertility rites that the **Canaanites** practiced in order to influence their deities **Baal** and **Asherah** to produce crops. Canaanite worship included bowing to idols. Since making statues and worshiping idols were activities clearly in violation of the Ten Commandments, the Hebrew religious leaders constantly denounced Hebrew participation in Canaanite worship.

> **Baal** [BAA-ul]
> A god or gods of Canaan. Baals were landlords or keepers of the land. Canaanites worshipped them to make crops grow.

For a very few centuries in Jewish history, human kings were chosen to give greater visibility to the nation among other nations, who were not always impressed by a theocracy led by a prophet or seer, such as Samuel.

> **Asherah** [ash-u-RAH]
> A goddess of Canaan and a counterpart to the male god, Baal. She was another example of the Mediterranean mother goddess.

(A seer is one who foretells the future through oracles.)[3] In succession, Saul, David, and Solomon built an expanded earthly kingdom by subduing ancient Hebrew enemies and forming alliances and trade agreements with many foreign powers.

David is a major figure in Judaism, a hero to his own age and a model of any deliverer of Israel. He defeated the Philistines who had plagued the Israelites and killed King Saul and his son Jonathan. He won Jerusalem and established it as the center of religion and government. He brought the Ark of the Covenant to the city and projected building the first temple to replace the sacred tent or tabernacle. In the collection of Psalms, the hymns of worship of Israel, many are labeled "A Psalm of David." He is credited not only with composing words and music but also with playing the harp and organizing musical groups who helped lead the worship of God.

Solomon, son of David and Bathsheba, built on his father's successes. In times of peace he reached out to neighboring countries to form alliances and trading partnerships. Wealth poured into his palace in Jerusalem. Judaism honors him for building the first temple in Jerusalem. He generously consecrated it by having priests and Levites sacrifice a staggering number of animals. Under Solomon, the Hebrews reached their height of political and economic power. To support beautiful architecture and a handsome lifestyle, Solomon instituted forced labor and heavy taxes. Rehoboam's continuation of Solomon's heavy tax program led to a revolt by the ten northern tribes, who established a rival capital for religion and state in Samaria. In the forsaking of a unified worship of God and a unified kingdom, many religious leaders foresaw disaster for the Hebrews.

The Hebrew Prophets

prophet [PROF-it] A person inspired by God to speak in his name. In Hebrew history, prophets in groups gave way to the messages of individual prophets such as Isaiah, Jeremiah, and Ezekiel.

Hebrew **prophets** established a pattern for a different kind of holy man in Hebrew life. The words they spoke were not their own; they were prefaced "Thus said the Lord." (Prophets are those men who feel called to speak for God.) In Judaism, their message was that the only way to avert national

David's Tomb. This sacred place on Mt. Zion in Jerusalem memorializes King David.

CHAPTER EIGHT

and personal disaster was through exclusive devotion to the God of Abraham, Isaac, Jacob, and Moses that was required in the Torah. Part of that devotion, emphasized by priests, entailed keeping the regulations of worship in the temple and observance of regulations on hygiene and diet in the home. Another part, emphasized by prophets, required a scrupulous application of laws on individual rights and social responsibilities.

The earliest prophets were men found in groups who stimulated ecstatic experiences. Later individuals stood apart from the groups and, in the name of God, criticized the immoral acts of monarchs. The prophet Elijah stirred revenge in Queen Jezebel by defeating Baal prophets and condemning King Ahab's murderous seizing of a vineyard belonging to his neighbor Naboth. Elijah performed dramatic public acts, such as a contest with Baal prophets on Mt. Carmel to demonstrate whose deity would send down fire from heaven to consume a prepared sacrifice. Baal failed to light a fire; God answered Elijah's prayers and consumed not only the sacrifice but also the stones on which it rested. Later, the voice of God came to Elijah not in earthquake, wind, or fire, but in the stillness of a mountain cave.

After King David had conspired to have Uriah the Hittite killed to cover up his adultery with Uriah's wife, Bathsheba, the prophet Nathan confronted his king. Nathan told a simple story of a rich man who slayed a neighbor's pet lamb to feed his guest. In a rage, King David said to Nathan, "As the Lord lives, the man who did this deserves to die!" Nathan answered, "That man is you." Nathan proceeded to tell David the word of God: "the sword shall never depart from your House" (II Samuel 12:1–12). The prophets believed that God's law was above prophets, priests, and yes, kings.

In the eighth century B.C.E., about 750, four prophets appeared with messages that left permanent imprints on Judaism. Amos, a prophet from the Southern Kingdom, prophesied in Bethel, of the Northern Kingdom, denouncing extreme inequalities among the economic classes of Hebrews. A nation could not survive such injustices among its people. Unless the people voluntarily restored justice in their relationships, God would use other nations as a scourge to discipline their rebellion against his law. Amos is remembered for his ringing challenge:

> But let justice well up like water,
> Righteousness like an unfailing stream. (Amos 5:24)

Hosea used his unfaithful wife as an illustration of Israel's unfaithfulness to God. As Hosea sought to restore his marriage by rehabilitating Gomer, so God, in strong love, sought to renew his marriage with Israel. Isaiah, in response to an awesome experience of God in the Jerusalem temple, challenged King Ahaz to avoid alliances with infidel kingdoms and meet an invasion threat with trust in the Lord. God told Isaiah not to follow the people but to trust only in God:

> None but the Lord of Hosts
> Shall you account holy;
> Give reverence to Him alone,
> Hold Him alone in awe. (Isaiah 8:13)

The nature of God and his relationship with Israel requires more than exact ceremonial observances, wrote the prophet Micah:

> He has told you, O man, what is good;
> And what the Lord requires of you:
> Only to do justice

And to love goodness,
And to walk modestly with your God;
Then will your name achieve wisdom. (Micah 6:8–9)

People listened to the prophets; some took their messages to heart. But many messages of the prophets remained unheeded at the time they were delivered. Some prophets were denounced by their contemporary leaders, only to be honored by most people in later generations. The destruction of the Northern Kingdom, followed a few decades later by the exile of leaders of the Southern Kingdom, caused the Jews who survived exile to have new respect for the old messages of the prophets.

Destroyed Kingdoms, Exiled Leaders

The destructions that came on the divided kingdoms left an enduring imprint on later Judaism. The ten northern tribes were conquered in 721 B.C.E by the Assyrians from Mesopotamia and carried away to be dispersed and replaced by immigrants of other peoples sent by the Assyrians. Only the Southern Kingdom survived. A few years later, in 701, they were besieged in Jerusalem. They were delivered when supernatural powers came to their aid.

> That night an angel of the Lord went out and struck down one hundred and eighty-five thousand in the Assyrian camp. . . . So King Sennacherib of Assyria broke camp and retreated, and stayed in Nineveh. (II Kings 19:35–36)

Jews interpret this deliverance of their pivotal city as God's fulfillment of his promise to King David.

However, survival was only for 115 years, and another Mesopotamian power, the Babylonians, conquered Judah and took Hebrew leaders and upper classes to settle in Babylon in two stages, 597 and 586 B.C.E. The temple was destroyed. Only a puppet state survived.

Life of Babylonian Exiles

In 597 B.C.E., Nebuchadnezzar, king of Babylon, exiled to Babylon the first group of Hebrew palace staff, military officers, aristocrats, and intellectuals, numbering approximately ten thousand, and their families. He returned for the remnant left in Jerusalem, except the poor, who were left to till the land. Spirits of the captives were very low, for they had been separated from their land and their temple.

Psalm 137:1–6 records the mood of the exiles:

1. By the rivers of Babylon,
      there we sat,
      sat and wept,
      as we thought of Zion.

2. There on the poplars
      we hung up our lyres,

3. for our captors asked us there for songs
      our tormentors, for amusement,
      "Sing us one of the songs of Zion."

4. How can we sing a song of the Lord
      on alien soil?

5. If I forget you, O Jerusalem,
      let my right hand wither;

Hebrew Book of Abraham. This first page was printed by Eliesser Toledano, in Lisbon, in 1489.

CHAPTER EIGHT

6. Let my tongue stick to my palate
   if I cease to think of you,
   if I do not keep Jerusalem in memory
   even in my happiest hour.

The Hebrew leaders were among them, however, and they soon found constructive ways to employ their time in a situation that would continue for generations.

Editing the Scriptures

With the temple destroyed, the priests favored the Torah. According to most scholars, the priests not only studied the scriptures but also revised them. There are some Bible scholars who believe that God dictated directly to Moses the Torah as it is today. But there is a strong scholarly movement, perhaps the mainstream of biblical scholarship, that takes a different view.

In their efforts to understand the Bible as deeply as possible, scholars have disputed not only the proper meaning of words and passages but also the nature of the literature itself. In the nineteenth century C.E., some scholars in Germany asked questions that led to a revolution in the interpretation of the Torah. How reliable is the Torah as a history of the Jewish people? Were the patriarchs, such as Abraham, real people, or were they fictional characters representing the ideals of later generations of Jews?

Wellhausen, a German scholar, saw the Genesis stories as unreliable history, reflecting the ideals of a period long after Moses. The effect of the Wellhausen approach to the Torah was to undermine its value as a reliable account of the persons and events of Jewish history.

A reaction to this doubting the Torah led to an opposite position—that the Torah is in every sense a reliable historical document. This position is represented by Yehezkel Kaufmann. Other scholars turned to archaeological evidence patiently gathered from sites in Mesopotamia, Egypt, the Sinai Peninsula, and the ancient land of Canaan. After considering both the text and archaeological evidence, Abraham Malamat writes,

> In examining the historical authenticity of the patriarchal traditions, one is instantly struck by their twofold nature, alluded to in our opening remarks on Israel's protohistory. On the one hand, they contain early, authentic material and, on the other, late, anachronistic conceptions.[4]

Torah materials, archaeology, and the study of epigrams enable scholars to construct a reliable history of the Jews. Archaeological excavations of sites have yielded evidence that supports many of the accounts in the Torah and other books of the Bible.

Although these scholars have differences of emphasis and interpretation, they agree that to form the Torah, priestly editors combined at least three documents. One is the *J* account or document, so labeled because the author refers to God as *Yahweh* (early German scholars used a *j* instead of a *y*). A second account used the term *Elohim* for God—it is labeled *E*. The third document, *D*, is Deuteronomy, found in the temple in the seventh century B.C.E. A fourth source of information is labeled *P*, for *priestly*, because it contains so much priestly legislation. The Torah is the edited account based on the three major documents. The accounts do not exist separately now; finding two accounts of the same event in the Bible gives some insight into the documents and the editing. In Babylon, much of the Torah was available to be used in instruction and in a new form of worship.

A few scholars think that Ezra, who arrived in Jerusalem in 458 B.C.E., completed the Torah.

An Alternative to Temple Worship

In Babylon, the seeds for the surviving tree of Judaism, which would last until the present day, were planted. An alternative to temple worship was instituted so that the exiles could worship in a strange land. The new institution took the form of a congregation. In later centuries congregations were housed in buildings that were known by the Greek term *synagogue*. Any group of ten Jewish men could form a congregation to worship God without the use of a priest or animal sacrifice. A layman could read the Torah and comment on it. A person who studied the Torah and commented on it was revered as a teacher, or **rabbi.** Prayers and hymns accompanied the reading and interpretation of the Torah, and Judaism emerged as a religion that could be practiced either with animal sacrifices in the Jerusalem temple or in congregations that met almost anywhere. The mode of worship was not an issue between rabbis and priests; their main concern was to find ways to unify the people.

Congregational worship was led not by priests but by laymen. Ritual focused not on a burning altar but on truth in a book. The Torah scrolls, God's words for Israel, were the visible and audible center of attention. Worshipers offered hymns and prayers to God; he spoke through the Torah as it was read by laymen and commented on by scholars of the scriptures. Those who worshiped were introduced to an experience similar to Isaiah's in the temple (Isaiah 6:1–13), praising God's holiness and being challenged to live as if on a mission from God.

Postexilic Judaism

Although exiles succeeded in worshiping God without the temple, they had serious questions about their loss of homes and temple. Preserving the

rabbi [RAB-eye]
In Judaism, a teacher. After 70 C.E., rabbis were ordained interpreters and leaders of Judaism.

Synagogue, Capernaum, Israel. This 4th century C.E. ruin in Galilee remained through the twentieth century.

Jewish faith required leaders to issue a **theodicy,** a rational explanation why in spite of their suffering Jews should still worship God. Some reasonable meaning for the national tragedy had to be given, or traditional faith in God would fade before the proven strength of Marduk, god of Babylon. Isaiah, Jeremiah, and Ezekiel were the names of prophets attached to scrolls that interpreted the sufferings of Judah. These prophets pictured God as being in charge of the vast international rise and fall of powers. He had not been overpowered by Marduk, but he used the Babylonians to discipline and purify his people, the Hebrews. He chastised the unreliable shepherds of Israel (their leaders) and would revive a people from the dead bones of the old nation (Ezekiel 37:3). Each person would answer to God for his or her own deeds, and the law would be internalized in human hearts rather than housed in vast social institutions:

theodicy [THEE-od-i-se]
A justification, in the presence of evil, of God's goodness, justice, and knowledge. How can an all-good, all-powerful, and all-knowing God allow evil?

> But such is the covenant I will make with the House of Israel after these days— declares the Lord: I will put my teaching into their inmost being and inscribe it upon their hearts. Then I will be their God, and they shall be My people. (Jeremiah 31:33)

When Cyrus of Persia defeated the Babylonians and permitted the Jews to return to Judea, the prophet Isaiah hailed him as the anointed of the Lord (Isaiah 45:1). Bearing the same name as the eighth-century prophet, this prophet of the sixth century is sometimes called the second Isaiah. Most scholars designate chapters 40 through 66 of Isaiah as Second Isaiah. In beautiful poetry, Isaiah challenges the exiles to prepare for return to their homeland:

> Comfort, oh comfort My people,
> Says your God.
> Speak tenderly to Jerusalem,
> And declare to her
> That her term of service is over,
> That her iniquity is expiated;
> For she has received at the hand of the Lord
> Double for all her sins. (Isaiah 40:1–2)

The theological view that God was in charge of history made the Jews more cosmopolitan in their understanding of international affairs and at the same time more determined than ever to maintain their distinctive heritage.

Ezra, a **scribe** (one who is a scholar of the Torah), and Nehemiah, a governor appointed by Artaxerxes of Persia, cooperated to reestablish Jerusalem and renew the covenant with God. Nehemiah succeeded in organizing Jews in Judah to rebuild the walls of Jerusalem. He selected people to move into the city, organized defenses against jealous non-Jews, and persuaded Jews of substance to offer interest-free loans to their Jewish neighbors in need. In 444 B.C.E., in the courtyard of the second temple, finished in 515 B.C.E., Ezra read the Torah to the congregation. The people agreed to keep all the commandments, ordinances, and statutes of the Lord. Through the renewal of the covenant between the Jews and God, the bitter years of Babylonian exile were replaced with a fresh hope for a better future in the homeland of the Jews.

scribe [SCRIIB]
From the centuries after the Babylonian captivity of the Jews, a scribe was a trained scholar, particularly in Torah studies.

The Greeks

Purity was almost impossible to maintain among people living in a corridor through which kings periodically marched to and from war. It was only a matter of time until the Greeks replaced the Persians as rulers of the area. In 332 B.C.E. Greek influence under Alexander the Great took the form of broad cultural changes identified as Hellenism. There was great attractiveness in the Greek way of doing things, and some permanent imprints were left. For example, a Greek translation of the Hebrew scriptures, the Septuagint, was made in Egypt and well served the Jews living outside the homeland, most of whom did not easily read Hebrew.

Wisdom Literature

Wisdom literature, scriptures that praise wisdom and learning, parallel Greek writings that elevate philosophy (love of wisdom), the use of reason to discover truth. Both Greek philosophy and Jewish wisdom literature break with traditional myths. The symbol of wisdom as a desirable woman to be pursued and loved, however, is present in both Jewish and Greek literature. Jewish wisdom literature generally maintains a strong faith in God, a feature present in some Greek literature. The writings of the Greek philosopher Aristotle on belief in God, when rediscovered in the medieval period, influenced not only Judaism but also Christianity and Islam.

Proverbs and Ecclesiastes, ascribed to King Solomon, are examples of wisdom literature. In Proverbs, the writer speaks as a father to a son, giving advice from experience:

> The beginning of wisdom is—acquire wisdom:
> With all your acquisitions, acquire discernment.
> Hug her to you and she will exalt you;
> She will bring you honor if you embrace her.
> She will adorn your head with a graceful wreath;
> Crown you with a glorious diadem. (Proverbs 4:7–9)

In Ecclesiastes, the writer also seeks wisdom, but he experiences disappointment in the supposed pleasures of life. His most famous lines are the following:

> Utter futility!—said Koheleth—
> Utter futility! All is futile!
> What real value is there for a man
> In all the gains he makes beneath the sun? (Ecclesiastes 1:2–3)

The pleasures of the body that had been a sign of God's blessings in Judaism were discovered to be meaningless. The dead were more fortunate than the living, and one not born was more fortunate than either (4:2–3). However, wisdom is more valuable than weapons of war (9:18). The book concludes,

> The sum of the matter, when all is said and done: Revere God and observe His commandments! For this applies to all mankind: that God will call every creature to account for everything unknown, be it good or bad. (12:13–14)

The Maccabean Revolt

In the hands of the Seleucids of Syria, Hellenism was a threat, for Antiochus IV (175–163 B.C.E.) prohibited possession of the Torah, observation of the Sabbath, and the practice of circumcision; he also desecrated the rebuilt temple of Jerusalem in 167 B.C.E. and rededicated it to the Greek god Zeus. The Maccabean revolt was the Jewish response that led to the defeat of the

Syrians and to the rededication of the temple in 164 B.C.E., an event celebrated in the Jewish festival of Hanukkah.

The revolt against Antiochus IV had begun in the city of Jerusalem; the popular leaders of a prolonged resistance movement began their work in a village northeast of Jerusalem, Modi'in. Jews were tired of being forced to eat pork, a food forbidden by the Torah, and being threatened with death for practicing their faith. When Syrian officers came to Modi'in, assembled the people, and attempted to force Jews, using threats of death, to desecrate their altar to God, the Jews faced an immediate crisis. Mattathias, a priest, refused to sacrifice an unclean animal on the altar. When a Jew came forward to obey the command of the king's officers, Mattathias killed him. In the fight, Syrians were killed. Mattathias and his sons escaped to the hills.

Supported by pious Jewish people, the Maccabees waged war on the Syrians with daily effect. Simon and Judas, the Maccabee (probably from the Hebrew word for hammer), became popular leaders. Judas, son of Mattathias, succeeded in controlling the temple area of Jerusalem so that devout priests could cleanse the corrupted temple and hold an eight-day festival to rededicate it to the worship of God. Rabbis today explain that the Jewish holiday **Hanukkah** is not so much a celebration of Judas's victory over the Syrians as it is a celebration of the miracle that a container of consecrated oil, which was enough to light the lamps for only one day, lasted eight days.

Hanukkah [khan-nu-ka]
The eight-day festival commemorating the rededication of the Jerusalem temple after the Maccabean revolt against the Syrians.

The Romans

The Romans, expanding their empire, eventually overcame the Jews as well. Pompey and the Romans came in 63 B.C.E. to settle a dispute between rivals for the post of high priest in Jerusalem; they stayed for centuries. Generally, the Romans were administrators who ignored Jewish peculiarities so long as the Jews paid their taxes and kept the peace. Jews had to work hard to meet Roman demands and at the same time maintain the purity of their culture and worship. Under the challenge, some Jews sought accommodation, some sought peace, and still others could not rest until they had driven the Romans from the land.

During the first and second centuries C.E., a variety of Jewish leaders and groups proposed their own ways to deal with Rome. The conservative **Sadducees,** who rejected prophetic writings and embraced only the first five books of the Bible (the Torah), found ways to cooperate with the Romans. At the other extreme were the **Zealots,** who sought a forceful overthrow of the Roman government in Palestine. In between were groups that had a variety of responses. The **Essenes,** for example, were intent on living purified lives apart from the troubles of the present world until God's final judgment should appear. Recent scholarly study of the Qumran community, near the Dead Sea, has given us a better understanding of these pious people who withdrew from society. The **Pharisees** believed that the Torah, both written and oral, should be applied to every aspect of daily life. They regarded as scriptural many books besides the Torah. Josephus, a Jewish historian, stated in his *The Antiquities of the Jews* (13.10.6), that Sadducees thought Pharisees required many observances not written in the Law of Moses.

A great many common people believed that the time for a deliverer—some sort of anointed one of God—to appear had drawn near. There was,

Sadducees [SAD-u-sees]
Jewish leaders who claimed allegiance to the priestly descendants of Zadok, a priest in the days of King David. These wealthier Jews followed only the Torah.

Zealots [ZEL-uts]
A party of Jews actively opposed to Roman occupation of Judea. They were active in the first century C.E., especially in the revolt that began in 66.

Essenes [ES-eens]
A group of pious Jews of the first century C.E. who lived in separate communities and practiced ritual washing and other acts for purity. Some scholars think that the inhabitants of the Qumran community, near the Dead Sea, were Essenes.

Pharisees [PHAR-i-sees]
A group of Jews who represented the piety of the common people in the centuries immediately after the Maccabean War.

however, much dispute about the qualifications and platform for any deliverer of the Jews. The expected deliverer was often referred to as the **Messiah.** The word, meaning "anointed," is used only twice in the Bible, both times in the book of Daniel (9:25 and 26). There are many references to the anointing of Hebrew kings, and one foreign king, Cyrus of Persia, was referred to as the Lord's anointed (Isaiah 45:1). In Daniel, however, "Messiah" is spoken of in Daniel's vision of Gabriel, who reveals the future. Scholars differ over whether the term applies only to a figure who will appear in the last days before judgment or may apply also to any kings or priests chosen by God.

The appearance of Judas the Galilean in 6 C.E. initiated the struggles of the first century which ended with the execution of Judas and perhaps two thousand other Zealots on crosses, the Roman instrument for capital punishment. John the Baptist, who worked beyond the Jordan River announcing that the kingdom of God was at hand and that everyone should repent, be baptized, and bear fruits of repentance, attracted large crowds and a group of devoted disciples. King Herod jailed and eventually beheaded him. Jesus of Nazareth, a cousin of John, announced the imminence of the kingdom of God, attracted large crowds, and had twelve apostles as well as numerous disciples. In spite of a large, popular following, he angered many scribes and Pharisees of the Jews and eventually disrupted the operation of their temple to the extent that he was arrested, tried before members of the **Sanhedrin,** the highest court, found guilty of blasphemy by the high priest, and then turned over to Pilate, the Roman prefect, who allowed him to be crucified by Roman soldiers. Disciples of both John the Baptist and Jesus of Nazareth continued the works of their masters and stirred people to the extent that they were of concern to the Sanhedrin. Their story will be told in the next chapter.

Rabbinic Judaism

The Judaism that had been expressed in both temple and synagogues was about to end. From the time of their return to Jerusalem under Persian rule, Jews had maintained synagogue worship, and when the building was completed, temple worship. Then, in 66 C.E., the temple's survival was threatened by a Jewish revolt in Jerusalem.

Many Jews, especially the Zealots, who had always opposed Roman rule of Palestine, found Roman administration unbearable. Romans controlled the temple and the high priest. They placed the burden of heavy taxes and duties on the population. In disputes between Jews and the Greco-Syrian population of Palestine, the Romans took the side of the foreigners. Roman administration had deteriorated to the point that the Romans could no longer guarantee peace and security.[5]

Already in turmoil because a Roman court decided in favor of foreigners against Jews in Caesarea, the crowds in Jerusalem were furious when Florus, the Roman procurator, took money from the temple. Jews in Jerusalem revolted, attacking Roman soldiers. In their battle with the Romans, the Jews gained control of the Temple Mount. In this opening revolt, Romans retained control of the Antonia fortress, but later lost control to the Jews. The Jews exterminated the Roman garrison. Jews in other cities, hearing news of the courageous fight of the Jerusalem Jews, attacked the Romans occupying their cities. The Jews disrupted the law and order so prized by Rome and challenged the authority of the strongest military power in the world.

The Western Wall, Jerusalem. This center of Jewish devotion is the platform of the former Temple, destroyed by Romans in 70 C.E. The lowest layer of stones is oldest, dating back more than 2,000 years.

It was a rebellion that the Romans could not ignore or settle by negotiation. Mobilizing sixty thousand troops, the Roman general Vespasian marched into Galilee and proceeded to conquer much of the country. When Vespasian returned to Rome to become emperor, his son Titus took charge of the siege of Jerusalem in 70 C.E. In the five-month siege, the Romans broke down the third wall and then the second wall until they reached the defenders in the Antonia fortress. Destroying the fortress, the Romans turned to the Temple Mount. Flavius Josephus, a historian of the period, described the destruction of the temple.

> While the holy house was on fire, everything was plundered that came to hand, and ten thousand of those that were caught were slain, nor was there a commiseration of any age or any reverence of gravity; but children and old men, and profane persons, and priests, were all slain in the same manner.[6]

To this day, the temple has not been rebuilt. Only the **Western Wall** of the platform survives. The Romans overcame the last resisting group in the Upper City. Only Machaerus and Masada, on the eastern and western banks of the Dead Sea, continued resistance.

The Western Wall, Jerusalem
The platform of the former Temple, destroyed by the Romans in 70 C.E.

Resisting from the top of Masada, a mountain stronghold, a group of Jewish patriots and their families stood off the Roman army for three more years. The historian Josephus praised the defenders, who braved repeated attacks from superior numbers. Under Flavius Silva, the Roman tenth legion built an earthwork against the side of the cliff and breached the walls of the fortress. They found no army to imprison or families to enslave because the 960 defenders had destroyed themselves by their own hands; the Romans gained only smoldering ruins and corpses.[7]

During the struggle for Jerusalem, a rabbi, Yohanan ben Zakkai, tricking the Zealot Jewish guards, had himself removed from the city in a coffin as part of a supposed funeral procession. Although some scholars regard that account as possible legend, they agree that Yohanan ben Zakkai reached Vespasian's officers and obtained Roman permission for the Sanhedrin to move to Yavneh. There he and his fellows established Jewish scriptures, prepared commentaries on the Torah, and developed a Jewish calendar so that wherever Jews happened to be, they could all celebrate the sacred festivals at the same time. Their work was a major achievement in helping Jews preserve their identity in widely dispersed communities. Again, as in Babylon, the congregations came to be the main institutions of Judaism other than the home. This time, the rabbis replaced the old priesthood as leaders of the religious life of the Jews.

Mishnah [MISH-na]
Teachings of the rabbis compiled about 200 C.E. The Mishnah records discussions of rabbis on how best to live according to the Torah.

Talmud [TAL-mud]
The collection of rabbinic teachings. It had deep influence over the lives of Jews from the beginning of the medieval period.

Hillel [hil-EL]
A prominent Jewish teacher and founder of the Hillel school of rabbis in the first century. He was considered more liberal in his views than the conservative Shammai.

Midrash [MID-rash]
(pl. *Midrashim*) Rabbinic exposition explaining the meaning of the scriptures. The root meaning is "to search out."

As important as the Bible is for Jews as a guide to living, it is the first word rather than the last of their developing faith. For Judaism did not stop changing and growing when the last official book of the Bible was certified by rabbis. The records of their adapting faith are contained in other books, such as the **Mishnah** and the **Talmud.** Although Judaism has changed significantly in the last two centuries, these two books and the Bible continue to guide Jews in their daily lives and in their aspirations for the future.

An even greater tragedy was in store for the Jews, if that could be imagined. Rabbi Akiba became convinced, about 130 C.E., that in a man named Bar Kokhba he had discovered the Messiah who would deliver the Jews from the oppression of Rome. Surely the time had come for God to raise up a deliverer for his people. The Romans, in spite of the destruction of the Jews' temple in Jerusalem, had continued to collect the temple tax from Jews. Now the Romans proposed to use the money to build a temple to Jupiter on the site of the old Jewish temple. Jews, led by Bar Kokhba and supported by Rabbi Akiba, revolted against Rome. About three-and-a-half years later, the Romans, under Hadrian, won their victory, and Jews were driven from political power in Jerusalem. The Romans rebuilt Jerusalem as a pagan city called Aelia Capitolina. Jews were not allowed to live in the city. Later they were permitted to approach the Western Wall (Wailing Wall) of the old Temple Mount on only one day each year. From that time it was referred to as the Wailing Wall, for Jews who went there bemoaned the loss of their temple. Since the restoration of the area to Jews in 1967 C.E., it has been referred to as the Western Wall.

With their hopes of reviving Jewish temple worship dashed, Jews embraced the work of the rabbis. Under Yohanan ben Zakkai and his successors at Yavneh, the teachings of the most learned and beloved rabbi, **Hillel,** were studied, and Judaism focused on books, learning, rituals, and moral life. Now that the temple was gone, keeping kosher, prescribed diets; pure Sabbath observances; and proper celebrations of the holidays— all required by the Torah—were elevated concerns. Jewishness had to be preserved even though dispersion was far and wide and the old center of faithful expression was lost.

By about 90 C.E., the canon of the Jewish Bible had been assembled. It included the Torah, which had been accepted as scripture at least since the Babylonian captivity, the writings of the major and the minor prophets as well as the preliterary prophets, and miscellaneous writings of the ancestors, such as Solomon. Other books were rejected as being instructive and helpful but not scriptures, for example, First and Second Maccabees, which describe the restoration of the temple in 164 B.C.E. after Syrian desecration. In the early centuries of Christianity some of these books, which were included in the Septuagint (Jewish scriptures in Greek), Christians accepted as part of their Old Testament, or Old Covenant. Scattered Jewish communities wanted further unity of their teachings. The interpretations of the rabbis needed to be gathered and preserved so that no matter where rabbis might be teaching, they would have continuity of opinion with the great rabbis, such as Hillel. There was a large body of unwritten Torah, and traditional commentaries by rabbis, **Midrash.** Rabbi Akiba had demonstrated that under six headings all these unwritten subjects could be gathered and grouped. It remained only for them to be written; the old fear that their written form might rival the Torah was no longer a primary concern.

Because Roman activities crushed the school at Yavneh, the surviving rabbis moved to Usha in Galilee. Under the influence of Rabbis Meir and Judah, the Patriarch, four thousand repetitions adapting the Torah to the second century were collected into the Mishnah. Thus, by about 220 C.E., Judaism had a book containing the assembled opinions of several generations of outstanding rabbis on how the Torah should be applied to daily life. A unity of Jewish opinions and practices in the **diaspora** was now possible.

The Jewish community in Babylon, continuous since the sixth century B.C.E., thought that it was desirable to expand the material of the Mishnah. Scholars gathered **Aggadah,** traditions of the rabbis, and **Halakhah,** juristic tradition, into the **Gemarah.** Then they combined the Gemarah and the Mishnah to make the exhaustive Babylonian Talmud, which was completed by 485 C.E. Although a smaller Talmud, the Palestinian, had been completed earlier, the Babylonian Talmud became the enduring standard for Judaism. Almost anything a Jew needed to know about keeping the faith under any circumstances could be found in the pages of the Talmud.

By the time the Western empire of Rome had fallen to the northern tribes of Europe, Judaism was prepared to maintain a continuity of distinctive existence, even though Jews were found in a great variety of cultures. Some societies honored Jews, others tolerated them, and still others persecuted them severely. Dress, food, marriage, family, death, holidays, Sabbath observance, subjects of study, prayers, and offerings—all distinguished the Jews as a particular community, giving them a common bond of identity in the face of cultures that varied according to time and geographical location. Ritual and legal observance, as well as Torah study, helped Jews preserve their identity and their pride as a separate people called by God. Rabbinic Judaism became the nucleus of modern Judaism. In the absence of a temple, the rabbis' interpretation of Torah became the only living Judaism.

Philo

Judaism outside Palestine avoided the bitter struggles of Jerusalem. In Alexandria, Philo Judaeus (30 B.C.E.–50 C.E.) attempted to reconcile Platonism with the teachings of Judaism.[8] Claiming that Plato's ideas could be found in the Torah, Philo began a philosophical explanation of scriptures. Already accustomed to using the **allegorical method** in interpreting scriptures, he was able to reconcile Jewish wisdom with Greek philosophy. The allegorical method assumes that scriptures have symbolic, or hidden, meanings as well as historical meanings. For example, in discussing Terah, the father of Abraham, Philo said that Terah was not only a historical person but also a symbol for Jews to "know thyself." For Greeks, Socrates was the symbol for this idea.[9] Once this premise has been granted, the interpreter can usually find hidden meanings that, astonishingly, parallel his favorite philosophical system. Using this approach, Philo thought Moses to be the teacher of Plato. Philo made a significant contribution to his generation and to later Jewish philosophers. Clement and Origen, Christian teachers of Alexandria, who came later, used a similar method to reconcile Platonic concepts with Christian teachings. Although Hebrew and Greek thought relied on human reasoning, Hebrews differed from Greeks by always identifying the source of wisdom as God.

diaspora [di-AHS-pe-ra]
A Greek word for the dispersion of Jews. These were the Jews who lived outside the Holy Land.

Aggadah [ug-GAHD-u]
The nonlegal, story aspect of rabbinic literature. It is distinguished from Halakhah, the legal side of Judaism.

Halakhah [ha-la-KAH]
The legal part of Jewish religion that was developed in rabbinic writings.

Gemarah [ge-MAHR-u]
The "learning" of the rabbis. It was combined with the Mishnah to form the Talmud.

allegorical method
Interpreting the symbols of an earlier age in meanings of a later age. Seeking the spiritual as well as the historical meaning of scriptures.

Medieval Judaism

Muslim [MUS-lim]
One who surrenders to God. A follower of the prophet Muhammad.

Medieval Judaism was Talmudic Judaism existing in cultures dominated by either Christians or **Muslims.** Although both of these religions acknowledged God's revelation to the Jews, both had quarrels with Jews. Jews had not accepted a later revelation by God either through Jesus as the Christ or through Muhammad as the reciter of the Quran. Except under threats of certain death, most Jews did not convert to another religion. Many Jews died rather than compromise their faith. Under generally good circumstances, Jews were permitted to live as second-class citizens among the persons of the dominant faith. A few Jews reached positions of great respect and reward as scholars, physicians, bankers, and merchants.

In any given place, conditions were only temporarily good for Jews. They had to seek the protection of holders of political power. From the thirteenth century on, they were labeled "king's serfs."[10] A king could charge them for the privilege of living in his territory or drive them out, confiscating their properties, whenever conditions in his territory supported drastic persecutions. Jews were severely restricted in occupations and property. They had to abide by the laws of the land as well as by the Talmud. Although they did not want to share in the social lives of Christians or Muslims—Jewish teachings restricted these relationships—they did desire equal protection and treatment under law. Every Jew had to remember that any offense he or she gave to a Christian or Muslim could invite wholesale persecution, even slaughter, of the entire Jewish community. Christian extermination of Jewish communities in medieval times was far too extensive to describe in this brief summary of Jewish history.

Two major traditions of Judaism predominated in the medieval period. The Babylonian tradition continued in the **Sephardic** tradition in southern Spain, and the **Ashkenazic** tradition, which developed from Latin roots, influenced northern Spain, France, and Germany. Although the two traditions competed in northern Spain, they were generally separated in geography.

Sephardim [se-fahr-DIM]
Jews who lived in medieval Spain until expelled in 1492. Those who refused to become Christians moved to North Africa, Italy, and especially Turkey, where Sultan Bayzid II admitted them gladly.

Ashkenazim [ahsh-ku-NAH-zim]
A Yiddish-speaking group of Jews who settled in central and northern Europe. The term in Hebrew referred to Germany.

Jewish Philosophy

A Jewish philosophy is one that explores humans in the universe in the light of the beliefs and practices of Judaism. The exploration is done with careful reasoning, but it stays within the context of the traditional faith.

SAADIA BEN JOSEPH

Among the scholars of medieval Judaism, Saadia ben Joseph (882–942), for part of his life Saadiah Gaon, or president, of the Sura Academy of Babylonia, is famous for combining Greek rationalism with Torah study in order to combat Karaism. Anan ben David led the Karaites, a group of Babylonian Jews, in their general resistance to rabbinic Judaism embodied in the Talmud. The Karaites were devoted to the study of the Torah and interpreted it in opposition to rabbis in the Talmud. They argued that the Geonim, leaders of the academy, led the people astray. The Karaites' biblical literalism struck at the authority of the rabbis and elevated revelation above reason in the Torah. Saadia responded that although revelation is the quickest route to truth and gives some information not available through reason alone, God has a purpose for endowing humans with reason. Through unaided reason, humans can reach metaphysical and moral truths.

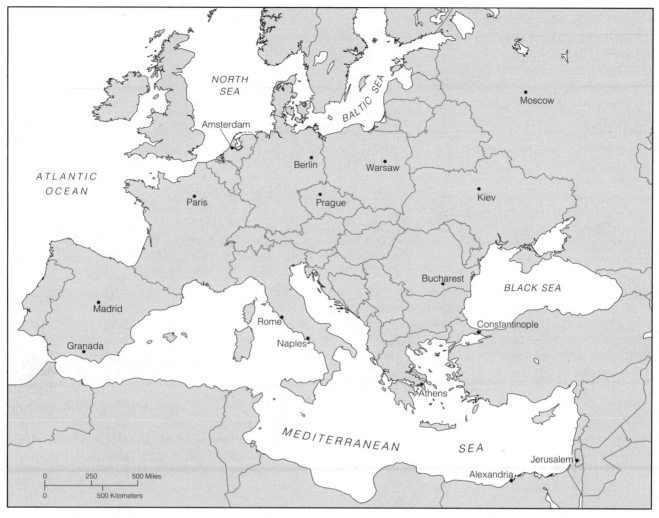

NORTH SEA

BALTIC SEA

Moscow

Amsterdam

Berlin

Warsaw

ATLANTIC OCEAN

Paris

Prague

Kiev

Bucharest

BLACK SEA

Madrid

Rome

Constantinople

Granada

Naples

MEDITERRANEAN SEA

Athens

Jerusalem

Alexandria

0   250   500 Miles

0   500 Kilometers

Major Centers of Judaism in Europe. Jews settled around the Mediterranean by the first century C.E. and soon became inhabitants of many of the cities in Europe.

Saadia initiated a project to translate Jewish scriptures into Arabic. He used Arabic works on Greek philosophy to show not only how reasonable the Talmud is but also how it agrees with the Torah. His combining Torah, Talmud, and Greek philosophy into a comprehensive system expressed in Arabic weakened the Karaites, and, at the same time, brought Judaism's intellectual views into the spheres of discussion of contemporary Muslim scholars. Saadia's influence traveled with Jewish scholars to Spain, where Jews, Christians, and Muslims helped develop a synthesis of Greek philosophy and revealed truth.

Jewish philosophers maintained the primacy of God, combining insights of Greek rationalists, such as Aristotle, with teachings of the Torah. Sometimes Jewish rationalism was warmed by a mystical love for God.

JUDAH HALEVI

Judah (Yahudah) Halevi of Spain (1075–1141) thought that Aristotle wrote about the same God as Torah, but the Torah revelation gave a more complete view of God. Halevi's memorable work, *The Kuzari*, is a fictional story about Bulan, king of the Kuzars, a Tatar people, who is seeking the right faith. The king calls in a philosopher who explains everything rationally, but the rationalism fails to convince him. Next he calls a Christian, but the argument has two flaws. The dogma runs contrary to reason and the faith keeps referring back to Judaism. The Muslim position is more reasonable, but it, too, refers to an earlier Judaism. The rabbi who comes describes God not as the subject of speculation but as one who appears in history to a multitude of people. In a public revelation, he called his people to action. Humans must respond to God not only with intellect but also with heart and soul. The Jewish tradition gives the only answer that is needed for life. God's choosing the Jews is a mystery; contrary to Saadia, not all things are discernible by reason. Bulan prefers the argument of the Jew.

Judah Halevi is also widely known in Judaism for his poetry of Zionism. Of his some eight hundred poems, the most famous are the *Shirei Ziyyon (Poems of Zion)*. In these thirty-five poems, he expresses the tension between love and pain, dream and reality. His intellectual basis was overcome by personal emotion.[11] Although most Jews were physically separated from the land of Israel, they were spiritually tied to it.

MAIMONIDES

In Cordoba, Spain, the young Jew Moses ben Maimon (1135–1204) began a comfortable life enjoying the library of his father, a rabbi. But with the arrival of the Almohads from North Africa, Muslim persecution of Jews affected his life. He migrated with his family to Morocco, then to Palestine, and then to Egypt. He settled, eventually, in Fostat, a suburb of Cairo. His reputation for Torah study and mastery of Aristotle brought him the title of "Nagid," or leader of Jewry in Egypt. Judaism was his love, but he supported his studies with a humanitarian trade, medicine. He made a dedicated study of pharmacy and methods of physicians. His reputation in that field led to his appointment as court physician to the emperor Saladin.[12] Maimonides, as he came to be known, declined an invitation from King Richard II to come to England.

Rambam, as he was respectfully known, gave first place in life to Jewish scholarship—in particular, reconciling the newer interpretations of Aristotle with his studies of the Torah. Although he liked Aristotle's proof for the existence of God, he preferred the creator in Plato's *Timaeus* to explain God's relationship to the world. His monumental works were the *Mishneh Torah*, a companion to the Torah written in Hebrew, and a *Guide for the Perplexed*, written in Arabic.

In the Torah commentary, he expressed the essential beliefs of Judaism in thirteen articles, including the existence, unity, spirituality, eternity, and omniscience of God; that God alone should be worshiped; that God bestowed the gift of prophecy; that Moses was the greatest prophet; that God gave the Torah and will never alter it; that he is omniscient; that he rewards the righteous and punishes the wicked; that he will send the Messiah; and that he will resurrect the dead. These articles were soon being repeated as a creed for Jews. In spite of objections by later scholars such as Hasdai Crescas (1405) and Moses Mendelssohn (eighteenth century), Jewish masses wanted these articles repeated as part of their expression of faith. From the fourteenth century, they were included in Jewish worship. The Yigdal, which expresses the articles in poetry, is part of the Siddur (Prayer Book) and is recited in the daily service. The following is a translation of the Yigdal (the Thirteen Articles of Jewish Faith) in metrical form:

We praise the living God,
For ever praise His name,
Who was and is and is to be
For e'er the same;
The One eternal God
Before our world appears,
And there can be no end of time
Beyond His years.

Without a form is He,
Nor can we comprehend
The measure of His love for us—
Without an end.
For He is Lord of all,
Creation speaks His praise.
The human race and all that grows
His will obeys.

He knows our every thought,
Our birth and death ordains;
He understands our fervent dreams,
Our hopes and our pains.
Eternal life has He
Implanted in our soul.
We dedicate our life to Him—
His way, our goal![13]

As did Philo centuries earlier, Maimonides interpreted the Genesis stories allegorically. He believed that revelation is reasonable, even when revelation gives truth that could not have been reached by unaided reason. He believed also that God can best be described in terms of what he is not, for denying limits to God indicates what God is. For his genius in combining reason and scholarship in philosophy with deep devotion and analysis of the Torah, Maimonides is recognized as the greatest of the Jewish philosophers.

THE KABBALAH

Revelation and rationalism in religions have been balanced by the esoteric. Hidden knowledge is not generally available to the masses but is available to a select few who are initiated into its mysteries. Behind the phenomena of the physical world are mysterious, irrational forces generated in a more powerful, unseen world. Those who have discovered special, secret knowledge can have access to codes that decipher information from the higher realm of being. Kabbalah is a Jewish form of the hidden knowledge that appeared in the medieval period and continued into the modern.

The best-known text of the Kabbalah is the *Zohar*, a text that scholars believe was written by Moses de Leon (1250–1305).[14] Through the practice of assigning numerical values to letters of the Hebrew alphabet, Kabbalists could exercise what appeared to be a more scientific deciphering of mystical truths in scriptures. The phenomenal world, that experienced by the five senses, is a corrupted product of the spiritual world, which can be encountered only mystically. Similar to Gnostic systems of earlier centuries, the Kabbalah has the absolute, named En Soph, at the top of a hierarchy of male and female pairs of emanations named Divine Will, Wisdom, Knowledge, Grace, and Power. Thus, the purity of God is safely removed from the corruption of the phenomenal world. Man—male and female—is a symbol that directly corresponds to the universe. Through proper knowledge, formulas, and rituals, humans can influence the forces of the universe.

The hidden powers are also in the human organism. Through a study of the physiology and psychology of humans and a proper application of that knowledge, humans can release the energies stored in the body and mind. Some find that there are similarities with the theories of Hindu yoga, in which energy centers are located along the spine. When the centers are activated, they produce a higher level of consciousness. Symbols, rather than arguments, are characteristic of Kabbalah. Kabbalists' belief that the Messiah could be recognized by a certain symbol led to a few incidents of Jews accepting messiahs who proved false.

Isaac Luria (1534–1572), of Spain, focused on the ideal human symbol, Adam. Adam embraced the universe; in his fall, he shattered into sparks of divine nature, illuminating souls. The goal of time is to unite these fragments into the ideal Adam. Reincarnation of the souls in plants, animals, and humans is part of the process of purification that enables souls to reach dimensions of higher union. Luria advocated ascetic living and recitation of formulas to help his followers experience direct union with highest reality. The goal of the hidden powers in Kabbalah is mystical union with God.

Judaism, Christianity, and Islam

Most societies have placed restrictions on Jews that made them permanent second-class citizens or subjects. Because their owning land was prohibited, Jews were seldom farmers. Excluded from Gentile institutions of learning, they were unable to enter most trades and professions. Segregated into ghettos, they turned inward to family, community, and study of the Torah. Forced to live by their wits, many Jews became astute in business. Because Muslims and Christians would not lend money for interest to members of their own religion, Jews discovered a service that they could render to kings, nobles, and merchants of other religions. Jewish money lenders became an indispensable part of later medieval society. Their services rewarded them well, but their success brought them envy and resentment from Gentiles. Powerful people who had difficulty paying debts were tempted to fan the ever-present sparks of prejudice among Christians. They stirred violent mobs to torture, kill, and seize the property of Jews. No debts remained to be paid. Destruction was justified by pious rationalizations based on general Christian contempt for Jews. Some of those claims were that Jews had murdered Christ, that Jews used the blood of Christian children in their rituals, and that Jews poisoned the wells of Christians.[15]

In 1492, any pleasant life for Jews in Spain ended. King Ferdinand and Queen Isabella, devoted Christian rulers, brought to a close the exemplary cooperation of Jews, Christians, and Muslims in Spain. Desiring their realm to be inhabited only by Christians, the monarchs gave Jews and Muslims a choice of converting to Christianity or leaving Spain. Devout Jews had no choice; they abandoned their properties and migrated to other countries. The Jews of Spain suffered a displacement similar to that of the Jews of France, who had been expelled in 1394. Many of the displaced Jews, especially those of Spain (the Safed) settled in the Jewish homeland (Israel), reviving it as a center of Jewish life.

Jews who converted to Christianity were under constant examination by the Inquisition. The Grand Inquisitor, Tomas de Torquemada, was especially devoted to rooting out heretical ideas. Both those Jews who left Spain and those who converted to Christianity suffered for their faith.

Judaism in the Modern Age

Judaism in the Middle Ages was excluded from full participation in Gentile society. In the modern age, some Jews found ways to escape from the ghettos and to participate in the intellectual and political life of their nations.

The Enlightenment, with its emphasis on human reason and scientific knowledge, deeply challenged the traditions of Judaism, Christianity, and **Islam.** Christian philosophers such as John Locke (1632–1704) of England and René Descartes (1596–1650) of France held the mind to be the measure of all things. Priority was assigned to reason over revelation and to science over tradition. God was relegated to a position of creator of the universe and establisher of its laws. The job of human beings was to discover the laws and to plan their lives to use them for their benefit. The philosopher replaced the theologian, the scientist the priest. Young men at the universities accepted views of the Enlightenment as proper for leaders.

Emphasis on reason over revelation is called **modernism.** In Judaism and Christianity, the emphasis on secular knowledge above traditional, revealed knowledge began to affect young people of the seventeenth century. In our time, it has also affected Islam. In response to these challenges, some religious groups changed their beliefs to accommodate new knowledge; others held more firmly to the teachings of their ancient traditions.

Islam [is-LAHM]
Like other religions of the family of Abraham, it emphasizes worship of one God. It believes that Muhammad is the last and most important of the prophets of God.

modernism [mod-ur-NIZ-um]
In religion, emphasis on reason in philosophy and science instead of traditional beliefs.

BARUCH SPINOZA

In Holland, a young Jew by the name of Baruch Spinoza (1632–1677) shocked Jews and Christians alike by his rational approach to religion. Although Spinoza believed that God is the only substance and can be known by intuition, he openly discussed ideas that were threatening to Orthodox Judaism and Christianity. Among other unpopular ideas, he suggested that angels may be imaginary and that the Old Testament does not teach a concept of immortality. Rabbis attempted to lead him back to orthodox ideas. Unsuccessful, in Amsterdam they excommunicated him from the synagogue in 1656.

Voltaire (1664–1778), of France, and Locke saw that valuing human reason had political implications. These implications led to political upheavals in the American and French revolutions. Young Jews discovered in the opinions of these philosophers opportunities to become citizens in the new order. Before participating fully, they reexamined the role of traditional Judaism in their lives.

MOSES MENDELSSOHN

The most influential Jew in this development was Moses Mendelssohn (1729–1786). The German playwright Lessing wrote *Nathan the Wise* about a character representing Mendelssohn. A Jew, a Christian, and a Muslim are represented in dialogues about their religions. The characters are presented as individuals with moral characteristics that can be separated from their religions. In showing a common origin for these religions, Lessing hoped to show the basis for a unity among their adherents. Bolstered by Lessing, Mendelssohn made his greatest contribution arguing that Jews should be freed from the ghettos and allowed equal participation in society. Mendelssohn used the German word *Mensch* to denote the common humanity of Jews and Christians.[16] Although he participated socially with a group of Christian intellectuals, his vision of a common humanity regardless of religion proved illusory.

Forms of Judaism

Jews who examined the traditions found different treasures. In the nineteenth century, Jews in Europe and the United States found new opportunities to express different interpretations of the traditional faith. In the United States, Jews enjoyed the rights of citizens. The first president, George Washington, wrote to Jews in Newport, Rhode Island, affirming religious freedom of citizens.

> The citizens of the United States of America have a right to applaud themselves for having given to mankind examples of an enlarged and liberal policy—a policy worthy of imitation. All possess alike liberty of conscience and immunities of citizenship.
>
> It is now no more that toleration is spoken of as if it were the indulgence of one class of people that another enjoyed the exercise of their inherent natural rights, for, happily, the Government of the United States, which gives to bigotry no factions [sanctions], to persecution no assistance, requires only that they who live under its protection should demean themselves as good citizens in giving it on all occasions their effectual support.[17]

In France, Great Britain, and Germany, Jews were granted rights as citizens to practice their religion without discrimination. Free to leave the ghettos and participate in civil and intellectual life of their countries, many Jews reexamined what Judaism meant to them. Forms of interpretation began to separate into movements or traditions, especially in Germany and then in the United States. Most traditional Jews, especially in Eastern Europe, wanted to keep all possible provisions of the Torah and Talmud. A few Jewish thinkers thought that ethical teachings were more important than ritual. Other Jewish scholars sought to compromise ancient and medieval customs with opportunities for life in a larger community. Certain persons emerged as leaders or spokespersons for various movements or traditions.

ABRAHAM GEIGER

Abraham Geiger (1810–1874) introduced a Reform Judaism, an emphasis on ethics, and a concession that Judaism does not rest on revealed doctrines. Although animal sacrifice, separation of men and women in services of worship, and dietary restrictions were appropriate to Judaism in ages past, Judaism had always changed through the centuries. In nineteenth-century Germany, among middle-class German Jews, such observances were no longer appropriate. The primary concern of those Jews was to bear witness to ethical monotheism, belief in one God who requires humans to moral principles as they interact with each other.

ZACHARIAS FRANKEL

Zacharias Frankel (1801–1875) had a conservative approach, which retained the Torah in tension with the modern needs of Jews. He sought to preserve many of the Jewish rituals that the Reform Jews had discarded as unnecessary. He thought that Jews should express their Judaism in ritual, keeping a traditional base on which they could slowly change to affirm Judaism in the modern world. Rabbis Geiger and Frankel both sought to make Judaism more compatible with the cultures of the modern world.

SAMSON RAPHAEL HIRSCH

Orthodox Jews, such as Samson Raphael Hirsch (1808–1888), disagreed with the movement to change the traditional practices of Judaism. Rabbi Hirsch insisted that Jews retain all laws of the Torah and Talmud and look to the restoration of Zion. He favored Jews participating in modern life and retaining their distinctions as Jews. Reform, Conservative, and Orthodox varieties of Judaism developed in Europe; they had parallels in the United States.

Theodore Hertzl. A portrait of the founder of Zionism.

REFORM JUDAISM

In the United States, Reform Judaism was inspired by David Einhorn (1809–1879) and Isaac Mayer Wise (1819–1900). In its Pittsburg Platform of 1885, the group of rabbis stated that the Torah is binding only in its moral teachings and that rabbinic teachings on diet, ceremonial purity, and dress are no longer binding in the new age. Orthodox and Conservative Judaism required Jews to abstain from all unclean foods, such as pork and shellfish, and to avoid eating meat and milk dishes at the same meal. Reform Judaism abandoned these kosher food laws. The Columbus Platform of 1937 gave stronger emphasis to the Torah and for the first time expressed the need for a Jewish homeland. In 1976, the Central Conference of American Rabbis emphasized religious practice, Sabbath observance, and keeping holy days, as well as a Jewish home. In Reform synagogues, most of the service is in English, and males are not required to wear hats. As in Conservative Judaism, Reform Judaism permits males and females to sit together. Women can be ordained rabbis.

CONSERVATIVE JUDAISM

Influenced by Frankel, Solomon Schechter (1850–1915) became the leader of Conservative Judaism. The Torah and Talmud must be followed. **Zionism,** a movement to establish a Jewish homeland, is important. **Mitzvot,** responses to God, must be followed as interpreted by congregations. They can vary in their practices, following a democratic spirit in America on such matters as whether to use organ music in their worship services. In Conservative synagogues, most parts of worship services are in Hebrew; males wear head coverings (*kippot* or *yarmulkes*); and members are encouraged to observe **kashruth, kosher** food laws, Shabbat, and holidays. Women have roles of leadership in the congregation; qualified women can be ordained rabbis.

RECONSTRUCTIONISM

In the twentieth century, a new, scientifically oriented view of Judaism appeared. Reconstructionism was a school of thought that has grown into a denomination.[18] In 1955, Mordecai Kaplan (1881–1983) established a Federation of Reconstructionist Congregations. Kaplan's concern was to revitalize Judaism for modern, scientifically oriented Jews. A naturalist,

Zionism [ZII-e-NIS-em]
A movement led by Jews to provide a home country for themselves. Theodor Herzl was a leader at the end of the nineteenth century.

mitzvah [MITZ-va]
(pl. *mitzvot*) In Judaism, a response in obedience to God according to the covenant. How to live in a covenant relationship with God is a central teaching of Judaism.

kashruth [KASH-root]
Jewish dietary regulations.

kosher [KO-sher]
In Judaism, meat that has been properly prepared for eating. One requirement is that most of the blood be removed from the meat.

A Blessing in Israel. An Orthodox rabbi blesses a man at the Western Wall in Jerusalem during the High Holy Days.

Kaplan rejected supernatural elements in Judaism. He emphasized the ethical values of Judaism and the importance of realizing these ethical values in the contemporary world. Rituals and holidays of the Jewish community should be observed, for if God is only an intellectual idea, people will not have the motives and strengths to live ethical lives. Kaplan's denying that Israel is a chosen people brought sharp criticism from Orthodox Judaism.

ORTHODOX JUDAISM

Orthodox Judaism retains as much as possible from the Torah and Talmud. Women and men do not sit together in worship. Men wear hats and prayer shawls. The service is in Hebrew. Members are expected to keep kashruth. Since 1948, a Jewish homeland has been generally supported. Orthodox Jews are free to participate as citizens in the modern world, but they are never to compromise their Jewish faith. In Israel, Orthodox Judaism is standard, and the American varieties of Reform Judaism and Conservative Judaism are not recognized as fully legitimate. For example, Orthodox rabbis in Israel do not accept Reform and Conservative rabbis as their equals in authority.

When speaking of Judaism outside Israel, it is desirable to indicate which group of congregations is being discussed, for groups vary considerably in their beliefs and practices, especially in the United States.[19] Ways of dress, observances of dietary restrictions, practices during synagogue worship, ways of keeping holidays, and attitudes toward the Torah and Talmud are areas where Jews can differ considerably and still be Jews. The differences occur in observances rather than in beliefs about God.

HASIDISM

The Hasidim, or "pious ones," of the modern world are devoted to the Torah and to pure lives. They are actively engaged in their societies, but, as a group, they maintain Judaism in the most ancient form possible. Purity can be kept with joy, even ecstasy. Israel Baal Shem (1700–1760) was so pure and exemplary in meditation that miracles were attributed to him. Elie Wiesel, whose grandfather was of the Hasidim, learned their traditional stories. One story that emphasizes Israel Baal Shem's power of meditation is that one morning he prayed so long that weary disciples left:

> Later he commented sadly: "Imagine a rare bird at the top of a tree. To reach it, men form a human ladder, thus allowing one of them to climb to the very top. But those at the bottom cannot see the bird and therefore lose patience and go home. The ladder falls apart, and up there the rare bird has flown away."[20]

In this tradition, a Zaddik, or holy man, can become a channel for God's saving power. He is a power in himself and can inspire enlightenment in others. The Hasidim prize humility and cultivate a love for every human that epitomizes the teachings of Judaism. Martin Buber (1878–1965), a Jewish philosopher, devoted his life to the study and interpretation of Hasidism. He emphasized that the world is waiting to be "hallowed" by devoted humans.[21] In his work *I and Thou*, he held that God is the eternal Thou.[22] Only in relationship with him can persons become fully human. In relationships with others, humans must relate to another "thou," a person, rather than to an "it" an object. In "I-and-Thou" relationships to God and others, people become fully human. In these relationships, the world, which has potential for more goodness, is hallowed.

Hermann Cohen (1842–1918), a German who was a professor of philosophy at the University of Marburg, defended Judaism against charges that it was a religion of foreign nationals, opposed to German and Christian ideals. A dedicated student of the philosophy of Immanuel Kant (1724–1804), Cohen began his own philosophy on a Kantian foundation. He developed an explanation of the role of Jews in the world and their relationship to Christianity.[23]

The great gift of Jews to the world is monotheism. Jews emphasize, also, that individuals are free; they must answer to God for their conduct. Above all, humans are creatures of reason. They can reason to sound conclusions about human conduct. The more humans learn, the more they want to know. They look forward to a world of the future that will be peaceful and good. That is what Jews mean by the Messianic Age, the kingdom of God. It is the age when humans will fulfill their highest ethical ideals. It will be life in harmony with God.

ZIONISM

Zionism was a Jewish movement of the late nineteenth century that intended to establish a Jewish homeland. Since 135 C.E., Jews had lost control of life in Jerusalem. Jews living in many different countries had no land of their own, a particular disadvantage in times of persecution. For example, although France had given Jews citizenship in the nineteenth century, the trial and sentencing of Capt. Alfred Dreyfus exhibited strong anti-Semitism. In 1896, Theodor Herzl published *The Jewish State*, a book that stimulated a determined migration of Jews to Palestine. The Balfour Declaration of 1917, obtained by efforts of Chaim Weizmann, a British chemist, lent support of the British government to migration. When Hitler came to power in Germany in 1933, approximately 220,000 Jews lived in Palestine. At the height of the **Holocaust,** the Nazis' systematic extermination of the

Holocaust [HOL-u-cost]
An offering brought to a deity and completely burnt. The term now refers to the Nazi extermination of Jews in occupied countries during World War II.

Death Camp at Belsen. This man barely survived the hardships that Nazis inflicted on Jews in Europe. Six million Jews were put to death.

Jewish population of Europe, Arab protests led the British to place a quota on Jewish immigrants to Palestine. In response to Nazi atrocities, Reform and Conservative congregations favored a permanent homeland for Jews in Palestine. Virtually all Jews now insist on Israel as a homeland for Jews.

Jews listened to the news of the Nazi invasion of Poland with the same shock as the rest of Europe and America. In the next few weeks, they were bombed, invaded, and occupied along with other citizens in European countries. In later months, as they were singled out with special registrations, passports, and clothing, they experienced a continuation of the persecutions that had increased in Germany since the rise of Hitler in 1933. They agonized over their families' being separated by force, some going to slave labor and others to "resettlement." Some Jews, for example those in Warsaw, were forced into a new ghetto. From ghettos and camps in Europe, Jews were selected for further "resettlement." Only when they were imprisoned in the death camps did most of them realize their horrible future.

A few Jews realized their peril of certain death. Risking their own lives, some Gentiles helped them hide. Anne Frank, who was thirteen years old in 1942, kept a diary of her years hiding in an office building in Amsterdam. In a closing entry she writes,

> It's really a wonder that I haven't dropped all my ideals, because they seem so absurd and impossible to carry out. Yet I keep them, because in spite of everything I still believe that people are really good at heart. I simply can't build up my hopes on a foundation consisting of confusion, misery, and death . . . I think that it will all come right, that this cruelty too will end, and that peace and tranquillity will return again.
>
> In the meantime, I must uphold my ideals, for perhaps the time will come when I shall be able to carry them out.[24]

The Gestapo found Anne and her family on August 4, 1944. After being moved to Auschwitz and then to Belsen, she died of illness in March 1945, a few weeks before the war ended.

In the Holocaust, 1933–1945, the Nazis exterminated six million Jews in Europe. Theodor Herzl had been right about the rising tide of anti-Semitism. In camps such as Auschwitz, they were gassed, and their clothes, possessions, and even their body parts were salvaged for the Nazi war effort. Bodies were burned in crematoriums. The Allied forces that liberated the camps produced photographs and eyewitness accounts that were, even in a time calloused to war atrocities, almost incredible. Records of the Nuremberg trials show widespread cooperation of the population of Europe with the scheme of Nazi officers for a "final solution" of the Jewish "problem." In spite of heroic efforts by individual Gentiles to save Jewish friends, almost no help came from the Christian church or from Allied governments.[25] Today, the extent of anti-Semitism shocks most people. The Holocaust has had an indescribable impact on every Jew. For Gentiles, it is a fact that counteracts any claim that with increased education humanity is becoming more humane. For many Jews and Christians it challenges traditional beliefs in the existence of a moral, knowing, and caring God.

Older and younger Jews emphasize different aspects of the Holocaust. Jews born before the Holocaust, such as Elie Wiesel and Emil Fackenheim, emphasize the suffering that Hitler imposed on Jews. Jews must remain faithful to Judaism lest they accomplish the work that Hitler began.[26] Jews born after the Holocaust, such as Marc Ellis, emphasize the implications of the Holocaust for Christians as well as Jews. Christians, too, are now bound historically to the tragedy of the Holocaust.

Israel

In 1948, in spite of determined Arab opposition, the state of Israel was carved out of the British Mandate. Initially, guerrilla bands fought each other constantly for control of city blocks, acres of farmland, and the water required for life in cities or on farms. In the twentieth century, Jewish immigrants established farms where families worked together to defend their land and produce crops. These cooperative farms, which people could enter or leave as they pleased, became known as *kibbutzim* (the singular form is *kibbutz*). Immigrants planted forests on hills and orchards in valleys. In cities, they built factories. Military service was made compulsory for males and females. Not only guerrilla attacks have been made but also international wars have been waged to dislodge the Jews from Palestine. Only a minority of Arabs agree that Israel should exist. A majority of Jews are willing to make sacrifices to see that Israel remains strong.

Through leaders such as David Ben-Gurion and Golda Meir, Israel has gained and retained the support of the United Nations. Nevertheless, although it is rocked by protests of Arabs within its borders and Palestinians seeking a nation for themselves, Israel still has to face forces in other nations that are devoted to its destruction. Having celebrated its fortieth anniversary, Israel is an established, recognized nation. It is, however, a very young nation still defining the course of its future.

David Ben-Gurion. A Polish immigrant in 1906, Ben-Gurion organized a Jewish army, and when Israel became a state, he served as its first prime minister.

The Roots of the Arab–Israeli Conflict

The tangled roots of the Arab–Israeli conflict cannot be summarized easily. Each side chooses which information to select, group, and explain. Historians who are neither Jews, Muslims, nor Palestinians, trace the Muslim control of Palestine in the seventh century through the Ottoman Empire that ended in the first quarter of the twentieth century. British rule ended in 1948, leaving American influence dominant after World War II.

Palestinians argue that their people tended the land under family ownership that endured for centuries. They believe that Israelis unfairly used military power, discriminatory laws, and influence of the United States to evict Palestinians from their land and force them into refugee camps.

Israelis argue that their occupation of the land goes back to Abraham. More recently, however, they bought land from Ottoman investors to whom Palestinians had defaulted on loans. Israelis cite, also, that when Arabs made war on them they repulsed the aggressors, acquiring in victory the territory of the West Bank, the Golan Heights, and the Gaza Strip.

In 1993 Israeli–Palestinian negotiations held in the United States produced what appeared to be the first experimental steps of Palestinian self-rule. A major step in the process was Israel's recognition of the Palestine Liberation Organization.

Who is a Jew? An answer from history after the Babylonian exile could trace a Jew to a descendant of the Southern Kingdom, from the area around Jerusalem. Before the Babylonian exile in the sixth century B.C.E., the ancestors were identified as Hebrews. In the time of the patriarchs, they were the children of Israel (Jacob) or the children of Abraham. An answer from Judaism is more precise.

Golda Meir. This woman served as prime minister of Israel.

The Halakhic definition is that a child born of Jewish parents or a convert to Judaism is considered a Jew, possessing the sanctity of the Jewish people and the obligation to observe the commandments.[27] From the Mishnah and the Talmud, in a mixed marriage the child's status is determined by that of the mother. The child of a Jewish mother is a Jew; the child of a non-Jewish mother is required to undergo ritual conversion even though the father is a Jew.

This straightforward answer has been particularly controversial in modern Israel. Converts to Judaism agree to follow 613 commandments, which most born Jews do not do. Many of the people exterminated by the Nazis as Jews did not meet the Halakhic standard for a Jew. Were these people who gave their lives for their Jewish identity not really Jews? The Rabbinate of Israel has opposed any secular definition of Jew. In the early days of the modern state of Israel, most Jews supported the rabbinical definition.

Since 1970, the national identity of a Jew may differ from the rabbinical definition. Conversions to Judaism under non-Orthodox rabbis and congregations can meet the standards of the Law of Return and automatic Israeli citizenship. On the other hand, a person born a Jew and who has converted to another religion cannot be accepted as a Jew. As one Reform rabbi expressed it, "There are no 'Jews for Jesus'; these *former* Jews are Christians." Non-Jews who marry Jews are not Jews by marriage alone; to become a Jew they must undergo a ceremony of conversion.

Israel faced a number of challenges. Of the Arab states, only Egypt had made formal peace with Israel. Most Arab states have argued that Israel should not exist. Palestinians have demanded self-rule, resettlement of refugees now in camps, and fair use of fresh water in agriculture. Israelis in the new cities in occupied territories have demanded security in the face of hostile neighbors. Reaching compromises that both Israelis and Palestinians will honor has required patient negotiations over many years.

A POINT
OF VIEW

CONSIDER THIS: AUTHENTIC OBSERVANCE

When Jews were not considered citizens of countries where they lived, they were usually united in their ghettos; now citizens where they live, they are divided in observances of their faith. Since the eighteenth century, when Jews began receiving civil rights in the United States and Europe, divisions have appeared between Orthodox observers and Jews who adjust their practices to cultures where they live. At the beginning of the twenty-first century, preferences of Orthodox Jews in Israel conflict sharply with preferences of Reform, Conservative, and Reconstructionist Jews in the United States. Because the generosity of Jews in other countries helps sustain Israel, the issues have financial as well as political and religious importance.

Orthodox rabbis, particularly in Israel, have difficulty respecting as rabbis those men and women ordained in non-Orthodox forms of Judaism. More recently, Orthodox rabbis in Israel have questioned whether converts to Judaism received by non-Orthodox rabbis are really Jews, entitled to the right of return to Israel as their homeland. Some non-Orthodox rabbis perceive Orthodox rabbis of Israel as asserting their authority over the lives of Jews in other countries, including the United States.

This controversy within Judaism is an example of the kind of conflict also affecting Islam and Christianity. How much should observances of a religion be limited to cultures of the past, and to what extent can they be adjusted to contemporary societies? "Fundamentalism" in Christianity and a somewhat different "fundamentalism" in Islam raise similar issues. Is authentic observance of a faith dependent on unchanging forms from past centuries, or can believers adjust their observances to contemporary conditions? What balance between past observances and present condition assures an optimum experience of a vital faith in the future?

WORLDVIEW

The worldview of Judaism today reflects about four millennia of God's interaction with the children of Abraham, Isaac, and Jacob. The worldview presented in the Bible has been foundational rather than final. Interactive experiences in rabbinic, medieval, and modern Judaism have produced other interpretations. Modern Judaism, then, comprises many living traditions that change as they interact with each other, with other religions, and with historical developments.

The Absolute

The creed of Judaism (the Shema) is brief: "Hear, O Israel! The Lord is our God, the Lord alone" (Deuteronomy 6:4). This is what every religious Jew believes. The next part of the creed is what a Jew does. "You shall love the Lord your God with all your heart and with all your soul and with all your might" (Deuteronomy 6:5). As part of the Torah, the creed comes from the most sacred part of the Bible.

Judaism has usually expressed the nature of the Lord, Adonai, in the analogy of a person. Where Greek philosophers preferred to conceive of God as unchanging and remote from the created world, the Bible is a record of God's involvement in changing seasons, the rise and fall of nations, and the activities of the families of his chosen people. Dialogues between the Lord and successive generations of humans are reported in detail. Yet as knowledge of the universe has increased, so has the concept of God.

As other religions developed from an animistic stage to personal gods and a God, so may Judaism have developed. A history-of-religions approach to the scriptures yields abundant examples of animism in the early stories of the Torah, the first five books of the Bible. Groves, springs, rocks, and hills are places where the divine is especially concentrated. His power is actually present in the symbol of the Ark of the Covenant, the box containing the stone tablets with the Ten Commandments. Only priests can touch the Ark; anyone else who touches it is subject to injury, death, or disease. The creation story of Genesis describes the Lord walking in his garden, Eden, in the cool of the evening, conversing with Adam and Eve. In the Exodus account, only Moses directly sees God. In other references, no person can see God and live. God speaks, however, to whomever he chooses.

Along with these stories, however, the Torah presents a very advanced concept of God. The whole world is his. He enters the lives of good people and makes covenants with them. He hears their cries when they need him and responds to deliver them. He guides and directs his people. He makes impotent toys of the greatest kings of the nations. He is compassionate to the fatherless, the barren woman, slaves, and prisoners. He is a warrior fighting for his people.

◆ **3760** First year of the Jewish calendar

◆ **2000** Abraham

◆ **1600** Amoses frees Egyptians from Hyksos rule

◆ **1300** Moses leads Hebrews to Promised Land

◆ **1004–965** King David reigns

◆ **965–928** King Solomon reigns

◆ **721** Assyria conquers Israel

◆ **597** Babylonians exile Jews

◆ **586** Nebuchadnezzar of Babylon destroys Jerusalem

◆ **538** Cyrus releases Jews from Babylon

◆ **515** Jews build second temple in Jerusalem

◆ **490** Greeks defeat Persians at Marathon

◆ **444** Ezra renews the covenant

◆ **332** Alexander the Great arrives

◆ **264–241** Punic Wars: Rome defeats Carthage

◆ **167** Antiochus IV provokes Jewish revolt

◆ **164** The temple rededicated

◆ **63** Pompey establishes Roman rule

◆ **30** Philo born

◆ **29** Christianity begins

70 Romans destroy Jerusalem temple ◆

73 Romans capture Masada ◆

90 Jewish Scriptures formed into canon ◆

135 Romans expel Jews from Jerusalem ◆

220 Rabbis complete the Mishnah ◆

480 Rabbis complete the Talmud in Babylon ◆

887 Saadia ben Joseph born ◆

BCE	2000	1500	1000	500	0	500	1000	1500	2000	CE

1000 Year 4760 of the Jewish calendar ◆

1075 Judah Halevi born ◆

1135 Maimonides born ◆

1250 Moses de Leon born ◆

1492 Spain expels Jews; Columbus sails for New World ◆

1700 Israel Baal Shem born ◆

1729 Moses Mendelssohn born ◆

1800 Napoleon becomes First Consul in France ◆

1842 Herman Cohen born ◆

1896 Theodore Herzl launches Zionism ◆

1917 Balfour Declaration ◆

1933 Nazis begin persecution of Jews ◆

1939–45 World War II fought; Jews suffer Holocaust ◆

1948 Israel becomes a state ◆
In India, Mohandas K. Gandhi assassinated

1956 Suez war between Israel and Egypt, Israel takes Gaza Strip ◆

1962 Lt. Col. John Glenn, Jr., first man to orbit the Earth ◆
Adolph Eichman hanged in Israel for his role in the Nazi persecution of the Jews

1967 Six Day War; Israel defeats enemies and expands its territory, holding ◆
Golan Heights, West Bank, Old City of Jerusalem, and Sinai

1979 Israel and Egypt, in cooperation with President Jimmy Carter, sign a final peace treaty ◆

1982 Israelis assault PLO forces inside Lebanon ◆

1987 Israeli occupied territories torn by civil disobedience ◆

1990 Jews and Muslims clash at Temple Mount, Jerusalem ◆

1993 Israel and Palestinians negotiate a peace treaty ◆

1994 Israel and Jordan negotiate a peace treaty ◆

1995 Rabbi Bea Wiler becomes Germany's first female rabbi since the Holocaust ◆

1996 Prime Minister Benjamin Netanyahu comes to power in Israel ◆

BCE 2000	1500	1000	500	0	500	1000	1500	2000 CE

In the prophets, the Lord is clearly God of all Hebrews and an effective contender with gods of other nations. Other gods, such as the Baals of the Canaanites, are not reliable or powerful when compared to the God of Elijah. In the eighth-century B.C.E. prophets, God controls the kingdoms of Israel and Judah. The Lord is the standard of justice, like a plumb line used by masons to test the perpendicular tolerance of walls. God is the source of forgiving, redeeming love, like a husband who forgives an unfaithful wife. The Lord is holy, set apart, high and lifted up. Above the petty ambitions of upstart kings, he preserves those who trust in him. The Lord is one who chose his servant while he was in his mother's womb. The Lord is ineffable, great beyond the power of words. He is one who saves remnants of his chosen people. He establishes peace on earth. David describes the Lord as a faithful shepherd.

A Psalm of David

The Lord is my shepherd;
    I lack nothing.
He makes me lie down in green pastures;
    He leads me to water in places of repose;
    He renews my life;
    As befits His name.
Though I walk through a valley of deepest darkness,
    I fear no harm, for You are with me;
    Your rod and Your staff—they comfort me.
You spread a table for me in full view of my enemies;
    You anoint my head with oil;
    my drink is abundant.
Only goodness and steadfast love shall pursue me
    all the days of my life,
    and I shall dwell in the house of the Lord
    for many long years. (Psalm 23:1–6)

Does Judaism ever indicate that God can be thought of in nonpersonal terms? There appear to be some exceptions to the personal analogies of the Lord. God, who speaks to Moses in the burning bush, identifies himself as Ehyeh-Asher-Ehyeh. Some writers believe that this reference means definitely that God is beyond limitations of a personal analogy. Other scholars emphasize that the name is not "I Am That I Am" but "I Am Who I Am." The En Soph of the *Zohar* is an absolute above the pairs of male and female emanations. In the philosophy of Baruch (Benedict) Spinoza (1632–1677), who was excommunicated from Judaism, God is identified with the totality of the cosmos, or universe.

A rabbi asked by a Gentile why God spoke to Moses from the midst of a bush answered:

To teach that there is no place void of the Divine Presence, not even so lowly a thing as a bush. The saying is attributed to God: "In every place where you find the imprint of men's feet there am I."[28]

Rudolph Otto describes God in his classic book *The Idea of the Holy* as one who is wholly other from the person who experiences him. God fascinates and draws humans to him, but he also is so awe inspiring that they feel the urge to flee his presence.[29] The human analogy gives the best conception of the Jewish God. Jews recognize, however, that the analogy must not lead to a cheap intimacy. Some devout Jews will not write all the letters of the name of God, preferring to write *G–d.* They refer to him as the Lord.

The World

The Genesis account of creation establishes the theme of the relationship of God and the world that is retained in the history of Judaism.

> When God began to create heaven and earth—the earth being unformed and void, with darkness over the surface of the deep and a wind from God sweeping over the water—God said, "Let there be light"; and there was light. God saw that the light was good, and God separated the light from the darkness. God called the light Day, and the darkness He called Night. And there was evening and there was morning, a first day. (Genesis 1:1–5)

The universe is subordinate to God and dependent on him; it is always less than God and other than God. Established in a thoughtful, systematic process, all its parts are good, and everything together is very good (Genesis 1:31). The phenomenal universe is not God, but it is evidence for God's creative power and love. Frightening oceans are balanced by fertile lands; unpleasant animals are balanced by tasty meats. The seasons change predictably; humans can plan their lives according to them.

Judaism celebrates the universe. The Psalms praise many features of the sky and the earth (Psalm 19:24).

> The heavens declare the glory of God,
>   the sky proclaims His handiwork.
> Day to day makes utterance,
>   night to night speaks out.
> There is no utterance,
>   there are no words,
>   whose sound goes unheard.
> Their voice carries throughout the earth,
>   their words to the end of the world.
> He placed in them a tent for the sun,
>   who is like a groom coming forth from the chamber,
>   like a hero, eager to run his course.
> His rising-place is at one end of heaven,
>   and his circuit reaches the other;
>   nothing escapes his heat. (Psalm 19:2–7)

Sun and rain cause the earth to yield food. The moon marks the seasons for thanksgiving and celebrating harvests. Increasing herds and crops are signs of God's blessings. In Judaism, the universe is made for humans; it is to be enjoyed with gratitude during a long life. Human suffering is not attributed to the created nature of the universe. Judaism rejects any worldview that sees nature as evil, a place to be escaped. The phenomenal world is God's world; he is present in the heavens, in the earth, and in the place of shadows (Sheol) under the earth. The world is other than God, but it is not opposed to God. In celebrating the nature of the universe, Jews praise the activity of God. Judaism's approach to ecology has always been based on the concept of humans as stewards of God's creation.

> The earth is the Lord's and the fullness thereof, the world and those who dwell therein. (Psalm 24:1)

As the story of Genesis explains, God created the world and everything in it; he entrusted Adam and Eve with its care. Only when humans act responsibly to God can they enjoy the bounty of the earth.

Humans

Genesis describes humans as God's highest creatures.

> And God created man in His image, in the image of God He created him; male and female He created them. God blessed them and God said to them, "Be fertile and increase, fill the earth and master it; and rule the fish of the sea, the birds of the sky, and all the living things that creep on the earth." (Genesis 1:27–28)

Male and female humans are created in the image of God. Each is a soul and body united. Each is created for fellowship with God. Humans should rule over all the earth, which has been given to them for food and pleasure. They are little less than gods (or angels); God has crowned them with glory and honor. How small and weak humans are in comparison to the vastness and power of the heavens and earth! Yet humans, rather than the impersonal universe, are the purpose of God's creation. God made humans good; in harmony with his plan for the universe, they are very good.

Humans are responsible. They are answerable to God for their conduct (Genesis 3:9–24). Unlike animals, which are governed solely by instincts, humans can evaluate situations and make choices. They can obey or disobey God, serve or reject God, live in harmony or in enmity with other humans, have nature for or against them. Humans can live any way they choose; they have only to bear the consequences.

Jews are part of the covenant people of God, having additional responsibilities in life. The covenant relationship between God and Israel was mediated by Moses. In the general obligation between two unequal parties, God and the children of Israel, God offers blessings to Israel on condition of its keeping his commandments. The covenant was sealed by a sacred meal and sacrifices.[30]

The women's movements of the twentieth century have inspired Jewish women to reconsider their roles in Judaism. Recognizing that Orthodox Judaism has supported not only the masculine concept of deity but also the subservience of women in a patriarchal system, some women in Reform and Conservative Judaism have offered alternative roles for women. They have compared themselves with Maimonides, who brought Judaism into harmony with his times. Women, they argue, can fulfill responsibilities beyond the traditional roles assigned in the home as wife and mother. They can serve as officers of congregations, study theology, and serve as rabbis. They can rework translations and liturgies in language that expresses feminine, as well as masculine, religious experience. Susannah Heschel outlined the agenda of Jewish women this way:

A Female Rabbi Blowing Shofar. In Greenberg, Mississippi in the mid-1980s, a rabbi in Reform Judaism blows the ram's horn trumpet.

> The most recent wave of Jewish feminism, beginning during the 1960s, is assuming the opposite posture: not breaking away from the community, but struggling to become full members of it. Feminists are calling today for changes within *halakhah* to end discrimination in areas from divorce laws to synagogue separation; for inclusion in secular leadership; for concrete changes in the structure of the community to accommodate changing life-styles of women, from day-care centers to greater community acceptance of single mothers. At the same time, new studies concerning various aspects of women and Judaism are being published: women in the Bible, women resistance fighters during World War II; images of women in aggadic literature.[31]

Jews are required to keep halakhah, the legal aspect of Judaism, which is distinguished from aggadah, the nonlegal aspect, particularly rabbinic literature. It now refers to the whole legal system of Judaism. The written law is that which God gave to Moses at Sinai; the oral law included the interpretations, or logical deductions, from written law.[32]

Each Jew is to keep mitzvot (plural of *mitzvah*), or religious duties. Traditionally, there are 248 positive and 365 negative mitzvot, a total of 613. Jewish boys are responsible for keeping them at age thirteen plus one day, and girls are responsible at age twelve plus one day. Mitzvot are performed as commanded by God; no reward follows immediately, but those who are obedient have confidence in the hereafter.[33]

The Problem and the Solution for Humans

Torah history describes the creation of Adam and Eve and their subsequent rebellion against God. Their exclusion from the Garden of Eden accounts for the miseries and frustrations humans must endure. God chose Noah and his family, righteous people, to survive a worldwide flood, forming a remnant of humans to repopulate the earth. The most righteous humans were soon involved in sinful acts; their children were no better than they. The biblical history of the Hebrews and their descendants, the Jews, relates God's ongoing endeavors to restore, for brief periods of time, a covenant relationship of loving-kindness and faithfulness.

Jews understand the teachings of Moses from Exodus through Deuteronomy as explanations of beliefs and practices that invite compliance with the covenant and permit restoration after human lapses. God, powerful and just, extends compassion to all generations.

> Have mercy upon me, O God,
>   as befits Your faithfulness;
>   in keeping with Your abundant compassion,
>   blot out my transgressions. (Psalm 51:3)

At various times, Jewish groups sought help from individuals other than priests. One group expected a descendant of King David to restore Judaism. Others expected someone in the prophetic tradition, such as the prophet Elijah, to help renew the covenant. Groups have identified one of their contemporaries as the Messiah, who would usher in a new age. Most Jews agree that although the Messiah is expected, he has not come. In this belief, Jews do not agree with Christians that Jesus is the Messiah.

Community and Ethics

Religious Jews consider themselves members of a family and of a larger community in covenant with God. The Passover observance reminds them of their membership in a community that God redeemed from bondage in Egypt and led to a land of promise. The community has often been severely persecuted, but God has always saved a remnant to fulfill his purposes. Jews may be of almost any nationality or race. There have been Ethiopian Jews since biblical times. Into modern times, these "falashas" continued to practice sacrifices in their temples. Israelis recognized them publicly as Jews by airlifting many of them to Israel. Those who claim to be Jews and who are accepted by the Jewish community are Jews.

In the age of universalism, or emphasis on a global community, the traditional Jewish idea of a chosen people strikes some non-Jews as an archaic concept. In the Bible, however, particularly in the writings of the

Deuteronomist, God rules universally, but he has chosen Israel as the people of God. God's election of Israel is based on its response to the covenant he has offered. Accepting the blessings of the covenant requires, in return, accepting its responsibilities. Israel is obligated to keep its law and statutes. Although God does not always approve of Israel's actions—he sometimes condemns the actions—he does not utterly reject Israel. In all history, he seeks to restore the covenant relationship with his people.

Beyond the age when the scriptures were written, rabbis have emphasized that God's choosing Israel is based on its accepting the Torah at Sinai. No other peoples on earth, except those who have become Jews, have accepted the conditions laid down in the Torah. In medieval Judaism, Judah Halevi advanced the idea that from the time of Adam, Jewish people were endowed with a special religious faculty. In modern Judaism, Moses Mendelssohn argued that Judaism is identical with a "religion of reason."[34]

Since the Holocaust, Jews have wrestled with developing a revised, up-to-date understanding of what it means to be a chosen people. Being chosen and set apart from other peoples brings suffering as well as the blessings of pleasant living.

The concept of chosen people is a part of Judaism that may be shared, in other forms, with other religions. Most of the religions that we have studied emphasized the special relationship of a people with a deity or with a particular discipline of life. Is there something in the nature of religion that reinforces particularity, even at the expense of universality?

Robert Gordis has written,

> Throughout its long history, Judaism kept in tension its particularistic origin and function and its universal vision and thrust. All the various modern interpretations of Judaism that possess any degree of authenticity recognize and share this preservation of a specific group loyalty linked to an attachment to universal values.
>
> This balance has always been natural to Jews but has often appeared as a stumbling block or a scandal to some and as a pretense or a contradiction to others. The sober, historical fact is, however, that both elements in this balance have survived in Jewish consciousness and thought for millennia. It is also the key to the understanding of the unique Jewish attitude toward national and religious loyalties outside of its own.[35]

Why did God choose the Jews? Reflecting pride and humility, Arthur Hertzberg has written,

> But why did God choose this people? There are several partial answers: the merits of their ancestors, chiefly Abraham, who accepted the One God and broke with idolatry; their comparative virtue; their humility and their faithfulness. The first reason, the argument based on the merit of Abraham, recurs everywhere in Jewish literature, and especially in the liturgy. The others (and more can be added) indicate that the question remained a question—and a source and guarantor of humility.[36]

Whatever the reason, Judaism thinks in terms of a community chosen to be responsible to God. Membership in a community of chosen people, however, requires commitment to universal values. Judaism promotes care for humans, animals, and the environment among all peoples. Ethical behavior is directed not only to Jews but to all peoples. It attends to both its particular origin and its universal vision.

One way that Jews have kept their separate identity is through food laws, *kashruth*. Arthur Hertzberg explains their purpose this way:

Essentially the traditional writings have produced two basic reasons for kashruth: that these laws represent a curbing of man's animal appetites and that they are ordained as a way of setting the Jews apart in their day to day life, so that they might be conscious of their responsibility as members of a priest-people. Ultimately, the laws of kashruth cannot be rationalized. The believer accepts them as part of a total system, the Jewish way to holiness, ordained by God. The nonbeliever may cling to kashruth out of sentiment or attachment to a cultural past, but this clinging has demonstrably seldom outlasted one generation of disbelief.[37]

The dietary laws of Judaism are directly related to the concept of a chosen people. The laws of kashruth, food that is fit or proper for preparation or consumption, are binding on Jews. In the Torah, all fruits and vegetables are permitted. Other laws describe which animals, birds, and fish may be eaten, how they may be prepared, and how they cannot be eaten with milk or dairy products.[38]

In the Pentateuch, ten clean animals are listed: ox, sheep, goat, hart, gazelle, roebuck, wild goat, ibex, antelope, and mountain sheep (Deuteronomy 14:4–5). Camels and pigs are forbidden. The Bible lists twenty-four unclean birds, especially birds of prey; it does not list any clean birds. Among Jews, pheasants and turkeys are disputed birds; goose and duck may be eaten. Although four kinds of locusts can be eaten, insects are forbidden; honey can be eaten. Fish must have at least one fin and one scale. Sturgeon and swordfish are disputed among Jews.

Slaughtering must be according to rules of **Shehitah** and carried out by a licensed **shohet.** An animal that died a natural death or one that was torn by a wild beast cannot be eaten. After the slaughter, the shohet must examine the meat for any signs of disease. If certain signs are present, the meat is forbidden. Neither the sciatic nerve nor fat attached to the intestines and the stomach can be eaten.

Because Jews are not permitted to eat blood, meat must be prepared so as to remove veinal blood. After proper slaughtering, which removes most of the blood, the remaining blood can be removed either by placing it in salt or by roasting the meat over an open flame. The proper preparation of meat is called koshering.

In the book of Exodus, Jews are forbidden to seethe a kid in its mother's milk (Exodus 23:19; Deuteronomy 14:21). Jews have interpreted this law to mean that milk and meat shall not be eaten in the same meal. The prohibition extends to cooking, eating, or deriving benefit from such a mixture. Prohibition on milk extends to all dairy products. To protect themselves from violation, Jews keep everything connected with preparation, serving, and eating meat separated from everything connected with preparation, serving, and eating milk and dairy products. In Orthodox Jewish homes there are complete, separate utensils for meat and milk preparation and consumption. Although fish, vegetables, and fruit are neutral, rabbis have prohibited eating meat and fish together. As only meat prepared by a Jew can be used, so also only milk production supervised by a Jew may be used.

Although Reform Judaism does not insist on observance of kashruth, other congregations emphasize compliance as highly desirable. Orthodox Jews insist on compliance.

Jews look to the ethical laws of the Torah to guide their relationships. The law requires them to love their neighbors as themselves. The Ten Commandments state the minimum requirements; the remainder of the Torah explains responsibilities in daily circumstances, especially in those where commandments have been violated. Widows, orphans, the poor, strangers,

Shehitah [she-HEE-tah]
The Jewish method of slaughtering permitted animals or birds for food. The method is to kill the living thing as swiftly and as painlessly as possible with one swift cut across the throat.

shohet [SHOW-het]
A Jewish slaughterer of animals, who kills according to ritually correct methods.

A Torah Scroll. The Scroll is removed from the ark in the temple (synagogue) and read to the congregation. Writings of Moses contain the central teachings of Judaism.

the homeless, and stray animals have always been given special compassion and aid.

The goal in ethics is to imitate the behavior of God. A person must love the Lord and walk in his ways, holding fast to him (Deuteronomy 11:22). "As the Holy One, blessed be He, is called righteous, be you also righteous; as He is called loving (Psalm 145:17), be you also loving" (Sifra Deuteronomy 49:85a). A. Cohen concludes,

> No finer summary of the Rabbinic teaching on the subject of brotherly love could be suggested than the pithy epigram: "Who is mighty? He who turns an enemy into his friend."[39]

Ethics for Jews are based on the entire halakhah. Jews have obligations of mitzvot, which include both the negative and the positive commandments. Although Orthodox Judaism considers halakhah absolutely binding, Reform Judaism rejects its absolute binding force.

Other than belief in one God and in the thirteen points of Maimonides, Judaism emphasizes deeds rather than beliefs. To be a practicing Jew is to participate in a lifetime of rituals using unique symbols. A Jew participates with hands and heart as well as with ear and mind. Rituals that mark the seasons and stages in each life work their way into the very fibers of practicing Jews' lives. Only a practicing Jew can grasp the full meaning of the rituals and symbols that have been a part of Judaism since the giving of the Torah.

Observances that mark important experiences for Jews are celebrated by both the community and individuals. The Sabbath is observed each week, beginning with sundown on Friday. Holidays are observed annually. The Jewish calendar is based on a lunar month, which means that each year holidays fall on different days of the solar calendar. There are regulations in the Jewish calendar, however, that keep the festivals in the same season. The new year begins in the fall.

In the month of Elul, a ram's horn (*shofar*) is sounded, calling the faithful to *teshubah*, openly confessing their sins against their neighbors. Prepared for the new year, Jews celebrate Rosh Hashana, New Year's Day.[40]

Rosh Hashana, the first of the Days of Awe, celebrates God's creation of the world. Although some cultures celebrate the new year with outpourings of joy and pleasure, Judaism marks the occasion with prayer, contemplation, and self-searching.[41] A period of repentance ensues to Yom Kippur, the holiest day of the Jewish calendar. It is the day of atonement, a twenty-four-hour period of fasting. During much of the evening and the next day, Jews spend their time either standing or kneeling in the congregation.

Hanukkah comes near the end of the solar year and celebrates the rededication of the Jerusalem temple in 164 B.C.E. The sacred oil that was enough for only one day miraculously lasted for eight days of celebration. The menorah of nine branches marks this special Feast of Lights. Hanukkah is a minor festival, as is Purim. A happy holiday observed as the days of winter lengthen, it recalls Queen Esther, who helped her people escape a sinister plot of genocide in Persia; the holiday of Purim celebrates the deliverance of Jews from their enemies.

In the spring, Jews celebrate two holidays. The most important holiday in the Jewish year is Passover, which marks God's deliverance of the Hebrews from slavery in Egypt through the leadership of Moses. The other holiday, Shavuot, marks an early harvest and calls attention to the giving (revelation) of the Ten Commandments.

During Passover, Jews eat a sacred meal, the Seder. The order of the meal is based on **Haggadah,** the Story. The words recited differ somewhat, according to the tradition of the family.[42] By custom, a child asks four questions about why the meal is different from all other meals.

Haggadah [hah-gah-DAH]
The story used at the Seder during the Jewish holiday of Passover. This term is distinguished from *aggadah*, nonlegal stories of rabbinic Judaism.

"Why is matzah eaten instead of bread?"
"It is the symbol of enslavement."

"Why are bitter herbs eaten?"
"They are symbols of enslavement."

"Why do we dip our bread (vegetables) in condiments?"
"They are symbols of freedom."

"Why do we sit in cushioned chairs (recline)?"
"It is a symbol of freedom."

Bar Mitzvah [bar-MITS-vu]
The ceremony that recognizes a thirteen-year-old Jewish boy as a son of the commandment. He is considered an adult responsible for religious duties.

Bat Mitzvah [bat-MITS-vu]
In Reform and Conservative Judaism, the ceremony that recognizes a daughter of the commandment, a Jewish female between twelve and fourteen years of age. She is considered an adult responsible for her religious duties.

Rituals also mark the most significant points of development in individual lives. Male infants are circumcised on the eighth day after birth; the ritual brings them into the covenant established with the patriarchs of Judaism. At age thirteen a boy is considered responsible for his religious acts. He becomes, on his birthday, a **Bar Mitzvah,** a son of the commandment. In recent times, a service in the synagogue celebrates the occasion. During the service, the boy reads from the Torah in Hebrew. Some congregations in America also hold **Bat Mitzvah** services, celebrating a girl's becoming responsible for her religious duties. A betrothal precedes the marriage service, which is held under a canopy, the *huppah*. The groom gives the bride a ring; she may also give him a ring. The bride and groom share a cup of wine. Although sharing the wine completes the marriage service, custom has added the breaking of a glass, symbolic of the fragile nature of supreme happiness. At death, the corpse is washed, simply clothed, and placed in a plain coffin. Family, members of the congregation, and friends express their grief and their faith in God. Judaism meets this important passage, as all others in a person's life, with distinctive ritual that reinforces identity with the community of believers.

Judaism has retained a fascinating balance between preserving its traditions and changing with the demands of the contemporary world. It has held its people to basic ideals of serving one God and maintaining high moral conduct. On the other hand, it has adapted to dress, language, laws, national loyalty, and educational and economic opportunities in a variety of geographical locations. It has a latitude that permits freedom of expression to different personality types and yet maintains a unity.

Life After Death

Judaism has emphasized a good life on earth more than the joys of heaven. In early Judaism, there was a belief that souls of the departed slept in Sheol, but most people did not find the prospect attractive. The Pharisees in the first century believed that the body is resurrected; the Sadducees denied it. Judaism today avoids embalming bodies and uses plain wooden boxes that will decay after burial. There are references in the Psalms to heaven and hell, concepts that some scholars believe were influenced by Zoroastrians. In reading Jewish services, there is an absence of specific descriptions of life beyond death. There is life with God in the age to come, and the joy of fellowship with God is more important than real estate, property, status, and activities. Isaac Luria taught that souls are reincarnated. But rabbis taught as a matter of faith that there is resurrection from the dead; to deny it is sinful. "Since a person repudiated belief in the Resurrection of the dead, he will have no share in the Resurrection" (Sanh. 90a).[43]

Judaism and Other Religions

Although Jews think of themselves as God's chosen people, that is, selected from among all others to live by the Torah, they believe that other peoples can worship God, overcome sin, and live according to his universal moral laws. From biblical times, converts have been welcomed to Judaism. Nevertheless, peoples can serve God in their own religions. In Hermann Cohen's view, the Messianic Age is a time when all peoples will live in peace under the rule of God. There are, nevertheless, significant differences between Judaism and major world religions. Jews cannot accept polytheistic forms of Hinduism, for Judaism condemns idolatry and worship of more than one God. They agree with the monotheism of Islam, but they cannot accept that Muhammad is the seal (last) of the prophets. To Jews, Trinitarian Christians are polytheists; calling Jesus God is blasphemous. Jesus, for Jews, is not the Messiah. For much of their history, Christianity and Islam have had strained relationships with Judaism. There have been some notable exceptions when Christians, Muslims, and Jews have lived together in harmony and mutual appreciation. Many examples of cooperation can be found in the United States in the twentieth century.

How do Jews view Christianity? Rabbi Leo Baeck (1873–1956), a brilliant scholar in Germany, survived the Gestapo's assault on his books and person. In his book of essays *Judaism and Christianity*, Rabbi Baeck describes Christianity as one of several postbiblical movements in Judaism.[44] The early followers of Jesus were Jews who drew heavily on the traditions of the fathers, especially in their expectations of a Messiah. After the destruction of the temple in 70 C.E., they formed the views that are presented in the gospels of the New Testament. They developed a romantic view of the world. By this term Rabbi Baeck meant that they abandoned the discipline of living ethical lives, preferring instead to give primacy to miracles and doctrines of a supernatural end of time. In a recent dialogue with a Christian, Pinchas Lapide advanced these theses for response: (1) Jesus did not present himself to his people as Messiah; (2) the people of Israel did not reject Jesus; and (3) Jesus never repudiated his people.[45]

The distinctive worldview of Judaism has developed from Jews' concept of themselves as a people in covenant with God. The events of history have helped them shape their particular identity. Although Jewish interpretation differs from that of all other peoples, it has influenced all culture of the West and, through Christianity and Islam, all peoples.

In the next chapter we will study Christianity. We will see how the Jewish worldview helped shape the response of people to Jesus of Nazareth as the Messiah. As a religion of the family of Abraham, Christianity shares many of the events of historical development and worldview with Judaism. Although acknowledging Judaism as preparation, Christians emphasize that Christianity is a separate, more acceptable religion. We will see how Christians have interpreted history and worldview to establish a different "chosen people."

✒ VOCABULARY

Aggadah [ug-GAHD-u]
allegorical method
Ark of the Covenant
Asherah [ash-u-RAH]
Ashkenazim [ahsh-ku-NAH-zim]
Baal [BAA-ul]
Bar Mitzvah [bar-MITS-vu]
Bat Mitzvah [bat-MITS-vu]
Canaanites [kay-nu-NIGHTS]
covenant [CUV-u-nunt]
diaspora [di-AHS-pe-ra]
Essenes [ES-eens]
Gemarah [ge-MAHR-u]
Haggadah [hah-gah-DAH]
Halakhah [ha-la-KAH]

Hanukkah [khan-nu-ka]
Hillel [hil-EL]
Holocaust [HOL-u-cost]
Islam [is-LAHM]
kashruth [KASH-root]
kosher [KO-sher]
matzah [MUT-za]
Messiah [mi-SIGH-u]
Midrash [MID-rash]
Mishnah [MISH-na]
mitzvah [MITZ-va]
modernism [mod-ur-NIZ-um]
Muslim [MUS-lim]
Passover [PASS-o-ver]
Pharisees [PHAR-i-sees]
prophet [PROF-it]

rabbi [RAB-eye]
Sadducees [SAD-u-sees]
Sanhedrin [san-HEED-rin]
scribe [SCRIIB]
Sephardim [se-fahr-DIM]
Shehitah [she-HEE-tah]
Shema [SHEE-ma]
shohet [SHOW-het]
Tanakh [ta-nak]
Talmud [TAL-mud]
theodicy [THEE-od-i-se]
Torah [TOR-ah]
Western Wall
Zealots [ZEL-uts]
Zionism [ZII-e-NIS-em]

QUESTIONS FOR REVIEW

1. What are two different ways of interpreting the history of Judaism?

2. What are the two major ways of interpreting the Jewish Bible?

3. List and describe ten of the most important leaders in the Bible.

4. Outline the steps that rabbis took in producing their written commentaries on Torah.

5. What beliefs and practices distinguish each major branch of Judaism?

6. List some of the obligations of Jews that distinguish them from other religions in the family of Abraham.

7. Name a half-dozen people who have helped form Judaism since the Bible and the Talmud. What contribution did each person make?

8. List some of the ways that practice of Judaism today differs from that in the Bible.

9. List some of the points of difference between Israelis and Palestinians. List some points on which both can agree.

10. Outline some steps that led to the Holocaust. What steps by people other than Nazis could have prevented it?

QUESTIONS FOR DISCUSSION

1. Since Hindus value a variety of forms of their gods, painting pictures of them and decorating carvings of them, why has Judaism had such a strong prohibition against idols?

2. Do Jews believe that God changes, or do they believe that their understanding of God changes?

3. What effect has Jewish suffering had on Jews' belief that they are a people chosen by God?

4. What qualifications must a person meet to be accepted as a Jew? How can a person not born a Jew become one?

5. How important is the state of Israel to the well-being of Judaism? What practical steps would you recommend for an enduring peace among the religions in the family of Abraham?

NOTES

1. From *The Tanakh, The New JPS Translation According to the Traditional Hebrew Text* (Philadelphia: Jewish Society, 1985). Copyright © 1985 by the Jewish Publication Society. Used by permission.

2. Ibid., p. 88.

3. A. Malmat, "Origins and the Formative Period," in *A History of the Jewish People*, ed. H. H. Ben-Sasson (Cambridge, MA: Harvard University Press, 1976), p. 91. Dates in this chapter are taken from this source.

4. Ibid., p. 33.

5. M. Stern, "The Period of the Second Temple," in *A History of the Jewish People*, ed. H. H. Ben-Sasson (Cambridge, MA: Harvard University Press, 1976), pp. 296–299.

6. Flavius Josephus, "The Wars of the Jews," in *The Works of Josephus*, trans. William Whiston (Peabody, MA: Hendrickson Publishers, 1987), p. 741.

7. *The Interpreter's Dictionary of the Bible*, vol. 3 (Nashville, TN: Abingdon Press, 1962), p. 294.

8. Samuel Belkin, *Philo and the Oral Law* (Cambridge, MA: Harvard University Press, 1940).

9. Leo Trepp, *A History of the Jewish Experience* (New York: Birman House, 1973), p. 131.

10. Jacob Katz, *Exclusiveness and Tolerance* (New York: Oxford University Press, 1961), p. 5.

11. See "Judah Halevi," in *Encyclopedia Judaica*, vol. 10, eds. Cecil Roth and Geoffrey Wigoder (Jerusalem: Keter, 1971), pp. 355–366.

12. Jacob S. Minkin, *The World of Moses Maimonides* (New York: Thomas Yosaloff, 1977).

13. *Gates of Prayer, The New Union Prayerbook* (New York: Central Conference of American Rabbis, 1975), pp. 732–733. For a different translation that makes clearer the points of Maimonides, see Bernard Martin, *Prayers in Judaism* (New York: Basic Books, 1968), pp. 84–85.

14. Daniel Chanan Matt, *Zohar* (New York: Paulist Press, 1983).

15. Katz.

16. Ibid., p. 170.

17. William W. Hallo, David B. Ruderman, and Michael Stanislawski, *Heritage, Civilization and the Jews: Source Reader* (New York: Praeger, 1984), p. 245. By permission of Greenwood Publishing Group, Westport, Conn.

18. Trepp, p. 397.

19. Bernard Martin, *Movements and Issues in American Judaism* (Westport, CT: Greenwood Press, 1978).

20. Elie Wiesel, *Souls on Fire,* trans. Marion Wiesel (New York: Random House, 1972), p. 30.

21. Martin Buber, *The Origin and Meaning of Hasidism,* trans. Maurice Friedman (New York: Harper & Row, 1960).

22. Martin Buber, *I and Thou* (New York: Scribner's, 1958).

23. Hermann Cohen, *Religion and Reason,* trans. Simon Kaplan (New York: Frederick Ungar, 1972).

24. Anne Frank, *The Diary of a Young Girl* (Garden City, NY: Doubleday, 1967), p. 287.

25. S. Ettinger, "The Modern Period," in *A History of the Jewish People,* ed. H. H. Ben-Sasson (Cambridge, MA: Harvard University Press, 1976), p. 1035.

26. Emil Fackenheim, *Quest for Past and Future* (Bloomington, IN: Indiana University Press), 1968.

27. See "Jew" in *Encyclopedia Judaica,* vol. 10, eds. Cecil Roth and Geoffrey Wigoder (Jerusalem: Keter, 1971), pp. 23–25.

28. A. Cohen, *Everyman's Talmud* (New York: Schocken Books, 1978), p. 9.

29. Rudolph Otto, *The Idea of the Holy* (London: Oxford University Press, 1924).

30. See "Covenant," in *Encyclopedia Judaica,* vol. 5, eds. Cecil Roth and Geoffrey Wigoder (Jerusalem: Keter, 1971), pp. 1012–1022.

31. Susannah Heschel, ed., *On Being a Jewish Feminist* (New York: Schocken Books, 1983), p. xv.

32. See "Halakhah," in *Encyclopedia Judaica,* vol. 7, eds. Cecil Roth and Geoffrey Wigoder (Jerusalem: Keter, 1971), pp. 1156–1158.

33. See "Mitzvah," in *Encyclopedia Judaica,* vol. 12, eds. Cecil Roth and Geoffrey Wigoder (Jerusalem: Keter, 1971), pp. 162–163.

34. See "Chosen People," *Encyclopedia Judaica,* vol. 5, eds. Cecil Roth and Geoffrey Wigoder (Jerusalem: Keter, 1971), pp. 498–502.

35. Robert Gordis, *The Root and the Branch* (Chicago: University of Chicago Press, 1962), p. 25.

36. Arthur Hertzberg, *Judaism* (New York: George Brazillier, 1962), pp. 27–28. Copyright © 1961 by Arthur Hertzberg. Reprinted by permission of Simon & Schuster, Inc.

37. Ibid., p. 100.

38. See "Kashruth," in *Encyclopedia Judaica,* vol. 6, eds. Cecil Roth and Geoffrey Wigoder (Jerusalem: Keter, 1971), pp. 26–45.

39. A. Cohen, pp. 211, 216.

40. Trepp.

41. Philip Goodman, *The Rosh Hashanah Anthology* (Philadelphia: Jewish Publication Society, 1970).

42. Ruth Gruber Fredman, *The Passover Seder* (Philadelphia: University of Pennsylvania Press, 1981).

43. A. Cohen, 357.

44. Leo Baeck, *Judaism and Christianity,* trans. Walter Kaufmann (New York: Atheneum, 1970).

45. Pinchas Lapide and Ulrich Luz, *Jesus in Two Perspectives,* trans. Lawrence W. Denef (Minneapolis: Augsburg, 1979).

✒ READINGS

Anderson, Bernard W. *Understanding the Old Testament.* Englewood Cliffs, NJ: Prentice Hall, 1986. A standard text in higher education for understanding the Old Testament.

Ben-Sasson, H. H. *A History of the Jewish People.* Cambridge, MA: Harvard University Press, 1976. A comprehensive volume that allows readers to examine particular events in their historical contexts.

Cohen, A. *Everyman's Talmud.* New York: Schocken Books, 1978. A readable, informative digest of some major teachings of the Talmud.

Fishbane, Michael. *Judaism.* Hagerstown, MD: Torch, 1987. A concise introduction to Judaism.

Greenberg, Irving. *The Jewish Way: Living the Holidays.* New York: Summit Books, 1988. For the general reader, a very helpful introduction to the meaning of Jewish holidays for Jews.

Halo, William, David Ruderman, and Michael Stanislawski, eds. *Heritage: Civilization and the Jews.* New York: Praeger, 1984. This volume accompanied a television series; it contains many primary sources needed for studying Judaism.

Holtz, Barry, ed. *Back to the Sources: Reading the Classical Jewish Texts.* New York: Summit Books, 1984. Helps readers understand Jewish texts from the Bible to the Prayer Book.

Neusner, Jacob: *Judaism's Theological Voice: The Melody of the Talmud.* Chicago: University of Chicago Press, 1995.

Plaskow, Judith. *Standing Again at Sinai: Judaism from a Feminist Perspective.* San Francisco: Harper, 1991.

Trepp, Leo. *Judaism.* Belmont, CA: Wadsworth, 1982. A general introduction to Judaism for a broad group of readers.

READINGS FOR RESEARCH AND REPORTS

Baeck, Leo. *Judaism and Christianity.* Translated by Walter Kaufmann. New York: Atheneum, 1970.

Bandstra, Barry L. *Reading the Old Testament.* Belmont, CA: Wadsworth, 1995.

Baskin, Judith R. *Jewish Women in Historical Perspective.* Detroit: Wayne State University, 1991.

Belkin, Samuel. *Philo and the Oral Law.* Cambridge, MA: Harvard University Press, 1940.

Ben-Gurion, David. *Israel.* New York: Funk & Wagnall's, 1971.

Berkovits, Eliezer. *Faith After the Holocaust.* New York: KTAV Publishing, 1973.

Bokser, Ben Zion. *The Wisdom of the Talmud.* New York: Philosophical Library, 1951.

Buber, Martin. *The Origin and Meaning of Hasidism,* trans. and ed. Maurice Friedman. New York: Harper Torchbooks, 1966.

———. *I and Thou.* New York: Scribner's, 1958.

Cantor, Norman E. *The Sacred Chain: The History of the Jews.* San Francisco: HarperSanFrancisco, 1994.

Cohen, Mark R., *Under Crescent and Cross: The Jews of the Middle Ages.* Princeton, NJ: Princeton University Press, 1994.

Danby, Herbert. *The Mishnah.* London: Oxford University Press, 1933.

Dimont, Max I. *The Jews in America.* New York: Simon & Schuster, 1978.

Donin, Hayim Halevy. *To Be a Jew.* New York: Basic Books, 1972.

Encyclopedia Judaica. Editors-in-chief Cecil Roth and Geoffrey Wigoder. Jerusalem: Keter, 1971.

Fackenheim, Emil. *Quest for Past and Future.* Bloomington: Indiana University Press, 1968.

Frank, Anne, *The Diary of a Young Girl,* trans. B. M. Mooyaart–Doubleday. Garden City, NY: Doubleday, 1967.

Fredman, Ruth Gruber. *The Passover Seder.* Philadelphia: University of Pennsylvania Press, 1981.

Friedman, Richard Elliott. *Who Wrote the Bible?* New York: Harper & Row, 1987.

Gates of Prayer, The New Union Prayerbook. New York: Central Conference of American Rabbis, 1975.

Gilbert, Martin. *The Holocaust.* New York: Holt, Rinehart and Winston, 1985.

Glatstein, Jacob, Israel Knox, and Samuel Margoshes. *Anthology of Holocaust Literature.* New York: Atheneum, 1980.

Golden, Hyman E. *A Treasury of Jewish Holidays.* New York: Twayne, 1952.

Goodman, Philip. *The Rosh Hashanah Anthology.* Philadelphia: Jewish Publication Society, 1970.

Gordis, Robert. *The Root and the Branch.* Chicago: University of Chicago Press, 1962.

Grossman, Susan, and Rivka Haut, eds. *Daughters of the King: Women of the Synagogue.* Philadelphia: Jewish Publication Society, 1992.

Halevi, Judah. *The Kuzari,* intro. H. Slonimsky. New York: Schocken Books, 1964.

Heschel, Abraham J. *The Circle of the Baal Shem Tov,* ed. Samuel H. Dresner. Chicago: University of Chicago Press, 1985.

Heschel, Susannah, ed. *On Being a Jewish Feminist.* New York: Schocken Books, 1983.

Josephus, Flavius. *The Complete and Unabridged Works of Josephus,* trans. William Whiston. Peabody, MA: Hendrickson, 1987.

———. *Selections from His Works,* intro. and notes Abraham Wasserstein; trans. William Whiston. New York: The Viking Press, 1974.

Katz, Jacob. *Exclusiveness and Tolerance.* New York: Oxford University Press, 1961.

Katz, Steven T. *Jewish Ideas and Concepts.* New York: Schocken Books, 1977.

Lapide, Pinchas, and Ulrich Luz. *Jesus in Two Perspectives,* trans. Lawrence W. Denef. Minneapolis: Augsburg, 1979.

Neusner, Jacob. *American Judaism: Adventure in Modernity.* Englewood Cliffs, NJ: Prentice Hall, 1972.

Novak, David. *Jewish Christian Dialogue: A Jewish Justification.* New York: Oxford University Press, 1989.

Oesterley, W. O. E., and T. H. Robinson. *A History of Israel.* London: Oxford University Press, 1932.

Price, James L. *The New Testament.* New York: Macmillan, 1987.

Rodkinson, Michael L. *New Edition of the Babylonian Talmud.* New York: New Talmud Publishing, 1900.

Rosenberg, David, ed. *Congregation. Contemporary Writers Read the Bible.* New York: Harcourt Brace Jovanovich, 1987.

Shanks, Hershel, ed. *Ancient Israel.* Englewood Cliffs, NJ: Prentice Hall, 1988.

Silberstein, Lawrence J. "Judaism as a Secular System of Meaning: The Writings of Ahad Haam." *Journal of the American Academy of Religion,* 52(3) (1984). Pp. 547–568.

Tanakh. Philadelphia: Jewish Publication Society, 1985.

Trepp, Leo. *A History of the Jewish Experience.* New York: Birman House, 1973.

Wiesel, Elie. *Messengers of God,* trans. Marion Wiesel. New York: Random House, 1976.

———. *Souls on Fire.* New York: Random House, 1972.

Wouk, Herman. *This Is My God.* Boston: Little, Brown, 1988.

Christianity

Baptism of Jesus. John the Baptist baptized Jesus in the Jordan River.

Introduction

Under Roman rule in Palestine, which began in 63 B.C.E., the house of Herod gained favor by helping keep peace and collect taxes. After the death of Herod the Great in 4 B.C.E., however, Jews were divided in their religious and political loyalties. Sadducees remained loyal to Torah, Temple, and Rome; Pharisees advocated innovations in Torah interpretation; the Essenes sought greater purity in religion; and Zealots stirred open revolt against Rome. Romans crucified followers of Judas the Galilean in 6 C.E., casting a shadow over subsequent advocates of religious and political change.

To ordinary people of Palestine, these revolutionaries may have seemed innocent, but they awakened in Jewish leaders a keen sense of impending collapse. Strong personalities stirred the simmering pot. John the Baptist, the son of a Jewish priest, baptized people for their sins in preparation for the imminent arrival of the Kingdom of God. His cousin, Jesus, was accused of blasphemy for forgiving people's sins and driving money changers from the Temple. Peter, James, and John, the fishermen from the Sea of Galilee who left their work to follow Jesus, helped organize and announce a new Way of life in Jerusalem. Mary the mother of Jesus would be honored as the mother of God. These troublemakers were exceeded only by another Jew who changed his name from Saul to Paul and brought Gentiles into the Way without requiring circumcision or observance of Torah.

Early Christians, nevertheless, played little part in the war that Vespasian and his son Titus waged to destroy the Temple in Jerusalem in 70 C.E. Earlier, many Christian leaders had been executed; their revolution of the Roman Empire was more protracted, not reaching a truce until the time of Constantine or victory until the reign of Theodosius. From these humble beginnings and an endorsement from a powerful Roman government, missionary-minded Christians tried faithfully to follow the Great Commission that Jesus gave his followers, "Go therefore and make disciples of all nations" (Matthew 28:19). In this chapter we will see how Jesus and his followers launched their teachings to all the world.

HISTORICAL DEVELOPMENT

As we examine the story of Christianity, we will see how these personalities within the Jewish religion so changed their views and emphases that they gave rise to a religion distinct from Judaism and all other religions. The term *Judeo-Christian religion*, sometimes used in the United States, emphasizes the common roots, beliefs, and practices of Judaism and Christianity. Nevertheless, both Jewish and Christian scholars know that in the twenty-first century Judaism and Christianity are two distinct faiths; they may cooperate, but they do not coalesce. As we emphasize the chronological development of Christianity, we will explain the unique view of Christian historiography.

Historiography

Christ [KRIIST]
The Greek word meaning "the anointed one." The Hebrew word for the concept was *messiah*. Christians believe that Jesus was the long-awaited Messiah.

Most Christians think of their history as a special plan of God that reached its apex in the birth, life, death, and resurrection of Jesus as **Christ**. All world events prior to him were but preparation for his coming; all events after him are but realization of God's plan that was clearly revealed. Early in their separate religions, Christians added to the Jewish concept of their history. Jews were God's chosen people, richly blessed by God until their leaders rejected Jesus as their Messiah. After that rejection, the old covenant was replaced by a new covenant for the new people of God, those who accepted Jesus as the Messiah, or Christ. These elements contribute to the particular "salvation history" of Christians. With these ideas in mind, we will outline the chronological development of contemporary Christianity. The central person of Christian history is, of course, Jesus of Nazareth, who is worshiped as the Christ, the Son of God.

Jesus of Nazareth

Our knowledge of Jesus is based on accounts in the Christian sacred writings, the New Testament. Except for the birth stories, which many scholars believe were the last sections of the gospels composed, we know little of Jesus' youth. The Gospel of Luke reports that he was related to John, who was known as "the Baptist." Although John was the son of a Jewish priest, Zechariah, he chose to preach outside the establishment, as had former Hebrew prophets. John announced that the kingdom of God was at hand. He challenged hearers to repent and believe the good news. Then he used water as a symbol of washing away the sins of those who repented and accepted the message. When Jesus was about thirty years old, he participated in one of the gatherings and received baptism from John. The Holy Spirit descended on Jesus as he came from the water, and a voice came from heaven saying, "Thou art my beloved Son, with thee I am well pleased" (Mark 1:11).[1]

Jesus did not appear in public immediately but spent a period of time in fasting and prayer. The gospels report that he engaged in a dialogue with Satan before returning to everyday life. When King Herod imprisoned

The Tomb of Christ. A Christian in devotion at the tomb within the Church of the Holy Sepulcher, Jerusalem, Israel.

John the Baptist, Jesus appeared in public announcing, "The time is fulfilled, and the kingdom of God is at hand; repent, and believe in the gospel" (Mark 1:15). Jesus chose disciples who would learn his teachings and help him in his work. Besides teaching, Jesus sometimes announced that a person's sin had been forgiven, or he sometimes performed mighty works **(miracles),** healing individuals or influencing natural phenomena. Luke emphasized that Jesus was concerned to help the poor, the ill, and "sinners" who did not measure up to rabbinical standards of piety. On occasion, he raised people from the dead. Stories of these deeds inspired wonder and awe among the common Jewish people; because Jesus seemed to perform them in his own name, the deeds raised deep concern and resentment among priests, scribes, and rabbis.

miracle [MIR-a-kul]
An event that is judged to be brought about by divine intervention in the ordinary events of history.

The Teachings of Jesus

The general theme of Jesus' teachings was the kingdom of God. He announced standards of human conduct that would prevail in the lives of

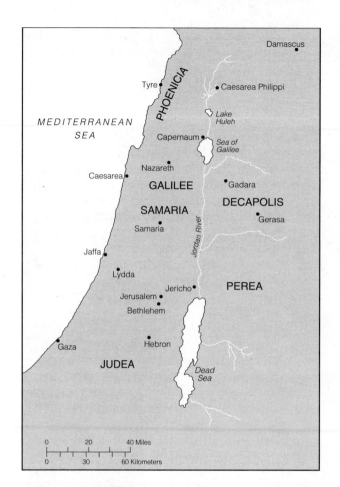

The Holy Land of the New Testament.
Judaism and Christianity share a reverence for the Holy Land of the first century, C.E. Christians have special reverence for Bethlehem, Jerusalem, Nazareth, and centers around the Sea of Galilee.

people who lived according to the will of God. Jesus established God's perfection as the only standard by which personal conduct could be measured. The generous mercy of God set the pattern for the kind of generosity with which people were to treat each other. The kingdom could begin with a few like-minded people at any one time and place, and increase as others freely chose to participate. The final, fullest participation in the kingdom under the direct rule of God could not be predicted in terms of time; it is a mystery known to God rather than to humans. Jesus taught that the kingdom of God had come and is coming when God chooses. Jesus emphasized the personal side of religion, referring to God as "our Father." He challenged men and women to fulfill their roles as children of the Most High. He welcomed children who came to him, saying that the kingdom of God was composed of people having childlike faith. He was content to eat with tax collectors, to talk with a prostitute in the home of a host, to defend a woman whom a crowd accused of adultery, to talk with a Samaritan woman at a public well, and to dismiss criticisms from the Pharisees with the words:

> Those who are well have no need of a physician, but those who are sick; I came not to call the righteous, but sinners. (MARK 2:17)

Although Jesus defended the letter of the Mosaic law in the Sermon on the Mount (Matthew 5:1–7:29), he argued that a righteous person would go beyond the letter of the law and fulfill the spirit as well. He supported the Mosaic law, which says that humans must not kill another human being, but he went beyond it, saying that humans must not even be angry with their brothers. He agreed with the Mosaic law that denounced adultery, but he disagreed with easy divorce, which, in his eyes, contributed to adultery. In the Gospel of Mark 10:9, he said that God joins man and woman in marriage; no one should break them apart. He denounced lust, which is a prelude to adultery. The Mosaic law teaches "eye for eye and tooth for tooth" (Exodus 21:24). Jesus said,

> Do not resist one who is evil. But if any one strikes you on the right cheek, turn to him the other also . . . and if any one forces you to go one mile, go with him two miles. (MATTHEW 5:39,41)

For Jesus, piety was an inner spirit that motivated good deeds, not a series of rituals that might win praise from religious people but disguise a mean spirit. God knows a person's heart, and a simple prayer for forgiveness of sins and for the coming of God's kingdom is more valued than elaborate prayers offered to gain praise from other religious people. If people cannot forgive their neighbors, they should not expect forgiveness from God. They must first be righteous before God before undertaking the correction of humanity and in the end, only God is the final judge of who is right and wrong. Jesus encouraged people to pray to God.

> Ask, and it will be given you; seek and you will find; knock, and it will be opened to you: For every one who asks receives, and he who seeks finds, and to him who knocks it will be opened. (MATTHEW 7:7–8)

Jesus summed up the law and the prophets with the words "So, whatever you wish that men would do to you, do so to them; for this is the law and the prophets" (Matthew 7:12).

The people who followed Jesus thought that he showed them the proper way of relating to God. Early Christians were known as members of the Way; John's gospel reported Jesus saying, "I am the Way" (John 14:16). Using a Jewish concept of Way in the Old Testament, Jesus and his followers emphasized it as God's preferred path for human conduct.

Jesus' teachings were memorable. Ordinary people called him rabbi. It was a title of respect, but Jesus had no formal rabbinic training. His hearers were aware that no one else spoke the way he did; he taught without giving references and quotations from Hillel or Shammai, leaders of rabbinic schools, or their disciples. Instead he told **parables,** or stories, that helped ordinary people consider profound religious questions. In the parable of the Good Samaritan, a Samaritan rescues the victim of highway robbery who had been passed by pious Jews who refused to help. The Samaritan, though despised by Jews, is a good neighbor (Luke 10:36). The Prodigal Son is a parable of universal appeal. A wayward son rebels against his father and leaves home to seek a more exciting, worldly life. Later, penniless and friendless, he comes to himself and returns to seek his father's forgiveness. The father, who sees him coming, runs to meet him, embraces him, and prepares a feast to celebrate his return, saying, "For this my son was dead, and is alive again; he was lost and is found" (Luke 15:24). Jesus used a very familiar situation to convey his concepts of God and human alienation and reconciliation. Sometimes he used paradoxes to drive home a point: "Why do you see the speck that is in your brother's eye, but do not notice the log that is in your own eye" (Matthew 7:3)? Or, "Woe to you, scribes and Pharisees, hypocrites! . . . You blind guides, straining out a gnat and swallowing a camel" (Matthew 23:23,24)!

parable [PARE-u-bul]
A simple story told to illustrate a religious truth or lesson.

Jesus' Authority

The question about the source of Jesus' authority was of utmost importance to Jewish officials in his day. How did he claim to know the truth of what he taught? He was not given to quoting authoritative rabbis or even to proving every point by citing scriptures. Had he been appointed by any Jewish officials? Was his forgiving sins blasphemous of God, an act inviting capital punishment under Jewish law? His measuring human conduct by God's perfection criticized Jewish religious leaders for falling short of the kingdom of God.

The disciples who accompanied Jesus, both men and women, recognized his authority as of God. He trained twelve of these disciples to convey his teachings and healings to villages that he could not immediately visit. Women from his family and families of his disciples helped support his work among the multitudes who followed him.

Trying to analyze Jesus' true identity stirred speculation among his hearers. The people of Nazareth, his hometown, saw him only as a son of Mary and Joseph, with brothers and sisters who lived in their midst. In Capernaum, he shocked people by his healing sick people on the Sabbath. His disciples, when he asked them at Caesarea Philippi, reported that people regarded him as Elijah returned, or one of the prophets, or as John the Baptist raised from the dead (Herod had beheaded John). Simon, son of Jonas of Capernaum and later known as Peter, which means "rock," said that Jesus was the **Messiah**—the anointed one the Jews had expected to be sent from God. Jesus told Simon not to tell anyone because he would be put to death.

The Teachings and Authority of Jesus in John, the Fourth Gospel

Although Christians have selected four gospels to present their official views of Jesus as the Christ, John, the fourth gospel, offers a perspective

Messiah [mi-SIGH-u]
The one whom the Jews expected to come and deliver Israel from oppression and establish a kingdom of righteousness.

The Last Supper. This engraving by Doré recalls the event that is commemorated by Christians in the Eucharist.

that is somewhat different from the first three gospels. The Gospel of John presents the teachings and authority of Jesus in impressive accounts, such as those that feature the "I am" sayings, or teachings, of Jesus. The person Jesus is presented as the believer's way to God: "I am the way, the truth, and the life" (John 14:6). These pronouncements are usually connected with a memorable event, such as John's account of Jesus' raising from the dead his friend Lazarus. Jesus arrived at the tomb of Lazarus four days after his entombment. Directing that the tomb be opened, Jesus, after praying to God, called, "Lazarus, come out!" The dead man came out wrapped in his burial clothes. Jesus directed bystanders to unbind him and let him go. Thus Jesus demonstrated the truth of his promise to Martha, "Your brother will rise again." He had also stated the reason why Lazarus would live again: "I am the resurrection and the life; he who believes in me, though he die, yet shall he live, and whoever lives and believes in me shall never die" (John 11:25,26). Other favorite sayings in John are "I am the bread of life" (6:35), "I am the light of the world" (8:12), "I am the door" (10:7), "I am the good shepherd" (10:11), and "I am the true vine" (15:1).

The Last Week of Jesus

The gospel accounts focus on the week before Jesus' death. The celebration of Palm Sunday recalls Jesus' entry into Jerusalem for the feast of the Passover. When he rode into the city on a small donkey, the crowds recognized the symbolism from Isaiah 62:11 and Zachariah 9:9:

Tell the daughter of Zion,
Behold, your king is coming to you,
humble, and mounted on an ass,
and on a colt, the foal of an ass. (MATTHEW 21:5)

Those who had known Jesus in Galilee waved palm branches in the air, spread their garments on the road before him, and shouted, "Hosanna to the Son of David! Blessed be he who comes in the name of the Lord! Hosanna in the highest!" (Matthew 21:9). Although his reception could have caused concern among religious leaders in Jerusalem, it was the next act of Jesus that sealed his doom. He went into the temple on the next morning and drove out those who bought and sold and the money changers, saying,

It is written, "My house shall be called the house of prayer";
but you make it a den of robbers. (ISAIAH 56:7; JEREMIAH 7:11; MATTHEW 21:13)

The last supper for Jesus and his disciples together has a special meaning for Christians. During the meal, Jesus took a piece of bread, blessed and broke it, saying, "Take, eat; this is my body" (Matthew 26:26). Then he took a cup of wine and, having blessed it, said, "Drink of it, all of you; for this is my blood of the covenant, which is poured out for many for the forgiveness of sins" (Matthew 26:27–28). These acts are recalled by most Christians in the sacrament of Holy Communion, the Lord's Supper, one of the most sacred occasions of worship for Christians. Jesus and his disciples ended the evening in the upper room by singing a hymn.

Jesus and eleven of his disciples then went to the garden of Gethsemane; they were to watch for him while he prayed. Later, a group carrying swords and clubs came from the priests and scribes to arrest him. Judas, the twelfth disciple, identified Jesus for them, an act making him the

Garden of Gethsemane. This garden outside the Old City of Jerusalem is the traditional site where Jesus was arrested as he prayed with his disciples.

betrayer of Christ. The group arrested Jesus and took him to the high priest's house, where he was given a hearing before members of the council.

The high priest, Caiaphas, said,

> "I adjure you by the living God, tell us if you are the Christ, the Son of God." Jesus said to him, "You have said so. But I tell you, hereafter you will see the Son of man seated at the right hand of Power, and coming on the clouds of heaven." Then the high priest tore his robes, and said, "He has uttered blasphemy. Why do we still need witnesses? You have now heard his blasphemy. What is your judgment?" They answered, "He deserves death." (MATTHEW 26:63–66)

The next morning, the high priest delivered Jesus to Pilate, the Roman prefect who governed Jerusalem at that time. The charge that the high priest brought against Jesus was that he claimed to be king of the Jews, a charge that caught the attention of Pilate, because insurrection, led by Zealots, had long been a threat to peace. Zealots were Jews who used force in an attempt to overthrow Roman rule in Palestine. Again, Jesus made no defense. Pilate asked the crowd what prisoner they would like to have released. They chose a man named Barabbas. Luke 23:19 identifies Barabbas as "a man who had been thrown into prison for an insurrection started in the city, and for murder." Pilate said to them,

> "Then what shall I do then with Jesus who is called Christ?" They all said, "Let him be crucified." And he said, "Why, what evil has he done?" But they shouted all the more, "Let him be crucified." (MATTHEW 27:23,24)

After torturing and scourging Jesus, the Romans led him outside the city to a place called Golgotha and fastened him to a cross, where he remained until he died, about three in the afternoon. The male disciples having forsaken Jesus, only the female disciples kept watch at the cross. An earthquake shook the region. It is reported that it tore the curtain from the Holy of Holies in the temple and that shortly afterward, many bodies of the saints were seen, resurrected from the dead. The centurion said, "Truly this was the Son of God!" (Matthew 27:54). A Roman speared Jesus in the side (John 19:34). The body was claimed by Joseph of Arimathea, a disciple of Jesus, who wrapped it in a linen shroud and placed it in his own new tomb (Matthew 27:60).

Easter, the day that God raised Jesus from the dead, is the most important day of the Christian calendar. Belief in Jesus' **resurrection** is based partly on stories of the tomb's being empty when female disciples returned on the morning after the Sabbath to finish preparing Jesus' body for burial. It is also based on stories that individuals and groups saw and visited with the resurrected Jesus. Sometimes he was readily identifiable; sometimes people took more time to make sure that they had encountered Jesus. At times he was clearly in a physical body; at other times he was a recognizable spirit—one who could enter through barred doors. There are accounts that mention that some of his followers doubted the resurrection, but most of those who remained in the fellowship believed. According to the accounts in the Acts of the Apostles, Jesus appeared on earth for forty days and then ascended into heaven on a cloud. Angels told his disciples that he would return in the same way that he had left them. For Christians, Jesus is not a dead prophet, but the living Son of God.

For Christians, Jesus of Nazareth is a person who is both human and divine. Considered in his human aspect, he was a carpenter, a Jewish layman who knew the scriptures and worshiped in synagogues and the temple. He attracted hundreds of ordinary people wherever he went; they wanted to hear him teach and watch him heal sick people. He was concerned for the last, the least, and the lost. He was critical of people who had set themselves up as models of Jewish piety, such as the scribes and the Pharisees. He spoke of a kingdom of God that was coming; indeed, it had already arrived. He taught the most profound lessons in terms that were easy to understand and remember. But this ordinary person was one in whom many people saw the presence of God. He had in him the power of God to heal broken bodies and sick minds—he could cast out demons. He could calm the waves of a stormy sea, walk on water, feed thousands of his followers with a few fish and loaves of bread, and appear, before the eyes of his closest apostles, in the presence of Moses and Elijah. He was surely the anointed one for whom the Jews waited to establish the rule of God on earth.

The high priest and his friends did not see a divine aspect to Jesus. He was a threat to the power they had received from Rome—it could be withdrawn if they failed to keep the peace. For these powerful Jews, Jesus was a rebel, a false prophet who had to be destroyed. Other Jews, named in the New Testament, regarded Jesus as a true prophet.

Three Thousand People Join the Church

Pentecost is a day of celebration for Christians. On that morning, a few days after Jesus' ascension into heaven, the Holy Spirit descended on the disciples. While **apostles** and disciples met in an upper room in Jerusalem, the Spirit descended on them in tongues of fire. The followers began speaking ecstatically in a spiritual language and went into the streets of

The Crucifixion of Jesus. This detail by Messina shows the women who watched as Romans crucified Jesus.

resurrection [RES-u-REC-shun]
A belief that a person who has been dead will be restored as a whole, living person.

Pentecost [PEN-ti-cost]
A festival in Judaism coming fifty days after Passover. The time when the Holy Spirit descended on the early Christian church.

apostle [a-POS-ul]
A person who was a disciple of Jesus sent out to proclaim the coming of the kingdom of God. Traditionally, there were twelve apostles chosen by Jesus.

◆ **44** Caesar Augustus begins reign

6 BCE Jesus born ◆

14 Caesar Augustus dies ◆

29 Romans execute Jesus; Pentecost ◆

34 Paul converted to Christianity ◆

64 Peter and Paul executed in Rome ◆

94 Domitian persecutes Christians; Revelation recorded ◆

200 St. Irenaeus dies; canon of scriptures formed ◆

213 Clement of Alexandria dies ◆

253 Origen of Alexandria dies ◆

325 Constantine presides over Council of Nicea ◆

354 St. Augustine of Hippo born ◆

407 St. John Chrysostom dies ◆

430 St. Augustine of Hippo dies ◆

543 St. Benedict dies ◆

596 Pope Gregory I sends Augustine to Kent, England ◆

1054 Roman Catholic and Eastern Orthodox Churches separate ◆

1099 Crusaders take Jerusalem from Muslims ◆

1157–1199 Richard the Lion-Hearted, crusader ◆

1170 Thomas à Becket, Archbishop of Canterbury, martyred ◆

1182 St. Francis of Assisi born ◆

1204 Roman Catholic troops sack Constantinople ◆

1215 King John of England signs Magna Carta ◆

1221 St. Dominic dies ◆

1225 St. Thomas Aquinas born ◆

1468 Johannes Gutenberg, inventor of moveable type, dies ◆

1484 Huldrych Zwingli born ◆

1491 St. Ignatius Loyola born ◆

1492 Columbus sails from Spain for the New World ◆

1506 Francis Xavier born ◆

1515 Teresa of Avila born ◆

| BCE | 2000 | 1500 | 1000 | 500 | 0 | 500 | 1000 | 1500 | 2000 | CE |

CHAPTER NINE

1517 Martin Luther posts 95 Theses in Wittenberg ◆

1542 John of the Cross is born ◆

1543 Copernicus's theory of heliocentric universe published ◆

1547 Henry VIII, King of England, dies ◆

1554–1618 Sir Walter Raleigh, colonizer of North Carolina ◆

1555 Peace of Augsburg ◆

1559 Calvin completes last version of *Institutes* ◆

1566 Pius VI is pope ◆

1588 Spanish Armada destroyed before reaching England ◆

1642 Galileo Galilei, astronomer and physicist, dies ◆

1647 George Fox preaches in England ◆

1734 Jonathan Edwards leads revival in Northhampton, Massachusetts ◆

1775 Bunker Hill, first major battle of American Revolution ◆

1786 Greek Orthodox Church in Florida ◆

1831 Joseph Smith organizes Church of Jesus Christ, Latter-day Saints ◆

1848 Marx and Engels publish *Communist Manifesto* ◆

1865 Lee surrenders to Grant at Appomattox, Virginia, ending Civil War ◆

1869 Vatican Council I ◆

1896 Gugliermo Marconi, Italian electrical engineer, patents first wireless receiver ◆

1946 Nag Hammadi codices discovered ◆

1954 Rev. Sun Myung Moon organizes Unification Church in Korea ◆

1965 Second Vatican Council ends ◆

1969 Martin Luther King, Jr. assassinated; First men walk on surface of Earth's moon ◆

1979 Margaret Thatcher is prime minister of the United Kingdom ◆

1989 Mikhail Gorbachev visits Pope John Paul II in Rome ◆

1990 Margaret Thatcher resigns as the prime minister of the United Kingdom ◆

1992 Religious liberties extended to religions in former Soviet Union ◆

1993 Pope John Paul II visits Lithuania ◆

1994 Anglican Church ordains women priests in England ◆

1995 Pope Paul II and Patriarch Bartholomew celebrate mass together in St. Peter's Basilica ◆

| BCE | 2000 | 1500 | 1000 | 500 | 0 | 500 | 1000 | 1500 | 2000 | CE |

Jerusalem to proclaim to Jewish pilgrims that Jesus was indeed the Christ, the long-awaited deliverer of God's people. This proclamation, or **kerygma,** of the **church** concluded,

> Let all the house of Israel therefore know assuredly that God has made him both Lord and Christ, this Jesus whom you crucified. (ACTS 2:36)

Jewish pilgrims had crowded the streets to celebrate the Feast of Weeks, which Greeks called Pentecost. About three thousand people joined the church. The movement that the chief priest had sought to eliminate now expanded rapidly.

The early church regarded speaking in tongues as a sign of the gift of God's Spirit. Wherever Christians gathered, this experience was part of worship. A few years later, a Christian leader, Paul, attempted to limit the practice by having only one or two people speak and by having interpreters translate for hearers. Nevertheless, through the centuries there have been recurrent movements to restore the practice of speaking in tongues.

Some Jews Feel Threatened by the Church

Persecution accelerated the expansion of "the Way," as the organized followers of the Christ were then known. Angry Jews, carrying out their penalty for blasphemy, dragged Stephen, a deacon of the Greek-speaking congregation in Jerusalem, into the street and stoned him to death. The stoning of Stephen became a signal for a general persecution of members of the Way. Those who could not flee were cast into prison, but many of those who could leave Jerusalem went to Galilee and even to Damascus. It was only a question of how seriously Jewish leaders wanted to take the threat to Judaism and how vigorously they wanted to prosecute members of the Way.

Saul of Tarsus

During this persecution, Christianity gained a convert who would transform it into a world faith. Saul of Tarsus, who had been present when Stephen was stoned in Jerusalem, volunteered to take writs to Damascus to find members of the Way, arrest them, and return them in chains to Jerusalem, where they would be tried. He was completely dedicated to eliminating the Christian influence within Judaism. However, as he approached Damascus, he was struck blind. Seeing a great light and falling to the ground, Saul heard a voice speaking to him.

> "Saul, Saul, why do you persecute me?"
> And he said, "Who are you, Lord?"
> And he said, "I am Jesus, whom you are persecuting; but rise and enter the city, and you will be told what you are to do." (ACTS 9:5,6)

Saul remained blind and had to be led into Damascus. Eventually a member of the Way, his former enemies, contacted him and helped him escape from the Jews, who sought his life because he had betrayed their cause. Saul recovered his sight and changed his Jewish name to the Greek form, Paul, in order to mark his change of commitment. For a time before becoming a missionary, he participated in the Jerusalem church.

kerygma [ke-RIG-ma]
The message or proclamation of the early Christians. Peter gave a proclamation on the day of the Pentecost.

church [CHURCH]
A congregation of Christians. All Christians considered together as the mystical body of Christ.

CHAPTER NINE

Paul was never completely at home with the Jewish Christians, who remembered his part in their persecution. There were Jews who would harass him all his remaining life for his rejection of their cause. Paul found it easier to work from Antioch, where members of the Way were first called Christians, as a missionary, one who is sent under sponsorship to win converts. His first efforts were in cooperation with Joseph Barnabas, who accompanied him on visits to synagogues in other regions to proclaim Jesus as the Christ. His success was usually interrupted by other Jews, who arrived to denounce him and to explain how the Jerusalem Jews had

The Conversion of St. Paul. Karel Dujardin has painted this interpretation of the dramatic event in the formation of Christianity as a worldwide religion.

rejected his positions. But Paul usually established a church that was separate from the synagogue. That church, under local leadership, continued to grow while Paul traveled abroad to establish other churches.

Paul's visit to Macedonia and Greece changed forever the religion of Greece and shaped the message of Christianity. Attracting non-Jews as well as Jews, Paul couched his message so that all could grasp the significance of Jesus as the Christ. Paying little attention to the gods and goddesses of the Olympian **pantheon,** Paul drew deeply on the reservoir of belief of Greek **mystery religions.** He presented the Christ as a dying and rising God who offered salvation and life after death to all who lived by faith in him. Paul's letters to Greek churches, such as those in Thessalonica and Corinth, are examples of his message.

The teaching that salvation comes through faith in God's gracious forgiveness and that because Christ lives, believers in him shall also overcome death was especially attractive. Paul rejoiced that Gentiles sought to become Christians. Their presence in the church created, however, a Gentile question. The question was whether Gentiles had to convert to Judaism to become Christians. In deciding the series of events, scholars debate over how to reconcile the account in Acts with the account in Galatians.[2] Most scholars conclude, on the basis of the account in Acts 15:19–21, that through negotiation with leaders in the Jerusalem church, Paul obtained permission to initiate Gentile members by baptism alone—circumcision was no longer required for male Christians. Kosher diets were not mandatory nor were Jewish liturgical laws. Christians were only to avoid eating meat offered to idols, meat that had been strangled, and blood. They were also to avoid the gross sexual excesses of some Gentiles. Indeed, Paul had to outline a new, Christian ethics for those who had not been raised under the Torah. Christianity under Paul became a religion for all nations and peoples, one that included Jews but did not require a convert to become a Jew or to keep the Jewish law. Recommending that Christians live according to the Spirit rather than according to the law, Paul wrote to the church in Rome,

1. There is therefore now no condemnation for those who are in Christ Jesus.
2. For the law of the Spirit of life in Christ Jesus has set me free from the law of sin and death.
3. For God has done what the law, weakened by flesh, could not do: sending his own Son in the likeness of sinful flesh and for sin, he condemned sin in the flesh,
4. in order that the just requirement of the law might be fulfilled in us, who walk not according to the flesh but according to the Spirit.
5. For those who live according to the flesh set their minds on the things of the flesh, but those who live according to the Spirit set their minds on the things of the Spirit.
6. To set the mind on the flesh is death, but to set the mind on the Spirit is life and peace.
7. For the mind that is set on the flesh is hostile to God; it does not submit to God's law, indeed it cannot;
8. and those who are in the flesh cannot please God. (ROMANS 8:1–8)

Judaizers, Jewish Christians who insisted that Christians first become Jews, openly denounced Paul's activities.

Paul's ethics emphasized purity of body and mind. Based on Judaism, he particularly denounced homosexual acts, fornication, incest, and adultery. He abhorred prostitution. Differing from Judaism, his ideal for men and women was virginity. Marriage was a concession for those who burned with passion. Once married, however, a person was to stay married, forgoing sex only when the spouse agreed. He condemned drunkenness and thievery. On the positive side, he challenged Christians to have in themselves the mind of Christ, to consider themselves as part of the body of Christ. Above all he challenged Christians to live by *agape*, self-giving love. He composed a beautiful hymn to love, recommending it to Christians as "a still more excellent way."

1. If I speak in the tongues of men and angels, but have not love, I am a noisy gong or a clanging cymbal.
2. And if I have prophetic powers, and understand all mysteries and all knowledge, and if I have all faith, so as to remove mountains, but have not love, I am nothing.
3. If I give away all I have, and if I deliver my body to be burned, but have not love, I gain nothing.
4. Love is patient and kind; love is not jealous or boastful;
5. It is not arrogant or rude. Love does not insist on its own way; it is not irritable or resentful;
6. It does not rejoice at wrong, but rejoices in the right.
7. Love bears all things, believes all things, hopes all things, endures all things.
8. Love never ends; as for prophecy, it will pass away; as for tongues, they will cease, as for knowledge, it will pass away.
9. For our knowledge is imperfect and our prophecy is imperfect;
10. but when the perfect comes, the imperfect will pass away.
11. When I was a child, I spoke like a child, I thought like a child, I reasoned like a child; when I became a man, I gave up childish ways.
12. For now we see in a mirror dimly, but then face to face. Now I know in part; then I shall understand fully, even as I have been fully understood.
13. So faith, hope, love abide, these three; but the greatest of these is love.
(I CORINTHIANS 13:1–13)

The apostles of Jesus, also, preached in other countries. Christian tradition describes the apostles as men who spread the good news, or gospel, to countries such as Ethiopia, Egypt, Italy, and India. Roman Catholics cherish the tradition that Peter reached Rome and became its first bishop. As the record in the Acts of the Apostles indicates, Christians were already active in Rome when Paul arrived for the first time, a prisoner of Rome who was awaiting action on an appeal to Caesar. Paul had been taken into custody in Jerusalem when a mob of Jews attempted to kill him. Traditions also indicate that violent deaths awaited many of the apostles; by tradition, Peter and Paul died during Nero's persecution of Christians after the great fire in Rome in 64 C.E.

Christians, drawing on precedents in Jewish literature, developed their own interpretation of religious persecution. The Book of Daniel established models for servants of God remaining true to their beliefs in times of severe persecution. In that story, divine intervention saved Daniel from a den of lions and three Hebrew youths from burning in a fiery furnace. A theme of Jewish and Christian literature is that God will deliver safely those who are faithful to him. The New Testament employs a similar theme in gospels and letters.

Romans Persecute Christians

Judaism was a recognized, legal religion in the Roman Empire. Jews informed the Romans that Christianity was not Judaism and not legally included within Judaism. Nero, after Rome burned in 64 C.E., accused Christians of starting the fire and labeled them enemies of the state. Romans began a history of persecuting Christians that lasted until Constantine came to power. Stories of Christian martyrs abound, but there are few more moving than that of Vibia Perpetua and her slave Felicitas. Not yielding to the pleas of her father, Perpetua, a twenty-two-year-old mother of a nursing infant was condemned to die in an arena in North Africa. Felicitas, her servant, who had recently given birth to a baby girl, joined her mistress. Refusing to wear clothes of pagan deities to the arena, the women were stripped naked to stand against a mad heifer.

> Even the crowd was horrified when they saw that one was a delicate young girl, and the other a woman fresh from childbirth, with milk still dripping from her breasts. And so they were brought back again and dressed in loose tunics.[3]

These women, though outwardly frail, were inwardly athletes seeking victory. Contesting the worst of their tormentors, they won victory for Christ.

Major Centers of Christianity in Europe. Having begun in the Holy Land, Christianity quickly spread to cities about the Mediterranean Sea. Soon missionaries carried Christianity to all major centers of Europe.

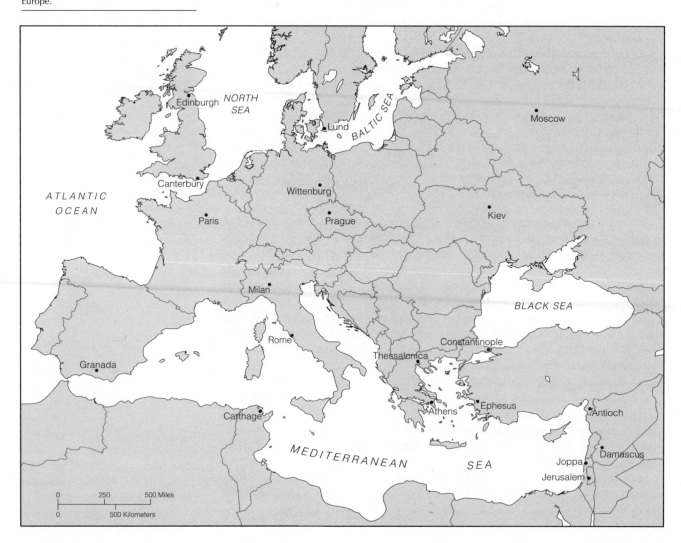

CHAPTER NINE

Perpetua is reported to have helped the executioner in her death. Perpetua, Felicitas, Saturus, Saturninus, and Revocatus died before Romans who saw no point in the new religion. But these martyrs and witnesses helped convert other people to the Christian faith.

Christians accepted persecution for a period of time as an inevitable testing. Because Jesus had been tortured and crucified, how could they who were but servants expect to escape the martyrdom of their master? They did not interpret persecutions to mean that they were wrong, that their cause was lost, or that God had abandoned them. They believed that God was always in charge of history and that after a period of testing them, he would deliver them. They had no doubt that the wicked people of the world would eventually be destroyed by God. They believed that Christ would at some point return from the heavens to which they had seen him ascend and usher in his kingdom. The righteous dead would be raised. Each person would have to stand before God to be judged according to his or her deeds, and more important, the contents of his or her heart.

> Then the King will say to those at his right hand, "Come, O blessed of my Father, inherit the kingdom prepared for you from the foundation of the world; for I was hungry and you gave me food, I was thirsty and you gave me drink, I was a stranger and you welcomed me, I was naked and you clothed me, I was sick and you visited me, I was in prison and you came to me." Then the righteous will answer him, "Lord, when did we see thee hungry and feed thee, or thirsty and give thee drink? And when did we see thee a stranger and welcome thee, or naked and clothe thee? And when did we see thee sick and in prison and visit thee?" And the King will answer them, "Truly, I say to you, as you did it to one of the least of these my brethren, you did it to me." (MATTHEW 25:34–40)

The wicked would be cast into fire, and the righteous would be gathered into the presence of God the Father. God would bring all of the persecutions, tears, and conflicts to an end, resolve all differences, and finally establish his will among humans, all creatures, and all creation.

The last book in the New Testament is an **apocalypse** that includes this vision:

apocalypse [u-POCK-u-lips]
A revelation. A prophetic vision of the destruction of evil and salvation of righteous people.

> Then one of the elders addressed me saying, "Who are these, clothed in white robes, and whence have they come?" I said to him, "Sir, you know." And he said to me, "These are they who have come out of the great tribulation; they have washed their robes and made them white in the blood of the Lamb.
>
> Therefore are they before the throne of God
> and serve him day and night within his temple;
> and he who sits upon the throne will shelter them with his presence.
>
> They shall hunger no more, neither thirst any more;
> the sun shall not strike them, nor any scorching heat.
>
> For the Lamb in the midst of the throne will be their shepherd,
> and he will guide them to springs of living water;
> and God will wipe away every tear from their eyes." (REVELATION 7:13–17)

Emperor Constantine, who ruled from 306 to 337 C.E., brought to an end Roman persecution of Christians. Under his leadership, Christianity became a legal religion, although not the only one. Constantine eventually became a **catechumen,** a student of Christianity, and helped it gain a measure of unity in the first ecumenical council held in Nicea in 325. His policy was a dramatic shift from the practices of Nero, Diocletian, Domitian, and others who had Christians killed for refusing to worship the emperor of Rome as divine. Christianity increased in acceptability and respectabil-

catechumen [KAT-i-KYOO-mun]
A convert to Christianity who received instruction in preparation for baptism.

ity until it had, by the end of the fourth century, gained a place as the official religion of the Roman Empire.

Forming the New Testament

During those centuries, the churches in countries near the Mediterranean Sea developed a **canon** of writings known as the New Testament, which they understood as a new covenant to amend the old covenant that God had made with Moses. These were the scriptures of a new people of God, called by him to believe in his Son whom he had sent to save the world.

The four **gospels,** or accounts of the life of Jesus, overlap and supplement each other so as to give a composite picture of the various churches' views of Jesus. Most New Testament scholars believe that the Gospel of Mark was the first written. Matthew and Luke used much of Mark in their gospels. Matthew added his special material, emphasizing that Jesus fulfilled prophecies of the Jewish scriptures. Luke added accounts that showed Jesus among the common people. In some passages, Matthew and Luke agree word for word on information not found in Mark. Scholars have a theory that they copied from a common source, *Q*, which stands for the German word *Quelle,* or "source." John is an independent account of the life of Jesus—it does not rely on the other three gospels. For example, instead of reporting Jesus' giving his disciples bread and wine at a supper, John reports Jesus' wrapping himself with a towel and washing his disciples' feet. He asked,

> Do you know what I have done to you? You call me Teacher and Lord; and you are right, for so I am. If I then, your Lord and Teacher, have washed your feet, you also ought to wash one another's feet. For I have given you an example, that you also should do as I have done to you. Truly, truly, I say to you, a servant is not greater than his master; nor is he who is sent greater than he who sent him. If you know these things, blessed are you if you do them. (JOHN 13:12–17)

Most scholars date the composition of the gospels after 70 C.E. Raymond Brown, a noted scholar of the Gospel of John, dates its completion about 90.[4]

The letters of Paul, called the **epistles,** are the oldest literature in the New Testament. Prior to 65, these letters of Paul were in circulation: Thessalonians, Corinthians, Galatians, Romans, Philippians, Philemon, and Colossians. After 65, other letters in a style similar to Paul's were written: Ephesians, Timothy, and Titus.[5]

The New Testament includes other kinds of literature. The Acts of the Apostles, a book written by Luke, describes the expansion of the church after the ascension of Jesus. Besides Paul's letters, there are the letters of Peter, James, John, and Jude. One book is Hebrews. The Revelation of John is an example of **apocalyptic literature,** a book that describes the end of time. It was probably composed during the persecution of Christians during the reign of Emperor Domitian, about 95.

The New Testament became the special, later word of God for Christians, although they continued to read and receive guidance from the Old Testament. The Old Testament spoke of God's covenant people, the suffering servant, and the anointed one. The liturgical and dietary laws of Judaism were no longer binding for Christians, but the moral law continued to have influence. Many other gospels and letters that were not chosen for the official canon had an influence on limited groups of Christians. These noncanonical writings played an important role in influencing not

Christian canon [CAN-on]
The list of books accepted as scriptures by Christians.

gospel [GOS-pul]
A message of good news. One of the four stories of the life of Christ found in the New Testament.

epistle [i-PIS-el]
A letter, particularly one that has become part of the New Testament scriptures. Many epistles of the New Testament were attributed to Paul and to the apostles who walked with Jesus.

apocalyptic literature
[u-POCK-u-LIP-tic]
Writings describing the last days, or the end of time. This literature inspires the faithful to stand firm in spite of the severe hardships of their time.

only Christians but also religious groups outside the church. Recently, scholars have studied other gospels found in 1947 near Nag Hammadi, Egypt. The Gospel of Thomas, for example, reported other sayings of Jesus that may supplement the four canonical gospels.

Christian Worship

Christian worship was patterned after synagogue worship. Singing psalms or hymns to God, offering prayers, reading scriptures and interpreting them, exhorting believers to live according to the teachings of the apostles, and receiving offerings for the needy were common activities. Baptizing converts and sharing the Lord's Supper commemorating Jesus' last supper with his apostles were **sacraments** in which Christians sought especially to identify with their Christ.

sacrament [SAK-ra-mint]
A rite instituted by Jesus as recorded in the New Testament to bestow a grace of God.

Christian teachings continued to develop beyond the canon of the New Testament through the works of church leaders and councils. Bishops were spiritual leaders and administrators in each city who supervised other leaders in the churches. Elders and presbyters are other church leaders.

Essentially two major traditions were at work within the Roman Empire. The churches at the eastern end of the Mediterranean Sea were basically Greek speaking. They developed liturgies and practices that tended to emphasize the theological or mystical union of believers with God. Churches at the western end of the Mediterranean Sea adopted Latin as the official language. They developed legal and administrative practices that reflected the genius of the Roman hierarchy. Greek and Roman were two different-colored strands that formed a cord binding traditions that became Christianity's main testimony. Intellectual, traditional, ethnic, and political concerns were always present as the churches communicated with each other to form agreements on orthodox doctrine and to expel **heretics,** those who insisted on continuing to teach what the main body of Christians officially rejected.

heretic [HER-i-tik]
A person who has been judged by the church to teach doctrine dangerously contrary to the teachings of the church.

Ethnic diversity among Christians was reflected in the major traditions of the Greek and Roman churches. From the first century, however, other ethnic traditions of Christianity were present. For example, the Coptic church, of Egypt, has had a distinguished record into the twentieth century. The Armenians have retained their traditions in spite of attempts of their conquerors to exterminate them. Arab Christians have persisted among Jews and Muslims as a faithful minority. They are active in many cities of Israel. Nestorian and Ethiopian Christians formed smaller churches, which were no less courageous in faithful service of their Lord.

Christian Platonists of Alexandria

Although Christians developed their own worldview, they lived among peoples whose worldviews were shaped by Greek philosophy and religions. Dialogues between these groups were essential if converts were to be won for Christ.

From its inception, Christianity was influenced by Greek thought. Hellenistic influence in Judaism dated from the time of Alexander the Great. Once Paul and other Christians launched their missionary journeys into Greece and adjacent territories, their messages incorporated Greek ideas.

Many Jewish concepts were recast in forms that Greeks could understand. Paul's sermon to the audience in the Areopagus of Athens is one example (Acts 17:22–31). In Alexandria, Egypt, a stronghold for Greek thought among Jews, Christian leaders relied on Greek philosophy for ideas that would lead able thinkers to respect and, perhaps, embrace Christianity.

In Alexandria, two outstanding Christian thinkers, Clement and Origen, sought to present Christian teachings as compatible with those of the Platonists, Plato and his followers.[6] They were aided in their task by the allegorical method, which enabled them to find spiritual and philosophical truths in the scripture of the Old Testament and the teachings of Christ. In Alexandria, philosophy was the "handmaiden" of Christianity.

Clement, who lived from about 150 to 213, had been a pupil of Pantaneus, a Stoic philosopher who converted to Christianity. Clement saw the Christ in terms of Logos, the Word, who came to earth to instruct humankind in the ways of salvation. A good Christian can begin in faith and proceed to intellectual knowledge of God. Knowing God is the highest good. The Christian who attains the highest good has an ideal Stoic life—one in which both pleasure and pain are absent.

Origen (180–253) was lay leader of the school for catechumens in Alexandria. As Philo, a Jew of the same city, had done earlier, Origen sought to combine scriptures with Greek philosophy, particularly Platonism and Stoicism. His ideas on the hierarchy of God and angels were presented in *De Principiis*. Origen saw the natural world, like Plato, as changing phenomena, less real than the unchanging spiritual reality behind it. Highly speculative in areas that had not been settled by Christian doctrine, he thought of God as highest, ruling the universe; of Christ, the Logos, ruling humans; and of the Spirit guiding the church. As had Paul, Origen emphasized that Christ died a sacrificial death in order to ransom humans from evil powers. He thought that souls may be eternal, preexisting birth and surviving death through reincarnation. All souls could be saved. A contemporary of Origen's, Bishop Methodius, denied reincarnation of the soul and emphasized the resurrection of the body. Some of Origen's teachings, such as that the created world has always been, that human soul had existed eternally, and that all souls will eventually be saved, were rejected later as official positions of the church.

Clement and Origen inspired later thinkers, such as Ambrose, bishop of Milan, and Augustine, bishop of Hippo, to examine how Christian beliefs are related to Greek philosophy. Although councils rejected some of their conclusions, they did not eliminate the quest to reconcile Christianity with secular philosophy. Ambrose employed the allegorical method of interpreting scriptures to reconcile them with the teachings of Plato and his followers, such as Plotinus. St. Augustine, in his early writings, employed many Platonist ideas in interpreting doctrines of the church. Centuries later, St. Thomas Aquinas studied Aristotle, a pupil of Plato. Using Aristotle's logic, St. Thomas helped develop an expression of Christian beliefs that employed many of Aristotle's philosophical ideas. Christian thinkers were loyal first to scriptures and the church, but they found that Greek philosophy helped them express their beliefs to intellectual leaders of their times.

Ecumenical Councils

Christians were free to study, believe, and teach until someone taught a doctrine that aroused serious objection from bishops of the church. The teachings of Arius, who argued that Christ is the highest creature made by God, aroused opposition from the bishop of Alexandria. Bishop Alexander argued that Christ, the Son, or Logos, is of the same divine nature as the Father, in Greek, *homoousia*.

Constantine, the Roman emperor, seeking the unity of his empire through unity of religion, called an **ecumenical** (whole household of faith) council in Nicea and paid the expenses of attending Catholic bishops, both Greek and Latin. Meeting in 325, they rejected the view of Arius and declared that the Son was begotten of the Father, not made by him. The Son of God was the same essence as God. For the remainder of the fourth century, the Arians appealed their defeat, but eventually supporters of the Arian position were driven out of the Roman Empire. From the second ecumenical council, in 381, is the Niceno-Constantinopolitan Creed, which states the position of the Catholics against the Arians:

> We believe in one God the Father All-sovereign, maker of heaven and earth, and of all things visible and invisible;
>
> And in one Lord Jesus Christ, the only-begotten Son of God, Begotten of the Father before all the ages, Light of Light, true God of true God, begotten not made, of one substance with the Father, through whom all things were made; who for us men and for our salvation came down from the heavens, and was made flesh of the Holy Spirit and the Virgin Mary, and became man, and was crucified for us under Pontius Pilate, and suffered and was buried, and rose again on the third day according to the Scriptures, and ascended into the heavens, and sitteth on the right hand of the Father, and cometh again with glory to judge living and dead, of whose kingdom there shall be no end:
>
> And in the holy Spirit, the Lord and the Life-giver, that proceedeth from the Father, who with Father and Son is worshiped together and glorified together, who spake through the prophets:
>
> In one Holy Catholic and Apostolic Church:
>
> We acknowledge one baptism unto remission of sins. We look for a resurrection of the dead, and the life of the age to come.[7]

The Council of Nicea defined Catholic beliefs about Christ. It also established precedent of bishops and monarchs working together in defining and enforcing doctrine. Christian emphasis on creeds is a departure from Judaism, which emphasizes observance over belief.

Other **heresies** developed concerning the person of Christ. Was he man or God? How were the divine and the human combined? **Adoptionists** claimed that Christ was essentially human; at Jesus' baptism, God had adopted him as his son. **Monophysites** claimed that he was essentially divine. Others thought he had a human body and a divine mind. The Council of Chalcedon in 451 settled the question with a compromise statement. Christ had to be God in order to have power to save sinful humans; he had to be man for his deeds to be effective for humans. The church's position is that he is fully God and fully man in one person.

How is Christ related to the Father and to the Spirit? The Bible speaks of God the Father; it says that those who have seen the Son have seen the Father. The Holy Spirit is also the Spirit of God; Jesus said that he would send the Spirit. How are these three related? How does a Christian who recognizes the reality of Father, Son, and Holy Spirit avoid polytheism?

The problem was explored by some of the greatest teachers in Christianity. The solution that Christianity accepted was set forth in a doctrine on the **Trinity.** One well-received solution was suggested by an earlier churchman from Carthage: Tertullian. He used the term *persona,* which

ecumenical [ek-yu-MEN-i-kul]
Refers to the whole household of faith. It is in contrast to matters of local or special interest.

heresy [HER-i-si]
A belief held by an adherent that is contrary to the accepted teachings of the religious organization.

adoptionist [a-DOPT-shun-ist]
A person who believes that at the baptism of the man Jesus, God adopted him as his Son.

monophysite [mu-NOF-u-SITE]
One who believes that in Christ there was only one nature—divine.

Trinity [TRIN-i-tee]
The Christian belief that three persons in union, Father, Son, and Holy Spirit, are one God.

could mean either a mask through which an actor spoke or a leading character in the state, such as Cicero. Father, Son, and Holy Spirit are three *personae* (persons) but only one essence. Where one is, the other two are fully present. They have their unity in the *economia,* or ruling, of God. The difference that eventually divided Greeks and Latins on the Trinity came later. The Roman Catholics added a teaching that the Holy Spirit proceeded from the Son *(filoque)* as well as from the Father. The Orthodox Church believed the Spirit proceeded only from the Father. Christians agree that God can be fully present in three ways, but there is never more than one God. Some Hindus, who believe that there is only one God who manifests himself through different persons, have few difficulties with the Christian Trinity; most Jews and Muslims find only polytheism in it.

Grace of God for the Sin of Man

St. Aurelius Augustine, bishop of Hippo (354–430), used the allegorical method of interpreting scriptures to reconcile the Bible with many of the insights of Neoplatonism. The allegorical method recognizes the historical, or literal, meaning of scriptures and also seeks their symbolic, or spiritual, meaning. Platonism held that through reason and choice, humans can overcome the evil world and ascend to the realm of pure ideas. But St. Augustine knew that in his youth his decision to forsake his love of sex for the love of wisdom had not borne fruit. For many years he earnestly sought a pure life but lived one that he found corrupt. After his conversion to Christianity, he believed that the grace of God, not his own will, had saved him from sin and damnation.

His classic book *The Confessions* reveals that Platonist philosophy helped him convert to Christianity. Through the excellent sermons of St. Ambrose, bishop of Milan, and through reading some Platonist books, Augustine discovered Christianity as a fulfillment of Plato's dream for a society governed by philosophy.[8] Humans are not evil; through their free will they can choose to move toward God or away from him. The good life is to know God. A person can turn away from the transitory world of senses and passions of flesh and find tranquility of soul in the presence of God. This idea is set forth in the beginning of *The Confessions,* in a prayer to God.

> For Thou madest us for Thyself, and our heart is restless, until it repose in Thee.[9]

Later in Augustine's life, a controversy with Pelagius sharpened his position on human choice. Pelagius argued that the human will is capable of choosing and receiving salvation. Augustine argued that man, originally good, was corrupted through Adam's fall. No one can effectively choose to be saved; only God's grace can lead a person to salvation. Augustine's position triumphed over that of Pelagius, who was condemned as a heretic. The Roman Catholic Church eventually softened St. Augustine's position, allowing for more human capabilities, but it is still anti-Pelagian.

St. John Chrysostom (347–407), of the Orthodox Church, differs with St. Augustine.[10] John Chrysostom's position is more representative of the Greek Orthodox view—human beings, although born sinners, after baptism can be good, can be trusted, and can achieve god-manhood. The grace of God is essential for salvation, but it is freely given and readily available. When a person turns toward God, God's grace assists his or her becoming more godlike.

Jews have found St. Augustine and St. Chrysostom particularly harsh. These church fathers thought that Jews should have become Christians.

Both fathers supported Christians placing harsh burdens on Jews to induce their repentance of Judaism and acceptance of Christianity. The fathers' dislike was for the Jewish religion; Jewish people who converted to Christianity were fully acceptable.[11]

Monasticism

While Christianity sought legal status in the Roman Empire and defined official theological positions, spiritual developments were taking place as well. For example, Christianity attracted men and women who wanted to deny the passions of the flesh and the comforts of the world to devote time to strengthening the spirit and praying for the kingdom of God. Some embraced poverty, celibacy, and obedience to the teachings of Christ. Some of them lived alone in caves or in wilderness areas and denied their bodies food, clothing, water, and ease from pain; some of them wanted to share the sufferings of Christ. Others sought a vision of Christ; others wanted to have the marks of the nail prints of his hands appear in theirs (stigmata), a sign of their identity with him. Others, however, were better satisfied to live together in groups, encouraging each other and learning how to live a more productive and rewarding life of the spirit. Separately, there were women who pledged themselves to virginity and to living all their lives dedicated to the service of Christ, carefully observing fasting and prayers.

From these expressions of personal preferences, Christianity developed rules, or ways of life, for monks and nuns. A person could deny the gross excesses of the sinful world and yet affirm a love for human beings. St. Ambrose of Milan (339–397) praised and established houses for women and men who maintained virginity. St. Augustine, also, supported orders for Christian men and women in North Africa.

St. Francis of Assisi. In a popular tradition, this painting from the school of Giunta Pisana surrounds the saint with scenes of events in his life.

Perhaps the most famous order was that developed by St. Benedict of Nursia (480–547) and instituted in Monte Cassino in Italy. Benedict's model was a garrison of Christ's soldiers.[12] The rule provided for periods of study and prayer alternating with periods of work necessary to maintain the life of the monastery. St. Benedict's Rule (way of life) attracted many men to monastic life.[13]

The famous Franciscan order had a fascinating founder, Francis, whose baptismal name was Giovanni Bernadone of Assisi (1182–1226).[14] His father, a businessman, disapproved of the wild, playboy life Francis enjoyed with his friends. He served in the military and spent time as a prisoner of war. Only a later illness made a difference in his attitude toward life. He spent his time meditating at a local grotto, encountered a leper, and experienced God's invitation to repair the abandoned chapel of San Damiano. Studying Matthew 10, he dedicated himself to imitating Christ and the kingdom of God. By 1208 other men had joined him, seeking to share his life in a brotherhood. In 1212, a noblewoman, Clare, put on religious clothing and began to share the monastic life at San Damiano. Soon other women joined her.

Francis was aware of the triune God in all his activities and teachings. In 1215, the Fourth Lateran Council promulgated reforms that he had advocated in his preaching. For his own companions, he emphasized using only what is needed, owning nothing, and engaging in fraternal service.[15] In every way, including poverty, he sought to imitate Christ. The famous Franciscans, or Gray Friars, minister to the poor and ill of society.

St. Dominic (1170–1221) formed, about the same time, the Dominicans, or Black Friars, who devoted their lives to preaching Christian doctrine and studying so that they could maintain the purity of teachings of the Catholic Church. Missionaries had to deny themselves and live in the kind of poverty the apostles had practiced. They had to beg for their daily food.

Besides men such as St. Augustine and St. Francis, whose lives included some dimensions of mysticism among their other practical interests and works, there were men and women who devoted most of their lives to contemplation, seeking direct communication with Christ.

Catherine of Siena (1347–1380) received her first vision of Christ when she was six years old. Pledging her virginity, she was devoted only to Christ, whom she often saw in visions. Her solitude was balanced by activities in the political world. She advocated that Popes Gregory XI and Urban VI unite Christendom in Holy War to oversee Palestine as a Christian trust. At the invitation of Pope Urban VI, she attempted to mediate his dispute with the anti-Pope, Clement VII. Catherine believed that knowledge of God in oneself and oneself in God is the foundation of all spiritual life.[16]

Governance in Roman Catholic and Greek Orthodox Traditions

Governance in the early church developed several different forms. The apostles were authorities from the beginning. Peter, mentioned often with James and John, was a conspicuous leader. James, the brother of Jesus, was a leader of the Christian church in Jerusalem. Paul was an authority for the churches that he founded. A distinction was gradually made between the churches of the Latin tradition and those of the Greek tradition. In both groups, the leader of a metropolitan district was an overseer of the priests who served the churches in the area. Deacons, presbyters, and bishops were established offices. Elders were mentioned too, as were widows. The churches of a metropolitan area were usually autocephalic, that is, they stood alone. When a council of the church, such as that at Nicea in 325, reached agreement on matters that all were required to believe, most churches conformed.

Over a long period, ecclesiastical power was concentrated in cities important to secular government. The center of the Latin power was in Rome; the center of Greek power became Constantinople. The Orthodox, or Greek, Church remained autocephalic, self-governing, but the patriarch of Constantinople had the status of first among equals. He was a symbol and a spokesman for the Greek Christian tradition. The Latin, or Roman Catholic, Church frequently looked to the bishop of Rome as its symbol of power. Initially, he was first among equals, but later popes claimed to be first without equal. As the civil government became weak and then abandoned Rome for Constantinople, the pope assumed more civil power in order to meet the great needs of Christians in the area. Gradually, the doctrine was affirmed that Jesus had appointed Peter his vicar for the church (Matthew 16:18) and that Peter, as the first bishop of Rome, appointed his successors to enter that office.[17] Only priests who had received the laying on of hands from Peter or those in his succession were regarded as clergy who could forgive sins or celebrate the Mass.

The Greek Orthodox and Roman Catholic traditions formalized their split in the year 1054. A controversy over doctrine and practice led a legate of Pope Leo IX to **excommunicate** Patriarch Cerularius. The patriarch, with his council, excommunicated the legate. Agreement on doctrine in the two traditions ended after the seventh ecumenical council; they went their separate ways. Some attempt at cooperation was made during the Muslim threat to Constantinople, but the crusaders—mostly Catholic—did more damage to the Orthodox center in 1204 than did the Muslims. Since 1054 most Christians have been divided between Greek Orthodox and Roman Catholic churches. Only after the sixteenth century did Protestant churches split from the Roman Catholic Church.

excommunicate
[ex-ku-MYUU-ni-caat]
The forced exclusion of a person from a religious organization, such as a church. People who continued, after warning, to practice errors, often were excommunicated from the church.

Greek Orthodox and Roman Catholic Paths of Service

Even though the Latin and the Greek churches agreed on the creeds of the first seven ecumenical councils, they differed in more than language and geography. They had a different view of humans and, thus, a different view of governance. They also had some different expressions of devotion. The Roman Catholic priests were in full view of the congregation throughout the service; the Orthodox priests were sometimes hidden behind an **iconostasis,** a screen composed of sacred pictures, or icons, that divided the laity from the most holy part of the church. Catholics had three-dimensional statues and two-dimensional paintings that reminded them of holy persons; Greek Orthodox worship featured two-dimensional paintings of holy persons, which some Greeks feared were worshiped. The Iconoclastic Controversy began when Emperor Leo III, in 726, forbade using icons in worship. Some Christians became **iconoclasts,** those who oppose the use of icons in worship. Other Christians were **iconodules,** those who favor the use of icons in worship. In the East, St. John of Damascus denied the emperor's right to legislate dogma. Monks and common people resisted until the emperor sent an army to enforce his decision. A synod during the reign of Pope Gregory II excommunicated those opposed to pictures. The controversy, according to one view, came about due to objections of Jews

iconostasis [ii-con-NOS-ta-sis]
A screen at the front of an Orthodox church that displays many precious icons.

iconoclast [ii-con-o-KLAST]
A person who was opposed to the use of icons in worship.

iconodule [ii-con-o-DOOL]
A person who favored the use of icons in worship.

Saints Boris and Gleb. These saints are credited with helping establish Christianity in Russia.

and Muslims, who found the practice of worshiping pictures idolatrous. Orthodox devotion developed, also, a practice of kissing the cross in worship. By themselves, these were small differences, but together they led Romans and Greeks to consider themselves to be from different traditions. The Roman Catholic troops' sack of Constantinople in 1204 left Christendom with two separate traditions.

Both Greek Orthodox and Roman Catholic traditions fostered missionary outreach. Pope Gregory I (the Great) became interested in England, perhaps due to some English slaves he saw in Rome. In 596, seeking to convert the English, he sent Augustine (not of Hippo) from Rome to the kingdom of Kent, where he baptized the king and thousands of his subjects. Consecrated in Arles, Augustine became Archbishop of Canterbury.

Hagia Sophia. This Christian church was started in 532 C.E. in Constantinople by the emperor Justinian. Muslim conquerors from Turkey turned it into a mosque. The building was secularized in 1934.

Europe and Scandinavia became part of the Roman tradition. The patriarch of Constantinople, supported by the pope, sent Cyril and Methodius, in the ninth century, to convert the Slavs. The story has circulated that Prince Vladimir of Kiev was asked, by Jews, Christians, and Muslims, in turn, to convert to their religions. All were part of his domain or his neighbors. He chose Christianity after his delegates reported the splendor of worship in the Cathedral of Saint Sophia in Constantinople. Later, in 988, Prince Vladimir of Kiev became a Christian and had most of his subjects baptized. In the sixteenth century, Moscow became one of six patriarchates, large territories governed by priests of the rank of patriarch in the Orthodox Church.

The missionary outreach of Christianity has remained alive in every century since its inception. This growth of new congregations has been balanced, periodically, with consolidations of theological beliefs, the worldview of Christians.

St. Thomas Aquinas

St. Thomas (1225–1274), son of the Count of Aquino, was a brilliant student. Having studied nine years at the abbey of Monte Cassino, St. Thomas decided to become a Dominican friar. His parents, furious, restrained him at home and tempted him with worldly pleasures to change his mind. Holding firm to his purpose, he proceeded, at the end of the year, to the University of Paris, where he studied with Albert the Great. In 1259, the outstanding student received an appointment as professor of theology in Paris. Soon afterward, he was invited to the court of the pope in Rome, where he taught until he returned to Paris in 1268. He died on the way to Lyons, where he had planned to attend a church council. His most famous writings are the *Summa Contra Gentiles* and *Summa Theologica*.[18]

St. Thomas Aquinas accomplished another reconciliation of philosophy and theology. **Scholasticism** was the name given to a type of education

scholasticism [sku-LAS-ti-siz-um] A medieval movement of education in which Christian schools taught particular methods of philosophy and theology.

that developed in the schools of France in the eleventh century. It applied logic and dialectics to theological questions. Scholasticism endeavored to draw logical implications from religious faith. St. Anselm (1033–1109) of Canterbury, as well as St. Augustine of Hippo, had found that faith and reason supported each other. St. Thomas Aquinas reinforced this position with his fresh knowledge of a rediscovered philosopher, Aristotle (384–322 B.C.E.). Aristotle's works had been translated from Greek to Arabic by Muslims and from Arabic to Latin by Christians in Cordoba. In the *Summa Theologica*, a classic work comprising several volumes, St. Thomas set forth a reconciliation of Aristotle and Christian theology. He reiterated that both faith and reason lead to truth. There are nevertheless, revealed truths that could not be discovered by reason alone. Once revealed, however, they are perfectly reasonable.

St. Thomas thought the existence of God could be proved by reason, apart from revelation. He wrote,

> *I answer that,* The existence of God can be proved in five ways.
>
> The first and more manifest way is the argument from motion. It is certain, and evident to our senses, that in the world some things are in motion. Now whatever is moved is moved by another, for nothing can be moved except it is in potentiality to that towards which it is moved; whereas a thing moves inasmuch as it is in act. For motion is nothing else than the reduction of something from potentiality to actuality. But nothing can be reduced from potentiality to actuality, except by something in a state of actuality. Thus that which is actually hot, as fire, makes wood, which is potentially hot, to be actually hot, and thereby moves and changes it. Now it is not possible that the same thing should be at once in actuality and potentiality in the same respect, but only in different respects. For what is actually hot cannot simultaneously be potentially hot; but it is simultaneously potentially cold. It is therefore impossible that in the same respect and in the same way a thing should be both mover and moved, i.e., that it should move itself. Therefore, whatever is moved must be moved by another. If that by which it is moved be itself moved, then this also must needs be moved by another, and that by another again. But this cannot go on to infinity, because then there would be no first mover, and, consequently, no other mover, seeing that subsequent movers move only inasmuch as they are moved by the first mover; as the staff moves only because it is moved by the first moved by the hand. Therefore it is necessary to arrive at a first mover, moved by no other; and this everyone understands to be God.[19]

In subsequent paragraphs, St. Thomas described proofs from the nature of efficient cause, from possibility and necessity, from the gradation found in objects, and from governance of the world.

The goal of theological inquiry for St. Thomas was to know God and the nature and destiny of humans. The scriptures, interpreted in the light of the church fathers and the councils, yield final authority. God is the highest substance and supreme good. God does only what is right. Humans make free choices, but only within the providence of God. Sin in the world often leads to virtues. Humans can return to God only through the grace he gives them. That grace became available through Christ, who accomplished what humans could not do for themselves.

With St. Thomas, Christian theology shifted from Platonism to Aristotelianism. Later, Protestant theologians as well as Catholics found inspiration in St. Augustine. But Thomism has dominated Roman Catholic theology into the twentieth century, as the teachings of St. Thomas have been required as part of the education of every priest.

The Crusades

Jews, Christians, and Muslims revered the Holy Land, Palestine, and the city of Jerusalem. Abraham had taken his son there as an offering to God. It was the site of the Temple. Jesus suffered and died there. The Dome of the Rock mosque was there. Peoples of three faiths sought to protect and control access to their holy places. Since the seventh century when Muslims occupied Jerusalem, they had controlled the area. In the eleventh century Muslim forces threatened trade in Byzantine territories and the city of Constantinople. For political, economic, and religious reasons, Christians sought a Holy War against Muslims.

Conflicts between Christians and Muslims deepened during crusades organized by Christians to free the Holy Land, particularly Jerusalem, from Muslim domination. The object of the crusaders was to place the Holy Land with its sacred places under Christian control so that pilgrims could freely visit them and carry out Christian devotions. Pope Urban II proclaimed the first crusade at a synod, an assembly of church officials, in Clermont in 1095. Several crusades were led by nobles of Europe. Jerusalem was liberated and, for a short while, controlled by Christians. Christian slaughter of Muslims in Jerusalem in July 1099 was extremely bloody, even for those times. Battles between Muslims and Christians during the crusades built a deep hatred on each side. Moreover, crusaders attacked Jewish quarters on their way to the Holy Land and persecuted Jews, claiming they were the murderers of the Christ.[20] In the fourth crusade, Christians from the Latin church turned on the populace of Constantinople in 1204 and plundered the city, using much of the loot, including Christian treasures, to pay their Venetian allies for use of their transport ships. Nicetas, a secretary to Isaac of Cyprus, who recorded the events of the crusades, accused the Latin Christians of numerous crimes in Constantinople:

> You have taken up the Cross, and have sworn on it and on the holy Gospels to us that you would pass over the territory of Christians without shedding blood and without turning to the right hand or to the left. You told us that you had taken up arms against the Saracens only, and that you would steep them in their blood alone. You promised to keep yourselves chaste while you bore the Cross, as became soldiers enrolled under the banner of Christ. Instead of defending His tomb, you have outraged the faithful who are members of Him. You have used Christians worse than the Arabs used the Latins, for they at least respected women.[21]

The crusaders generated many tales of heroism that circulated in Western Christendom, but in the process, they deepened divisions among Christians, Muslims, and Jews.

The Arts

Christians employed arts that Jews and Muslims avoided because of their religions' prohibition of idolatry. Jewish arts did not include sculpting and painting. Architecture was limited, and art objects associated with Torah copying, scroll reading, and feast paraphernalia were minimal. Jews following biblical tradition could, however, excel in music. Muslims concentrated on designs in weaving and mosaics that featured subjects in nature rather than humans. Christians seeking to convert Jews and Muslims had opposed the use of icons in worship. The Greek Orthodox Church saw no

Martin Luther. Luther's protest was based on his serious studies of the scriptures.

idolatry in using pictures of sacred people to inspire worship of God and faithful living. Through its popes and bishops, the Catholic Church became a patron of the arts. Michelangelo (1475–1564) was a master carver of statues. His *Pietà*, Mary holding on her lap the crucified Jesus, shows Michelangelo's mastery in depicting the human body. Pope Julius II commissioned him to paint the Sistine Chapel in the Vatican. Among the scenes completed by 1511 is a fresco showing God creating the sun and the planets. Michelangelo's inspiring paintings on the ceiling of the Sistine Chapel made him famous.

In the late medieval period, painting, sculpting, weaving, and music developed rapidly in promoting praise to God. Architecture, borrowing the pointed arch from Muslims, soared to new heights in the Gothic cathedrals of France. Orthodox churches promoted icon painting. Churches became repositories for art and inspired new schools of expression. But there were holy men who would challenge the means used to finance these rich displays and, eventually, the arts themselves.

Christians sought God's grace in their rites of passage through their seven sacraments and in material forms dedicated to his glory. Scriptures could inspire those educated in Latin. Ordinary people, and clergy who could not read Latin well, learned through lessons in fine and performing arts. Paintings, carvings, music, and actions of ritual and drama conveyed the essential messages of faith.

Protestant and Reformed Churches

A third major division in Christianity, the Protestant, became distinct in the sixteenth century. The rift occurred in Germany, France, and Switzerland; soon most countries of Europe had participants. England and Scotland were deeply involved.

Numerous interests and forces converged to inspire Christian Reformation. Many people were sick, angry, and fearful over corruption in the priesthood, waste of revenue from local parishes, and conflicts between princes of the world and princes of the church. The conflict of authorities was between the papacy and all others; the authority of the papacy was also disputed. Many reformers sought to revive earlier forms of holy life, inner piety expressed in good deeds. A few reformers challenged the basic authority of the medieval church, preferring scripture over tradition. Seeing a religious solution to secular problems, many secular princes supported the reformers.

MARTIN LUTHER

theology [THEE-ol-e-jee]
The discipline that describes and explains God and his relationship to the world. Theology is a formal, reasoned explanation of the beliefs of the faithful people of a religion.

indulgence [in-DUL-jens]
A remission of temporal punishment for sin that has already been pardoned. Indulgences became a subject of debate for Martin Luther.

On October 31, 1517, in Wittenberg, Germany, Professor Martin Luther (1483–1546) of the local university announced a meeting to discuss openly some urgent questions of **theology.** He posted on the door of the castle church his Ninety-Five Theses for academic debate. The theses pertained to the ecclesiastical practice of **indulgences,** which had not been dogmatically defined.[22] In the Roman Catholic Church, an indulgence remitted temporal punishment after the sin had been forgiven. The debate was introduced as a probing inquiry. At the same time, Luther cited a number of popular grievances against the Roman church. Luther was not prepared for the situation that developed. The list of issues for a quiet, academic debate in Wittenberg was copied, using the latest technology—printing presses—and distributed over much of Europe. Horrified by the issues, Tetzel—a promoter of the sale of indulgences—and others sent copies to Pope Leo X, Giovanni d'Medici. The pope recognized at once that Luther raised the question of authority. In Roman Catholicism, authority for doctrine rested on the Bible and its interpretation by the fathers of the church, the ecumenical councils, and popes. As Luther argued about the legitimacy of the church's sale of indulgences, the proceeds being used to finance the building of St. Peter's Basilica in Rome, he advanced the idea that the Bible is the main source of authority for a Christian. Moreover, as he was threatened by the church, he argued that each layperson is free to read the Bible without aid from a priest. To reinforce his views, Luther translated the Bible into everyday German. Luther, his creative genius stimulated by opposition, published many small books, amply illustrated with cartoons, attacking the pope and sundry other people he thought to be sinful. Luther's emphasis on scripture led him to declare that a Christian is free, for being justified by faith before God, he is no longer subjected to the law of works. He is in a new personal relationship with God, free to serve both God and his neighbor.

The pope swiftly excommunicated Luther and placed him under ban of empire; anyone finding him was to arrest him. The German princes were divided in their support for the pope and Luther, so the pope was never able to punish Luther. In the Peace of Augsburg in 1555, Germans were assigned to Protestant or Catholic churches according to the faith of their prince.

The Roman Catholic Church did not compromise its principles. In the Council of Trent, the church affirmed several positions that were opposed to Protestant doctrine. The council held that the Bible is only one source of authority among others for Christians. The fathers, the councils, and the popes cannot simply be dismissed as worthless. Moreover, the Vulgate, a Latin Bible, was the only official scripture. It was to be interpreted by the church and not by any untrained layperson. The Roman Catholic Church retained seven sacraments, Baptism, Eucharist, Confirmation, Marriage, Holy Orders, Penance, and Anointing of the Sick. Luther recognized, on the basis of scriptures, only two sacraments: Baptism and the Lord's Supper. Luther and his followers were still considered heretics. They were also denounced by Rome because some monks and nuns who followed Luther renounced their vows of chastity. Luther and many of his followers married and raised families, establishing a precedent among Protestant clergy.

JOHN CALVIN

The reform movement was centered in Geneva, Switzerland. John Calvin (1509–1564) differed from Luther in temperament. Luther had abandoned his intent to study law; Calvin was well trained in law. In 1533, Calvin, until then a **humanist,** experienced God speaking to him through the scriptures. King Francis of France attacked Lutheranism, a reformed ideology Calvin had expressed. Later, the king charged French Protestants with anarchy. Safe in Basel, Calvin began work on his *Institutes of the Christian Religion*. It was a systematic presentation of Protestant theology that was revised several times before its final edition in 1559. Calvin sent a cover letter to King Francis, pointing out that his early edition would show that the charges the king was making were baseless. Calvin was immediately recognized as the leader of the French Protestants. One of Calvin's milder criticisms of the papacy reads,

humanist
A person who believes the values of humans are the highest in the universe. Humans are "on their own" in the universe.

John Calvin. This leader of the Reformation in Geneva was known for his clear exposition of the Christian faith as it is found in the Bible.

Now, if any one will closely observe and strictly examine this whole form of ecclesiastical government, which exists at the present day under the Papacy, he will find it a nest of the most lawless and ferocious banditti in the world. Every thing in it is clearly so dissimilar and repugnant to the institution of Christ, so degenerated from the ancient regulations and usages of the Church, so at variance with nature and reason, that no greater injury can be done to Christ, than by pleading his name in defence of such a disorderly government.[23]

Calvin's leadership came to fruition in Geneva, Switzerland. Responding to an invitation, he helped establish a theocracy governed by the scriptures. Calvin, as did Luther, emphasized that human sinners cannot save themselves through good deeds but must rely on the grace of God, who gives faith to those whom he has predestined to be among the elect.[24] Calvin's position was based on the letter of St. Paul to the Romans. Calvinists denounced the whole system of indulgences and penance of the Roman church. Under Calvin and John Knox of Scotland, Presbyterian churches developed. In them, a republican form of government replaced the episcopal form, which is based on monarchy.

HULDRYCH ZWINGLI

Huldrych Zwingli (1484–1531), of Switzerland, was also convinced that only the Bible is binding authority. The Christian community is the human authority that should direct duly constituted civil government. Christian life conforms to the will of God in the Bible.

WILHELM RÖUBLI

In 1525, Wilhelm Röubli, a priest, disagreed that all children in an area of Switzerland should be baptized. He and his supporters taught that believers, rather than infants, should be baptized. Because most people had been baptized as infants, baptizing adults was a second baptism. Those who practiced baptism of believers were known as Anabaptists. Relying on the authority of the Bible and that of the congregation of believers, Anabaptists initiated a free church tradition or, as they saw it, recovered the tradition of the New Testament.

KING HENRY VIII

Henry VIII (1491–1547), of England, forged yet another kind of Protestantism. The king, outraged when the pope declined to grant him a divorce from Catherine of Aragon so that he could marry Anne Boleyn, separated the Church of England from the authority of the pope. Henceforth, the monarch of England would be head of the church in England. Services of worship had a Catholic form, and the episcopal structure remained in place. The services were conducted in English. Nobility, at least, could read the English Bible. The church published a Book of Common Prayer to be used in all services and a confession of faith.

Although the reformers agreed on a break with the authority of the pope, they did not agree on the expression of Christian faith. Luther, a hearty participant in family and community life, enjoyed good food and drink, conversation, and singing. He relied on support from the state. Calvin, a systematic scholar with legal training, was more guarded against the pleasures of the world, such as dancing and alcohol. Calvinists preferred a theocracy under the leadership of reformed clergy and laity. Henry

VIII was a dedicated Catholic who had no serious doctrinal dispute with Catholicism—he wanted to retain Catholic beliefs and practices. He insisted only on his political and economic control of the church; his allowing scriptures to be read by nobles was not an invitation to the doctrinal and political reforms found in Switzerland and Germany. Other reformers appeared before the Reformation reached full flower.

These main divisions from Rome—the Lutheran, the Presbyterian, and the Church of England—stimulated smaller divisions. When laypeople could read the Bible and develop doctrine as the Holy Spirit might lead them, dozens of groups formed in England, Scotland, France, Belgium, Holland, and Germany. Although unity among Christians weakened, most Protestants thought that the principle of individual interpretation of God's revelation was fully justified. Congregational form of government, a kind of town-meeting democracy, permitted small groups of members to organize and appoint their own leaders.

George Fox

George Fox began preaching in England in 1647. His Society of Friends (known as Quakers) emphasized that the Inner Light of Christ dwells in ordinary people. Not satisfied with a formal university education in religion, Fox sought a direct experience of God. He wrote in his journal,

> And one day when I had been walking solitary abroad and was come home, I was taken up in the love of God, so that I could not help but admire the greatness of his love. And while I was in that condition it was opened up to me by the eternal Light and power, and I therein saw clearly that all was done and to be done in and by Christ, and how he conquers and destroys this tempter, the Devil and all his works, and is atop of him, and that all these troubles were good for me, and temptations for the trial of my faith which Christ had given me.[25]

Ordinary people can live by the guidance of the Holy Spirit. In worship, Friends preferred long periods of silence during which the Spirit might move individuals to speak its message. Regarding all life as sacramental, they did not observe any special sacraments. Other Protestant leaders in different countries developed Christian communities with similar ideals.

The Catholic Reformation

Forces that produced the Protestant and Reformed churches inspired reform within the Catholic Church. Because the Catholic Reformation was contemporaneous with the Protestant Reformation, it is less often discussed. The Roman Catholic Church, however, reformed as it responded to challenges from individuals with exemplary holy lives. Both women and men became role models for higher Christian spirituality and morality.

The Society of Jesus, which began in Spain, expressed the work of two men who helped change Catholic education and missions. Ignatius of Loyola (ca. 1491–1556) and Francis Xavier (1506–1552) met while they studied theology in Paris. Their zeal, however, exceeded that of most academics.

St. Ignatius was a man not only of deep spiritual devotion but also of superb administrative abilities. Born in 1491 in Azpeitia, Spain, he served in a military force until he was wounded in a battle with the French army. While he was convalescing, he read the *Life of Christ* and the *Lives of the Saints*. Subsequently, he had a vision of the Virgin Mary with the child

Jesus. Breaking with his former sins, he devoted himself to prayer and to writing about Christ and Our Lady. Besides an account of his life, St. Ignatius wrote the *Spiritual Exercises*, a guide to a disciplined spiritual life under command of God, and the *Constitutions*, an outline for administering the Company of Jesus (later known as the Society of Jesus, or Jesuits).[26] Pope Julius III recognized the company in 1550. The Jesuits played a major role in church reform and missionary activities. The Society members were scholarly, well-disciplined students in the spiritual life. Their goal was missionary outreach rather than military conquest.

Francis Xavier, of the Society of Jesus, introduced Christianity to Japan in 1549. By the end of the century, the number of churches had reached about 200, and membership was about 150,000. The harsh treatment of Christians under Hideyoshi reversed the liberal policy of Nobunaga, a cycle that was often repeated in Japan. Throughout these periods, "hidden Christians" operated underground to keep faith alive.

In the late nineteenth century, when Japanese feudalism gave way to industrialization, proscriptions against Christianity were removed in 1873. Catholic, Orthodox, and Protestant missionaries became active. As Japan came into conflict and wars with Russia, China, European countries, and eventually America, the Japanese weakened ties with outside churches and developed their own finances and leadership. Although Japanese churches were small, they were free of imperialistic encroachments from other nations.

When the Jesuits arrived in China under the leadership of men such as Alessandro Valignano and Matteo Ricci, they sought to adapt Christianity to Chinese culture. Nestorian Christians had been in China since the eighth century. But now an orthodox Christianity was introduced along with Western academic knowledge. So that Christianity would be acceptable to Chinese scholars, Jesuits combined it with studies of Chinese classics. Successful with the Chinese, the Jesuits were opposed by Dominicans and Franciscans for giving too much honor to Chinese religions.

Mystics, also, set examples of Christian piety. Teresa of Ávila (1515–1582), an aristocrat, lived as a Carmelite nun and suffered paralysis. Eventually she experienced visions, voices, and revelations that culminated in an image of the wounded Christ. In her renewed piety, she developed a stricter life for nuns of her order. Her devotion reformed religious lives for both women and men; she founded thirty-two reformed houses of devotion.[27]

John of the Cross (1542–1591) was inspired by Teresa, his elder example. While imprisoned by monks who opposed his efforts at reform, John experienced visions. Escaping from his imprisonment, he reformed monasteries and founded houses for exemplary religious life.

Popes, also, sought reforms in Rome. Catholic leaders were painfully aware that some popes had been excessive in the ways of the world. New popes had opportunities to set examples of pious living. Pius V (1566–1572), a Dominican, lived as an ascetic in the Vatican. He and his court rejected the more flagrant abuses that had marred the Vatican in favor of exemplary spiritual and moral lives.

Although the lines between Protestants and Catholics were drawn and reinforced, Christianity had undergone a renewal of faith and morals. Members of the divided churches debated vigorously who was the real church and who had departed from it.

John of the Cross. With St. Teresa, he founded the Decalced Carmelites. He was renowned for his poetry in mystical theology.

The earliest missionaries in North America were Roman Catholics, who had organized forty missions with twenty-six thousand Indian converts before Protestants reached Virginia and New England. Protestants, having multiplied rapidly since Luther's debate in Wittenberg in 1517, were represented in a variety of denominations. They found the new colonies in North America attractive for economic reasons as well as for liberty to develop, without threat of persecution, the full implications of doctrines they had fashioned from fresh studies of the Bible. The new colonies, states, and territories in North America permitted even more fragmentation of the Christian churches and doctrines than had been possible since the earliest centuries of Christianity.

Anglicans, descending from the Church of England under Henry VIII, settled in Jamestown, Virginia, in 1606. They were the forerunners of the Protestant Episcopal Church. **Puritans** and **Separatists** departed further from Roman Catholic practices than Anglicans cared to go. These English people settled in Massachusetts. **Anne Hutchinson** (1591–1643), dissenting from these groups, settled with her children in Rhode Island.[28] **Baptists** emphasized a gathered community of believers who had been baptized by immersion. In Pennsylvania, **Quakers** were given a safe haven under William Penn, as were Catholics and Jews. **Presbyterians** from Scotland and Switzerland, adherents of Calvin's views, settled along the coast of several colonies, one being North Carolina. **John Wesley** (1703–1791), who inspired clergy to ride circuits on the frontier, was a **Methodist.** Immigrants from Germanic states and Scandinavian countries brought **Lutheran** churches based on the Augsburg Confession of 1530. These Protestant groups blazed a trail for hundreds of other forms of Protestant Christianity that developed in the next century.

Camp and evangelistic meetings were often nondenominational or independent, producing numerous varieties of Christian doctrines and practices. In the settled community of Northampton, Massachusetts, in 1734, Pastor Jonathan Edwards led a spiritual revival that reverberated throughout New England. In 1739–1740, George Whitefield's evangelistic tour of the American colonies stirred people in the North and South. The Great Awakening, as it came to be known, sharply divided Christians. Outdoor preaching by itinerant clergy, "sudden" conversions, and dramatic evidences of the outpouring of the Holy Spirit troubled members of established parishes. Were the new spiritual experiences "proper" for Christians? They continued as part of American religious life.

Some people saw in the famous revival meeting of Cane Ridge, Kentucky, in August 1801 an outpouring of the Holy Spirit similar to Pentecost. In the excitement of the meeting, people screamed and dropped to the floor as if dead. Others, while standing, jerked back and forth, almost touching the floor. Some of those who were jerking danced back and forth until they fell to the floor, exhausted. Loud, hearty laughter possessed some of the believers, but it did not spread to others.[29] Some Christians prefer this kind of religious experience over formal worship in traditional churches.

Responding to French activities in Canada, in 1670 the English formed the Hudson Bay Company. The first Anglican Church met in Halifax, Nova Scotia, in 1750. In 1832 the Anglican Church became the established church

Anglicans [ANG-gli-cuns]
Members of the Church of England. Their church government is episcopal, having clergy directed by bishops.

Puritans [PYOOR-i-tuns]
Former members of the Church of England who sought to purify the church. They settled in Massachusetts and sought to establish a theocracy, a government under rule of God.

Separatists [SEP-ar-a-tists]
Former members of the Church of England who settled in Massachusetts. Believing the Church of England to be beyond reform, they separated to form a new church. They sought a theocracy.

Anne Hutchinson
A dissenter banished in 1637 from Massachusetts Bay Colony. She and her children found more freedom in Rhode Island.

Baptists [BAP-tists]
Members of the Baptist tradition. Baptists believe that adherents should be baptized when they are old enough to choose Christ as their savior. Immersion is the preferred, often required, form of baptism. Baptist government is by members of each congregation.

Quakers [KWAY-kurs]
Members of the Society of Friends. The group was established in England by George Fox. Quakers are led by the Inner Light, through democracy.

Presbyterians [PREZ-bit-tir-ee-uns]
In the tradition of the teachings of Calvin's *Institutes of the Christian Religion,* Presbyterians base their beliefs primarily on the Bible. Governance of the church is through elected representatives. One governing body is the Presbytery.

John Wesley
An Anglican priest who formed the Methodist Church. Methodist circuit riders ministered to frontier families in America.

Methodists [METH-u-dists]
Members of the church that followed the "method" of John Wesley, former Anglican clergyman. The church's government is episcopal, that is, through bishops.

Lutherans [LOO-ther-ans]
Members of a major Protestant denomination based on the teachings and practices of Martin Luther (1483–1546). Lutherans base their beliefs primarily on the Bible rather than on teachings of the church fathers, ecumenical councils, or the pope.

Eastern Orthodox Church
[OR-tha-dox]
The Christian church of the Greek tradition. The churches of the eastern Mediterranean countries retained a more democratic form of governance.

of Canada. The Anglican Church, the Roman Catholic Church, and the United Church of Canada comprise two-thirds of religious memberships in Canada. Jews, Greek Orthodox Christians, and Protestant groups comprise the remainder.

Eastern Orthodox Christianity in the New World

Although Greeks arrived in a new colony in New Smyrna, Florida, in 1786, the community did not endure. The first Orthodox community that lasted began in Alaska with Russian explorers. The Russian Imperial Missionary Society helped support the **Eastern Orthodox Church** in Alaska and adjoining islands. In the next century, Orthodox centers appeared in San Francisco and in New York City.

Religious Diversity in the United States

Peoples in the geographical area that became the United States have always exhibited religious diversity. The early settlers who arrived in different places at different times brought different religions. Protestants, Catholics, and Jews have always practiced their own faiths. Although sporadic episodes of discrimination and intolerance have marred the history of religions in the territories or states, no widespread religious wars have

A Greek Orthodox Service on Good Friday. In New York City members of this major branch of Christianity observe the traditional rituals recalling Jesus' crucifixion.

CHAPTER NINE

been fought. The Constitution of the United States, in the First Amendment, has prevented governmental establishment of any religion. The principle of separation of church and state has encouraged religious liberty to express itself in numerous varieties of organizations. Although Christianity has been the religion of the majority, immigration has brought citizens who practice each of the world religions. Diversity of religion, present with early settlers, has continued to multiply.

The Age of Reason

Peoples who formed the colonies that became the United States sought to avoid the religious wars that had plagued Europe. In the writings of philosophers they found an emphasis on reason, which allowed them to transcend the clerical disputes of Europe.

The traditional Christian view of the world, already affected by the new sciences, was further influenced by the Enlightenment, also known as the Age of Reason. In the late 1600s, the empirical emphasis of the English philosopher John Locke (1632–1704) and the rational emphasis of the French philosopher René Descartes (1596–1650) found expression among more popular thinkers. These thinkers used the spirit of free investigation of reasonable people to challenge the traditional monarchies and the doctrines of the churches. In France, Voltaire (the pen name of François-Marie Arouet, 1694–1778) inspired such devotion that his remains were transported on July 11, 1791, to the Pantheon, a former church. With great ceremony, he was enshrined in the building that the French government had dedicated to brilliant human achievements. The archbishop of Paris abdicated on November 7, 1793. On November 10, 1793, in the Cathedral of Notre Dame, a great procession of citizens led Mademoiselle Maillard, a singer of the opera, inside to ascend a "mountain" atop which was a temple inscribed "To Reason." Clergy suffered diminished powers, answering often to groups of laity. Although the Enlightenment in other European countries was less dramatic, it produced enduring changes for Christians. The emphasis on orderliness in nature challenged the miracles of Christianity. Reason was prized above the revelation of scriptures. **Deism,** the belief in a Supreme Being who created the world and its laws and then left them alone, often replaced **theism,** belief in a personal God who continually responds to prayers.

Many of the people who formed the Constitution of the United States were influenced by deism. Allowing free practice of traditional theism, they ensured the freedom of citizens who held other religious beliefs or who avoided any traditional form of religion.

Emerging Forms of Protestant Christianity

In the United States, especially, the environment of freedom of religious thought helped major denominations of Protestant Christianity produce many other denominations. Leaders who could find followers were free to break away from parent bodies and form new denominations. Some sought to be known simply as Christian. Others emphasized the second advent of Christ, holiness of life, or being disciples of Christ. All were free to form new organizations, beliefs, practices, and missions. All were still Americans and supporters, for the most part, of American **civil religion.**

deism [DEE-iz-ŭm]
The belief that a Supreme Being created the law-abiding universe and does not interfere with its operation to answer prayers and perform miracles.

theism [THEE-iz-um]
The belief that a personlike God created a law-abiding universe, but sometimes he answers prayers and performs miracles.

civil religion [SIV-ul]
A term used by Jean-Jacques Rousseau (1712–1778). Now, in the United States, it refers to religious terms and practices used in celebrations of national events and holidays.

AFRICAN-AMERICAN CHURCHES

One new movement in America was the African-American church. Slaves brought from Africa against their wills had their own religions. There were parts of the Christian religion and Judaism, however, to which they could relate. The story of Moses and the Exodus of Hebrew slaves from Egypt struck a sympathetic chord in their experience. The idea of the survival of a remnant was important. A belief that suffering in this life can be rewarded with a good life in the next appealed at least as much to blacks as it did to whites.

Although African-Americans participated in some of the established denominations, they soon developed churches and groups of churches of their own. They were free to choose their own leaders and practice their own forms of worship and social responsibility. Many of these groups have become part of the traditional Protestant denominations. Others have remained distinctively black. The church was a center of community life for African Americans, and it helped shape community ideals and achievements. Clergy demonstrated that inner piety expresses itself in good works. African Americans have looked to some of their clergy for leadership in education, welfare, and social and political reform. On the national scene, the names and contributions of men such as Ralph Abernathy, Jesse Jackson, **Martin Luther King, Jr.** (1929–1968), and Andrew Young are very well known. Each region has other men who, although not so widely known, have helped improve life in the United States. Through their efforts to improve life for members of the African-American community, they have brought dignity to people of other minorities.

INDEPENDENT EVANGELISTS

Another distinctive feature of American Protestantism has been the freedom of individuals to form their own evangelistic crusades and movements. These movements have often begun with an evangelist "led by the Spirit" to operate outside denominational churches. Evangelists have appealed to people of all denominations to follow the living Spirit. In frontier days, evangelists preached their gospel in tent meetings. In more recent times, they have preached in city stadiums. Billy Graham is one example of a person who has his own ministry, which he exercises in cooperation with many established churches. The advent of radio and television gave evangelists access to hearers and money from all over the nation and abroad. More recent examples included the ministries of Oral Roberts and M. G. "Pat" Robertson. Although these ministries have been largely free from government interference, at the close of the twentieth century the federal government has chosen to investigate some issues pertaining to the finances, investments, and political activities of some evangelical organizations.

THE CHURCH OF CHRIST, SCIENTIST

Another example of the freedom of establishing new churches is the work of **Mary Baker Eddy** (1821–1910), founder of Christian Science. Appealing to the new interest in science, Mary Baker Eddy sought to combine insights of science with the gospel. In particular, she was concerned with alleviating suffering and promoting healing. She established the practice of healing through reading the Bible, interpreting it through her principles in *Science and Health with Key to the Scriptures*. Although the Church of Christ,

Martin Luther King, Jr.
African-American Baptist clergyman who led the civil rights movement in the United States. Adopting Gandhi's methods, King's followers used nonviolent demonstrations to awaken American consciences to racial injustice.

Mary Baker Eddy
Founder of the Church of Christ, Scientist. She was the author of *Science and Health with Key to the Scriptures*.

Mary Baker Eddy. She organized the Church of Christ, Scientist. Its mother church is in Boston, Massachusetts.

The Vatican, Rome. Roman Catholic Christians have their spiritual center in a state within the city of Rome. The Church of St. Peter is at the center of this picture.

Scientist, has local congregations, Eddy wanted all Christian Scientists to belong to the mother church in Boston. Since her death, the church has continued as a highly respected institution. In the late twentieth century, however, practicing Christian Scientists have lost some court cases in which the state prosecuted parents who, because of their beliefs, have failed to provide customary medical treatment for their sick children.

Cooperation Among Protestants

A nineteenth-century Christian missionary impetus taught Christians that diversity can go too far, even among Protestants. By some estimates, there were thousands of denominations. In almost every country of the world, especially China, Japan, and India, and on the continent of Africa, Protestant missionaries carried their particular brands of denominationalism. Denominations vied for growing numbers of converts. This enthusiasm produced a flood of money donations that helped missionaries win thousands of converts to Protestant doctrines. By the early twentieth century, some Protestant missionaries reached the same conclusion that Catholics had arrived at in the sixteenth century. Too much competition can become self-defeating, with potential converts confused and cynical, duplicated efforts by missionaries, and large areas of potential converts unreached. Missionary conferences were called by Christians in various locations to bring order, respect, and cooperation into an effort that had become chaotic. This movement became, after World War II, a World Council of Churches. It was a movement for mutual respect rather than a reunion of all Protestant bodies. However, in the same period, a number of Protestant groups whose doctrines were essentially the same did unite. Through the National Council of Churches of Christ in the United States of America, a number of denominations cooperate in their Christian witness.

Mormon Tabernacle. The Mormon Temple and Tabernacle in Salt Lake City, Utah, is a sacred center for adherents of the Church of Jesus Christ of Latter-Day Saints.

Joseph Smith
Founder of the Church of Jesus Christ of Latter-Day Saints.

Book of Mormon
A book revealed to Joseph Smith.

Brigham Young
Joseph Smith's successor, who led Mormons to Salt Lake City, Utah.

Rev. Sun Myung Moon
Founder of the Unification Church. Born in Korea, he became a well-known religious leader in the United States.

Joseph Smith. The founder of the Church of Jesus Christ of Latter-Day Saints reported that he was motivated by a primary experience of the divine.

Newer Forms of Christianity

In the nineteenth and twentieth centuries, two worldwide churches appeared independent of the major traditions. In the nineteenth century **Joseph Smith** (1805–1844) formed the Church of Jesus Christ of Latter-Day Saints, and in the twentieth century, the Rev. Sun Myung Moon formed the Unification Church. Each new church embraced, in addition to traditional Christian scriptures, a special revelation received by its founder.

Joseph Smith organized the Church of Jesus Christ of Latter-Day Saints in 1831 in response to a revealed word of God recorded in the *Book of Mormon.* He emphasized Christian beliefs in the Bible, supplementing them with insights revealed to him in the *Book of Mormon.* Finding no churches pure enough, Smith organized his own congregation of believers. Smith led members of the church to the Midwest, where a group of local citizens assassinated him. His successor, **Brigham Young** (1801–1877), led a large body of the Mormons to Salt Lake City, Utah, the church's present headquarters. Having renounced its nineteenth-century practice of multiple marriages, the church has now been well received in the United States and in the many countries where it has missionaries.

The **Rev. Sun Myung Moon** launched the Unification movement in Korea in 1954. His particular revelation is an interpretation of the Bible entitled the **Divine Principle.** The foundation of a proper society is God–father–mother–child, the basic family unit. Reverend Moon attracted worldwide attention in performing mass marriage ceremonies for couples he had selected. Combining Asian and Western values in one church, he initially encountered strong resistance among American Christians. The more established church has gained tolerance in the United States and has expanded its international influence through missionary work in many countries.

Major Roman Catholic Reforms

Two Vatican Councils have had major impact on twentieth-century Roman Catholicism. Concerned about the church's role in the world, at two different times popes called councils at the Vatican. The first Vatican Council (1869–1870) developed a syllabus of errors and the dogma of papal infallibility. Catholicism's vitality as a rapidly expanding church stimulated lively discussions among clergy and laypeople in new countries. Among the issues that were advocated for serious discussion were ecumenism, Eastern churches, religious life, missions, Christian education, the relationship of the church to non-Christian religions, and religious freedom. In response to these discussions, Pope John XXIII issued a call for the Second Vatican Council (1963–1965) to let in "a little fresh air."[30] The major achievement of the Second Vatican Council was its emphasis that the church is the light of Christ in the world rather than an institution existing for itself. Some of the changes that ensued from the council were permission to have translations of the Bible other than the Latin Vulgate, to say Mass in the language of the country where it was celebrated, to have priests participate in Christian services of worship with other Christians in Protestant churches on occasion, and to have nuns wear street clothes other than the uniform habits of their orders. The Index of Prohibited Books was abolished. Protestants were acknowledged as Christians, as were members of the Eastern Orthodox Church. Jews were no longer held to be the murderers of Christ.[31] Yet Roman Catholics are divided on many points of authority and doctrine, especially in the United States. These include issues of marriage and the family as well as of the proper role of women in the church.

Brigham Young. After the assassination of Joseph Smith, he led the Mormons to Salt Lake City, Utah.

Divine Principle [di-VIINE]
Rev. Sun Myung Moon's book interpreting the teachings of Christian scriptures.

Christianity and Liberation

Jesus' teachings emphasized that piety was an inner spirit that motivated good deeds, and many people who have read his words have sought to change the world. When Christians read the New Testament with a focus on the life of Christ, ordinary values become reversed. Jesus began his Sermon on the Mount with Beatitudes, a list of people who will be happy in the kingdom of God (Matthew 5:1–12). The people who will be happy are those that society has considered too low to be of value: the poor in spirit, those who mourn, the meek, those who hunger and thirst for righteousness, the merciful, the pure in heart, the peacemakers, and those persecuted for righteousness' sake. In Nazareth, Jesus identified his mission with these people when he quoted from the prophet Isaiah:

liberation theology
A presentation of Christian teachings that emphasizes Jesus' role in elevating people who had been neglected or oppressed.

> The Spirit of the Lord is upon me, because he has anointed me to preach good news to the poor. He has sent me to proclaim release to the captives and recovering of sight to the blind, to set at liberty those who are oppressed, to proclaim the acceptable year of the Lord. (LUKE 4:18–19)

Readers who identify themselves as the people in these words rejoice that Christ established a better place for them among humans.

In recent years, some of these readers have been the peoples of Third World nations. Particularly in South America, priests have stirred poor people, many of whom are Indians, to struggle for social justice. This struggle has threatened the status quo of church and state cooperation, because the Christian thinkers who have formed a **liberation theology** think that

Rev. Sun Myung Moon.

Mass Wedding Performed by Rev. Sun Myung Moon. In Madison Square Garden, New York, Moon married 2,200 couples.

governments must be forced to change. They challenge the church to change the government. They challenge, also, the church to change its emphasis from supporting the rich and powerful, who then gave charity to the poor, to championing the poor and the weak. Liberationists have changed crusades for charity to crusades for justice. Liberation clergy and laypeople have not been deterred when opponents have tried to label them Marxists. They see themselves as Christians who follow the example of Christ. Two of the spokespeople for liberation theology have been Juan Luis Segundo of Uruguay and Gustavo Gutierrez of Peru.[32]

Bishop Desmond Tutu, of the Anglican Church, has sought to move whites of the world to help blacks of South Africa attain full rights as citizens. A less conspicuous effort is that of Father Naim Ateek, who has written a call for justice in Palestinian liberation theology.

> A theology of liberation is a way of speaking prophetically and contextually to a particular situation, especially where oppression, suffering, and injustice have long reigned. God has something very relevant and very important to say to both the oppressed and the oppressors in the Middle East.[33]

Blacks, also, have found in the life of Christ an example for their liberation. Black theology, formal statements about God, emphasizes that black peoples, having a different history from whites, require a theology fashioned to their special needs and their struggle for equal places in the social order. Retaining their cultural traditions, they want to be free to participate fully in all of modern life. Authors writing about black theology include James H. Cone and J. Deotis Roberts.

In the twentieth century, the women's movement has stimulated a comprehensive examination of the Christian worldview of humans. Growing out of a patriarchal religion and forming its own theological doctrines in societies where decent women were expected to keep silent in public and defer to directions of fathers, brothers, or husbands, Christianity has viewed women as less qualified than men for religious leadership or responsibility. More recently, women have studied theology, been odained,

Ordination of a Woman Priest to the Church of England. In 1995, in Canterbury Cathedral, England, a woman was ordained to the Anglican priesthood.

and written liturgies in language less gender specific. They have been hampered by old sources of authority: scriptures, church fathers, councils, and the pope. A liberation approach to the problem has been suggested by Rosemary Radford Ruether:

> We read canonical, patriarchal texts in a new light. They lose their normative status and we read them critically in the light of that larger reality that they hide and deny. In the process, a new norm emerges on which to construct a new community, a new theology, eventually a new canon. That new norm makes women as subjects the center rather than the margin. Women are empowered to define themselves rather than to be defined by others. Women's speech and presence are normative rather than aberrant.[34]

Ruether proposes, then, that a Christian understanding of humans move women to the center in documents that will become governing standards for all Christians.

The development of Christianity resembles the growth of a gigantic tree, extending its welcome shade against a harsh sun. Its roots extend deep into the fertile soul of Judaism, drawing nourishment from rich experiences of Jewish people. Its solid trunk is dedicated to the life and teachings of Jesus, who unites believers into one body. The main branches of the tree are the traditions of Greek, Roman, Protestant, and other churches. These branches multiply the historical forms of authority, flourishing most recently in the women's movements and in churches of peoples in the Third World.

At the beginning of the twentieth century, Christianity's worldview, although different from New Testament, medieval, or modern times, still shares basic beliefs with earlier Christians. Sources of religious authority divide adherents, but all agree that the ultimate head of the church is Jesus Christ. The worldview section outlines only a few of the widely shared views of Christians; interpretations of other Christians are also valuable.

The Absolute

Christians believe in one God. God has no partners or rivals; idolatry is strictly prohibited. Nevertheless, the most complete revelation of God has been through God the Son, who was incarnate in Jesus of Nazareth. He is coeternal with God the Father and was born in human form through the Virgin Mary. He is both God and man. He is God in respect to revealing God; he is man in bearing all human afflictions except sin. God also reveals himself as the Holy Spirit, who bestows on human beings power, comfort, peace, and love. Although God appears in three persons, Christians insist that there is only one God. On the doctrine of the Trinity, then, Christians have an understanding of God that is rejected by Jews and Muslims.

CHRIST

The role of Jesus of Nazareth is subject to various interpretations among Christians. All agree on the importance of his teachings through words, examples, and the excellence of his life. Jesus' sermons, parables, and miracles set him above all other men and women. In every way, he reveals the power and love of God. The majority of Christians have always gone beyond this understanding of the role of Jesus. The New Testament emphasizes that Jesus was crucified in order to demonstrate the depths of God's love for humans. Even as the blood of lambs sacrificed to God removed sin for Jews, so the blood of Christ has removed sin from those who believe in him. Christians believe that Jesus died on the cross and was buried. On the third day he rose again to life, and he ascended, after forty days, to heaven, where he lives with God the Father.

The gospels give several views of how Jesus was the Son of God. In Matthew, he is shown to be born of the virgin, Mary. He is the fulfillment of the expected Messiah in the Jewish scriptures. In Mark, at the baptism of Jesus, God announces that Jesus is his Son. In Luke, Jesus is born of the virgin, Mary, and angels announce his coming to shepherds in the field. In the Gospel of John is the idea of a preexistent Christ who came to the earth to live among humans as the **incarnation** of God:

incarnation [in-cahr-NA-shun]
To invest God in human flesh. Christians consider the Christ as God in human form.

> In the beginning was the Word, and the Word was with God, and the Word was God. He was in the beginning with God; all things were made through him, and without him was not anything made that was made. In him was life, and the life was the light of men. The light shines in the darkness, and the darkness has not overcome it. (JOHN 1:1–5)

> And the Word became flesh and dwelt among us, full of grace and truth; we have beheld his glory, glory as of the only Son from the Father. . . . And from his fullness have we all received, grace upon grace. For the law was given through Moses; grace and truth came through Jesus Christ. No one has ever seen God; the only Son, who is in the bosom of the Father, he has made him known. (JOHN 1:14, 16–18)

Writers in the New Testament describe several ways that Christ has meaning for Christians. The Gospel of John provides a favorite quotation for many Christians in 3:16:

> For God so loved the world that he gave his only son, that whoever believes in him should not perish but have eternal life.

Paul has another description that emphasizes the importance of Jesus' death and resurrection. One form of expression is given in I Corinthians 15:19–20:

> If in this life we who are in Christ have only hope, we are of all men most to be pitied. But in fact Christ has been raised from the dead, the first fruits of those who have fallen asleep.

Although liberation theologies draw inspiration from examples in the life of Jesus, most Christians have turned from the quest for the historical Jesus that occupied earlier writers, such as Albert Schweitzer. The writings of Karl Barth and Emil Brunner, called neo-orthodox theologians because they returned to views of Christ held by theologians of earlier centuries, minimized the need for trying to reconstruct a detailed biography of Jesus.

The World

Christians draw on the Genesis account and the Psalms for their view of the world in its original form. God created a good universe and good humans. But many Christians find that nature and humans have gone awry since the rebellion of Adam and Eve. St. Paul speaks of the whole universe groaning in pain (Romans 8:22). Influences from Platonist and Manichaean (Persian dualism) thought reinforced Christian ideas that the human body is not good and that the soul should, as far as possible, deny the desires of the body. From early days, there was a theme in Christianity that the world, with its life in the human body, is an environment of suffering to be escaped or overcome with spiritual discipline. For many Christians, heaven is their home; they are only pilgrims passing through the desolation of earthly existence. St. Francis sometimes minimized the importance of physical pleasures, but he rejoiced in the world of nature. There are Christians who rejoice in the goodness of nature and humans, but the majority think that humans and nature have become alienated from God and require his assistance in effecting reconciliation.

Activities of scientists have sometimes intimidated Christian leaders. Theologians emphasize truths learned through revelation, philosophers emphasize truths learned through reason, and scientists emphasize truths arrived at through observations of phenomena. Some theologians have found serious conflicts between revelation, which is special, individual, and private, and empirical knowledge, which is accessible for public scrutiny. Luther was upset by Nicholas Copernicus's observation that the planets revolve around the sun. Some scientists think that the Catholic Church labeled itself an enemy of scientific investigations when it placed under arrest the creative astronomer Galileo Galilei. Cotton Mather, a Congregational clergyman of Boston, was an exception to the Christian church's opposition to the sciences. He fought the medical establishment and supported, during a smallpox epidemic, experiments with inoculation. More often, clergy saw in the conclusions of scientists only threats to ecclesiastical authority and dogmas. Scientists increasingly came to conclusions that challenged biblical stories of miracles; they preferred inexorable laws of nature to divine intervention in the affairs of humans.

Belatedly, Christians have generally accepted the insights of Copernicus, who wrote that the earth travels around the sun; of Galileo, who found that contrary to Aristotle's beliefs, the moon only reflects the light of the sun; and of Newton, who found that bodies are attracted to each other by

Cotton Mather. This engraved portrait is of the congregational minister of Boston who supported controversial smallpox inoculations in Massachusetts Bay Colony.

universal gravitational force. Many Christians are still divided over Darwin's theory of evolution, some accepting it as absolutely essential, even if the views of Genesis must be dismissed as myth. Others insist on the verbal inspiration of God's word in Genesis and reject any scientific theory that seems to question it. Christians who seek to accommodate scriptures and science are called liberals. They regard scriptures as largely human products recording spiritual insights, many of which have been subsequently outmoded. Christians who insist that all scriptures are the revealed word of God and that any theory that seems to conflict with them must be dismissed as erroneous are known as fundamentalists. The Roman Catholic and Eastern Orthodox Christians sometimes have problems bringing teachings of past centuries into accord with rapidly developing scientific theories. Generally, the main body of Christian teachings and practices lags behind the scientific theories currently being taught in major universities.

The Reformation, Counterreformation, and conquest of North and South America launched Christianity on expeditions to conquer the world, natural and human. With almost unlimited frontiers and resources, Christians repeatedly moved to newer horizons. Preparing to live for centuries in the same environment was unnecessary. In the last half of the twentieth century Christians have begun to realize that stewardship applies to natural resources, animals, minority humans, and communities. In the twenty-first century more churches may increase short resolutions on the environment to a formal theology, bringing together Christian insights and scientific descriptions.

Humans

Christians believe that humans are created "in the image of God." Differing on details of the concept, they agree that humans are different from all other animals in that they have responsibility to God. Humans are accountable for how they live their lives.

Two traditions have influenced Christian views of humans. One tradition teaches that since the time of Adam and Eve, humans have been influenced by sin so pervasive that only God can overcome it. That sin is present in every infant, and deliverance from it can be accomplished only by baptism. The other tradition is that humans have a capacity for both good and evil; through family nurture and individual devotion to God, humans can live with God's approval. Although both traditions emphasize that God's grace is essential, the second view assigns a greater responsibility to each person. Grace is the power of God affecting human lives. Present in all human situations, it is especially available in the sacraments and rites of the church.

The Problem and the Solution for Humans

Christians believe that God has replaced his old covenant expressed in the Torah with a new covenant based on faith in Christ. The new covenant is necessary because humans, due to the sin of Adam, are unable by their efforts alone to fulfill the law. Only by God's effective action in human lives can the results of Adam's sins be overcome. As Paul has shown in his letter to Christians in Rome, salvation is through the grace of God, who bestows faith on those whom he would save. Christians believe that they are saved by grace through faith in Christ. Good deeds alone cannot save sinful humans. Good deeds that are the evidence of repentance are possible only after a person has been saved through faith in Christ. A person who has been saved will live an exemplary life in love to God and fellow humans. Christians believe that those who have been saved by grace through faith in Christ will desire to have fellowship with those who are called to be saints, the church, which is the body of Christ.

The doctrines of the Trinity, the Incarnation, Resurrection of the dead, and the Atonement provide Christianity with ideas that are, in their full depths, mysteries. They can be understood sufficiently by humans for the purpose of salvation, but they cannot be completely understood by human reason. Human reason is good and leads to truth, said St. Augustine, just as surely as does the authority of the scriptures. Nevertheless, scriptures and faith are more reliable guides than reason, which is more or less limited in humans. Individuals can read and interpret scriptures and reason from their contents to individual conclusions. However, individual reason and interpretation serve Christians better when they balance their interpretations with the teachings of the traditional church.

Most Christians believe that evil is real. Unnecessary suffering of humans and other animals is evil. The world of nature is good, for it is a gift of God that should be received with gratitude and used with care. Humans should do what they can to avoid harm to others, for Jesus said, "And as you wish that men would do to you, do so to them" (Luke 6:31). It may be necessary, under some circumstances, for Christians to endure suffering rather than escape it. Theodicy is an attempt to explain how a good God can allow unnecessary suffering. Why should innocent people suffer? Christianity has taught that through the suffering of some innocent people other people have been saved. Jesus Christ accepted torture and death on the cross in order to effect salvation for humankind. Martyrs of the church have endured suffering so that testimony to the value of the Christian faith can be demonstrated. Other human suffering may be the result of punishment for the sin of Adam, taught St. Augustine.[35] St. Irenaeus taught that suffering helps humans learn how to live as children of God.[36]

Community and Ethics

A person becomes part of the Christian community through baptism—it is a matter of choice rather than of birth. The Christian community is a gathered community of those who believe that Jesus is the Christ and that they have salvation in his name. It is open to men and women of any age, race, or nationality. A Christian is normally affiliated with a particular parish or congregation that is under the care of a particular clergyperson. A believer is usually accepted as a Christian by all Christians everywhere; however, there may be some additional requirements to meet if a person transfers to a church of a different tradition.

Giving money and goods needed by others has long been a part of Christian living. Some Christians engage in tithing, the donation of 10 percent of their income to support the work of the church, which includes charitable services to those in need. Other Christians give smaller amounts of their income to the church but contribute either directly to those in need or to organizations that serve human beings or other animals.

Although some Christians believe that the world will continue to become more evil until Christ returns to earth, many others think that they are obliged to improve the world. Christian service to God means, to them,

Rev. Martin Luther King, Jr. In the United States and abroad peoples of all races honor this leader of the civil rights movement.

not only charity to meet current needs but also altering institutions and structures of society in order to alleviate poverty, illness, and injustices. For some Christians, the social implications of the gospel are religious. John Woolman visited slaveholders in the United States to persuade them to free their slaves. Henry Ward Beecher openly supported a campaign to free all slaves. Walter Rauschenbusch labored to improve living and working conditions for poor people in cities. Albert Schweitzer brought modern medicine to peoples in Africa. Martin Luther King, Jr., used the nonviolent resistance methods pioneered by Mohandas K. Gandhi to win recognition of civil rights for African-American people of the United States. Mother Teresa worked to save abandoned children in Calcutta. These few examples give some idea of the variety of activities Christians have fostered to improve the living conditions of their fellow humans.

Divisions in Christianity express differences in sources and channels of authority. Other than God—Father, Son, and Holy Spirit—Christians recognize value in both scriptures and tradition. The scriptural foundation is the Bible, writings of the Old and the New Testaments. Tradition supplies three other foundations. A second foundation is the teaching of church fathers. A third foundation is the record of decisions by ecumenical councils. A fourth foundation is the pope. Although Roman Catholics use four foundations, the Greek Orthodox Church omits the fourth, the pope. The Anglican Church omits the fourth foundation, substituting the monarch of England. Many Protestant churches often recognize as binding authority only the Bible. The Society of Friends gives primacy to guidance of the

Mother Teresa. The work of this nun with children in India has brought international support for her mission.

Inner Light, some Protestant churches follow only the teachings of Jesus, and Unitarians emphasize God as authority, omitting the Son and the Holy Spirit.

Another way to classify authority is by channels through which it flows. Episcopal organization depends on authority flowing from the top, God, down through Peter, his successors, and various orders of clergy who have been ordained by the laying on of hands from the time of Peter, the first bishop of Rome. In the Roman Catholic Church, the pope is an essential successor of Peter, heading the hierarchy to the present day. In the Orthodox Church, patriarchs of major groups of churches provide leadership; there is no pope. Presbyterial organizations channel authority from church members through elected representatives of the congregation, a number of congregations—the Presbytery—and a larger body of churches, the Synod. Congregationally organized churches, such as Baptists, recognize the congregation of members as highest authority; however, congregations may delegate authority to organizations that represent larger numbers of churches, such as a Convention. In congregational and presbyterial forms of government, the Holy Spirit, acting continuously, as in the Bible, is credited with guiding decisions of official meetings. Protestant churches generally emphasize the Bible and the Holy Spirit above ecumenical councils and church fathers. They are skeptical of assigning spiritual authority to a pope.

The historical development of Christianity influenced the ways that Christians viewed the world. Although they received a rich heritage from Judaism, Christians drew on the resources of Greek religion and philosophy and the administrative genius of the Romans. As they attracted converts of other cultures, Christians added new understandings of the universe and moral obligations. The twentieth-century worldview of Christians is still rooted in New Testament experiences, but it also reflects the continued guidance of the Holy Spirit in new endeavors among minorities and the Third World.

CHRISTIANITY

An Interpretation of History

Christians believe that all history, from the creation of the world to its end, is subject to the Christ. The Son was present with the Father and the Holy Spirit at the creation of the world. The teachings of Moses and the teachings of the prophets prepared the way for the Father to send the Son into the world. The coming of the Christ was the apex of history, separating all time into before and after the incarnation of the Christ. Since the ascension of the Son to join the Father in heaven, people who are reconciled to God actively participate in the earthly body of Christ, which is the church. Those who reject salvation through the Christ bring judgment on themselves. Although people good and bad live in the same world, at the time of the last judgment they will be separated. Good people will enter heaven and evil people will enter hell. At the end of history, God will defeat all evil.

Rituals and Symbols

Coming to be identified as a Christian is to choose a fellowship with over a billion people of all nations and races who believe that Jesus is the Christ, the Son of God, and the Savior from sin for inclusion in God's kingdom. With baptism, a person joins the church, a fellowship of believers organized to continue learning about Christian living, to support each other in living a Christian life, to worship God, and to serve him in the name of Christ by acts of love to fellow human beings, both Christian and non-Christian.

After affirming their identity in the social group, Christians can choose a number of different lifestyles. Working in commerce or in professions or serving in politics is encouraged. A person can be a good Christian in any of these pursuits. A Christian may marry and raise a family in a stable relationship for a lifetime, similar to the Jewish model, or choose a life of celibacy, living as a single person in the secular world. Some may choose to live a life of celibacy, poverty, and obedience within one of the many orders for men or women within churches. Catholics, Orthodox, and some Protestant groups make provisions for monastic living for those who desire it. Christians may become scholars or mystics whether they are in an order or in the secular world. In most Protestant groups, both men and women may aspire to become clergy. Currently in Catholicism and Orthodoxy, only men can become clergy. Other roles are open to women in all these churches.

WORSHIP

Christians are urged to participate in congregational worship every Sunday and on several weekdays. Christian worship services have similarities in their themes, but there are differences in their emphases. Roman Catholic services have as their central ritual the Mass, the Holy Eucharist, in which the sacrifice of Christ on the cross is recalled in the bread and wine. Orthodox churches focus on the divine liturgy, a cooperation of priests and laity in the praise of God. Protestant services, on the whole, give greater emphasis to reading and interpreting the Bible in a sermon. Charismatic groups depart from these formal structures and focus on the gift of the Holy Spirit, evidenced in healings, testimonials, and speaking in tongues. All these forms have developed over many centuries and are shared across national boundaries.

The Christian year has several occasions that all Christians celebrate and many others that are celebrated by the Orthodox, Catholic, or Episcopal churches. Most Christians celebrate Palm Sunday, the occasion when Jesus entered Jerusalem in triumph. Many Christians also observe Maundy Thursday, the last supper Jesus shared with his disciples, and Good Friday, the day of Jesus' crucifixion. Easter is the most important day of celebration in the Christian year, for it expresses joy that God has raised Jesus from the dead, and it renews the Christian hope that God will also raise from the dead followers of Christ. The meaning of Easter is the same in Western and Eastern churches, but the days of the year on which it is celebrated are different. The same is true of Christmas, which commemorates the birthday of Jesus of Nazareth. Pentecost comes after Easter and marks the day when the Holy Spirit descended on the apostles in Jerusalem and when, through inspired preaching, they added about three thousand members to the church.

SACRAMENTS

Points of passage in a Christian's life are marked by sacraments. A sacrament is a sign that was instituted by Christ so that believers might receive God's grace for their salvation. Baptism is a sacrament that a Christian shares with Jesus, who was baptized. For the believers, it is a symbol of dying to the old life of sin and of being resurrected to a new life in Christ. If a person receives baptism as an infant, it is followed by Confirmation, when, at the age of discretion, he or she freely chooses to identify with the Christian church. First Communion may follow—the participation of the believer in the last supper of Jesus and his disciples.

Believers who marry in the church promise before God and the congregation to remain married until their spouse dies. Only on the death of a spouse is a person free to remarry. In the Catholic Church, marriage is a sacrament, but in the Protestant churches it is not. Although the Catholic Church has recently broadened grounds that may lead to annulment of marriage, its stand against divorce has remained firm. People who divorce in secular courts and who remarry are not welcome to receive the sacraments of the Catholic Church. The Catholic Church does not remarry divorced people. Protestant churches generally recognize divorce, although they discourage it. Many Protestant churches now permit Christian marriage of divorced people, although particulars differ according to various denominations.

Holy Orders is a sacrament in the Catholic Church. Ordination in Protestant churches is a sacred occasion, but it is not a sacrament.

Christians are expected to visit the sick and those in prison. Prayers are said for healing the sick, and in Catholic and Orthodox churches, the ancient rite of anointing the sick with holy oil may be practiced. Christians who are near the point of death are encouraged to make a final confession of sins and to receive forgiveness so that they can enter death with a clear conscience. Christians are taught that death is a part of God's plan for human life, and that beyond death, those who have lived a Christian life have hope of living from age to age in the presence of God. Heaven is a state of bliss, free from suffering and death. Most Christians believe that the unrighteous will suffer in hell, which is commonly thought to be a place of flames and extreme pain.

Christianity, then, provides for all personality types and for every major transition in human life. It takes care of personal anxieties and gives

Communion. Worshipers at an Episcopal Church in Philadelphia receive the sacrament of Holy Communion.

support and guidance. It gives people ways to live beyond themselves and also to contribute to the welfare of social groups. It balances self-interest at every stage of life with a larger social interest that builds up other individuals and groups. Christians view world peace and world welfare as being in their own best interest and therefore worth working for throughout their lives.

Life After Death

Christianity teaches that those who believe in Christ as their savior will be resurrected from death. They will become a unity of soul and spiritual body that can recognize and be recognized by other resurrected people. Most Christians believe that those who have lived righteous lives will live happily in the presence of God in heaven; those who are wicked will endure hell. The kingdom of God will not be completed before Christ comes again to earth.

There are also some minority views on life after death. Immortality of the soul, the soul's living on without need of any physical manifestations, is a belief from Greek thought that has been shared by many Christians. Some early Christian writers entertained possibilities that the soul may be reincarnated in another human body. These ideas are overshadowed by the belief in the resurrection of the body held by a majority of Christians:

> Therefore the Christian belief in the resurrection, as distinct from the Greek belief in immortality, is tied to a divine total process implying deliverance. Sin and death must be conquered. We cannot do this. Another has done it for us; and he was able to do it only in that he betook himself to the province of death—that is, he himself died and expiated sin, so that death as the wages of sin is overcome. Christian faith proclaims that Jesus has done this and that he arose with body and soul after he was fully and really dead. Here God has consummated the miracle of the new creation expected at the end. Once again he has created life as in the beginning. At this one point, in Jesus Christ, this has already happened! Resurrection, not only in the sense of the Holy Spirit's taking possession of the inner man, but also resurrection of the body. This is a new creation of matter—an incorruptible matter. Nowhere else in the world is there this new spiritual matter. Nowhere else is there a spiritual body—only here in Christ.[37]

Christianity and Other Religions

Christian views of other religions have emphasized that all people should be considered children of God who ought to become Christians. As a missionary religion, Christianity has sought converts among all peoples. Missionaries have studied thousands of dialects, reduced them to writing, and translated the Bible into them. People who have not had a chance to make a decision for Christ are the responsibility of Christians; those who have declined an opportunity to convert bear responsibility for their decisions.

In *Nostra Aetate*, the Second Vatican Council addressed relationships with other world religions. Speaking for tolerance and against persecution, the document advocates brotherly attitudes toward all people. At the same time,

> as the Church has always held and continues to hold, Christ in his boundless love freely underwent His passion and death because of the sins of all men, so that all might attain salvation. It is therefore the duty of the Church's preaching to proclaim the cross of Christ as the sign of God's all-embracing love and as the fountain from which every grace flows.[38]

Based on their belief that a new revelation was given in Jesus Christ, Christians see all history in terms of before and after Christ, *anno Domini*, "in the year of the Lord." His appearance has interpreted all faith before his time and has influenced all faith since his time. God continues to reveal himself through the Holy Spirit who leads to truth, but Christians believe that the more complete revelation will not contradict the revelation through Jesus Christ but bring to light and understanding what has been given through him.

CONSIDER THIS: WHAT SEPARATES JEWS AND CHRISTIANS?

Although Jews and Christians share many scriptures, personalities, rituals, and ethics, most of them deny that there is a common Judeo-Christian faith. Judaism has long had a vision that other religions will join Jews in worshiping one God. Christians have long believed that God intends Jews to unite with Christianity. Why do Jews and Christians not agree that they share one faith?

Jews and Christians disagree about Jesus. In Jewish tradition the Messiah would help Jews defeat their enemies, reestablish their kingdom, and restore their Temple. Jesus did not meet these expectations of Jews; they do not accept him as their Messiah. For Jews, Jesus—as any other Jew who has made the claim—was a false Messiah. In light of Jesus' life and teachings, Christians developed a different set of criteria for their Messiah, or Christ. Jesus met and exceeded their expectations. Many Christians do not understand why Jews do not believe that the prophecies of the Bible prove that Jesus is the one promised to deliver Israel.

Can Jews and Christians establish a common basis for greater dialogue and understanding? Some rabbis and some Christian theologians think that a common basis is possible. How could Jews and Christians increase their mutual understanding?

✍ A POINT OF VIEW

✍ VOCABULARY

adoptionist [a-DOPT-shun-ist]
Anglicans [ANG-gli-cuns]
Anne Hutchinson
apocalypse [u-POCK-u-lips]
apocalyptic literature
    [u-POCK-u-LIP-tic]
apostle [a-POS-ul]
Baptists [BAP-tists]
Book of Mormon
Brigham Young
Christian canon [CAN-on]
catechumen [KAT-i-KYOO-mun]
Christ [KRIIST]
church [CHURCH]
civil religion [SIV-ul]
deism [DEE-iz-um]
Divine Principle [di-VIINE]
Eastern Orthodox Church
    [OR-tha-dox]
ecumenical [ek-yu-MEN-i-kul]

epistle [i-PIS-el]
excommunicate
    [ex-ku-MYUU-ni-caat]
gospel [GOS-pul]
heresy [HER-i-si]
heretic [HER-i-tik]
humanist
iconoclast [ii-con-o-KLAST]
iconodule [ii-con-O-DOOL]
iconostasis [ii-con-NOS-ta-sis]
incarnation [in-cahr-NA-shun]
indulgence [in-DUL-jens]
John Wesley
Joseph Smith
Judaizers [JOO-day-iiz-ers]
kerygma [ke-RIG-ma]
liberation theology
Lutherans [LOO-ther-ans]
Martin Luther King, Jr.
Mary Baker Eddy

Messiah [mi-SIGH-u]
Methodists [METH-u-dists]
miracle [MIR-a-kul]
monophysite [mu-NOF-u-SITE]
mystery religions
pantheon [PAN-the-on]
parable [PARE-u-bul]
Pentecost [PEN-ti-cost]
Presbyterians
    [PREZ-bit-tir-ee-uns]
Puritans [PYOOR-i-tuns]
Quakers [KWAY-kurs]
resurrection [RES-u-REC-shun]
Rev. Sun Myung Moon
sacrament [SAK-ra-mint]
scholasticism [sku-LAS-ti-siz-um]
Separatists [SEP-ar-a-tists]
theism [THEE-iz-um]
theology [THEE-ol-e-jee]
Trinity [TRIN-i-tee]

QUESTIONS FOR REVIEW

1. How do Jews and Christians differ on historiography of their religions?

2. Was the life of Jesus devoted to preserving Torah and the prophets, or did Jesus intend to introduce new beliefs and practices for his people? Explain.

3. Are there basic differences between the views of the synoptic gospels and John, or are they essentially telling the same story of Jesus? Discuss.

4. What did Paul (Saul) contribute to Christianity as a major world religion?

5. How did the major divisions among Christians arise?

6. Outline some important events in developing the essential scriptures and doctrines of Christianity.

7. Compare and contrast the Orthodox, Roman Catholic, and Protestant forms of Christianity.

8. Describe ten people who seem to have made the greatest contributions to the development of Christianity. Give reasons for your choices.

9. How does Christianity of the twenty-first century differ from Christianity of the first century?

10. What beliefs and practices are shared by Judaism and Christianity? How do they differ?

QUESTIONS FOR DISCUSSION

1. What are the advantages and disadvantages of the various forms of governance among Christian churches?

2. Should Christians seek to convert all peoples to Christianity, or should they sometimes seek only friendly dialogue with peoples of other religions?

3. Have views of Jesus as the Christ changed significantly between early Christianity and today? In what ways are they similar or different?

4. Do you think Christians are seeking greater unity or practicing more diversity? Cite examples to support your answer.

5. What are the most significant issues facing Christians at the beginning of the twenty-first century? How do you think Christians will respond?

NOTES

1. This quotation and others in this chapter are from the Revised Standard Version of the Bible (New York: Thomas Nelson, Old Testament Section, 1952; New Testament Section, 1946).

2. James L. Price, *The New Testament: Its History and Theology* (New York: Macmillan, 1987), pp. 283–287.

3. *Passio Perpetua,* as quoted in *Adam, Eve, and the Serpent: Changing Patterns of Sexual Morality,* by Elaine Pagels (New York: Random House, 1988), p. 35.

4. Raymond E. Brown, *The Community of the Beloved Disciple* (New York: Paulist Press, 1979), p. 59.

5. Price, pp. 309–397.

6. Charles Bigg, *The Christian Platonists of Alexandria* (Oxford: Clarendon Press, 1886).

7. Henry Bettenson, ed., *Documents of the Christian Church* (New York: Oxford University Press, 1947), p. 37.

8. Peter Brown, *Augustine of Hippo* (Berkeley: University of California Press, 1967).

9. Augustine, *The Confessions of St. Augustine,* trans. Dr. E. B. Pusey (New York: Dutton, 1951), p. 1.

10. Elaine Pagels, *Adam, Eve, and the Serpent* (New York: Random House, 1988).

11. Rosemary Radford Ruether, *Faith and Fratricide: The Theological Roots of Anti-Semitism* (New York: Seabury Press, 1974), pp. 173–174.

12. Williston Walker, *A History of the Christian Church* (New York: Scribner's, 1952), p. 139.

13. John Chapman, *Saint Benedict and the Sixth Century* (Westport, CT: Gatewood Press, 1971).

14. Omer Englebert, *St. Francis of Assisi,* trans. E. M. Cooper (Chicago: Franciscan Herald Press, 1965).

15. R. J. Bucher, "Francis of Assisi," in *Encyclopedia of Religion,* vol. 5, ed. Mircea Eliade (New York: Macmillan 1987), pp. 408–410.

16. Suzanne Noffke, O. P. "Catherine of Siena," in *Encyclopedia of Religion,* vol. 3, ed. Mircea Eliade (New York: Macmillan, 1987), pp. 120–121.

17. J. T. Shotwell and J. R. Loomis, eds., *The See of Peter* (New York: Octagon Books, 1965).

18. Josef Pieper, *Guide to Thomas Aquinas,* trans. R. and C.

Winston (New York: New American Library of World Literature, 1962).

19. St. Thomas Aquinas, *Summa Theologica*, part I, question 2, art. 3, as quoted in Anton C. Pegis, *Basic Writings of St. Thomas Aquinas* (New York: Random House, 1945), p. 22. This translation is based on that of the English Dominican translation that began in 1911. It was the work of Father Laurence Shapcote, O.P.

20. H. H. Ben-Sasson, ed., *A History of the Jewish People* (Cambridge, MA: Harvard University Press, 1976), pp. 413–414.

21. As quoted in Edwin Pears, *The Fall of Constantinople* (New York: Cooper Square Publishers, 1975), p. 346.

22. Hans J. Hillerbrand, "Luther," in *The Encyclopedia of Religion*, vol. 9, ed. Mircea Eliade (New York: Macmillan, 1987), pp. 57–61.

23. John Calvin, *Institutes of Christian Religion*, trans. John Allen, 7th ed. (Philadelphia: Presbyterian Board of Christian Education), pp. 360–361.

24. Ibid.

25. George Fox, *Journal* (Cambridge: University Press, 1952), p. 14.

26. Ignatius Loyola, *St. Ignatius' Own Story*, trans. Young (Chicago: Loyola University Press, 1956). James Broderick, *The Origin of the Jesuits* (Westport, CT: Greenwood Press, 1971).

27. Kenneth Scott Latourette, *A History of Christianity* (New York: Harper, 1953), p. 851.

28. Gaius Glenn Atkins and Frederick L. Fagley, *History of American Congregationalism* (Boston: The Pilgrim Press, 1942), p. 89.

29. A description based on Rev. Barton W. Stone. Found in Sydney Ahlstrom, *A Religious History of the American People* (New Haven, CT: Yale University Press, 1972), pp. 434–435.

30. Walter M. Abbott, S. J., ed., *The Documents of Vatican II* (New York: Herder and Herder), 1966, Contents.

31. Ibid.

32. Gustavo Gutierrez, *A Theology of Liberation*, trans. Sister Caridad Inda and John Eagleson (Maryknoll, NY: Orbis Books, 1973). Juan Luis Segundo, S. J., *Theology and the Church: A Response to Cardinal Ratzinger and the Whole Church*, trans. John W. Dierksmeier (New York: Winston Press, 1970).

33. Naim Ateek, *Justice and Only Justice* (Maryknoll, NY: Orbis Books, 1989), p. 6.

34. Rosemary Radford Ruether, *Womanguides: Readings Toward a Feminist Theology* (Boston: Beacon Press, 1985), p. xi.

35. St. Augustine, "The City of God, XIII, 14." *A select History of the Nicene and Post Nicene Fathers of the Christian Church*, vol. 2, ed. Philip Schaff (Grand Rapids, MI: Eerdmans, 1983), p. 251.

36. St. Irenaeus, *Against Heresis*, 4, 37–38. *The Anti-Nicene Fathers*, vol. 1, eds. Alexander Roberts and James Donaldson (Grand Rapids, MI: Eerdmans, 1980), pp. 518–522.

37. Oscar Cullmann, "Immortality of the Soul or Resurrection of the Dead," in *Immortality and Resurrection*, ed. Krister Stendahl (New York: Macmillan, 1965), pp. 29–30.

38. Abbott, p. 667.

✐ READINGS

Ehrman, Bart D. *The New Testament*. New York: Oxford University Press, 1997. A recent overview of the New Testament for students.

Frankel, Sandra S. *Christianity*. Hagerstown, MD: Torch Publishing, 1985. A concise introduction to Christianity.

Kee, Howard Clark, et al. *Christianity: A Social and Cultural History*. New York: Macmillan, 1991. A survey of Christian development in the early centuries.

Price, James L. *The New Testament*. New York: Macmillan, 1987. A scholarly introduction to the writings of the New Testament.

Spivey, Robert A., and D. Moody Smith. *The Anatomy of the New Testament*. Englewood Cliffs, NJ: Prentice Hall, 1995. A concise introduction to the New Testament.

Walker, Williston. *A History of the Christian Church*, rev. Norris, Lotz, and Handy. New York: Scribner's, 1985. A revised, concise history of Christian doctrines and institutions.

Weaver, Mary Jo. *Introduction to Christianity*. Belmont, CA: Wadsworth, 1991. A brief overview of Christianity.

READINGS FOR RESEARCH AND REPORTS

Albanese, Catherine L. *American Religions and Religion*. Belmont, CA: Wadsworth, 1981.

Aquinas, Thomas. *Summa Theologiae*. 60 vols. New York: McGraw-Hill, 1963.

Augustine, St. Aurelius. *Basic Writings of St. Augustine*. 2 vols. Ed. Whitney J. Oates. Grand Rapids, MI: Baker Books, 1994.

Bainton, Roland H. *Here I Stand: A Life of Martin Luther*. New York: Abingdon Press, 1991.

———. *Women of the Reformation*. Minneapolis: Augsburg Publishing, 1971.

Barth, Karl. *Church Dogmatics: A Selection*. Ed. and trans. Geoffrey W. Bromily. Louisville, KY: Westminster John Knox Press, 1994.

Bettenson, Henry, ed. *Documents of the Christian Church*. New York: Oxford University Press, 1970.

Bigg, Charles. *The Christian Platonists of Alexandria*. Oxford: Clarendon Press, 1986.

Calvin, John. *Institutes of the Christian Religion*. 2 vols. Ed. John T. McNeill. Library of Christian Classics. Louisville, KY: Westminster John Knox Press, 1960.

Carmody, Denise L., and John T. Carmody. *Roman Catholicism: An Introduction*. New York: Macmillan, 1990.

Chapman, Dom John. *St. Benedict and the Sixth Century*. Westport, CT: Greenwood Press, 1971.

Cone, James H. *Black Theology and Liberation*. Philadelphia: Lippincott, 1970.

Dillenberger, John, and Claude Welch. *Protestant Christianity Interpreted Through Its Development*. New York: Macmillan, 1988.

Fischer, Kathleen. *Women at the Well*. New York: Paulist Press, 1988.

Goguel, M. *The Life of Jesus*. Trans. Olive Wyon. New York: Macmillan, 1945. Reprinted by A.M.S. Press.

Haight, Roger. *An Alternative Vision: An Interpretation of Liberation Theology*. Maryknoll, NY: Paulist Press, 1985.

Hick, John, and Paul Knitter, eds. *The Myth of Christian Uniqueness, Toward a Pluralistic Theology of Religions*. Albany: State University of New York Press.

Hick, John, and Edmund S. Merter. *Three Faiths—One God: A Jewish, Christian, and Muslim Encounter*. Albany: State University of New York Press.

Loyola, Ignatius. *The Spiritual Exercises of St. Ignatius Loyola*. Trans. Anthony Mottola. Garden City, NY: Image Books, 1964.

Luther, Martin. *Luther's Works*. 55 vols. St. Louis: Concordia Publishing, 1958.

Marty, Martin E. *Protestantism in the United States*. New York: Scribner's, 1986.

McArthur, Harvey K. *Understanding the Sermon on the Mount*. Westport, CT: Greenwood Press, 1978.

Pagels, Elaine, *The Origins of Satan*. New York: Vintage Books, 1995.

Roberts, Deotis. *Black Theology in Dialogue*. Philadelphia: Westminster Press, 1987.

Ruether, Rosemary Radford. *Womenguides: Readings Toward a Feminist Theology*. Boston: Beacon Press, 1985.

———. *Faith and Fratricide: The Theological Roots of Anti-Semitism*. New York: Seabury Press, 1974.

Segundo, Juan L. *The Liberation of Dogma*. Maryknoll, NY: Orbis Books, 1992.

Teresa of Ávila. *Perfect Love: The Meditations, Prayers, & Writings of Teresa of Ávila*. New York: Doubleday (Image Books), 1995.

Young, Josiah U. *Black and African Theologies*. Maryknoll, NY: Orbis Books, 1986.

Islam

Introduction

When Muhammad, the Messenger of God, appeared in Arabia in the seventh century of the Common Era, Judaism had already completed the Bible and the Babylonian Talmud. The Christians, now leaders of the official religion of the Roman Empire, had long ago agreed on the collection of their New Testament. Although Rome had fallen to the Visigoths, Constantinople thrived as the center of the Byzantine empire. Muhammad's recitations of God's word to him would set in motion dynamic religious and political fervor that threatened or toppled Jewish and Christian strongholds around the Mediterranean Sea.

Inspired by God, Muhammad combined religious, military, and administrative genius to unify the tribes of Arabia into one people, Muslims. God's revelation to him affirmed the tradition of Abraham and Ishmael as builders of the Ka'bah in Mecca. Prophets to Israel were also honored in Islam; John the Baptist and Jesus were accepted as true prophets of God. Muhammad's recitations, uttered after inspiration by God, were piously written down by his followers, later to be combined into the Holy Quran, who accepted it as the final, flawless revelation of God's will for humankind.

Always known as a reverent, admirable person, Muhammad endured attacks from some factions within his city of Mecca and from polytheists of the countrysides. Persevering despite an assassination attempt on his life, he established a rival holy city in Medina that eventually reaffirmed Mecca as the preeminent center of Islam. When Muhammad died, Arabs were unified in one faith and prepared to promoted their religion in the Byzantine empire.

Muhammad's closest family and associates included influential women as well as the men who would become his successors.

Arab Muslims Kneeling in Prayer. A Muslim is required to participate in required prayer (salat) five times a day.

Quran [KUR-an]
The sacred scriptures of the Muslims, regarded as the word of God dictated to Muhammad by God through the archangel Gabriel. The Prophet received and recited the messages over a period of approximately twenty years.

Khadijah, his sympathetic and supportive older wife; Aishah, his younger wife, married after the death of Khadijah; and his four daughters undoubtedly influenced his reforms initiated on behalf of all women in Islam. Although his marriages evoked criticism from Jews and Christians, Muslims interpreted them as evidence of his compassion for women, particularly for the widows of his fallen comrades.

The youngest of the world's major religions, except Sikhism, which appeared among Muslims and Hindus in India, Islam exhibited a vigor that was unabated in the twentieth century. The third sibling among the children of Abraham continues to hold its place as a worldwide, missionary faith.

HISTORICAL DEVELOPMENT

Islam's record of expansion is filled with impressive accomplishments. Like any record, however, it is open to interpretation by those who preserve it and those who read and apply it. Within the first century, two sharply different ways of telling the story appeared.

Historiography

Although Islam is largely unified in its own view of its historical development, Jews, Christians, and secular historians see things differently. Focusing on God's revelation to Muhammad, Muslims believe that the central fact of Islam is the Quran. Aware that there are divine and human forces at work in the dynamics of their faith, they deny that their Prophet adapted social influences from Jews and Christians. Peoples of those religions, however, were skeptical of the "revelation" that set aside their own scriptures as erroneous and antiquated. Ever ready to denigrate Muhammad, they often pointed out his social experiences in his travels that led to his "erroneous" revelation about their beliefs and practices. Secular historians, although more tolerant of Muhammad's religious experiences and sociological practices, have tried to explain his religious teachings as a result of social, historical, and political influences.

In the ensuing account I try to present the facts of history with respect for the Muslim views that Muhammad's actions, words, and teachings were inspired by his own religious experiences. Nevertheless, other forces interacted with his recitations of the Quran and his actions based on them. In the history of this religion, as I have with others, I try to present a sympathetic, understanding account of the religion's beliefs about its origin and development.

The Background of Islam

Islam emerged in Arabia, specifically in the city of Mecca, in the seventh century C.E. A peninsula that had some fertile land on the coasts and some scattered oases of excellent agriculture, Arabia also had vast stretches of barren hills and valleys and an immense area of desert sands. There were some well-established cities, such as Mecca, but the inhabitants of the open spaces were the bedouin, who moved their tents and flocks as necessary to find food and water. In both situations, the key organization was the tribe, and within the tribe, the clan. The tribal identities superseded any loyalty

Grand Mosque, Mecca. The Ka'bah, center, has remained the central shrine of Islam from the time of Muhammad.

to geographic area or city. Survival depended on water and vegetation, to be sure, but just as surely it depended on the strength of the tribe. An isolated individual or even family had little chance of survival in a natural and human environment that was usually hostile.

Economically, there was some interdependence among the desert tribes and the city tribes. The bedouin were largely independent, but they could trade their sheep, goat, and camel wool to peoples of oases for products of their trees and fields. Farmers could gain through trading their dates and wheat for the wool used in making clothes, carpets, and tapestries. Then there were peoples such as the Meccans, who produced little but made a business of buying and selling and providing markets where the various tribes could come together and exchange goods. Mecca also had individuals who could organize large caravans and trade with other population centers, among which were Damascus, in Syria; South Arabia; and Ethiopia. Although poor in natural resources themselves, the Meccans managed to maintain a level of commercial activity that brought them economic and political importance.

The Meccans had something even more important than most oases had. The famous **Ka'bah** was located there.[1] The cubic building possessed the Black Stone in its southeast corner, which was a symbol of divine power. The building contained some 360 idols, many of them representing forces of nature and celestial beings. Every Arab tribe could find its deities there, and religious pilgrimages could be combined with caravans organized for trade within the city limits. Mecca also had an established tradition of truce for pilgrimages during part of the year; tribes that were normally at war with each other could enter an area of safety and carry on trade for a period of time without being in constant fear of a surprise raid on their persons and possessions.

The keepers of the Ka'bah were members of the Quraysh tribe. They had considerable status among Arabs due to their stewardship of this most sacred precinct. It is obvious that they also had considerable economic advantage from the pilgrims and traders who came to their city to conduct religious rituals and business activities. They were also aware that theirs was not a monopoly, for there were other centers where goods could be

Ka'bah [KUH-bah]
The cube-shaped building of stone in the open court of the Grand Mosque of Mecca. In Islamic tradition, the first Ka'bah was built by Abraham and Ishmael.

exchanged. So the Quraysh were always alert to anyone or anything that could undermine their social position or livelihood.

The Life of Muhammad

The child Muhammad, born to a powerful but impoverished clan, was not to inherit wealth. Muhammad's father, Abdullah, died in Yathrib before he was born to Aminah, his mother. Any inheritance that Abdullah might have received would have passed to brothers, not to his son. Pious Muslims tell stories of the holy birth of Muhammad. God willed his truth to a fixed abode, transferring the Purified One to Aminah. She had become pregnant with one of the Lights of Essence. All nature informed the Quraysh of his being expected. At his birth many strange and miraculous signs proclaimed heaven's triumph over satanic spirits.[2]

Following the custom of the time, Muhammad was sent to the country to live with a wet nurse and her family until he was six years old. Because Halimah, a member of the tribe of Banu-Asad, was married to a shepherd, Muhammad spent his earliest childhood roaming the countryside with this family that spent most of its days looking for sustenance for themselves and their flocks. After Halimah returned Muhammad to his mother, she took him on a journey to see her family in Yathrib, the city where his father had died on a trading mission when he was only twenty-five years old. Unfortunately, his mother did not survive the return journey, and Muhammad was an orphan when he reached Mecca again. Now he was entirely dependent on his grandfather and, after his grandfather's death, his uncle Abu Talib.

The time between Muhammad's birth in 570 C.E. and his marriage to Khadijah at the age of twenty-five is only sketched in outline, except for some stories circulated by some of the pious that are by no means accepted by the majority of Muslims. At some point, Muhammad had accepted employment from the well-to-do widow Khadijah and had led some caravans for her. Tradition reports that she was about forty years old when Muhammad married her. The marriage was successful; Muhammad did not have another wife as long as Khadijah lived. In the twenty-five years they lived together, they had at least two sons, who died in infancy, and four daughters, Zaynab, Ruqayyah, Umm-Khulthum, and Fatima, all of them except Fatima dying before their father. Khadijah was a counselor and companion to her husband, and her wealth enabled him to spend some of his time in religious meditation. Always a moral person, he sought now to deepen his spiritual life. He sometimes wandered outside the city to meditate among the hills.

Muhammad's spiritual quest led to results that were absolutely startling for him. While he was meditating in a cave on Mt. Hira about 610, the angel Gabriel confronted him and delivered a message from Allah (Arabic for "the God"). Gabriel challenged Muhammad to read or recite the message of God.

> In the Name of God, the Merciful, the Compassionate
> Recite: In the Name of thy Lord who created,
>   created Man of a blood-clot.
> Recite: And thy Lord is the Most Generous,
>   who taught by the Pen,
>   taught Man that he knew not. (QURAN 96:1–5)[3]

Far from ecstatic, Muhammad was anxious as he described his experience to Khadijah. Was he becoming possessed? Khadijah consulted a cousin of hers, a **hanif** (worshiper of one God), Waraqa Ibn Nawfal, who had become a Christian; he assured her that the experience of Muhammad was in line with the experience of other prophets recognized by Jews and Christians. He was not possessed by **jinn.** Khadijah supported him from the beginning of his revelations until the time of her death.

Once Muhammad was sure that it was really God speaking through him, he did his duty and recited the messages exactly as he received them. That took exceptional courage, for the message that God gave him to recite was one of social and religious reform. At its heart was emphasis on God as the only deity and the absolute requirement that all the idols of the Arabs be destroyed. The people to whom Muhammad was to recite these words of God were the people of Mecca, including the tribe of Quraysh. There was not much resistance to the idea that Muhammad was a prophet; there was immediate resistance to the message that all idols had to be destroyed. The Quraysh did not take a long time to see that following the message could jeopardize their traditional means of livelihood. They could not very well assail God, but they could ridicule Muhammad to the point that no one socially acceptable to the Meccans would take him seriously, let alone identify with his beliefs. A tradition reporting that Muhammad received certain "satanic verses" is regarded by many Muslims as untrue.[4] The account states that two verses that he received, permitting Arabs to worship three traditional goddesses, were rejected as inspired by the "satan." Sura 53 of the Quran now describes these goddesses as only imaginary, deserving no worship.

The first converts came from his own household. Besides Khadijah and his cousin 'Ali, son of the Abu Talib, Zayd Ibn Horithah, his adopted son, accepted him. The first convert outside his household was Abu Bakr, who, although a little younger than Muhammad, was a man of some wealth and influence in Mecca. Two other converts, Khalid Ibn Said and 'Uthman Ibn Affan, came from the rival branch of the Quraysh, the Ummayads. These first converts were to figure significantly in the development of the organization of the new religion. Eventually Muhammad gave daughters in marriage to 'Ali and 'Uthman. Muhammad married Abu Bakr's daughter Aishah after the death of Khadijah. Early Islam was maintained with strong family ties.

Other converts came slowly from ranks of young people and slaves. Tremendous pressure was placed on the converts to renounce their new faith and return to traditional Arab polytheism. Yet they persisted and were even successful in making converts of some of the persecutors, for example, 'Umar. Eventually, several Muslim families had to emigrate to Ethiopia to seek safety; even there the enemies of Muhammad sought their deportation. To bring further pressure, leaders of the Quraysh placed a boycott on the house of Hashim, Muhammad's clan. Abu Talib did not give in to their threats, nor did he ask Muhammad to compromise the message of God. With the deaths of Abu Talib and Khadijah within a period of a year, Muhammad became even more desolate.

In the year 620, Muhammad had contact with representatives from Yathrib who were seeking someone to arbitrate conflicts there and serve as an impartial leader. Muhammad accepted the challenge on condition that the Medinans embrace Islam. Some of them returned and agreed to practice a rigid monotheism. Muhammad sent a teacher with them when they returned to Yathrib and helped them prepare a body of Muslims in their own city. Later, Muhammad chose twelve leaders from the Khazraj and the

hanif [HA-neef]
In Arabia, prior to Muhammad's recitations, a person who worshiped one God. Waraqa Ibn Nawfal, a kinsman of Khadijah, was a hanif.

jinn [JIN]
In Arabia, a race of beings created from fire, distinguished from humans, who were created from clay. Some jinn are good; others are bad.

553 Justinian's missionaries smuggle silkworms out of China; ◆
Europe begins silk industry

560 Buddhism in Japan ◆

570 Muhammad born ◆

610 Muhammad receives first revelation ◆

620 Muhammad meets representatives from Yathrib ◆

622 The Hijrah; Muhammad moves from Mecca to Yathrib ◆

624 The Battle of Badr ◆

625 The Battle of Uhud ◆

628 Agreement at al-Hudaybiyyah between Muhammad and Meccans ◆

630 Muhammad controls Mecca ◆

632 Muhammad dies at Medina; Abu Bakr succeeds him ◆

634 Umar succeeds Abu Bakr ◆

635 Muslims conquer Damascus ◆

638 Muslims conquer Jerusalem ◆

641 Muslims take Egypt ◆

644 'Uthman succeeds 'Umar ◆

656 'Uthman assassinated ◆

661 'Ali assassinated ◆

680 Husayn killed at Karbala ◆

697 Arabs destroy Carthage ◆

716 Arab empire extends to China ◆

732 Charles Martel turns back Muslims near Tours ◆

802 Rabia dies ◆

935 Al-Ash'ari dies ◆

982 Eric the Red establishes Viking colony in Greenland ◆

1055 Seljuk Turks conquer Baghdad ◆

1099 Crusaders conquer Jerusalem ◆

1111 Al-Ghazali dies ◆

1126 Ibn Rushd born ◆

| BCE | 2000 | 1500 | 1000 | 500 | 0 | 500 | 1000 | 1500 | 2000 | CE |

1165 Ibn Arabi born ◆

1183 Genghis Khan invades Russia ◆

1244 Muslims gain control of Jerusalem after crusades ◆

1251 Kublai Khan governs China ◆

1258 Mongols sack Baghdad, ending Abbasid caliphate ◆

1347 Black Death (Bubonic plague) begins to afflict Europe ◆

1453 Constantinople falls to Turks ◆

1492 Spain expels all Muslims ◆

1497 Vasco da Gama sails around Africa to India ◆

1570 Japan permits visits of foreign ships ◆

1703 Ibn Abd al-Wahhab born ◆

1798 Napoleon extends rule to Egypt ◆

1817 Sayyid Ahmad Khan born ◆

1833 Slavery abolished in British Empire ◆

1838 Jamal al-Din al-Afghani born ◆

1849 Muhammad Abduh born ◆

1928 Amir Ali dies ◆

1938 Sir Muhammad Iqbal dies ◆

1946 First General Assembly of United Nations, London ◆

1947 Pakistan independent from India and Great Britain ◆

1949 Indonesia independent of Netherlands ◆

1956 Gamel Abdel Nasser takes Suez Canal ◆
Indonesia abrogates its union with the Netherlands

1966 Arab-Israeli war ◆

1973 Anwar Sadat has October war with Israel ◆
Arabs cut oil supplies to supporters of Israel

1979 Ayatullah Khomeini returns to Iran ◆

1988 Benazir Bhutto leads Pakistan ◆

1993 Benazir Bhutto, having left office, returns ◆
Israel and Palestine Liberation Organization sign peace accord

1995 Vatican welcomes opening of mosque in Rome; forms joint committee ◆
for better understanding between Christianity and Islam

| BCE | 2000 | 1500 | 1000 | 500 | 0 | 500 | 1000 | 1500 | 2000 | CE |

Aws, tribes of Yathrib, and set them apart to become the leaders of his religious community in Yathrib. Muhammad counseled his adherents in Mecca to get their affairs in order and leave the city to make a new life in Yathrib. Muhammad's enemies in Mecca looked on this development as a new threat. They wanted him and his converts where they could keep an eye on them and, if possible, control them.

Forty men, representing several different clans in Mecca, excluded the house of Hashim from a secret meeting called to discuss the fate of Muhammad. Because the forty would act as one person to kill Muhammad, the Hashimites could not afford to attack all of the various clans in blood revenge. The forty men guarded Abu Bakr's house, where Muhammad was supposed to be staying. However, 'Ali took the place of the prophet in bed, and Muhammad and Abu Bakr slipped out of the city and hid in a cave to the south of Mecca. The enemies conducted a rigorous search, but eventually Muhammad and Abu Bakr escaped and made their way north to Yathrib. 'Ali escaped as well. Yathrib became the new home of the Prophet. The **Hijrah,** the migration, was in 622, which became the beginning year of the Muslim calendar.

Muhammad's move to Yathrib added a new dimension to the story of Islam. Until that point, the life of the Prophet was parallel to the calling of several different leaders of world religions, including Jesus and Gautama. But Muhammad had to add, almost at once, an administrative element to his leadership without diminishing at all his spiritual leadership; indeed, the two had to be inseparable if the new religion was to survive. An element of that administrative leadership that has been widely misunderstood outside Islam was the necessity in Arabia of military leadership. The tribes of Arabia lived by honor and retaliation; individuals who were also tribe members were expected to defend not only themselves and their property but also their honor and other

Hijrah [HEJ-rah]
Muhammad's migration from Mecca to Yathrib (Medina) in 622. He and Abu Bakr made the journey in less than the normal eleven days.

Important Cities in Muslim Expansion.
From its base in Arabia, Islam spread rapidly through the Middle East, North Africa, Europe, and Asia.

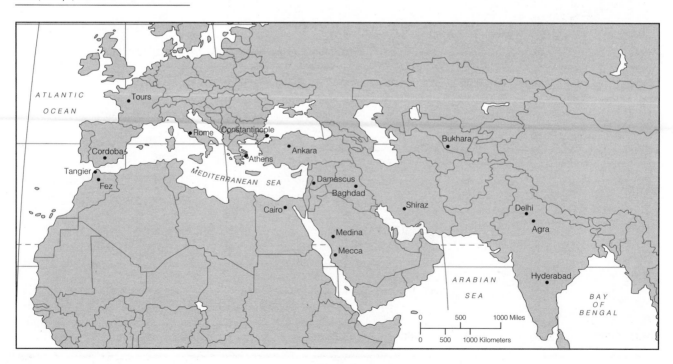

CHAPTER TEN

members of their tribe. To identify with Muhammad in Islam was, in a sense, to give allegiance to a new type of tribe. Thrust upon Muhammad were the responsibilities of a sheik to lead, defend, and avenge the members of his tribe. To fail in that responsibility would have made him in the eyes of Arabs not worthy of respect as a person. Muhammad from this point may seem very different from Jesus; they lived in very different societies. Muhammad's course, however, would not be unheard of for those who have studied the history of Judaism, for there are several precedents for leaders who combined administrative, military, and spiritual leadership roles. The Sikh gurus had to take a similar stance to survive among Muslims and Hindus.

When Yathrib became Medina, the city of the Prophet, not all inhabitants shared with equal enthusiasm Muhammad's leadership. The **ansar** (helpers), who had helped him come to the city of Medina, welcomed him, and the **muhajirun** (companions), who came from Mecca to make their new homes with Muhammad, welcomed a chance to live without persecution for their new faith. But a third group, which included many Jews, was composed of those who did not honor Muhammad as a prophet and who wished that he and his followers would get out of their lives and stay out. Tensions were present from the beginning of his stay, and they grew as it became necessary for Muhammad to make new rules for the lives of the faithful. As Muhammad built his house and the main mosque and as his supporters acquired places to live and took such jobs as were available, frictions developed that added to the smoldering resentments that carried over from earlier conflicts among the various tribes and clans. The startling revelations of the Quran continued to stir the Prophet. An illiterate man, Muhammad received the messages during periods of withdrawal from his surroundings. His periods of reception were filled with awe. Later, he would recite the message he had received. He then applied the messages to developing law and practices.

ansar [AN-sahr]
Helpers; Medinans who helped Muhammad relocate from Mecca to Medina. They were joined by Muhammad and his companions after the Hijrah.

muhajirun [mu-HAJ-i-roon]
The emigrants from Mecca who joined Muhammad in Medina. These early converts to Islam lost their property and income when they followed Muhammad.

> It belongs not to any mortal that
> God should speak to him, except
> by revelation, or from behind a veil,
> or that He should send a messenger
> and he reveal whatsoever He will,
> by his leave; surely He is All-high, All-wise.
> Even so We have revealed to thee a
> Spirit of Our bidding. Thou knewest
> not what the Book was, nor belief;
> but We made it a light, whereby We
> guide whom We will of Our servants. And thou,
> surely thou shalt guide unto a straight path—
> the path of God, to whom belongs whatsoever is in
> the heavens, and whatsoever is in the earth. Surely unto God all things come
>   home. (QURAN 42:50–53)

Muhammad's role was, indeed an awesome responsibility, as Fazlur Rahman has written:

> Muhammad, like all other prophets, is a "warner and giver of good tidings" and his mission is to preach—constantly and unflinchingly. Since this message is from God and is direly needed by men for survival and success, it has to be accepted by man and implemented. His preaching, therefore, is no conventional speechmaking but has to "bring home" the crucial message.[5]

The Meccans were not satisfied with having Muhammad free in Medina building a rival faith. Abu al-Hakam, the chief of Muhammad's main enemies, and others sought ways to cause difficulties for the Muslims beyond confiscating their properties. The Muslims were sending out armed parties to various territories; sometimes these were led by Muhammad, but often they were led by lesser persons. Many times these expeditions were well received in peace, and Muhammad's cause gained friends, if not military allies. Eventually, a Muslim raid on a Meccan caravan south of Mecca incited a retaliatory raid from the Meccans that took place at Badr in 624. To their surprise, the Meccans were soundly defeated, and the Muslims gained not only more wealth but also more respect among the sheiks whose alliance they sought. Abu Sufyan of the Meccan Ummayads raised money for an army to avenge the defeat that they had suffered at Badr. Things were reversed at Uhud in 625, and the Meccans defeated the Muslims, even wounding Muhammad. The Meccans failed to finish the war, however, and the Muslims were able to recoup their losses and make preparations for the next encounter. The next attack was on Medina itself by a superior force of Meccans led by Abu Sufyan, including numerous other tribes they enlisted along the way. Medina survived for two reasons: Muslims had gathered in provisions from the fields that the Meccan force would have needed to sustain a siege, and they borrowed a Persian expedient of digging a trench on the north or open side of the city, the other sides being protected by hills. These unexpected developments and unseasonably cold and stormy weather eventually led Abu Sufyan to lift the siege and return to Mecca.

In March of 628, Muhammad took sixteen hundred men and set out for Mecca, intending to make a religious pilgrimage. The Meccans were upset, and some of them under Khalid Ibn al-Walid, the budding military genius, set about to block Muhammad's progress. Taking a different route, the prophet arrived at al-Hudaybiyyah, a few miles from Mecca. Both sides were divided over whether to fight. The upshot was a truce that Muhammad negotiated with the Quraysh that was to give ten years of peace and permit the Muslims to return the next year to make a pilgrimage to the Ka'bah. The truce worked to the advantage of Muhammad in that as Muslims and Meccans intermingled in peace, some of the brightest and most able Meccans, Khalid Ibn al-Walid among them, decided to become Muslims.

Muhammad continued to seek converts among Arab tribes, Christians, Jews, and foreign leaders. Sometimes he was successful and sometimes not. The Jews of Khaybar to the north of Medina were relentless in their opposition to Muhammad, so he marched on the city to defeat it. The Jews who continued to live there had to give half of their produce each year to the Muslims. In revenge for the loss of her husband at Khaybar, a Jewish captive, Zaynab Bint al-Harith, gave Muhammad some poisoned meat to eat. Although the poison killed a companion of Muhammad, he detected it in time to escape death. Muhammad and Jews had reached a parting of the ways; even earlier in Medina the Prophet had changed the direction that Muslims faced in prayer from Jerusalem to Mecca. His approaches to Arab tribes asking them to join him in Islam were successful, and the Meccans were losing support month after month.

The next year brought the Muslims some success and a notable failure. The success was in a long-delayed pilgrimage to Mecca. The Muslims had three days to perform their religious duties at the Ka'bah, something they had not been allowed to do for about ten years. The failure was an expedition under Khalid sent into the Christian territory to the north of Medina. The Byzantine army was too strong for the Muslim force, and after losing some very important men, the Muslims were fortunate to escape with their lives. The humiliation hurt, but Muhammad did not abandon his hopes of making inroads to the north.

The year 630 was the year of triumph for the Muslims. Their eight-year exile from Mecca ended when Muhammad judged that the Meccans had broken their truce by fighting a tribe in alliance with the Muslims. Ten thousand men marched with Muhammad as he approached the holy city. When Abu Sufyan saw the force, he tried to negotiate as much safety as possible for the inhabitants. Muhammad granted amnesty to those who did not resist his invasion.

The only military opposition seems to have been in the southern quarters, advanced upon by Khalid. The real destruction Muhammad carried out was on the idols of the Ka'bah. The polytheism he had denounced for nearly twenty years was crushed for all time from the sacred city of the Arabs. Seven persons were executed. Within a month, he moved to crush two remaining tribes who opposed him, the Hawazin and the Thaquf.

Although Muhammad had control of Mecca, he continued to make Medina the place of his residence. It was there during the remaining years of his life that he received the stream of delegations seeking alliance with him. He made his farewell pilgrimage to Mecca in the spring of 632, and he delivered a final sermon there during his ten-day sojourn. He returned to Medina and continued his leadership in administration and religion in spite of problems with his health. Tradition reports that he went to the mosque on the morning of the day that he died in 632.

An orphan without property, a prophet denounced by many leaders of his own tribe, Muhammad persevered through faith in God until most of the tribes of Arabia joined him in Islam and made Mecca the center of pure monotheism. For the first time, someone had succeeded in unifying the peoples of Arabia into a powerful nation. As yet, Arabia was untried against the other nations of the world, but Muhammad had sown the seeds, and expeditions to spread the faith were already planned. Muhammad died a revered prophet of a new religion that embraced nearly all Arabs and was ready to make converts in all parts of the world.

The Teachings of Muhammad

What was the teaching of this prophet who moved so many proud men to join him in service to God? If his teachings were so different that they were rejected by a majority of his own tribe, how could they be embraced by people who would be persecuted for their allegiance? The profundity of Muhammad's message and the intricate implications of his revelations were carried out in acts that could be performed by the simple shepherd or his wife, by warriors, by merchants, scholars, and saints. Five requirements are made of all Muslims: First, they have to declare in the **Shahada,** witness, that there is no god but Allah and that Muhammad is his **rasul,** or messenger. Second, they must participate in five periods of prayer each day. Third, they must pay an obligatory tax, called **zakat,** to the needy. Fourth, they must fast during the daylight hours in the month of Ramadan. Fifth, if they are able, they should make a pilgrimage to Mecca, a **Hajj,** once during their lifetime. These are acts that even the simplest person can

Shahada [sheh-HAH-da]
Means "witnessing." The Muslim profession of faith. There is but one God and Muhammad is his rasul or messenger.

rasul [ra-SOOL]
"Messenger." One who recites for God. Muhammad was the rasul of God.

zakat [za-KAHT]
In Islam, the payment of a due to support the community. It is an act of purification through giving.

Hajj [HAHJ]
The pilgrimage to Mecca, expected of all Muslims who are able.

understand and practice; they are the five Pillars of Islam. That is not to say, however, that the full understanding of the beliefs behind the practices is easy or that keeping all of the practices is always convenient.

There is only one God, without partners or descendants **(Tawhid).** Angels and Shaytan, adversaries to God and tempters of humans, are clearly lesser beings than God, for they do not share his essence. The Christian belief in a Trinity or in a Son of God is clearly denounced in Islam. Muhammad is the spokesman of God, a prophet in the tradition of the Jewish prophets but in no way a divine being. The Quran is the revealed word of God and as such is not a creation of humans, even Muhammad. God is merciful and compassionate to those who repent and submit to him. But he is just in his law and requires justice in social relations. At the end of time, God will judge every person and every deed. Rewards will be given to the righteous and punishments will fall on the liars and hypocrites. There will be a resurrection of the dead and a final judgment. Paradise and hell are places of physical reward and punishment. These are just a few of the beliefs outlined in the Quran and related to the Shahada.

Prayer is encouraged and can be volunteered at any time. At a bare minimum, every Muslim is required to participate in prescribed prayer **(salat)** five times a day. Although these prayers can be said alone or with groups, there seems to be special benefit in reciting them in groups. Noon on Friday is the time of community prayer in the mosque. Dawn, noon, midafternoon, nightfall, and evening are the five times of prayers that consist of prescribed **rak'as,** or postures and recitations. The faithful in the community are called to prayer by a **muezzin,** and there is a sense of the community at prayer at one time even though individuals are not gathered into a physical congregation for prayer. One of the prayers repeated more than a dozen times a day is the opening *surah* (section) of the Quran.

> In the Name of God, the Merciful, the Compassionate
> Praise belongs to God, the Lord of all Being,
> the All-merciful, the All-compassionate, the Master of the Day of Doom.
> Thee only we serve; to Thee alone we pray for succour.
> Guide us in the straight path,
> the path of those whom Thou has blessed,
> not of those against whom Thou art wrathful, nor of those who are astray.
> (QURAN 1:1–7)

Giving alms may take the form of a direct gift of compassion from one believer to another. This is called "charity" **(sadaqa)** and should be given frequently. But there is a more organized concept of giving *(zakat)* to a common treasury from which the needs of the community can be met. In a sense, alms are to be voluntary, but in another sense they are obligatory, like a tax. In any case, alms are different from the *jizyah* exacted from the non-Muslims and used for administration and military expenses. Alms are related to the nature of God, who is merciful and requires mercy in his worshipers toward each other. Compassion toward weak and defenseless persons of the community is a reflection of the compassion of God. Widows, orphans, and females in general are of particular concern in the words of Muhammad, and believers are exhorted to be compassionate to them in administering their trusts or permitting them to live through infancy, particularly unwanted females.

Tawhid [TAHW-heed]
The Muslim doctrine of the unity of God. Islam denies any partners to God such as Christians are believed to have in their Trinity.

salat [sa-LAHT]
In Islam, the prescribed prayer.

rak'a [RAK-ah]
Each complete cycle of ritual movements that is part of Muslim prayer. During prayer Muslims stand, bow, kneel, and touch their foreheads to the ground.

muezzin [mu-EZ-in]
One who calls Muslims to prayer. Muhammad preferred the human voice to the Christian use of bells.

sadaqa [sah-DAH-ka]
Informal charity between Muslims.

The month of Ramadan is set aside to recall the month in which God began to reveal the Quran to Muhammad. Although Islam does not despise the human body or advocate a rigid asceticism, it does recognize the value of fasting for clearing a person's spiritual perception. The fast, then, is enjoined on able-bodied believers for one month each year, but only during the daylight hours. After sunset, nourishment can be taken; believers can even celebrate with friends while taking much food and non-alcoholic drink.

Muhammad set the precedent for pilgrimages to Mecca while he was at Medina. All Muslims should make a pilgrimage to Mecca at least once in a lifetime if they can afford it and health permits. The journey is to be made in the period of the Hajj, and pilgrims are to remain in the state of *ihram*, or purity, for the two-week period of activities that center around Mecca but also involve Arafat and Mina. The most sacred place, of course, is the Ka'bah, which includes the Black Stone. Muslim tradition ties the Ka'bah to Abraham, who built the first building.

Muhammad's formation of Islam involved two sources, the Quran and the **Sunna.** The first, and most important, was the Quran. This revelation from God came to the prophet over many years and was given in suras, or chapters, applicable to specific situations in the life of the prophet and the community. The lines came in the poetic form of the Arabs, so beautiful that Muhammad challenged any poets to try to duplicate it. Indeed, the Quran is the one miracle in Islam; it is not at all the product of Muhammad's efforts or prior experiences. As Sheik Muhammad Abduh wrote,

Sunna [SUN-na]
The custom or tradition of Muhammad. It supplements the Quran as a source for the Shari'a.

> The mighty Book was vindicated as being speech *par excellence,* and the judgments superior to all others. Is not the appearance of such a Book, from the lips of an illiterate man, the greatest miracle and clearest evidence that it is not of human origin? Is it not rather the light that emanates from the sun of divine knowledge, the heavenly wisdom coming forth from the Lord upon the illiterate Prophet?[6]

Muslims have the Quran in Arabic; they believe that it cannot be translated into other languages. According to tradition, the book that Muslims have today was transcribed by Zayd Ibn Thabit, secretary to Muhammad, who collected the scraps on which followers had written oral messages. Muhammad did not write the messages he received. Nor did he seek the revelations; on the contrary, they came to him sometimes during periods of extreme physical ordeal, in which he broke out in a sweat and heard a loud ringing like a bell in his head.

hadiths [had-EETHS]
Reports of what Muhammad said or did; examples for faithful Muslims to follow. The *Sunna* are the traditions of the prophet in the literary form of *hadith*—reports.

The second source of guidance was Muhammad's word and practice. During his long period of political and religious leadership, the prophet was called on hundreds of times to make decisions and take actions that were not at the time clearly covered by revelation from God. His personality was so charismatic that his followers honored his words and examples, regarding them as binding on themselves. Given a chance to mingle with his followers and to observe and hear him, even his worst enemies sometimes joined his religion. These **hadiths,** or traditions of the prophet, once collected and evaluated as to their authenticity, became guides to the practice of Islam along with the Quran and comprise the literary form of the Sunna. The Quran and the Sunna, or custom of Muhammad, together form the guidelines for the beliefs and practices of the Muslim community.

The Quran. This page is from a Quran of the 13th century.

The Successors of the Prophet

caliph [KAA-lif]
A successor of the prophet Muhammad. The first caliph was Abu Bakr. The ideal of Islam is that religion and state are not separated.

Muhammad died without announcing to the whole community of Muslims his choice of successor. The disagreement over what principle should be employed in naming a successor threatened to divide the community at once; within a short time, it led to the major division that continues until the present time with little signs of healing. The person first chosen as successor, or **caliph** (khalifah), of the prophet was Abu Bakr, one of his oldest companions. Although he was the father of Muhammad's wife Aishah, he was not of his immediate family as was 'Ali, his cousin, the son of his uncle Abu Talib. When Abu Bakr died after two years, the next successor was 'Umar. Under 'Umar, Islam expanded rapidly into other countries. After 'Umar's murder, 'Uthman, a son-in-law of the prophet, succeeded him and ruled for about ten years. 'Uthman was from the rival faction of Mecca, and the original supporters of Muhammad regarded him as a usurper. He was murdered in Medina.[7] The old division culminated with the choice of the fourth caliph. 'Ali was the choice of the community at Medina, but Mu'awiyah, governor of Syria, refused to acknowledge him and held out to be the caliph himself. To the old guard at Medina, this suggestion was impossible, for Mu'awiyah was from the Ummayad branch of the Quraysh, the clan that had opposed Muhammad in his early years and made the Hijrah necessary, who refused him entrance to Mecca for a pilgrimage until he had the military strength to crush the Meccans. Now a descendant of that infamous clan was claiming to be the successor of the Prophet. The assassination of 'Uthman and the problem of choosing a successor weighed heavily on the community.

Sunni and Shi'a

Shi'a [SHE-a]
Members of the "party" of 'Ali, who believed that he should have been the fourth leader.

Sunni [SOON-e]
The traditional, majority, Muslims who accepted Mu'awiyah as the fourth leader.

The details of the story vary somewhat between the accounts of the **Shi'a,** the partisans of 'Ali, or the **Sunni,** the traditionalists who accept the outcome that left Mu'awiyah the fourth leader. 'Ali agreed to submit the dispute between himself and Mu'awiyah to arbitration. A group, the Kharijites, seceded from 'Ali. These puritans thought that the community had a right to select any morally pure Muslim as caliph and that any true successor would let God settle the issue through battle. 'Ali was assassinated in 661, and Mu'awiyah retained power. 'Ali's son Hasan served briefly in Iraq, but he renounced his claim and returned to Medina. 'Ali's son Husayn attempted to establish a caliphate in 680, but he was intercepted on his way to Iraq near the town of Karbala. The Ummayad troops killed and beheaded him and sent his head to Damascus. This deed is regarded as an act of martyrdom by Shi'ites who fervently recall it in a passion play each year during the month of Muharram.

The Shi'ites hold to the institution of *imam,* the spiritual leader of the community, and regard 'Ali as the first imam. Although 'Ali had the ideal of temporal power as well as spiritual, other imams have had only spiritual power. For the Shi'a, 'Ali and those who succeeded him—not Mu'awiyah and his successors—are true imams.

Two branches of Shi'ites, the Zaydis and the Ismailis, separated from the main group, which is known as the Twelvers or Imamis. The Twelvers recognize 'Ali, son of Abu Talib, as first imam, and continue the succession to the twelfth imam, Muhammad al-Mahdi al-Hujja. He disappeared in 873 in a cave in Samarra, near Baghdad, but continued to appear to chosen deputies from time to time. Although since 940 he has been concealed, the Twelvers think that God has prolonged his life. He will finally reappear as the **Mahdi** during the reign of the last imam and usher in a golden age of Shi'a Islam. Until then, the Mahdi illumines the religious scholars of the Twelvers. The Zaydis think the proper fourth imam was Zayd, a grandson of Husayn; the Ismailis accept only the first six imams, for the proper seventh imam was Ismail rather than Musa al-Kazim.

What principles separate Sunnis and Shi'ites? Sunnis, about 85 percent of Muslims, believe that successors of the Prophet were correctly chosen by consensus of the community. Family relationships to the Prophet were not of primary importance. The Shi'ites think that Muhammad announced at Ghadir al-Khumm, on his return from his last pilgrimage to Mecca, that 'Ali was to be his successor. Sunnis acknowledge the event but interpret it differently. The Shi'ites see the role of imam as spiritual; he is a moral, theological, and even mystical leader. Sunnis have been more pragmatic in seeing the caliph as the head of a religious institution that comprises all life, including government. Although Shi'ites think that the imam is alive now, he is not visible on earth but rules through a representative. For Sunnis, an imam is simply one who leads services in a mosque. The Shi'a recall the death of Husayn, a grandson of the prophet Muhammad, at the hand of enemies of Karbala in 680. This event is dramatically reenacted annually by pious Shi'a, as was noted, who sometimes wound their bodies until their blood flows.

> In fact, it may safely be stated that, at least for later *Shī'ī* piety, this great universal drama which began before creation with Husayn as its chief character will end with him. What follows on the Day of Resurrection will be simply a foregone conclusion of his final judgment. Through his death, Husayn provided the final proof or contention (*hujjah*) of God over and against His creation. Hence, it will be his prerogative to pronounce the divine judgment over all men. Thus the sixth *Imām* is supposed to have boldly asserted, "The one who shall conduct the final reckoning (*hisāb*) of men before the Day of Resurrection is Hysayn Ibn'Ali. As for the Day of Resurrection itself, it shall be a day of sending forth (ba'th) to the Garden or to the Fire."[8]

The Expansion of Islam

The phenomenal spread of Islam beyond Arabia is one of the most rapid expansions of a religion in the history of the world. From the dates alone, it would appear that this marching of Muslim armies was an idea of the first caliphs that developed after the death of Muhammad. Other sources, however, indicate that Muhammad had already contemplated expeditions to the north, such as the first encounter with the Byzantine armies that led to Muslim reverses, salvaged only by the abilities of Khalid Ibn al-Walid. Apparently Muhammad had already mapped out another campaign and appointed a leader, Usamah, the son of Zayd. Abu Bakr simply carried out the plans of the Prophet when he sent Usamah out into Byzantine domains. This first expedition after the death of the Prophet was not a disaster, but it was not followed up immediately. Some tribes of Arabia considered that their alliance was with Muhammad and that it ended with his death. Only with force could the caliphs maintain the unity of the Arabs until they realized that they were part of a new community of Islam, committed to the Muslim way and not just to the man Muhammad.

Under 'Umar, the second caliph from 634 to 644, the Arab armies moved in a series of rapid thrusts that captured most of the Middle East. Damascus,

Mahdi [MAH-di]
In Islam, the expected one. Twelvers believe that an imam is in occultation and will return as a messianic figure.

Dome of the Rock, Jerusalem. This building, also known as the Mosque of Omar, dates from 691 to 2 C.E. The rock covered by the dome has been sacred from the time of Abraham.

the capital of Syria, fell after a siege of six months in the year 635. Khalid offered the inhabitants security of person, property, and churches so long as they did not resist and paid the required tax. The Byzantines lost battle after battle with the horse- and camel-mounted warriors of the Arabs. The population of Syria welcomed the overthrow of the harsh Byzantine rulers by Semitic forces more similar to themselves. Jerusalem was a religious prize that fell into Muslim hands in 638. Its importance to Muslim religion came only after Mecca and Medina, for many of the events of the Hebrew Bible were shared in the accounts of the Quran. In the beginning of Muhammad's prophecy, he had enjoined Muslims to face Jerusalem in prayer. Egypt fell in 641, and soon the other North African countries to the west fell. Religious zeal motivated the soldiers: converting idolaters (which did not include Christians and Jews) to Islam was an act of merit that aided others as well as themselves. Worshipers of one God could be tolerated, but believers waged war on all idolaters. Fighting that cost believers their lives could lead directly to paradise, another religious motive. Wealth that could be shared by the warriors and sent back to the treasury of Islam to help the needy of the community also was a motive.

After the time of 'Umar, the expansion continued rapidly until about 750. Muslim forces moved into Spain and even into France until turned back by Charles Martel in 732. To the east, Muslim forces entered Persia, eventually making it a center for Islam. Other campaigns moved Muslims to Turkestan and Mongolia and even into India. The Mogul Empire was established by descendants of Mongols, the most enlightened of whom was Akbar, the grandson of Babur. Constantinople survived many threats before it fell to the Muslim Turks in 1453. The success of Muslims in gaining territory limited Christians in their travels for trade and religious pilgrimages.

Muslim victory did not mean, however, that everyone in a territory became a Muslim. It is true that people without a book of religion were sometimes given a choice of conversion or death. Nevertheless, Jews and Christians could retain their faith by paying a tax. They were offered the status of **dhimmis,** or persons protected by Muslims, so long as they abided by agreements with their conquerors, remaining submissive as second-class citizens. The relations between these people of the Book and Muslims varied greatly from time to time and place to place. Occasionally, they lived together in creative cooperation, as in medieval Spain. More often, there were conflicts and oppressions, with Jews and Christians managing to survive but not able to live very well. Where Muslims ruled, there was great incentive for converting to Islam.

The Shari'a

As Muslims expanded their rule to other countries, they had to extend their administrative and legal structure. The law that would govern the life of Muslims in all countries was the **Shari'a.** It included the revealed law of the Quran, of course, but it was more than that alone. The Sunna had to be considered. Also, the consensus of the community, **ijma',** had to be assessed; in practice, this consensus contained the considered judgments of the scholars of jurisprudence. To a lesser extent, and somewhat more controversial, the fourth dimension was the employment of **qiyas,** or analogy. When a circumstance arose that was not clearly covered in the other three sources, reasoning from known cases could be applied to the new situation, and it could be determined how the case would have been handled if it had been considered by Muhammad. Eventually, four different Sunni schools of interpretation of the Shari'a emerged as dominant. The Hanifite school is somewhat liberal in that it also employed **ra'y,** or personal opinion, in some decisions, which could lead to forsaking even the commands of the Quran in some applications. The law was formulated primarily for Iraq and is still employed there and in Turkey, Pakistan, and India. The Malikite school developed in Medina and relied heavily on ijma', or consensus, of the Medina community. It is still followed in eastern Arabia, West, Central, and North Africa, and parts of Egypt. The Shafi'ite school rejected all forms of opinion and tended to elevate hadiths even above the Quran. This school tends to prevail in Cairo and in the southern areas of Arabia and in Malaysia and Indonesia. The Hanbalite school is the most conservative of all. Founded in Baghdad by a student of al-Shafi, Hanbal rejected opinion and gave primary emphasis to the Quran with secondary place to hadiths. This school is prevalent in Saudi Arabia. Where Muslim governments control countries, the Shari'a can still carry weight. In countries that have secular governments in spite of large Muslim populations, it is still influential in the lives of the faithful.

Greek Influences on Islam

When Byzantine governments gave way to Islam, the interest of Greek philosophers turned to discussions of Islam. One Muslim problem arose from differences between puritanical Kharijites, who wanted only morally pure adherents accepted in Islam, and the Murjites, who accepted all who expressed faith. Murjites believed that God will decide the outcome for each believer at the day of judgment. Two other problems were how much people's actions are based on their own choice and how much they are based on God's predestination and whether the Quran is eternal or created by God.

The Mu'tazilites gave credit to human reason and choice. Faith and decision are within human power. The Quran cannot be eternal, for if it were,

dhimmi [THIM-mi]
A client of the Muslims. In exchange for protection, non-Muslims agreed to certain conditions of subservience to Muslims. Jews and Christians were often dhimmis of Muslim rulers.

Shari'a [SHA-ree-a]
The duties that God has placed on the Muslim community. It is sometimes translated as "law."

ijma' [IJ-mah]
The consensus of Muslim religious leaders on matters of practice.

qiyas [KEE-yas]
In Islam, analogies used in applying the Quran and the Sunna to other practical situations.

ra'y [RAA-ee]
In Muslim law, the considered opinion of Muslim leaders acting for public good.

it would be a second god. It is, therefore, created by God. God does not have human qualities; words that suggest his having a human form are only metaphors.

Al-Ash'ari (d. 935) gave the orthodox response to Mu'tazilites. Combining the positions, he said that God is absolute and different from humans. The qualities that humans ascribe to God are there in some form. God directs all human actions, but by participating in acts, humans become morally responsible for them—deserving reward or punishment. The Quran is eternal, but the words that humans read and recite are not eternal. Al-Ash'ari rejected Greek rationalism, but he formulated orthodox Islamic doctrine in ways that met some serious objections from philosophy.[9] A little over a century later, al-Ghazali used similar tactics.

Muslim Spiritual Experiences

Islam is more than institutions; for Muhammad and his early converts there were religious experiences of God. To experience the presence of God was always an aim of Muslim worshipers, although to submit to God was even higher in priority. The majesty of God comes through clearly in the earliest experiences of the Muslim community. Although he is compassionate to repenting sinners and those in need, God is also just and requires justice in believers' conduct toward himself and fellows. Both awe and fascination are characteristic of the worship experience of Muhammad and his close companions.

The importance of worship was never lost in Islam. The very rapid influx of converts during the period of military expansion challenged Muslims to maintain consistently deep spiritual lives in spite of worldly success. There were gentle souls who wanted to move away from the constant strife of the world and focus on a closer walk with God. Although Islam developed its own models in time, looking to Muhammad who could live simply even when wealth was pouring into the community treasury, some Muslims also found help among the Christians and even among the Buddhists. Asceticism was not a rule for Muslims or Jews, but some of them, as well as early Christians, gave it an important place in expressing their faith. Muslims in northern Arabia encountered Christian monks and sometimes shared their asceticism as an approach to the holy life. Others realized that denial of the body was not the main goal of the holy life but an experience of the reality of God and being in his presence. The practice of devotion involved ritual, but it also led to speculation about the nature of God, the Quran, Truth, Being, and the nature of destiny and freedom. Although some theology was devoted in Islam to apology and legalism, other theology developed to explain the life of devotion of the mystics.

Sufis

The Sufis are associated with Muslim mysticism.[10] They took their name from the clothing they wore—rough woolen garments.[11] Their organizations sometimes paralleled those of Christian mystics, and their theology shared insights with Neoplatonism and Gnosticism.[12] Their goals varied somewhat, but their direction was toward experiencing in this life the union of the soul with God. Through various leaders, such as Ibn Arabi (1165–1240), a body of knowledge developed that outlined steps toward union with God. Perhaps their turning from the world was regarded by

Dervishes. In Syria, dervishes of Sufism whirl to reach a state of mystical ecstasy.

some Muslims as selfishness, for to the more worldly believers, Sufis seemed to look only to their own experience and not to the well-being of the larger Muslim community. Indeed, their concentration on meditation and the mystical experience led them away from rigid concentration on everyday ritual and legalism.

Was mysticism selfishness? After reading the works of Rabia, a woman mystic of Basra who died in 802, it is hard to come to that conclusion. Her words do focus on the individual's relationship to God, but they deny seeking any rewards other than knowing God:

> O God! If I worship Thee in fear of Hell, burn me in Hell; and if I worship Thee in hope of Paradise, exclude me from Paradise; but if I worship Thee for Thine own sake, withhold not Thine Everlasting Beauty.[13]

Many other mystics wrote in the same spirit, thirsting to know and worship God, but asking nothing beyond that experience itself. The Persian poet Jalal al-Din Rumi (1207–1273) used the analogy of lover and beloved.[14]

> Lovers, lovers, whoever sees His face, his reason become distraught, his habit confounded.
> He becomes a seeker of the Beloved, his shop is ruined, he runs headlong like water in his river.[15]

But what of those who experienced union with God? How could that loss of self and the ascendancy of God in human life be expressed? That problem became acute for mystics and ordinary orthodox believers alike. Three centuries after the Hijrah, a Persian Sufi, Hosayn ibn Mansur al-Hallaj (d. 922), cried out that he was the True (ana al-Haqq). Misunderstanding him, thinking that he had claimed to be God, orthodox Muslims tortured and then crucified him for his blasphemy. Other mystics understood the message that the orthodox community had sent and decided to find other ways of expressing the experience of the soul and God being in union. Sufis had a bad reputation with the orthodox, and legalism made mysticism seem heretical.

The larger Muslim community has always balanced the Law and the Way, the Shari'a and the Tariqah (spiritual path). Seyyed Hossein Nasr has employed the symbol of the walnut to illustrate their relationship. The Shari'a is the shell that protects and permits growth. The kernel is the Tariqah, which gives it end and purpose. Both are necessary for the walnut to subsist and manifest itself.[16]

Al-Ghazali

The person who helped most to overcome the division between orthodox practices of Islam and the mystics was Abu Hamid al-Ghazali, who died in 1111. A brilliant young student of jurisprudence, he was invited to become a professor at the Nizamiyah, a new university in Baghdad, where he attracted some three hundred students. From his twentieth year, he tells his readers, he had pursued every kind of dogma or belief so as to understand as many as possible. Ascetics, Sufis, theologians, and philosophers all attracted him as much as jurisprudence. He was well established as a professor with acclaim and income. However, he became dissatisfied in his work and was deeply concerned to prepare his soul for the final judgment. He was more concerned to be right with God than to have the approval of humanity. He had already read thoroughly the theoretical works on mysticism and therefore had gone as far as he could progress without actually leaving the university and his ties to the world to practice the disciplined life of a mystic. Eventually, he found the courage to leave his teaching post, and for eleven years he made an in-depth practice of the mystical life. He did respond favorably to the request of his sultan and returned to teaching for a few years, combining intellectual disciplines with his practices of the mystical life.

Al-Ghazali did not become anti-intellectual in his total outlook, but he did see the limitations of human intellectual activity in the light of the importance of the mystical experience of God. Theology, he concluded, was directed toward preserving the creed of orthodoxy against heretical ideas. In philosophy, he found that the materialists (those who believe only in atoms and space), the naturalists (those who believe that nature is the highest reality), and the theists (those who believe in a supreme God), including Plato and Aristotle, were all affected with unbelief. They believed the world is eternal, that God knows only universals, and they denied the resurrection of the body.[17] He also lumped with them in their unbelief their Muslim followers Ibn Sina and al-Farabi as well as others who employed a Neoplatonic framework in understanding the world. Works in mathematics, logic, and natural sciences in general he found outside any religious controversy; they were sciences that Muslims could accept as readily as they could medicine. He did insist that the material world is created by God and does not exist of itself alone. In the end, he rejected those ideas from any secular knowledge that contradicted the revelation of the Quran and generally accepted knowledge that was not superstitious or did not threaten the essential revelation of God. To submit to God and his revelation was to be placed first beyond all human knowledge and practices, no matter what rewards might be attached to them.

Sufism gained considerable respectability after al-Ghazali; it was not automatically regarded as heretical or anti-orthodox. However, the established orders of Sufis did not escape the kind of decline that seems to manifest itself in all such groups, regardless of the religion. The high ideals and practices of the founders were relaxed in subsequent generations to provide a more comfortable and rewarding livelihood for members. The kinds of doctrines and practices that win enthusiasm from the masses who despise intellectual rigor and prefer credulity were adopted by various holy men and orders. Here and there, however, individual saints and groups continued to practice the presence of God in human life and to keep doctrines and practices that were intellectually respectable.

Philosophy After Al-Ghazali: Ibn Arabi

Practicing the kind of speculation that al-Ghazali had denounced, Ibn Arabi startled many philosophers, theologians, and Sufis.[18] He conceived of God as the only reality. That commitment meant that everything else in human experience is a manifestation of God, not as created by God but as words of God. Whether this view is understood as pantheism (God is all) or monism (only one reality), it brings God, creation, and humans together in a way frightening to orthodox Islam. This Muslim view however, fulfills the desire of many mystics, for it overcomes the chasm between God and humans.

Ibn Arabi was no less creative with other concepts. Muhammad was a perfect manifestation of reality, an example for creation. But every person is a manifestation of reality; Christians were wrong in claiming that only Jesus was God. Desiring to be known, God manifests himself both in nature and in humans. Humans are potentially full manifestations of God. Through mystical experiences, they can perfect that manifestation. In his emphasis on the unity of all Being, Ibn Arabi saw unity in all religions; he could write that love alone was his religion.

Although it brought a mixed response, Ibn Arabi's influence was lasting. His description of Muhammad's night journey to heaven is believed to have influenced Dante's description of paradise. But Ibn Arabi's emphasis on spiritual experience lessened the importance of theology and law, offending theologians and scholars. Sufis were enthusiastic for human spirits to experience God, but many of them denied that God and the soul ever become one. The implication that he was the seal of the saints as Muhammad was seal of the prophets was especially dangerous in orthodox Islam.

Islam's Relationship with Other Religions

From the beginning, Islam's relationship with other religions has been somewhat ambiguous. Muslims have no doubts about Islam's being the final revelation of God through Muhammad. Nor is there any doubt that polytheism is to be stamped out and Islam substituted for it, as was the practice when Muhammad took control of Mecca. The problem is complicated in Islam's relationship to Judaism and Christianity. In the Quran, there are favorable references to the prophets of Judaism and the personalities of the New Testament. There is also the idea that peoples of the Book are to be treated with more respect than pagans, those without a sacred literature. Jews and Christians were not forced to convert to Islam but were allowed to keep their religions as long as they paid a tax. But Muhammad obviously changed in his relationship to Jews in Arabia when they opposed theocracy in Medina. The Muslim clashes with Byzantine forces, who were nominally Christian, added to some problems of theology the conflicts of military enemies. Muslims had problems with the Christian doctrine of the Trinity, which seemed to add partners to God. This was also a problem with the Christian doctrine of the Incarnation, holding that Jesus was very God. Islam could regard Jesus as a true prophet, but it had to denounce the idea that Jesus was the Son of God or God. Add to these problems the more complete and final revelation from God, and there are the makings of tense relationships among these religions in spite of their sharing certain stories, personalities, and beliefs in ancient times.

Territories occupied by Muslims tended to become predominantly Muslim. The Jews and the Christians who remained firm in their faith had to make considerable sacrifices. How severe these sacrifices were depended on the time and place and the wishes of the ruler. The pattern was sometimes based on the old Arab concept of a client people; that is, Jews or Christians had to place themselves under the protective custody of a strong Muslim who could guarantee them certain privileges of survival and practice in exchange for compensation. Although the tradeoffs might make sense in terms of making the best of a bad situation, there was usually a measure of humiliation involved for the client peoples.

THE CRUSADES

The patriarch of Constantinople was always concerned about the Muslim threat on his doorstep. When Muslims in control of Jerusalem and other Christian holy places became particularly harsh to Christian pilgrims during medieval times, there was an additional reason for Roman Catholic Christians to be concerned about the Muslim occupation of so much land at the eastern end of the Mediterranean Sea. Statements of concern from Constantinople and tales of horror from Jerusalem pilgrims began to add up, and eventually sentiments in Europe favored doing something to alter the situation. A pope took leadership in calling for crusades of Christian soldiers to journey to the Holy Land and free the Christian places of worship from the so-called Muslim infidels. A variety of motives—including, perhaps, both piety and economic gain—moved monarchs in Britain and Europe to respond to the call and raise armies to assault Jerusalem and other places of importance to pilgrims.

Pope Urban II responded to the appeal for help from Alexius I by calling for a crusade at a synod in Clermont in 1095. Any Christians falling in battle would be forgiven their sins and win immediate entrance into eternal life. The response was enthusiastic, if sometimes misdirected against Jews and others living along the way. The nobility of Europe, however, eventually captured Jerusalem on July 15, 1099. When the Muslims were united under Saladin in the twelfth century, he defeated the Latin army at Hattin and soon recovered the city of Jerusalem and other territory for the Muslims. A fifth crusade under Holy Roman Emperor Frederick II gave

Jerusalem, Bethlehem, and Nazareth to Christians for a while, together with access to the coast, beginning in 1229. But the area was lost to the Muslims again in 1244.

There are stories of chivalry and horror on both sides of the struggle. For example, T. A. Archer, in his account of the crusade of Richard I, the Lion-Hearted, gives a Christian account and a Muslim account of Christians killing Muslim hostages. A Christian account says that Saladin, the Muslim leader, waited past the deadline for redeeming Turkish hostages. Besides, according to Roger of Howden, Saladin had, two days earlier, already beheaded all his Christian prisoners; thus King Richard was completely justified in having 2,700 Turks led outside the city of Acre and beheaded.[19] A Muslim account by Beha-ed-Din (Bohadin) reports that Saladin had arranged a payment in three parts over a month's time to redeem Muslim hostages. King Richard had promised the Muslims that on surrender they could go free with their families if Saladin redeemed them; otherwise they

The Alhambra. This view of the Court of Lions shows the Muslim influence on architecture remaining in Granada, Spain.

would become slaves. Those were the conditions they accepted in surrender. Seeing Saladin's delays, King Richard did what he planned to do if he had received payment: He had the Franks kill the Muslim hostages. Beha-ed-Din concludes,

> The motives of this massacre are differently told; according to some, the captives were slain by way of reprisal for the death of those Christians whom the Musulmans had slain. Others again say that the king of England, on deciding to attempt the conquest of Ascalon, thought it unwise to leave so many prisoners in the town after his departure. God alone knows what the real reason was.[20]

The Christian massacre of Jews and Muslims and eventually even their sack of their own city of Constantinople cannot be pointed to as the finest examples of Christian behavior. Considerable bitterness built up on all sides among the three religions, with stories told to justify behavior and condemn the cause of the enemy. These examples have circulated through the centuries and have done their parts to nourish suspicion and mistrust among the three religions.

COOPERATION

These horror stories can be balanced, however, with other instances. It was not unheard of for a Jewish physician to serve a Muslim monarch; Maimonides so served Saladin in Cairo. Muslims also provided services to Christians—one example is the Muslim discovery of Aristotle and the translations and commentaries that were shared with Christians. Muslim intellectual influence was very strong in Spain, particularly Cordoba. A Christian, Alvaro, wrote in 854,

> My fellow-Christians delight in the poems and romances of the Arabs; they study the works of Mohammedan theologians and philosophers, not in order to refute them, but to acquire a correct and elegant Arabic style. Where today can a layman be found who reads the Latin commentaries on Holy Scriptures? Who is there that studies the Gospels, the Prophets, the Apostles? Alas! the young Christians who are most conspicuous for their talents have no knowledge of any literature or language save the Arabic; they read and study with avidity Arabian books; they amass whole libraries of them at a vast cost, and they everywhere sing the praises of Arabian lore. On the other hand, at the mention of Christian books they disdainfully protest that such works are unworthy of their notice. The pity of it! Christians have forgotten their own tongue. . . .[21]

Ibn Rushd

Ibn Rushd (1126–1198) was known to Christian Europe as Averroës. He worked in Cordoba, Spain, writing learned commentaries on the works of Aristotle. They were so prized by Christian theologians that they were used in the University of Paris. St. Thomas Aquinas knew them from his studies with Albert the Great. Although Aquinas benefited from Ibn Rushd's studies, he differed with his conclusion that there is no immortality of the individual because all individuals participate in one soul. In Islam, Ibn Rushd continued speculative philosophy after the effective attacks on it by al-Ghazali, but the spirit of al-Ghazali triumphed. Ibn Rushd was the last philosopher in the speculative tradition. In Spain, the fruitful interplay between Jews, Christians, and Muslims ended in 1492, when the Christian monarchs Ferdinand and Isabella intervened. These monarchs prized strict orthodoxy above doctrines and practices that might be tainted with the strange ideas of other religions.

Islam in India

Islam reached India through three different sources—conquest, immigration, and conversion.[22] Conquest started in 712 with the Arab takeover of Sind. Arabs and Turks continued their conquest through the centuries. But these invading armies were relatively small, and they customarily built garrison cities outside the cities of the local population. The invading warriors were not numerous enough to win sweeping allegiance to a religion. Muslim ideas and customs were borrowed by Hindus, but complete abandonment of Hinduism was not typical. Nevertheless, Muslims from central and western Asia, seeking new opportunities, arrived to settle in the new land.

In South India, the earliest Muslims were Arab traders and settlers who arrived in the seventh century.[23] These Muslims settled among Hindus and practiced the faith of Islam. In this region there were Hindus who embraced Islam, but others adapted Islam to their Hindu heritage. There were many situations where Islam and Hinduism lived together in harmony.

Other Hindus were converted to Islam by missionaries who lived exemplary spiritual lives. By the eleventh century, Ismaili missionaries from Yemen arrived in Gujarat. In the fifteenth and sixteenth centuries, many conversions came through the influence of Muslim mystics. Lower castes of Hindus and outcastes found that Islam's emphasis on the unity of all

Baha'i Shrine, Haifa Israel. Mt. Carmel rises sharply to the Shrine.

Abdul-Baha. In 1912 he attended the laying of the cornerstone of the beautiful Baha'i house of worship in Wilmette, Illinois.

Muslims opened new opportunities for them. Although force sometimes played a role in conversions, many conversions came about voluntarily. Some Hindus were attracted to the high spiritual teachings and examples of Islam.

Through the Moguls and other groups, Islam made a lasting impression on India. The most famous building in India for outsiders, the Taj Mahal, is a monument to the wife of Shah Jahan, a Muslim ruler. The Moguls related to Hindus in several ways, ranging from tolerance, to appreciation, to persecution for their polytheism. Sikhism, which attempted to harmonize Islam and Hinduism, was largely rejected by Hindus and Muslims, and Sikh gurus were sometimes severely tortured by Moguls in an attempt to return them to orthodox Islam.

The Baha'i Religion

After asserting that the Baha'i faith is an independent religion, William S. Hatcher and J. Douglas Martin further assert that the religious matrix of the Baha'i faith was Islam.[24] The expectation of Shi'a Islam that a manifestation of God would appear was fulfilled for many people in the declaration of Baha'u'llah (1817–1892) of Persia. He declared that he was the expected one. He emphasized unity of humans, religions, races, and knowledge. The response of those faithful to him has led to a worldwide representation of the Baha'i faith. Muslims, however, have denied that Baha'u'llah was the expected one. The Baha'is have gone their own way as an independent religion.

Modernism in Islam

Islam could not escape the waves of modernism any more than could Judaism or Christianity. The new ways of looking at the universe that developed after Copernicus and the new ways of looking at human beings after the writings of Darwin could not be avoided, for Islam was often thrown against its will into contact with European colonial powers. Young Muslim scholars who encountered ideas from European university faculties had to make some sort of accommodation between their secular, scientific views and the theology and practices of the Prophet, his companions, and medieval institutions.

The educational problems brought to Islam by the pure and social sciences were serious. Although young Muslims could learn technology and engineering without challenging the Quran studies and theologies that prevailed in their societies and their *madrasas* (religious schools), other branches of learning were not easily assimilated. Studies of order in the universe in themselves did not attack order in creation established by God. Order in society, the philosophy of the Europeans, ethics, and law were difficult to study in the languages of Europe. More serious than the limited resources in textbooks was their secular orientation, which seemed to undermine the **'ulama'** (clerical scholars) in each country. In countries where the 'ulama' were excluded from the formal educational system, secularism threatened to bring the social problems familiar to Muslims observing the immoralities of the West. Where the 'ulama' had a good working relationship with the state they were able, to a great extent, to limit the development of any scholarship that challenged their very conservative traditions.

'ulama' [UL-ah-mah]
Muslim clerical scholars.

Muslim Responses to Modernism

Islam offered a variety of responses to modernism. One response, the **Wahhab,** rejected not only Western innovations but also many of the popular practices of medieval Islam. Muhammad Ibn 'Abd al-Wahhab (1703–1792) was a purist for his faith. He wanted a faith based on only the Quran and

Wahhab [WAH-hab]
One of the 99 names of Allah. 'Abd al-Wahhab means "The Servant of the Bestower."

The Taj Mahal. The Muslim mausoleum in Agra, India, not only is an example of Muslim architecture, but also is widely regarded as one of the most beautiful buildings in the world.

the Sunna of the Prophet. This radical fundamentalism attacked Sufism, philosophies of monism and pantheism, worship at tombs of saints, beliefs that Muslim saints could pray for sinners, and schools of law other than the Hanbalite. In spite of resistance by the 'ulama', Wahhabism had widespread political, economic, and religious impact. It gained political support from the Saudi family, which continues at this time as protector of the Wahhabis and enforcer of the puritan movement. Through a Syrian disciple of 'Abd al-Wahhab, Rashid Rida, the Salafiya movement spread to Africa, India, and Indonesia.

Jamal al-Din al-Afghani (1838–1897) agitated throughout the Muslim world for a Pan-Islam movement that would stand against Western colonialism. He supported Abd al-Hamid II of the Ottoman Empire, who claimed to be the true caliph of Islam. Weak governments and minority Muslim communities were inspired by the theme of strength through unity.

A disciple of al-Afghani, Muhammad Abduh (1849–1905), with British support became chief legal consultant of Islam in Egypt and an administrator of al-Azhar, the famous Islamic school in Cairo. He argued that the advance of modern sciences and scholarship is in keeping with the Quran. Long before Christians did, Muslims who understood the Quran led the way in sciences and medicine. Abduh urged that animosity to rationalism, freedom, and scientific studies be changed and that Islam regain its leadership in education.

In spite of their minority among Hindus, Muslims in India sought a position of strength. Sayyid Ahmad Khan (1817–1898) thought that in order for young Muslims to be kept in the faith, the excesses of medieval Islam would have to be replaced with modern rationalism and the sciences. God is creator of the world; studying his creation is not threatening to his majesty. When he advocated that Muslims remove some practices that offended many unbelievers—polygamy (having more than one spouse) and *purdah* (veiling and seclusion of women)—Ahmad Khan met strong resistance.

Amir Ali (1849–1928), a Shi'ite, stirred Muslims in India and beyond with his book *The Spirit of Islam.* He presented Muhammad as an enlightened moral reformer who instituted government that protected the rights of women, children, and orphans. The Quran teaches an enlightened, liberal view of humans and society. Amir Ali's religious liberalism ran parallel to a similar movement in Christianity.

Another Shi'ite of India, Muhammad Iqbal (1877–1938), brought together poetry and spirit. He argued that Islam supports philosophical thought on the immanence of God. The human spirit that is rational and free draws strength from God to help create a wonderful world. Educated in Western philosophy, Iqbal saw the philosophies of Bergson, Nietzsche, and Whitehead as expressions of the spirit of the greatest Muslim thinkers. Many writers, including Hamilton A. R. Gibb, credit Muhammad Iqbal with preparing the way for Pakistan as a Muslim state in 1947. It is acknowledged that Iqbal is Pakistan's "spiritual father."

Muslims, as do other peoples, want the benefits of scientific studies without the moral corruption of the societies that first developed them. Whether the spirit of free inquiry that promotes creative sciences can be joined to traditional Quran and hadith interpretations is still an open question for Muslim educators such as Fazlur Rahman.[25] If tradition does not permit free inquiry in Muslim countries and stifles students who have studied in universities of the West, Islam will have a majority of adherents

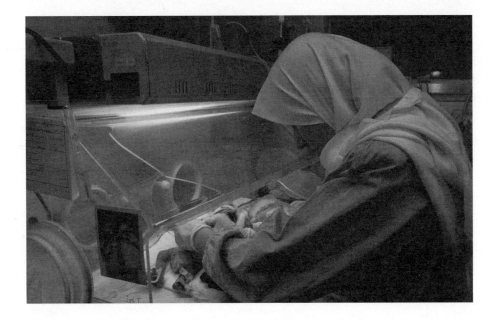

Doctor Checks Newborn Baby. In an Arab hospital in Jerusalem, in 1995, a doctor examines a newborn baby in an incubator.

who are isolated from the fruitful educational achievements of the most advanced countries in science, technology, manufacturing, and trade. Much of the ferment in Muslim countries arises from the conflicting views on educational ideals to be supported in the next century.

Islam in the Last Half of the Twentieth Century

In the last half of the twentieth century, Muslims have concentrated on creating Islamic states. In their thinking, an Islamic state is based not on Western culture or codes but only on the Quran and the Sunna. The law of the country must be the Shari'a. Each nation must be independent of Western or other influence, for Islam must be the dominant religion. All Islamic nations should be in league with each other in a worldwide community, or Islamic brotherhood. There is no particular Islamic economic or political system. There can be flexibility in these areas; what matters is that all practices be worked out in the light of early Muslim traditions based on the Quran and the prophet Muhammad.

PAKISTAN

Muhammad Iqbal's concept of the Islamic state was anchored in the doctrine of Tawhid, the absolute unity of God. Besides the Shari'a, another pillar of the state is the absolute equality of the members of the community, **ummah.** Iqbal awakened the need for the Islamic state to be separate from the Hindus of India. But his theoretical dreams had to be carried out by others.[26] Much of the work on the constitution was inspired by Abul Ala Mawdudi. Pakistan has, since 1958, been dominated almost exclusively by military leaders, such as the late Zia ul-Haq. His successor was Benazir Bhutto. She left office in 1990 but became prime minister again in 1993.

ummah [UM-mah]
The Muslim community.

EGYPT

With the rise of Gamal Abdel Nasser in Egypt in 1952, Muslims found an ideal hero. He emphasized both nationalism and a United Arab Republic.

His seizing of the Suez Canal on July 26, 1956, rocketed him to the position of a star in the Muslim world. He defied Britain, France, and Israel, and eventually reopened the canal under Egyptian management. Nasser's status plunged, however, when he was defeated in a war with Israel in 1967. His brand of Islamic state did not provide the religious leadership that Sayyid Qutb and the Muslim brotherhood advocated. Challenged by Qutb, Nasser eventually executed him and had him buried secretly.

President Anwar Sadat used Muslim symbols to rally Egyptians in the October war (1973) against Israel. Although Israel won the war, Arabs felt vindicated for their 1967 defeat, and the oil embargo of 1973 against countries supporting Israel threw the West into such an economic panic that Arabs believed that they had found their rightful political power in the modern world. But Sadat lost stature in making peace with Israel and in resisting making Egypt an Islamic state under religious leaders. Those concerns helped lead to his assassination. His successor, President Mubarak, has not yielded to the idea of turning over the reins of government to religious leaders.

LIBYA

Col. Muammar al-Qaddafi of Libya replaced Nasser of Egypt as the best hope for leading an Islamic state after the 1967 war with Israel. Coming to power in 1969, Colonel Qaddafi represented the conservative Islam of the Libyan tribes, the poor, ordinary people of the country. He graduated from the military academy and studied in Britain, but he was identified with the Islam of the people. He instituted religious leadership within the government, abolished churches and synagogues, banished alcohol, and reinstituted Quranic punishments for crimes. On the other hand, he kept the religious leaders under his control. His own views of the Islamic state were presented in his *Green Book*.[27] Colonel Qaddafi was replaced as the hope of many Muslims by the hero of Iran, the Ayatollah Khomeini, who died in June 1989.

IRAN

Ruhullah Musavi Khomeini eclipsed the other Muslim leaders in fulfilling the ideal of the Islamic state. He was obviously a qualified religious interpreter of Quran, Sunna, and Shari'a. Despite exile from Iran by the shah, Imam Khomeini carried on a relentless attack on the government that he thought compromised too many Islamic ideals for Western military and economic success. He accused the shah of being on the side of Israel. With the fall of the shah from power, Ayatollah Khomeini returned to Iran on February 1, 1979. After Khomeini's death, the Islamic Republic of Iran came under the leadership of President Hashemi Rafsanjani.

The Islamic Republic in Iran was clearly under the control of Ayatollah Khomeini, as the Islamic idealists envisioned. He eliminated people who openly opposed rule by the Shari'a. The military and any civilian government representatives were clearly subordinate to the religious leaders. The government claimed to be for the people, but anyone in dissent from the religious leaders was in constant danger. Whether this last condition is a necessary feature of the Islamic state ideal is debatable. A long, costly war with Iraq led to severe suffering among the Iranians. On the other hand, they developed a national pride as well as Islamic pride in defying the United States and inspiring idealists among Muslims of many nations. Tra-

Ayatollah Khomeini.

CHAPTER TEN

ditional Muslim governments, such as the very conservative one in Saudi Arabia, have felt deep concern about the model that gives ultimate power to religious leaders. When representatives of the ideal Islamic state seized the Grand Mosque in Mecca in 1979, the Saudis were served notice of opposition to their more traditional rule.[28]

The variety of expressions in Islam today make any attempt to place it in a system unacceptable to many Muslims. Turkey and Egypt have developed states that are somewhat independent of the 'ulama'. In Indonesia and Pakistan, the 'ulama' still have a conservative influence. In Iran, the clerical group has the firm support of the state. Although oil production and trade with many industrialized societies is brisk, Saudi Arabia retains the conservative influence of Wahhabis. All Muslim theorists speak of retaining the important teachings of the Quran, the Sunna, and the Shari'a; they seriously disagree on how these teachings are to be applied in contemporary world society.

Islam in the United States

Only recently have many Americans become aware that Islam is a significant religion in the United States. Islam is represented by two major groups. One group comprises immigrants who voluntarily came to the United States seeking a better life. Although Syrian and Lebanese immigrants were the first Muslims, now large groups have come from Pakistan, Iran, Afghanistan, Turkey, and Eastern Europe.[29] Another major group comprises African Americans who sought a religion more congenial to their experience than the Christianity of most whites. There are approximately six hundred mosques and Islamic centers in the United States. Estimates of membership vary widely; some Muslim groups avoid letting outsiders know statistics of their organization. The various groups have associations of mosques and Islamic centers. The oldest is the Federation of Islamic Associations, headquartered in Detroit, Michigan. More recently, the Muslim World League, of Mecca, has a Council of Masajid at the United Nations which helps fund building mosques and distributing Qurans. There is a Muslim Student Association with members on many campuses. The Islamic Society of North America (ISNA) is the largest Muslim "umbrella" organization.

MUSLIMS OF THE MIDWEST

The Muslims of the Midwest are primarily Arabs, most from Syrian and Lebanese descent, from families that have been in the United States for many years. These immigrants from the Middle East, coming from areas controlled by the Ottoman Empire, began arriving in the late nineteenth century and continued, in waves, until World War II. They brought their Islamic observances with them, but over time they have modified their practices until they have some parallels with the practices of Christians and some Jews. For example, mosques are more than places of worship. They are also social and educational centers. Their imams do more than lead worship. They are counselors to members of the congregation, conductors of funerals and weddings, and general administrators of Islamic laws and principles. They perform functions that in other countries would be conducted by other people in Muslim communities.

Muslims of the Midwest have become part of the American scene. They participate fully in social, economic, and civil religion activities of their

Minister Louis Farrakhan. The leader of the Nation of Islam, in his Chicago office, ca. 1985.

Timothy Drew
In 1913, in New Jersey, he taught that blacks are Asians, or Muslims. He was a contributor to the Black Muslim movement in the United States.

Elijah (Poole) Muhammad
Founder of the Black Muslim movement, the Nation of Islam. Dissatisfied with Christianity, which appeared to be a white religion, Poole organized a religion for blacks.

Nation of Islam
The branch of Black Muslims that struggles with Christianity and whites. It is not accepted by orthodox Muslims as Islam, which welcomes all races.

Malcolm X, or **Malcolm Little**
Formerly of the Nation of Islam, he formed his own group in 1964 in the tradition of Sunni Islam. A major change in his teaching was that all people are brothers and sisters, whites as well as blacks.

American Muslim Mission
A Muslim group formed for African Americans by Wallace Deen Muhammad. World Islam accepts these adherents as Muslims.

communities. Criticism of their Islam comes from members of other faiths and from newly arrived Muslims from countries that practice a more conservative Islam. Many Muslims from Pakistan now live near Chicago.

MUSLIMS OF THE EAST COAST

Many Muslims on the East Coast have arrived more recently. They comprise highly educated professionals and semiprofessionals who have entered the United States to pursue higher education, economic opportunities, and a better life for their families. Coming from Pakistan, Iran, Saudi Arabia, and other countries where conservative Islam is the rule, they prefer a more rigorous practice of traditions than their fellow Muslims in the Midwest. For example, they are more likely to reserve the mosque for worship only. Their dress and economic and social activities are limited by their Muslim heritage. They reject jobs associated with serving alcohol or taking interest on money. They are more likely to have imams who insist on practices that prevail in the "old country."

Although Muslim men are permitted to marry women of other faiths, Muslim women are supposed to avoid marrying anyone other than a Muslim. The goal is that children of Muslims should be raised as Muslims. These positions lead many Muslims to keep their children from practicing the American custom of dating. Unmarried men and women should socialize, if at all, only when it may lead to marriage. Arranged marriages are considered preferable to those entered into by the choice of the couple alone.

BLACK MUSLIMS

Black Muslims have their own history. **Timothy Drew** (1886–1929), who called himself Noble Drew Ali, the Prophet, taught in New Jersey, in 1913, that blacks were really Asiatics, or Muslims. His teachings were only remotely Islamic, and his Quran bore little resemblance to the Muslim Quran. Another prophet, W. D. Fard, began a temple in Detroit. His movement linked Islam with antiwhite activities. After his disappearance, leadership of the temple was taken by **Elijah (Poole) Muhammad** (1897–1975). He formed the **Nation of Islam,** which was antiwhite and anti-Christian. Part of the story of the Black Muslim movement centered around an account of Mr. Yakub that a superior black race once ruled the world. Mr. Yakub, an evil scientist, created an inferior white race through genetic engineering. The whites were devils and their religion was Christianity. The religion of original black people was Islam. Through trickery, the whites gained power over the black race. In their view of last things, Black Muslims saw the extermination of "white devils" and the black race's proper restoration to dominance.

Malcolm X (Little; 1925–1965), who was converted to the Nation of Islam in prison, rose to leadership of a Harlem temple. Malcolm X broke with the movement in 1964 after a pilgrimage to Mecca. He converted to Sunni Islam, which rejected racial discrimination. Malcolm X was assassinated in 1965.

TWO BLACK MUSLIM ORGANIZATIONS

The successor of Elijah Muhammad, Wallace Deen Muhammad, espoused traditional Islam. To signify the new position, he named the group the **American Muslim Mission.** A dissenting group, led by Louis Farrakhan, known as Louis X, retained the title the Nation of Islam and the antiwhite position of Elijah Muhammad. Thus, there are two main Muslim groups among African Americans. One group continues the tradition of rejecting the white race and the Christian religion, whereas the other participates in worldwide Islam, which is inclusive of all races and considers Christians and Jews as people of the Book.

Muslims in the United States generally participate in the civil religion of America. Fourth of July, Thanksgiving, Memorial Day, and Halloween pose no serious problems. The most liberal Muslims participate to some extent in the parts of Christmas that include a decorated tree, Santa Claus, and presents. In their business and social activities, Americans commonly serve pork and alcohol. Their work schedules regularly include Friday, which makes it difficult for Muslims to attend congregational worship. Young Americans regularly date without chaperons, and Muslims oppose their young people dating after the American practice. Many Muslims in the United States think that the press is unfriendly to Islam. Terrorism abroad has led many Americans to be suspicious of Islam in general and to resist any large influence of Muslims in the United States.

WORLDVIEW

In the worldview of Muslims, symbols, rituals, and actions are important. But confessing the proper beliefs is the foundation on which a life of exemplary action is built. In the Pillars of Islam, action overshadows belief. Reflection shows, however, that actions are based on a few fundamental beliefs. The most important belief is the nature of God; the second is the nature of everything created by God.

The Absolute

Islam is a firm monotheism. The Shahada recited by every Muslim emphasizes that there is no god but God. God is great; God is merciful (Quran 1:1). Muslims attribute ninety-nine most beautiful names to God, but he is beyond human ability to comprehend. God has been pleased to reveal through his prophet Muhammad that he is a just God, requiring each person to live according to his will and to act justly toward other members of the community. He will require every person to stand before him for a final judgment.

God communicates with humanity through the Quran, through prophets, through prayers of individuals, and through direction of individual lives. All Muslims agree on the sovereignty of God over human life; the question is only how much choice individuals have in directing their own affairs. Some Muslims hold to a rigid predestination of human lives. Others believe that God allows humans to exercise great freedom. The middle position is most widespread—God plans human lives, and individuals become responsible for their deeds by assenting to participate in them.

The absolute singleness of God leads Islam to denounce every form of idolatry. Muslims retain, however, a belief in angels as messengers of God. Gabriel delivered the words of the Quran to Muhammad. The Prophet spoke by the Spirit of God. But the Quran denounced any references to a son of God. Muslims also believe in Iblis, the personification of evil. There are other beings, such as jinn. According to Muslims, none compromise the absolute unity of God.

> He who created the heavens and earth, and sent down for you out of
>   heaven water;
> and We caused to grow therewith gardens full of loveliness whose trees you
>   could never grow.
> Is there a god with God?
> Nay, but they are a people who assign to Him equals! (QURAN 27:60)[30]

The World

Muslims think God created a good world. Having been created, it is not eternal. It was made by God, but it is not God. It is sustained by the will of God, but God is not coursing through it as sap through a vine. Orthodox

Muhammad on Buraq, Rising to Meet God. This version of Muhammad's ascent to heaven dates from the fifteenth century (Freer Gallery).

CHAPTER TEN

Islam has rejected the pantheism of philosophers who influenced certain Sufis. Al-Ghazali rejected Neoplatonist influences on Muslim philosophers. On the other hand, study of mathematics, astronomy, and all sciences of the natural world should be pursued in the spirit of appreciating God's great handiwork.

The world is made for humans to enjoy. Food is good. Drink, other than alcohol, is generally good. Comfortable clothing and shelter are good. Marriage is expected. Sex and procreation are good. Having property and wealth is good, so long as believers remember to share with those in need. The world is a wonderful place, a kind of preview of conditions that can be found in even purer form in the next life.

It is proper for Muslims to reflect in their fine arts the beauties of God's creation. Themes of nature can be expressed in carpets and mosaics. Manuscripts can show the beauty of forms. Architecture and landscaping can help humans appreciate natural beauty. Muslims generally avoid, however, pictorial representation of human and animal forms in a religious context, such as in a copy of the Quran or a mosque. Islam never encouraged its adherents to turn their backs on the world to pursue some supposed spiritual reality.

Islamic Carpet. The subject of this Persian carpet is the Tree of Life.

Humans

Islam has a story of Adam and Eve, the first humans created by God. Humans are above all other creatures in the order of nature, for they have the moral responsibility to live according to the commandments of God.

> And recite to them the tiding of him to whom
> We gave Our signs, but he cast them off,
> and Satan followed after him, and he became one of the perverts.
> And had We willed, We would have raised him up
> thereby; but he inclined towards the earth
> and followed his lust. So the likeness of him
> is as the likeness of a dog; if thou attackest it
> it lolls its tongue out, or if thou leavest it
> it lolls its tongue out. That is that people's likeness
> who cried lies to Our signs. So relate the story; haply they will reflect.
> (QURAN 7:174,175)

When possible, humans are to live at peace with each other, recognizing that all humans of any race or location are called to submit to God. All who submit to God are brothers and sisters and part of one community.

Islam brought considerable improvement in the status of females. Eve was created by God to be a helper and companion for Adam. Islam does not permit infanticide or abuse of women. Wives should be properly treated. Women are able to inherit and own property, but they are dependent on men. Their roles are not separate from men's roles but supportive of them. Once the supportive relationship is understood, life for both men and women becomes more pleasant and rewarding.

> Mankind, fear your Lord, who created you
> of a single soul, and from it created
> its mate, and from the pair of them scattered
> abroad many men and women; and fear God
> by whom you demand one of another
> and the wombs; surely God ever watches over you.

Give the orphans their property, and do not
exchange the corrupt for the good; and devour
not their property with your property; surely that is a great crime.
If you fear that you will not act justly
towards the orphans, marry such women
as seem good to you, two, three, four;
but if you fear you will not be equitable,
then only one, or what your right hands own;
so it is likelier you will not be partial.
And give the women their dowries as a gift
spontaneous; but if they are pleased
to offer you any of it, consume it with wholesome appetite.
But do not give to fools their property
that God has assigned to you to manage;
provide for them and clothe them out of it,
and speak to them honourable words.
Test well the orphans, until they reach
the age of marrying; then, if you perceive
in them right judgment, deliver to them
their property; consume it not wastefully and hastily
ere they are grown. If any man is rich,
let him be abstinent; if poor, let him consume in reason.
And when you deliver to them their property,
take witnesses over them; God suffices for a reckoner.
To the men a share of what parents and kinsmen
leave, and to the women a share of what
parents and kinsmen leave, whether it be
little or much, a share apportioned;
and when the division is attended by
kinsmen and orphans and the poor,
make provision for them out of it,
and speak to them honourable words. (QURAN 4:1–9)

In Islamic beliefs, body and soul are strongly united. Except in Sufism, the soul is not emphasized apart from the body. The whole person communicates with God and answers to him for conduct. The person carries out the duties of the Pillars of Islam. The practice of mortifying the flesh to release the spirit has not been well received in Islam. Responsibilities of benevolence, defense, and witnessing for the faith require whole persons, not spirits.

The Problem for Humans

Islam acknowledges the sin of Adam and Eve, but it does not see the effects as extending to all other humans.

And when thy Lord took from the Children of Adam,
from their loins, their seed, and made them testify
touching themselves, "Am I not your Lord?"
They said, "Yes, we testify—lest you should say
on the Day of Resurrection, 'As for us, we were heedless of this,'
or lest you say, 'Our fathers were idolaters
aforetime, and we were seed after them.'
What, wilt Thou then destroy us for the deeds of the vain-doers?"
(QURAN 7:172,173)

Sin is refusal to submit to the will of God revealed through his prophets, especially his final one, Muhammad.

The Solution for Humans

Salvation comes in acknowledging that there is no god but God and that Muhammad is his prophet. When a person can recite the Shahada without reservation and live according to the direction of the Quran, he or she has success. Offering prayers five times each day, giving alms to the poor, keeping the fast of Ramadan, and making a pilgrimage to Mecca if circumstances permit as well as reciting the Shahada comprise Muslims' obligations. When Muslims have fulfilled these religious duties and refrained from prohibited actions, they can trust that God will find them acceptable in the day of judgment. Most students of world religions find Islam's teachings of alienation and reconciliation the easiest of all religions to understand.

Community and Ethics

The term for a Muslim community is *ummah*. Although Islam attacked many tribes from the deserts, its beginnings were in cities. Muslim cities are built around a mosque, a symbol for a community centered on God. An individual apart from family and community is an anomaly in Islam. The unity of Muslims, regardless of race, economic status, or location, has long been the ideal.

> It is not piety, that you turn your faces
> to the East and to the West.
> True piety is this:
> to believe in God, and the Last Day,
> the angels, the Book, and the Prophets,
> to give of one's substance, however cherished,
> to kinsmen, and orphans,
> the needy, the traveller, beggars,
> and to ransom the slave,
> to perform the prayer, to pay the alms.
> And they who fulfill their covenant
> when they have engaged in a covenant,
> and endure with fortitude
> misfortune, hardship and peril,
> these are they who are true in their faith,
> these are the truly godfearing. (QURAN 2:172)

Alms include an individual's giving not only to a beggar but also to a common treasury used to support the welfare of all in the community—even slaves and strangers—who have need. Individuals may offer prayers anywhere, but special value is given to praying with other Muslims in a mosque, especially on Friday at noon.

Personal ethics of Islam require that believers avoid certain prohibited things. Among them are gambling, drinking alcohol, lying, and stealing. For religious reasons, believers must not eat pork. The Quran teaches against being an aggressor; however, when an injustice has been done, fighting to avenge it is required. Aggression is to be met with force until the enemy ceases to resist. Usury is prohibited, but Muslims may be compensated by sharing profits if risk is entailed.

Although marriage is usually between one husband and only one wife, Islam makes provision for up to four wives for a man who can support them adequately and treat them equally.[31] Brides may have property, and if they are divorced, they may keep their dowries. Divorced men and women may remarry, either each other or other partners. In the days when slavery was common, Islam maintained an elaborate system of laws governing a Muslim's relationship to slaves and concubines. For several reasons, one being economic, polygamy has declined.

Rituals and Symbols

Muslim tradition has rites of passage for individuals and annual holidays for the community. Beliefs of Islam support well-established acts or rituals.

Islam welcomes children as signs of God's blessing. Male infants are usually circumcised, a practice of Semitic peoples prior to Muhammad. Many children, especially boys, memorize the Quran, which means that they memorize in Arabic. A few young people continue their studies until they have memorized every surah, but most know selective stories, characters, and teachings.

Marriages are usually arranged by parents or guardians. A young woman must freely give consent before she is married. Usually she receives a dowry that can support her in event of divorce. Marriage is a contractual arrangement rather than a sacrament. Divorce can be initiated by men, but the husband may take the wife again up to a third marriage. After a third divorce, he cannot marry her again until she has been married to another man.

Funerals provide opportunities for mourning and burial of the body. Muslims believe that the person will be resurrected and live after death in either paradise or hell.

In the daily prayers, there are prescribed cycles of kneeling, touching the forehead to the ground, and standing while reciting appropriate formulae. Men use the mosques more than women do. Women in the mosque must be kept out of the sight of men. A mosque is a place of prayer, although there are provisions for pulpits so that an imam may address the adherents. In each mosque is a **mihrab,** or niche, indicating the direction of Mecca, which the congregation faces in prayer.

Some of the annual observations are Ramadan, followed by Id al-Fitr (the festival of breaking the fast), and the birthday of the Prophet. The month of Ramadan recalls the appearance of Gabriel to Muhammad to give him the Quran. During the daylight hours, able-bodied Muslims are to refrain from food, drink, sex, and acts that take their attention from God. In the hours of darkness, they may enjoy what he has denied them by day. Deep suffering is avoided, but when the fast falls in a hot season it is especially trying. Muslims claim benefits from identifying with the needs of the poor and suffering of humanity. The feast of rejoicing after Ramadan lasts for three days.

Charity may be extended in alms at any time. But Muslims are expected to give annually approximately 2.5 percent of their wealth to the needs of the community. It is sinful for some Muslims to have so much and others to suffer for lack of necessities. Distributing gifts to the poor acknowledges God's mercy and the unity of Islam.

The holy city that all Muslims face in prayer five times a day is Mecca (Makkah). Every Muslim who is financially and physically able is expected

mihrab [MIH-rahb]
The niche in a mosque that signifies the direction of Mecca. Muslims face Mecca when they pray.

CHAPTER TEN

to make a pilgrimage to Mecca. Only a small percentage of Muslims can attend in a given year. But the gathering of more than a million faithful assembled from all over the world is an impressive display of the universal appeal of the prophet Muhammad and his call to worship Allah, or God. Dressed in clothes that show their unity, the pilgrims wear two seamless pieces of white cloth sewn together, emphasizing that before God all believers are equal. For the duration of the pilgrimage, no Muslims (women and children can also participate) cut their hair or nails or engage in sex.

Participating in rituals that recall the faithful acts of their father Abraham, pilgrims do things that are extraordinary. In the Haram Mosque of Mecca, Muslims walk around the Ka'bah seven times. The cubic stone building, usually covered by a **kiswah,** a black cloth, is a replacement of one that Muslims believe was built by Abraham, whose footprint remains nearby. Muslims begin by kissing the sacred Black Stone that they believe was given to Abraham by the angel Gabriel. They then run between two low hills, imitating Abraham's concubine Hagar, who frantically searched for water in the desert to save their child, Ishmael, after Sarah had them excluded from her camp. At noon on the ninth day, the pilgrim stands on the Mount of Mercy facing Mecca, fourteen miles distant. Here, on the Plain of Arafat, Muhammad recited verses on his last pilgrimage indicating that God had completed the Islamic religion.

kiswah [KIS-wa]
The robe, or covering, usually placed over the Ka'bah in Mecca.

> Today I have perfected your religion
> for you, and I have completed My blessing
> upon you, and I have approved Islam for your religion. (QURAN 5:5)

On the tenth day, during a stop at Mina, the pilgrim joins others in throwing stones at three stone pillars representing devils that tried to persuade Abraham to disobey God and refuse to sacrifice his son Isaac. In the 'Id al Adha, any pilgrims who can afford it sacrifice animals and share the meat with the poor, recalling that God allowed Abraham to sacrifice a ram instead of his son. Only after returning to Mecca and circumambulating the Ka'bah are pilgrims allowed to cut hair and nails, ending the state of purity, **ihram.** Pilgrims who can arrange it continue north to Medina to visit the tomb of the prophet Muhammad, the greatest and last of all God's prophets. Having completed the Hajj, the pilgrim is a changed person, remembering his or her experience and bearing the title *hajji* (for men) or *hajjiyah* (for women).

ihram [IH-rahm]
The consecrated state in which Muslims perform the Hajj. Muslims abstain from sex, perfume, hunting, and other things during the pilgrimage to Mecca.

Life After Death

Islam believes in life after death. Each person will be resurrected to appear before God and judged according to his or her deeds on earth (Quran 56). God will decide who will be rewarded in paradise or punished in hell:

> And those who believe, and do deeds
> of righteousness—We charge not any
> soul, save according to its capacity;
> those are the inhabitants of Paradise, therein dwelling forever;
> We shall strip away all rancour that is in their breasts;
> and underneath them rivers flowing and they will say,
> "Praise belongs to God, who guided
> us unto this; had God not guided
> us, we had surely never been guided.
> Indeed, our Lord's Messengers came with the truth."

And it will be proclaimed: "This
is your Paradise; you have been
given it as your inheritance for what you did."
The inhabitants of Paradise will call
to the inhabitants of the Fire:
"We have found that which our Lord
promised us true; have you found
what your Lord promised you true?"
　　"Yes," they will say.
And then a herald shall proclaim
between them: "God's curse is on the evildoers
who bar from God's way, desiring
to make it crooked, disbelieving in the world to come." (QURAN 7:40–44)

Paradise is a pleasant oasis where a man's every desire, according to popular tradition, is satisfied either by his wife or by beautiful houris, or virgins. Hell is a place of burning and heat where excruciating pains are perpetual (Quran 104).

Islam and Other Religions

Because God has sent his prophet and revealed the Quran, all humans should become Muslims. Polytheists and idolaters have never had a proper knowledge of God and should convert at once. Jews and Christians have received through the prophets, including Jesus, a proper, although incomplete, knowledge of God. Muslims cite the errors of Jews in worshiping Elijah and Christians in worshiping a Trinity and in claiming that Jesus is God's son. Jesus gave many wonderful signs that he was a great prophet, born of the virgin Mary. He will come again before the last judgment. But Jesus is not in any way divine. Muhammad has recited God's word that corrects the erroneous beliefs of Jews, Christians, and all other religions. Although they can be tolerated as people of the Book, Jews and Christians should convert. The Quran requires that Muslims denounce all idolaters. It directs Muslims not to choose friends among Christians and Jews rather than Muslims (Quran 3:25ff).

Considering the Quran and the traditions of Islam, what view of Jesus do Muslims have today? Kenneth Cragg, a Christian who is a scholar of Islam, wrote,

> Through all we have reviewed there runs a great tenderness for Jesus, yet a sharp dissociation from his Christian dimensions. Islam registers a profound attraction but condemns its Christian interpretation. Jesus is the theme at once of acknowledgement and disavowal. Islam finds his nativity miraculous but his Incarnation impossible. His teaching entails suffering but the one is not perfected in the other. He is highly exalted, but by rescue rather than victory. He is vindicated but not by resurrection. His servanthood is understood to disclaim the sonship which is its secret. His word is scripturised into the incidence of the Quran fragmentarily. He does not pass as personality into a literature possessing him communally. Islam has for him a recognition moving within a non-recognition, a rejectionism on behalf of a deep and reverent esteem.[32]

From time to time, Muslims have cooperated with Jews, Christians, and even Hindus. In many countries they have learned to live with other religions—India is one example. In some former republics of the Soviet Union, Muslims often predominate over Orthodox Christians. Granted religious as well as political freedom, these Muslims have recently participated fully in the community of world Islam. Cooperation with other religions, although sometimes practiced by Muslims, is not as high a priority as making converts to Islam. It is a missionary religion that seeks adherents among all peoples. Contrary to popular beliefs of other religions, Islam does not teach aggression:

> And fight in the way of God with those
> who fight with you, but aggress not: God loves not aggressors. (QURAN 2:187)

> No compulsion is there in religion.
> Rectitude has become clear from error.
> So whosoever disbelieves in idols
> and believes in God, has laid hold of
> the most firm handle, unbreaking; God is All-hearing, All-knowing. (QURAN 2:256)

Islam and the Future

The Islamic state is a primary issue, not only for outsiders but also for Muslims. Are Muslims to establish rules under religious leaders, return to the Shari'a, and seek to live under customs similar to those at Mecca and Medina during the time of Muhammad? Or are they to take the course of some liberal reformers of the late nineteenth and early twentieth century? Will Muslims participate fully in the new global community, keeping only the essential religious and moral principles of their faith? The answer seems to lie with the political power of various national factions. Fervent movements for governments that give religious leaders the upper hand stimulate strong resistance among governments that keep religious leaders in subservient positions to ruling families or parliamentary governments.

Many Muslims cannot accept the existence of the state of Israel. Writing in 1968, Maxime Rodinson observed,

> The Arabs have never, at any stage, accepted the *fait accompli* carried out at their expense and without their agreement by Israeli power, backed up by the support of the European and American world.[33]

Writing fifteen years later, Ismail R. al-Faruqi states the problem this way:

> Islam is not opposed to Judaism but regards it as the religion of God. . . . Rather, Islam is opposed to Zionism, to Zionist politics and conduct. . . . For its crimes against the individual Palestinian men and women, against the corporate existence of the Palestinians, against the individual Arabs of the surrounding countries as well as the *ummah*, Islam condemns Zionism. Islam demands that every atom's weight of injustice perpetrated against the innocent be undone. Hence, it imposes upon all Muslims the world over to rise like one man to put an end to injustice and to reinstate its sufferers in their lands, homes, and properties. . . . Therefore, the Islamic position leaves no chance for the Zionist state but to be dismantled and destroyed, and its wealth confiscated to pay off its liabilities.[34]

Some states that are predominantly Muslim have accepted United Nations resolutions granting Israel the right to exist. Some Palestinian groups are adamantly opposed to anyone who accepts those conditions, including Yasir Arafat.

To some women outside Islam, it appears that the Muslims should liberate women. Some nations, such as Egypt and Syria, have given women considerable freedom and equality in education and participation in

Muslim Teacher and Students. A muslim Madrasa school in Jakarta, Indonesia, 1995.

public life. Saudi Arabia has preferred to keep women from public view and in roles close to those of early Islam. Iran, under Ayatollah Khomeini, placed women in purdah, reversing some of the trends that had developed prior to the deposal of the late shah. Malaysian women are allowed to attend universities in the same classes with men, but their dress and their conduct are closely regulated to prevent easy social interaction with men.

Women may live exemplary lives, even becoming saints, but their devotional lives are separated from men in the mosque. In Egypt and the Sudan women may engage in *zar* ceremonies to rid them of supposed spirit possession, and in Iraq women may be hereditary religious teachers, reading in public stories of the life of Imam Hussayn.[35]

Although many of the old questions for Islamic women abide—polygamy, child marriages, the veil, inheritance, and testimony against men—many women of Islam have initiated changes. From her studies, Yvonne Yazbeck Haddad has concluded,

> What we can see now is therefore a new generation of Muslim women, many of whom are not only educated in the liberal arts and sciences, but have also acquired an Islamic literacy—through study of the Qur'āan and the Hadīth—that their husbands who are actively working to build society through new careers in technology, are not able to attain. These women are taking as their models the founding mothers of Islam—the Prophet's wives 'A'isha, Hafa, and Umm Salāma—as well as others of the early women believers who both participated actively in the struggles of the early Muslim community and helped keep the men accountable to the tenets of the faith.[36]

Another issue for Islam is its relationship to black peoples. At times, in spite of its idealism of welcoming all converts, Muslims engaged in slave trade that alienated blacks from Islam. In the twentieth century, Muslims have made determined efforts to win converts in the new African nations. In the United States, Elijah Muhammad started the Black Muslim movement as an alternative to Christianity, which he regarded as a white religion. His teaching that all whites are devils was at odds with orthodox Islam. Malcom X, however, was accepted by Muslims of Arabia and allowed to participate in the pilgrimage to Mecca. A growing body of African Americans participate in the movement of worldwide Islam.

It is difficult to predict what Islam will become in the twenty-first century. But statistics show that in many nations Muslim converts increase—Islam is a vital, growing religion.

CONSIDER THIS: WHAT SEPARATES JEWS, CHRISTIANS, AND MUSLIMS?

Because Islam is a religion of the family of Abraham, one may be inclined to think of it as naturally friendly to Judaism and Christianity. It can be pointed out that Muslims have given Jews and Christians special status as "People of the Book." Many of the prophets honored by Jews and Christians are also honored by Muslims. Unlike Jews, Muslims have honored as prophets both John the Baptist and Jesus. These facts would seem to support cooperative relationships among the religions of Abraham.

Other facts, however, indicate a strong sibling rivalry among the religions, one that sometimes erupts into open conflict. Muslims ascribe worship of Moses to Jews and decry Christians' ascribing "Son of God" status to Jesus. Since they deny that God has any partners, they reject the Christian doctrine of the Trinity. They regard the scriptures of Jews and Christians, once based on revelation, as now erroneous. These scriptures have been supplanted by the Quran, revealed by God to Muhammad, the last true Prophet; they are to be followed above all others.

Historically, conflicts have usually separated the three religions. Nevertheless, in certain times and places, such as in Cordoba, Spain, in medieval times, scholars of the three religions developed appreciation and cooperation. Is it possible for these three religions to draw closer together in a more cooperative approach to the faith of Abraham? Can they work together to meet present needs of the peoples of the world? Try to think of arguments that would support your conclusion. What specific steps would you suggest for each religion in order to increase a spirit of appreciation and cooperation?

◇ A POINT
OF VIEW

◇ VOCABULARY

American Muslim Mission	kiswah [KIS-wa]	salat [sa-LAHT]
ansar [AN-sahr]	Mahdi [MAH-di]	Shahada [sheh-HAH-da]
caliph [KAA-lif]	Malcolm X (Malcolm Little)	Shari'a [SHA-ree-a]
dhimmi [THIM-mi]	mihrab [MIH-rahb]	Shi'a [SHE'a]
Elijah (Poole) Muhammad	muezzin [mu-EZ-in]	Sunna [SUN-na]
hadiths [had-EETHS]	muhajirun [mu-HAJ-i-roon]	Sunni [SOON-e]
Hajj [HAHJ]	Nation of Islam	tawhid [TAHW-heed]
hanif [HA-neef]	qiyas [KEE-yas]	Timothy Drew
Hijrah [HEJ-rah]	Quran [KUR-an]	'ulama' [UL-ah-mah]
ihram [IH-rahm]	rak'a [RAK-ah]	ummah [UM-mah]
ijma' [IJ-mah]	rasul [ra-SOOL]	Wahhab [WAH-hab]
jinn [JIN]	ra'y [RAA-ee]	zakat [za-KAHT]
Ka'bah [KUH-bah]	sadaqa [sah-DAH-ka]	

QUESTIONS FOR REVIEW

1. List some of the reasons why leaders of the Quraysh opposed Muhammad's recitations of the Quran.

2. How did Muhammad use Medina to overcome resistance in Mecca?

3. What evidence would support a view that early leadership in Islam was "within the family"?

4. Describe the Shari'a and its function in Islam.

5. Compare the Pillars of Islam with requirements in Judaism and Christianity.

6. Trace the conflicts among successors of the Prophet that led to Sunni and Shi'a Islam.

7. List the major steps in the worldwide spread of Islam.

8. List outstanding achievements of Islamic cultures in medieval times.

9. What evidence would support a description of Muhammad as a "liberator" of women? What evidence would negate such a title?

10. What are some of the major religious conflicts among Muslims today?

QUESTIONS FOR DISCUSSION

1. Are Western religions partial to theocracy, monarchy, or democracy? Do they function equally under all forms of government?

2. What disputes in Islam arise from the belief that the Quran is the final revelation of God?

3. In your opinion, what ideals of Islam attract universal respect? Which ideals of Islam interfere with people's embracing it?

4. How do you interpret Islam's ideal status of women?

5. In the Americas of the twenty-first century, which forms of Islam do you think will be most successful? What facts and trends support your opinions?

NOTES

1. Harry B. Partin, "Ka'bah," in *The Encyclopedia of Religion*, vol. 8, ed. Mircea Eliade (New York: Macmillan, 1987), pp. 225–226.

2. Andrew Rippen and Jan Knappert, *Textual Sources for the Study of Islam* (Chicago: University of Chicago Press, 1990), pp. 66–67.

3. Reprinted in the U.S. with the permission of Simon & Schuster from *The Koran Interpreted*, trans. Arthur J. Arberry. Copyright © 1955 by George Allen & Unwin, Ltd. Reprinted outside the U.S. by Permission of Unwin Hyman, an Imprint of HarperCollins Publishers Limited. Copyright © 1955 by Unwin Hyman, an Imprint of Harper-Collins Publishers Limited.

4. Karen Armstrong, *Muhammad: A Biography of the Prophet* (New York: HarperCollins Publishers, 1992), p. 111.

5. Fazlur Rahman, *Major Themes of the Qur'an* (Minneapolis: Bibliotheca Islamica, 1980), p. 83.

6. Muhammad Abduh, *The Theology of Unity*, trans. Kenneth Cragg (London: Allen & Unwin, 1965), pp. 118–122, as quoted in Kenneth Cragg and R. Marston Speight, *Islam from Within* (Belmont, CA: Wadsworth, 1980), pp. 19–20.

7. Alfred Guillaume, *Islam* (Hammondsworth, Middlesex, England: Penguin Books, 1954), pp. 80, 81.

8. Mahmoud Ayoub, *Redemptive Suffering in Islam* (The Hague: Mouton, 1978), p. 229.

9. Majid Fakhry, *A History of Islamic Philosophy* (New York: Columbia University Press, 1970), pp. 228–235.

10. Annemarie Schimmel, *Mystical Dimensions of Islam* (Chapel Hill: University of North Carolina Press, 1975), p. 3.

11. Idries Shah, *The Way of the Sufi* (London: Octagon Press, 1980), pp. 13–14.

12. Fazlur Rahman, *Islam* (Chicago: University of Chicago Press, 1979), p. 131. His view is that Sufism began and developed in Islam, following the example of the Prophet.

13. Arthur J. Arberry, *Sufism* (London: Unwin Paperbacks, 1979), pp. 42–43. Copyright © 1979 by Unwin Hyman, an Imprint of HarperCollins Publishers Limited. Reprinted by Permission.

14. Jalal al-Din Rumi, "*Divan-e Shams*," in *Mystical Poems of Rumi*, trans. Arthur J. Arberry (Boulder, CO: Westview Press, 1979).

15. Arberry, *Mystical Poems of Rumi*, p. 53, no. 268.

16. Seyyed Hossein Nasr, *Ideals and Realties of Islam* (London: Unwin Hyman, 1988), p. 124.

17. Fakhry, p. 250.

18. Seyyed Hossein Nasr, *Three Muslim Sages* (Cambridge, MA: Harvard University Press, 1964), p. 91.

19. T. A. Archer, *The Crusade of Richard I 1189–92* (New York: Putnam's, 1889), p. 126.

20. Ibid., pp. 130–131.

21. Gustave E. Von Grunebaum, *Medieval Islam* (Chicago: University of Chicago Press, 1953), pp. 57–58.

22. M. Mujeeb, *The Indian Muslims* (London: Allen & Unwin, 1967), p. 20.

23. Peter Hardy, "Islam in South Asia," in *The Encyclopedia of Religion*, vol. 7, ed. Mircea Eliade (New York: Macmillan, 1987), pp. 390–404.

24. William S. Hatcher and J. Douglas Martin, *The Baha'i Faith: The Emerging Global Religion* (New York: Harper & Row, 1989), p. 1.

25. Fazlur Rahman, *Islam and Modernity* (Chicago: University of Chicago Press, 1982), pp. 145–162.

26. John L. Esposito, "Muhammad Iqbal and the Islamic State," in *Voices of Resurgent Islam*, ed. John L. Esposito (New York: Oxford University Press, 1983), pp. 175–190.

27. Lisa Anderson, "Qaddafi's Islam," *Voices of Resurgent Islam*, ed. John L. Esposito (New York: Oxford University Press, 1983), pp. 134–149.

28. Ali E. Hillal Dessouki, ed. *Resurgence in the Arab World* (New York: Praeger, CBS, 1982), p. 190.

29. Yvonne Yazbeck Haddad and Adaire T. Lummis, *Islamic Values in the United States* (New York: Oxford University Press, 1987), p. 3.

30. Suggestions for passages from the Quran in the "Worldview" given in Rahman.

31. Hammudah Abdalati, *Islam in Focus* (Indianapolis: American Trust Publications, 1975), p. 117.

32. Kenneth Cragg, *Jesus and the Muslim* (London: Allen & Unwin, 1985), pp. 278–279.

33. Maxime Rodinson, *Israel and the Arabs*, trans. Michael Perl (New York: Pantheon Books, 1968), p. 227.

34. Ismail R. al Faruqi, "Islam and Zionism," in *Voices of Resurgent Islam*, ed. John L. Esposito (New York: Oxford University Press, 1983), pp. 261–262.

35. Jane I. Smith, "Islam," in *Women in World Religions*, ed. Arvind Sharma (Albany: State University of New York Press, 1987), p. 245.

36. Yvonne Yazbeck Haddad, "Islam, Women, and Revolution," in *Women, Religion, and Social Change*, ed. Yvonne Yazbeck Haddad and Ellison Banks Findly (Albany: State University of New York Press, 1985), p. 295.

READINGS

Armstrong, Karen. *Muhammad: A Biography of the Prophet.* New York: HarperCollins, 1992. A recent biography of Muhammad.

Cragg, Kenneth. *The House of Islam.* Belmont, CA: Dickinson, 1969. A short, readable introduction to Islam.

Cragg, Kenneth, and Marston Speight. *Islam from Within.* Belmont, CA: Wadsworth, 1950. A collection of accounts showing how Muslims view their religion.

Denny, Frederick Mathewson. *An Introduction to Islam.* New York: Macmillan, 1993. A recent survey of Islam. Good scholarship, but easy to read.

Denny, Frederick M. *Islam.* San Francisco: Harper and Row, 1987. A concise introduction to Islam.

Esposito, John L. *Islam, The Straight Path.* New York: Oxford University Press, 1988. For beginners, an excellent introduction to Islam.

———, ed. *Voices of Resurgent Islam.* New York: Oxford University Press, 1983. An exploration of more recent issues in Islam.

Guillaume, Alfred. *Islam.* Hammondsworth, Middlesex, England: Penguin Books, Ltd., 1954. A respected, older account of Islam.

Nasr, Seyyed Hossein. *Ideals and Realities of Islam.* London: Unwin Hyman Limited, 1988.

Rahman, Fazlur. *Islam.* Chicago: University of Chicago Press, 1979.

———. *Major Themes of Qur'an.* Minneapolis: Bibliotheca Islamica, 1980.

Rippin, Andrew, and Jan Knappert, eds., *Textual Sources for the Study of Islam.* Chicago: University of Chicago Press, 1990.

Rodinson, Maxime. *Mohammed.* Translated by Anne Carter. New York: Pantheon Books, 1971. An excellent source of the Prophet.

Watt, W. Montgomery. *Mohammed at Mecca.* Oxford: Clarendon Press, 1953. A detailed account of the early life of the Prophet.

———. *Muhammed at Medina.* Oxford: Clarendon Press, 1956. A detailed account of Muhammad's leadership in Medina.

READINGS FOR RESEARCH AND REPORTS

Abdalati, Hammudah. *Islam in Focus.* Indianapolis: American Trust Publications, 1975.

Al-Tabataba'i. *Shi'ite Islam*, trans. Seyyed Hossein Nasr. New York: State University of New York, 1975.

Arberry, Arthur J. *Discourses of Rumi.* London: Murray, 1961.

———. *Revelation and Reason in Islam.* London: Allen & Unwin, 1957.

———. *Sufism.* London: Allen & Unwin, 1950.

———, trans. *Mystical Poems of Rumi.* Boulder, CO: Westview Press, 1979.

Archer, T. A. *The Crusade of Richard I 1189–92.* New York: Putnam's, 1889.

Ayoub, Mahmoud. *Redemptive Suffering in Islam.* The Hague: Mouton, 1978.

Bowen, Donna Lee, and Evelyn A. Early, eds. *Everyday Life in the Muslim Middle East.* Bloomington and Indianapolis: Indiana University Press, 1993.

Brend, Barbara, *Islamic Art.* Cambridge, MA: Harvard University Press, 1991.

Caplan, Lionel, ed. *Studies in Religious Fundamentalism.* Albany: State University of New York Press, 1987.

Corbin, Henry. *Avicenna and the Visionary Recital,* trans. Willard R. Trask. New York: Bollingen Foundation, 1960.

Cragg, Kenneth. *Jesus and the Muslim.* London: Allen & Unwin, 1985.

Dawood, N. J., trans. *The Koran.* New York: Viking Penguin, 1974.

Dekmejian, R. Hrair. *Islam in Revolution.* Syracuse, NY: Syracuse University Press, 1985.

Deninger, Johannes. "Revelation," trans. Matthew J. O'Connell. In *The Encyclopedia of Religion,* vol. 12, pp. 356–362. Ed. Mircea Eliade. New York: Macmillan, 1987.

Dessouki, Ali E. Hillal, ed. *Islamic Resurgence in the Arab World.* New York: Praeger, CBS, 1982.

Esposito, John L., ed. *Islam in Asia.* New York: Oxford University Press, 1987.

Esposito, John L., ed.-in-chief, *The Oxford Encyclopedia of the Modern Islamic World,* 4 vols. New York and Oxford: Oxford University Press, 1995.

Fakhry, Majid. *A History of Islamic Philosophy.* New York: Columbia University Press, 1970.

Gaudefroy-Demonbynes, Maurice. *Muslim Institutions,* trans. J. P. Macgregor. London: Allen & Unwin, 1954.

Gibb, H. A. R. *Modern Trends in Islam.* New York: Octagon Books, 1972.

———. *Mohammedanism.* New York: The New American Library of World Literature, 1955.

Haddad, Yvonne Yazbeck, and Ellison Banks Findly. *Women, Religion, and Social Change.* Albany: State University of New York, 1985.

Haddad, Yvonne Yazbeck, and Adaire T. Lummis. *Islamic Values in the United States.* New York: Oxford University Press, 1987.

Haneef, Suzanne. *What Everyone Should Know About Islam and Muslims.* Chicago: Kazi, 1982.

Hardy, Peter. "Islam in South Asia." In *The Encyclopedia of Religion,* vol. 7, pp. 390–404. Ed. Mircea Eliade. New York: Macmillan, 1987.

Hatcher, William S., and J. Douglas Martin. *The Baha'i Faith: The Emerging Global Religion.* New York: Harper & Row, 1989.

Hick, John, and Edmund S. Meltzer, eds. *Three Faiths—One God: A Jewish, Christian, Muslim Encounter.* New York: State University of New York Press, 1989.

Hourani, Albert Habib. *A History of the Arab Peoples.* Cambridge, MA: Belknap Press of Harvard University Press, 1991.

Iqbal, Muhammad. *Poems from Iqbal,* trans. V. G. Kiernan. London: Murray, 1955.

Kandiyoti, Deniz, ed. *Women, Islam, and the State.* Philadelphia: Temple University Press, 1991.

Kepel, Gilles. *Muslim Extremism: The Prophet and the Pharaoh.* Berkeley and Los Angeles: University of California Press, 1993.

Long, David Edwin. *The Hajj Today.* New York: State University of New York Press with the Middle East Institute, 1979.

Madoodi, Sayed Abdul Ala. *Towards Understanding Islam.* Leicester, England: Islamic Foundation, 1988.

Marty, Martin E., and R. Scott Appleby, *Fundamentalisms Observed.* Chicago: University of Chicago Press, 1991.

Mujeeb, M. *The Indian Muslims.* London: Allen & Unwin, 1967.

Nasr, Seyyed Hossein. *Sufi Essays.* Albany: State University of New York Press, 1972.

———. *Three Muslim Sages.* Cambridge, MA: Harvard University Press, 1964.

Peters, F. E. *Muhammad and the Origins of Islam.* Albany: State University of New York Press, 1994.

Pickthall, M. M. *The Meaning of the Glorious Koran.* London: Allen & Unwin, 1979.

The Quran, trans. T. B. Irving. Brattleboro, VT: Amana Books, 1985.

Rahman, Fazlur. *Islam and Modernity.* Chicago: University of Chicago Press, 1982.

Rodinson, Maxime. *Israel and the Arabs.* Trans. Michael Perl. New York: Pantheon Books, 1968.

Rumi, Jalal al-Din. "Divan-e Shams." In *Mystical Poems of Rumi,* trans. Arthur J. Arberry. Boulder, CO: Westview Press, 1979.

Schimmel, Annemarie. *Islam: An Introduction.* Albany: State University of New York Press, 1992.

———. *Mystical Dimensions of Islam.* Chapel Hill: University of North Carolina Press, 1975.

Shah, Idries. *The Way of the Sufi.* London: Octagon Press, 1980.

Sharma, Arvind, ed. *Women in World Religions.* Albany: State University of New York Press, 1987.

Stoddard, Philip H., et al. *Change in the Muslim World.* Syracuse, NY: Syracuse University Press, 1981.

Stowasser, Barbara Freyer. *Women in the Qur'an, Traditions and Interpretation.* New York: Oxford University Press, 1994.

van der Leeuw, G. *Religion in Essence and Manifestation.* 2 vols. New York: Harper & Row, 1963.

von Grunebaum, Gustave E. *Medieval Islam.* Chicago: University of Chicago Press, 1953.

Watt, W. Montgomery. *The Faith and Practice of Al-Ghazali.* London: Allen & Unwin, 1953.

Wolfson, Harry Austryn. *The Philosophy of the Kalam.* Cambridge, MA: Harvard University Press, 1976.

CHAPTER TEN

Conclusion

I hope that <u>World Religions</u> has helped answer some of your important questions about the charismatic leaders of religions and the beliefs, rituals, and organizations that they established. In your experiences with the Buddha, Confucius, Moses, Jesus, and Muhammad, you have learned that the giants among religious peoples differ in how they view the world and respond to its challenges. As you have examined beliefs and practices of peoples in religions large and small, ancient and recent, you have seen many options for your own understanding of religion.

Your study of the historical development and worldview of many religions has prepared you to continue your study of religions. Although you may pursue formal study of a few religions, you can also participate in informal study. You have learned how to read about religions and how to discuss them with peoples of those faiths. You have learned how to find similarities and differences among religions and how to recognize what is new or different in religions that you encounter for the first time. With many other students of world religions, you have learned how to explore the common ground of religions while respecting their diversity.

DIVERSITY AND COMMON GROUND

A few scholars have tried to make sense of diversity and shared experiences. We can consider the insights of Ramakrishna, Frithjof Schuon, Wilfred Cantwell Smith, John Hick, and Mircea Eliade. Each person has offered a way to understand how diverse experiences and expressions may point toward a unity of religions. Their views represent three different ways of relating similarities and differences.

One group emphasizes that there is one Absolute experienced through a variety of different traditions. Ramakrishna, the Hindu priest of Kali, you will recall, said that different creeds are but different paths to the Almighty. Different ways lead to Calcutta. Different ways lead to the Lord. Every religion is one of those paths to God. Because he had experimented with Hindu, Muslim, and Christian paths and found God, Ramakrishna spoke from his own experience.[1]

A second group theorizes that in their ideal forms religions agree on one Absolute. According to Huston Smith, an authority on world religions, Frithjof Schuon has argued that although religions differ at their exoteric, or everyday practice, level, in their ideal, esoteric, level they approach the apex of a triangle where all agree.[2] John Hick, a philosopher of religion, borrows from the philosopher **Immanuel Kant** (1724–1804) to argue that although God, as God, is unknown, we do know God through our experiences in the **phenomenal** world. Because our phenomenal experiences are imperfect and conditioned by individual, social, and cultural differences, our experiences of the Absolute are different. Our differing phenomenal experiences, however, point toward one Absolute behind all experiences.[3]

Immanuel Kant
A Prussian philosopher who advanced a theory of knowledge that a knower can know an object only subjectively, not as it is in itself. John Hick uses Kant's theory to help exlain how religions that differ in concepts of god may be experiencing the same Absolute.

phenomenal [fi-NOM-u-nal]
In Kant's theory of knowledge, a subject's experience of an object that is different from the object itself. A person can know only subjective experiences, not the object as it is in itself (*an sich*).

We could include in the second group Wilfred Cantwell Smith.[4] The common ground of religious experience is the self-consciousness of humans that expresses itself, among other ways, as faith. Faith is expressed in terms of traditions. Differing religious traditions are not compartmentalized experiences. Throughout history, traditions have shared ideas with each other. The constant among these practices is faith, which expresses itself in a particular tradition.

A third group can be represented by Mircea Eliade. These scholars are not sure that there is one Absolute behind all experiences or one Absolute ideal that unifies different traditions. They know, however, that some phenomena of the sacred appear in many different cultures. Peoples speak of sacred time, space, and myths. They speak of sacred nature, sacred cosmos, and sacred human life. In a diversity of terms and descriptions, cultures share many ways of organizing time, space, and human lives. Amid diversity, there are ways of presenting similarities of belief and practice.

LEARNING MORE ABOUT WORLD RELIGIONS

You have made a good start in understanding world religions, and you may want to consider how you can broaden and deepen your knowledge. Bibliographies for each religion in the text offer opportunities for more reading. Your reading may seem more relevant, however, if it is related to your daily experiences with peoples of diverse religious traditions. Through your interaction with other people, issues and questions will arise to motivate your reading. How can you learn more about peoples of other faiths?

The Campus

You can begin where you are. Students and members of faculties in most colleges and universities represent many of the world religions. You have opportunities in academic activities and in the related social environment to become acquainted with adherents of other world religions. You share with these fellow members of an academic community many common concerns of scholarship. It is easy to build on that interest through sharing informal social occasions. In the process of discussing holidays, travels, diets, and personal preferences, members of the academic community have opportunities to learn about religions of other people. When people sense toleration of their most cherished values, they are more willing to explain their larger system of beliefs.

Dialogue

Dialogue can be a prelude to participation. When you show a desire to read the scriptures of another faith and to read and discuss pamphlets and books explaining the essentials of the faith, you will find that its adherents are willing, even eager, to share ideas. Adherents of many faiths are delighted to invite others as guests to their student organization. Or you may ask that the members of another faith accompany you to their place of worship and explain the symbols and rituals. Many students find that adherents of other religions welcome them to their services and show an interest in helping them obtain a favorable knowledge of their religion.

You may choose to attend a formal dialogue among representatives of world religions. Dialogues between leaders of world religions can be enlightening to adherents of each faith. These dialogues can occur in large, specially convened conferences on world religions, or they may be an occasional program of a campus religious group. You can supplement these events with readings of position papers presented at conferences that have emphasized dialogue between leaders of world religions.[5] These discussions help you learn which issues are of greatest concern to leaders of world religions.

Travel

Travel can bring you into relationships with people of many other religions. Whether you travel for leisure or pursue business or professional assignments, you have opportunities for observing other religions and meeting their adherents. Those who can live abroad for a period of time have many opportunities to discuss the worldviews of adherents of world religions.

Discovery of Values

You do not have to become an adherent of another religion to appreciate it or benefit from it. Your appreciation increases for certain aspects of another religion. Those who examine their own religious tradition—or lack of one—may discover dimensions of values that were beyond their knowledge. The Buddhist and Christian views on suffering can supplement each other. Christians become aware of saints whose prayer life is all consuming when they learn of the Muslim appreciation of prayer. Hindu yoga helps outsiders see that discipline in spiritual progress is beneficial; other religions have developed similar approaches to elevation of the soul. The Daoist concern for living with nature and the Jain reverence for life can awaken others to similar concerns in Shintoism and Judaism. Studying other religions helps people appreciate the tradition with which they are most familiar.

One important result of a study of world religions is that it leads to self-discovery. What are your most cherished values? In a world of plural value systems, how do you choose to live?

World religions express themselves continually in new forms. Old temples decay; old traditions are abandoned. New prophets and sages declare their latest visions and insights. Young men and women, inspired by a new leader, gather to follow a fresh path. New symbols appear, adorning new sanctuaries that house the latest words of the Absolute. The communicated message reaches many people who have felt lost or rejected. They come to themselves. Having been lost, now they are found. In gratitude, they offer their praise and reorder their lives. They enter workplaces, government, and institutions of learning. Through them their culture changes, expressing the values of their new religion. While tourists visit the archaeological sites of religions of the past, eager students of world religions consult teachers of the emerging faith. Through international trade and travel, the new values enter other societies. These developments form a drama that is older than the pyramids of Egypt; it is a drama that is as fresh as stories in tomorrow's newspaper. We are privileged participants in that perpetual drama.

VOCABULARY

Immanuel Kant   phenomenal [fi-NOM-u-nal]

NOTES

1. *The Gospel of Sri Ramakrishna*, trans. Swami Nikhi-lananda (New York: The Ramakrishna-Vivekananda Center, 1970). Quotation appears in this text, Chapter 3, "Hinduism."

2. Huston Smith, Introduction, in *The Transcendent Unity of Religions* by Frithjof Schuon, trans. Peter Townsend (New York: Harper Torchbooks, 1975), pp. xi and xii.

3. John Hick, *Philosophy of Religion*, 4th ed. (Englewood Cliffs, NJ: Prentice Hall, 1990), chapter 9. See also *God Has Many Names* (Philadelphia: The Westminster Press, 1982), p. 53.

4. Wilfred Cantwell Smith, *Towards a World Theology* (Philadelphia: Westminster Press, 1981).

5. Hans Kung, *Christianity and the World Religions*, trans. Peter Heinegg (Garden City, NY: Doubleday, 1986).

READINGS

D'Costa, Gavin. *Theology and Religious Pluralism*. Oxford: Basil Blackwell, 1986.

Hick, John. *An Interpretation of Religion*. New Haven, CT: Yale University Press, 1989.

———. "Religious Pluralism." In *The Encyclopedia of Religion*, vol. 12, ed. Mircea Eliade. New York: Macmillan, 1987, pp. 331–333.

———. *God Has Many Names*. Philadelphia: The Westminster Press, 1982.

Kung, Hans. *Christianity and the World Religions*, trans. Peter Heinegg. Garden City, NY: Doubleday, 1986.

Smith, Wilfred Cantwell. *Towards a World Theology*. Philadelphia: Westminster Press, 1981.

———. *The Meaning and End of Religion*. New York: Macmillan, 1962, 1963.

Appendix: Charts

MEMBERSHIP OF RELIGIONS

MEMBERSHIP OF CHURCHES IN CANADA

Anglican Church in Canada	780,897
Canadian Baptist Ministries	130,000
Evangelical Lutheran Church	198,751
Orthodox Church in America (Canada Section)	1,000,000
Roman Catholic Church	12,498,605
United Church of Canada	1,867,500

Source: Yearbook of American and Canadian Churches. Ed. Kenneth B. Bedell. Nashville, TN: Abingdon Press, © 1997, pp. 248–258. Used by permission. Only a few groups discussed in the text have been selected here.

MEMBERSHIP OF CHURCHES IN THE UNITED STATES

African Methodist Episcopal Church	3,500,000
Assemblies of God	2,387,982
Church of God in Christ	5,449,875
Church of Jesus Christ, Latter-Day Saints	4,711,500
Episcopal Church	2,536,550
Evangelical Lutheran Church in America	5,190,489
Orthodox Church in America	2,000,000
Lutheran Church, Missouri Synod	2,594,555
National Baptist Convention in America, Inc.	3,500,000
National Baptist Convention, U.S.A., Inc.	8,200,000
Presbyterian Church (USA)	3,669,489
Roman Catholic Church	60,280,454
Southern Baptist Convention	15,663,296
United Methodist Church	8,538,662
United Church of Christ	1,472,213

Source: Yearbook of American and Canadian Churches. Ed. Kenneth B. Bedell. Nashville, TN: Abingdon Press, © 1997, pp. 248–258. Used by permission. Only a few groups discussed in the text have been selected here.

MEMBERSHIP OF MAJOR RELIGIONS

Baha'is	6,104,000
Buddhists	323,894,000
Christians	1,927,953,000
Confucians	5,254,000
Jews	14,117,000
Muslims	1,099,634,000
Sikhs	19,161,000
Shintoists	2,844,000

Source: Eight religions in the text. The *1996 Britannica Book of the Year,* © 1996, p. 298. Encyclopedia Britannica, Inc., Chicago, Illinois.

BASIC TENETS OF RELIGIONS

1. RELIGIONS OF THE AMERICAS

Absolutes

North America

A. Naskapi

Mantu Soul (soul in living things)

Mista'peo Great Man (individual soul)

Tsaka'bec (trickster)

B. Powhatans

Okeus (wrathful deity)   Ahone (beneficent deity)

C. Cherokees

Wild Boy   Water Beetle (creator)

D. Zuni

Awanawilona (god of the wide sky)

E. Dakota

Wakan tanka (collective name for "the sacred ones")

Mesoamerica and South America

A. Religion of the Aztecs
Huitzilopochtli (sun)
Tezcatlipoca (night sky)
Tlaloc (earth and rain)

B. Religion of the Incas
Inti-Viracocha (creator and sustainer)
Peaks of the Andes (mother earth)

2. RELIGIONS OF AFRICA

A. Ancient Egyptian Religion

Devourer	Sun Amon-Re, Aton, Hathor		
Seth	Iris	Osiris	Horus

B. Basongye of Zaire

Kafilefile (evil deity)   Efile Mukulu (beneficent deity)

C. Zulu

Inkosi Yezulu (god of the sky)

Inkosazana (princess of heaven)

Izinyanga Zezulu (weather deity)

D. Yoruba

Obatala (creator of earth)

Olorun (supreme deity of the sky)

Orunmila (god of Ifa divination)

3. HINDUISM

Gods of the Rig-Veda

Indra (storms, monsoons)

Mitra (faith keeping, loyalty)

Rudra (mountain storms, plants)

Savitar, Surya (sun)

Varuna (the high-arched sky)

Gods of the Sacrifice

Agni (god of fire)   Soma (drink of communion)

Principle of Order

Rita [Ṛta]

Gods of Popular Hinduism

Brahma (creator)

Shiva (destroyer)	Vishnu (preserver)
	(Lakshmi)
Devi or Shakti	*Avatars of Vishnu*
Durga (avenger)	Krishna [Radha]
Kali (wrathful goddess)	
Parvati (young lover)	Rama [Sita]
Umma (protecting mother)	
Sons	
Ganesha	
Kumara or Karttikeya	
Adherents	*Adherents*
Shaivites	Vaishnavites

4. BUDDHISM

Theravadin	Mahayana	Tibet
(Sthaviravadins)	(Mahasanghikas)	Gelugpa
China	Japan	Nyingyapa
Tian Tai	Tendai	
Hua-Yen	Kegon	
Chan	Zen	
Jingtu	Shingon	
Chen Yen	Jodo Shin Shu	
	Nichiren	

5. JAINISM AND SIKHISM

A. Jains
Main Groups

Digambaras   Shvetambaras

Tirthankaras
Mahavira (twenty-fourth)

B. Sikh Gurus
Nanak (first)
Adi Granth (current)

6. RELIGIONS OF CHINA AND JAPAN

A. China

Daoism	*Confucianism*	*Mohism*	*Fajia*
Laozi	Confucius	Mozi	Han Feizi
Zhuangzi	Mengzi		

Neo-Confucianism
Zhuxi

B. Japan

Izanagi   Izanami

Amaterasu	Susanoo	Tsukiyomi
(sun)	(storms)	(moon)
Ninigi		
Jimmu		
(first emperor)		

Japanese Religious Groups

Traditional Shinto	*Mountain Sects*	*Revelation Sects*	*New Religions*
Shinto Taikyo	Ontakekyo	Kurozumikyo	P. L. Kyodan
Izumo Oyashirokyo	Fusokyo	Konkokyo	Seicho-no-le
Shinto Shuseiha	Jikkokyo	Misogukyo	Soka Gakkai
Shinto Taiseikyo		Omoto	
Shinshukyo		Tenri-kyo	
Shinrikyo			

7. ANCIENT RELIGIONS OF IRAQ AND IRAN

A. Iraq
Ancient Religion of Babylon

Erishkegal   Gilgamesh

Tiamat–Marduk

Inanna   Damuzi

B. Iran
Zoroastrianism

Angra Mainyu (evil spirit)   Ahura Mazda (god of light)

Vohu Manu (good thought)

8. JUDAISM

Forms of Judaism

Reform	Conservative	Orthodox
Abraham Geiger (1810–1874) Germany	Zacharias Frankel (1801–1875) Germany	Samson Raphael Hirsch (1808–1888) Germany

Isaac Mayer Wise
(1819–1900)
(United States)

Soloman Schechter
(1850–1915)

Reconstructionism

Mordecai Kaplan (b. 1881)

Hasidism

Israel Baal Shem (1700–1760)

THE BOOKS OF THE JEWISH BIBLE (The *Tanakh*)

Torah The Five Books of Moses	*The Twelve* Minor Prophets	*Kethuvim* The Writings
Genesis	Hosea	Psalms
Exodus	Joel	Proverbs
Leviticus	Amos	Job
Numbers	Obadiah	The Song of Songs
Deuteronomy	Jonah	Ruth
Nevi'im The Prophets	Micah	Lamentations
	Nahum	Ecclesiastes
Joshua	Habakkuk	Esther
Judges	Zephaniah	Daniel
I Samuel	Haggai	Ezra
II Samuel	Zechariah	Nehemiah
I Kings	Malachi	I Chronicles
II Kings		II Chronicles
Isaiah		
Jeremiah		
Ezekiel		

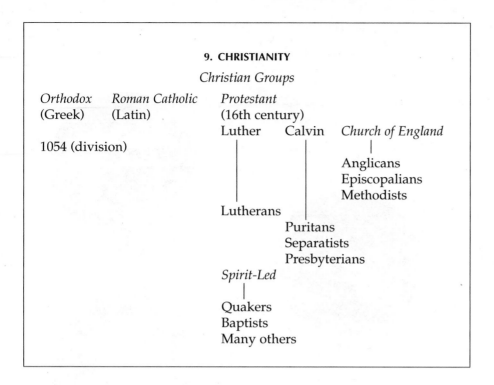

9. CHRISTIANITY

Christian Groups

Orthodox (Greek)	*Roman Catholic* (Latin)	*Protestant* (16th century)		
		Luther	Calvin	*Church of England*
1054 (division)				
				Anglicans Episcopalians Methodists
		Lutherans		
			Puritans Separatists Presbyterians	
		Spirit-Led		
		Quakers Baptists Many others		

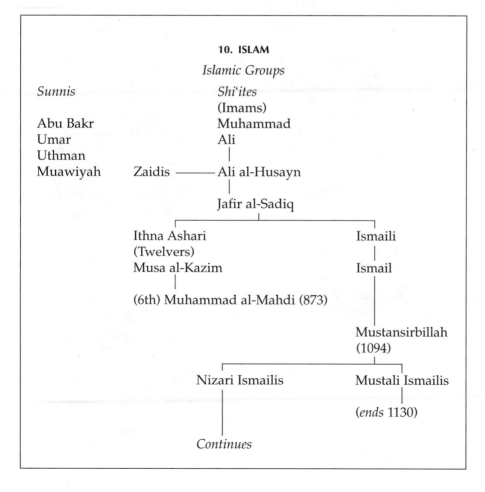

10. ISLAM

Islamic Groups

Sunnis		*Shi'ites* (Imams)
Abu Bakr		Muhammad
Umar		Ali
Uthman		
Muawiyah	Zaidis ————	Ali al-Husayn
		Jafir al-Sadiq

Ithna Ashari
(Twelvers)
Musa al-Kazim

(6th) Muhammad al-Mahdi (873)

Ismaili

Ismail

Mustansirbillah
(1094)

Nizari Ismailis

Mustali Ismailis

(*ends* 1130)

Continues

SOME COMMON SYMBOLS OF VARIOUS RELIGIONS

Hinduism

Sikhism

Shinto

Buddhism

Daoism

Judaism

Jainism

Confucianism

Christianity

Zoroastrianism

Islam

442

APPENDIXAPPENDIX

GLOSSARY

abathakati [u-bah-TAH-kah-ti] In Zulu society, a person who uses spiritual forces for evil ends. A witch or wizard.

Adi Granth [AH-di-grunth] The scriptures and perpetual guru of the Sikhs. Hymns by the Sikh gurus are recorded in the Adi Granth.

adoptionist [a-DOPT-shun-ist] A person who believes that at the baptism of the man Jesus, God adopted him as his Son.

Agamas [AH-ga-mas] The collection of Jain scriptures. These writings divide according to the deity worshiped in each. It is subdivided into three categories: *Purva, Anga,* and *Angabahya.* Scripture from tradition.

Aggadah [ug-GAHD-u] The nonlegal, story aspect of rabbinic literature. It is distinguished from Halakhah, the legal side of Judaism.

Agni [AG-ni] Fire. The Vedic god of fire.

ahimsa [u-HIM-su] The Sanskrit word that is translated "nonviolence." In Jainism, it is a reverence for all living things.

Ahone [A-hone] The beneficent deity of the Powhatans, whose powers were of less concern than those of the malevolent Okeus.

Ahura Mazda [u-HOOR-u MAZ-du] The Zoroastrian god of light; the Wise Lord who is the highest deity.

ajiva or non-jiva [AH-JEE-va] Category of existence that is insentient; lacking soul.

akh [AHK] or **ikhu** A part of the soul of a person. It was the ghost that went to the land of the blessed.

allegorical method Interpreting the symbols of an earlier age in meanings of a later age. Seeking the spiritual as well as the historical meaning of scriptures.

Amaterasu [AH-MAH-te-RAH-su] In Shinto, the goddess of the sun, created by purification of Izanagi. She is sister to Susanoo, the god of storms.

American Muslim Mission A Muslim group formed for African Americans by Wallace Deen Muhammad. World Islam accepts these adherents as Muslims.

Amesha Spentas [u-MEE-shu SPIN-tas] In Zoroastrianism, the higher spirits directly under Ahura Mazda. They are modes of divine being that bear names of ethical virtues, such as "Good Thought."

Amitabha (Amida) [a-mee-TAH-ba] The Buddha who presides over Western Paradise. Hozo Bosatsu is the Japanese name for a legendary monk who long ago took a vow to become a Buddha if his merits could be used to help others. After fulfilling 48 vows, he became Amitabha.

Amon-Re [AH-mun-ray] A sun god of Egypt. His symbol was the obelisk, a ray of the sun. Amon, originally the god of Thebes, became highest god in 2000 B.C.E., when Thebes dominated all Egypt.

Anahita [anna-HEE-tu] In later Zoroastrianism, a mother goddess who was worshiped with fertility rites.

Anglicans [ANG-gli-cuns] Members of the Church of England. Their church government is episcopal, having clergy directed by bishops.

Angra Mainyu [ANG-gra MIIN-yu] In Zoroastrianism, the evil spirit who opposes Ahura Mazda.

Anicca [a-NICH-cha] Impermanence. The Buddhist doctrine that there are no permanent entities. All phenomena continuously change.

ankh [ankh] In Egypt, the circle-topped cross representing life. Some forms incorporate a cat on top of the circle.

Anatta (Anatman) [a-NAT-ta] The Pali word for no soul or Sanscrit no Atman.

Anne Hutchinson A dissenter banished in 1637 from Massachusetts Bay Colony. She and her children found more freedom in Rhode Island.

ansar [AN-sahr] Helpers; Medinans who helped Muhammad relocate from Mecca to Medina. They were joined by Muhammad and his companions after the Hijrah.

antyesti [un-TYES-ti] Funerals. Last rites.

apocalypse [u-POCK-u-lips] A revelation. A prophetic vision of the destruction of evil and salvation of righteous people.

apocalyptic literature [u-POCK-u-LIP-tic] Writings describing the last days, or the end of time. This literature inspires the faithful to stand firm in spite of the severe hardships of their time.

apostle [a-POS-ul] A person who was a disciple of Jesus sent out to proclaim the coming of the kingdom of God. Traditionally, there were twelve apostles chosen by Jesus.

Aranyakas [ah-RAN-yu-kuz] A philosophical section interpreting ritual of the Vedas for ascetics living in the forest.

arhat [UR-hut] An enlightened, holy person.

Ark of the Covenant A box containing the Ten Commandments. Priests carried it in processions and then housed it in the tabernacle.

Aryans [AHR-yuns] Indo-Europeans who entered the Indus Valley prior to 1000 B.C.E. They expressed their evolving religion in the hymns of the Rig-Veda.

Asanga [a-SANG-a] Made famous in the fourth century C.E., the Yogacara school of Buddhist philosophy that was founded by Maitreyanatha.

ase [AH-se] Spiritual forces of the Yoruba; divine energy.

asha [ASH-u] In Zoroastrianism, spiritual truth. Some scholars equate Asha with the Hindu Rita.

Asherah [ash-u-RAH] A goddess of Canaan and a counterpart to the male god, Baal. She was another example of the Mediterranean mother goddess.

Ashkenazim [ahsh-ku-NAH-zim] A Yiddish-speaking group of Jews who settled in central and northern Europe. The term in Hebrew referred to Germany.

Ashoka [a-SHOW-ka] This king, who reigned in India 27–232 B.C.E., sponsored Buddhist missionary activities.

Atman [AHT-man] The essence of Brahman that is present in individuals. The universal self.

Aton [AHT-un] In Egypt, this god´s symbol was a disk, represneting the sun. After Akhenaton established his throne in Akhetaton, Aton was the only god worshiped.

avidya [a-VID-ya] In Hinduism, the term means "ignorance," or not seeing things as they are.

Awanawilona [u-WAH-nah-wi-LOW-nu] The Zuni god of the wide sky.

awon iya wa [a-WON-I-YAH-wa] Yoruba term for "the mothers."

aworo [a-WOH-roh] A priest of the Yoruba.

ba [BAH] In Egypt, a kind of human consciousness. It is sometimes described as the soul.

Baal [BAA-ul] A god or gods of Canaan. Baals were landlords or keepers of the land. Canaanites worshiped them to make crops grow.

Babalawo [bah-BAH-lah-wu] The one who practices Yoruba, Ifa divination.

Baptists [BAP-tists] Members of the Baptist tradition. Baptists believe that adherents should be baptized when they are old enough to choose Christ as their savior. Immersion is the preferred, often required, form of baptism. Baptist government is by members of each congregation.

Bar Mitzvah [bar-MITS-vu] The ceremony that recognizes a thirteen-year-old Jewish boy as a son of the commandment. He is considered an adult responsible for religious duties.

Bat Mitzvah [bat-MITS-vu] In Reform and Conservative Judaism, the ceremony that recognizes a daughter of the commandment, a Jewish female between twelve and fourteen years of age. She is considered an adult responsible for her religious duties.

bhais [BA-iz] The brothers of a Sikh gurdwara who assist in worship. It is also the title used for a Sikh priest.

bhakti yoga [BAHK-ti] Personal devotion to deity. In Hinduism, a path that leads to salvation.

Bodhgaya [BOHD-GAH-ya] A temple that commemorates the grove where the Buddha found enlightenment.

Bodhidharma [BOW-dee-DAHR-ma] The monk who brought meditative Buddhism to China. His example inspired Chan (Zen) Buddhism.

bodhisattvas [bow-dhee-SAT-tvas] In Buddhism, people who have qualified to enter Nirvana, but who, out of compassion for others, remain available to help others.

Bon [PAIN] The ancient animistic religion of Tibet.

Book of Mormon A book revealed to Joseph Smith.

Brahma [Bram-HAH] Ultimate reality; the creator.

Brahman [bram-MUN] In Hinduism, the name of the highest deity, the Absolute.

Brahmanas [BRAH-muh-nus] Commentaries and manuals prepared to instruct priests in the rites associated with the Vedas.

Brahmin [BRAH-men] In Hinduism, the name of the highest, priestly caste. After the Aryans were settled in India, the priests became more important than the warriors of the Kshatriya caste.

Brigham Young Joseph Smith's successor, who led Mormons to Salt Lake City, Utah.

bushido [bu-shi-DOOH] A code of honor for Japanese warriors. It incorporated both Daoist and Zen Buddhist concepts and governed the samurai, the feudal military class.

butsudan [bu-tsu-DAH-NAH] A Buddhist altar. Tablets commemorating ancestors are kept on it.

caliph [KAA-lif] A successor of the prophet Muhammad. The first caliph was Abu Bakr. The ideal of Islam is that religion and state are not separated.

Canaanites [kay-nu-NIGHTS] The people among whom the Israelites settled on their return from slavery in Egypt. Canaan comprised the area bordered by the Sea of Galilee, the Jordan River, and the Dead Sea.

caste [CAST] In Hinduism, the permanent social group into which a person is born. Social and religious obligations are determined for a lifetime by caste.

catechumen [KAT-i-KYOO-mun] A convert to Christianity who received instruction in preparation for baptism.

Chan (Ch'an) [CHAHN] The Chinese Buddhist school of meditation founded by Bodhidharma.

Chiang K'ai Shek [CHUNG-kai-SHEK] The leader of Nationalist China who established a government in Taiwan. He was driven from mainland China by Mao Zedong.

Chinvat Bridge [CHIN-vaht] In Zoroastrianism, the bridge of judgment that a soul must walk over after death.

Christ [KRIIST] The Greek word meaning "the anointed one." The Hebrew word for the concept was *messiah.* Christians believe that Jesus was the long-awaited Messiah.

Christian canon [CAN-on] The list of books accepted as scriptures by Christians.

church [CHURCH] A congregation of Christians. All Christians considered together as the mystical body of Christ.

civil religion [SIV-ul] A term used by Jean-Jacques Rousseau (1712–1778). Now, in the United States, it refers to religious terms and practices used in celebrations of national events and holidays.

Confucius [kun-FYOO-shus] Kongfuzi, the Chinese founder of Confucianism. Primarily a teacher, he sought to develop good government through a responsible ruler and ethical people.

covenant [CUV-u-nunt] The binding agreement between God and his chosen people. The covenant was repeatedly renewed. Unlike a contract, the covenant had no date of expiration.

cuneiform [kyoo-NEE-a-form] Wedge-shaped writing found on clay tablets in ancient Mesopotamia.

dakhma [DAHK-ma] A Zoroastrian Tower of Silence used for disposal of corpses of the faithful. It is believed to be necessary because a corpse cannot be allowed to contaminate either soil or fire.

Damuzi [du-MU-zi] (Tammuz) The Mesopotamian god of fertility, who gave life to vegetation and children to women.

Dao (Tao) [DOW] In China or in Daoism (Taoism), the path, course, or way of the universe. Although its influence is in nature, the eternal Dao is believed to be hidden from empirical experience.

Dao De Jing (Tao Te Ching) [dow-du-JING] *The Way and Its Power.* A book attributed to Laozi, founder of Daoism.

Daoists (Taoists) [DOW-ists] Followers of a philosophy or religion expressed in the *Dao De Jing,* attributed to Laozi, a sage of ancient China.

deism [DEE-iz-um] The belief that a Supreme Being created the law-abiding universe and does not interfere with its operation to answer prayers and perform miracles.

dharma [DAR-ma] Law. Religion. One's support. Religious duty or merit. In Buddhism, law. It can be the law of the universe or the law or tradition taught by the Buddha.

dhimmi [THIM-mi] A client of the Muslims. In exchange for protection, non-Muslims agreed to certain conditions of subservience to Muslims. Jews and Christians were often dhimmis of Muslim rulers.

Dhyana [DYAH-na] In Buddhism, mental concentration. It is the term for Buddhist meditation.

diaspora [di-AHS-pe-ra] A Greek word for the dispersion of Jews. These were the Jews who lived outside the Holy Land.

Digambaras [di-GAHM-ba-ras] The Jains who believe that a true monk is "sky clad." These monks think that women cannot become liberated until they are reborn as men.

Divine Principle [di-VIINE] Rev. Sun Myung Moon's book interpreting the teachings of Christian scriptures.

diviner [di-VII-nur] A person, man or woman, who is spirit-possessed and knows how to discover people's destinies.

Dravidians [drah-VID-e-uns] Dark-skinned inhabitants of India. They differed from the light-skinned Aryans who entered from the Northwest.

dukkha [DUK-kah] The Buddhist term for the suffering of humans and other sentient beings.

Ea [eah] A water god. He was sometimes known as Enlil.

Eastern Orthodox Church [OR-tha-dox] The Christian church of the Greek tradition. The churches of the eastern Mediterranean countries retained a more democratic form of governance.

ecumenical [ek-yu-MEN-i-kul] Refers to the whole household of faith. It is in contrast to matters of local or special interest.

Efile Mukulu [E-fu-le mu-KOO-loo] Among the Basongye of Congo [Zaire], the chief god of good. His counterpart is the evil god, Kafilefile.

Eightfold Path The fourth Noble Truth, the path of deliverance in Buddhism.

Elijah (Poole) Muhammad Founder of the Black Muslim movement, the Nation of Islam. Dissatisfied with Christianity, which appeared to be a white religion, Poole organized a religion for blacks.

Enkidu [IN-ki-du] In Mesopotamian tradition, a wild man befriended by Gilgamesh. He was killed by Enlil for slaying the monster Huwawa.

epic [EP-ic] A narrative poem celebrating the acts of a traditional hero.

epistle [i-PIS-el] A letter, particularly one that has become part of the New Testament scriptures. Many epistles of the New Testament were attributed to Paul and to the apostles who walked with Jesus.

Essenes [ES-eens] A group of pious Jews of the first century C.E. who lived in separate communities and practiced ritual washing and other acts for purity. Some scholars think that the inhabitants of the Qumran community, near the Dead Sea, were Essenes.

Esu [ES-zoo] A Yoruba god who is amoral; he is a trickster deity and a messenger.

excommunicate [ex-ku-MYUU-ni-caat] The forced exclusion of a person from a religious organization, such as a church. People who continued, after warning, to practice errors, often were excommunicated from the church.

Fajia (Fa-Chia or Legalists) [fah-JEE-a] In China, the Legalist school of philosophy that taught governance by reward and punishment. An example of a Fa-Chia philosopher is Han Feizi.

Gelugpa [ge-LUG-pa] The Buddhists of Tibet known as Yellow Hats. They reformed the practices of the Nyingmapa, or Red Hat Buddhists.

Gemarah [ge-MAHR-u] The "learning" of the rabbis. It was combined with the Mishnah to form the Talmud.

Genku (Honen Shonin) [GEN-koo] Twelfth-century C.E. founder of the Jodo Buddhist sect in Japan. He was the monk Genku, who had been trained at Tendai monasteries on Mt. Hiei.

Gilgamesh [GIL-gu-mesh] A Mesopotamian king of Uruk about 2600 B.C.E. He searched for immortality, found the plant that was its source, and lost it to a serpent.

gospel [GOS-pul] A message of good news. One of the four stories of the life of Christ found in the New Testament.

Guan Yin (Kwan-yin) [GUAHN-YIN] Guanyin, bodhisattva of mercy, is also known is Avalokiteshvara. In Pure Land Buddhism, he is placed beside Amitabha as his attendant.

gurdwara [GUR-dwah-ra] A place of Sikh worship, fellowship, and hospitality. It is a temple, the dwelling of the guru.

Guru [GU-RU] or [GOO-ROO] A Hindu teacher of religious duties. For a student, the guru represents the divine in human form.

Guru [GU-ru] or [GOO-ROO] In Sikhism, one of ten early spiritual leaders or, after their times, the Adi Granth. God is the one, true Guru.

hadiths [had-EETHS] Reports of what Muhammad said or did; examples for faithful Muslims to follow. The *Sunna* are the traditions of the prophet in the literary form of *hadith*–reports.

Haggadah [hah-gah-DAH] The story used at the Seder during the Jewish holiday of Passover. This term is distinguished from aggadah, nonlegal stories of rabbinic Judaism.

Hajj [HAHJ] The pilgrimage to Mecca, expected of all Muslims who are able.

Halakhah [ha-la-KAH] The legal part of Jewish religion that was developed in rabbinic writings.

Han Feizi (Han Fei Tzu) [hahn-FAY-dzi] A representative of the Fajia, or Legalist, school of philosophy in China. He taught that people were governed best by a ruler who harshly enforced rigid laws.

Hanif [HA-neef] In Arabia, prior to Muhammad's recitations, a person who worshiped one God. Waraqa Ibn Nawfal, a kinsman of Khadijah, was a hanif.

Hanukkah [khan-nu-ka] The eight-day festival commemorating the rededication of the Jerusalem temple after the Maccabean revolt against the Syrians.

Haoma [HOE-mu] In late Zoroastrianism, the divinity of the sacred elixir prepared during Zoroastrian ritual.

hara-kiri (seppuku) [HAH-RAH-kee-ree] In Japan, a ritual suicide to preserve or to restore a person's honor. It is considered an act of bravery rather than cowardice.

Hathor [HAH-thor] The Egyptian goddess who created the world. Her symbol was a woman's body with the head of a cow.

henotheism [HEN-o-the-ISM] A belief that affirms one deity without denying the existence of others, or that one deity is supreme over other deities.

heresy [HER-i-si] A belief held by an adherent that is contrary to the accepted teachings of the religious organization.

heretic [HER-i-tik] A person who has been judged by the church to teach doctrine dangerously contrary to the teachings of the church.

hieroglyphics [HII-er-u-GLIF-iks] A system of writing used in ancient Egypt. Pictorial symbols representing sounds or sounds and meanings.

Hijrah [HEJ-rah] Muhammad's migration from Mecca to Yathrib (Medina) in 622. He and Abu Bakr made the journey in less than the normal eleven days.

Hillel [hil-EL] A prominent Jewish teacher and founder of the Hillel school of rabbis in the first century. He was considered more liberal in his views than the conservative Shammai.

Holocaust [HOL-u-cost] An offering brought to a deity and completely burnt. The term now refers to the Nazi extermination of Jews in occupied countries during World War II.

Horus [HOR-us] In Egypt, the son of Isis and Osiris who opposed his uncle, Seth. Horus was also the sun, symbolized by a falcon.

Hozo Bosatsu [ho-zo-bo-SAHT-soo] In Shinran Buddhism, a meritorious person who became Amida Buddha.

Hua-Yen [HWAH-YEN] The Chinese Buddhist sect whose primary Buddha is Vairocana. The school had a holistic view of Buddha nature and the universe.

huacas [HUAH-cas] In Inca religion, natural phenomena that provide unusual manifestations of the holy. Unusual rocks, for example, could symbolize the presence of the holy.

Huitzilopochtli [HWEET-zi-low-POK-tli] The chief god of the Aztecs. He was god of the sun who led his people, the Aztecs, to their home in Tenochtitln.

humanist A person who believes the values of humans are the highest in the universe. Humans are "on their own" in the universe.

huskanaw [HUS-ka-now] The Powhatan rite of passage for adolescent boys. They left their families, "died," and returned as warriors who were under command of their weroances and Powhatan.

iconoclast [ii-con-o-KLAST] A person who was opposed to the use of icons in worship.

iconodule [ii-con-o-DOOL] A person who favored the use of icons in worship.

iconostasis [ii-con-NOS-ta-sis] A screen at the front of an Orthodox church that displays many precious icons.

Ife [IF-fe] The most sacred city of the Yoruba peoples of Nigeria.

ihlambo [ih-LAHM-boh] The ceremony of washing spears after mourning the death of a Zulu chief.

ihram [IH-rahm] The consecrated state in which Muslims perform the Hajj. Muslims abstain from sex, perfume, hunting, and other things during the pilgrimage to Mecca.

ijma' [IJ-mah] The consensus of Muslim religious leaders on matters of practice.

Immanuel Kant A Prussian philosopher who advanced a theory of knowledge that a knower can know an object only subjectively, not as it is in itself. John Hick uses Kant's theory to help exlain how religions that differ in concepts of god may be experiencing the same Absolute.

Inanna [in-AHN-nu] In Mesopotamia, the goddess who was wife of Damuzi (Tammuz). She descended into the underworld to seek her husband's release.

incarnation [in-cahr-NA-shun] To invest God in human flesh. Christians consider the Christ as God in human form.

Indra [IN-dra] In Hinduism, a god of the Rig-Veda. The creator and ruler of the universe.

indulgence [in-DUL-jens] A remission of temporal punishment for sin that has already been pardoned. Indulgences became a subject of debate for Martin Luther.

Inkosazana [in-KOH-sa-ZAH-na] The Zulu princess of heaven who assists women and girls.

Inkosi Yezulu [in-KOH-si ye-ZOO-loo] In Zulu religion, one name for the God of the Sky.

Inti [IN-ti] An early god of the Incas, probably symbolized by a hummingbird. Inti was a creator god who was later combined with Viracocha.

isangoma [i-san-GO-ma] A Zulu woman who is a diviner.

Ishatpragbhara [ee-shut-PRAHG-bu-ru] The Jain state beyond life and death.

Ishtar [ISH-tar] In Babylonia, a mother goddess who descended into the underworld. She was also known as Inanna.

Isis [II-sis] In Egypt, the wife of Osiris, god of the dead, and the mother of their son, Horus. She was the giver of life.

Islam [is-LAHM] Like other religions of the family of Abraham, it emphasizes worship of one God. It believes that Muhammad is the last and most important of the prophets of God.

Itihasa-Purana [iti-HAHT-sah poo-RAH-na] Ancient. Eighteen *puranas* honor Brahma, Shiva, and Vishnu.

Izanagi [ee-zah-NAH-gee] In Shinto, the male-who-invites. Cocreator, with Izanami, of Japan.

Izanami [ee-zah-NAA-mee] In Shinto, the female-who-invites. Cocreator, with Izanagi, of Japan.

izinyanga zezulu [iz-in-YAN-ga ze-ZOO-loo] The deity in Zulu religion who herds weather or sky as boys herd cattle.

Jade Emperor A mythical emperor of ancient China. In 1012 C.E., the emperor (Chen Tsung) claimed to have received revelation from Huang Di (Yu Huang), the Jade Emperor.

jan'u [JAN-eu] The sacred thread worn by the three upper castes.

Japji [JAP-ji] A Sikh hymn recited in devotions every morning. A guide for Sikh conduct.

Jatakas [JAH-ta-kas] Stories of the previous lives of the Buddha, which were collected and used in the teachings of Theravadin monks.

jhana [JHAH-na] Buddhist meditation, or the states reached in Buddhist meditation.

Jimmu [jee-moo] In Shinto, the first human emperor, a descendant of the gods. As part of the Shinto religion, the emperor of Japan has been revered.

Jina [JI-na] In Jainism, a person who has conquered rebirth. Mahavira wasa jina.

Jingtu (ching-tú) [JING-too] Pure Land, or Western Paradise, Buddhism. It believes in Sukhavati, which is ruled by Amitabha Buddha. [In Japan the sect is Jodo.]

Jinn [JIN] In Arabia, a race of beings created from fire, distinguished from humans, who were created from clay. Some jinn are good; others are bad.

jiva [JEE-va] In Jainism, the soul. The term is opposite of ajiva, body. A monad is a single unit of basic substance.

jnana yoga [JYNAH-na] Jnana means knowledge or wisdom. The Hindu path of release based on intellectual knowledge. Jnana yoga appeals to people who emphasize rational understanding of religious beliefs.

Jodo [JO-DO] The Japanese sect of the Pure Land. It was founded in the twelfth century C.E. by the monk Genku. Salvation comes by grace, through faith.

John Wesley An Anglican priest who formed the Methodist Church. Methodist circuit riders ministered to frontier families in America.

Joseph Smith Founder of the Church of Jesus Christ of Latter-Day Saints.

Judaizers [JOO-day-iiz-ers] Persons who advocated the practice of Jewish observances for all Christians. They opposed Paul's emphasis on freedom from the law.

junzi (chun-tzu) [JUN-dzi] In Confucianism, the gentleman or superior man. He was a role model for the conduct of the Chinese people.

ka [KA] In Egypt, divine breath that supported life. It is sometimes referred to as the soul.

Ka'bah [KUH-bah] The cube-shaped building of stone in the open court of the Grand Mosque of Mecca. In Islamic tradition, the first Ka'bah was built by Abraham and Ishmael.

Kabir [ku-BEER] 1440–1518. A Muslim who believed that God can save anyone of any caste from the Law of Karma.

kachinas [ka-CHI-nas] Among the Hopi, masked, costumed dancers that represent gods, ancestors, or spirits.

Kafilefile [kah-FI-le-FI-le] In Congo, Zaire, among the Basongye, the god of evil. His counterpart is the good god, Efile Mukulu.

Kalachakra [kah-lah-CHAK-ra] The space–time doctrine in Tibet. The whole universe is related in its flow to the vital currents of the human body.

kalpa [KAL-pa] In Hinduism, a long period of the created world. One world ends and a new period begins with another creation.

kami [KAH-mee] Natural and supernatural persons and powers worshiped in Shinto. Kami are present everywhere, in nature and in people.

kami-dana [KAH-mee-DAH-NAH] In Japanese homes, a center of symbols honoring the kami. Sometimes the center is a shelf.

Karma [KAHR-ma] The law that a person's thoughts and deeds are followed eventually by deserved pleasure or pain. In Hinduism, it is an explanation for caste. In Buddhism, karma is primarily psychological; in Jainism, it is understood in primarily physical terms.

kashruth [KASH-root] Jewish dietary regulations.

kerygma [ke-RIG-ma] The message or proclamation of the early Christians. Peter gave a proclamation on the day of the Pentecost.

kikudu [ki-KOO-doo] The soul of a human being that may live after the death of the body.

kiswah [KIS-wa] The robe, or covering, usually placed over the Ka'bah in Mecca.

kivas [KEE-vas] Underground chambers used by the Hopi for religious ceremonies.

koan [KO-an] A problem used by Zen Buddhists to reduce dependence on ordinary ways of thinking about self and the universe.

kosher [KO-sher] In Judaism, meat that has been properly prepared for eating. One requirement is that most of the blood be removed from the meat.

Krishna [KRISH-na] An incarnation of Vishnu, who is also the chariot driver of the warrior Arjuna of the Bhagavad Gita.

Kshatriya [KSHA-tri-ya] A Hindu caste of warriors and administrators. Originally, this caste was the highest, but it was later subordinated to the Brahmins.

Kukai (Kobo Daishi) [KOO-KAI] The ninth-century C.E. founder of the Japanese Buddhist Shingon sect. All Buddhas are emanations of the great sun, Vairocana or, in Japan, Dainichi.

kusti [KOOS-ti] A sacred thread worn to indicate initiation into a religion. Hindus and Zoroastrians use the symbol.

lama [LAH-mah] The term means "supreme being," comparable to the term *guru* in Indian Buddhism. A priest in Tibetan Buddhism.

Laozi (Lao Tzu) [LAHOW-dzi] The sage of China once believed to have been the author of the *Dao De Jing (Tao Te Ching)*. He is regarded as the founder of Daoism.

Law of Karma [KAHR-ma] The inexorable principle in Hinduism that a person's thoughts and deeds are followed eventually by deserved pleasure or pain.

Laws of Manu A Hindu code of conduct compiled about 200 B.C.E. to 200 C.E.

liberation theology A presentation of Christian teachings that emphasizes Jesus' role in elevating people who had been neglected or oppressed.

Li Ji (Li Chi) [LEE-jee] The Chinese classic on rites supposedly edited by Confucius. Although it is one of five Confucian classics, it is now regarded as coming from a period later than Confucius.

li [LEE] The Confucian principle of righteousness or propriety. Li can refer to ritual and correct conduct in society.

loka [LOW-ka] The universe where categories of sentient beings are reborn.

Lutherans [LOO-ther-ans] Members of a major Protestant denomination based on the teachings and practices of Martin Luther (1483–1546). Lutherans base their beliefs primarily on the Bible rather than on teachings of the church fathers, ecumenical councils, or the pope.

Madhyamika [ma-DYAM-ee-ka] The Buddhist philosophy that the phenomenal objects that one experiences are not ultimately real. Nagarjuna was the founder of the Madhyamika school.

Magi [MAY-jii] Among the ancient Persians, priests. Their doctrine reduced Ahura Mazda from a transcendent principle to a good spirit, opposed by an evil spirit.

Mahabharata [ma-HAH-BAH-ra-ta] A long epic poem featuring activities of the god Krishna.

Mahayanists [ma-HAH-YAH-nists] Those of the great vehicle, who emphasized universal Buddhist enlightenment.

Mahdi [MAH-di] In Islam, the expected one. Twelvers believe that an imam is in occultation and will return as a messianic figure.

Maitreya [mi-TRAY-ya] In the tradition of East Asia, the next Buddha to appear on earth.

Makiguchi (Tsunesaburo) [MAH-ke-GOO-chee] Founder of Soka Gakkai (Value Creation Society) of Japan in 1937.

Malcolm X, or **Malcolm Little** Formerly of the Nation of Islam, he formed his own group in 1964 in the tradition of Sunni Islam. A major change in his teaching was that all people are brothers and sisters, whites as well as blacks.

Mamanatowick [ma-ma-na-TOW-wick] The supreme king or chief of the Algonquian-speaking peoples of eastern Virgina. Powhatan was the first mamanatowick that the English settlers dealt with at Jamestown.

mandala [MAN-da-la] A geometric pattern used in worship.

Mani [MAH-nee] A Persian teacher of religious dualism; he considered himself the Holy Spirit.

mankishi [man-KI-shi] Among the Basongye of Congo (Zaire), a small carved figure used to represent a child desired by a couple. The figure can also be used to effect good fishing and to protect homes and people from bad magic.

Mantra [MAN-tra] A special formula of words recited in worship.

Mantu [MAHN-too] Among the Naskapi, the soul of nature, animals, and humans. The soul of a person is referred to as the "Great Man."

Manu [MAH-noo] In Hinduism, the first man.

Mao Zedong (Mao Tse-Tung) [MAOW-tse-DONG] The Marxist leader of China who overthrew the Nationalist government of Chiang K'ai Shek in 1949. He established the People's Republic of China.

Mara [MAH-rah] The evil one who tempted the Buddha at Bodhgaya.

Marduk [MAHR-dook] The Babylonian god of creation. To create the world, he defeated the goddess of chaos, Tiamat.

Martin Luther King, Jr. African-American Baptist clergyman who led the civil rights movement in the United States. Adopting Gandhi's methods, King's followers used nonviolent demonstrations to awaken American consciences to racial injustice.

Mary Baker Eddy Founder of the Church of Christ, Scientist. She was the author of *Science and Health with Key to the Scriptures.*

matzah [MUT-za] (pl. matzot) Unleavened bread eaten by Jews during the Passover. During Passover, no leaven should be present in a Jewish home.

Maya (queen) [MAH-ya] The mother of Siddhartha Gautama, the Buddha.

Maya [MAH-ya] Appearance or illusion; power of creation.

Mayet [MU-yut] (Maat) The Egyptian goddess of order and truth, who prompted the deceased at the time of judgment.

Mengzi (Mencius) [MENG-dzi] A later disciple of Confucius who emphasized an inborn goodness of humans. He differed from Xunzi (Hsun Tzu), who argued that men are born evil.

Messiah [mi-SIGH-u] The one whom the Jews expected to come and deliver Israel from oppression and establish a kingdom of righteousness. It can refer to a historical person or to a supernatural being.

Methodists [METH-u-dists] Members of the church that followed the "method" of John Wesley, former Anglican clergyman. The church's government is episcopal, that is, through bishops.

Midrash [MID-rash] (pl. Midrashim) Rabbinic exposition explaining the meaning of the scriptures. The root meaning is "to search out."

mihrab [MIH-rahb] The niche in a mosque that signifies the direction of Mecca. Muslims face Mecca when they pray.

Miki Nakayama [MI-ki NAH-KAH-YAH-MAH] In Japan, founder of the new religion, Tenrikyo. She experienced divine healing through the kami of Divine Reason.

mikishi [mi-KI-shi] Among the Basongye of Congo (Zaire), these are human spirits bent on doing harm. Sorcerers can control them.

miracle [MIR-a-kul] An event that is judged to be brought about by divine intervention in the ordinary events of history.

Mishnah [MISH-na] Teachings of the rabbis compiled about 200 C.E. The Mishnah records discussions of rabbis on how best to live according to the Torah.

Mista'peo [mis-TAH-pe-oh] Among the Naskapi, the Great man—an individual's soul that lives in the heart; it is a person's essential self. It reveals itself in dreams.

Mithra [MITH-ra] The god of light in Zoroastrianism.

Mitra [MI-tra] A Hindu deity of the Vedas. A god of faithfulness and keeping promises.

mitzvah [MITZ-va] (pl. mitzvot) In Judaism, a response in obedience to God according to the covenant. How to live in a covenant relationship with God is a central teaching of Judaism.

Modernism [mod-ur-NIZ-um] In religion, emphasis on reason in philosophy and science instead of traditional beliefs.

Mohists [MOW-hists] Followers of Mozi (Mo Tzu). They advocated curing the ills of society by practicing mutual love among people. Confucians objected to Mohist universal love because it did not allow for special feelings for kin.

Moksha [MOWK-sha] In Hinduism, the release of the soul from a cycle of rebirths. It is one of the four acceptable goals of life for Hindus.

monophysite [mu-NOF-u-SITE] One who believes that in Christ there was only one natureÑdivine.

monotheism [MON-u-the-IS-um] A belief that there is only one deity.

Mozi (Mo Tzu) [MOW-dzi] Founder of the Mohist philosophy, which advocated brotherly love. Brotherhood meant sharing equally the essentials of food, clothing, and shelter.

mudras [MUD-dras] Special positions of hands used in worship.

muezzin [mu-EZ-in] One who calls Muslims to prayer. Muhammad preferred the human voice to the Christian use of bells.

muhajirun [mu-HAJ-i-roon] The emigrants from Mecca who joined Muhammad in Medina. These early converts to Islam lost their property and income when they followed Muhammad.

Muslim [MUS-lim] One who surrenders to God. A follower of the prophet Muhammad.

mystery religions Greek religions that practiced secret rites guaranteeing initiates immortality.

myth [MITH] A story of gods acting in a different time. Creation myths are stories of how the gods acted before humans were created, how they created humans, and how they communicate with humans. The word *myth* in religious studies does not mean untrue.

Nagarjuna [NAH-GAHR-ju-NAH] The Buddhist philosopher of the second century C.E. who established the Madhyamika school of philosophy.

Naozot [NAY-ow-zot] Zoroastrian vesting of a child with a sacred shirt.

Nation of Islam The branch of Black Muslims that struggles with Christianity and whites. It is not accepted by orthodox Muslims as Islam, which welcomes all races.

Nichiren [NEE-chee-REN] A monk in Japan who established a school based on the Lotus Sutra.

nihangs [NI-hangs] The Sikhs with military skills who are always ready to fight for the community.

nirguna Brahman [NIR-goo-na] In Hinduism, Brahman as he is in himself, beyond attributes. Nirguna Brahman is impersonal.

Nirvana [ner-VAH-na] In Buddhism, the state of being free of egocentrism and the suffering that it causes. Positively, it is joy and peace.

Nubians [NOO-bay-ans] People of the southern Nile valley; neighbors of the ancient Egyptians. Their leaders formed the twenty-fifth dynasty of Egyptian pharaohs.

Nyingmapa [ning-MAH-pa] The Red Hat Buddhists of Tibet. Their Buddhism retained an element of pre-Buddhist beliefs and practices.

oba [OH-ba] A chief or king of the Yoruba.

Obatala [OH-bah-TUH-lu] Creator of earth, according to the Yoruba, who brought to it sixteen people created by Olorun.

Odudwa [oh-DOO-doo-wah] A Yoruba creation god associated with the city of Ife.

Okeus [OH-kee-us] Among the Powhatans, a god, or group of gods, that caused suffering. His counterpart is the beneficent deity, Ahone.

Olodumare [oh-LOH-du-MA-ree] In Yoruba religion, the sky.

Olorun [OH-lu-roon] Supreme deity of the sky in Yoruba religion.

orisha [oh-REE-sha] Various Yoruba spirits.

Orisha-nla [oli-REE-sha-nla] A Yoruba creation god.

Orun [OH-roon] In Yoruba religion, the supreme king; the sky. Also known as Oldumare.

Osiris [oh-SI-ris] In Egyptian myth, a king who became lord of the underworld. With his wife, Isis, he fathered Horus, the king of Egypt.

pantheon [PAN-the-on] All the gods or a temple dedicated to them.

parable [PARE-u-bul] A simple story told to illustrate a religious truth or lesson.

Pentecost [PEN-ti-cost] A festival in Judaism coming fifty days after Passover. The time when the Holy Spirit descended on the early Christian church.

Pharisees [PHAR-i-sees] A group of Jews who represented the piety of the common people in the centuries immediately after the Maccabean War.

phenomenal [fi-NOM-u-nal] In Kant's theory of knowledge, a subject's experience of an object that is different from the object itself. A person can know only subjective experiences, not the object as it is in itself (*an sich*).

potlatch [POT-lach] A practice among Kwakiuti peoples of distributing gifts at ceremonial feasts according to social order.

Prakriti [pra-KRI-ti] In Hinduism, it refers to matter, as opposed to *purusha*, spirit.

pratitya-samutpada [pra-TEET-ya sam-ut-PAH-da] The Buddhist doctrine of dependent origination. It explains the experienced universe without resorting either to lawlessness or a first cause.

Presbyterians [PREZ-bit-tir-ee-uns] In the tradition of the teachings of Calvin's *Institutes of the Christian Religion*, Presbyterians base their beliefs primarily on the Bible. Governance of the church is through elected representatives. One governing body is the Presbytery.

profane [proh-FANE] Nonreligious. Outside the sphere of religion. Contemptuous of religion.

prophet [PROF-it] A person inspired by God to speak in his name. In Hebrew history, prophets in groups gave way to the messages of individual prophets such as Isaiah, Jeremiah, and Ezekiel.

puja [POO-ja] Hindu worship of deities. The ritual of worship in India.

Puranas [pu-RAHN-as] "Ancient Lore" treatises or the deities of popular Hinduism.

Puritans [PYOOR-i-tuns] Former members of the Church of England who sought to purify the church. They settled in Massachusetts and sought to establish a theocracy, a government under rule of God.

Purusha [PU-roo-sha] Primal spirit, or soul of an individual.

qiyas [KEE-yas] In Islam, analogies used in applying the Quran and the Sunna to other practical situations.

Quakers [KWAY-kurs] Members of the Society of Friends. The group was established in England by George Fox. Quakers are led by the Inner Light, through democracy.

Quetzalcoatl [KWETT-zal-coatl] The Aztec god known as the Plumed Serpent. He was god of civilization, teacher of the arts and priestcraft.

Quran [KUR-an] The sacred scriptures of the Muslims, regarded as the word of God dictated to Muhammad by God through the archangel Gabriel. The Prophet received and recited the messages over a period of approximately twenty years.

ra'y [RAA-ee] In Muslim law, the considered opinion of Muslim leaders acting for public good.

rabbi [RAB-eye] In Judaism, a teacher. After 70 C.E., rabbis were ordained interpreters and leaders of Judaism.

rak'a [RAK-ah] Each complete cycle of ritual movements that is part of Muslim prayer. During prayer Muslims stand, bow, kneel, and touch their foreheads to the ground.

Ramayana [rah-MAH-ya-na] An epic of the ideal man, Rama, and Sita, the ideal woman.

rasul [ra-SOOL] "Messenger." One who recites for God. Muhammad was the rasul of God.

reincarnation [REE-in-cahr-NAY-shun] A belief, widely shared among world religions, that a soul that has departed a body can, after a period of respite, return in the body of a newborn child. Although bodies are replaced, the soul remains essentially the same.

ren (jen) [RUN] In Confucianism, the humane principle, based on fellow-feeling. It is having deep empathy or compassion for other humans.

resurrection [RES-u-REC-shun] A belief that a person who has been dead will be restored as a whole, living person.

Rev. Sun Myung Moon Founder of the Unification Church. Born in Korea, he became a well-known religious leader in the United States.

Rita [RI-ta] The Hindu god of order and principles.

rites of passage [riits-ov-PAS-ij] A prescribed ceremonial act or series of acts. The sign that a person is passing from one stage of life to another.

rituals [RICH-oo-als] Prescribed religious ceremonies.

Ryonin [RYO-neen] In the early twelfth century C.E., founder of Amida worship in Japan.

sacrament [SAK-ra-mint] A rite instituted by Jesus as recorded in the New Testament to bestow a grace of God.

sacred [SAY-crid] Set apart for worship of a deity or as worthy of worship.

sadaqa [sah-DAH-ka] Informal charity between Muslims.

Sadducees [SAD-u-sees] Jewish leaders who claimed allegiance to the priestly descendants of Zadok, a priest in the days of King David. These wealthier Jews followed only the Torah.

saguna Brahman [SA-goo-na] In Hinduism, Brahman as he is known with his attributes. This form of Brahman has personlike qualities.

Saicho [SAI-CHOH] (Dengyo Daishi) The monk who introduced Tendai (T'ien-T'ai) Buddhism in Japan. He helped the Emperor Kwammu establish a new capital at Kyoto, diminishing the power of Buddhists at Nara.

salat [sa-LAHT] In Islam, the prescribed prayer.

sallekhana [sal-lek-HAN-na] In Jainism, a holy death achieved by fasting.

samadhi [sa-MAH-di] Concentration that unifies; absorption.

samsara [sam-SAH-ra] The Hindu concept of the wheel of rebirth that turns forever. Souls are reborn until they reach perfection.

Samskaras [sam-SKAHR-as] The sacraments or rites by which a Hindu is fully integrated into the community.

Sangha [SANG-ha] The Buddhist monastic order. Buddhism accepted both monks and nuns. The term can also include laity.

Sanhedrin [san-HEED-rin] In times of the temple, the supreme judicial body of the Jews.

sannyasin [san-NYAH-sin] One in the last stage of renunciation or detachment.

Sant [sant] A Punjabi tradition based on Bhakti worship of Vishnu.

satori [SAH-TOW-ree] The Japanese term for the Zen Buddhist experience of enlightenment.

scholasticism [sku-LAS-ti-siz-um] A medieval movement of education in which Christian schools taught particular methods of philosophy and theology.

scribe [SCRIIB] From the centuries after the Babylonian captivity of the Jews, a scribe was a trained scholar, particularly in Torah studies.

scriptures [SKRIP-churs] Sacred writings. A sacred scroll or book.

secular [SEK-u-lur] Worldly. Not spiritual or religious.

Separatists [SEP-ar-a-tists] Former members of the Church of England who settled in Massachusetts. Believing the Church of England to be beyond reform, they separated to form a new church. They sought a theocracy.

Sephardim [se-fahr-DIM] Jews who lived in medieval Spain until expelled in 1492. Those who refused to become Christians moved to North Africa, Italy, and especially Turkey, where Sultan Bayzid II admitted them gladly.

Seth [seth] In Egyptian myths, the wicked brother of Osiris. He stole the third eye from Osiris. Horus, the son of Osiris, fought Seth and recovered the third eye, symbol of kingship in Egypt.

Shahada [sheh-HAH-da] Means "witnessing." The Muslim profession of faith. There is but one God and Muhammad is his rasul or messenger.

Shakyamuni [SHAH-kya-MOO-nee] The sage of the Shakya clan, Siddhartha Gautama, the Buddha. The term is widely used in China and Japan.

shaman [SHAH-man] A Siberian term for people who have been initiated in rituals that enable them to control spirits. Shamanlike men were found among Indians of North America. In Asia, some shamans were women. Today, the term is applied to persons of many cultures.

Shang Di [shang-DI] In China, the lord of heaven. Ancestors are believed to be obedient to Shang Di as living persons are to the emperor.

Shari'a [SHA-ree-a] The duties that God has placed on the Muslim community. It is sometimes translated as "law."

Shehitah [she-HEE-tah] The Jewish method of slaughtering permitted animals or birds for food. The method is to kill the living thing as swiftly and as painlessly as possible with one swift cut across the throat.

Shema [SHEE-ma] Hear. The beginning word of Deuteronomy 6:4, "Hear, O Israel!" A declaration of God's unity, it is recited twice daily.

Shi'a [SHE-a] Members of the "party" of 'Alis, who believed that he should have been the fourth leader.

Shingon [SHIN-GOHN] Japanese for the Chinese Chen Yen school of Buddhism. It taught that matter and other Buddhas emanate from Vairocana.

Shinran [SHIN-RAN] Genku's disciple, who established the Jodo-Shin sect of Buddhism in Japan.

Shinto [SHIN-TOOH] The Japanese religion of *kami no michi*, the way of the gods. Japanese people participate in Shinto, a combination of religion and patriotism.

Shiva [SHEE-va] The Auspicious. Ultimate Lord; the destroyer.

shogun [SHOW-GOON] In Japan, a military ruler serving, ostensibly, under the emperor.

shohet [SHOW-het] A Jewish slaughterer of animals, who kills according to ritually correct methods.

Shotoku (Shotuku Taishi) [SHOOH-TOH-ku] The Japanese prince who supported the establishment of Buddhism in his country.

shouyi (Shou-i) [shoo-yi] In Daoism, to preserve the One or to meditate on the One. It includes methods of meditation on the One.

shraddha [SHRAD-dha] Last rites. The prescribed rituals for the deceased.

shruti [SHROO-ti] Sacred writings, such as the Vedas, based on what Hindu writers "heard" in revelation. These writings are revealed knowledge.

shu [SHOO] In Confucianism, reciprocity; individuals treating others as they would like to be treated. They do not do to others what they would not want done to themselves.

Shudra [SHOO-dra] In Hinduism, the fourth caste, the caste of laborers. Shudras were not permitted even to hear the reading of the Vedas.

Shvetambara [SHVAY-TAHM-ba-ra] Jains who follow the tradition that allows monks to wear clothes. Shvetambaras believe that women can obtain release from life without being reborn as a man.

Singh [sing] A "lion" of the Sikhs. The term was initiated by Guru Gobind, the tenth guru, in 1699 C.E.

smriti [SMRI-ti] Writings based on what their human authors "remembered" of revelations to Hindus. These works are less authoritative than revealed scriptures.

Soka Gakkai [SOH-ka GAHK-kai] In Japan, a group of Buddhist laypeople known as the Value Creation Society.

Soma [SOW-ma] The Hindu deity of a plant that was intoxicating. In the Vedas, soma was used in worship.

Sthanakvasis [STAHN-AK-va-sees] A group of Jains that separated from the Shvetambaras over use of idols in worship.

Suddhodana [SUD-DHOH-da-na] The king who was father of Siddhartha Gautama. He is said to have kept Siddhartha ignorant of human suffering.

sudreh [SHOOD-reh] The sacred shirt used in vesting a Zoroastrian child.

Sun Yat-sen The first leader of the republic in China after the fall of the Manchus. He reasserted Confucian virtues.

Sunna [SUN-na] The custom or tradition of Muhammad. It supplements the Quran as a source for the Shari'a.

Sunni [SOON-e] The traditional, majority, Muslims who accepted Mu'awiyah as the fourth leader.

Susanoo [su-SAH-NOOH] In Shinto, the storm god, who was brother of Amasterasu, the sun goddess.

Taiji (Tai Chi) [tai-JEE] The Great Ultimate in Zhuxi's (Chu Hsi's) Neo-Confucian philosophy. It is the rational law, or li, that works within everything.

taixi (T'ai-hsi) [tai-SHEE] In Daoism, the art of embryonic breathing, a method of holding one's breath in contemplation.

Talmud [TAL-mud] The collection of rabbinic teachings. It had deep influence over the lives of Jews from the beginning of the medieval period.

Tammuz [TAM-muz] The Babylonian version of Damuzi, the Mesopotamian god of springtime. He was a god of fertility.

Tanakh [ta-NAK] The complete Jewish Bible, comprising three parts: Torah, the five books of Moses; Nevi'im, the prophets; and Kethuvim, the writings. The first letters of the three terms yield Tanakh.

tanha [TAN-ha] In Buddhism, the thirst or craving that leads to suffering. In the second Noble Truth, it is identified as the cause of suffering.

tantras [TUN-trus] Religious treatises for developing latent powers in persons. Dialogues between Shiva and Shakti.

Tara [TAH-rah] The popular mother goddess of Tibet, associated with Avalokitesvara, the Lord Who Looks Down.

Tathagata [ta-TAH-ga-ta] A title of the Buddha, meaning: one who has thus gone.

tawhid [TAHW-heed] The Muslim doctrine of the unity of God. Islam denies any partners to God such as Christians are believed to have in their Trinity.

Tenochtitlán [TEN-ok-TIT-lan] The Aztec island city on Lake Texcoco. Hernando Cortez called it the Venice of the New World. It was the site of the major temple to the Aztec god Huitzilopochtli.

Tenrikyo [TEN-ree-KYOOH] A new religion of Japan based on the teachings of Miki Nakayama. It reveres the kami of Divine Reason.

Tezcatlipoca [tez-CAT-li-POH-ca] The Aztec lord of the night sky.

theism [THEE-iz-um] The belief that a personlike God created a law-abiding universe, but sometimes he answers prayers and performs miracles.

theodicy [THEE-od-i-se] A justification, in the presence of evil, of God's goodness, justice, and knowledge. How can an all-good, all-powerful, and all-knowing God allow evil?

theology [THEE-ol-e-jee] The discipline that describes and explains God and his relationship to the world. Theology is a formal, reasoned explanation of the beliefs of the faithful people of a religion.

Theravadins [ter-a-VAH-din] The elders, monks who imitated the Buddhas ascetic life to attain enlightenment.

Three Purities In China, three deities of Daoism: Ling Bao, the Jade Emperor, and Laozi.

Tiamat [TYU-mut] The Babylonian goddess of chaos. She was defeated by the god Marduk, who created the world.

Tian Tai (Ti'en-T'ai) [TYIAN-TAI] The Mahayana Buddhist sect of China (and Japan) that is based on the Lotus Sutra. All beings can actualize their Buddha nature and become Buddhas.

tianming (t'ien-ming) [TYIAN-MING] In Confucianism, the mandate of heaven. Zhou and Han emperors claimed to rule successfully because they followed the mandate of heaven.

Timothy Drew In 1913, in New Jersey, he taught that blacks are Asians, or Muslims. He was a contributor to the Black Muslim movement in the United States.

Tirthankara [ter-TAN-ka-ra] In Jainism, a spiritual leader who has found the crossing to the farther shore.

Tlaloc [TLAH-loc] The Aztec god of earth and rain.

Tonatiuh [TOE-na-TI-uh] An Aztec sun god.

Torah [TOR-ah] Teachings that comprise the first five books of the Bible: Genesis, Exodus, Leviticus, Numbers, and Deuteronomy.

torii [TOH-RE-EE] In Shinto, a formal gate to a shrine. It marks the entrance to sacred space.

totem [TOW-tem] An animal, plant, or object serving as the symbol of a traditional people's clan or tribe.

trickster [TRIK-stur] A male character found among stories of North American Indians. Although the trickster was not the creator, he audaciously performed deeds that latered creation. He represents the canniness admired by nonliterate peoples.

Trikaya [tre-KAH-ya] According to Buddhist doctrine, the three bodies of Buddha. The first body was indescribable, the second body is the almost divine body in which the Buddha appeared to the Mahayana faithful, and the third body was his appearance as a human being.

triloka [tri-LOW-ka] The areas of the universe considered together: upper, middle, and lower.

Trinity [TRIN-i-tee] The Christian belief that three persons in union, Father, Son, and Holy Spirit, are one God.

Tripitaka [TREE-PI-ta-ka] The "three baskets" collection of Buddhist scriptures. It is comprised of the "Vinaya Pitaka" (monastic rules), the "Sutta Pitaka" (discourses), and the "Abhidhamma Pitaka" (supplement to the doctrines).

Tsaka'bec [tsah-KAH-bec] Among the Naskapi, a hero figure. He was a trickster who altered the natural world. He exhibited a craftiness admired by the Naskapi.

Tsukiyomi [tsoo-ki-yoh-mi] In Shinto, the moon god. He is related to Amaterasu and Susanoo.

U Nu [U-NOO] A twentieth-century Buddhist leader of Burma, who was active in the United Nations.

u mueling angi [oo-MWE-ling-AHN-gi] In the creation story of Zulus, the first "comer out," followed by humans, animals and nature.

ubuthongo [oo-boo-THON-go] Zulu term for the deep sleep of persons in which ancestors can appear.

ukubuyisa idlozi rite [oo-KOO-boo-YI-sa id-LOH-si] The Zulu ritual of bringing home the ancestor after a period of mourning.

'ulama' [UL-ah-mah] Muslim clerical scholars.

ummah [UM-mah] The Muslim community.

umnayama [oom-nay-YAH-ma] Zulus use this term for a weakened state that makes a person vulnerable to environmental influences.

umnumzane [oom-nam-ZAH-ni] The head of the kraal in Zulu society.

umsamo [oom-SAH-mo] In Zulu religion, the place where ancestors are communicated with.

untouchable In Hinduism, a person, often a Shudra, who is considered by upper castes to be too impure to allow physical contact. Untouchability has been abolished.

upanayana [oo-PA-na-YAH-na] The initiation rite indicating that a boy is a twice-born person.

Upanishads [oo-PA-ne-shads] Sitting closely to a teacher; the last of the Vedas.

Utnapishtim [OOT-nu-PISH-tim] In Mesopotamia, a just man whom the gods saved from the world flood and gave immortality. He informed Gilgamesh where he could find the plant of immortality.

Vairocana [vai-ROH-cha-na] In Japanese Buddhism, the Sun, who is also the Buddha. It is also Dainichi and Amaterasu.

Vaishyas [VAI-shyas] The third Hindu caste, that of merchants and artisans. Its members participate in the Vedic practices of religion.

varna [VAR-na] Color once associated with caste.

Varuna [VA-roo-na] In Hinduism, the Rig-Veda god of the high-arched sky.

Vedanta [ve-DAHN-ta] The end of the Vedas. A name for schools of philosophy founded on teachings of the Upanishads.

Vedas [VAY-daz] Knowledge or wisdom. Scriptures of the Hindus.

Viracocha [VI-rah-COH-cha] A creator god of the Incas. He symbolized the sun.

Vishnu [VISH-noo] The Supreme Lord; the preserver.

vivaha [vi-VA-ha] Marriage. The rite of entry into the second stage or ashram, that of householder.

Vohu Manah [VOH-hoo-MAH-nu] In Zoroastrianism, Good Thought, one of the Amesha Spentas.

Wahhab [WAH-hab] One of the 99 names of Allah. 'Abd al-Wahhab means "The Servant of the Bestower."

Wakan tanka [WAH-kan-TAHN-ka] Among the Dakota peoples, the collective name of "the sacred ones," a hierarchy of spirits.

weroances [WEH-row-ance] The subchiefs, or commanders, of the Powhatan empire. Female commanders were known as **weroansquas**.

The Western Wall, Jerusalem The platform of the former Temple, destroyed by the Romans in 70 C.E.

wisakon [WI-sa-kon] The Powhatan term for medicine and substances tasting like medicine. The priests controlled all medicines of significance.

wuwei (wu wei) [WOO-WAY] The Daoist principle of accomplishing tasks without assertion. Individuals in harmony with the flow of the Dao can accomplish more than individuals who assert themselves.

Xunzi (Hsun Tzu) [SHUN-dzi] A Confucian who argued that humans are evil by nature and must be taught good rather than evil. He differed from Mengzi (Mencius), who believed that humans are born good.

Yang [YAHNG] In China, the male side of the Dao. It is exemplified in bright, warm, and dry conditions. Its opposite is Yin, the female side of the Dao.

Yashodhara [ya-SHOW-dha-ra] The wife of Siddhartha Gautama and mother of Rahula. She is said to have been a neighboring princess chosen for Prince Siddhartha.

yi [YEE] In Confucianism, internalized li, or righteousness; li as it has become a part of an individual's conduct.

Yijing (I Ching) [YEE-jing] An ancient book of China that assists people in deciding how to plan their lives in accord with the forces of the universe. The *Yijing* influenced both Daoism and Confucianism.

Yin [YIN] In China, the female side of the Dao. It is exemplified in dark, cool, and moist conditions. Its opposite is Yang, the male side of the Dao.

Yoga [YOH-ga] In Hinduism, a path of discipline. Four disciplines lead to release from rebirth.

Yogacara [YOH-ga-CHAH-ra] The Buddhist school of philosophy that teaches that neither the phenomenal world nor the mind is real. Founded by Maitreyanatha in the third century C.E., it was made famous in the fourth by Asanga.

zakat [za-KAHT] In Islam, the payment of a due to support the community. It is an act of purification through giving.

Zaoshen (Tsao Shen) [ZOW-SHEN] In Daoism, the god of the stove. The stove was essential in family life and in work of the Daoist alchemists.

Zealots [ZEL-uts] A party of Jews actively opposed to Roman occupation of Judea. They were active in the first century C.E., especially in the revolt that began in 66.

Zen [ZEN] The Japanese Buddhist meditation sect (in China, Chan) that was based on the practices of the Indian Buddhist, Bodhidharma.

Zhiyi (Chi-kai or Chi-i) [ZHIR-YEE] The monk who founded the Tian Tai sect of Buddhism in China.

zhongyong (chung yung) [JONG-YONG] In Confucianism, the doctrine of the constant mean, the path between extremes of conduct. Confucius taught that a superior man avoids excesses in his conduct.

Zhuangzi (Chuang Tzu) [JYAHNG-dzi] A later Daoist. Zhuangzi wrote, in part, to distinguish Daoism from Confucianism.

Zhuxi (Chu Hsi) [JYOO-SHEE] The leader of the Neo-Confucian revival in the twelfth century.

ziggurats [ZIG-gu-rats] In Mesopotamia, pyramidlike structures used in worship. The brick- or stone-covered mounds were topped by a house that represented the court of the deity.

Zionism [ZII-e-NIS-em] A movement led by Jews to provide a home country for themselves. Theodor Herzl was a leader at the end of the nineteenth century.

Zulu [ZOO-loo] A member of the Bantu peoples of southeast Africa. Inhabitants of South Africa.

Zurvan [ZUR-van] Among a minority of Zoroastrians, boundless time. It embraces both Ahura Mazda and Angra Mainyu.

INDEX

Abathakati, **69**
Abd al-Hamid II, 412
"Abd al-Wahhab," Muhammad
    Ibn, 411–12
Abduh, Muhammad, 412
Abdullah, 388
Abernathy, Ralph, 366
Abraham, 264, 275, 279, 280, 282,
    283–84, 291, 299, 311, 385
  family of religions, 274,
    279–426, 427
Absolute, 10–11, 431, 432
  African religions, 74
  Aztec religion, 42
  Buddhism, 11, 165–66
  Christianity, 10, 372
  Confucianism, 10, 231–32
  Daoism, 10, 216
  Egyptian religion, 56–58
  Hinduism, 10, 112–13
  Inca religion, 46
  Islam, 417–18
  Jainism, 11, 183–84
  Judaism, 10, 313–16
  Mesopotamian religion, 259–60
  North American religions, 24,
    37
  reconciliation with, 115–16
  Shinto, 244
  Sikhism, 200
  symbols and, 13
  Zoroastrianism, 270–71
Abu al-Hakam, 394
Abu Bakr, 389, 392, 398, 399
Abu Sufyan, 394, 395
Abu Talib, 388, 389, 398
Acaranga, 183
Adam, 317, 350, 374, 375, 419, 420
Adi Granth, 194, 197, **198**, 199,
    201, 202, 203
Ado, 151
Adonai, 313
Adoptionists, **349**
Advaita Vedanta, 103–4, 111
Advishta, 104

African-American churches, 366
African religions, 53–77, 437
  common features, 73–76
Afterlife. *See* Life after death.
Agama, **182**
Agamas, **85**
Agape, 343
Agemo, 72
Age of Reason, 365
Aggadah, **299**, 318, 323
Agni, 81, **85**, 85–86, 87, 89
Ahab, 289
Ahaz, 289
Ahimsa, 107, 181, **186**, 279
Ahone, **30**, 31, 37
Ahura Mazda, **267**, 268, 269, 270,
    272, 274
Ahuras, 267
Aishah, 386, 389, 398
Aiye, 73
Ajiva, 183, **185**
Akbar, 400
Akh, **61**
Akhenaton, 56, 59, 279
Akiba, 298
Akkadians, 259, 262
Al-Afghani, Jamal al-Din, 412
Alara Kalama, 131
Al-Ash'ari, 402
Albert the Great, 355, 408
Alchemy, Daoism and, 215
Alexander, Bishop, 349
Alexander the Great, 148, 259,
    294, 347
Alexius I, 406
Al-Farabi, 404
Al-Faruqi, Ismail R., 425
Al-Ghazali, Abu Hamid, 402,
    404–5, 408, 419
  philosophy after, 405
Al-Hallaj, Hosayn ibn Mansur,
    404
'Ali, 389, 392, 398, 399
Ali, Amir, 412
Ali, Noble Drew, 416

Alienation
  Shintoism, 245
  Sikhism, 200
  Zoroastrianism, 272
Allah, 388
Allegorical method, **299**
Allione, Tsultrim, 164
Almohads, 302
Alms, 396, 421
Alvaro, 408
Amar Das, 197
Amaterasu, 153, **237**, 238, 242,
    244, 248
Amaushumgalana, 263
Ambipali, 142
Ambrose, 348, 350, 351
Amenhotep IV, 56
Ameretat, 268
American Muslim Mission, **416**
Ames, Rev. Samuel, 28
Amesha Spentas, **268**, 269
Amida Buddha, 150, 153, 154
Aminah, 388
Amitabha Buddha, **150**, 152, 153,
    166
Amon-Re, **56**
Amos, 289
An, 260
Anabaptists, 360
Anahita, **270**
Analects, 221, 222
Analogy in Islam, 401
Anan ben David, 300
Ananda, 134, 138, 141, 143
Anarchy, Daoist, 225
Anatta, 165
Ancestor veneration
  Confucian, 235
  Hindu, 99
  Shinto, 248
  Yoruba, 72
  Chinese folk religion, 230
  North American religions, 40
Ancestral spirits, 66, 69, 71
Angabahya, 182

Angad, 195, 196–97
Angas, 182, 183
Anglican Church, 363–64, 376
Anglicans, **363**
Angra Mainyu, **267**, 268, 269, 270, 271, 272, 274
Anicca, 165, **165**
Animism, 157
Ankh, **58**
Anointing the Sick, sacrament of, 359
Ansar, **393**
Antiochus IV, 294, 295
Anti-Pope, 352
Anti-Semitism, 309, 310
Antyesti, **117**
Anula, 149
Anunnaki, 262
Aparagraph, 187
Apocalypse, **345**
Apocalyptic literature, **346**
Apostles, **337**
Apsu, 260
Arab Christians, 347
Arab-Israeli conflict, 311, 312, 425
Arafat, Yasir, 425
Aranyakas, **85**, 89
Archer, T. A., 407
Arhats, **133**, 144, 149, 169
Aristotle, 225, 294, 301, 302, 348, 356, 373, 404, 408
Arius, 349
Arjan, 197, 202
Arjuna, 94, 96, 97, 119
Ark of Covenant, **286**, 288, 313
Armenian church, 347
Arouet, Marie. *See* Voltaire.
Artaxerxes, 293
Artha, 98
Artharva-Veda, 85, 88
Arya Samaj, 106, 122
Aryans, 82, **84**, 85, 86, 106, 113, 191, 255, 267
Asanga, **147**
Ascetic(s)
    Buddha as, 131–32
    five, 132, 133
    Moslem, 402
    wandering, 131, 139
Ase, **72**, 73
Asha, **272**
Asha Vahista, 268
Asherah, **287**

Ashkenazim, **300**
Ashoka Maurya, 127, 143, **148**, 148–49, 158
Assyrians, 255, 259, 290
Asteya, 187
Asuras, 84
Atahualpa, 44, 45, 46
Ateek, Naim, 370
Atheism, 3
    Maoism and, 151, 159
Atman, **89**, 92, 93, 99, 100, 104, 115, 116
Aton, **56**, 58, 59
Atonement, 375
    day of, 323
Auatta, **167**
Augsburg Confession, 363
Augustine, Archbishop of Canterbury, 354
Augustine of Hippo, Saint, 348, 350, 351, 356, 375
Authentic observance, 312–13
Authoritarianism, Confucian, 234
Avalokita, 154
Avalokiteshvara, 146, 157, 166
Avatamsaka Sutra, 150
Averroës. *See* Ibn Rushd.
Avesta, 268, 272
Avidya, 100, **104**, 115
Awajale, 72
Awanawilona, **35**
Awon iya wa, **72**
Aworo, **71**
Aws, 392
Aztecs, 41–44

Ba, **61**
Baal, **287**, 289, 316
Babalawo, **20**
Babylonian exiles, 290–91
Babylonians, 255, 259, 290
Babylonian Talmud, 256, 260, 281, 299, 385
Baeck, Leo, 325
Baha'i religion, 410
Baha'u'llah, 410
Bal Gangadhar Tilak, 108
Banares, first sermon at, 132–35
Banu-Asad, 388
Baptism
    Christian, 330, 347
    sacrament of, 359, 379
    Sikh, 198

Baptists, **363**
Barabbas, 336
Bar Kokhba, 298
Bar Mitzvah, **324**
Barth, Karl, 373
Basham, A. L., 112
Basongye people, 63–67
Bast, 58
Bathsheba, 280, 288, 289
Bat Mitzvah, **324**
Beatitudes, 369
Beecher, Henry Ward, 376
Beha-ed-Din, 407, 408
Bel-Marduk, 264
Benedict, Saint, 352
Benevolence, Confucian, 222
Ben-Gurion, David, 311
Berger, Peter, 17, 209
Bergson, Henri, 412
Beyer, Stephan, 157
Bhagavad Gita, 4, 17, 82, 94–97, 99, 100, 101, 102, 120
Bhais, **202**
Bhai Gurdas, 197
Bhakti movement, 122
Bhakti yoga, **97**, 100–102, 115, 116
Bhavabhuti, 101
Bhikkus, 141
Bhutto, Benazir, 413
Bible
    interpreting, 281–82
    Mesopotamia in, 265
    Persians in, 270
    as word of God, 283
Birrell, Annie, 230
Birth rituals
    Hindu, 117
    Islamic, 422
    Jewish, 324
    North American religions, 39
    Zoroastrian, 272–73
    Zulu, 69–70
Blacker, Carmen, 236
Black Muslims, 416–17, 426
Black Stone, 387, 397, 423
Black theology, 370
Blasphemy, 334, 340
Blavatsky, Helena Petrovna, 122
Bliss, Body of, 166
Bodde, Dirk, 234
Bodhgaya, **132**
Bodhi tree, 132, 149
Bodhidharma, **150**, 154

Bodhisattvas, **145**, 146, 154, 157, 169, 171
  of mercy, 150, 154
Body of Bliss, 166
Body of Essence, 166
Bohadin. *See* Beha-ed-Din.
Bon, **157**
Book of Mormon, **368**
Boris, Saint, 354
Bowes, Pratima, 191
Brahma, **100**
Brahmacarya, 187
Brahmacharya, 97
Brahman, **89**, 91, 92, 93, 97, 99, 100, 104, 113, 116
  nirguna, **93**
  saguna, **93**
Brahmanas, **85**, 89, 104
  Satapatha, 89
Brahman-Atman, 178, 187
Brahmins, **88**, 89, 93, 94, 98, 102, 106, 118, 119, 139
Brahmo Samaj, 105, 106, 116
Brown, Raymond, 346
Brundage, Burr C., 47
Brunner, Emil, 373
Buber, Martin, 308
Buddha, 11, 81, 127, 128, 280
  compassion, 146
  first sermon, 132–35
  four passing sights, 131
  life of, 130–35, 141–42
  metaphysics and, 140–41
  ways of experiencing, 143–44
Buddhism, 94, 127–73
  absolute, 165–66
  after Buddha, 142–43
  basic tenets, 438
  in Burma, 159
  in China, 149–51, 154–55
  community and ethics, 170–71
  compassion, 170, 171
  historical development, 128–65
  historiography, 128
  humans, 167–70
  in India, 102, 132–49, 158
  in Japan, 151–57, 161–62
  in Korea, 151
  life after death, 172–73
  Mahayana, 128, **144**, 144–47, 148, 149, 159, 164, 166, 172
  Missionary, 148–49, 162
  other religions and, 173

  recent, 158–62, 164–65
  rituals, 171–72
  schools, 147–48, 149–51, 152–57
  science and, 167
  in Sri Lanka, 149
  suffering, 136, 138–39, 167–68
  symbols, 171–72
  Theravadin, 128, 140, 146–47, 148, 149, 152, 156, 159, 163, 164, 166, 172
  Three Jewels, 135
  in Tibet, 157–58
  time line, 160
  in Vietnam, 159–60
  West and, 162–64
  women, 164
  world, 166–67
  worldview, 165–73
Buddhist councils, 143
Buddhist scriptures, 142–43
Buddhist Virha Society, 163
Budge, Sir Wallis, 61
Bunjiro, Kawate, 242
Burial
  Islamic, 422
  among Naskapi, 26
Burland, Cottie, 37
Burma, Buddhism in, 159
Bushido, **239**
Butsudan, 164, **240**

Caiaphas, 336
Caliph, **398**, 399
Calvinists, 360
Calvin, John, 359–60
Campbell, Joseph, 4
Canaanites, **287**, 316
Canon, **346**, 347
Caribou Man, 25, 26
Carnarvon, Lord, 56
Carter, Howard, 56
Caste system, 81, **85**, 133
  Buddhism and, 171
  four classes within, 98
Catechumen, **345**, 348
Catherine of Siena, Saint, 352
Catholic Reformation, 361–62
Celestial Master, 215
Cerularius, Patriarch, 353
Chajang, 151
Chaldean empire, 259
Ch'an school, **150**, 154, 155, 169
Chandogya Upanishad, 91

Charismatic Christian groups, 378
Charity in Islam, 396, 422
Chatterji, Gadadhar, 106
Chau, Thich Tam, 159
Chen Yen school, 153
Cheops, 54, 56, 63
Cherokees, 31–35, 37
Chiang K'ai Shek, **229**
Chichimec, 42
China
  Buddhism, 149–51, 154–55
  Christianity, 362
  religions, 207–35, 439
  time line, 246–47
Chinvat Bridge, **269**, 273
Chosen people
  Christians, 325
  Jews, 320, 321, 324, 330
Christ, 330, 341. *See also* Messiah.
Christianity, 279, 329–81
  absolute, 372
  arts, 357–58
  basic tenets, 441
  canon, 346
  Christ's role, 372–73
  community and ethics, 375–77
  ecumenical councils, 348–50
  governance, 352–53
  Greek Orthodox, 352–55
  growth, 337–40
  historical development, 330–71
  historiography, 330
  humans, 374–75
  in India, 105, 109
  and Islam, 405–8
  and Judaism, 300, 304–5, 381
  and liberation, 369
  life after death, 380
  missionary, 279, 362, 363–64, 380
  monasticism, 351–52
  mystical, 362
  neo-orthodox, 373
  new forms, 368
  noncanonical writings, 346–47
  other religions and, 380–81
  persecution, 340, 344–46
  Protestant, 358–61, 363–67
  rituals and symbols, 378–80
  Roman Catholic, 352–55, 361–62, 369
  sacraments, 335, **347**, 379–80

time line, 338–39
women, 370–71
world, 373–74
worldview, 371, 372–81
worship, 347
Christian Platonists, 347–48
Christian Reformation, 358
Christian Science, 366–67
Christmas, 379, 417
Chuang Tzu. *See* Zhuangzi.
Chu Hsi. *See* Zhuxi.
Chung-ying Cheng, 209
Chung yung. *See* zhongyong.
Chun-tzu. *See* Jungzi.
Church, **340**
Church of Christ, Scientist, 366–67
Church of England, 360, 361, 363, 371
Church of Jesus Christ of Latter-day Saints, 368
Cicero, 350
Circumcision, 324, 342
Civil religion, **365**
Clark, Walter H., 17
Clement, 299, 348
Clement VII, anti-Pope, 352
Clothing in Jainism, 179–80, 182
Coatlicue, 42
Cohen, A., 322
Cohen, Hermann, 309, 324
Columbus, Christopher, 178
Communion, 6, 379
Communism, Buddhism and, 158–59
Community, 12
    Buddhist, 12, 170
    Christian, 12, 375–77
    Confucian, 233–34
    Daoist, 218
    Hindu, 12, 116
    Islamic, 421–22
    Jain, 187
    Jewish, 12, 319–22
    North American religions, 38–39
    Sikh, 201
Compassion, 170, 171, 222
Cone, James H., 370
Confession of sins, final, 379
Confirmation, sacrament of, 359, 379
Confucianism, 209, 210, 219–35

absolute, 231–32
after Confucius, 225–26
community and ethics, 233–34
Daoism and, 211, 225
example in, 221
Five Relations, 241
historical development, 219–31
historiography, 219–20
human goodness, 220
in Korea and Japan, 228–29
life after death, 235
Neo-, 227–28
rituals and symbols, 234–35
under Mao Tse-tung, 229–30
world, 232
worldview, 231–35
Confucius, 5, 11, 208, 211, **219**, 231, 280
    challenges to, 223–25
    life, 220
    teachings, 220–22
    view of heaven, 231
Congregational organizations, 377
Congregational worship, 292, 378
Consensus of community, 401
Conservative Judaism, 307, 308, 312, 318
Constantine, 329, 349
Contemplation in Daoism, 217
Copernicus, Nicholas, 373, 410
Coptic church, 347
Coricancha, 46, 47
Cortez, Hernando, 42, 44
Council of Chalcedon, 349
Council of Nicea, 349
Council of Trent, 359
Counterreformation, 374
Covenent, **284**, 320, 325
    Ark of, **286**, 288, 313
    new vs. old, 374
Coyote, 38
Cragg, Kenneth, 424
Craving, 136, 137–38
Creation stories, 4
    Cherokee, 33, 37
    Hebrew, 313, 317, 318
    Japanese, 236–37
    Mesopotamian, 260
    Zulu, 70
    Zuni, 37
Creed of Judaism, 313. *See also* Shema.

Cremation, 248
Crescas, Hasdai, 302
Crow, Carl, 220
Crusades, 357, 406–8
Cuneiform, **9**
Cyril, 355
Cyrus the Great, 255, 259, 268, 269, 293, 296

Dainichi, 153
Dakhma, **273**, 275
Dakota peoples, 36
Dalai Lama, 127, 159
Damuzi, **259**, 260, 261, 263
Dance
    lord of, 112, 114
    sacred, 6, 37, 73, 112
Daniel, 265, 296, 343
Dante, 405
Dao, **209**, 212, 225
Dao De Jing, 208, 210, 212, 213, 214, 216, 218
Daoism, 209, 210–19
    absolute, 216
    community and ethics, 218
    Confucianism and, 211, 225
    historical development, 211–16
    historiography, 211
    humans, 216–18
    in Korea and Japan, 228–29
    rituals and symbols, 218–19
    sectarian, 215–16
    Three Purities of, 216
    world, 216
    worldview, 216–19
Daoists, **214**, 225
Darius, 269
Darmesteter, J., 269
Darwin, Charles, 374, 410
Dasas, 86
David, 280, 288, 289, 290, 316, 319
Day of atonement, 323
Days of Awe, 323
Death, life after. *See* Life after death.
Death rites
    Christian, 379
    Egyptian, 61
    Hindu, 117–18
    Jewish, 324
    North American religions, 39
    Zoroastrian, 273

Zulu, 70
De Bary, Wm. Theodore, 150
Deborah, 280
Deepavali, 119
Definitions, types of, 17
Deism, **365**
De Leon, Moses, 303
Dengyo Daishi, **152**, 156
Dervishes, 403
Descartes, René, 305, 365
Descriptive definitions, 17
Destiny, 138
Devadatta, 135
Devas, 84, 267
Dhamma, 141
Dharma
    Buddhist, **128**, 133, 142, 143,
       146, 148, 171, 172
    Hindu, **98**
Dharmakaya, 166
Dharma Shastras, 105
Dharma Wheel, 171–72
Dhyana, **154**
Dhimmis, **401**
Diaspora, **299**
Dietary laws. See Kashruth.
Digambaras, **179**, 180, 181, 182,
    184, 186
Dinesen, Isak, 5
Dinka people, 74
Diocletian, 345
Disharmony, 217, 233
Divali, 117
Diversity in religion, 431–32
Divination, 20, 26, 29, 30, 67, 71
Divine Principle, 368, **369**
Divine Reason, kami of, 243, 244
Divorce, 379, 422
Domitian, 345, 346
Dosho, 155
Drama, religious, 6–7
Dravidians, **84**, 85, 191
Dreaming, Daoism on, 214–15
Drew, Timothy, **416**
Driver, Harold E., 36
Dualism
    Hindu, 92–93, 104
    Manichaean, 270, 373
    Zoroastrian, 269, 270, 274
Duchesne-Guillemin, Jacques,
    269
Dughdhova, 267
Dukkha, **136**, 136–37, 165

Durga, 101
Durkheim, Emile, 17

Ea, **260**
Earnestness, Confucian, 222
Easter, 7, 379
Eastern Orthodox Church, **364**,
    374. See also Greek Orthodox
    Church.
Eating as symbol in Sikhism, 202
Ecclesiastes, 294
Economia, 350
Ecumenical, **349**
Ecumenical councils, 348–50
Eddy, Mary Baker, **366**, 367
Education, need for, 233
Edwards, Jonathan, 363
Efile Mukulu, **64**, 65, 66
Egyptian religion, 54–63
    absolute, 56–58
    Hebrews and, 284–85
    historical development, 55–56
    life after death, 61–63
    other religions and, 63
    rituals and symbols, 58
    worldview, 56–63
Egypt, Islam in, 413–14
Eightfold Path, **136**, 139, 168. See
    also Middle Path.
Eight mirrors, 169
Einhorn, David, 307
Ek Oankar, 195
Eliade, Mircea, 2, 431, 432
Elijah, 289, 319, 334, 337, 424
Ellis, Marc, 310
Ellwood, Robert, 245
Elohim, 291
Emerkur, 264
Emerson, Ralph Waldo, 122
Enki, 260, 261
Enkidu, **262**
Enlightenment, 132, 138, 169, 365
Enlil, 260, 262
En Soph, 303, 316
Enuma Elish, 260
Epic, **4**
Episcopal Church, 363, 377
Epistles, **346**
Equality, Mohist, 225
Ereshkigal, 261, 262
Essence, Body of, 166
Essenes, **295**, 329
Essential definitions, 17

Esther, 280, 323
Esu, **71**
Ethics, 12
    Buddhist, 170–71
    Christian, 375–77
    Confucian, 12, 233–34
    Daoist, 12, 218
    Hindu, 116
    Islamic, 421–22
    Jain, 12, 187
    Jewish, 319–22
    North American religions,
       38–39
    Sikh, 201
Ethiopian Christians, 347
Ethiopian Jews, 319
Eucharist, sacrament of, 359, 378
Evangelists, independent
    Protestant, 366
Eve, 317, 374, 419, 420
Ewing, Joan, 164
Excommunicate, **353**
Ezekiel, 265, 280, 293
Ezra, 293

Fa-Chia. See Fajia.
Fackenheim, Emil, 310
Fajia, 210, **224**, 224–25
Falashas, 319
Family
    Hinduism, 116
    Shinto, 245
Fard, W. D., 416
Farrakhan, Louis, 416
Fatima, 388
Fa Zang, 150, 169
Feast of Lights, 323
Feast of Weeks, 340
Felicitas, 344, 345
Final confession, 379
First Communion, 379
Five ascetics, 132, 133
Five Ks, 198
Five Pillars of Islam, 396, 417
Five Relations of Confucianism,
    241
Flame, sacred, 257, 272
Flavius Josephus, 297
Flavius Silva, 297
Florus, 296
Flower Garland Buddhism, 149,
    150
Folk religion, Chinese, 230–31

Food laws. *See* Kashruth.
Four Apes, 62, 63
Four Noble Truths, 12, 127, 128, 133, 135, **136**, 139
Fourth Lateran Council, 352
Fox, George, 361
Fox, Richard G., 203
Francis, King, 359
Francis of Assisi, Saint, 351, 352, 373
Frank, Anne, 310
Frankel, Zacharias, 306–7
Frederick II, 406
Free church tradition, 360
Freud, Sigmund, 13, 17
Friedman, R. E., 282
Frugality, 218
Functional definitions, 17
"Fundamentalism"
    Christian, 313
    Islamic, 313, 412
Fung Yu-Lan, 223
Fusokyo, 242

Galilei, Galileo, 373
Gandhi, Indira, 111, 119, 203
Gandhi, Mohandas K., 81, 82, 107–8, 186, 376
Ganesh, 101
Gathas, 267, 268
Gautama, 104
Geertz, Clifford, 17
Ge Hong, 215
Geiger, Abraham, 306, 307
Gelb, Saint, 354
Gelede festival, 72
Gelugpa, **158**, 159
Gemarah, **299**
Genku, **153**
Gentiles, 342
Geonim, 300
Ghose, Sri Aubindo, 81, 108–9, 116
Gibb, Hamilton A. R., 412
Gilgamesh, **260**, 262–63
    epic of, 258, 260, 262, 263
Gnostic systems, 303, 402
Gobind Rai, 198. *See also* Gobind Singh.
Gobind Singh, 198, 201, 202
God
    Judaism, 281–82, 285–87, 313–16

Sikhism, 192–94, 195, 196
    proof of existence, 356
    union with, 196, 200–201
Golden Rule, 224
Golden Temple, 119, 178, 197, 201, 203
Gomer, 289
Good Friday, 379
Good ruler, 225
Good Samaritan, parable of, 333
Gordis, Robert, 320
Gospel, **346**
    of John, 333, 334–35, 346, 372
    of Luke, 330, 331, 336, 346, 372
    of Mark, 333, 346, 372
    of Matthew, 346, 372
    of Thomas, 347
Grace
    Christian view, 350–51, 374
    Sikh view, 196
Graham, A. C., 226, 233
Graham, Billy, 366
Great Awakening, 363
Great Plains peoples, 36, 37
Great Soul, 82
Great Sun, 153
Great Ultimate, 228
Greek Orthodox Church, 364. *See also* Eastern Orthodox Church.
    governance, 352–53, 376, 377
    path of service, 353–55
    patriarch, 353
Greek influence
    on Islam, 401–2
    on Judaism, 293–94
Gregory I, Pope, 354
Gregory II, Pope, 353
Gregory XI, Pope, 352
Guanyin, 146, **150**, 166. *See also* Kwannon.
Guan Zhong, **224**
Gurdwaras, 201, **202**, 203
Guru, **90**, 90–92
    in Sikhism, **194**
Gutierrez, Gustavo, 370

Haddad, Yvonne Yazbeck, 426
Hadiths, **397**, 401
Hadrian, 298
Hagar, 279, 284, 423
Haggadah, **323**
Hajj, **395**, 397, 423

Halakhah, **299**, 318, 322
    standard for Jewishness, 312
Halevi, Judah, 301–2, 320
Halimah, 388
Hammurabi, 5, 260
    law code of, 257, 260
Hanbalite school, 401, 412
Han Fe Tzu. *See* Han Feizi.
Han Feizi, **224**
Hanif, **389**
Hanifite school, 401
Hanukkah, **295**, 323
Han Yu, 227
Haoma, 87, **270**, 273
Hara-kiri, **239**
Haran, 283, 284
Har Gobind, 197
Haribhadra, 185
Harijans, 107
Harkishan, 197
Harmony, 233
    in Japan, 244
    of mean, 221
    of opposites, 212
    in social relationships, 12, 231
    universal, 235
    with nature, 12, 216
Har Rai, 197
Hasan, 398
Hashim, 389, 392
Hasidism, 308
Hatcher, William S., 410
Hatha Yoga, 157
Hathor, **56**, 58
Hawazin, 395
Heart Sutra, 154
Heaven
    Chinese view, 209
    Christian view, 379, 380
    Confucian view, 231
    mandate, 222, 231
    Muslim view, 423, 424
Hebrew history, 284–91
Hebrew prophets, 280, 288–90, 316, 385
Heilsgeschichte, 282
Hell
    Christianity, 379, 380
    Islam, 423, 424
Henotheism, **37, 113**
Henry VIII, 360–61, 363
Heresies, **349**
Heretics, **347**

Herod, 296, 329, 330, 334
Hertzberg, Arthur, 320
Herzl, Theodor, 306, 307, 309, 310
Heschel, Susannah, 318
Hideyoshi, 362
Hieroglyphics, **9**
Hick, John, 431
Hijrah, **392**, 398, 404
Hillel, **298**, 333
Hinayana, 144
Hinduism, 82–122
   absolute, 10, 112–13
   basic tenets, 437
   community and ethics, 116
   four goals, 97–98
   historical development, 83–112
   historiography, 83
   humans, 115–16
   monogamy, 117
   origins, 83–85
   orthodox philosophical sys-
      tems, 103–4
   other religions and, 121–22
   reincarnation, 119–20
   response to Western influence,
      105
   rituals and symbols, 117–19
   time line, 110
   in the United States, 122
   women, 111
   world, 113–15
   worldview, 112–22
Hinnells, J., 274, 275
Hirsch, Samson Raphael, 307
Historiography, 8
   Buddhist, 128–29
   Christian, 330
   Confucianist, 219–20
   Daoist, 211
   Hindu, 83
   Islamic, 386
   Jewish, 282–83
   Mesopotamian religion, 258
   Shinto, 236
   Sikh, 190–91
   Zoroastrian, 267
History. *See* Interpretation of his-
   tory; Time line.
Hitler, Adolf, 309, 310
Holi, 119
Holocaust, **309**, 310–11, 320
Holy Orders, sacrament of, 359,
   379

Holy Spirit, 330, 337, 348, 361,
   363, 377, 378
Holy War, Christian, 357
Honen Shonin, **153**
Honmichi, 243
Honor in Shinto, 245
Hopi, 35
Horus, **56**, 60, 285
Hosea, 289
Hourvatat, 268
House of Growth, 243
Hozo Bosatsu, 150, **153**, 154
Hsuan-tsang, 155
Hsun Tsu. *See* Xunzi.
Huacas, **46**
Huanacauri, 47
Huang Di, 215
Huang Tsung-hsi. *See* Zongzi.
Huan Tui, 220
Huascar, 46, 47
Hua-Yen, **150**, 169
Huitzilopochtli, **41**, 42, 43
Humaneness, 222
Humanist, **359**
Humans, 11
   Buddhism, 167–70
   Christianity, 374–75
   Confucianism, 233
   Daoism, 216–18
   Hinduism, 115–16
   Islam, 419–21
   Jainism, 185–86
   Judaism, 318–19
   North American religions, 37
   problem for. See Problem for
      humans.
   Shinto, 245
   Sikhism, 200–201
   solution for. See Solution for
      humans.
   sub-Saharan African religions,
      75
   Zoroastrianism, 272
Human sacrifice
   among Aztecs, 41, 42–43, 44
   among Pawnee, 36
Humility, 218
Humphries, Christmas, 155
Hunting, 25–26, 38
Husayn, 398, 399, 426
Huskanaw, **31**
Hutchinson, Anne, **363**
Huwawa, 262

"I and Thou" relationships, 308
Iblis, 417
Ibn Arabi, 402, 405
Ibn Rushd, 408–9
Ibn Sina, 404
I Ching. *See* Yijing.
Iconoclast, **353**
Iconodule, **353**
Iconostasis, **353**
'Id al-Adha, 423
Id al-Fitr, 422
Idowu, Bolaji, 72
Ife, 20, **71**, 73
Ignatius of Loyola, 361–62
Ihlambo, **70**
Ihram, 397, **423**
Ijma', **401**
Ikeda, Daisaku, 161, 163
Imam, 398, 399
Imamis, 398
Inaction, 218
Inanna, **259**, 260, 261, 262, 263
Incarnation, **372**, 375
Inca peoples, 44–49
Index of Prohibited Books, 369
India
   Buddhism, 102, 132–49, 158
   Christianity, 105, 109
   Islam, 104, 409–10, 412
   independent, 109–11
   religions, 81–204
Indra, 81, **86**, 86–87, 182
Indrabhuti Gautama, 182
Indulgences, **358**, 359
Infanticide, 38
Initiation rituals
   Hindu, 117
   Jewish, 324
   Powhatan, 31, 39
   Sanpoil, 39
   Sikh, 198
   Zulu, 70
Inkosazana, **70**, 74
Inkosi Yezulu, **70**, 74
Inner Light of Christ, 361, 377
Inquisition, 305
International Society for Krishna
   Consciousness, 119, 122
Interpretation of history, 12–13
   Buddhism, 171
   Christianity, 12–13, 378
   Hinduism, 12, 117
   Judaism, 12

North American religions, 39
Zoroastrianism, 274
Inti, **46**, 47
Iqbal, Muhammad, 412, 413
Iranian religion. *See* Zoroastrianism.
Iran, Islam in, 414–15
Iraqi religion, ancient, 258–66, 439
Irenaeus, Saint, 375
Isaac, 279, 280, 284, 289
Isaiah, 269, 280, 289, 293, 369
Isaiah (Second), 293
Isangoma, **71**
Ishatpragbhara, **182**, 184
Isha Upanishad, 107
Ishmael, 279, 280, 284, 385, 423
Ishtar, **260**, 261, 262
Isis, 56, **60**, 63, 285
Islam, 279, **305**, 385–427
  absolute, 417–18
  background, 386–88
  basic tenets, 441
  Christianity and, 405–8
  community and ethics, 422–23
  expansion, 399–401
  Five Pillars of, 396
  future of, 425–27
  Greek influence, 401–2
  historical development, 386–417
  historiography, 386
  humans, 419–21
  in India, 104, 409–10, 412
  Judaism and, 304–5, 406
  life after death, 423–24
  missionary, 279
  modernism, 410–13
  monotheism, 396, 417
  mysticism, 402–4, 409
  Nation of, **416**, 417
  other religions and, 405–8, 424–25
  recent decades, 413–15
  rituals and symbols, 422–23
  Shi'a, **398**, 399, 410, 412
  spiritual experiences, 402
  Sunni, **398**, 399
  time line, 390–91
  women, 419, 425–26
  world, 418–19
  worldview, 417–27
Ismail, 399

Ismailis, 398, 399
Israel [Jacob]. *See* Jacob.
Israel [nation], 310
  Arab conflict, 311, 312, 425
Israel Baal Shem, 308
Itihasa-Purana, **85**, 94
Izanagi, **236**, 237, 241
Izanami, **236**, 237, 241
Izingyanga zemithi, 67
Izinyanga zezulu, **69**
Izumo Oyashirokyo, 241

Jackson, Jesse, 366
Jacob, 284, 289, 311
Jacobsen, Thorkild, 259, 260
Jade Emperor, **215**, 216
Jaimini, 104
Jainai, 223
Jainism, 94, 178–89, 204
  absolute, 183–84
  basic tenets, 438
  community and ethics, 187
  historical development, 179–83
  humans, 185–86
  nonviolence, 186–87
  other religions and, 189
  rituals and symbols, 188–89
  scriptures, 182–83
  time line, 193
  world, 184–85
  worldview, 183–89
James, 329, 352
James, William, 17
Janamsakhi, 191
Janëu, **117**, 191
Japan
  Buddhism, 151–57
  Christianity, 362
  foreign influence and, 239–40
  Korean visitors, 236
  myths, 236–38
  new religions, 243
  religions, 235–49, 439
  time line, 246–47
Japji, **192**, 192–94
Jatakas, **144**
Jatis, 106
Jen. *See* Ren.
Jeremiah, 280, 293
Jesuits, 362
Jesus, 102, 279, 296, 319, 325, 329, 385
  first appearance, 330–31

last week, 335–37
  teachings, 331–33, 334–35
Jewels of Buddhism, 135, 144
Jewish identity, 311–12
Jewish philosophy, 300–304
Jezebel, 289
Jhana, **136**
Jikkokyo, 242
Jimmu, **237**, 238
Jina, **182**, 183, 188
Jinasena, 184
Jingtu, **150**
Jinn, **389**
Jiva, 183, **184**, 184–85
Jizyah, 396
Jnana yoga, **96**, 100, 115, 116
Jnatrputra Vardhamana, 180, 181
Jodo school, **153**, 163
John XXIII, Pope, 369
John Chrysostom, Saint, 350
John, Gospel of, 333, 334, 346, 372
John of Damascus, Saint, 353
John of Galilee, 329, 352
John of the Cross, 362
John the Baptist, 296, 329, 330, 331, 334–35, 385
Jonathan, 288
Jordan, David K., 230
Joseph Barnabas, 341
Joseph [father of Jesus], 334
Joseph [son of Jacob], 280, 284
Joseph of Arimathea, 337
Josephus, 295
Joshua, 280, 287
Judah the Patriarch, 299
Judaism, 279, 280–325
  absolute, 313–16
  basic tenets, 440
  Christianity and, 300, 304–5, 381
  community and ethics, 319–22
  Conservative, 307, 308, 312, 318
  Greeks and, 293–94
  Hasidic, 308
  historical development, 282–313
  historiography, 282–83
  Holocaust, 309, 310–11
  humans, 318–19
  Islam and, 304–5, 406
  Israel and, 310
  Kabbalah, 303–4
  life after death, 324–25

medieval, 300
modern age, 305–6
Orthodox, 282, 307, 308, 312, 318, 321, 322
Reconstructionist, 307–8
Reform, 282, 307, 308, 312, 318, 321, 322
rituals and symbols, 323–24
Romans and, 295–99
Talmudic, 300
time line, 314–15
wisdom literature, 294
world, 317
worldview, 313–25
Judaizers, **342**
Judas Iscariot, 335
Judas Maccabee, 295
Judas of Galilee, 296, 329
Judgment of dead, Egyptian, 61–63
Julius II, Pope, 358
Julius III, Pope, 362
Jung, C. G., 209
Junzi, **221**, 222, 225, 234, 239
Justinian, 355

Ka, **61**
Ka'bah, 6, 194, 385, **387**, 394, 395, 423
Kabbalah, 303–4
Kabir, 104, **191**, 195
Kachinas, **35**
Kafilefile, **65**, 66
Kaghi, Soryu, 163
Kalachakra, **157**
Kali, 101
Kalpa, 93, 113
Kalupahana, David, 148
Kama, 98
Kamasutra, 98
Kami, **235**, 237, 238, 239, 240, 241, 242, 244
of Divine Reason, 243
Kami-dana, **240**
Kami no michi, 235
Kanada, 104
Kanishka, 143
Kanjur, 142
Kant, Immanuel, 309, **431**
Kapalakundala, 101
Kapila, 103
Kaplan, Mordecai, 307–8
Karaites, 300, 301

Karbala, 399
Karma
  Buddhist, **139**, 139–40, 167, 172
  eight types, 186
  Hindu, 81, 93, 94, 115, 194
  Jain, 185, 186
  Law of, **93**, 104, 112, 115, 116, 170, 183, 185, 187, 189
  samsara and, 93–94
  Sikh, 195, 200
Karma yoga, 94, 96, 99–100, 116
Karuna, 170
Kashruth, **307**, 308, 320, 321
Kashyapa, 133, 150
Kaufmann, Yehezkel, 291
Kelleher, Theresa, 234
Kerygma, **340**
Kew, J. E. Michael, 21
Khadijah, 386, 388, 389
Khalid Ibn al-Walid, 394, 395, 399, 400
Khalid Ibn Said, 389
Khalsa, 198, 201
Khan, Sayyid Ahmad, 412
Kharijites, 398, 401
Khazraj, 389
Khomeini, Ruhullah Musavi, 414, 426
Khshatra Vairya, 268
Kibbutzim, 311
King, Martin Luther, Jr., **366**, 376
King, Noel, 75
Kingsu, 260
Kirpan, 198, 202
Kirtana, 122
Kisagotami, 141, 142
Kiswah, **423**
Kivas, **35**
Klostermaier, Klaus K., 92
Knox, John, 360
Koans, **155**
Kobo Daishi, **152**
Ko Hong. *See* Ge Hong.
Kojiki, 236, 241
Kokobunji, 238
Kongfuzi. *See* Confucius.
Konjin, 242
Konko Daijin, 242
Konkokyo, 242
Korea
  Buddhism, 151
  Confucianism and Daoism, 228–29

Kosher food laws, 307, **308**, 342. *See also* Kashruth.
Koshering, 321
Krishna, **94**, 95, 96, 97, 99, 101, 106, 113, 119, 122
Krishna Consciousness, International Society for, 119, 122
Kshatriyas, **94**, 98
Kuan Chung. *See* Guan Zhong.
Kueiken sect, 171
Kukai, **152**, 153
Kurozumikyo, 242
Kusti, **273**
Kwakiutl people, 26–27
Kwannon, 154. *See also* Guanyin.
Kyodan, P. L., 243
Kyomik, 151

Lakshmi, 101
Lama, **158**
Lankavatara Sutra, 150
Lao Tzu. *See* Laozi.
Laozi, 5, 208, **211**, 211–14, 216, 217, 219, 225
Lapide, Pinchas, 325
Lau, D. C., 219
Law of Karma, **93**, 104, 112, 115, 116, 170, 183, 185, 187, 189
Laws of Manu, 89, **98**, 98–99, 102–3, 109
Law of Moses, 295, 332, 333
Law of Return, 312
Layard, Sir Austin Henry, 258
Lazarus, 335
Leaf, Murray J., 202
Legalists. *See* Fajia.
Leo III, Emperor, 353
Leo IX, Pope, 353
Leo X, Pope, 359
Lessing, Gotthold, 305, 306
Letting go, 138–39
Levites, 288
Li, **221**, 222
Liberal Christians, 374
Liberation theology, **369**, 369–71, 373
Libya, Islam in, 414
Li Chi. *See* Li Ji.
Life, four stages of, 98–99
Life after death
  ancient Egypt, 13, 61–63
  Buddhism, 172–73

Christianity, 380
Confucianism, 13, 235
Hinduism, 13, 119–20
Islam, 13, 423–24
Judaism, 324–25
North American religions, 30, 40
Shintoism, 13, 248
Sikhism, 202–3
sub-Saharan African religions, 76
Zoroastrianism, 273–74
Li Ji, **221**
Lin Chi, 155
Ling Bao, 216
Little, Malcolm. *See* Malcolm X.
Living things, respecting, 183, 186–87
Locke, John, 305, 365
Logos, 348
Loka, **184**
Lord's Supper, 335, 347, 359
Lot, 284
Lotus Buddhism, 149–50
Lotus Sutra, 149
Love, universal, 223
Luckmann, Thomas, 17
Luke, Gospel of, 330, 331, 336, 346, 372
Lumumba, Patrice, 64
Luria, Isaac, 304, 324
Lutheranism, 359, 361
Lutherans, 363, **364**
Luther, Martin, 358–59, 360, 373

Maat. *See* Mayet.
Maccabean revolt, 294–95
Machiavelli, Niccolo, 224
Machu Picchu, 46
Madhyamika school, **147**
Madrasas, 411
Magi, **269**
Magic, 30, 64, 66
    Daoism and, 215
Magnanimity, Confucian, 222
Mahabharata, 82, **85**, 94
Mahajapati, 135
Mahakashyapa, 133, 141, 142
Mahapadma, 143
Mahasanghikas, 143, 144. *See also* Mahayanists.
Mahavibhasa, 143
Mahavira, 81, 94, 179–82, 183,

186, 188, 189, 280
Mahayanists, 128, **144**, 144–46, 148, 159, 164, 168, 172
    in China, 149–50
    idea of absolute, 166
    idea of world, 166
    in Japan, 151–54, 155–57
    in Korea, 151
    Theravadins and, 146–47
Mahdi, **399**
Mahendra, 149
Mahisha, 101
Maimonides, 281, 302–3, 318, 323, 408
Maitreyi, 90, 91, 144, **171**
Ma Jnanananda, 111
Makiguchi Tsunesaburo, **161**
Malamat, Abraham, 291
Malananda, 151
Malatimadhava, 101
Malcolm X, **416**, 427
Malikite school, 401
Mallowan, Sir Max, 258
Malunkyaputta, 140, 141
Mamanatowick, **28**
Mandala, **153**, 157
Mandate of heaven, 222, 231
Mandela, Nelson, 67
Mani, **270**, 271
Manichaeism, 270, 373
Mankishi, **66**
Mantra, **153**, 157
Mantu, **23**
Manu, **85**, 89, 98–99, 102–3, 109
Maoism, 151, 158–59
Mao Tse-tung, 15, 158, 159, **229**, Confucianism under, 229–30
Mao Zedong, **229**. *See also* Mao Tse-tung.
Mara, **132**, 148
Mardana, 178, 194, 195
Marduk, **260**, 264, 293
Mark, Gospel of, 333, 346, 372
Marriage ceremonies
    Hindu, 117
    Jewish, 324
    Muslim, 422
    North American religions, 39–40
    Zulu, 70
Marriage sacrament, 359
Martel, Charles, 400
Martin, J. Douglas, 410

Marx, Karl, 158
Marxism, 158. *See also* Communism; Maoism.
    liberation theology and, 370
Martha, 335
Mary, 329, 334. *See also* Virgin Mary.
Masaharu, Taniguchi, 243
Masakane, Inoue, 242
Masamochi, Yoshimura, 242
Masani, Rustom, 267, 268, 269, 272
Mather, Cotton, 373
Mattathias, 295
Matthew, Gospel of, 346, 372
Matzah, **286**
Maundy Thursday, 379
Mawdudi, Abul Ala, 413
Maya, **89**, 92, 104, 115
Maya people, 41, 44
Maya [Queen], 127, 130, 131, 135
Mayet, **56**, 61
Mbiti, John S., 64
McCrary, Ben C., 27, 30
Mean, 225
Meditation
    Buddhist, 147
    Sikh, 196
Meditation Buddhism, 149, 150, 154–55
Meir, Golda, 281, 311
Meir, Rabbi, 299
Membership of religions
    in Canada, 435
    in United States, 435
    worldwide, 436
Mencius, 223, **226**. *See also* Mengzi.
Mendelssohn, Moses, 302, 305–6, 320
Mengzi, **226**, 226, 233. *See also* Mencius.
Menes, 55
Mercy, 218
Merriam, Alan P., 64, 66, 67
Mesoamerican religions, 41–44, 436
    common features, 49–50
Mesopotamia, 257, 258
    in Bible, 265
Mesopotamian religion, 258–66, 439
    absolute, 259–60

historical development, 258–59
historiography, 258
myths, 260–62
other religions and, 264–65
rituals and symbols, 263–64
time line, 266
worldview, 259–65
Messiah, **296**, 319, 325, 330, **334**
false, 381
Messianic Age, 309, 324
Methodists, **363**
Methodius, Bishop, 348
Methodius of Russia, 355
Micah, 289
Michelangelo, 358
Middle Path, 133, 139, 147, 189.
See also Eightfold Path.
Midrash, **298**
Mihrab, **422**
Mikishi, **66**
Miko, 236
Ming, 222
Miracle, **331**
Mishnah, **298**, 299, 312
Misogi harai, 242
Misogikyo, 242
Missionary Buddhism, 148–49,
162
Missionary Christianity, 279, 362,
363–64
Mista´peo, **24**
Mithra, **270**
Mitra, **88**
Mitzvot, **307**, 319, 322
Model person, 221
Modernism, **305**
Islam and, 410–13
Moguls, 104, 410
Mohists, 210, **223**, 223–24, 225
Moksha, **93**, 98, 182, 188
Monasticism
Buddhist, 156, 172
Christian, 351–52
Monism, 92–93, 103
Monophysites, **349**
Monotheism, **37**, 74, 104
of Akhenaton, 56, 279
Islamic, 389, 417
Jewish, 309, 320, 323
Sikh, 199–200
Zoroastrian, 268, 270
Montezuma, 44
Mooney, James, 33, 35

Moral code, Hindu, 116
Morality, Buddhist, 170–71
Morley, S. G., 44
Mormon, Book of, **368**
Moses, 280, 285–87, 291, 313, 316,
318, 319, 323, 337, 366, 378
Law of, 295, 332, 333
Mo Tzu. *See* Mozi.
Mountain worship sects, 241, 242
Mou Tzu, 149
Moyers, Bill, 4
Mozi, **223**
Mu, 151
Mu'awiyah, 398
Mubarak, Hosni, 414
Mudang, 151
Mudras, **153**, 157
Muezzin, **396**
Muhajirun, **393**
Muhammad, 102, 279, 325, 385,
386, 402, 405, 421, 423, 424,
425
life, 388–95
teachings, 395–98
Muhammad Abduh, 397
Muhammad al-Mahdi al-Hujja,
398
Muhammad, Elijah, **416**, 417, 426
Muhammad, Wallace Deen, 416
Muharram, 398
Mummification, 61
Munetada, Kurozumi, 242
Murjites, 401
Musa al-Kazim, 399
Muslim brotherhood, 414
Muslims, **300**
Black, 416–17, 426
Mu'tazilites. 401, 402
Myrdal, Jan, 119
Mystery religions, **342**
Mysticism
Christian, 362
Muslim, 402–4, 409
Myth, **4**, **33**

Naboth, 289
Nagarjuna, **147**
Nagasena, 140
Nagid, 302
Nakayama, Miki, **243**
NAM, 200
Nanak, 81, 104, 178, 190, 197, 198,
202, 203

life, 191–95
teachings, 195–96
Nandi, 101
Nao, Deguchi, 242
Naozot, **273**
Naskapi people, 21–26
Nasr, Seyyed Hossein, 404
Nasser, Gamal Abdel, 413, 414
Nataraja, 112
Nathan, 289
Nationalism
Shinto, 240
Zoroastrian, 269
Nation of Islam, **416**, 417
Native American Church, 40
Natural force, 228. *See also* Qi.
Natural order, 228. *See also* Li.
Nature in Daoism, 214, 217
Natyasastras, 98
Navjote ceremony, 274
Nebuchadnezzar, 260, 265, 290
Nefertiti, 58
Nehemiah, 293
Nehru, Jawaharlal, 81, 82
Neo-Confucianism, 227–28, 229,
230, 231, 232, 239
Neo-orthodox Christian theology,
373
Neoplatonism, 402, 419
Nero, 343, 344, 345
Nestorian Christians, 256, 347
Neufeldt, R, W., 203
Nevi'im, 281
New Testament, 337, 343, 345,
360, 376, 372, 377
formation, 346–47
Newton, Isaac, 373
Nibanna, 165
Nichiren Buddhism, **156**, 156–57
Nichiren Shoshu Sokagakkai,
161, 163
Nietzsche, Friedrich, 412
Nihangs, 201, **202**
Ninhursaga, 260
Ninigi, 237
Nirgal, 263
Nirguna Brahman, **93**, 195, 200
Nirmanakaya, 166
Nirvana, 100, 135, 139, **140**, 144,
145, 154, 166, 168, 169, 170
in Jainism, 182
Noble Truths. *See* Four Noble
Truths.

Nobunaga, 362
Nonattachment, 187
Nondualism, 103
Nonviolence, 107
  Christian, 376
  Jain, 181, 186–87
Norito, 248
Normative definitions, 17
North American religions, 21–40, 436
  common features, 36–40
Nubians, **55**
Nuer people, 74
Nyaya, 104
Nyberg, H. S., 269
Nyingmapa, **158**, 159

Oba, **71**, 72
Obatala, **73**
Occultation, 399
Odudwa, **73**
O'Flaherty, Wendy, 90
Okeus, **30**, 31, 37
Okuninushi no Kami, 237, 241
Old Testament, 282, 346, 376
Olodumare, **72**, 74
Olorun, **71**, 72, 73, 74
Omoto, 242, 243
Onisaburo, 242
Onishi, 243
Ontakekyo, 242
Opinion, personal, 401
Oral traditions, 4
Ordination, 379
Organ, Troy W., 116
"Orientalists," 83
Origen, 299, 348
Original sin, 350, 374, 375
Orisha, **72**, 73
Orisha-nla, **71**, 73
Orthodox Judaism, 282, 307, 308, 312, 318, 321, 322
Orun, **72**
Osiris, 56, **60**, 61, 62, 63
Otto, Rudolph, 316

Padma-Sambhava, 157
Pakistan, Islam in, 413
Palestinian Talmud, 299
Palm Sunday, 335, 379
Pangborn, Cyrus, 269
Pan-Islam movement, 412
Pantaneus, 348

Pantheon, **342**
Parable, **333**
Paradise in Islam, 423, 424
Parshva, 178, 179, 182
Parvati, 101
Passover, 6, **285**, 285–86, 319, 323, 335
Patanjali, 102
Paul, Saint, 279, 329, 340, 341–43, 346, 347, 373, 374
Paul, Diana Y., 164
Pawnee, 36
Pelagius, 350
Penance, sacrament of, 359
Pentateuch, 321
Pentecost, 7, **337**, 340, 363, 379
Perpetua, 344, 345
Persian dualism. *See* Manichaeism.
Persians, 255
  in Bible, 270
Persona, 349–50
Peter, 329, 334, 343, 352, 353, 377
Peterson, Joseph, 275
Pharisees, **295**, 296, 324, 329, 332, 333, 337
Phenomenal, **431**
Philo Judaeus, 299, 303, 348
Pilate, 336
Pilgrim, Richard, 245
Pilgrimages, 245
Pillars of Islam, 396, 417
Pius V, Pope, 362
Pizarro, Francisco, 44, 45
Plato, 299, 302, 348, 350, 404
Platonism, 348, 373
  Christian, 347–48
  neo-, 402, 419
Plotinus, 348
Plumed Serpent, 44
Pocahontas, 31
Podok, 151
Poe, 230
Polygamy in Islam, 412, 422
Polytheism
  traditional Arab, 389, 395
  Trinitarianism vs., 349, 350
Pompey, 295
Poole, Elija. *See* Muhammad, Elijah.
Popes, 352, 353, 362
Potlatch, **26**, 27
Pourushaspa, 267

Powhatan [chief], 28, 31
Powhatan people, 27–31
Prakriti, **92**, 93, 103
Pratittya, 147
Pratitya-samutpada, **138**, 147, 165
Prayer
  Christian, 379
  Islamic, 395, 396, 422
  Shinto, 248
Prayer wheels, 164
Prebish, Charles, 163
Presbyterial organizations, 377
Presbyterianism, 360, 361
Presbyterians, **363**
Problem for humans, 11
  Buddhism, 11, 167–68
  Christianity, 11, 374–75
  Confucianism, 11, 233
  Daoism, 11, 217
  Hinduism, 11, 115
  Islam, 11, 420–21
  Jainism, 185–86
  Judaism, 11, 319
  North American religions, 24–25, 37–38
  Shinto, 245
  Sikhism, 200
  sub-Saharan African religions, 75
  Zoroastrianism, 272
Prodigal Son, parable of, 333
Profane, **2**
Prophet(s), **288**, 378
  false, 337
  Hebrew, 280, 288–90, 316, 385
  Muhammad, 393, 396
  true, 337
Protestant churches, 358–61
  foundations, 376–77
  cooperation among, 367
  emerging forms, 365–67
  evangelical, 366
Protestant Reformation, 358–61
Protestants, 361
Proverbs, 294
Psalms, 280, 288, 290, 316, 317, 324, 373
Ptolemies, 56
Puberty rituals. *See* Initiation rituals.
Pueblo peoples, 35
Puja, **118**, 122, **157**
Puranas, 99, **100**

Purdah, 412
Pure Land Buddhism, 149, 150, 153, 163, 169, 172, 239
Purification rites, Shinto, 237, 241
Purim, 323
Puritans, **363**
Purusha, **85**, 92, 103, 115
Purusha Sukta, 85
Purvas, 182, 183
Purva-Mimamsa, 104

Qaddafi, Muammar al-, 414
Qi, 228
Qiyas, **401**
Quakers, 361, **363**. *See also* Society of Friends.
Quang, Thich Tri, 159
Quetzalcoatl, **44**
Qumran community, 295
Quran, 300, **385**, 386, 389, 393, 396, 397, 400, 401, 405, 411, 412, 413, 414, 417, 421, 427
Quraysh tribe, 387, 388, 389, 394, 398
Qutb, Sayyid, 414

Ra. *See* Amon-Re.
Rabbi, **292**
Rabia, 403
Radha, 101
Radhakrishnan, Sarvepalli, 109, 119
Rafsanjani, Hashemi, 414
Rahat Maryada, 199
Rahman, Fazlur, 393, 412
Rahula, 131, 134
Raja yoga, 97, 99, 102, 104, 106, 115
Rak'as, **396**
Raksabandhana, 118
Rama, 101, 102, 106, 111, 118
Ramadan, 395, 397, 421, 422
Ramakrishna, 106, 113, 122, 431
Ramayana, 4, 7, **85**, 100, 101
Rambam, 302. *See also* Maimonides.
Ram Das, 197
Ram Mohan Roy, 105–6
Ramses II, 285
Rasul, **395**
Rauschenbusch, Walter, 376
Ravana, 119
Ra'y, **401**

Reason, scriptural revelation vs., 365
Rebekah, 280
Rebirth, Wheel of, 81, 93–94, 96. *See also* Samsara.
Reciprocity, Confucian, 222, 233
Reconciliation
    four paths, 115–16
    Shinto, 245
    Zoroastrian, 272
Reconstructionist Judaism, 307–8, 312
Red Buddhism, 158
Reformation, 374
    Catholic, 361–62
    Christian, 358
    Protestant, 358–661
Reform churches, 358–61
Reform Judaism, 282, 307, 308, 312, 318, 321, 322
Rehoboam, 288
Reincarnation, **26**, 81, **93**
    Christian, 348
    Jain, 186
    Naskapi, 24, 26
    North American religions, 40
    Sikh, 202
Reischauer, A. K., 152
Reiyukai, 243
Ren, **222**
Renunciation
    Buddha's, 131–32
    Hindu, 96
Renzai, 155, 163, 164
Resurrection, **337**
    Christian view, 337, 348, 375, 380
    Jewish view, 324
Return to Root sect, 171
Revelation
    in Hinduism, 85
    of John, 346
    of Muhammad, 386
Ricci, Matteo, 362
Richard I, 407, 408
Rida, Rashid, 412
Rig-Veda, 4, 100, 178, 267, 280
    gods of, 85–88
Rissho Koseikai, 243
Rita, **87**, 108, 116
Rites of passage, **5**. *See also* Birth rituals; Death rites; Initiation rituals; Marriage customs;

Purification rites.
Rituals, **5**, 5–6, 13
    against demons, 268
    Aztec, 42–43
    Buddhist, 171–72
    Christian, 378–80
    Confucian, 234–35
    Daoist, 218–19
    Egyptian religion, 58, 61
    Hindu, 117–19
    Inca, 46–49
    Islamic, 422–23
    Jain, 188–89
    Jewish, 323–24
    Mesopotamian religion, 263–64
    North American religions, 39–40
    Shinto, 245–48
    Sikh, 201–2
    sub-Saharan African religions, 75–76
    Zoroastrian, 272–73
Roberts, J. Deotis, 370
Roberts, Oral, 366
Robertson, M. G. "Pat," 366
Rodinson, Maxime, 425
Roger of Howdon, 407
Role model, 221
Roman Catholic Church
    governance, 352–53, 376, 377
    indulgences, 358
    path of service, 353–55
    popes, 352, 353, 362
    reformation, 361–62
    seven sacraments, 359
    world, 373, 374
Romans
    Christianity and, 344–46
    Judaism and, 295–99
Rosh Hashana, 323
Roshi, Jiyu Kennett, 164
Röubli, Wilhelm, 360
Rountree, Helen C., 27, 30, 31
Rshabha, 182, 188
Ruether, Rosemary Radford, 371
Rumi, Jalal al-Din, 403
Ruqayyah, 388
Ryonin, **153**

Saadia ben Joseph, 300–301
Sabbath observance, 299
Sacraments, 335, **347**, 379–80
Sacred, **2**

Sacred dance, 6
Sacred flame, 257, 272
Sacred space, 3
Sacred stories, 3–4
Sacrifice
    human, 36, 41, 42–43, 44
    in Judaism, 284
Sadaebu, 228
Sadaqa, **396**
Sadat, Anwar, 414
Sadducees, **295**, 324, 329
Safed, 304
Sage, 212–13, 217, 235
Saguna Brahman, **93**, 195, 200
Saicho, **152**, 153
Sakhmet, 56
Saladin, 281, 302, 406, 407, 408
Salafiya movement, 412
Salat, **396**
Sallekhana, **187**
Salvation, 12
    four ways of, 99–102
Samadhi, **99**, 102, 106
Sama-Veda, 85, 88
Sambhogakaya, 166
Samhitas, 88
Samsara, **93**, 94, 119, 169, 172, 194
    karma and, 93–94, 139–40, 185
Samskaras, **117**
Samutpada, 147
Sangha, **133**, 135, 142, 146, 170, 172
Sanghamitta, 149
Sanhedrin, **296**, 297
San I. *See* Sanyi.
Sankhya system, 10, 103, 104
Sannyasin, **99**, 106
Sanpoil, 39
Sant tradition, **191**
Sanyi, 217
Sarah, 279, 280, 284
Sarasvati, Swami Dayananda,
    106, 122
Sariputra, 154
Sassanians, 269
Sataniv verses, 389
Satapatha Brahmana, 89
Sat-chit-ananda, 108
Satori, **155**
Satya, 187
Satyagraha, 107
Saul, 288
Saul of Tarsus, 329, 340–43. *See
    also* Paul.

Schechter, Solomon, 307
Scholasticism, **355**, 356
Schuon, Frithjof, 431
Schweitzer, Albert, 373, 376
Scribe, **293**
Scriptures, **4**, 4–5
    Buddhist, 142–43
    Christian, 375
    Hebrew, 291–92
    Jain, 182–83
Secret Teachings, 153
Secular, **2**
Seder, 323
Segundo, Juan Luis, 370
Seicho-no-le, 243
Seleucids, 294
Selfless mind, 165
Self-sacrifice in Shinto, 245
Separatists, **363**
Sephardim, **300**
Septuagint, 294, 298
Sermon on the Mount, 332, 369
Seth, **60**
Shabbat, 307
Shafi'ite school, 401
Shahada **395**, 396, 417, 421
Shah Jahan, 410
Shakra, 181
Shakti cults, 158
Shaku, Soyen, 163
Shakyamuni, 127. *See also*
    Buddha.
Shaman, **23**, 23–24, 236, 242
Shamash, 260
Shang Di, **215**
Shammai, 333
Shankara, 103
Shantarakshita, 157
Shari'a, 397, **401**, 404, 413, 414,
    415, 425
    schools interpreting, 401
Sharma, I. C., 118
Shavuot, 323
Shaytan, 396
Shehitah, **321**
Shema, **287**, 313
Sheol, 317, 324
Shi'a, **398**, 399, 410, 412
Shingon school, 152–53, **153**, 169
Shingyo, 154–55
Shinran school, **153**, 153–54, 156
Shinrikyo, 242
Shinshukyo, 242

Shinto, 152, **235**, 235–44
    absolute, 244
    Buddhist influence, 238–39
    community and ethics, 245
    Confucian influence, 239
    historical development, 235–44
    historiography, 236
    humans, 245
    life after death, 248
    mountain worship sects, 241,
        242
    other religions and, 248
    recent, 240
    revelation sects, 241, 242–43
    rituals and symbols, 245
    sectarian, 240–43
    state, 240
    traditional sects, 241–42
    world, 244
    worldview, 244–48
Shinto Shuseiha, 241
Shinto Taiseikyo, 241
Shiva, 81, 85, **100**, 101, 112, 113,
    114, 116
Shofar, 318, 323
Shogun, **240**
Shohet, **321**
Shoshone people, 39
Shotoku, **238**
Shouyi, **217**
Shraddha rites, 99, **117**, 117–18
Shreyamsa, 188
Shruti, **85**, 93
Shu, **222**
Shudras, **94**, 98, 107, 119
Shvetambaras, **179**, 180, 181, 182
Shvetasvatara Upanishad, 92
Siddhartha, 180
Siddhartha Gautama, 81, 94, 102,
    127, 128, 144, 166, 171, 208.
    See also Buddha.
    birth, 130–31
    death, 141–42
    life, 130–35, 141–42
Siddur, 302
Sikhism, 104, 190–204, 386, 410
    absolute, 200
    basic tenets, 438
    community and ethics, 201
    historical development,
        190–200
    historiography, 190–91
    humans, 200–201

life after death, 202–3
militarism, 197, 198, 201, 203
other religions and, 203–4
rituals and symbols, 201–2
time line, 193
world, 200
worldview, 200–204
Sima Quin, 220
Simon [Maccabee], 295
Simon [son of Jonas], 334. *See also* Peter.
Sin [Mesopotamian god], 260
Sin, 11, 12
forgiveness of, 334
in Islam, 420–21
in Sikhism, 196
original, 350, 374, 375
Sincerity, Confucian, 222
Singh, **198**
Sita, 101, 102, 106
Situa, 47
Skandhas, 137, 165, 167
Sky clad, 179, 180, 181
Smith, George, 258
Smith, Huston, 431
Smith, John, 28, 30, 31
Smith, Joseph, **368**
Smith, Robert J., 248
Smith, Wilfred Cantwell, 431, 432
Smriti, **85**, 93
Society of Friends, 361, 376. *See also* Quakers.
Society of Jesus, 361, 362
Socrates, 90, 299
Soka Gakkai, **161**, 161–62, 243
Solomon, 280, 288, 294, 298
Solution for humans, 12
Buddhist, 12, 168–70
Christian, 12, 374–75
Confucian, 12, 233
Daoist, 12, 217–18
Hindu, 12, 115–16
Islamic, 12, 421
Jain, 186
Jewish, 12, 319
North American religions, 38
Shinto, 245
Sikh, 200–201
sub-Saharan African religions, 75
Zoroastrian, 272
Soma, 86, **87**
Soto, 155, 164

South American religions, 44–50, 436
common features, 49–50
Speck, Frank G., 21, 23, 26
Spelman, Henry, 28
Spenta Armaita, 268
Sphinx, 55, 63
Spinoza, Baruch, 305, 316
Spirit. *See* Holy Spirit.
Sri Aurobindo, 81, 108–9, 116
Sri Lanka, Buddhism in, 149
Srong Tsan Gampo, 157
Stephen, 340
Sthanakvasis, **188**
Sthaviradins. *See* Theravadins.
Sthaviras, 143, 144
Stigmata, 351
Stoicism, 348
Stone of the Sun, 43
Strachey, William, 28, 30
Submitting to God, 12
Sub-Saharan African religions, 63–76
common features, 73–76
Suddhodanna, 127, 131, 134, 135
Sudreh, **273**
Suffering, 12, 136, 138–39, 167–68, 317
Sufis, 402–4, 405, 412, 419, 420
Suicide, ritual, 239
Sujata, 132
Sukhavati, 150
Sumerians, 258, 259
Sundo, 151
Sun Myung Moon, **368**, 369
Sunna, **397**, 401, 412, 413, 414, 415
Sunni, **398**, 399, 416
Sun Yat-sen, **229**
Surah, 396, 422
Susanoo, **237**
Sutra, 142
Sutta. *See* Sutra.
Suzuki, D. T., 162
Svetaketu, 91, 92
Swami Vivekananda, 106
Sweat house, 29
Symbols, 13, 442
Aztec religion, 42–43
Buddhist, 171–72
Christian, 378–80
Confucian, 234–35
Daoist, 218–19
Egyptian religion, 56, 58

Hindu, 117–19
Inca religion, 46–49
Islamic, 422–23
Jain, 188
Jewish, 323–24
Mesopotamian religion, 263–64
North American religions, 39
Shinto, 245–48
Sikh, 201–2
Zoroastrian, 272–73
Synagogue, 292
Synod, 353, 377, 406

Tagore, Debendranath, 106
Tagore, Rabindranath, 81, 106–7
Tai-hsi. *See* Taixi.
T'ai Hsu, 167
Taishang Laojun, 215
Taixi, **217**
Talmud, **298**, 299, 300, 301, 307, 308, 312
Babylonian, 256, 260, 281, 299, 385
Palestinian, 299
Tammuz, **260**, 263, 265. *See also* Damuzi.
Tanakh, **281**
Tanha, **136**, 137–38
Tanjur, 142
Tantras, 99, **101**
Tantric Buddhism, 151, 157, 169, 170
Tantrism, 101, 157
Tao. *See* Dao.
Tao Te Ching. *See* Dao De Jing.
Tara, **157**
Tariqah, 404
Tathagata, **141**
Tawhid, **396**
Teaching of Heavenly Reason, 243
Tegh Bahadur, 198
Temple of the Sun, 46
Temple worship, 288, 292
Ten Commandments, 286–87, 313, 321, 323
Tendai school, 152, 153
Tenochtitlán, **41**, 42, 43
Ten Precepts, 135
Tenrikyo, **243**, 244
Terah, 279, 283, 299
Teresa, Mother, 376, 377
Teresa of Ávila, Saint, 362

Tertullian, 349
Teshubah, 323
Tezcatlipoca, **43**, 44
Thanksgiving, 7, 417
Thaquf, 395
Theism, **365**
Theocracy, 360
Theodicy, **293**, 375
Theodosius, 329
Theology, **358**
   black, 370
   liberation, **369**, 369–71
   neo-orthodox, 373
   Protestant, 359
Theosophy, 119, 122
Theravadins, 128, 140, 143, **144**,
      148, 152, 156, 159, 163, 164,
      168, 172
   idea of absolute, 166
   idea of world, 166
   in India, 102, 132–49, 158
   Jainism and, 189
   Mahayanists and, 146–47
   in Sri Lanka, 149
Thomas Aquinas, Saint, 228, 348,
      355–56
Thomas Church of India, 105
Thomas, Gospel of, 347
Thoreau, Henry David, 122
Three fires, 169
Three Jewels of Buddhism, 135,
      144
Three Purities, 216, **216**
Three refuges, 172
Tiamat, **260**, 264
Tianming, **231**
Tian Tai, **149**, 149–50, 152, 169
Tibet, Buddhism in, 157–58
T'ien-ming. *See* Tianming.
Tillich, Paul, 17
Time line
   Buddhism, 160
   Christianity, 338–39
   Hinduism, 110
   Islam, 390–91
   Jainism, 193
   Judaism, 314–15
   religions of Africa, 57
   religions of Americas, 48
   religions of China, 246–47
   religions of Japan, 246–47
   Sikhism, 193
Tirthankaras, 81, 94, 178, 179, **180**,

181, 182, 189
Titus, 329
Tlaloc, **42**
Toda, Josei, 161
Tokuchika, Miki, 243
Tonatiuh, **43**
Topley, Marjorie, 171
Torah, **281**, 283, 287, 289, 291, 292,
      293, 294, 295, 297, 298, 299,
      301, 302, 303, 307, 308, 313,
      321, 324
Torah Scroll, 322
Torii, **235**
Torquemada, Tomas de, 305
Totem, **26**
Tower of Silence, 273
Toxcotl festival, 43
Traditions, oral, 4
Transformation Body, 166
Transformation of things, 215
Transmigration of soul, 40
Tree of enlightenment, 132, 149
Trickster, **24**, 38
Trikaya, **166**
Triloka, **184**
Trimurti, 100
Trinitarian Christians, 325
Trinity, **349**, 349–50, 372, 375, 396,
      406, 424, 427
Tripitaka, **143**, 164
Trishala, 180, 181
True Name, 194
True Word Buddhism, 153
Tsaka´bec, **24**, 38
Tsao Shen. *See* Zaoshen.
Ts'ao-tung, 155
Tsukiyomi, **237**
Tusita heaven, 144
Tutankhamen, 3, 56
Tutu, Desmond, 370
Twelvers, 398, 399

Ubuthongo, **71**
Uddaka Ramaputta, 131
Uddalaka Aruni, 81, 91–92
Ukubuyisa idlozi rite, **70**
'Ulama', **411**, 415
'Umar, 389, 398, 399, 400
Ummah, **413**, 421, 425
Ummayads, 394, 398
Umm-Khulthum, 388
Umnayama, **70**
Umnumzane, **67**

Umsamo, **67**, 69
U mueling angi angi, **70**
Unification Church, 368
Unitarianism, 105, 377
United Church of Canada, 364
United States
   Islam in, 415–17
   religious diversity, 364–65
Universal harmony, doctrine of,
      235
Universal love, 223
Untouchable, **107**. *See also*
      Shudras.
U Nu, **159**
Upali, 143
Upanayana rite, 116, **117**
Upanishads, **85**, 89–93, 100, 103,
      105, 113, 208
   alternatives, 94–97
   Chandogya, 91
   Isha, 107
   Shvetasvatara, 92
Uprightness, Confucian, 222
Urban II, Pope, 357, 406
Urban VI, Pope, 352
Uriah, 289
Uruvela Kashyapa, 133
Usamah, 399
'Uthman Ibn Affan, 389, 398
Utnapishtim, **262**

Vairocana, 150, **153**, 166
Vaisheshika philosophy, 104
Vaishyas, **94**, 98, 119
Valignano, Alessandro, 362
Varley, H. Paul, 243
Varna, **85**, 115
Varuna, **87**, 87–88
Vasettha, 165, 166
Vasubandhu, **148**
Vatican Councils, 369, 380
Vedanta, **85**, 103
   Advaita, 103–4, 111
Vedanta Sutra, 104
Vedas, **83**, 85, 88, 90, 93, 94, 98,
      99, 104, 106, 112, 113, 116,
      117, 128, 158, 194
   alternatives, 94–97
   collections, 88–89
   Rita, 108, 116
Vespasian, 297, 329
Vietnam, Buddhism in, 159–61
Vijayadasami, 118

Vinaya school, 143, 151, 172
Vindevdat, 268
Violence, Jain view of, 187
Viracocha, **46**, 47
Virgin Mary, 361, 372, 424
Vishnu, 81, 96, **100**, 113, 116
Vishtaspa, 268
Vision quest, 39
Visperad, 268
Vivaha, **117**
Vivekananda, Swami, 106, 122
    Vedanta of, 109
Vohu Manah, **267**, 268
Voltaire, 305, 365
Vritra, 86
Vulgate, 359, 369

Wahhab, **411**
Wahhabis, 415
Wakan tanka, **36**
Wandering ascetic, 131, 139
Wang Wei, 211
Waraqa Ibn Nawfal, 389
Washington, George, 306
Watson, Burton, 224, 226
Way of Devotion, 100–102. *See
    also* Bhakti yoga.
Way of Knowledge, 100. *See also*
    Jnana yoga.
Way of Physical Discipline, 102.
    See also Raja yoga.
Way of the gods, 235
Way of Works, 99. *See also* Karma
    yoga.
Weizmann, Chaim, 309
Wellhausen, 291
Weroances, **28**, 30, 31
Weroansquas, **28**, 30
Wesley, John, **363**
West, Buddhism and, 162–64
Western Wall, **297**
Wheel of becoming, 138
Wheel of law, 171–72
Wheel of Rebirth, 81, 93–94, 96.
    See also Samsara.
    Buddha and, 131
Whitehead, Alfred North, 412
Whitefield, George, 363
Wiesel, Elie, 308, 310
Wing-Tsit Chan, 230
Wisakon, **29**
Wise, Isaac Mayer, 307
Witches, Basongye, 66–67

Women
    in Buddhism, 164, 171
    in Christianity, 370–71
    in Confucianism, 234
    in Hinduism, 111
    in Islam, 419, 425–26
    in Judaism, 307, 318
    in Sikhism, 201
Woolman, John, 376
Word of God, 196
Work as deliverance from sam-
    sara, 94–95
World
    in Buddhism, 166–67
    in Christianity, 373–74
    in Confucianism, 232
    in Daoism, 216
    detachment from, 166
    in Hinduism, 113–15
    in Islam, 418–19
    in Jainism, 184–85
    in Judaism, 317
    in North American religions, 37
    in Shinto, 244
    in Sikhism, 200
    in sub-Saharan African reli-
        gions, 74–75
    in Zoroastrianism, 271
World Council of Churches, 367
World Soul, 166
Worldview, 9–15
    ancient Egyptian, 56–63
    Aztec, 43–44
    Basongye, 64–65
    Buddhist, 165–73
    Christian, 371, 372–81
    Confucian, 231–35
    Daoist, 216–19
    Hindu, 112–22
    Jain, 183–89
    Jewish, 313–25
    Mesopotamian religion, 259–65
    Muslim, 417–27
    Shinto, 244–48
    Sikh, 200–204
    sub-Saharan African, 74–76
    Zoroastrian, 270–75
    Zulu, 67–71
Wuwei, **213**

X, Malcolm, **416**, 417
Xavier, Francis, 361, 362
Xerxes, 269

Xunzi, **226**, 226–27, 228, 233

Yahweh, 291
Yajnavalkya, 82, 90–91, 113
Yajur-Veda, 85, 88
Yakub, Mr., 416
Yamabashi healer, 243
Yamaga-Soko, 239
Yang, **209**, 218
Yashodhara, **131**, 135
Yashts, 268
Yasnas, 267, 268, 269, 271
Yi, **221**
Yigdal, 302–3
Yijing, **209**
Yin, **209**, 218
Yi-Pao Mei, 223
Yoga, **94**, 104
    bhakti, **97**, 100–102, 115, 116
    hatha, 157
    jnana, **96**, 100, 115, 116
    karma, 94, 96, 99–100, 116
    raja, 97, 99, 102, 104, 106, 115
Yogacara school, **147**, 147–48, 155,
    169
Yoga Sutra, 102
Yohanan ben Zakkai, 281, 297,
    298
Yom Kippur, 323
Yoruba peoples, 71–73
Young, Andrew, 366
Young, Brigham, **368**, 369

Zaddik, 308
Zaehner, R. C., 267, 268
Zakat, **395**, 396
Zaoshen, **216**
Zarathustra, 257, 271
    life, 267–68
    teachings, 268–69
Zar ceremonies, 426
Zayd, 399
Zayd Ibn Horithah, 389
Zayd Ibn Thabit, 397
Zaydis, 398, 399
Zaynab, 388
Zaynab Bint al-Harith, 394
Zealots, **295**, 296, 297, 329, 336
Zechariah, 330
Zen Buddhism, **150**, 154–55, 156,
    163, 166, 169, 239
Zeus, 294
Zhang Daoling, 215

Zhiya, **149**, 152
Zhongyong, **225**
Zhuangzi, 213, **214**, 214–15, 217, 225
Zhuxi, **227**, 227–28
Zia ul-Haq, 413
Ziggurats, 257, **258**, 263, 264
Zionism, 302, **307**, 309–10, 425
Zohar, 303, 316
Zongzi, 228

Zoroastrianism, 255, 256, 267–75, 324
absolute, 270–71
after Zarathustra, 269–70
basic tenets, 439
historical development, 267–70
historiography, 267
humans, 272
life after death, 273–74
principles, 268–69

scriptures, 268
symbols and rituals, 272–73
world, 271
worldview, 270–75
Zulu peoples, **67**, 67–71
Zuni, 35, 37
Zurvan, **270**
Zurvanism, 270
Zwingli, Huldrych, 360

PHOTO CREDITS

CANADA

NORTH
PACIFIC
OCEAN

UNITED STATES

NORTH
ATLANTIC
OCEAN

Tropic of Cancer

MEXICO

CUBA

HAITI

DOMICAN
REPUBLIC

PUERTO RICO

BELIZE

JAMAICA

GUATEMALA
EL SALVADOR
NICARAGUA
COSTA RICA
PANAMA

HONDURAS

TRINIDAD & TOBAGO

GUYANA
SURINAME
FRENCH
GUIANA

VENEZUELA
COLOMBIA

Equator

ECUADOR

PERU

B R A Z I L

WESTERN
SAMOA

TONGA

BOLIVIA

PARAGUAY

Tropic of Capricorn

CHILE

ARGENTINA

URUGUAY

SOUTH
PACIFIC
OCEAN

SOUTH
ATLANTIC
OCEAN

Antarctic Circle